EVENT-CITIES 2

Event Cities, published in 1994 on the occasion of Bernard Tschumi's exhibition at The Museum of Modern Art in New York, was an expanded version of *Praxis Villes-Événements,* produced in French in November 1993 (Le Fresnoy and Massimo Riposati, Editeurs, Paris). *Event-Cities 2* documents work done from 1994 to 1999.

Book Design and Production: Bernard Tschumi, Johanne Riegels Oestergaard, Anne Save de Beaurecueil, Andrea Day, Kate Linker, and Massimo Riposati with the assistance of Stephen Perrella.

Library of Congress Cataloging-in-Publication Data:

Tschumi Bernard, 1994-
Event-cities 2 / Bernard Tschumi.
p. cm
Includes bibliographical references,
ISBN # 0-262-70074-3 (pb : alk, paper)
1. Tschumi, Bernard, 1944-. 2. Architecture, Modern–20th century.
3. Architectural design–Philosophy. 4. Public spaces–Designs and plans.
I. Title: Event-cities two. II. Title.
NA2707.T73A4 2000
724'.6–dc21 00-027644

The MIT Press, Cambridge, Massachusetts/London, England
Printed and bound in Italy - Diagonale - Rome

BERNARD TSCHUMI

EVENT-CITIES 2

The MIT Press
Cambridge, Massachusetts
London, England

Acknowledgements
Bernard Tschumi would like to thank all whose assistance and collaboration have been crucial to the development of the projects in this book, in particular (for the Parc de la Villette) Jean-François Erhel, Colin Fournier, Ursula Kurz, and Luca Merlini, who also was associated architect for the Lausanne Interface project and for the Geneva OMM competition. Hugh Dutton played a key role in several projects, in particular for the Lerner Hall glass ramps, but also in the technology of glass and metal enclosures for Rouen, Marne-la-Vallée, and Lausanne. So did Peter Samton and Tim Schmiderer of Gruzen Samton Architects, associated with us on the Lerner Hall project.

Tom Kowalski, Kim Starr, Megan Miller, Ruth Berktold, Mark Haukos, Kevin Collins, Greg Merryweather, Peter Cornell, Rhett Russo, Anne Save de Beaurecueil, Johanne Riegels Oestergaard, Robert Holton, Joel Rutten, Encarnita Rivera, and Andrea Day have been essential figures in the New York office of Bernard Tschumi Architects.

For the Paris part of the operation, I would like to thank Véronique Descharrières, who gave strength and coherence to many of our endeavors; Sylviane Brossard, whose administrative intelligence has allowed an office to operate for now over a decade on both sides of the Atlantic; Alex Reid, whose responsibilities in construction supervision of the Marne-la-Vallée and Rouen projects have turned into major contributions; and Yves Dessuant, Jean-Hughes Manoury, Christian Biecher, Cristina Devizzi, Laurane Ponsonnet, and Emmanuel Ventura for valuable assistance.

Also to be noted are client body representatives whose support and foresight have made several projects built realities, in particular, François Barré and Serge Goldberg for the Parc de la Villette, and George Rupp, Emily Lloyd and Jonathan Cole at Columbia University for Lerner Hall.

I also would like to thank the students and faculty at Columbia for their encouragement, as well as Roger Conover and Terry Riley for their early support. Last but not least, I wish to thank Kate Linker, whose support and resilience made much of this enterprise possible.

Contents

Introduction

Event-Cities 2 is a documentation of urban projects designed for the early 21st century. As in the first volume,[1] the book makes intentional use of rough, photocopy-quality documents, avoiding the lush color of photographs and computer-generated images. Not only do we like its black and white abstraction; we also aim at emphasizing concepts, notations, and strategies rather than their representation—hence, the hard plans, sections, axonometrics, and volumetric perspective views presented here. It is important to reiterate that this roughness is not due to "bad printing." It is exactly the way we want it to be.

The Materialization of Concepts

In the same way as the book tries to avoid the pre-eminence of the formal or visual, the work shown deals with ideas and strategies, rather than chiefly with the production of forms. As opposed to many architects' work, none of the projects described in these pages starts with an image or form, not even with a formal strategy. The projects always begin from an urban condition and a program. They then try to uncover potentialities hidden in the program, site, or circumstances, whether economic, social, or cultural. Dynamic forces and/or intensely public spaces are encouraged; a concept is identified; and, eventually, a form arrived at, so as to reinforce or qualify the concept. Often, the "place" of the concept will also be the place of technological innovation: much as the invention of long-span steel structures and elevators changed 19th-century architecture, so structural glass, glue, digital space, and microchips are changing architecture today. This is explored—to cite only a few projects—in the ramps at Lerner Hall, the covered galleries at La Villette, and the building envelope at Rouen. Formal debates are never the starting point of these projects. Architecture is seen as the materialization of concepts, as opposed to the materialization of form.

If architecture is the materialization of concepts, these concepts also need to be closely associated with site, program, and/or technology. (Concepts or theories from other disciplines rarely are susceptible to literal translation.) Hence, none of the projects presented here starts with a theory per se. Architecture is not there—or here—to illustrate theory on a one-to-one basis.

Design, however, cannot be too "innocent," either. The point, instead, is to be aware of theoretical issues and to start from a project, aiming at making connections with important ideas of our time. This was our concern at La Villette. Theory is not intended to defend, justify, or promote design. *Architecture and Disjunction,*[2] written parallel to several architectural projects, was published as a separate book, so as not to confuse questions of theory and design. In this publication, in a similar manner, we have kept texts to a minimum. Plans, sections, and three-dimensional views are employed to show each project extensively, in contrast to a "media-bite" architectural approach.

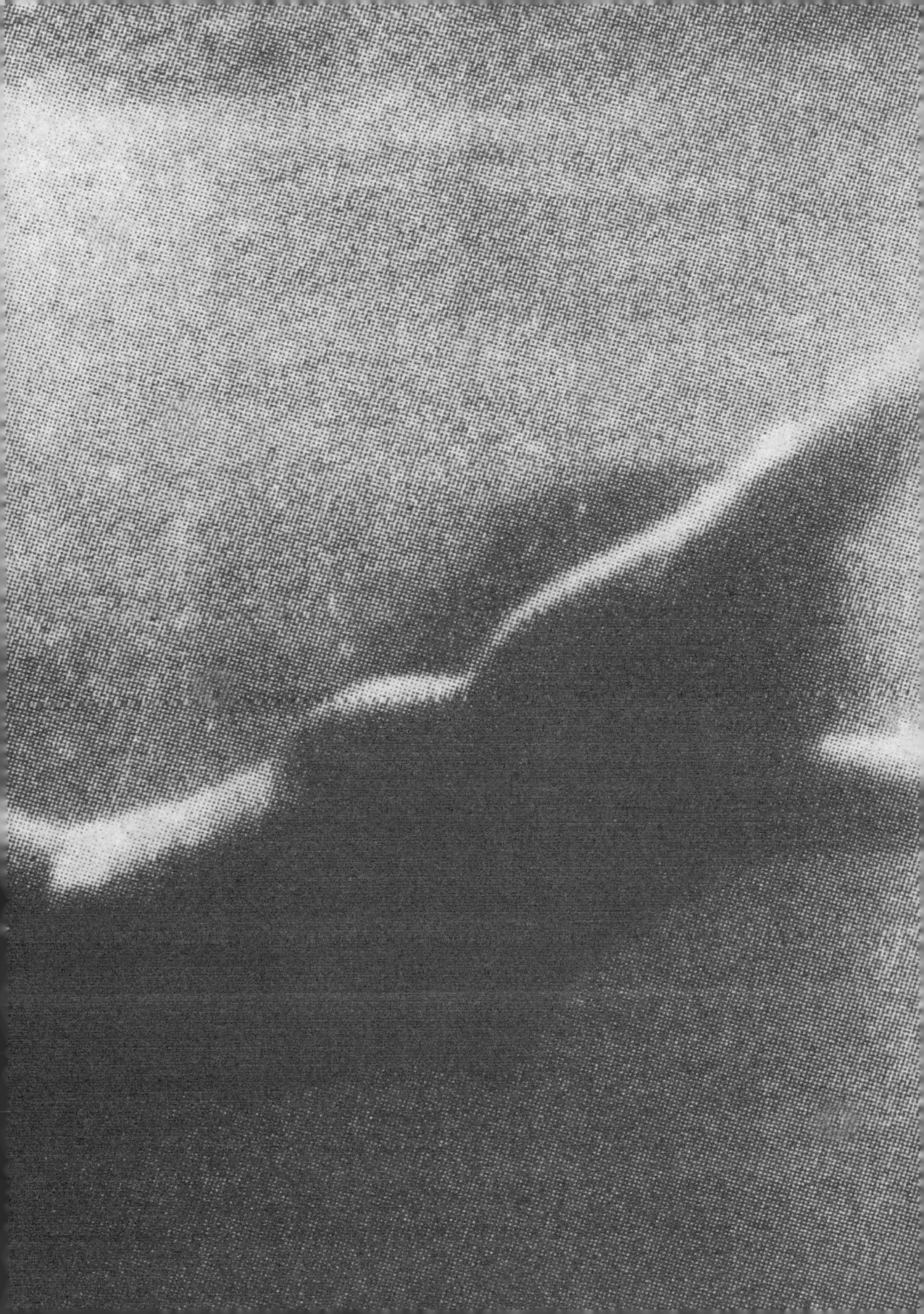

A.
Space, Event, Movement (sem)

"Rituals" and the Parc de la Villette in Paris are two architectural propositions at very different scales. "Rituals" measures 8 by 8 inches, or 1/25 of one square meter. La Villette is 125 acres, or 550,000 square meters, in size. "Rituals" took three dollars worth of photocopies and a night of work to complete, and remained private. La Villette took $300 million and fifteen years to complete, and became intensely public. Both, however, address the same issue: the interaction between space, movement, and event. "There is no architecture without program, no architecture without movement" is a leitmotif of the work presented here. Yet the relation between architecture and program intentionally can be one of indifference, reciprocity, or conflict. "Rituals" deals with reciprocity, the Park with all three.

Rituals, 1978

Movement as Generator

Preface

A few years ago, during a long winter evening, the film director Eric Rohmer, the actor Boris Karloff, and I spent intense hours discussing the architectural spaces contained in Murnau's Faust, about which Rohmer had just finished writing his Ph.D. thesis. The philosophical—and architectural—speculations during that dark and windy night inevitably led us to reminisce about the film Frankenstein, which had revealed Karloff to the cinema audiences of 1932. The clumsiness of James Whale's film encouraged us to try to rediscover the original spirit of Mary Shelley's story, and especially of the spaces it suggested. Towards four o'clock in the morning, a bizarre construction began to emerge from the often complex and sometimes confused argument. Boris suggested that this construction could become his house. The following pages retrace our discussion.

August 1978

The difficulty of relating events and spaces does not lie on the theoretical level. In fact, the very nature of architecture would make it easy to demonstrate that conceptual space and real space, abstract parameters and the depths of human experience are "architecturally" independent. The difficulty lies in the practical application. If you wonder whether the spaces you design are affected by the events that take place in them; if you wonder whether the experience of a certain space will be altered by, say, a birthday party as opposed to a rehearsal for a wake; then you will want to carry such questions to their ultimate consequences by taking temporary events (as opposed to permanent functions) and merging them in architectural spaces. Of course, people do not let themselves be manipulated the way spaces are. There are ceremonies that determine space, and spaces that determine ceremonies. "Rituals" treats the former, for the latter still carry reminiscences of early twentieth-century behaviorism. Here, the ceremonies, or rather these rituals (after all, a ritual is a formalized event in the same way that architecture is a formalized space) determine a set of spaces. They *regulate* these spaces. The spaces are determined by a "rituel régulateur" in the same way that other periods of architectural history have talked of a "tracé régulateur." In this example, three banal rituals have been isolated - and three subsequent spaces defined.

Ritual 1. The Dance

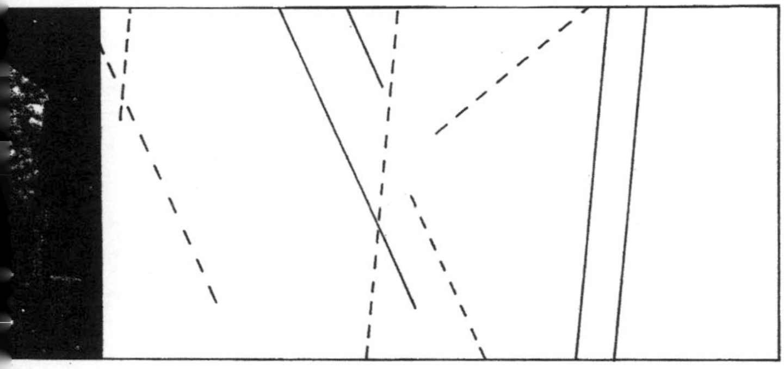

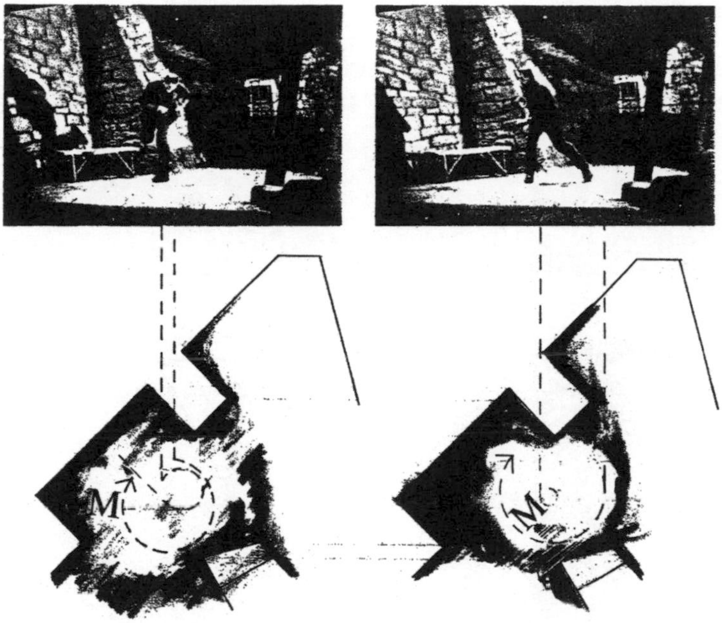

Heterogeneity: architecture and film, architecture from film

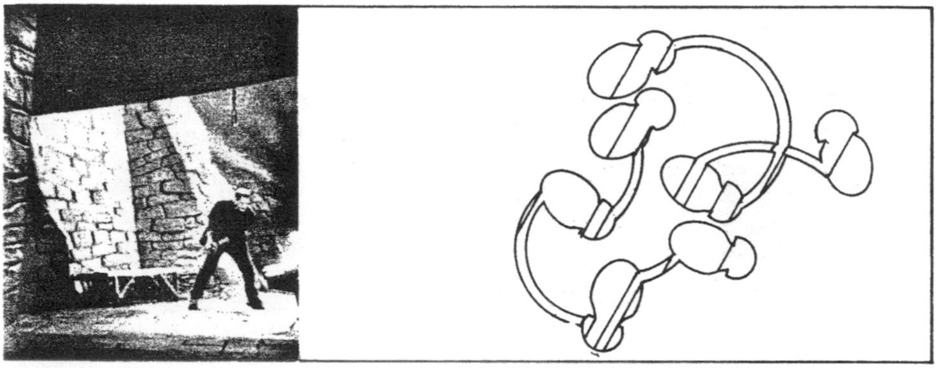

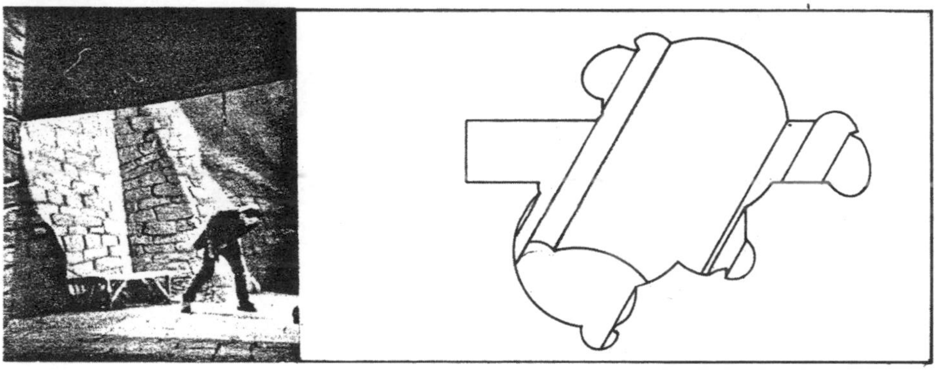

Carving into matter as if it were clay or butter

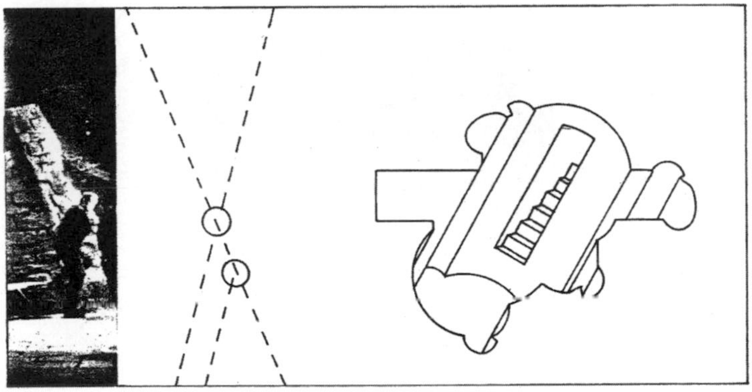

Ritual 2. The Chase

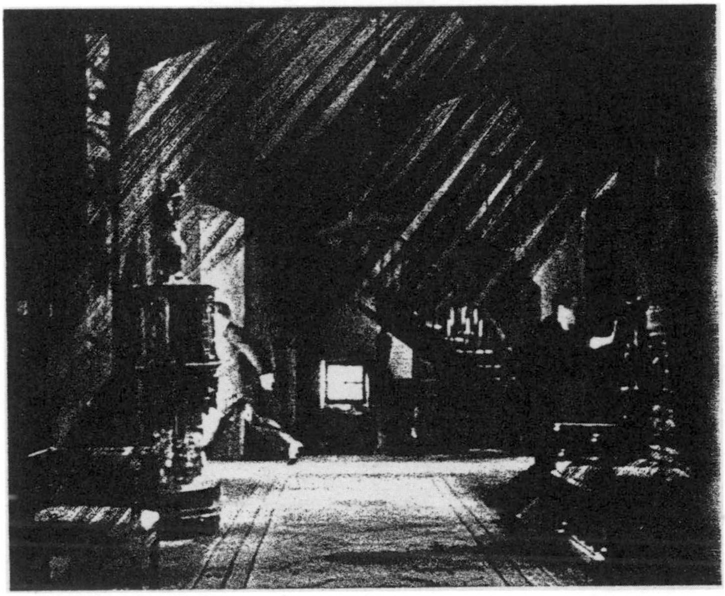

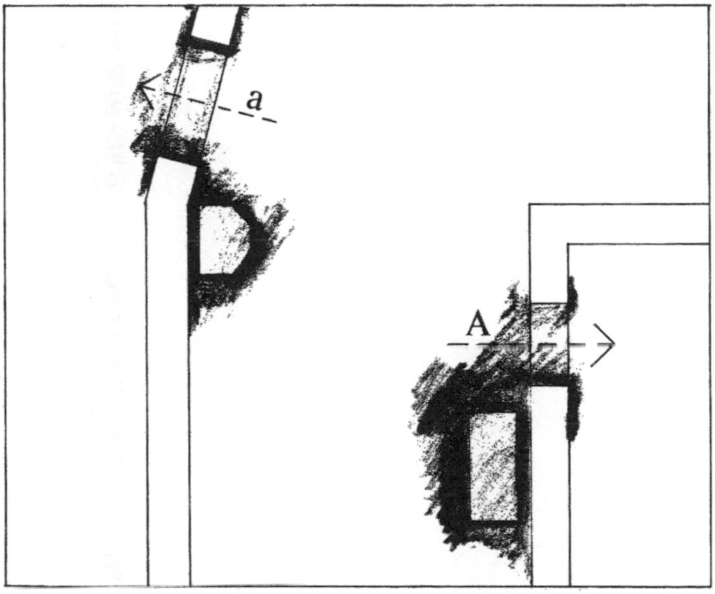
a
A

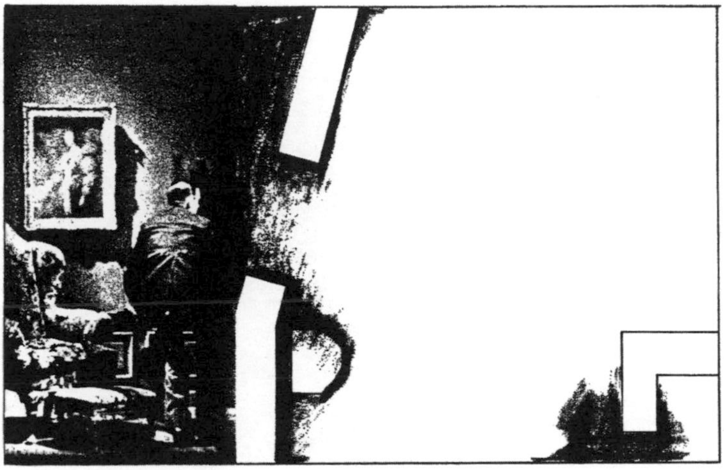

a
a
A

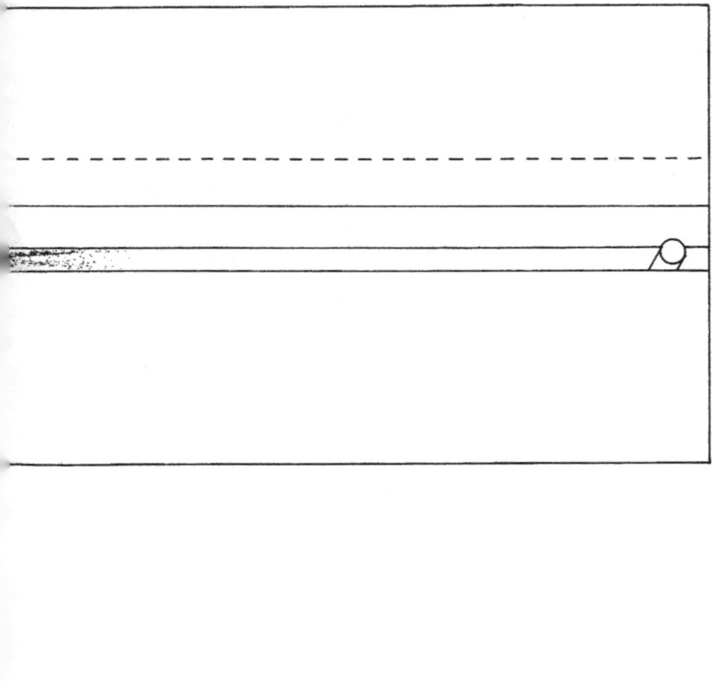

Ritual 3. The Fight

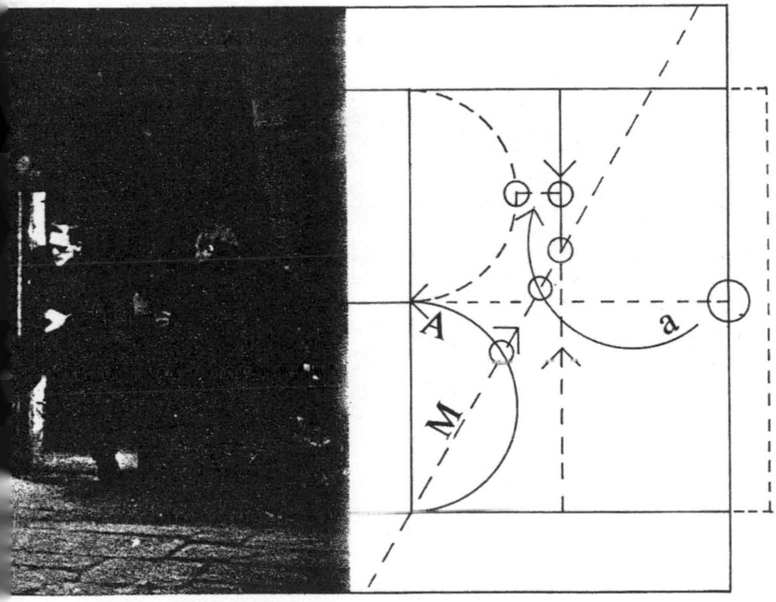

Movement notation

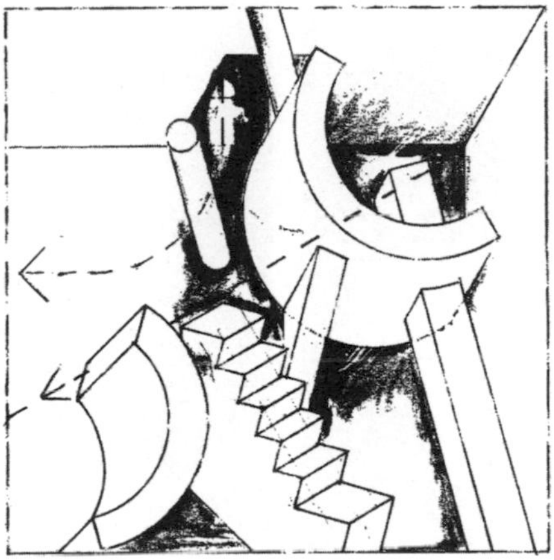

Solidifying movement (frozen motion)

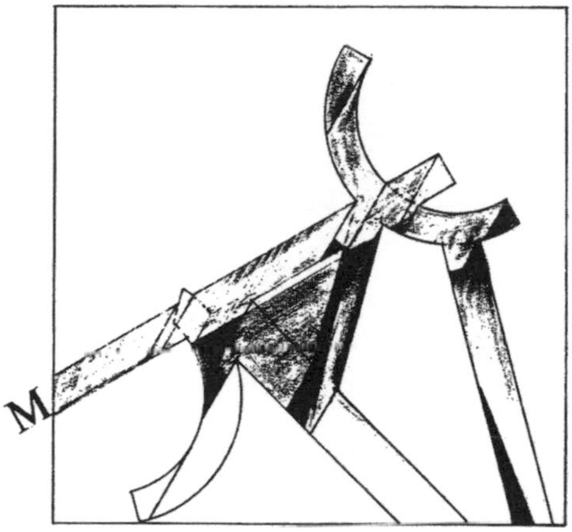

Vectors generate spaces

The House

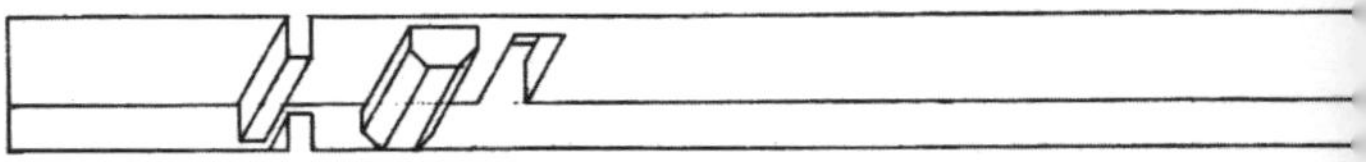

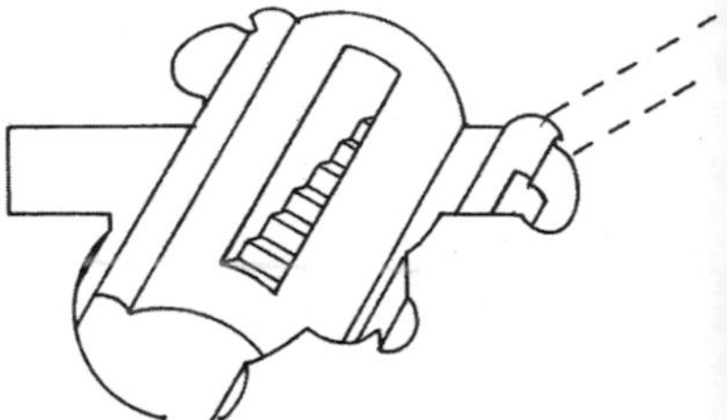

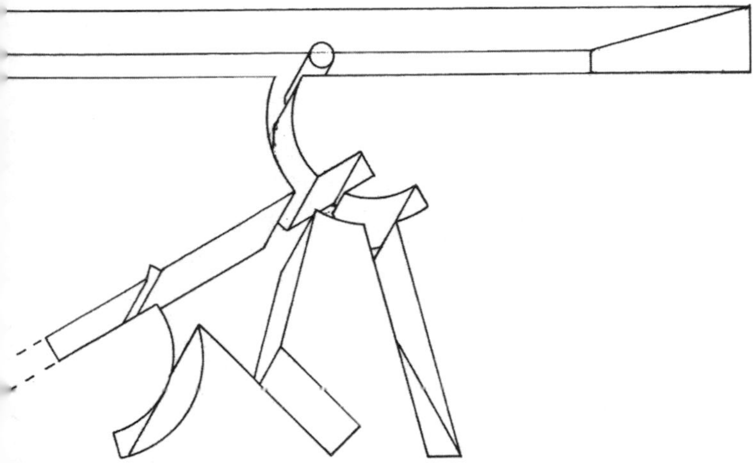

A movement diagram becomes architecture

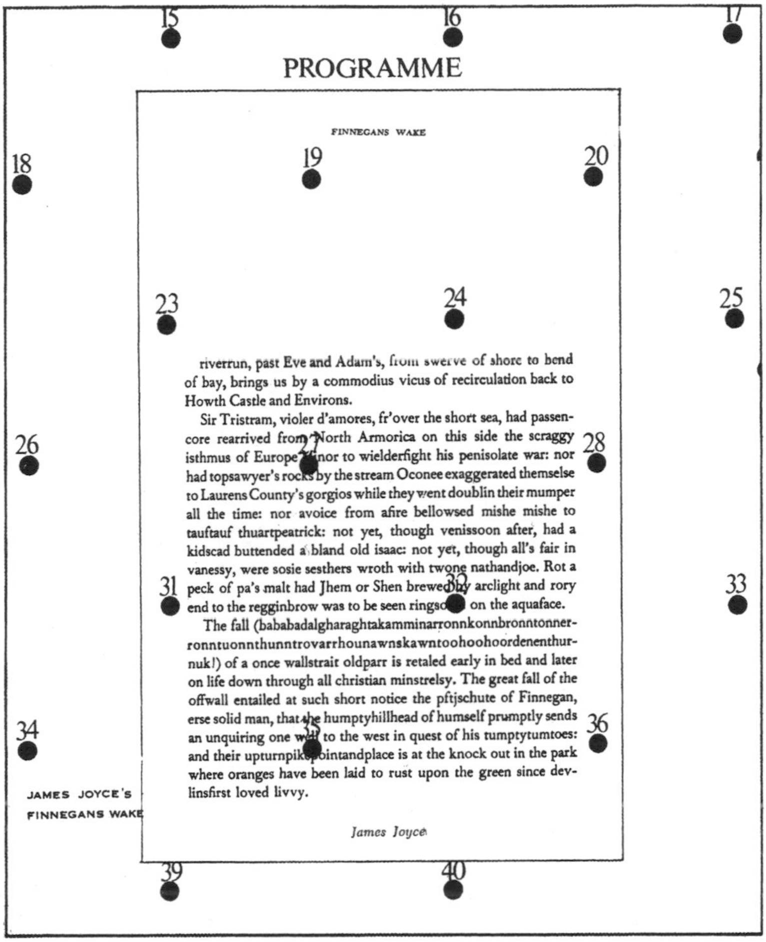

Joyce's Garden, 1976-77: a literary text, *Finnegans Wake*, was used as the program. An abstract point grid functioned as a mediator between the text and the site—the precedent for La Villette's point grid

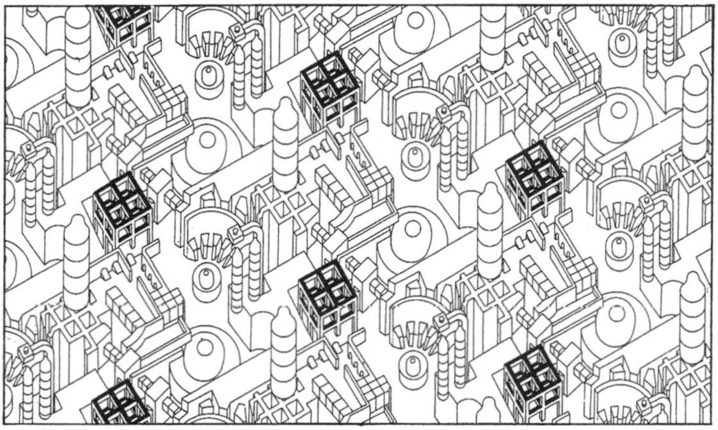

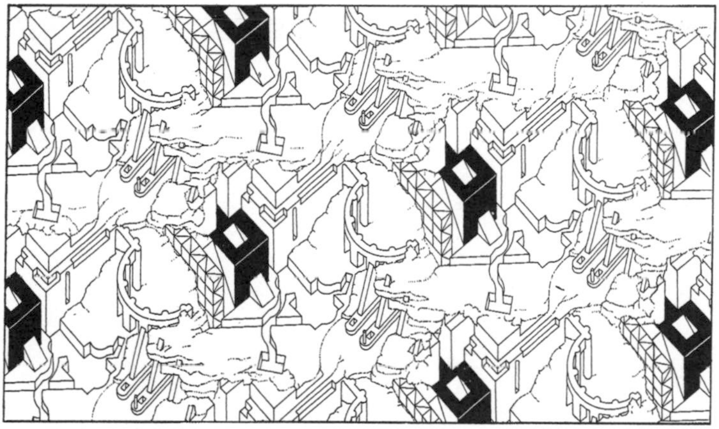

Paris, Parc de la Villette, 1982–98

Superimpositions / Juxtapositions / Permutations

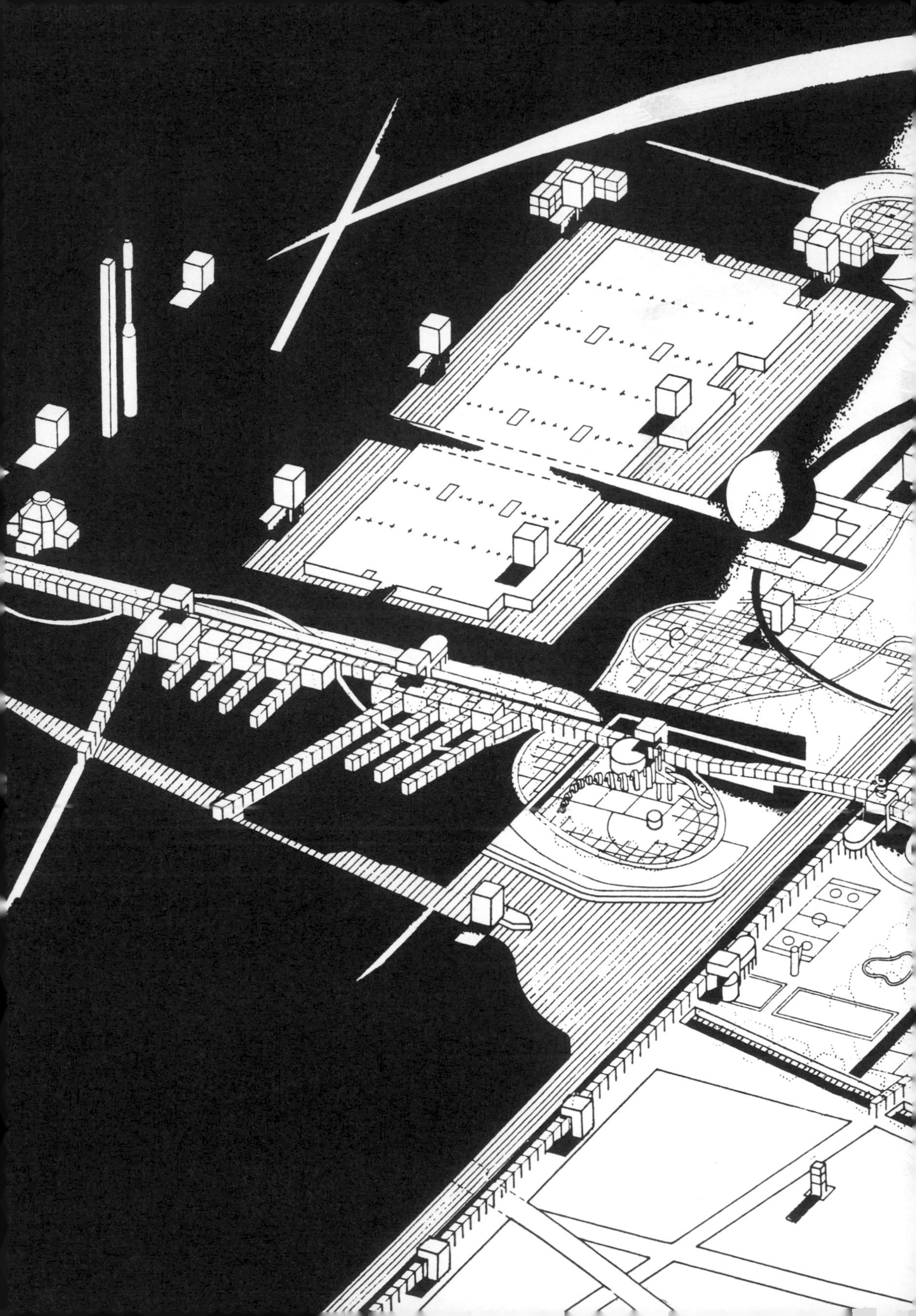

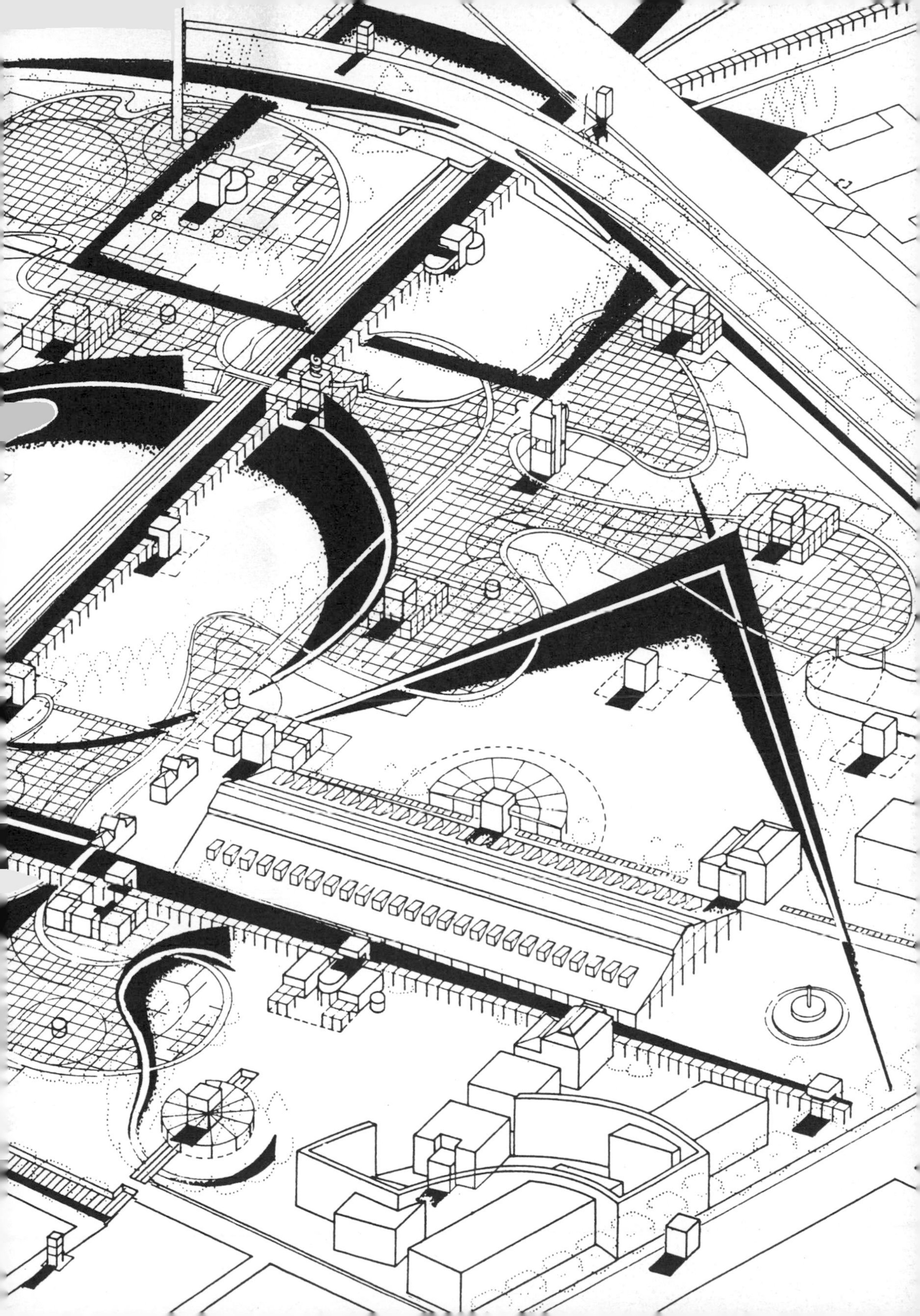

Concepts of large scale organization (city scale)

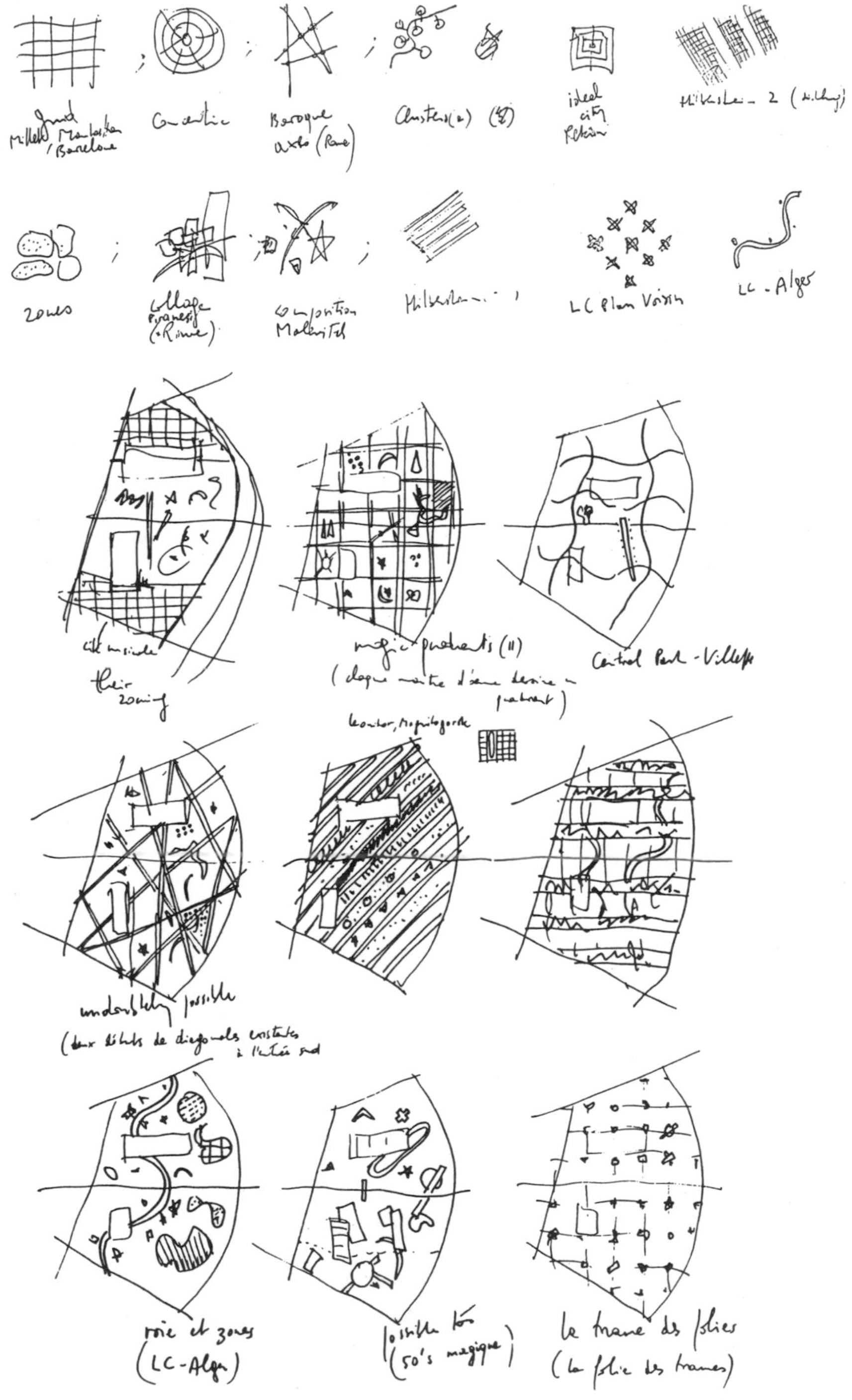

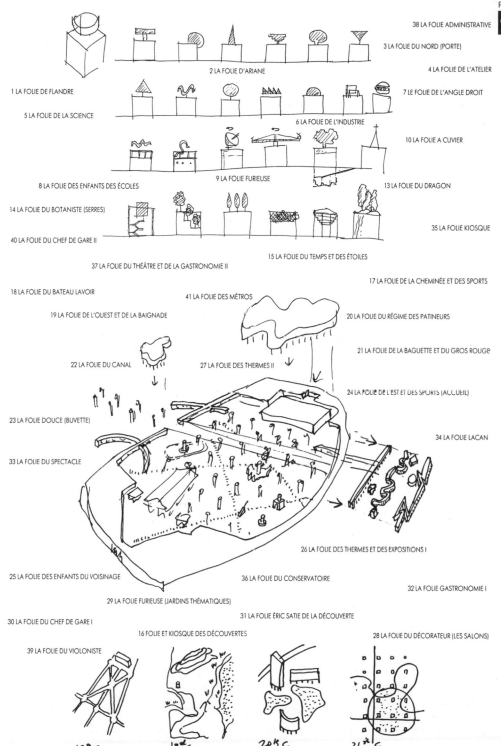

38 LA FOLIE ADMINISTRATIVE

3 LA FOLIE DU NORD (PORTE)

2 LA FOLIE D'ARIANE

4 LA FOLIE DE L'ATELIER

1 LA FOLIE DE FLANDRE

7 LE FOLIE DE L'ANGLE DROIT

5 LA FOLIE DE LA SCIENCE

6 LA FOLIE DE L'INDUSTRIE

10 LA FOLIE A CUVIER

9 LA FOLIE FURIEUSE

8 LA FOLIE DES ENFANTS DES ÉCOLES

13 LA FOLIE DU DRAGON

14 LA FOLIE DU BOTANISTE (SERRES)

35 LA FOLIE KIOSQUE

40 LA FOLIE DU CHEF DE GARE II

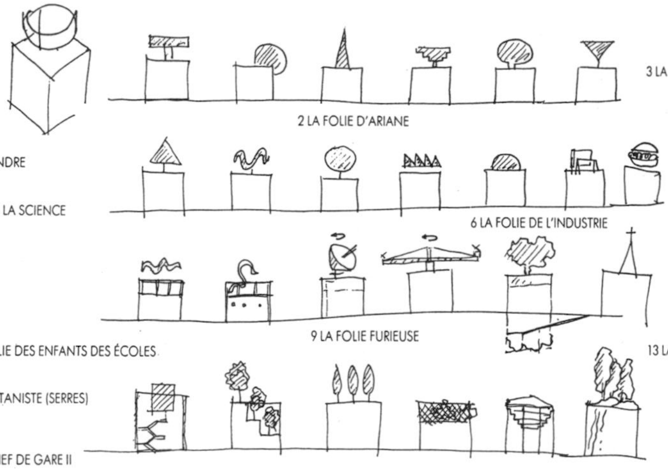

15 LA FOLIE DU TEMPS ET DES ÉTOILES

37 LA FOLIE DU THÉÂTRE ET DE LA GASTRONOMIE II

17 LA FOLIE DE LA CHEMINÉE ET DES SPORTS

18 LA FOLIE DU BATEAU LAVOIR

41 LA FOLIE DES MÉTROS

19 LA FOLIE DE L'OUEST ET DE LA BAIGNADE

20 LA FOLIE DU RÉGIME DES PATINEURS

21 LA FOLIE DE LA BAGUETTE ET DU GROS ROUGE

22 LA FOLIE DU CANAL

27 LA FOLIE DES THERMES II

24 LA FOLIE DE L'EST ET DES SPORTS (ACCUEIL)

23 LA FOLIE DOUCE (BUVETTE)

34 LA FOLIE LACAN

33 LA FOLIE DU SPECTACLE

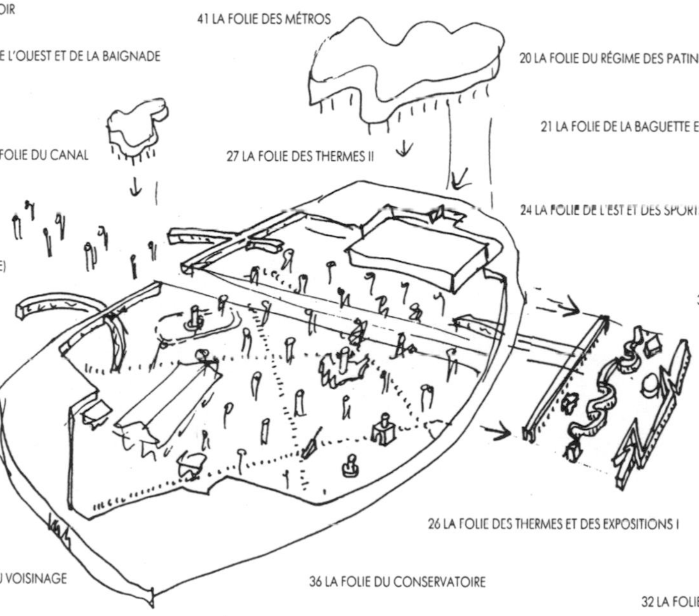

26 LA FOLIE DES THERMES ET DES EXPOSITIONS I

25 LA FOLIE DES ENFANTS DU VOISINAGE

36 LA FOLIE DU CONSERVATOIRE

32 LA FOLIE GASTRONOMIE I

29 LA FOLIE FURIEUSE (JARDINS THÉMATIQUES)

31 LA FOLIE ÉRIC SATIE DE LA DÉCOUVERTE

30 LA FOLIE DU CHEF DE GARE I

16 FOLIE ET KIOSQUE DES DÉCOUVERTES

28 LA FOLIE DU DÉCORATEUR (LES SALONS)

39 LA FOLIE DU VIOLONISTE

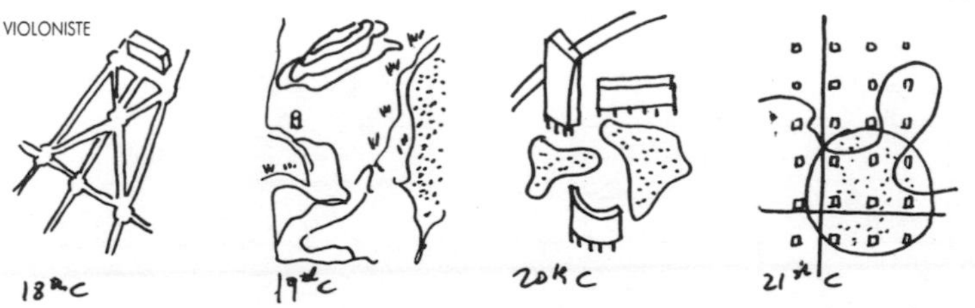

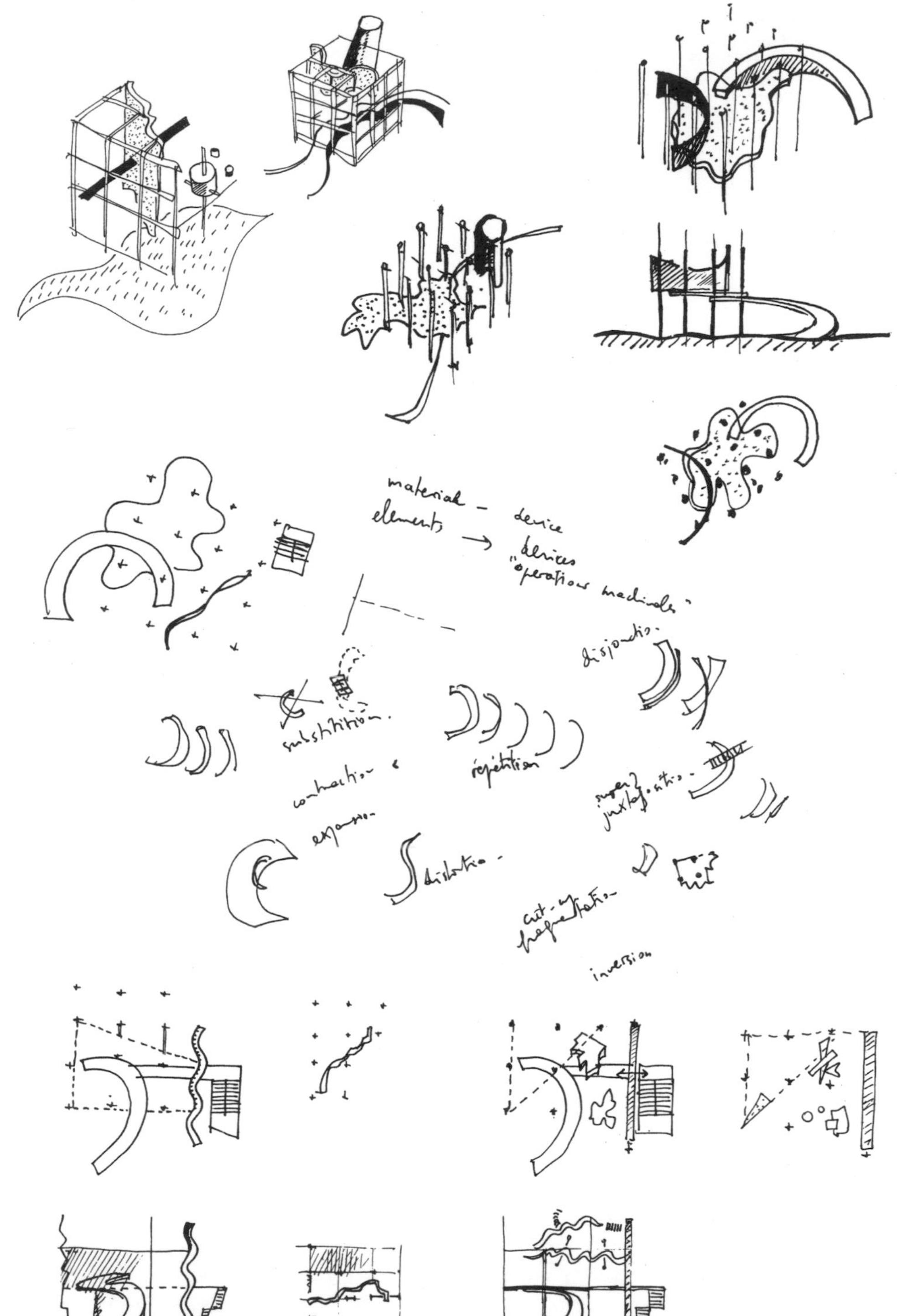

material
device
devices
substitution
répétition
inversion

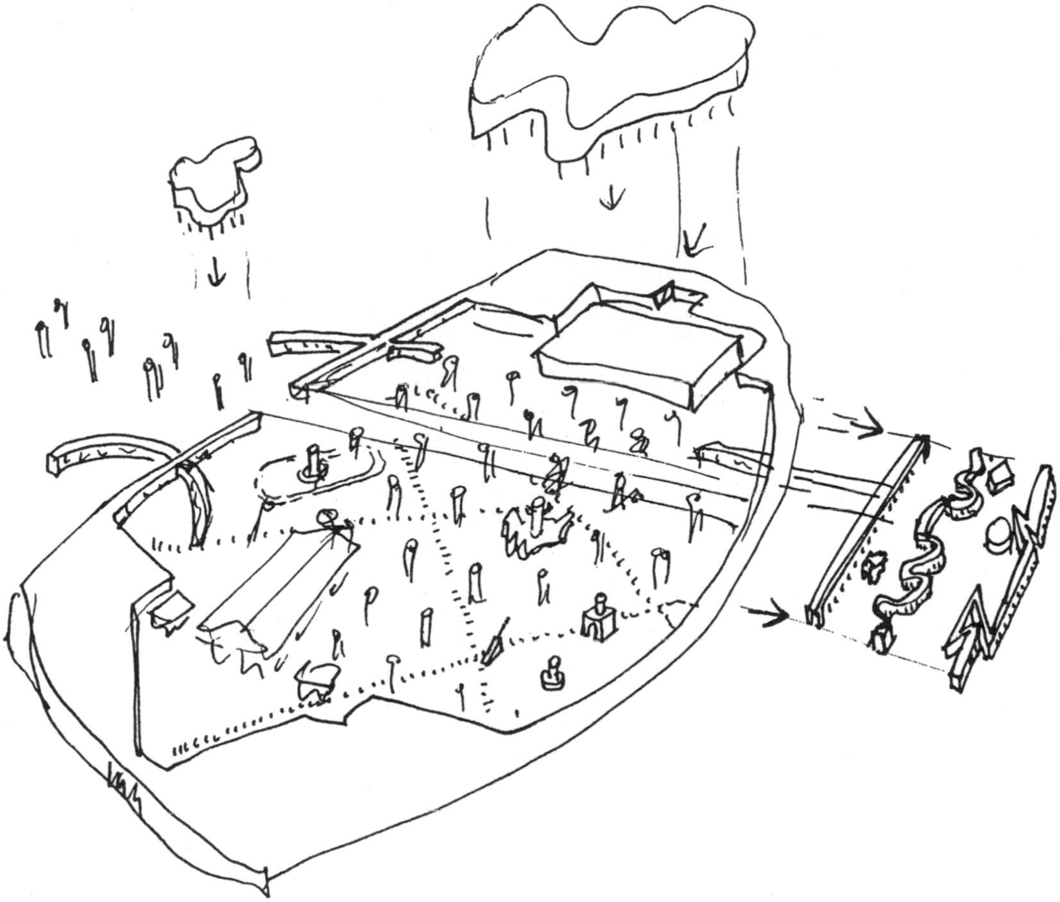

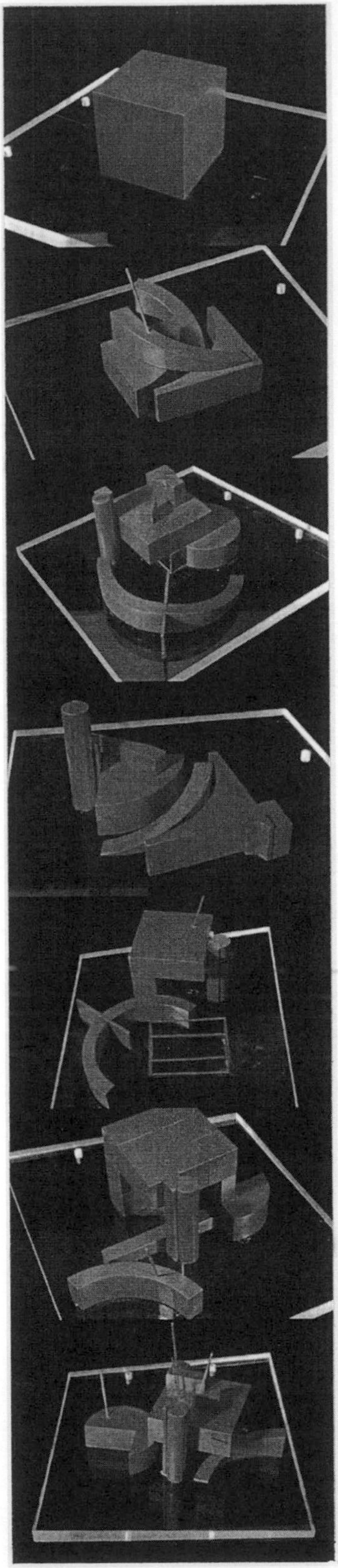

Parc de la Villette

The competition for the Parc de la Villette was organized by the French Government in 1982. Its objectives were both to mark the vision of an era and to act upon the future economic and cultural development of a key area in Paris. As with other "Grands Projets" such as the Opera at Bastille, the Louvre Pyramid, or the Arch at Tête-Défense, the Parc de la Villette was the center of numerous polemics, first at the time of the competition, when landscape designers violently opposed the challenges of architects, then during governmental changes and various general budgetary crises.

The Parc de la Villette is located on one of the last remaining large sites in Paris, a 125-acre expanse previously occupied by the central slaughter houses and situated on the northeast corner of the city, between the Metro stations Porte de Pantin and Porte de la Villette. Over one kilometer long in one direction and seven hundred meters in the other, La Villette appears as a multiple programmatic field, containing, in addition to the park, a large Museum of Science and Industry, a City of Music, a Grande Halle for exhibitions, and a rock concert hall.

Despite its name, the park as designated in the competition was to be no simple landscape replica. On the contrary, the brief for this "Urban Park for the 21st Century" develops a complex program of cultural and entertainment facilities, encompassing open-air theaters, restaurants, art galleries, music and painting workshops, playgrounds, video and computer displays, as well as the obligatory gardens where cultural invention, rather than natural recreation, was encouraged. The object of the competition was to select a chief architect who would oversee the master plan and also build the structuring elements of the park. Artists, landscape designers, and other architects were to contribute a variety of gardens or buildings.

Systems and Superimpositions

Our project was motivated by the fact that the site is not "virgin land," but is located in a populated semi-industrial quarter, and includes two enormous existing structures, the Museum of Science and Technology and the Grande Halle. Rejecting the idea of introducing another mass, even of a linear character, into an already encumbered terrain and respecting the extensive requirements of the program, we proposed a simple structural solution: to distribute the programmatic requirements over the total site in a regular arrangement of points of intensity, designated as *Folies*. Deconstructing the program into intense areas of activity placed according to existing site characteristics and use, this scheme permits maximum movement through the site, emphasizing discoveries and presenting visitors with a variety of programs and events.

Developments in architecture are generally related to cultural developments motivated by new functions, social relations, or technological advances. We have taken this as axiomatic for our scheme, which aims to constitute itself as image, as structural model, and as a paradigmatic example of architectural organization. Proper to a period that has seen the rise of mass production, serial repetition, and disjunction, this concept for the park consists of a series of related neutral objects whose very similarity allows them to be "qualified" by function. Thus, in its basic structure each *Folie* is bare, undifferentiated, and "industrial" in character; in the specialization of its program it is complex, articulated, and weighted with meaning. Each *Folie* constitutes an autonomous sign that indicates its independent programmatic concerns and possibilities while suggesting, through a common structural core, the unity of the total system. This interplay of theme and variation allows the park to read symbolically *and* structurally, while permitting maximum programmatic flexibility and invention.

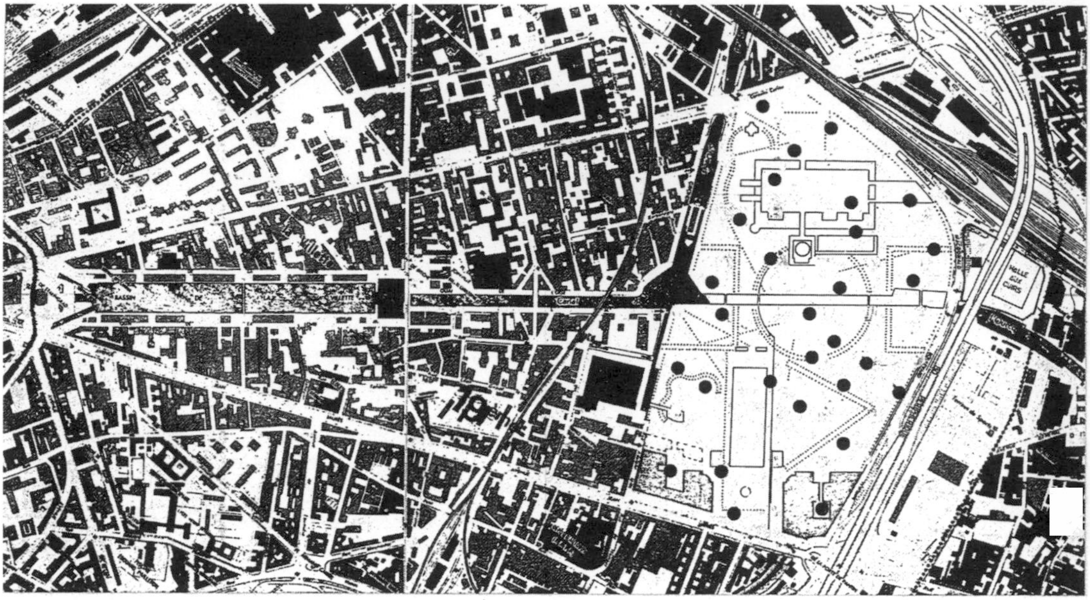

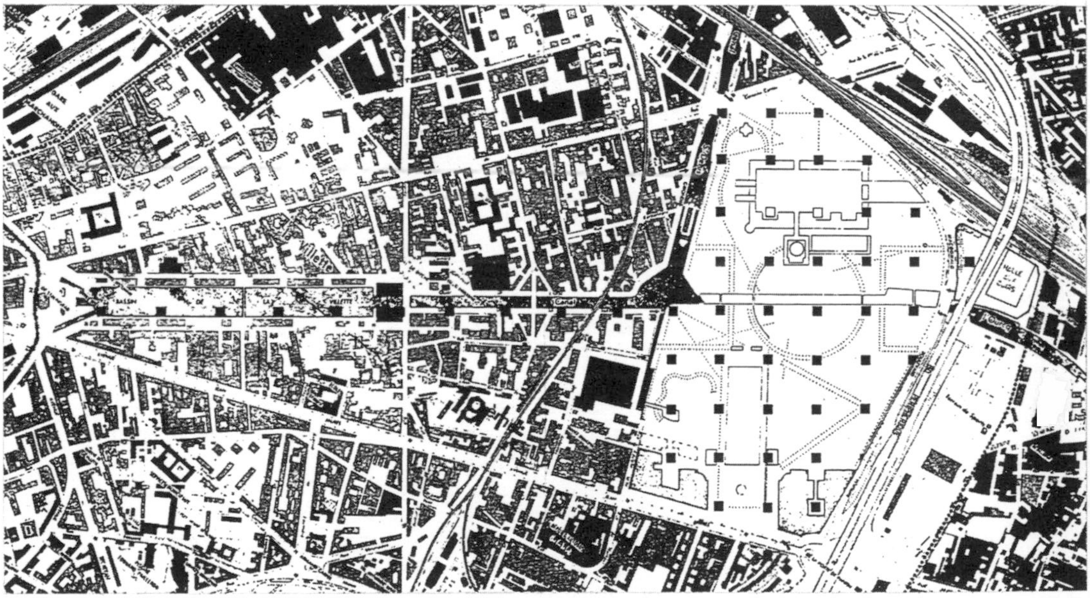

Points of intensity

An Urban Park for the 21st Century (Competition Document)

The competition for the Parc de la Villette is the first in recent architectural history to set forth a new program—that of the "Urban Park," proposing that the juxtaposition and combination of a variety of activities will encourage new attitudes and perspectives. This program represents an important breakthrough. The 70s witnessed a period of renewed interest in the formal constitution of the city, its typologies and morphologies. While developing analyses focused on the history of the city, this attention was largely devoid of programmatic justification. No analysis addressed the issue of the activities that were to occur in the city. Nor did any properly address the fact that the organization of functions and events was as much an architectural concern as the elaboration of forms or styles.

The Parc de la Villette, in contrast, represents an open-air cultural center, encouraging an integrated programmatic policy related both to the city's needs and to its limitations. The program allocates space for workshops, gymnasium and bath facilities, playgrounds, exhibitions, concerts, scientific experiments, games and competitions, in addition to a Museum of Science and Technology and a City of Music. The park could be conceived as one of the largest *buildings* ever constructed—a discontinuous building, but nevertheless a single structure, overlapping in certain areas with the city and existing suburbs. It forms an embryonic model of what the new programs for the 21st century will be.

During the 20th century we have witnessed a shift in the *concept* of the park, which can no longer be separated from the concept of the city. *The park forms part of the vision of the city.* The fact that Paris concentrates tertiary or professional employment argues against passive "esthetic" parks of repose in favor of new urban parks based on cultural invention, education, and entertainment. The inadequacy of the civilization vs. nature polarity under modern city conditions has invalidated the time-honored prototype of the park as an image of nature. It can no longer be conceived as an undefiled utopian world-in-miniature, protected from vile reality.

What we see, then, is the exhaustion of the "open space" concept faced with the *reality* of the cultural park. Hence we oppose the notion of Olmsted, widespread throughout the 19th century, that "in the park, the city is not supposed to exist." To create false hills hiding the Périphérique ignores the power of urban reality.

A New Model

We propose, instead, a distinctive and innovative kind of park, embodying a change in social context. Extending the radical shift in ideology implicit in the program, our ambition goes beyond producing a variation on an existing type by altering one of its components. We aim neither to change styles while retaining a traditional content, nor to fit the proposed program into a conventional mold, whether neo-classical, neo-romantic, or neo-modernist. Rather, our project is motivated by the most constructive principle within the legitimate "history" of architecture, by which new programmatic developments and inspirations result in new typologies. Our ambition is to create a new *model* in which program, form, and ideology all play integral roles.

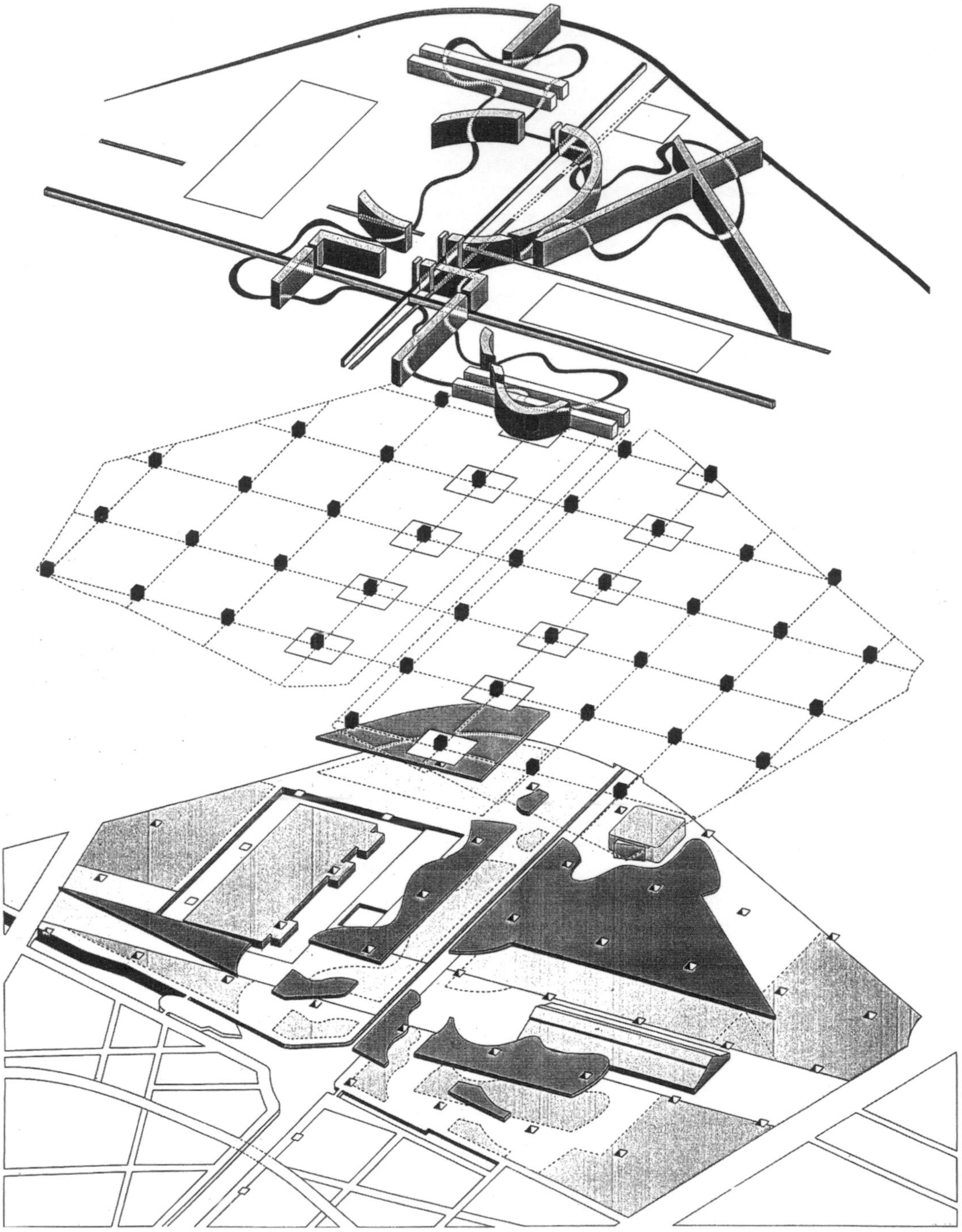

Points Lines Surfaces

(a)	Points	point-like activities
(b)	Lines	linear activities
(c)	Surfaces	surface activities

1. Points

The *Folies* are placed according to a point-grid coordinate system at 120-meter intervals. They provide a common denominator for all events generated by the program. Each is essential to the program. Each is basically a 10 x 10 x 10 meter cube, or a three-story construction of neutral space, that can be transformed and elaborated according to specific programmatic needs.

The strict repetition of the basic 10 x 10 x 10 meter *Folie* is aimed at developing a clear *symbol* for the park, a recognizable identity as strong as the British telephone booth or the Paris Metro gates.

The advantages of this grid system are manifold. It is by far the simplest system establishing territorial recognition and one that is easily implemented. It lends itself to easy maintenance. The structure provides a comprehensive image or shape for an otherwise ill-defined terrain. The regularity of routes and positioning makes orientation simple for those unfamiliar with the area. The advantage of the point-grid system is that it provides for the *minimum adequate equipment* of the urban park relative to the number of its visitors.

2. Lines

The *Folie* grid is related to a larger coordinate structure (the Coordinates), an orthogonal system of high-density pedestrian movement that marks the site with a cross. The North-South Passage or Coordinate links the two Paris gates and subway stations of Porte de la Villette and Porte de Pantin; the East-West Coordinate joins Paris to its suburbs. A five-meter-wide, open, covered structure runs the length of both Coordinates. Organized around the Coordinates so as to facilitate and encourage access are *Folies* designated for the most frequented activities: the City of Music, restaurants, Square of the Baths, art and science displays, children's playgrounds, video workshops and Sports Center.

The Line system also includes the *Path of Thematic Gardens*, the seemingly random curvilinear route that links various parts of the park in the form of a carefully-planned circuit. The Path of Thematic Gardens intersects the Coordinate axes at various places, providing unexpected encounters with unusual aspects of domesticated or "programmed" nature.

3. Surfaces

The *surfaces* of the park receive all activities requiring large expanses of horizontal space for play, games, body exercises, mass entertainment, markets, etc. Each surface is programmatically determined. So-called left-over surfaces (when every aspect of the program has been fulfilled) are composed of compacted earth and gravel, a park material familiar to all Parisians. Earth and gravel surfaces allow for complete programmatic freedom.

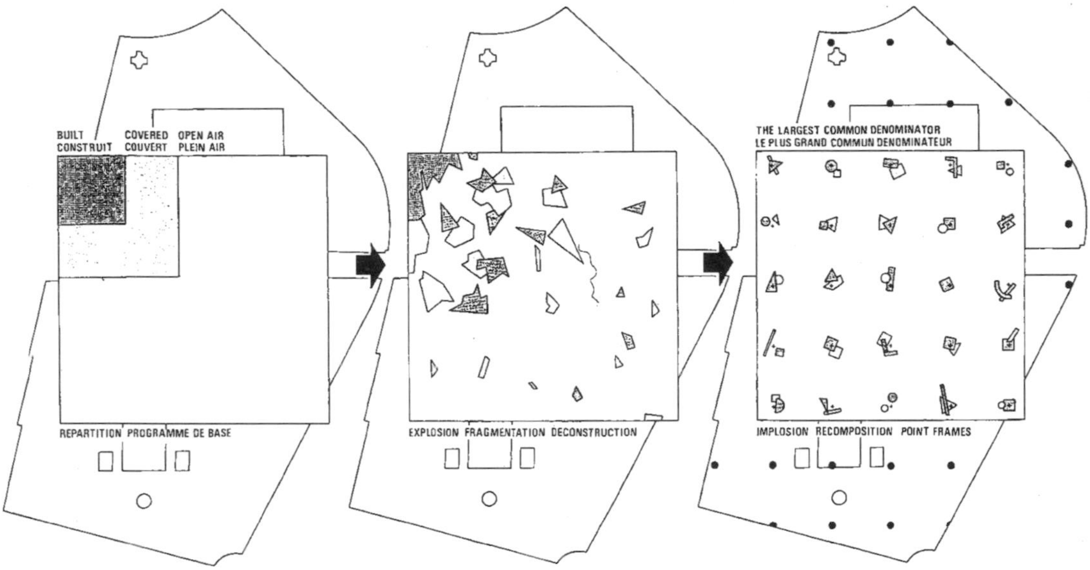

DECONSTRUCTION PROGRAMMATIQUE: LE PLUS GRAND COMMUN DENOMINATEUR = LA FOLIE

A simple structural solution: exploding programmatic requirements throughout the site onto a regular grid of points of intensity. Hence, the different types of activities are first isolated and then distributed on the site, often encouraging the combination of apparently incompatible activities. (e.g., "The running track passes through the piano-bar inside the tropical greenhouse.")

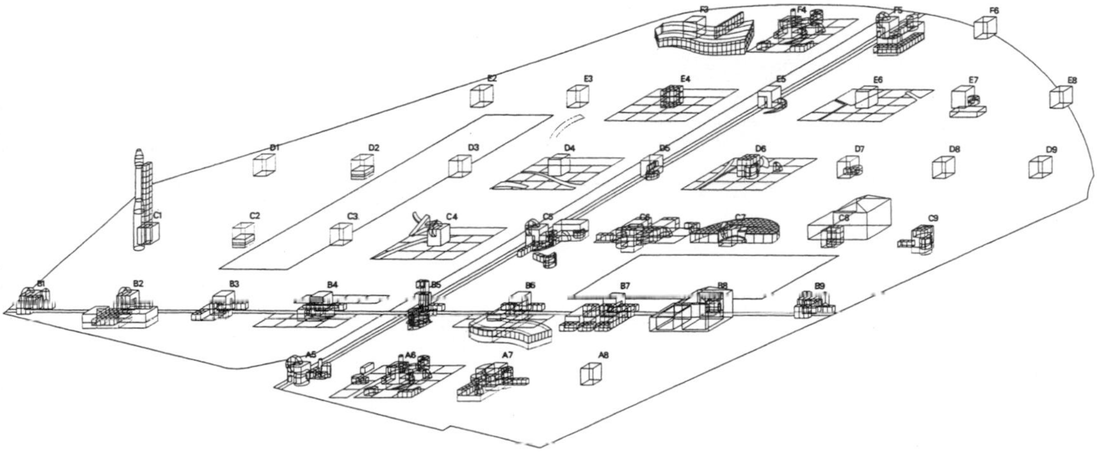

Distribution of built masses throughout the site: the folies are both singular points and anchoring points of possible future constructions

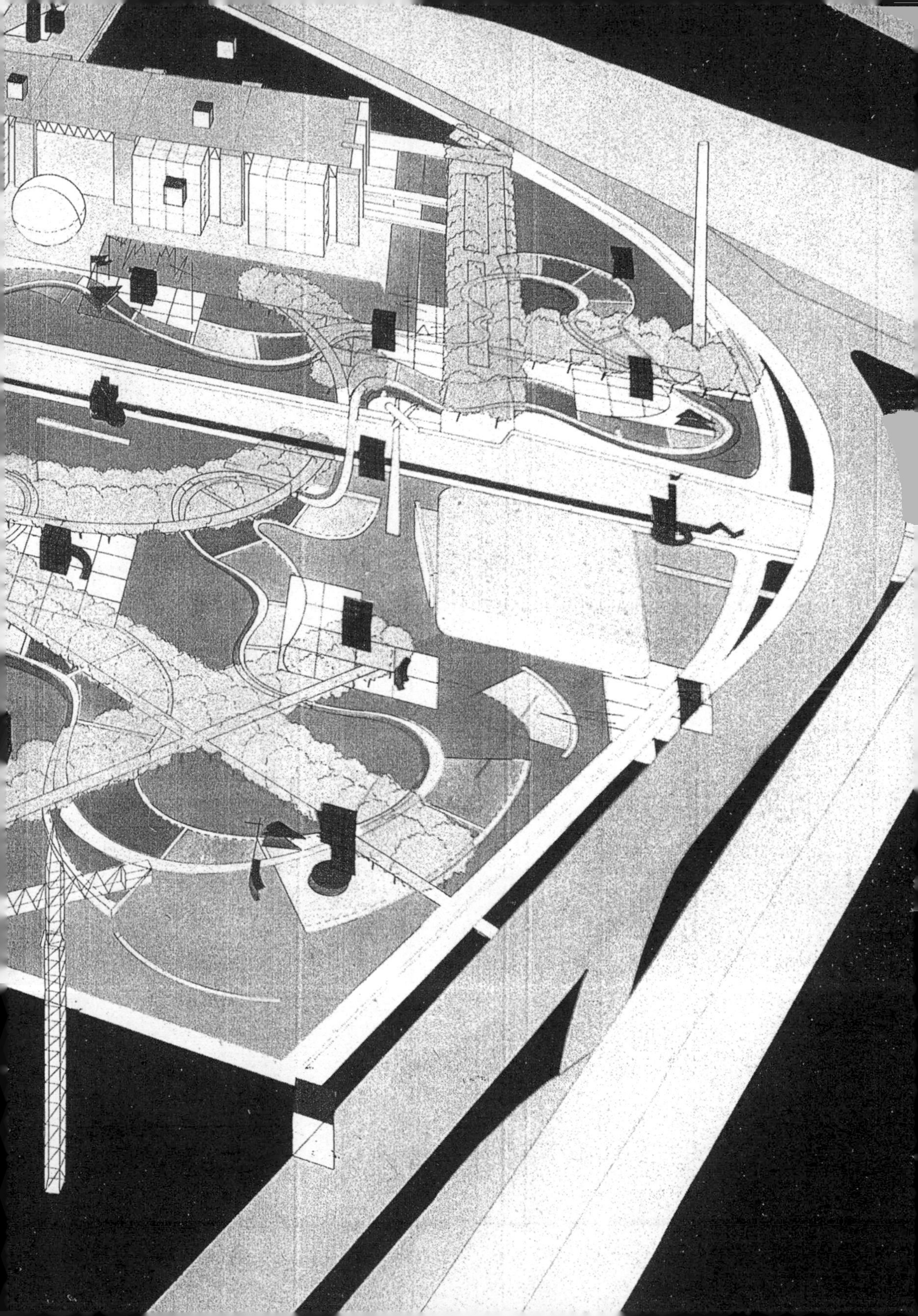

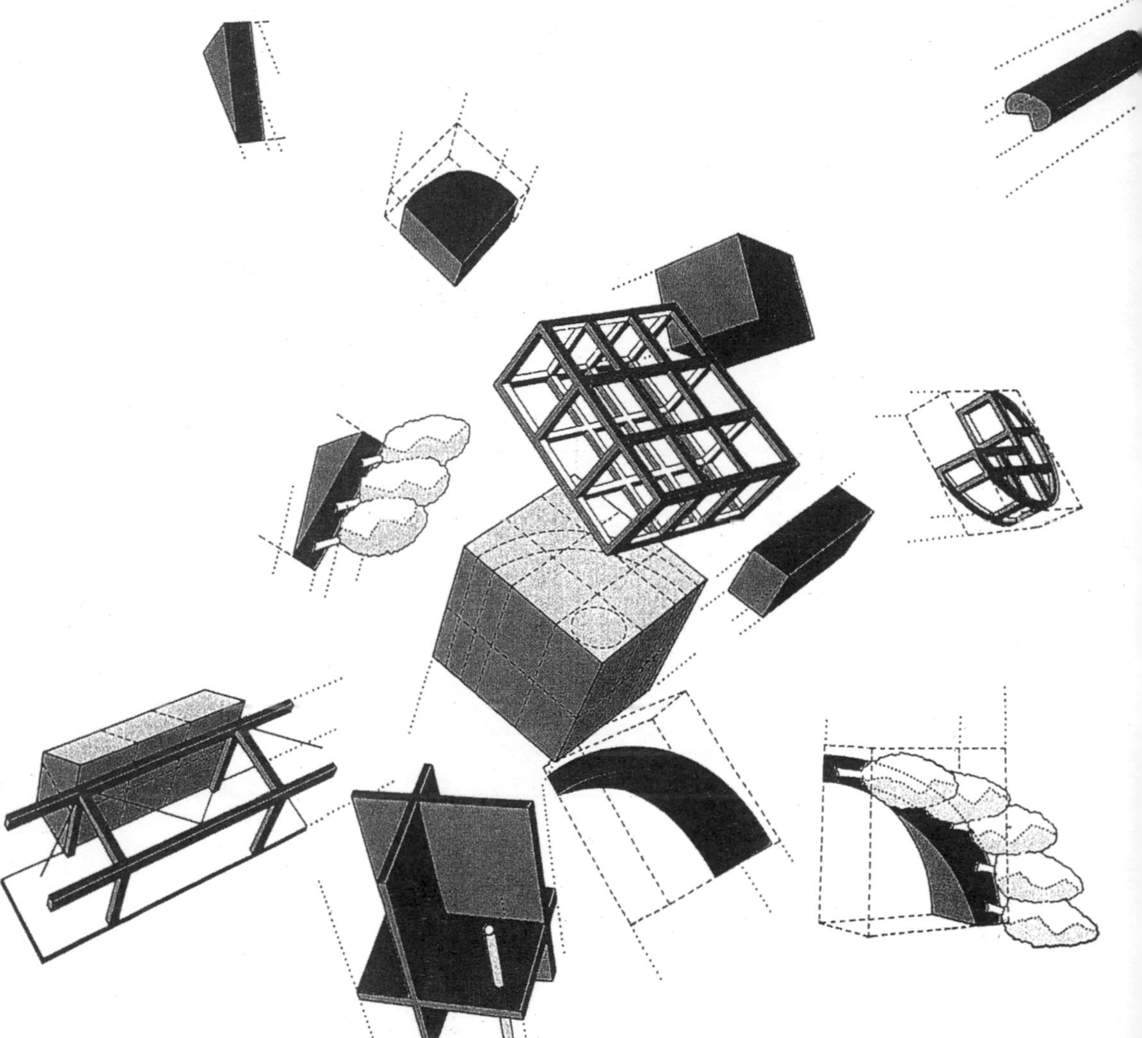

Structural System of the Folies

All of the *Folies* use the same repetitive system, based on a 10.8 meter by 10.8 meter (36 x 36 x 36 foot) cube. The cube is then divided in three in each direction, forming a cage with 3.6 meters (12 feet) between bars.

The cage can be decomposed into fragments of a cage, or extended through the addition of other elements (one- or two-story cylindrical or triangular volumes, stairs, ramps) according to a variety of combinatory principles, while simultaneously (and independently) confronting specific programmatic requirements. The primary structure (the cage) is composed of a frame that can be concrete or steel—or any other material, for that matter. The selection of the structural material is made according to fire code requirements or economic conditions. A red enameled-steel envelope covers every part of the structural frame. It is designed so as to solve every interior or exterior corner, cantilever or edge condition.

Although the *Folies* proceed from a simple construction principle, deviation alters the relationship to the structural grid. The grid then becomes a simple support around which a transgressive architecture can develop in relation to the original norm. The relationship between normality and deviation suggests a method for the elaboration of the *Folies*. First, requirements and constraints derived from the program are confronted with the architectonic combination and transformation principles of the project. The confrontation results in a basic architectural state: the "norm." Then, the norm is transgressed—without, however, disappearing. A distortion of the original norm results: deviation.

Deviation is both the excess of rationality and irrationality. As a norm, it contains the components of its own explosion. As a deviation, it frees them. Normality tends towards unity; deviation, towards heterogeneity and dissociation. This is not a coupling of opposites but, instead, a matter of degree. How are these degrees of deviation determined? Through economy, time, money, circumstances, client demands. A "normal" *Folie* is not built in the same manner as a "deviant" one.

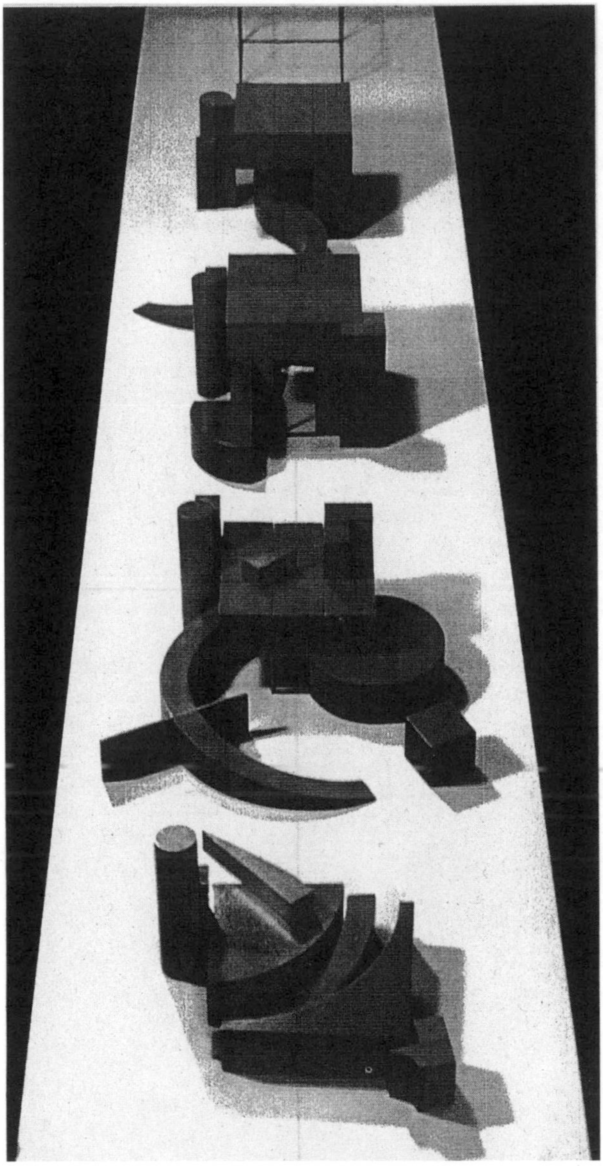

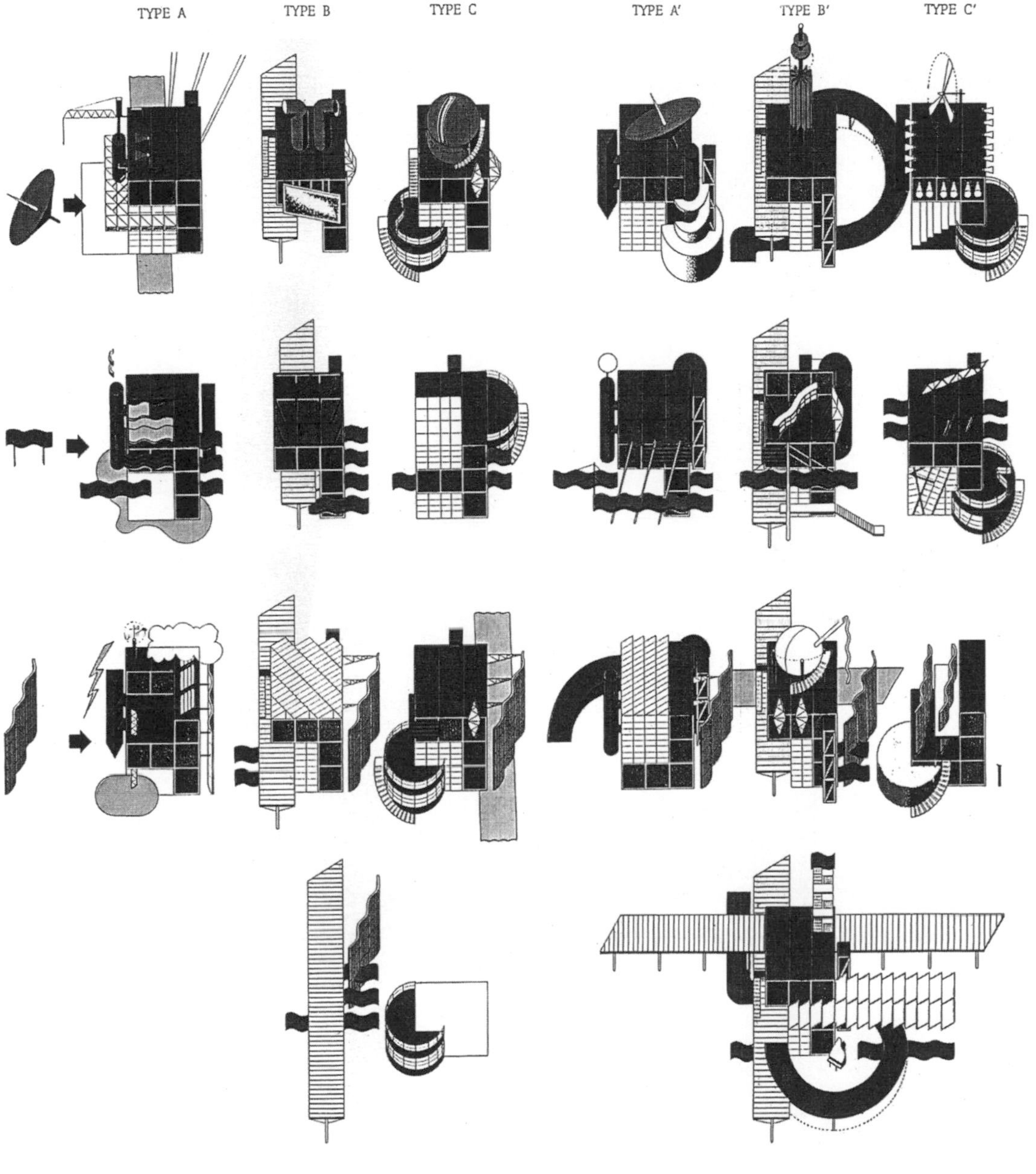

The normative

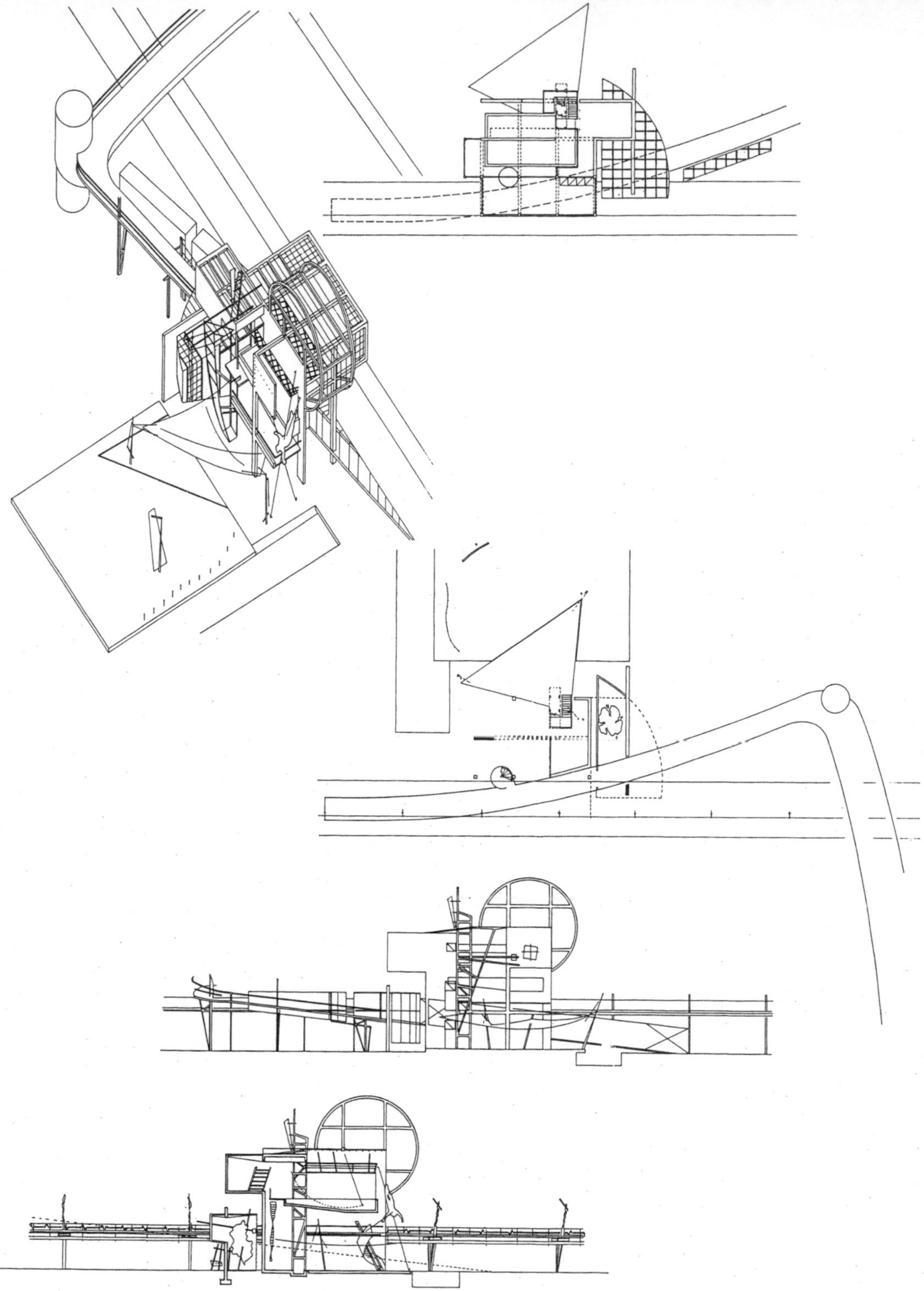

The derivation

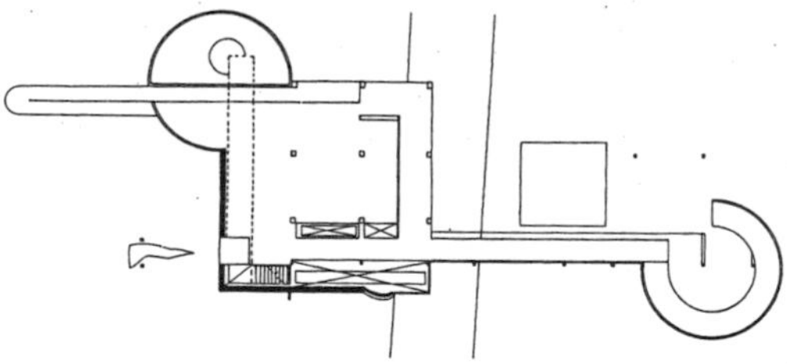

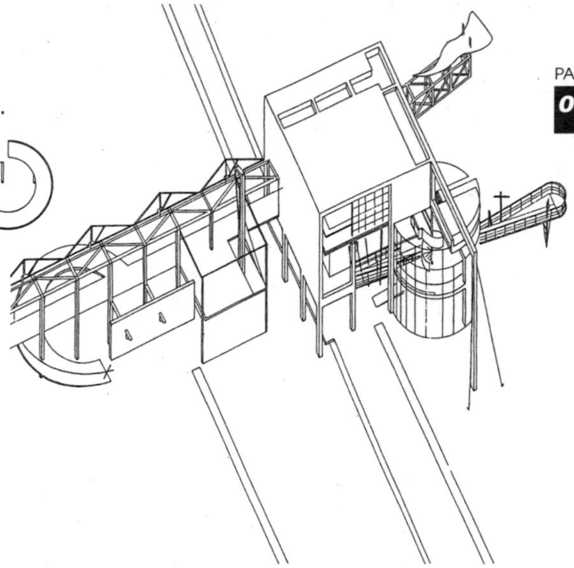

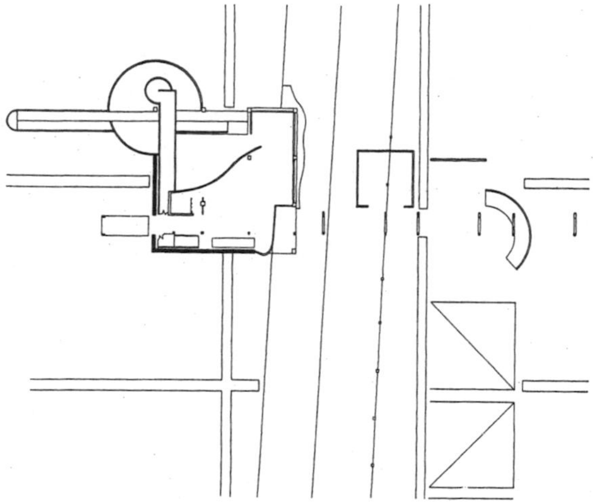

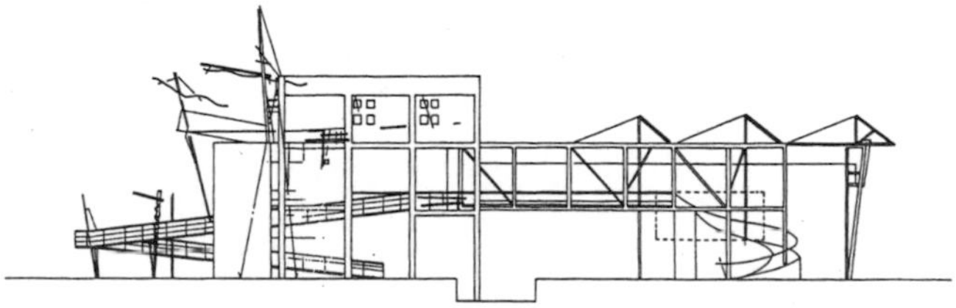

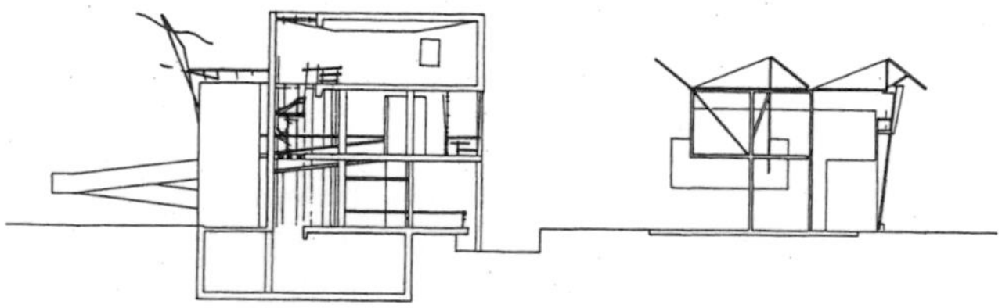

Folies: envelope, vectors, structure—a combinative

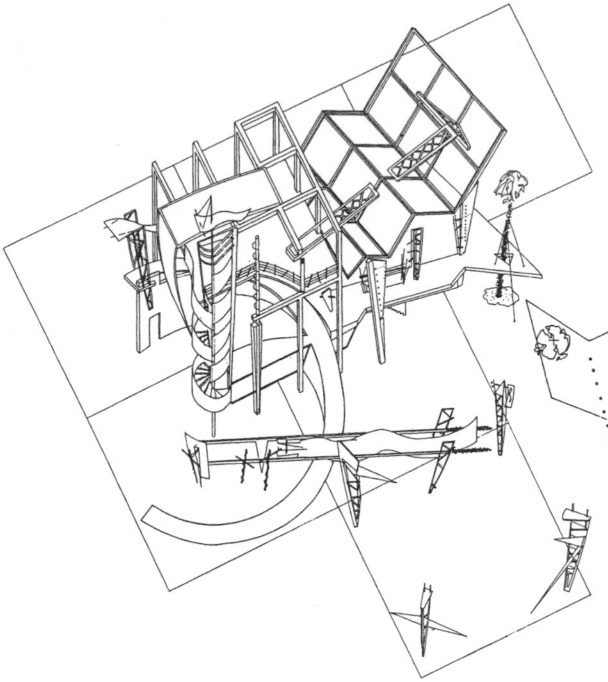

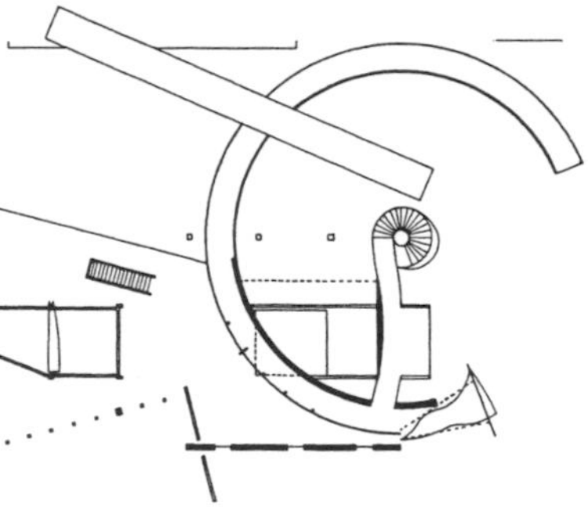

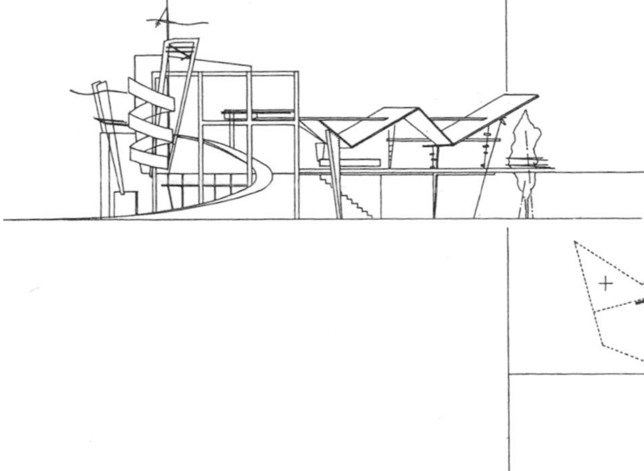

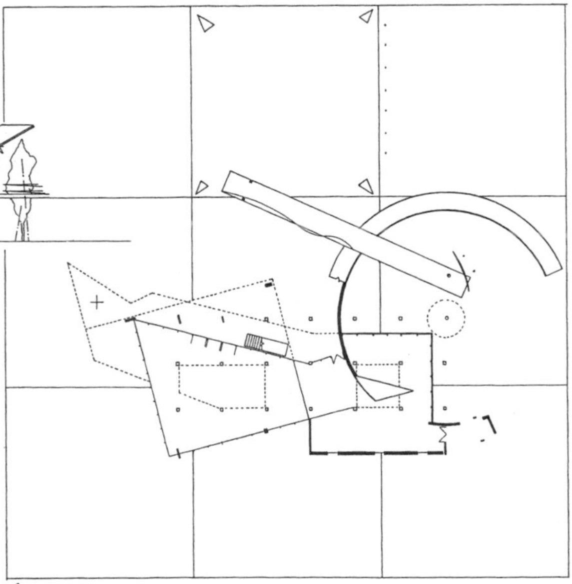

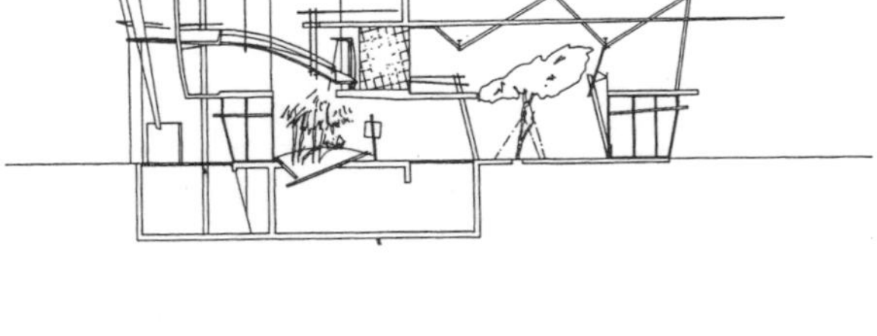

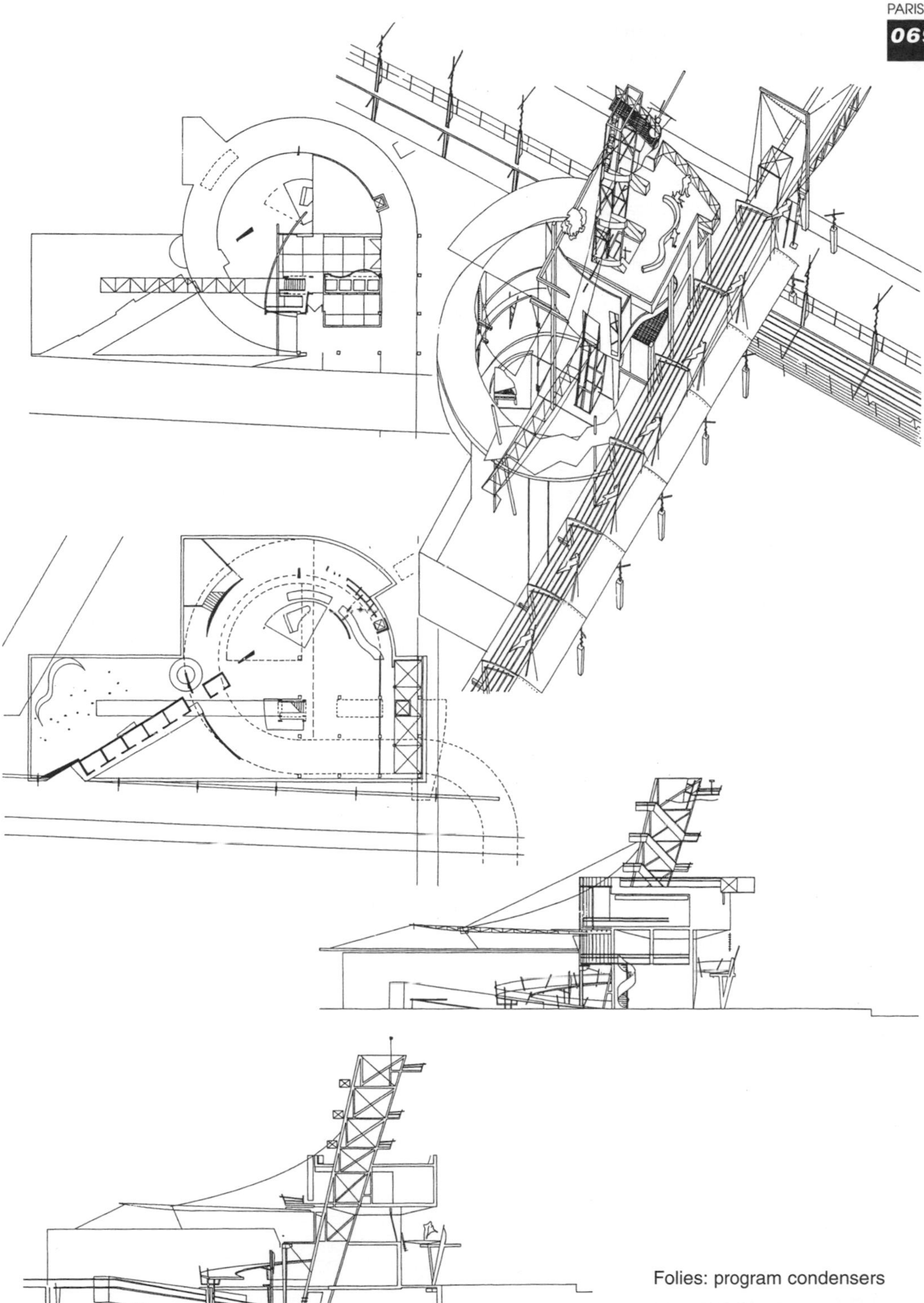

Folies: program condensers

Frames and Sequences

The Cinematic Promenade is one of the key features of the park. It is conceived along the analogy of a film strip, in which the sound-track corresponds to the general walkway for visitors and the image-track corresponds to the successive frames of individual gardens. The linearity of sequences orders events, movements, and spaces in a progression that either combines or parallels divergent concerns. Each part, each frame of a sequence qualifies, reinforces, or alters the parts that precede and follow it. The associations thus formed allow for a plurality of interpretations rather than a singular fact. Each part is thus both complete and incomplete. If the general structure of the sequence of gardens requires the indetermination of its content (hence the role of the chief architect as film director, overseeing the montage of sequences), its specific content implies determinacy (through the particular designs of individual designers). The park is also inhabited: sequences of events, use, activities, incidents are inevitably superimposed on those fixed spatial sequences. It suggests secret maps and impossible fictions, rambling collections of events all strung along a collection of spaces, frame after frame, garden after garden, episode after episode.

At La Villette, a frame means each of the segments of the sequence: in the cinematic promenade, each frame defines a garden. Each of these frames can be turned into a single piece of work.

The framing principle permits the arrangement of each part of the sequence since, as with the cinegrams of a film, each frame can be mixed, combined, superimposed, etc., infinitely. Moreover, the content of each frame can be shown from above or from below, producing unusual viewpoints. The spatial sequences at La Villette also can be seen independently from the meanings they may suggest. Their signification can be deduced directly from the events occurring in the sequence. (A row of slides, a sand box, and a roller-skating space undoubtedly imply a children's sequence.)

In literature and in the cinema, the relations between frames or sequences can be manipulated through devices such as flashbacks, jumpcuts, dissolves, and so on. Why not in architecture or in landscape? At La Villette, the cut between two garden sequences is established by means of an intersecting line of trees.

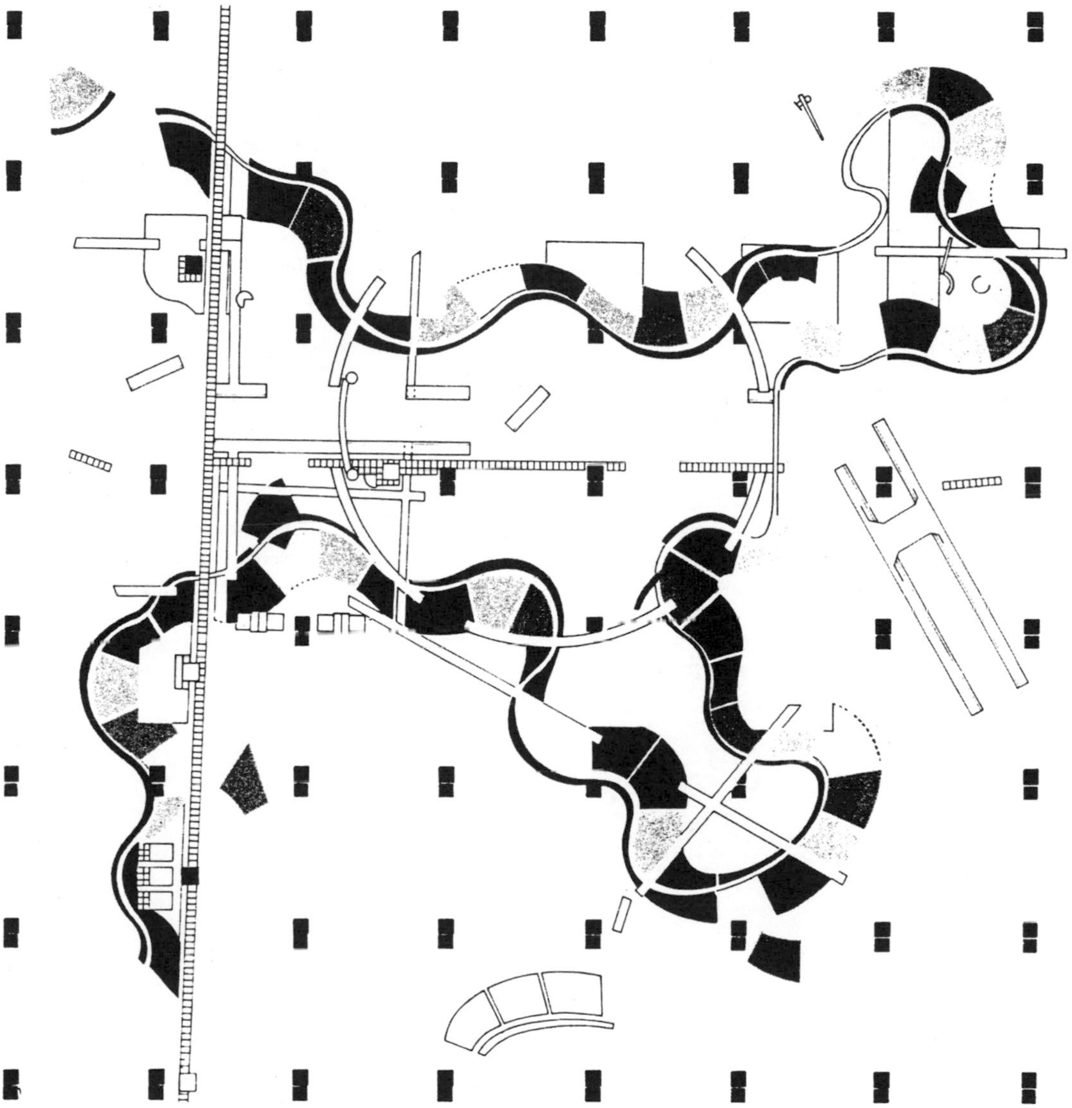

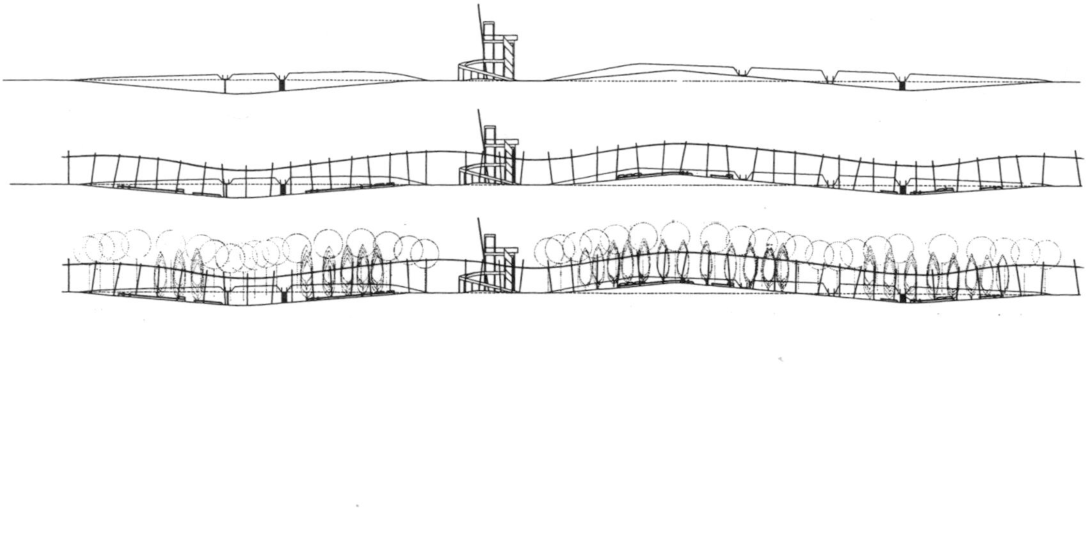

Vectors cutting through landscape

Accelerated movement, distended movement, slow time

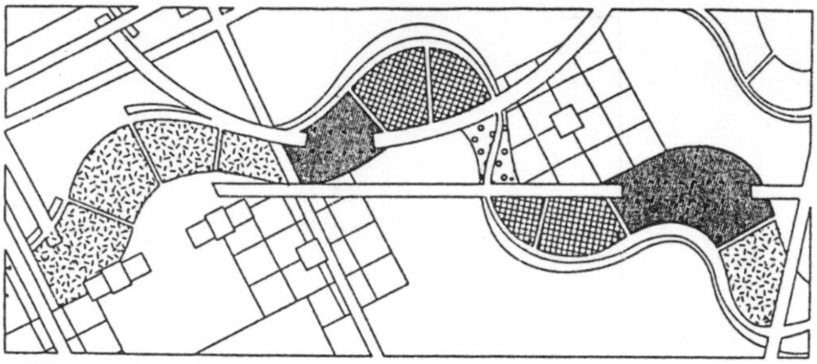

AMBIANCE
SPECTACLE
CENTRE DE JARDINAGE
JEUX

USAGE

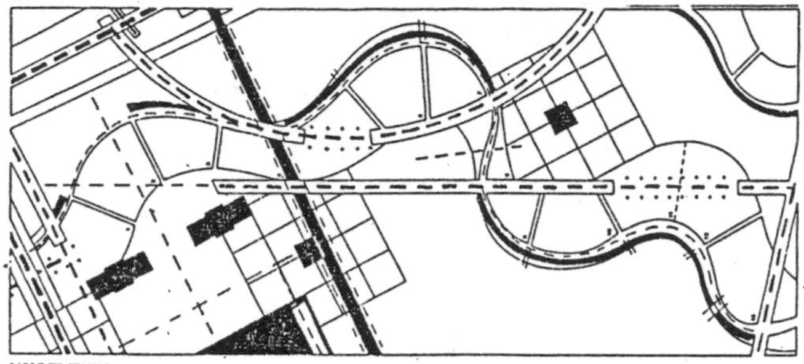

MOUVEMENTS
BARRIERES

MOUVEMENTS

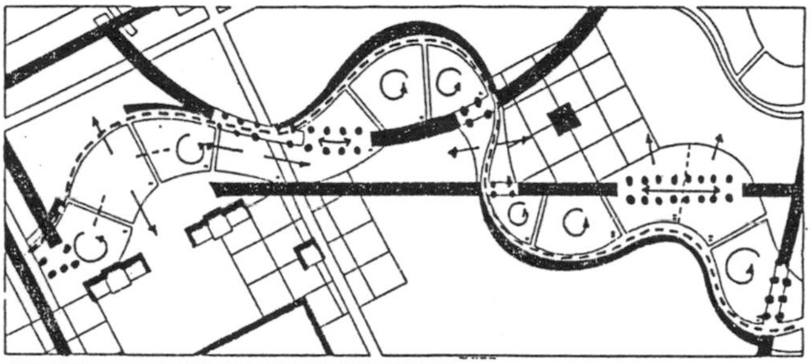

CONDITIONS SPATIALES DES JARDINS THEMATIQUES

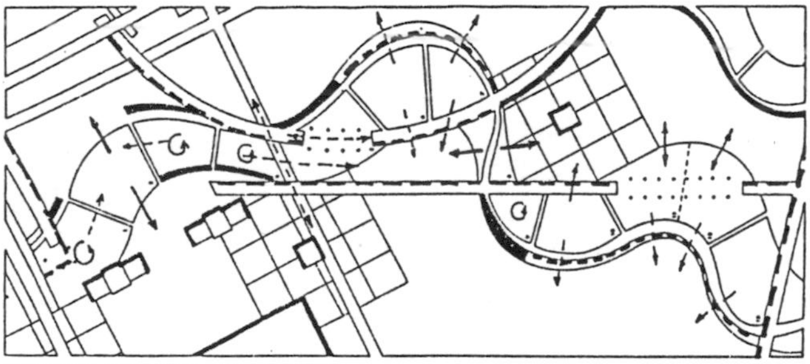

BARRIERES VISUELLES
TRANSPARENCES

RELATIONS VISUELLES INTERSPATIALES

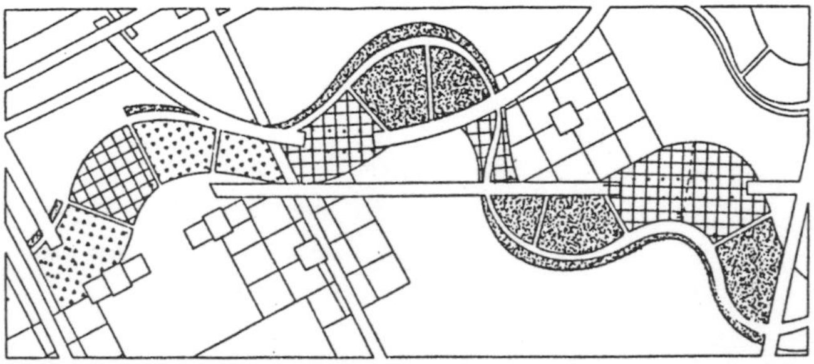

MINERAL
VEGETAL
MIXTE

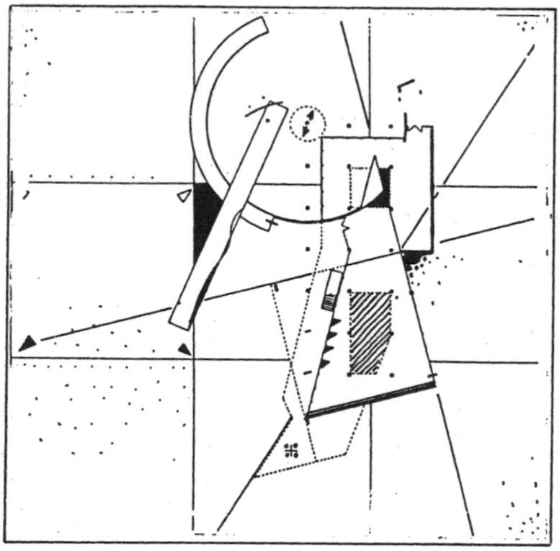

Superimpositions

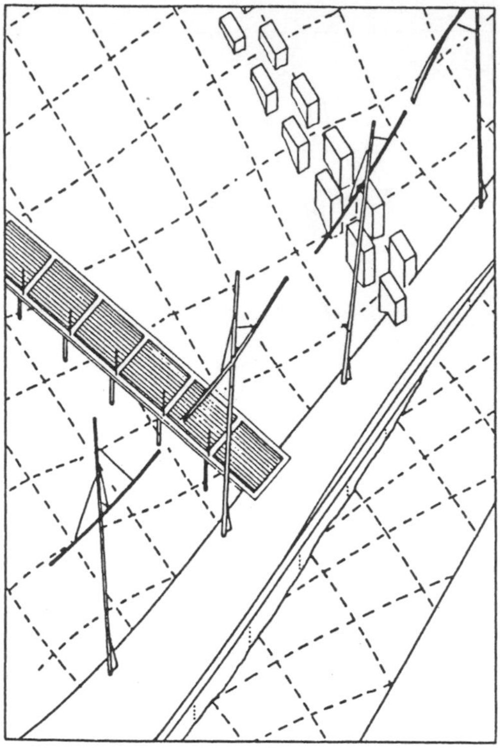

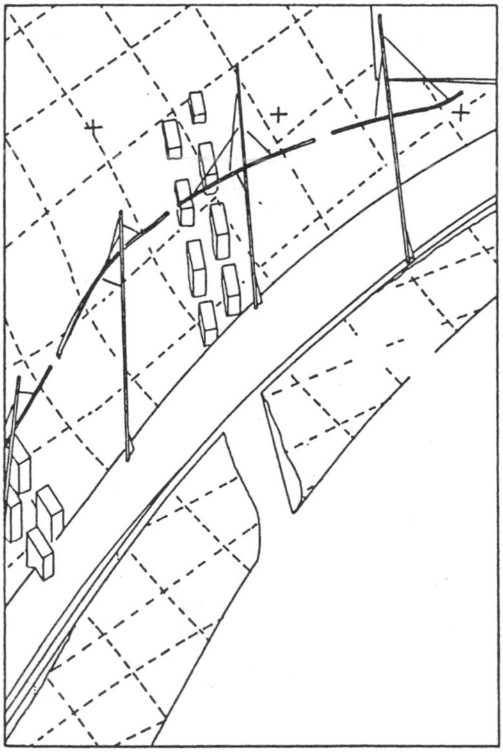

Juxtapositions

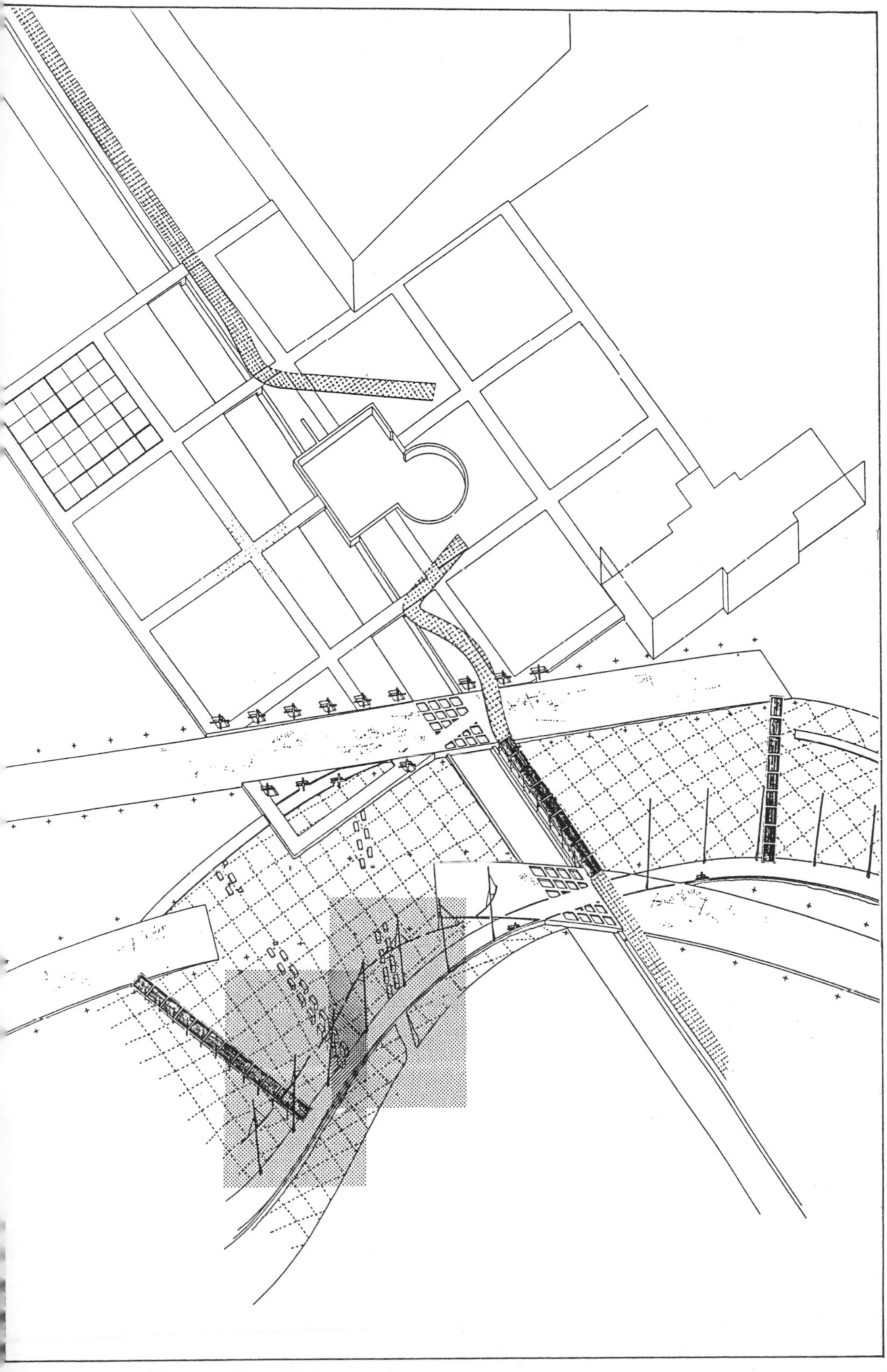

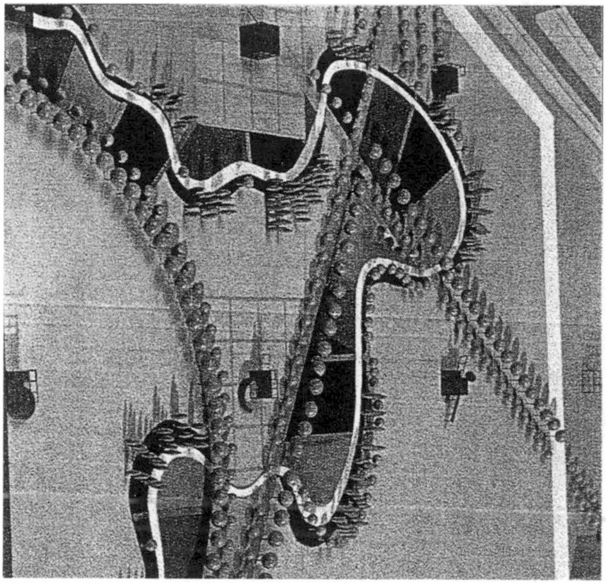

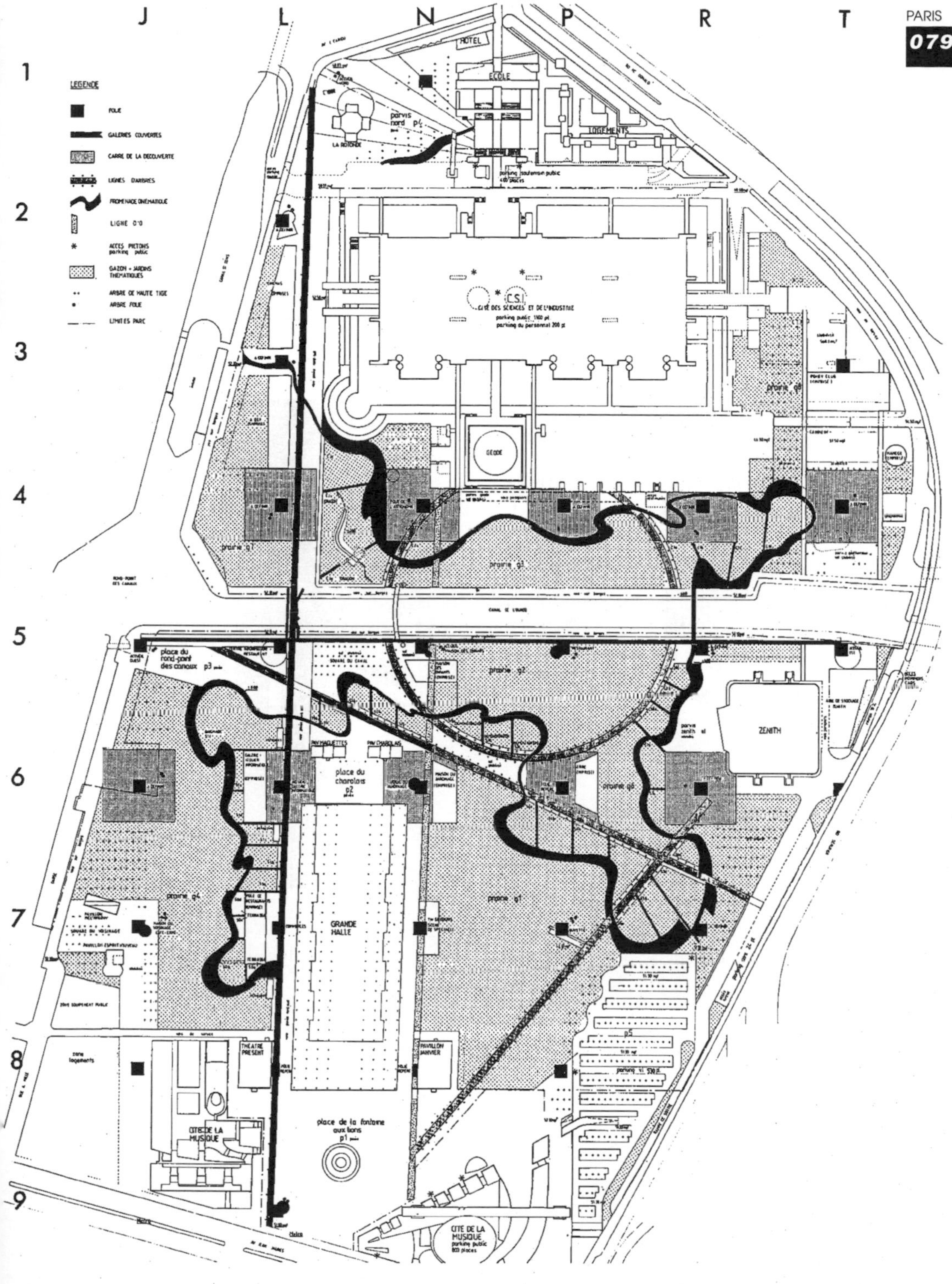
J
L
N
P
R
T
1
2
3
4
5
6
7
8
9
LEGENDE
FOLIE
GALERIES COUVERTES
CARRE DE LA DECOUVERTE
LIGNES D'ARBRES
PROMENADE CINEMATIQUE
ACCES PIETONS
parking public
GAZON + JARDINS THEMATIQUES
ARBRE DE HAUTE TIGE
ARBRE FOLIE
LIMITES PARC
HOTEL
ECOLE
LOGEMENTS
parvis nord p4
LA ROTONDE
C.S.I.
CITE DES SCIENCES ET DE L'INDUSTRIE
parking public 1600 pl
parking du personnel 200 pl
GEODE
prairie g3
prairie g7
CANAL DE L'OURCQ
place du rond-point des canaux p3
prairie g2
ZENITH
PAV MAQUETTES
PAV CHAROLAIS
place du charolais p2
prairie g4
prairie g1
GRANDE HALLE
zone logements
THEATRE PRESENT
PAVILLON JANVIER
p5
CITE DE LA MUSIQUE
place de la fontaine aux lions p1
CITE DE LA MUSIQUE
parking public
800 places

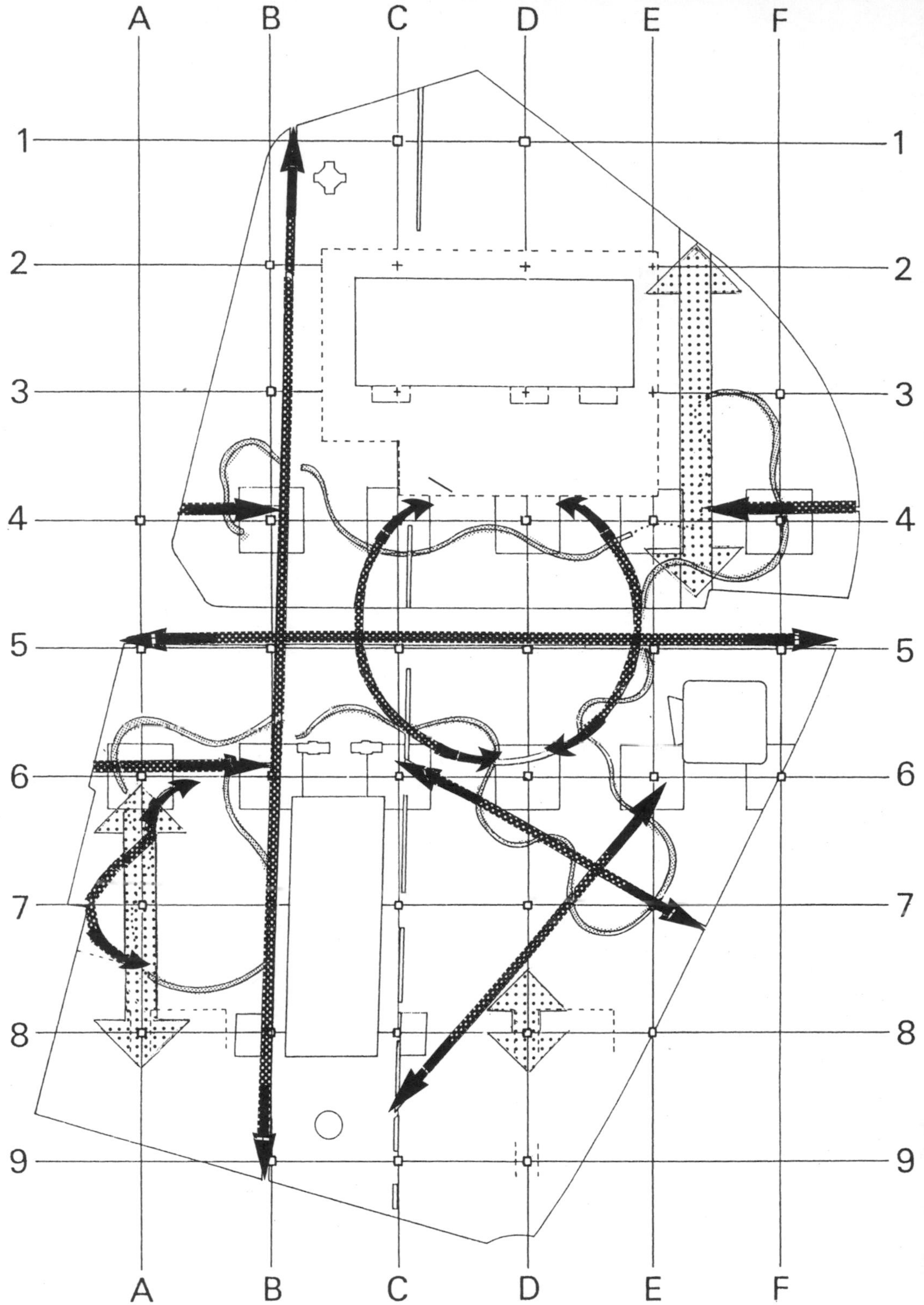

System of lines: vectors

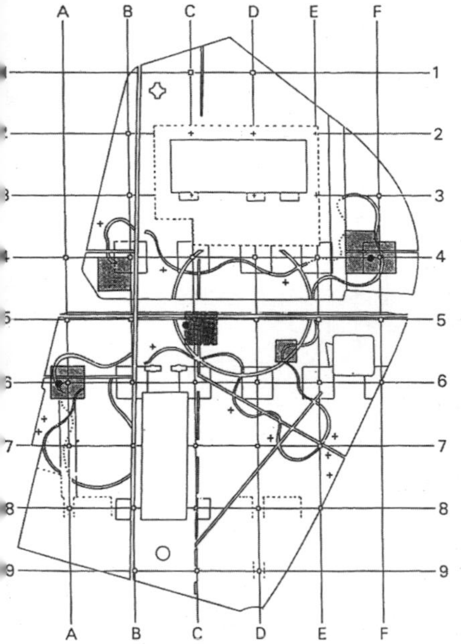

● MAISON DES ENFANTS

A6 : Quartier
C5 : Parc
F4 : Sésame Place

ESPACES JEUX ENFANTS

ESPACES JEUX D'EAU

+ JEUX D'ENFANTS PONCTUELS
(emplacement exact à étudier)

ENFANTS

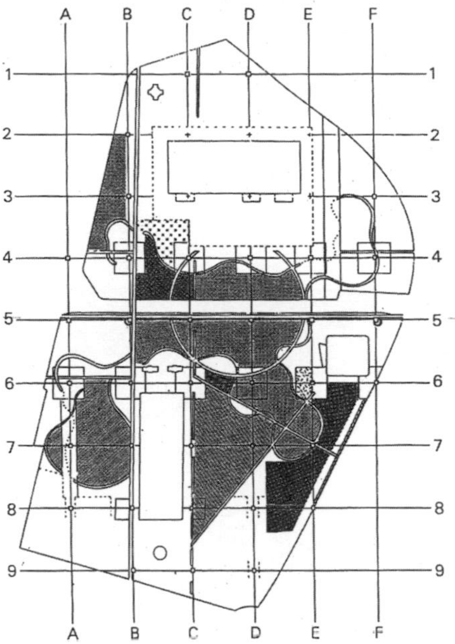

PISTE DE JOGGING

PRAIRIES

SURFACES SPORTIVES

PATINOIRE

PATIN À ROULETTES

ACTIVITES DE PLEIN-AIR

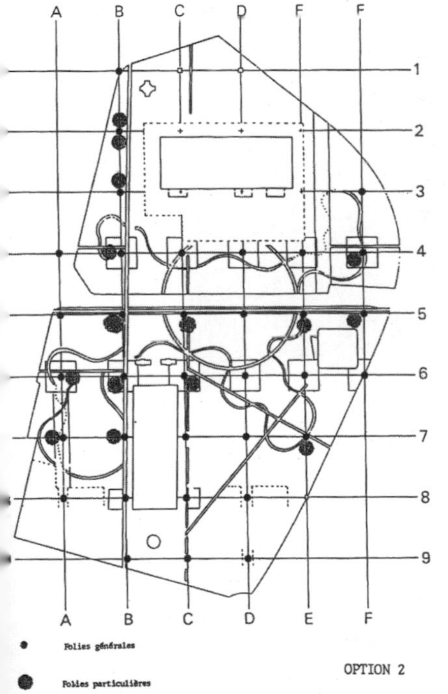

● Folies générales

● Folies particulières

● Folies particulières .
évent. réalisées par la MOG

OPTION 2

Dans le cas de l'Option 2.
nous pouvons considérer 13 à 17 MOP.

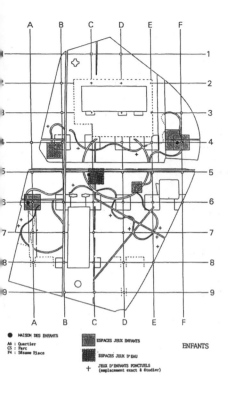

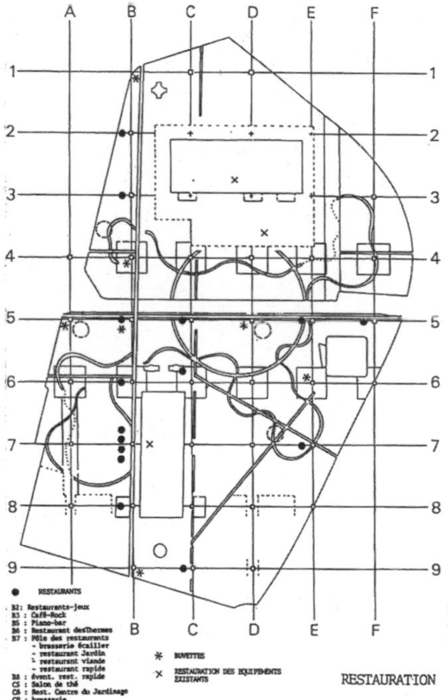

● RESTAURANTS

B2: Restaurants-jeux
B3 : Café-Rock
B5 : Piano-bar
B6 : Restaurant desThermes
B7 : Pôle des restaurants
- brasserie écailler
- restaurant Jardin
- restaurant viande
- restaurant rapide
B8 : évent. rest. rapide
C5 : Salon de thé
C6 : Rest. Centre du Jardinage
C9 : brasserie
E5 : Café-vidéo
E7 : év. centre des cuisines diversifiées

* BUVETTES

× RESTAURATION DES EQUIPEMENTS EXISTANTS

RESTAURATION

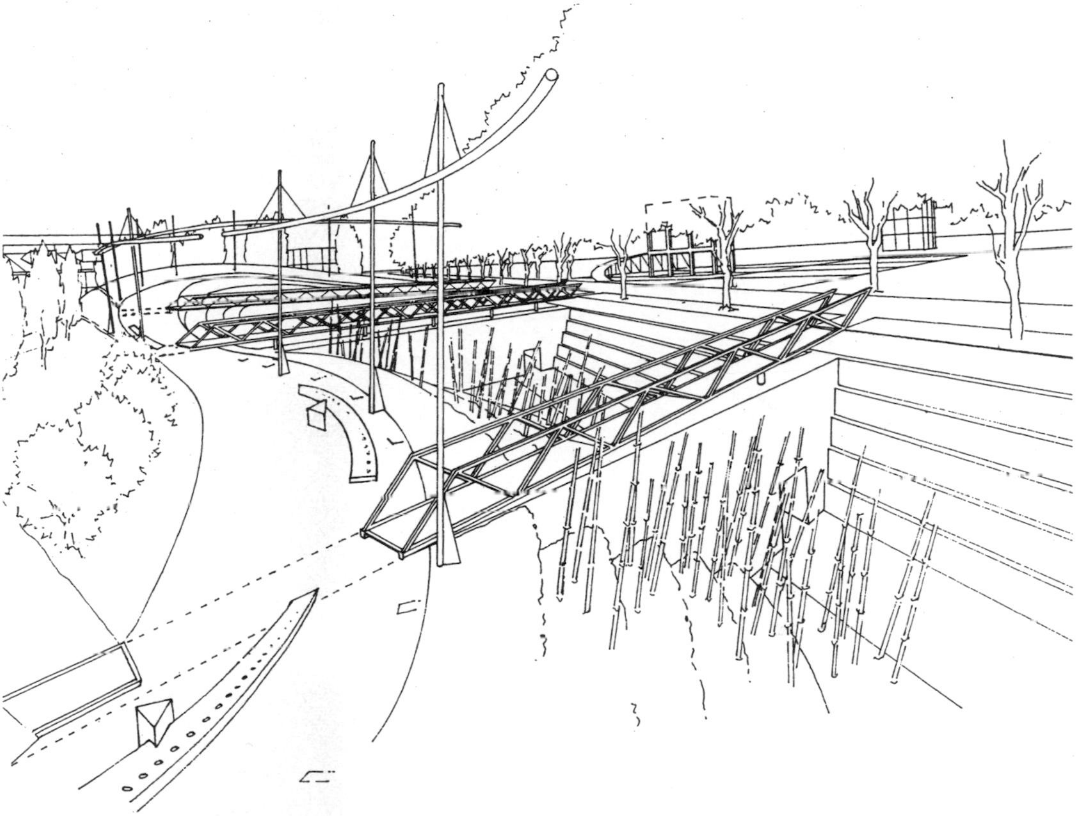

Sequence 4 (Bamboo Garden)

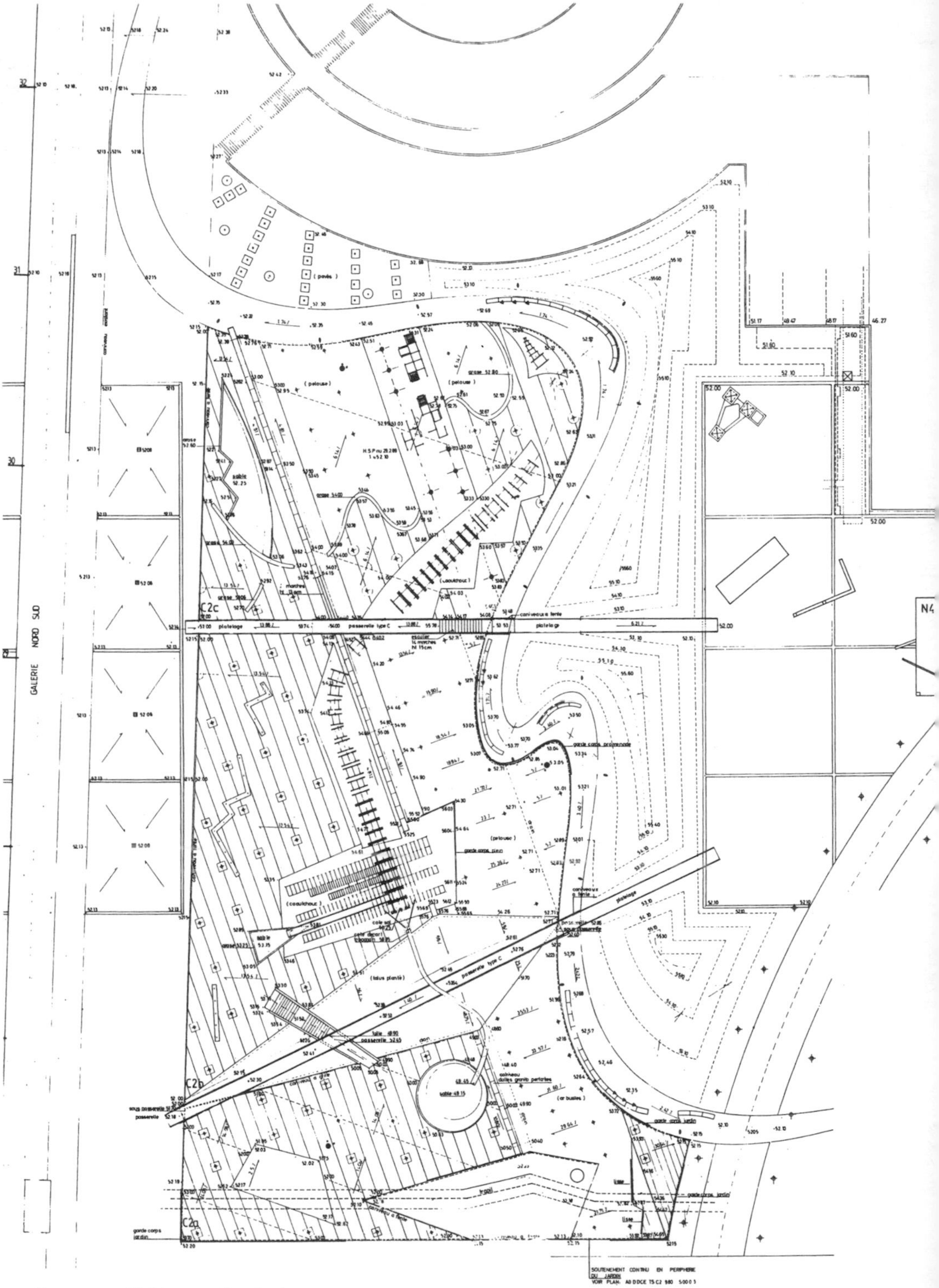

Sequence 10 (Dragon Garden)

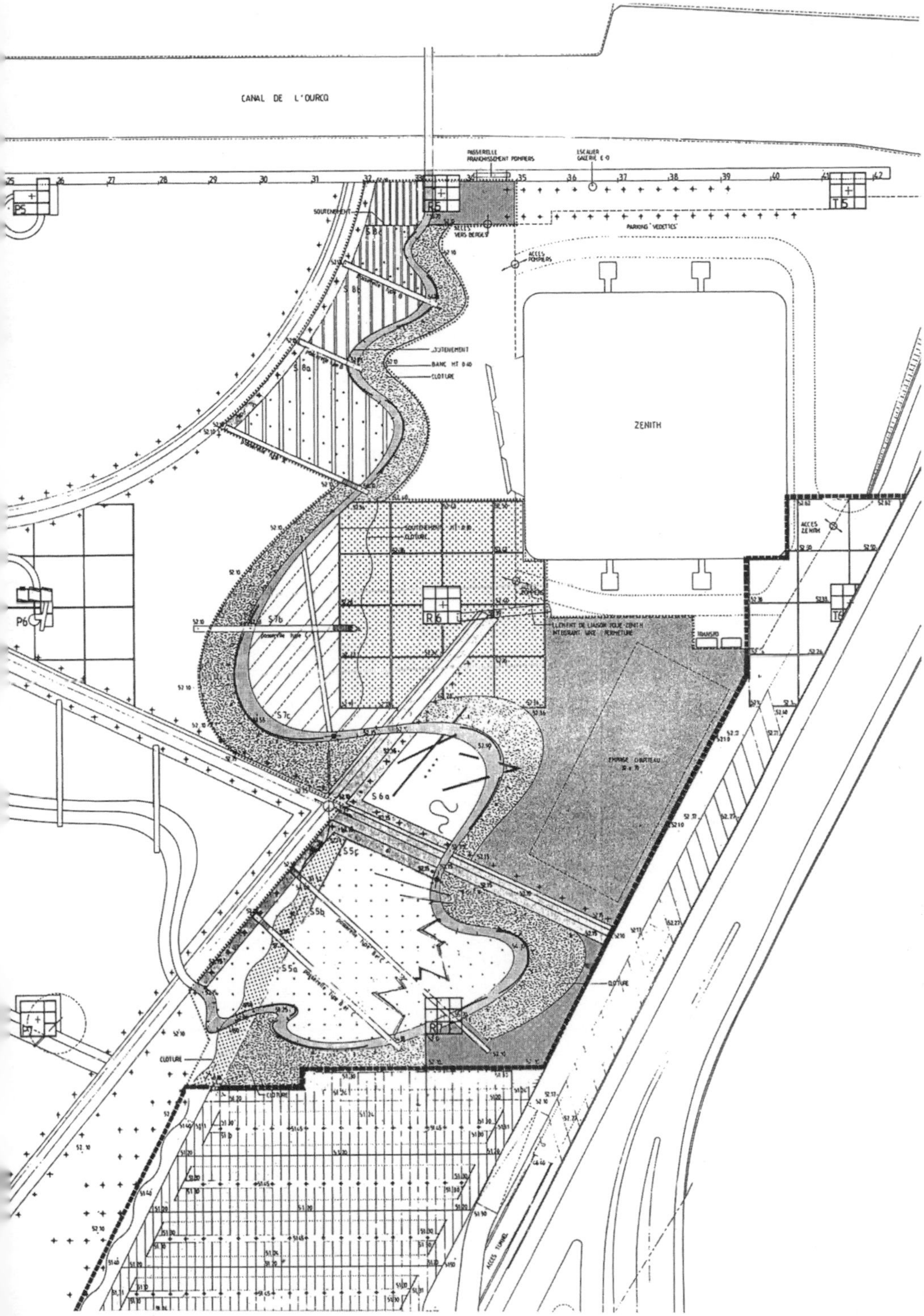

Sequences 6 and 7

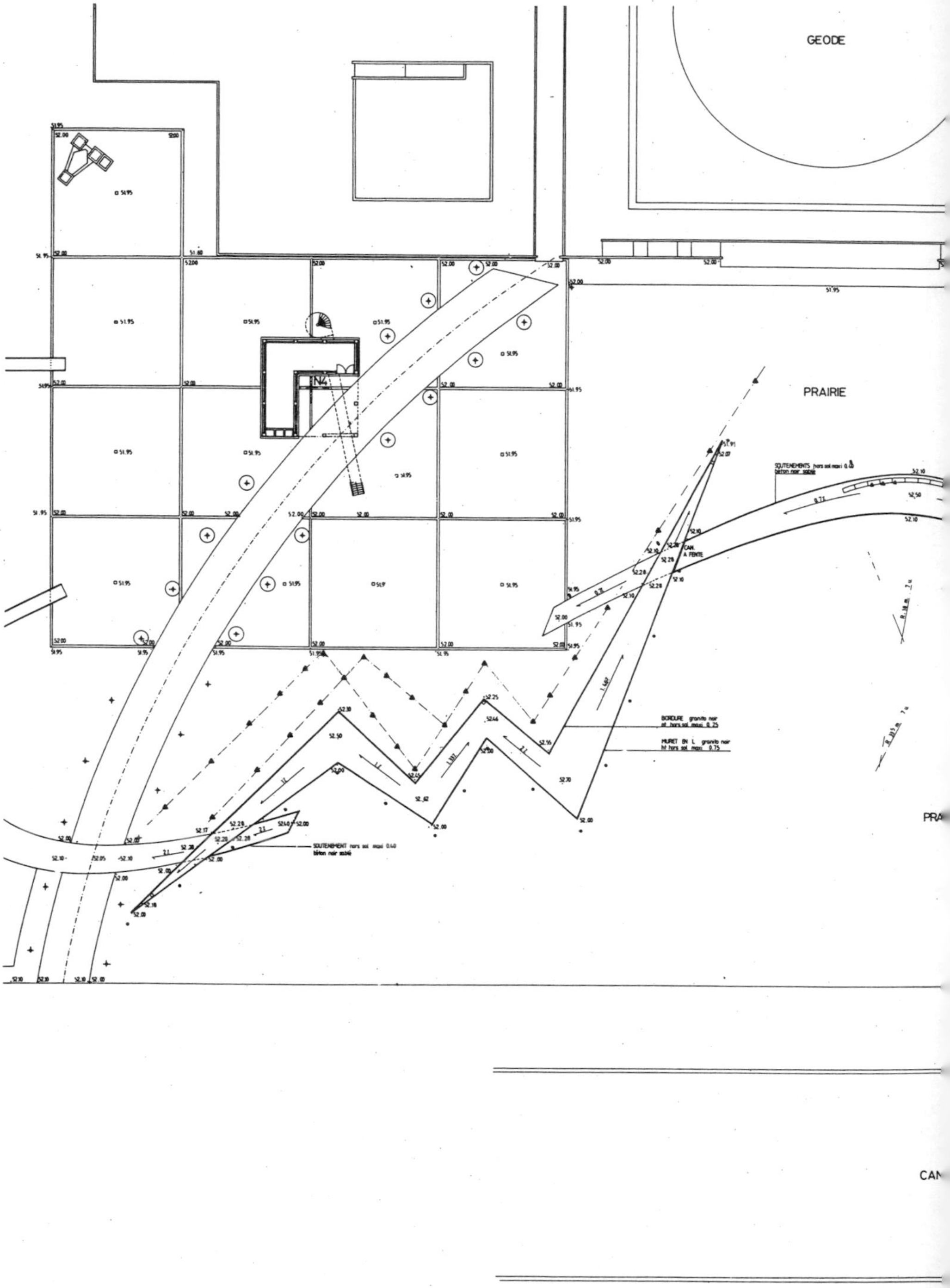
GEODE
PRAIRIE
SOUTENEMENTS hors sol maxi 0.40
béton noir sablé
CAN.
A FENTE
BORDURE granito noir
ht hors sol maxi 0.25
MURET EN L granito noir
ht hors sol maxi 0.75
SOUTENEMENT hors sol maxi 0.40
béton noir sablé
N4
PRA
CAN

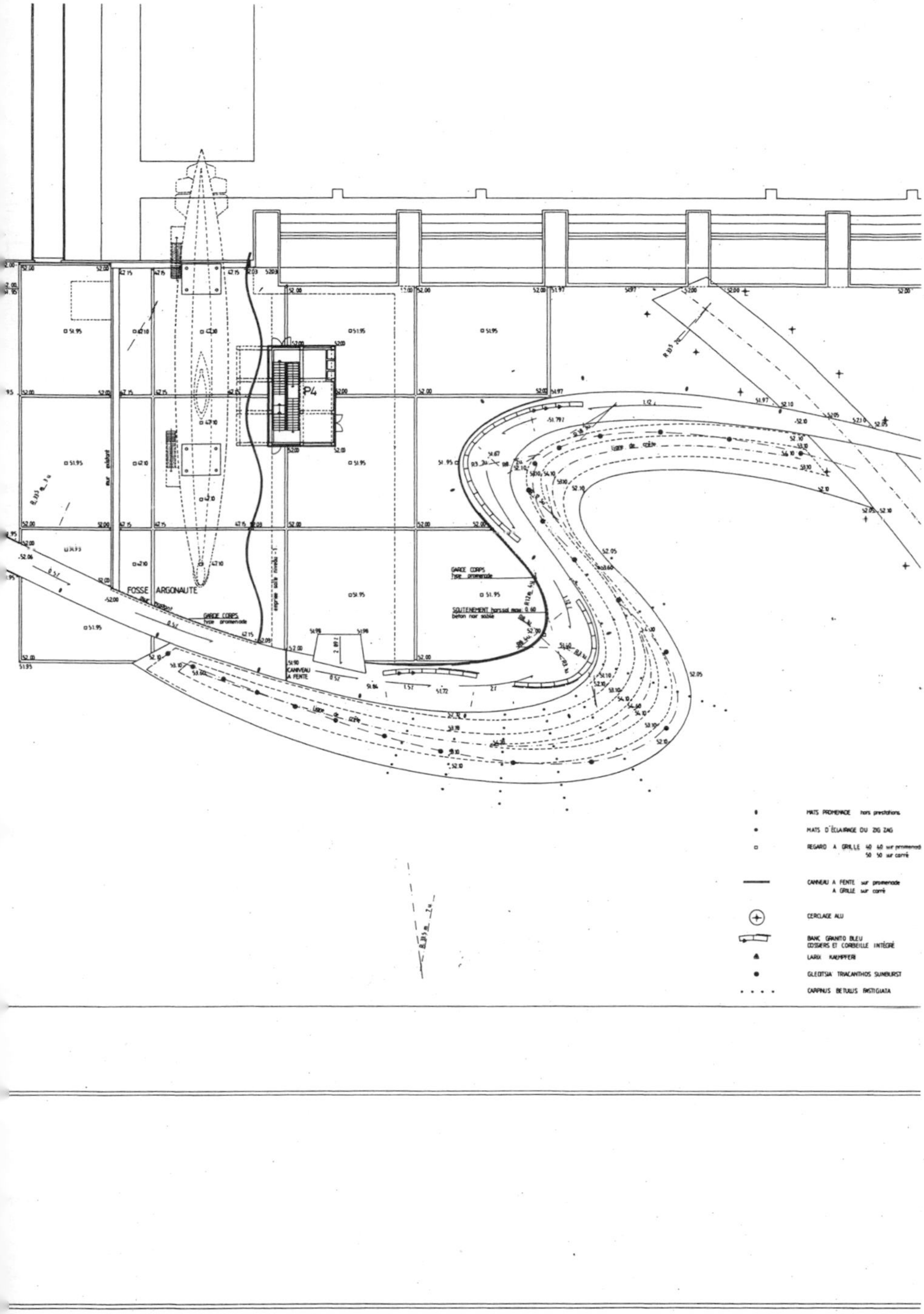
P4
FOSSE ARGONAUTE
GARDE CORPS type promenade
SOUTENEMENT hors sol max 0.60 beton noir sablé
CANIVEAU A FENTE
MATS PROMENADE hors prestations
MATS D'ÉCLAIRAGE DU ZIG ZAG
REGARD A GRILLE 40 40 sur promenade
50 50 sur carré
CANIVEAU A FENTE sur promenade
A GRILLE sur carré
CERCLAGE ALU
BANC GRANITO BLEU
DOSSIERS ET CORBEILLE INTÉGRÉ
LARIX KAEMPFERI
GLEDITSIA TRIACANTHOS SUNBURST
CARPINUS BETULUS FASTIGIATA

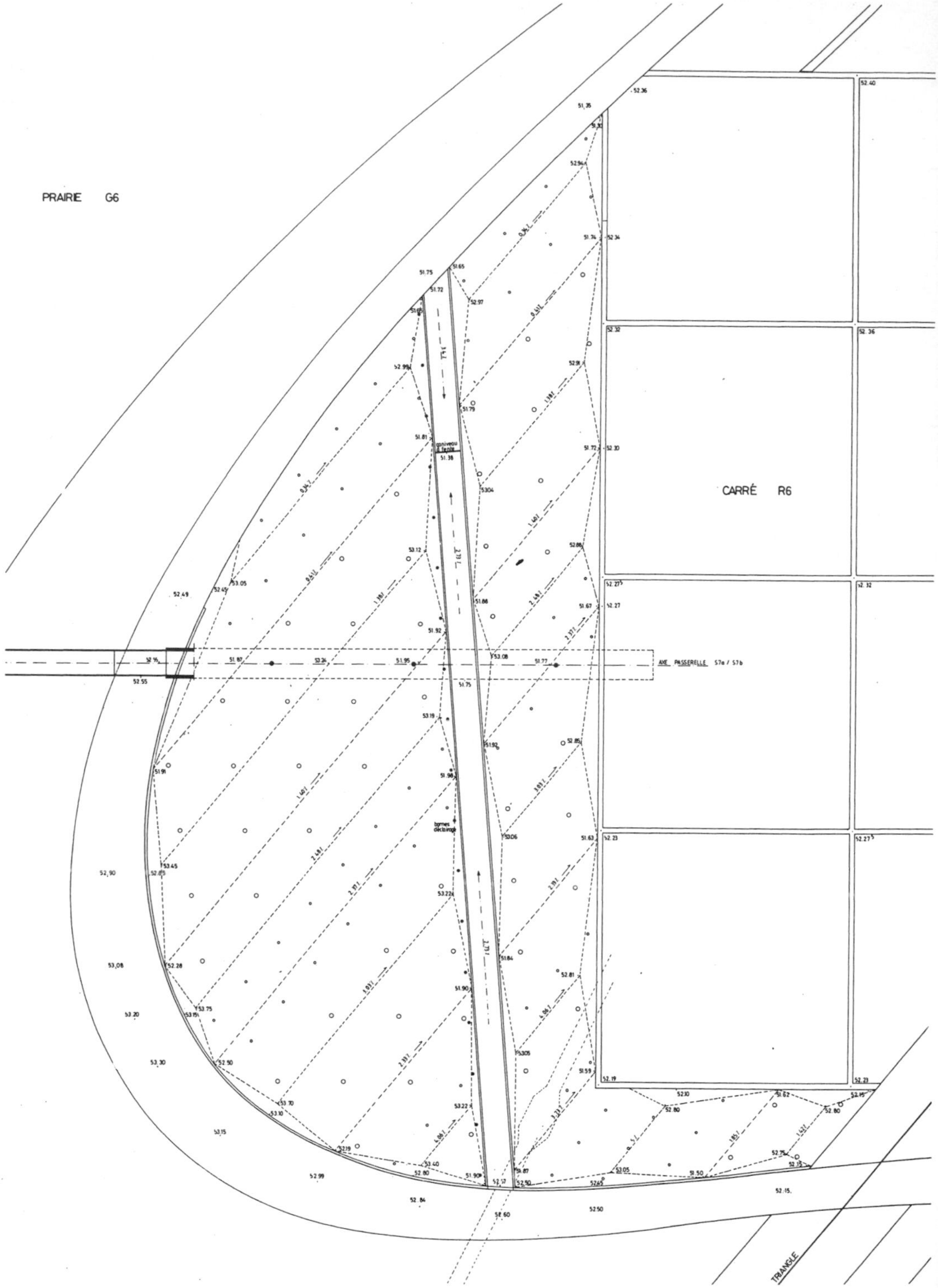

Sequence 6 (Garden of Childhood Frights)

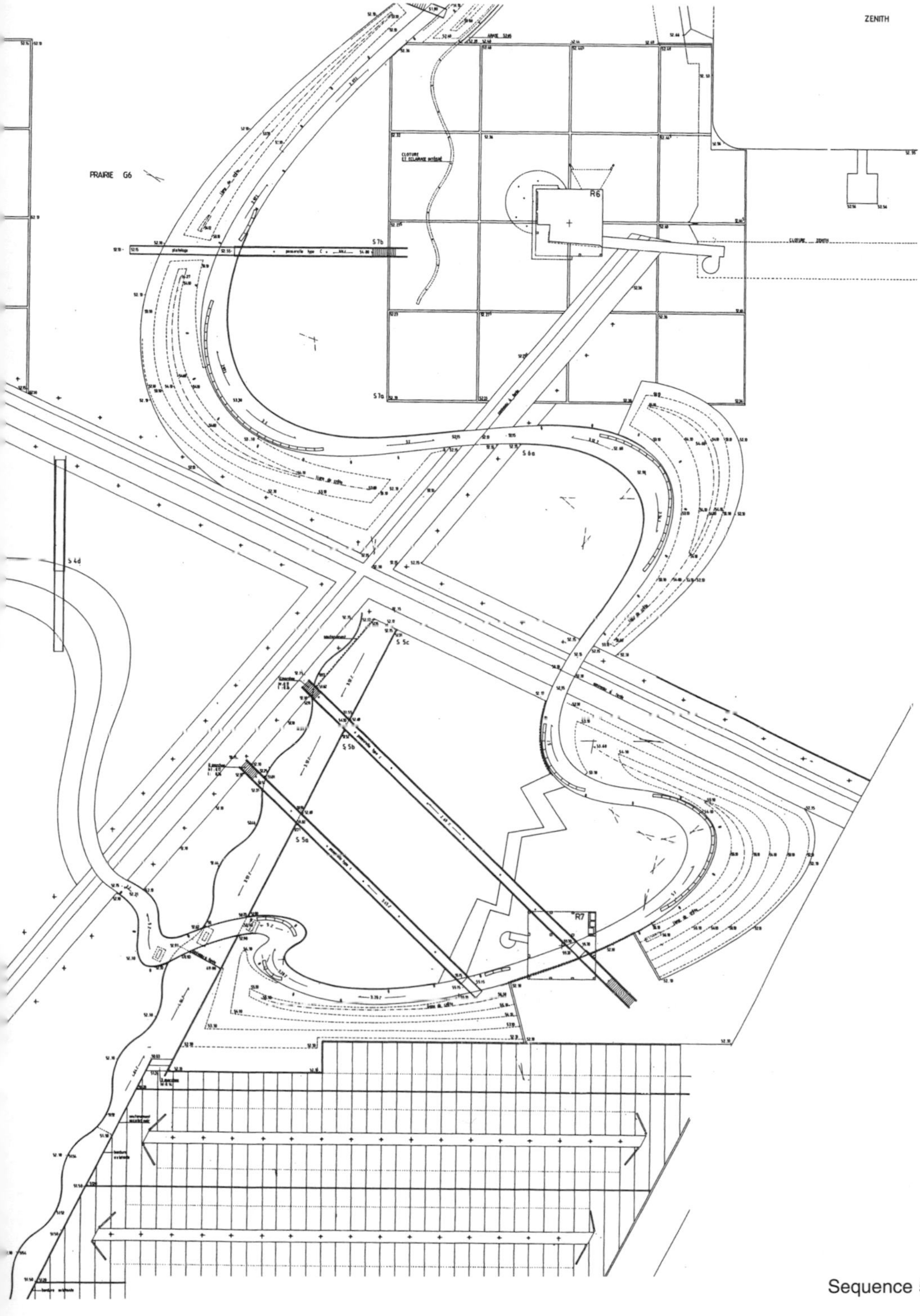

Sequence 5

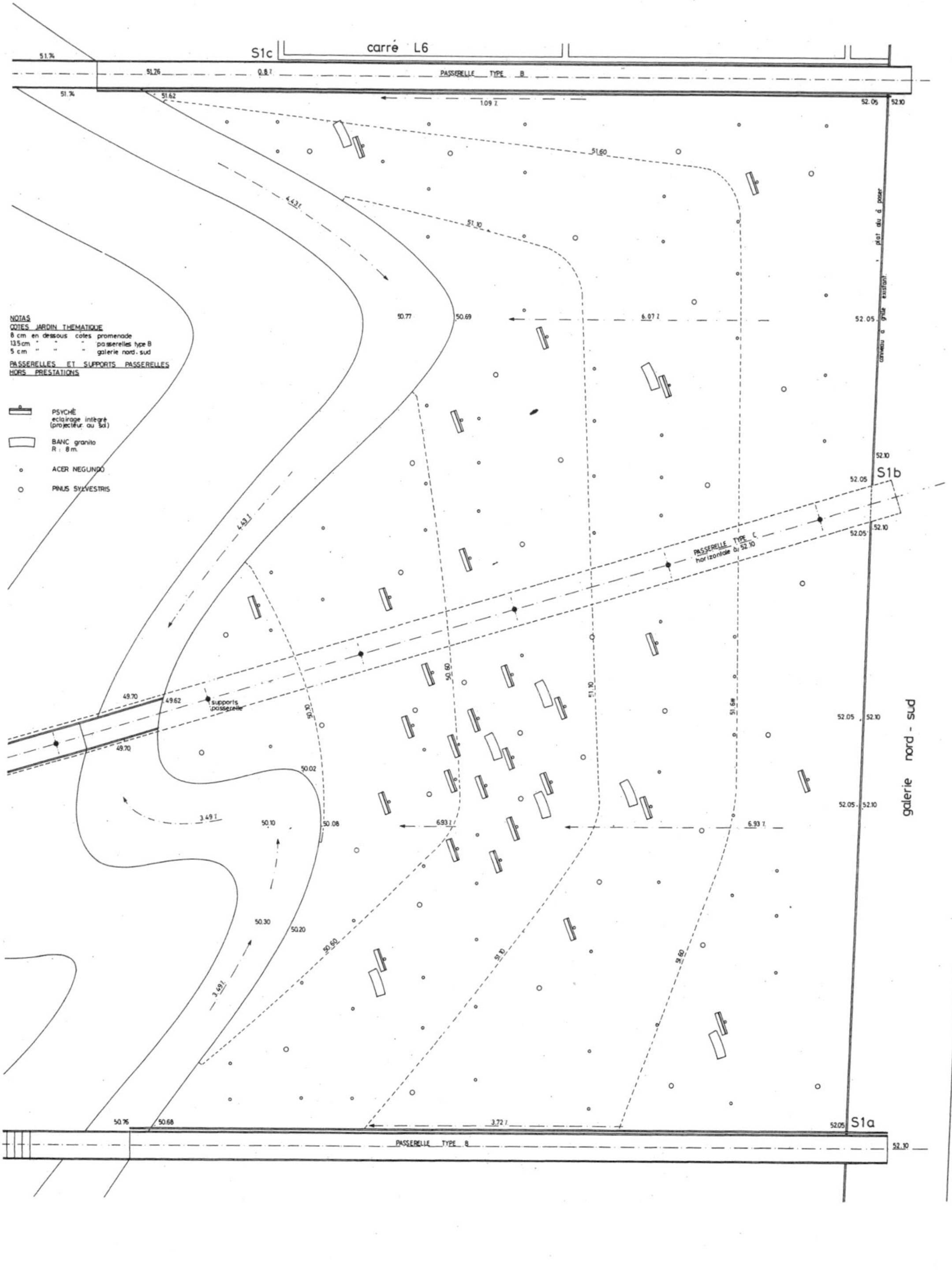

Sequence 16 (Garden of Mirrors)

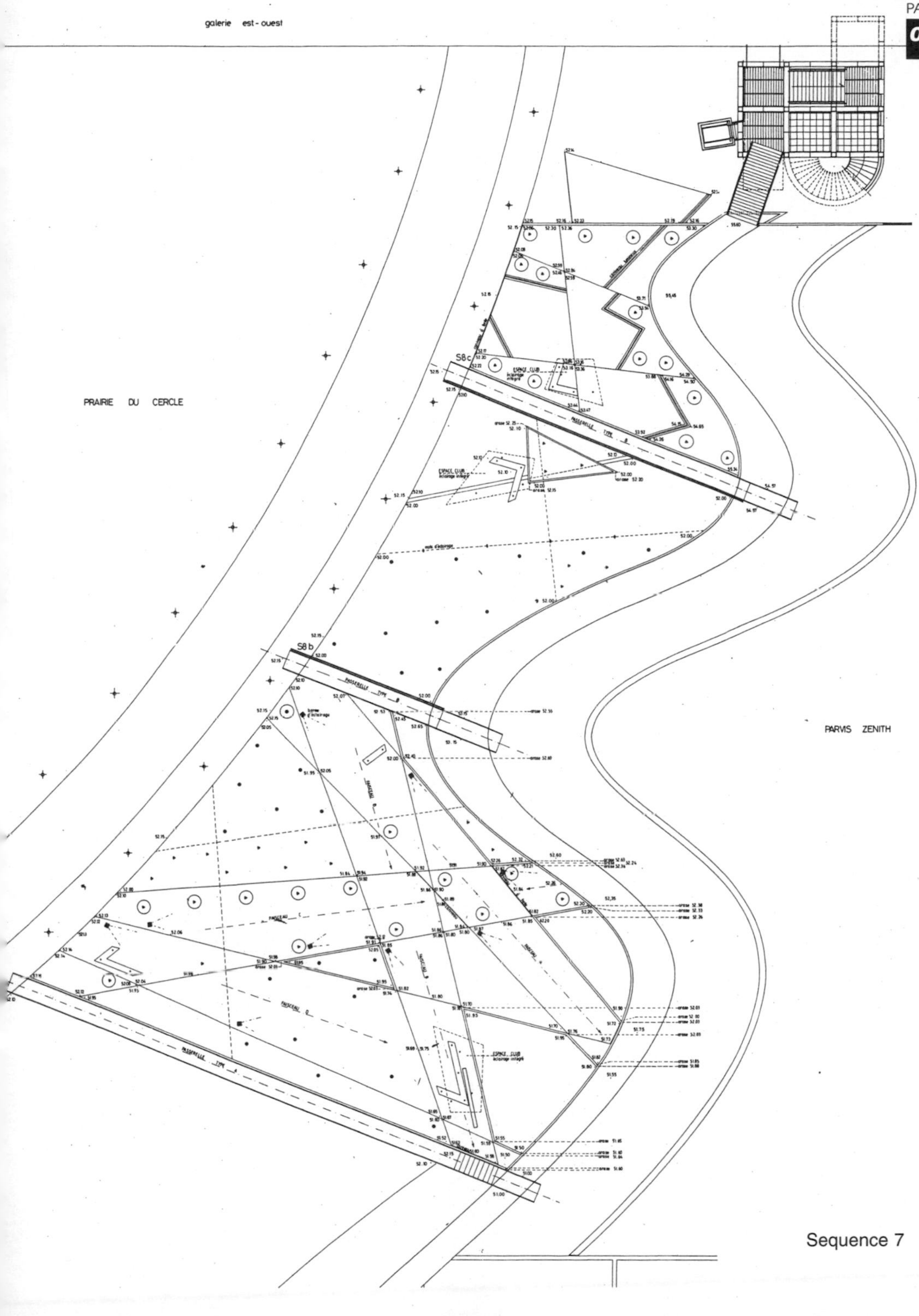
galerie est-ouest
PRAIRIE DU CERCLE
PARVIS ZENITH
S8c
S8b
ESPACE CLUB

Sequence 7

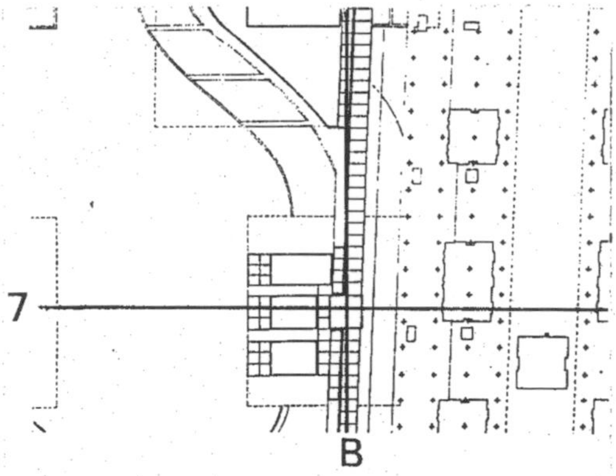
7
B

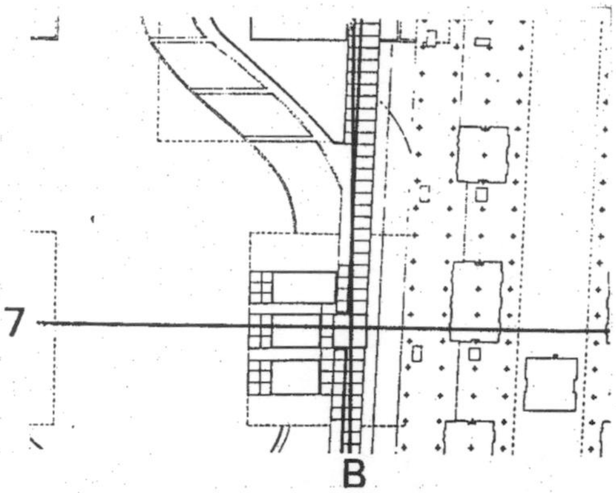
7
B

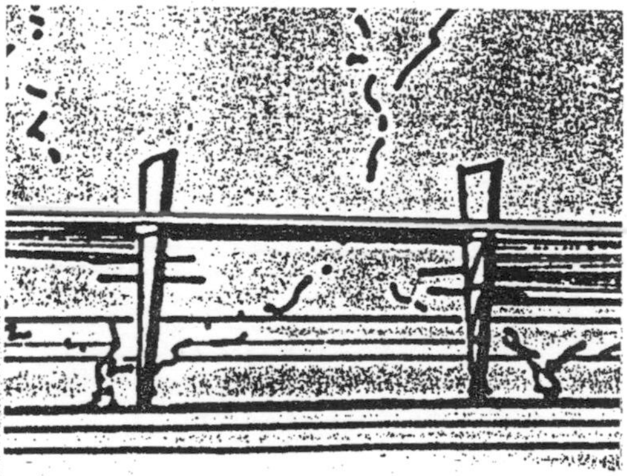

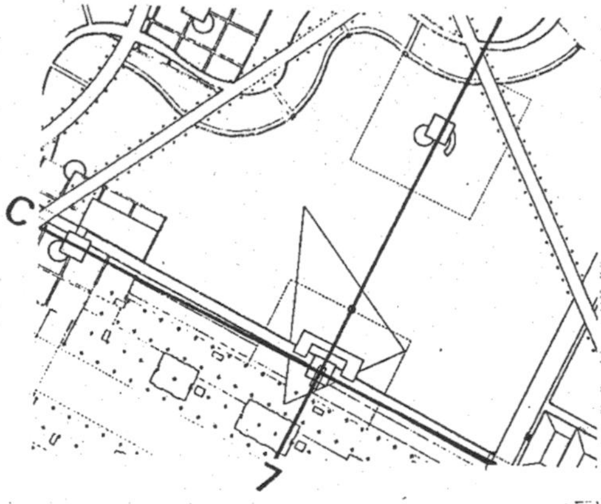
C
7

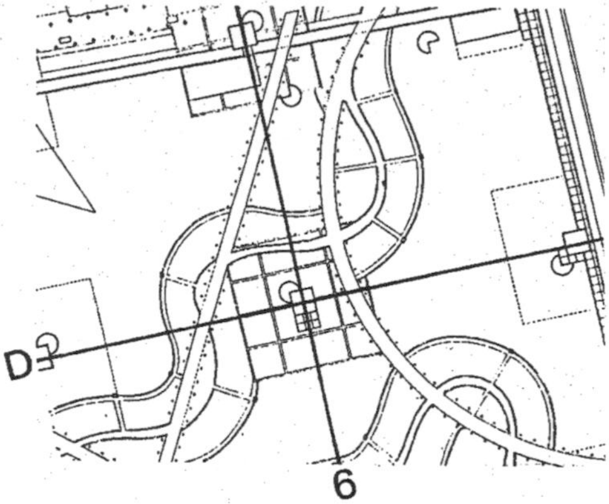
D
6

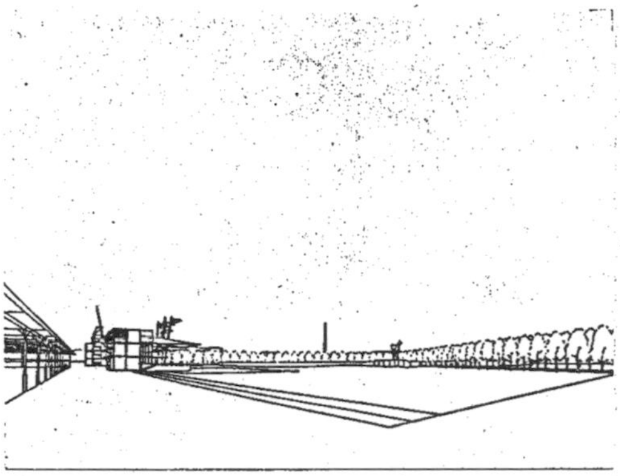

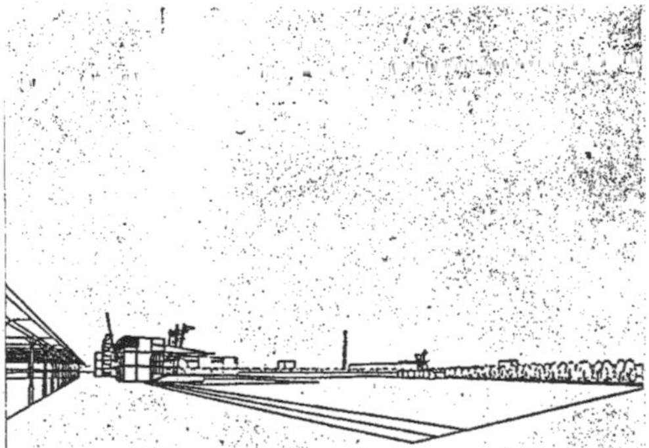

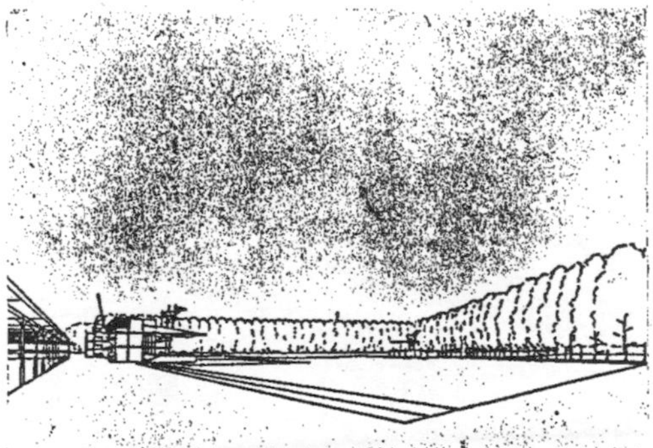

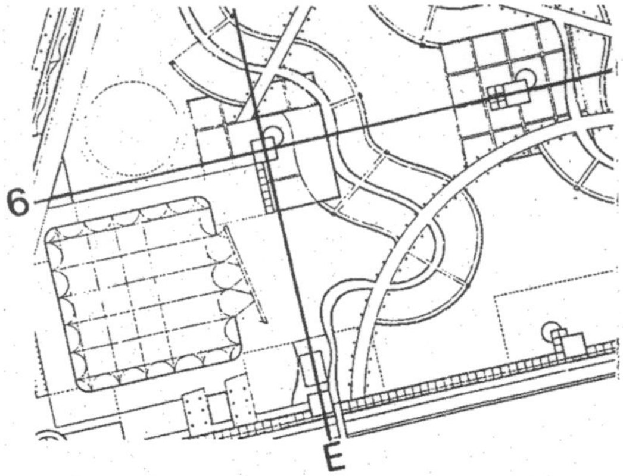
6
E

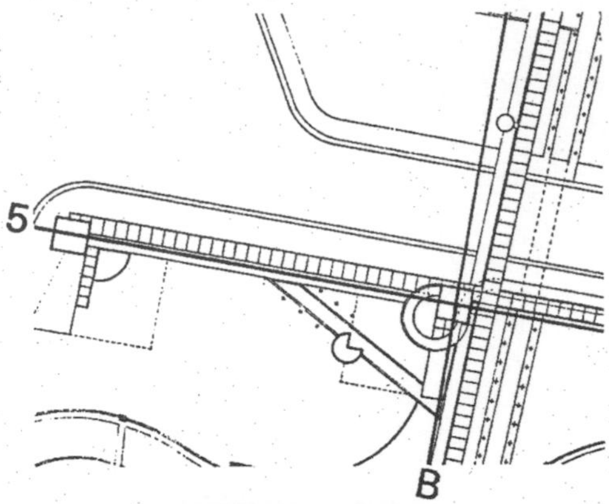
5
B

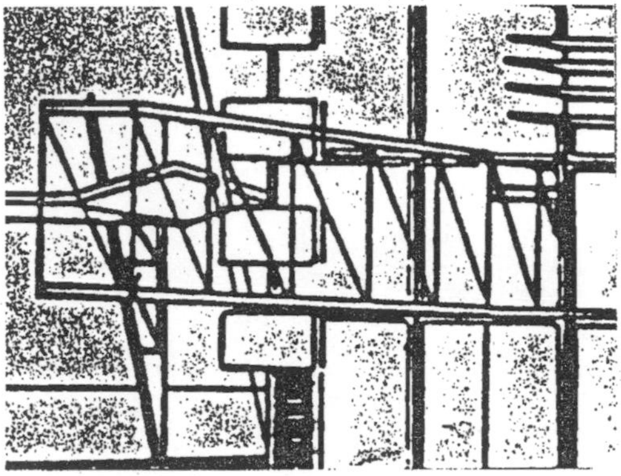

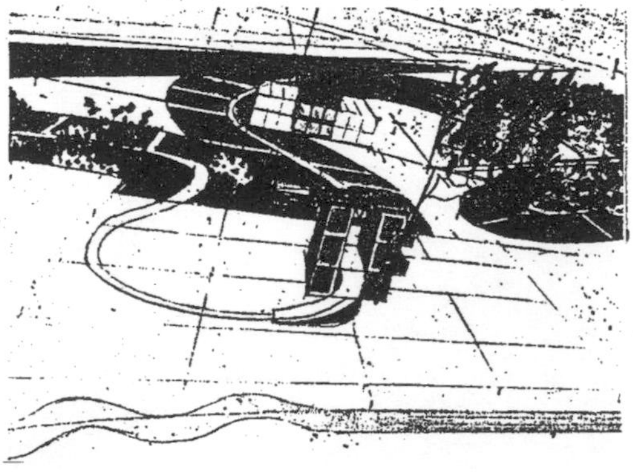

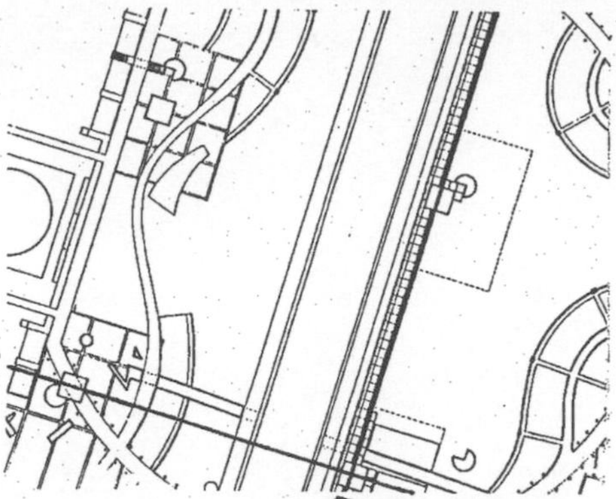

5

4

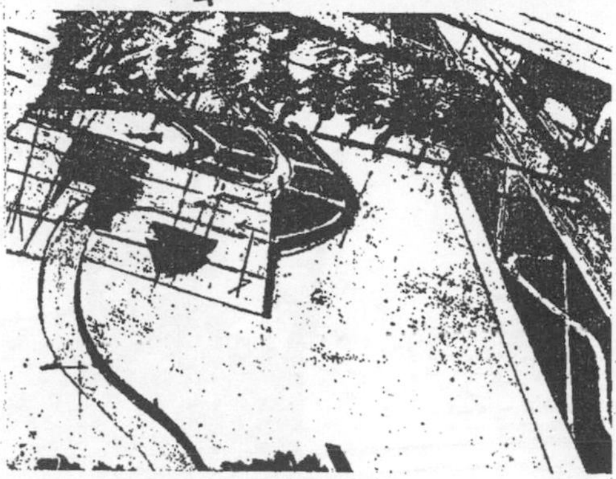

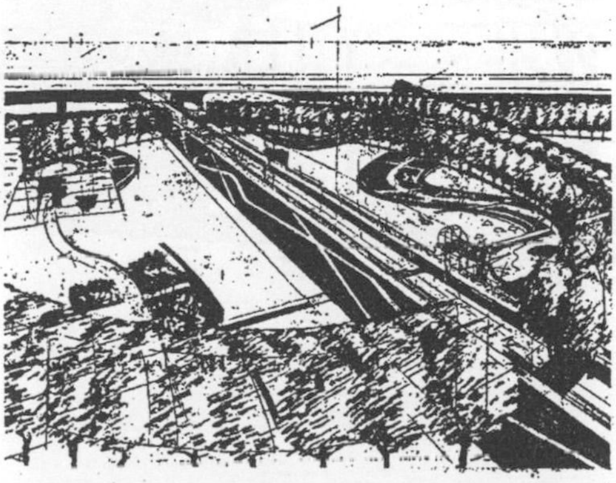

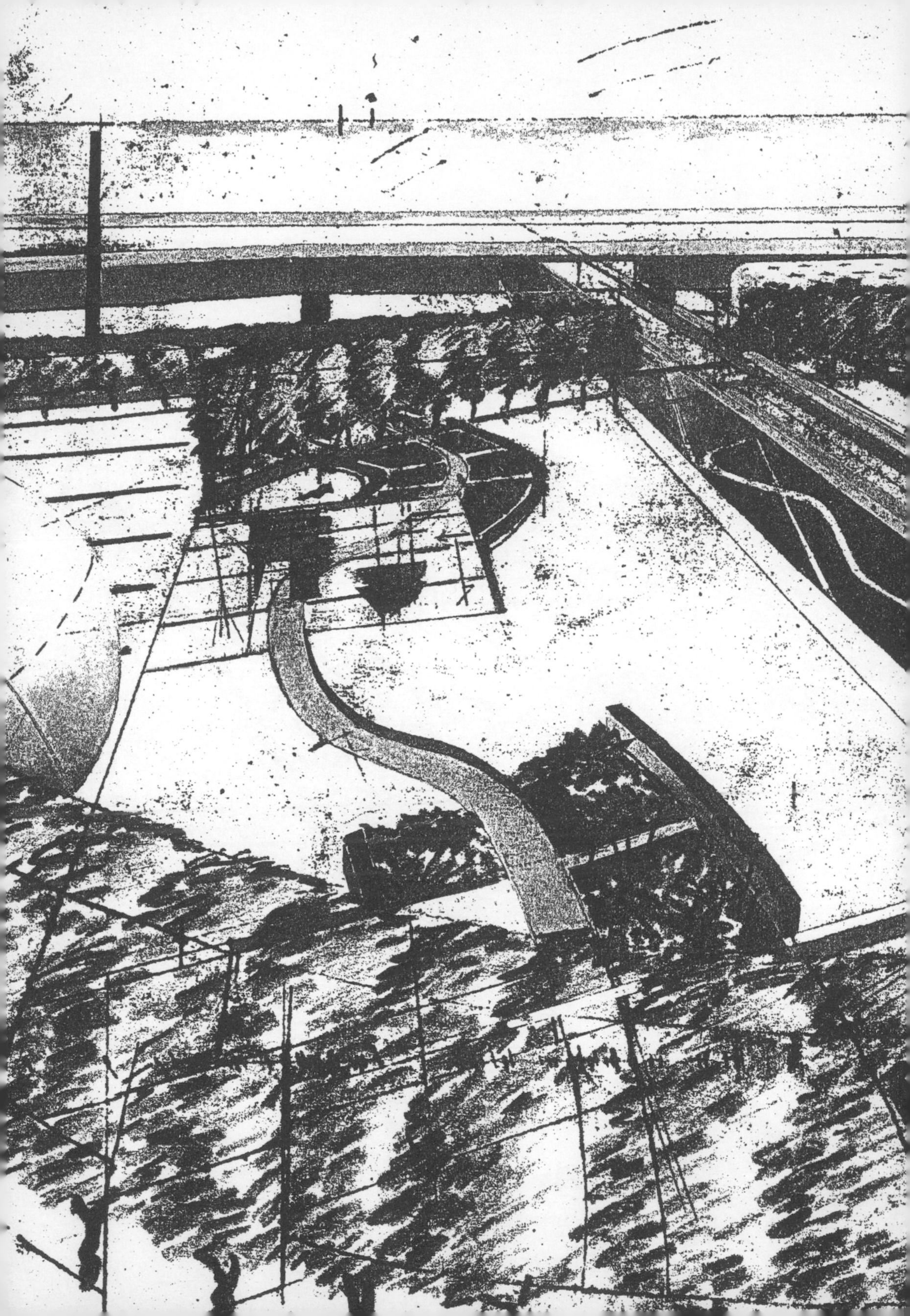

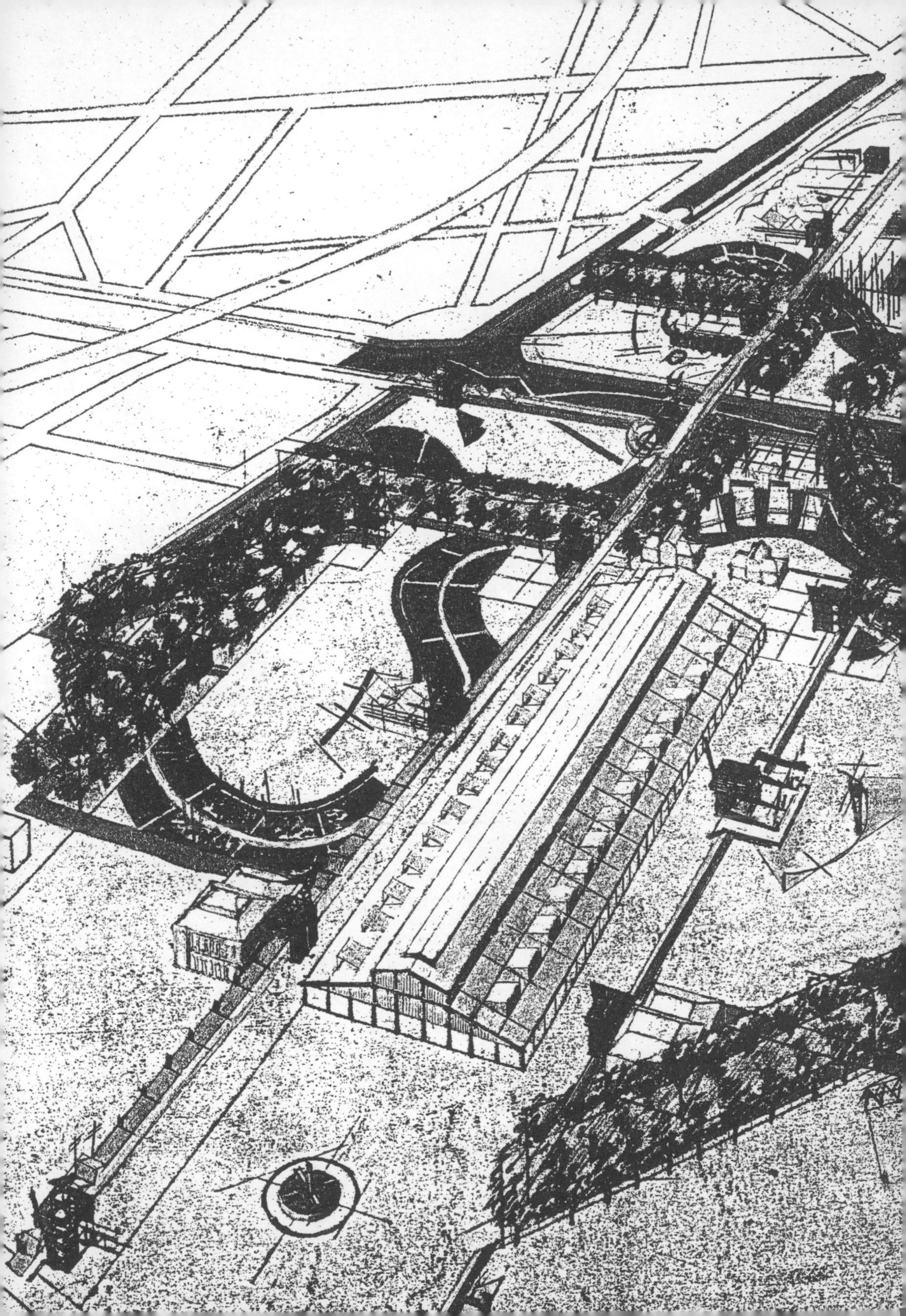

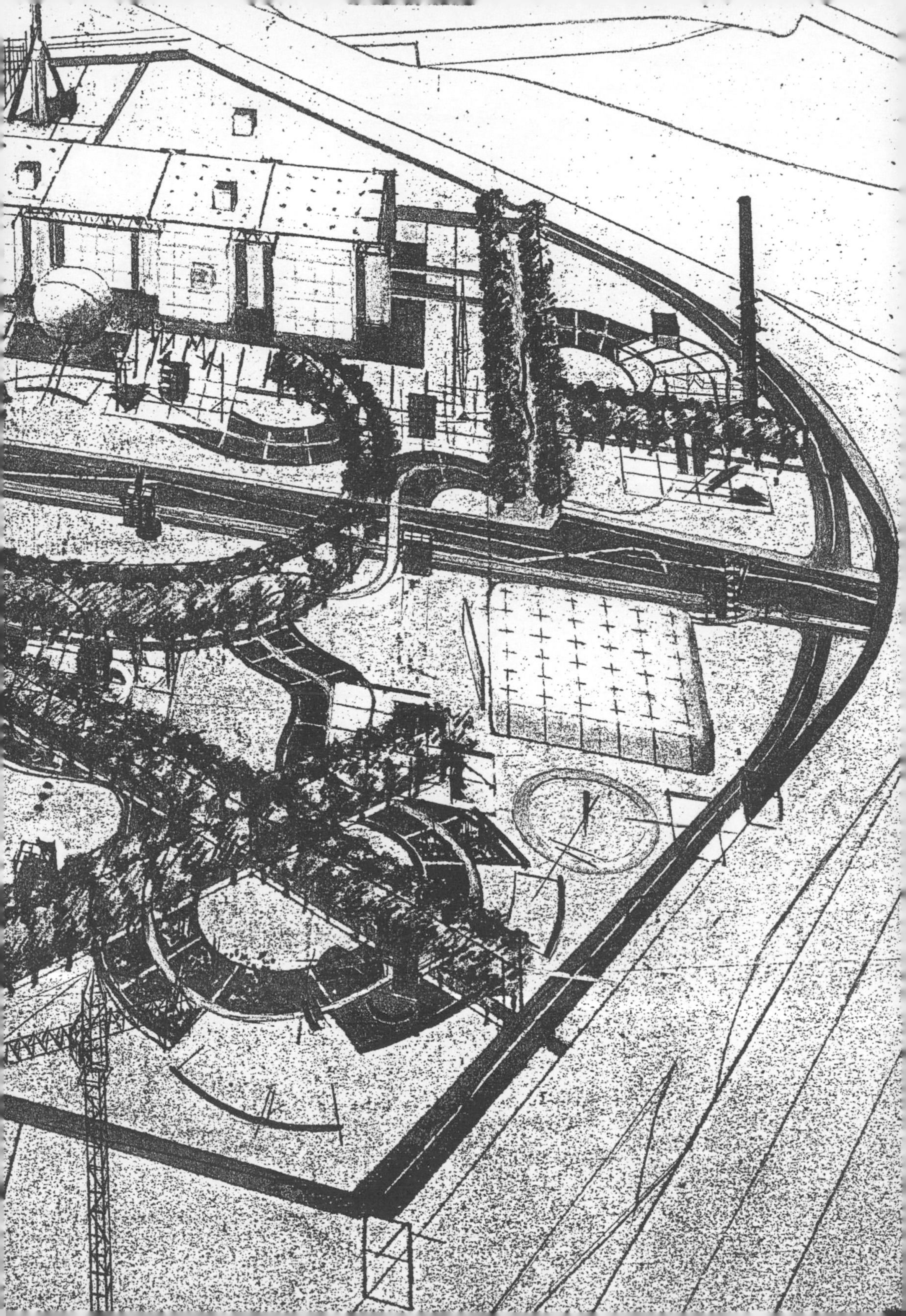

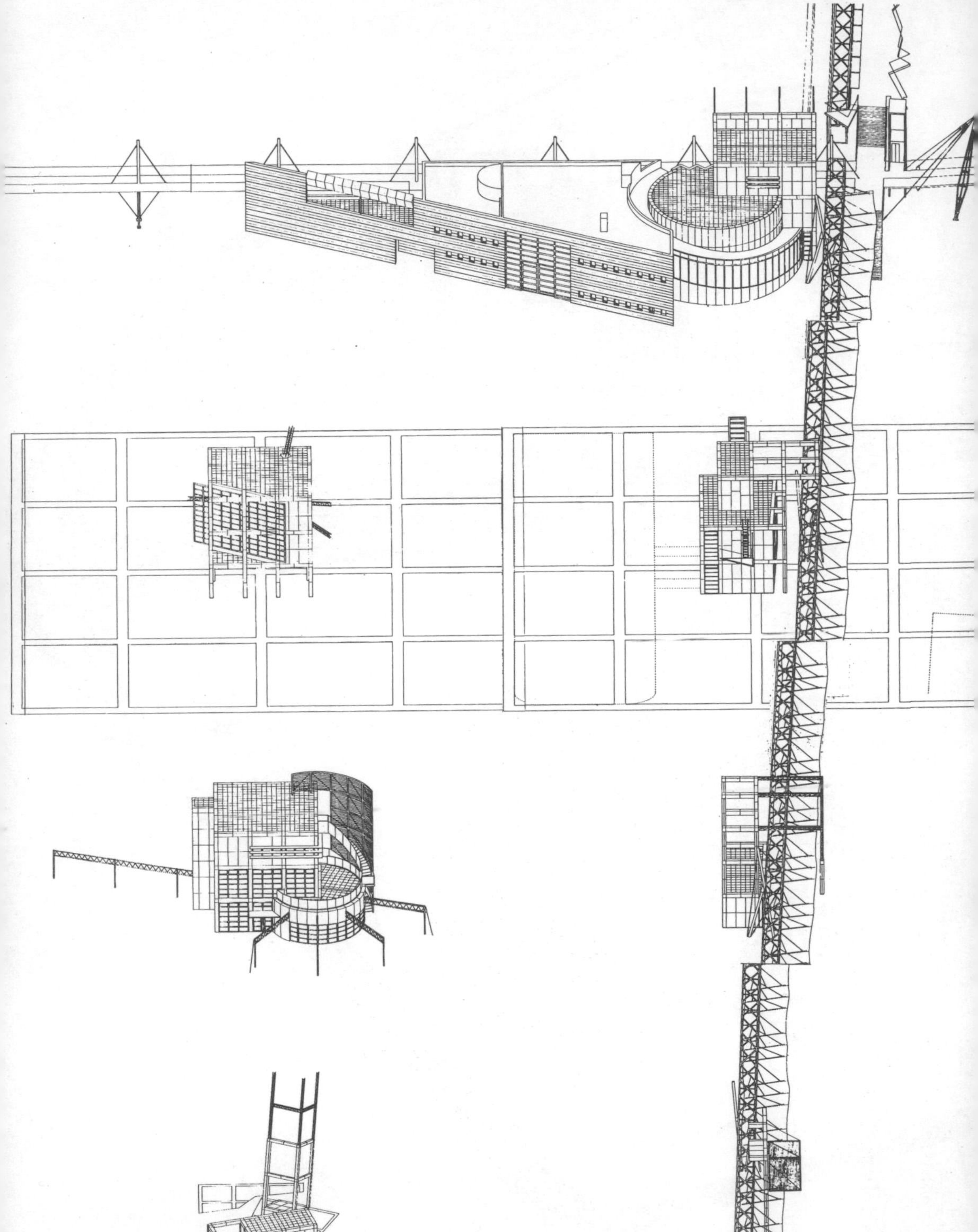

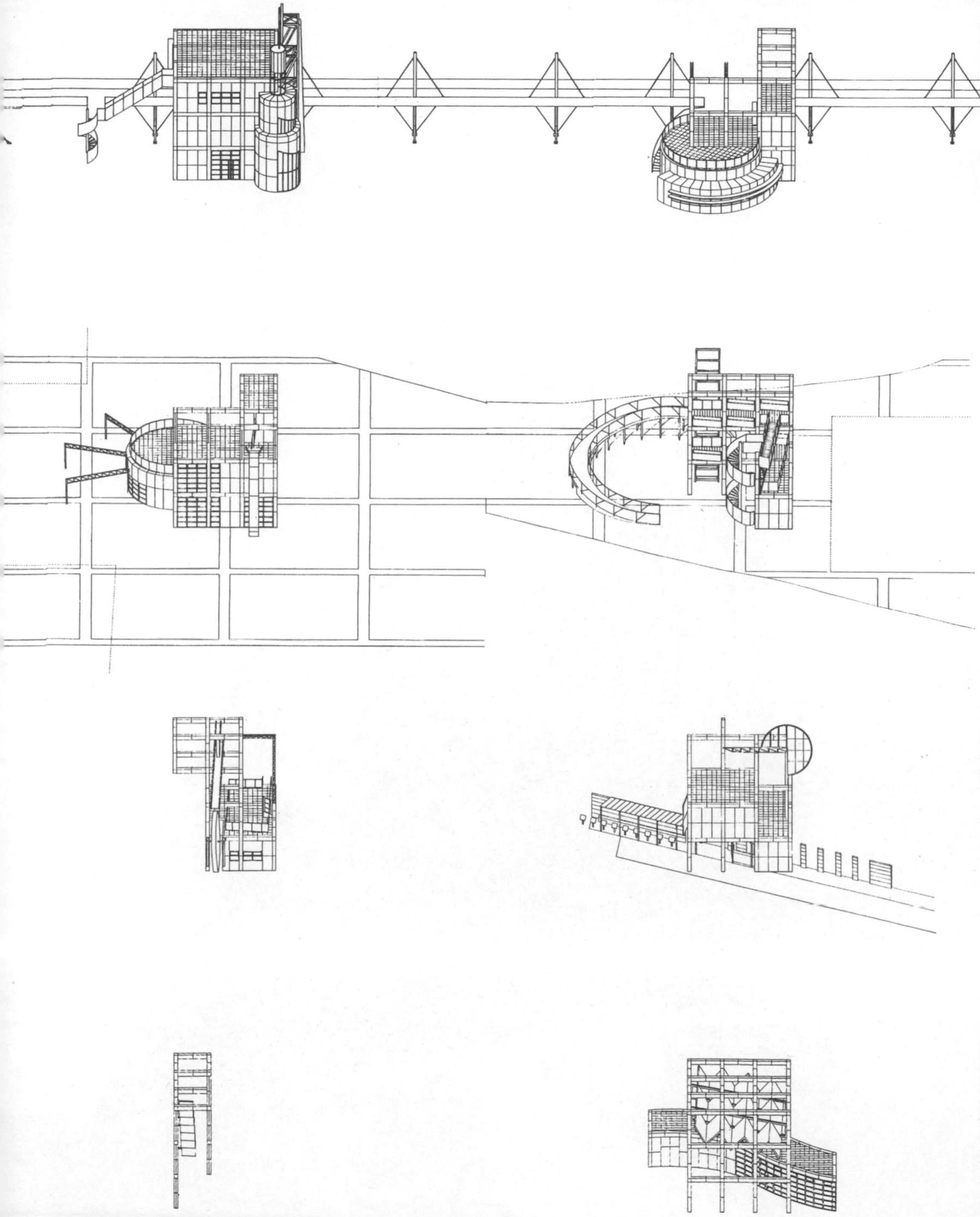

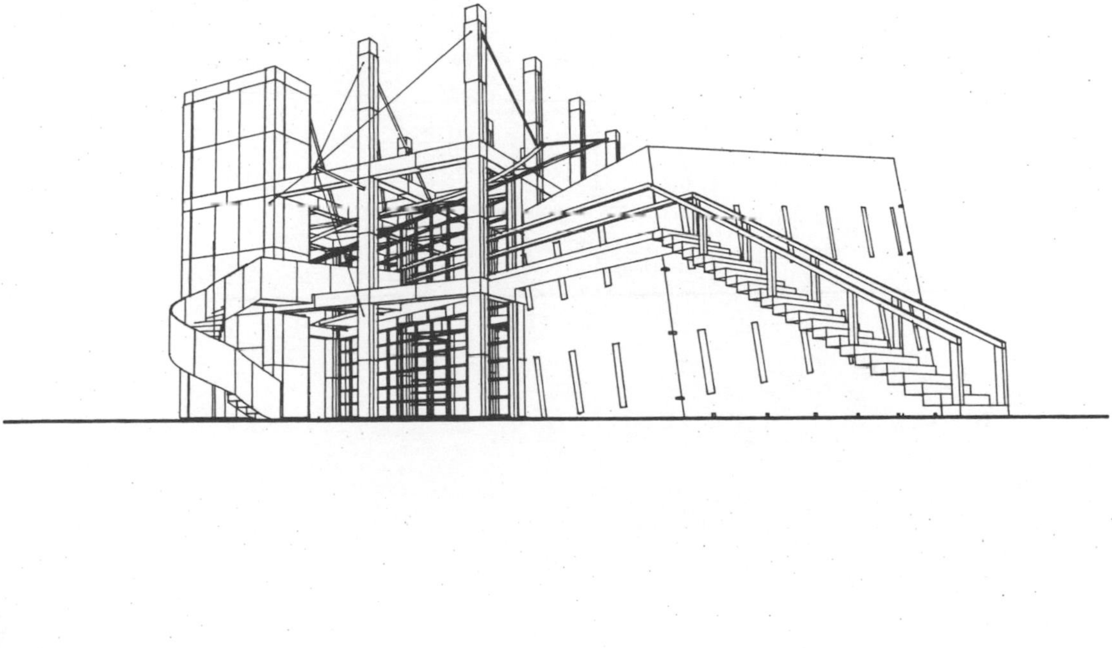

Folie P8 (Folie de la Musique) Program: recording studio, small music auditorium, conference room, music room, atelier for the construction of musical instruments, information booth, waiting area

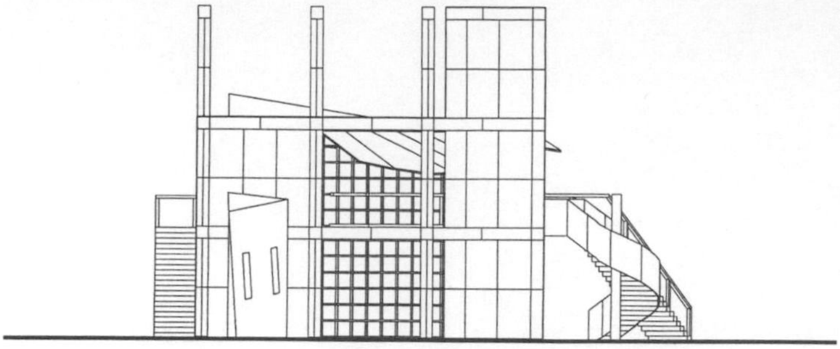

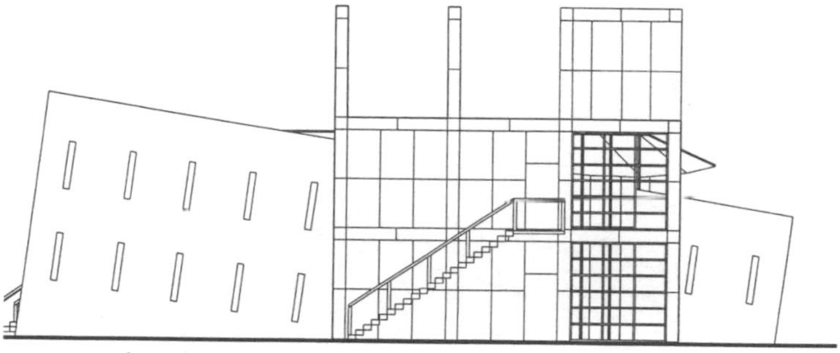

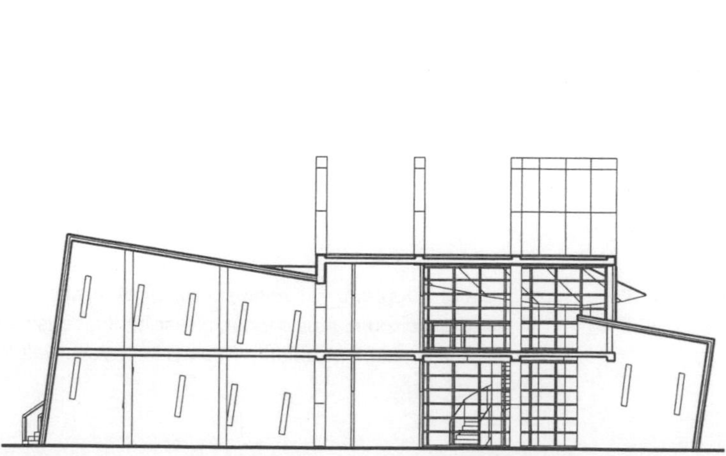

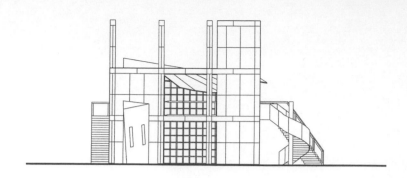

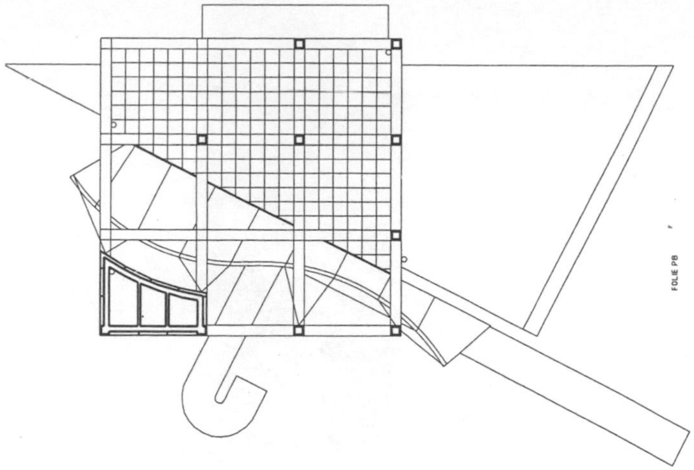
FOLIE P8

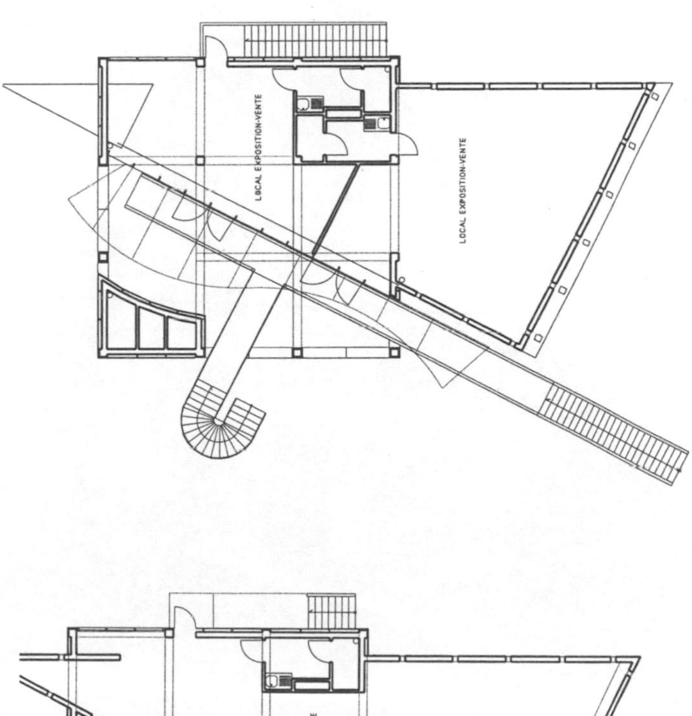
LOCAL EXPOSITION-VENTE
LOCAL EXPOSITION-VENTE

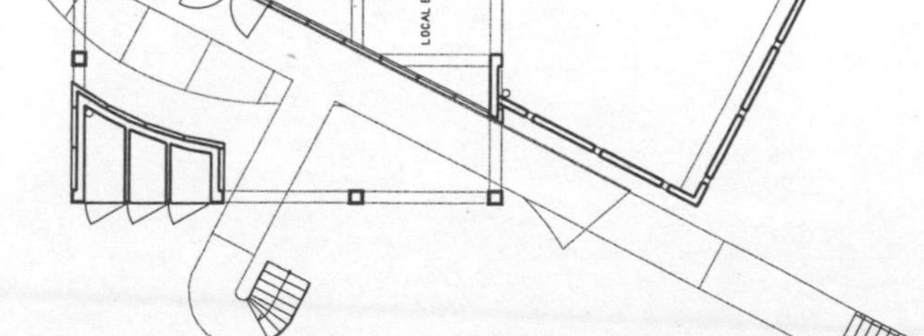
LOCAL EXPOSITION-VENTE

BRASS

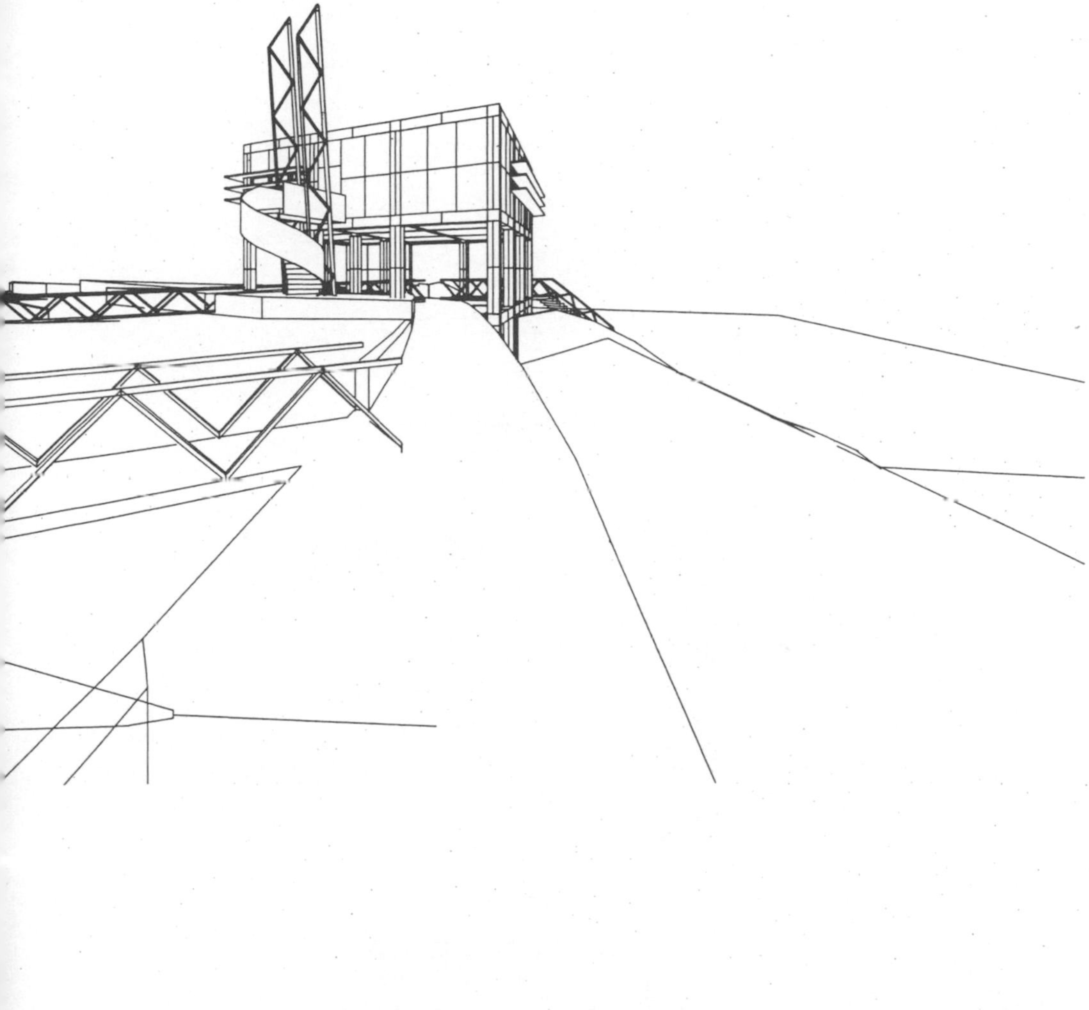

Folie R7 Program: upper level with offices for jazz club, intermediate level with gardens and waiting area. Lower level with jazz club, stage, bar, changing rooms, coatcheck

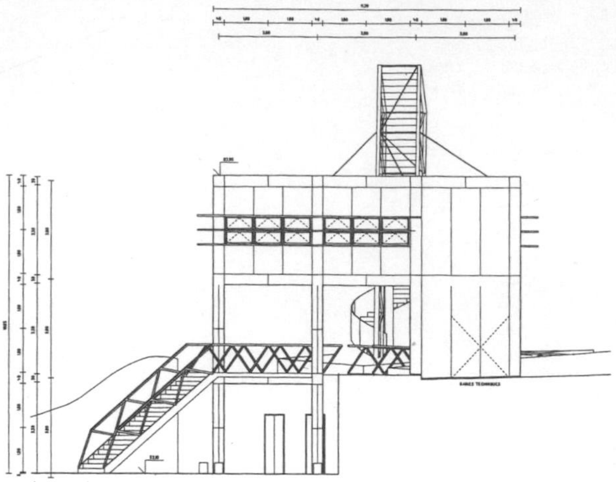

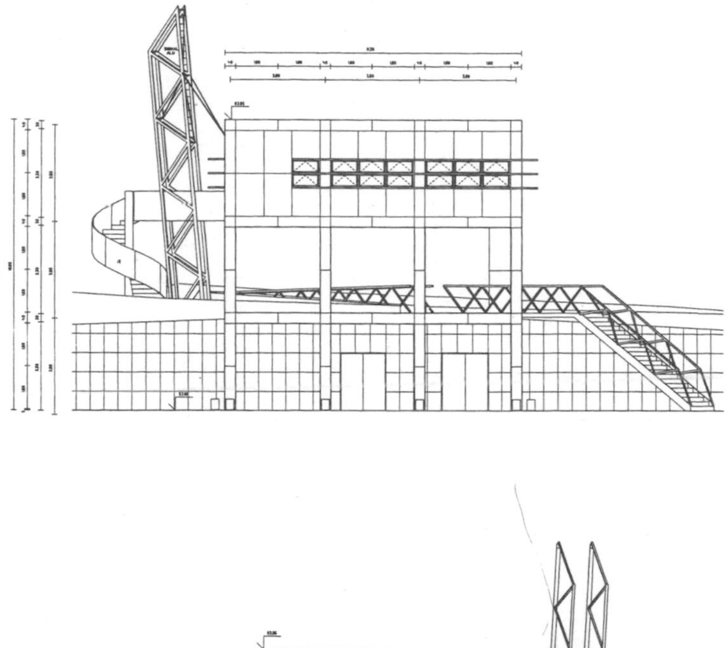

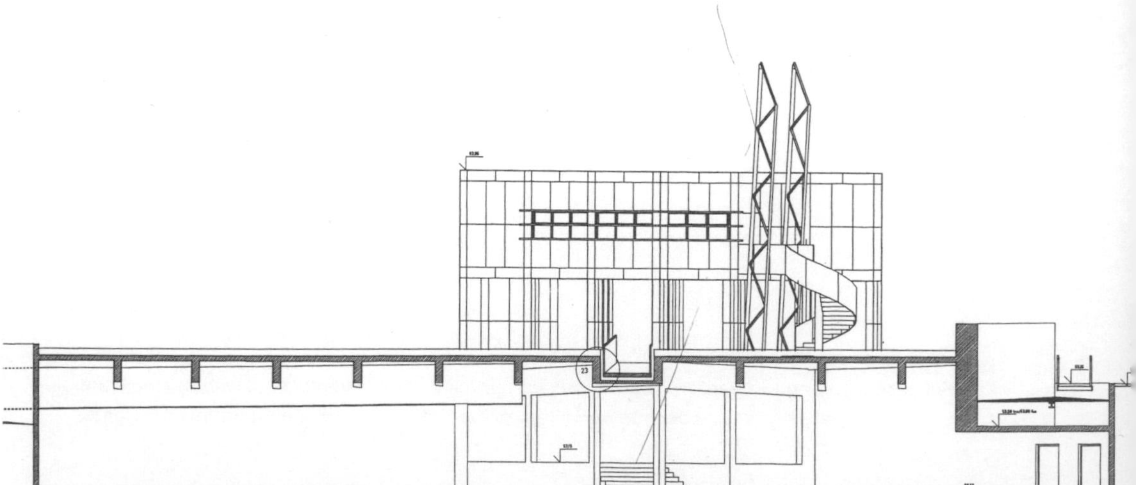

FOLIE R7

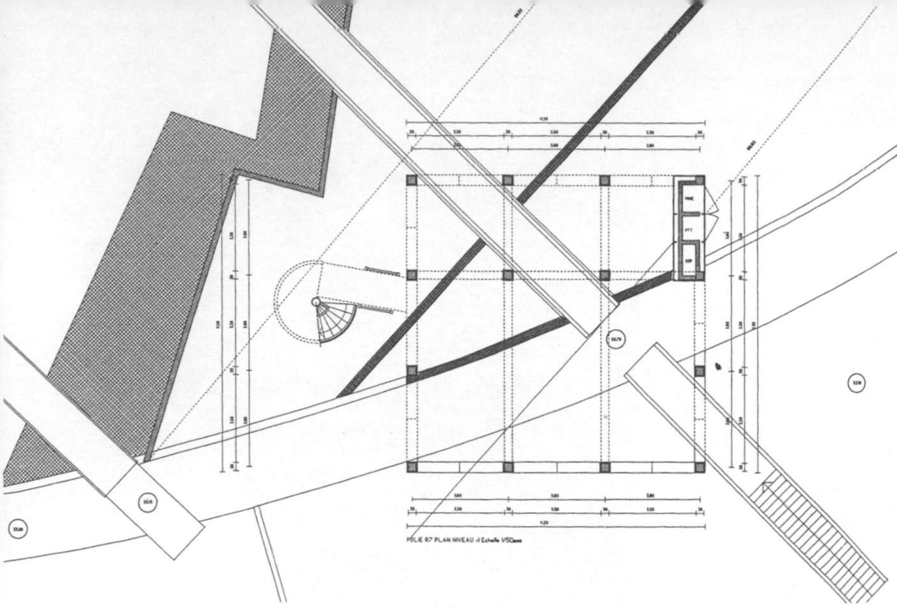

FOLIE R7 PLAN NIVEAU -1 Echelle 1/50eme

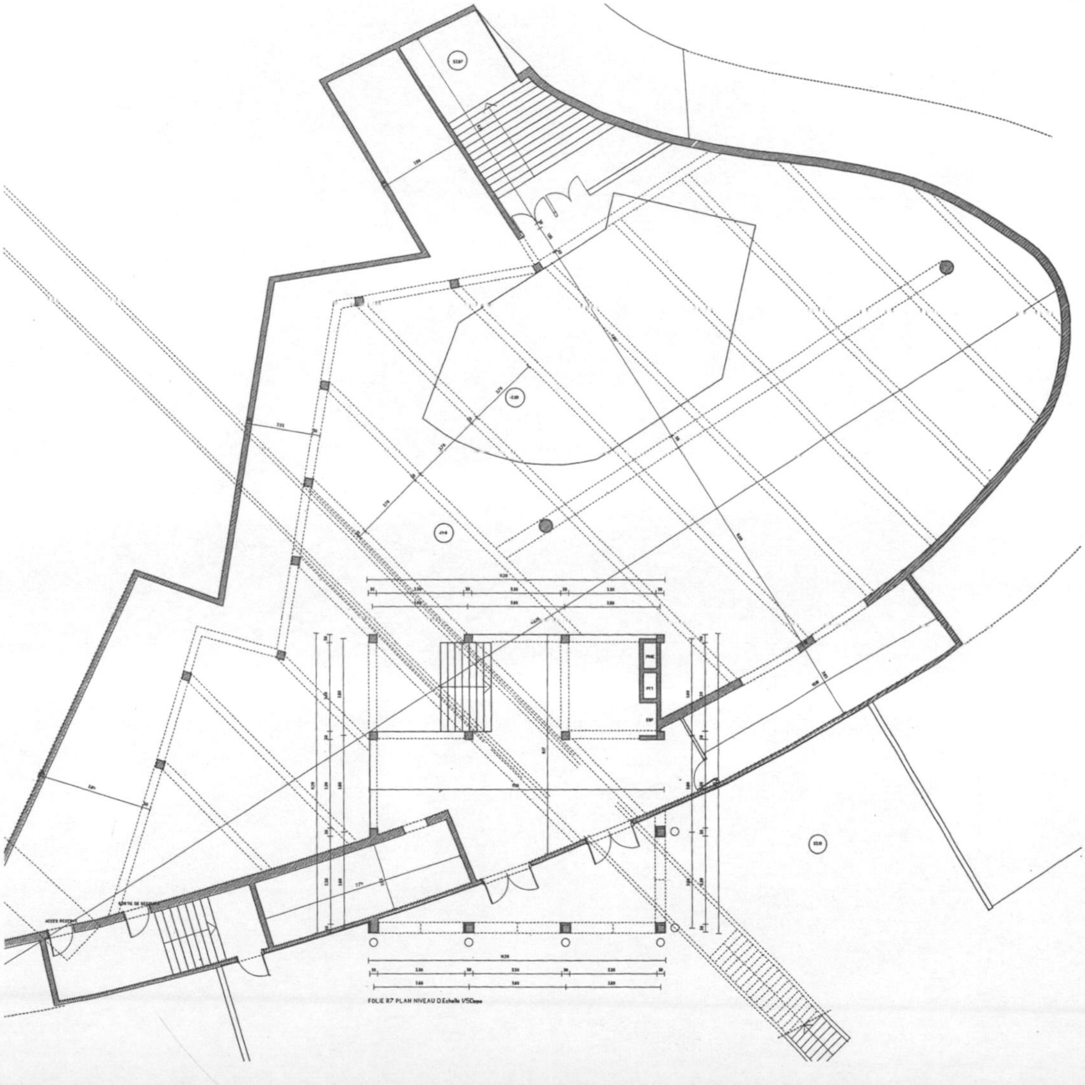

FOLIE R7 PLAN NIVEAU 0 Echelle 1/50eme

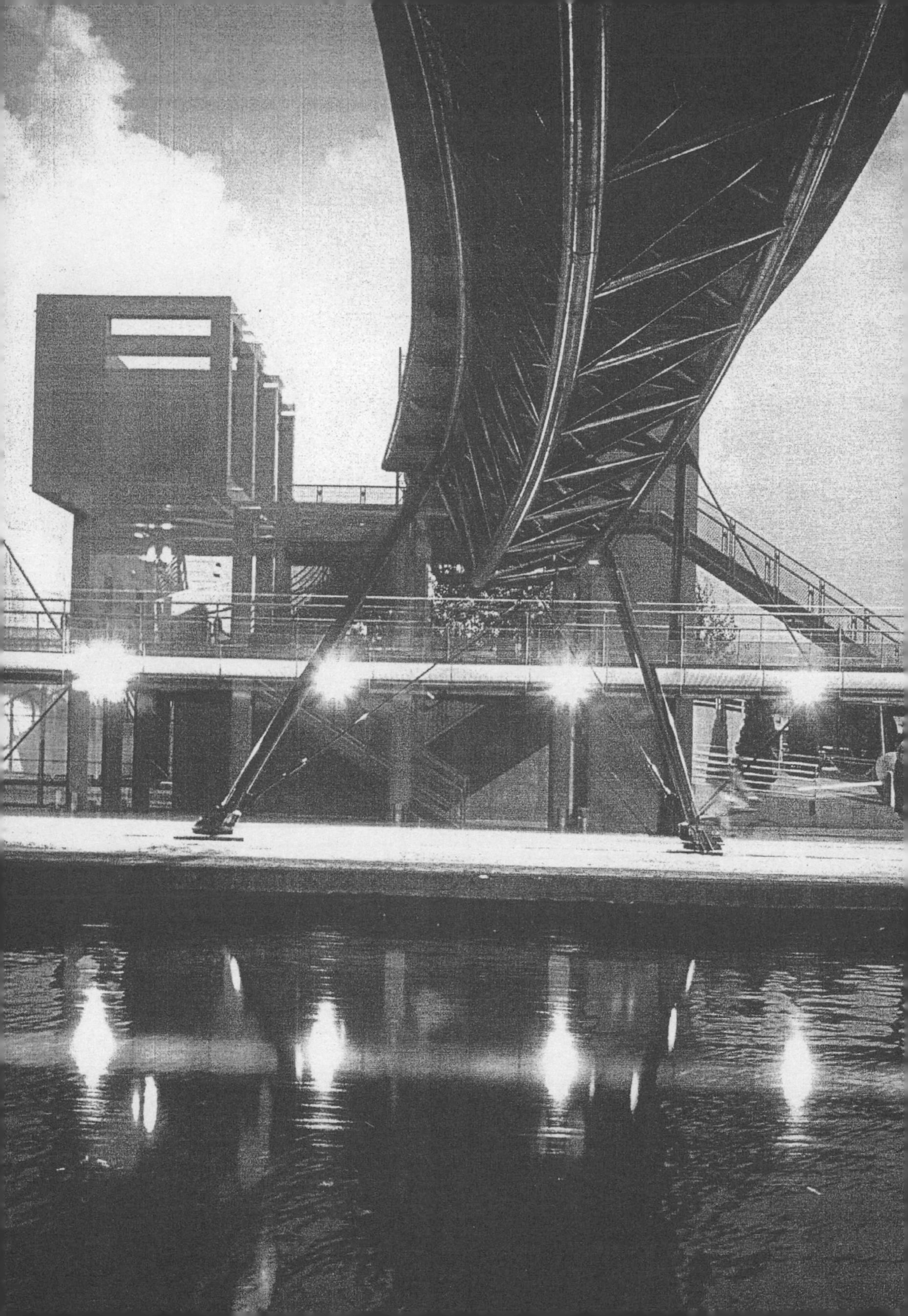

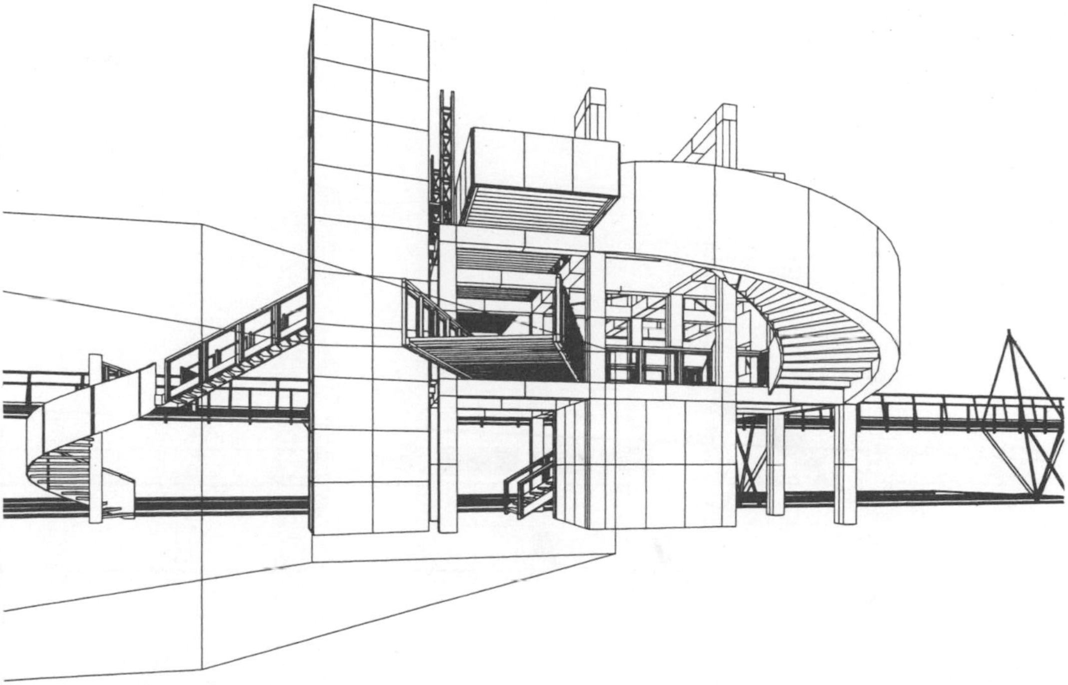

Folie R5 Program: intersecting three levels a) bridge over canal extending cinematic promenade
b) east-west gallery with elevated walkway along canal
c) ground level—elevators, stairs, bridge

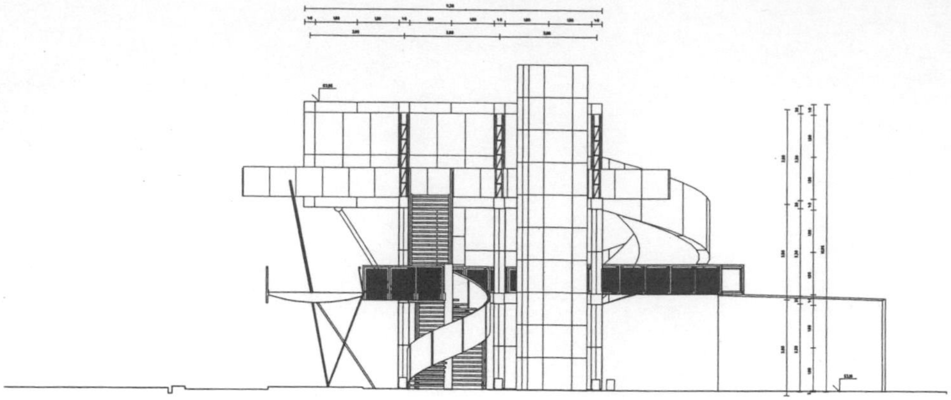

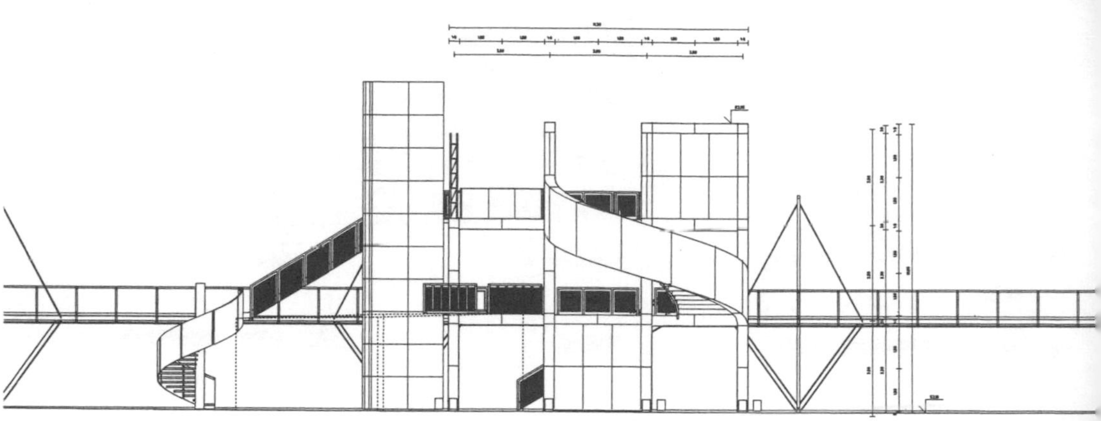

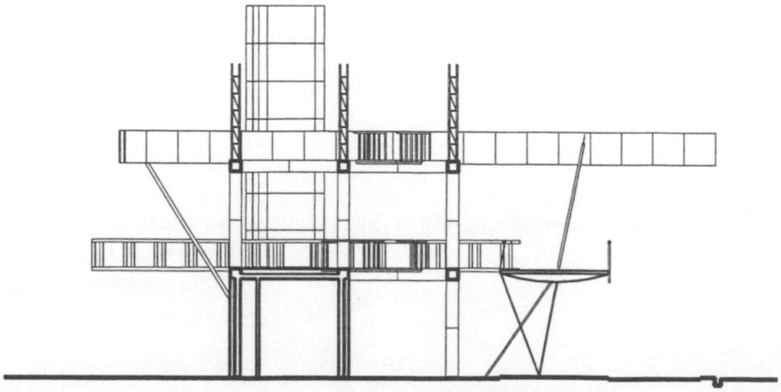

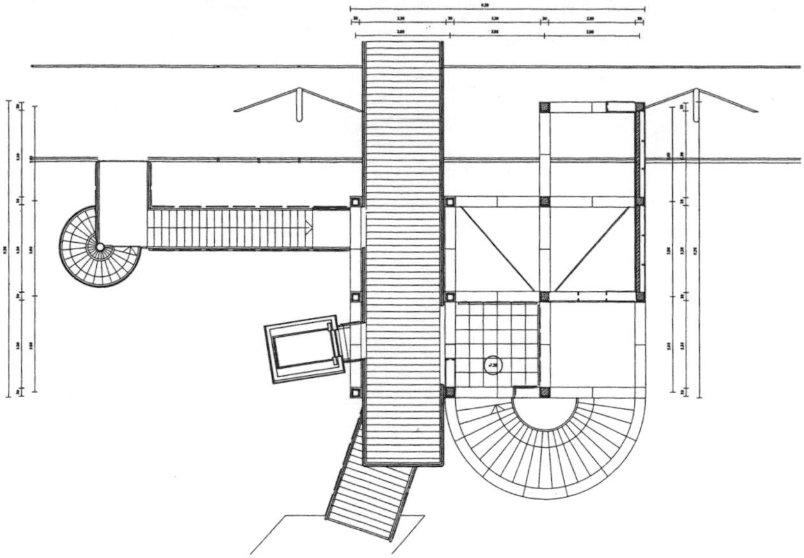

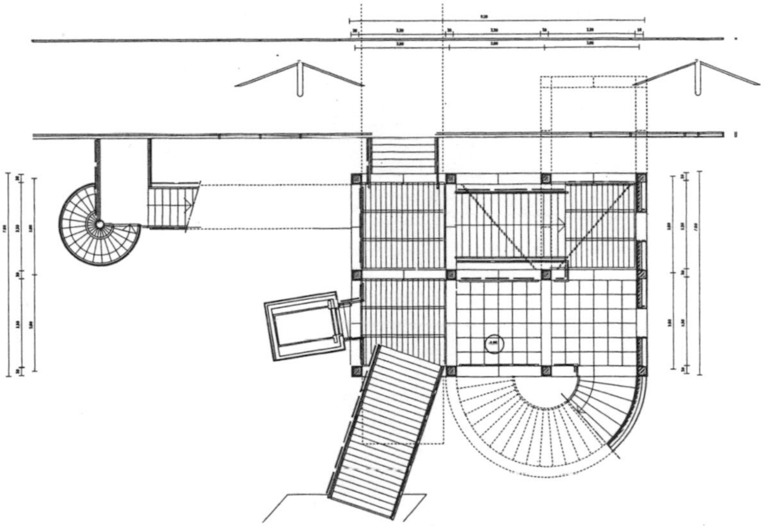

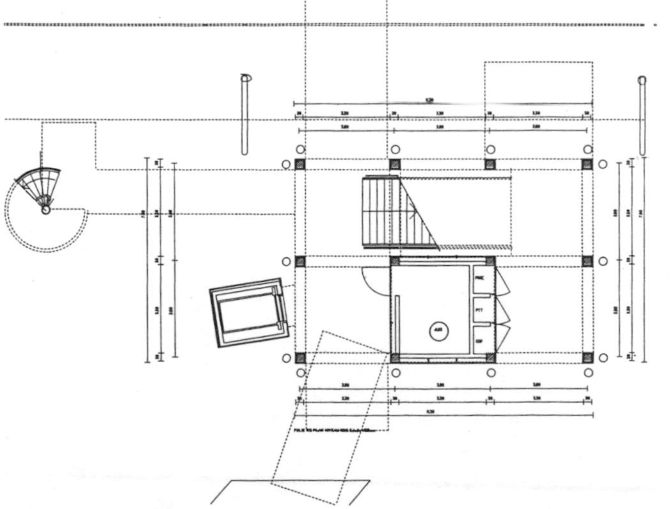

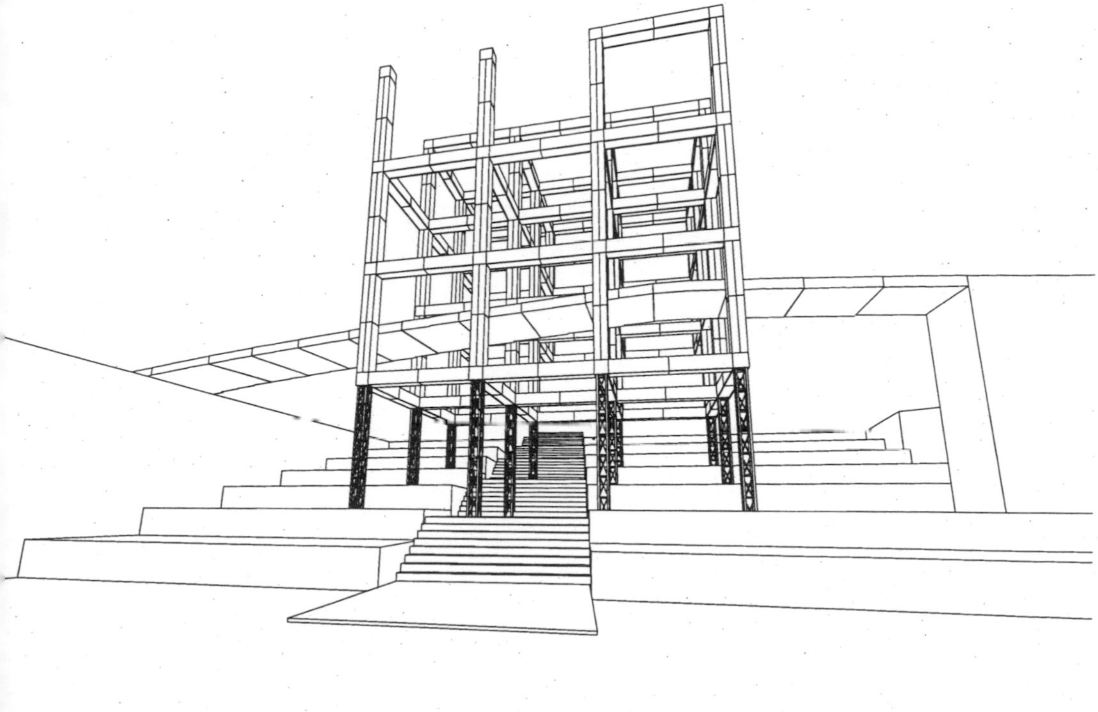

Folie R4 Folies are like mirrors: you project your own fantasies on them

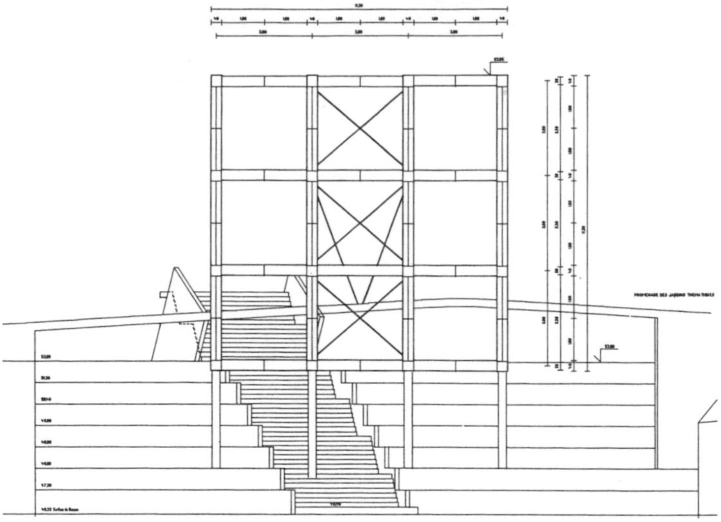

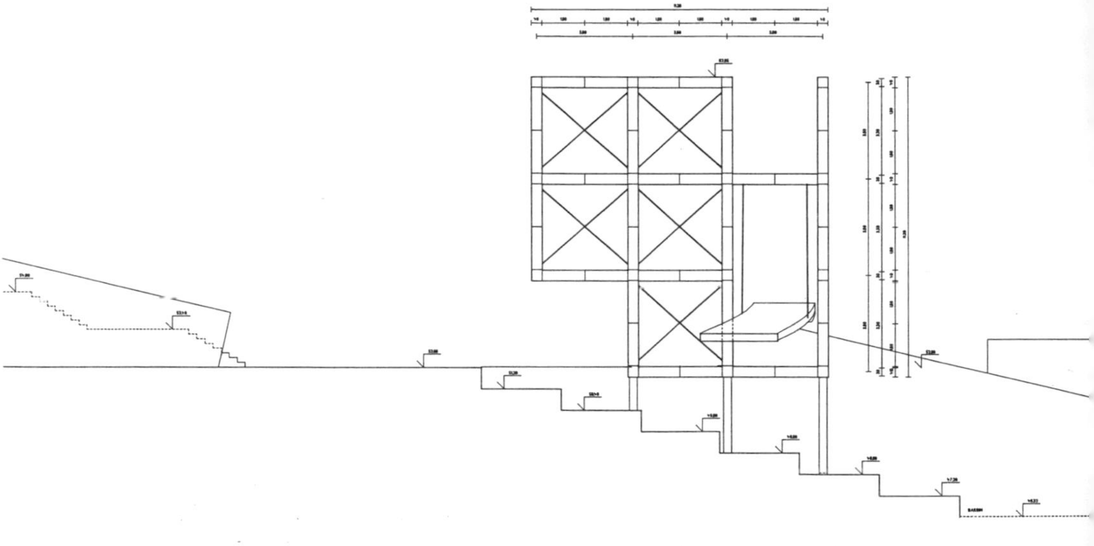

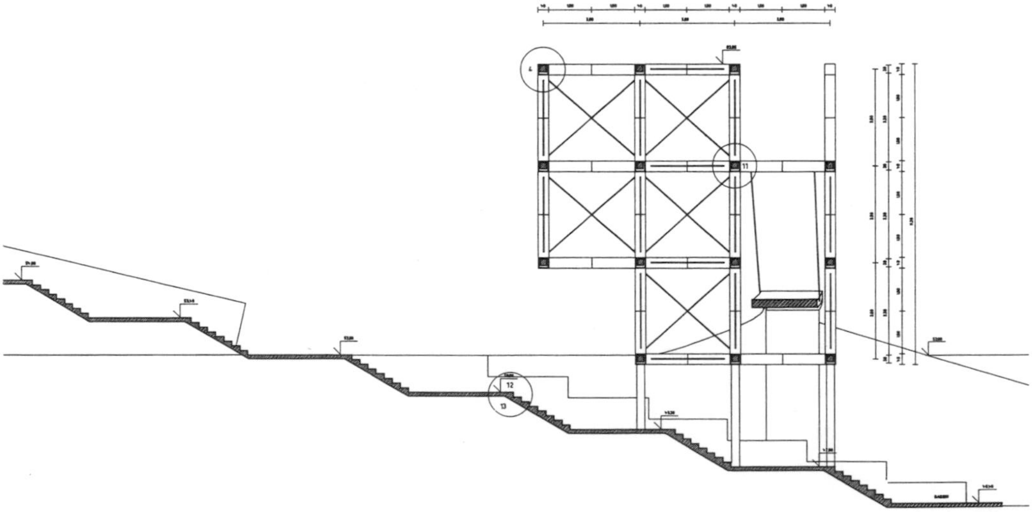
4
11
12
13

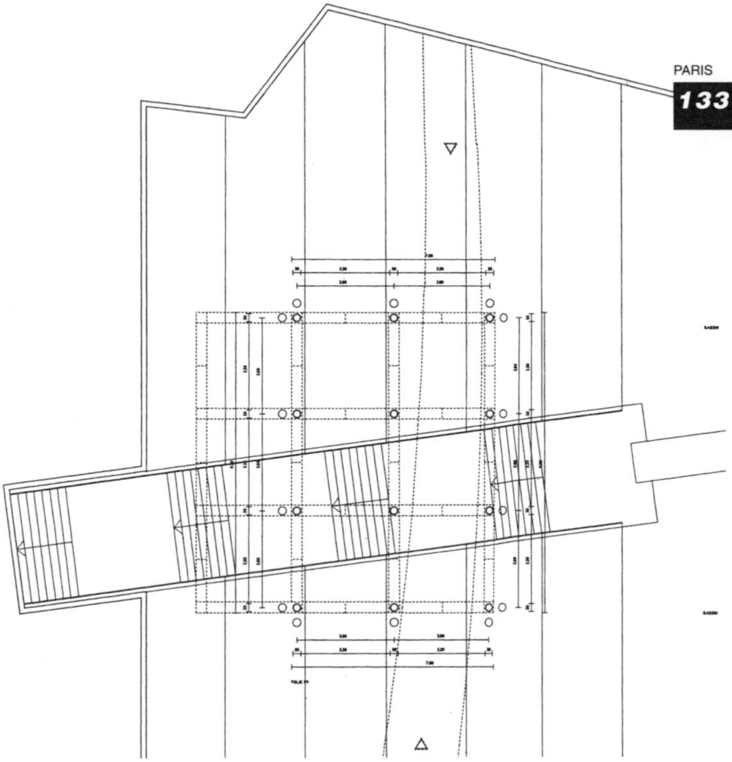

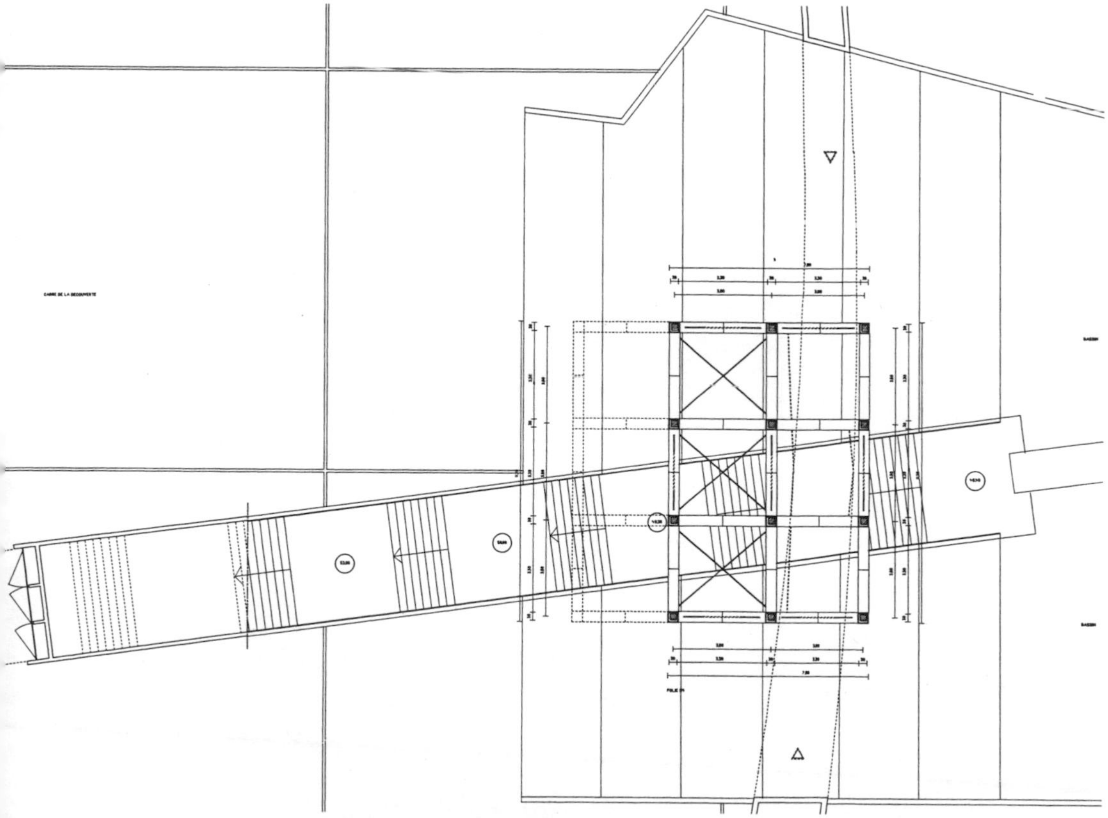

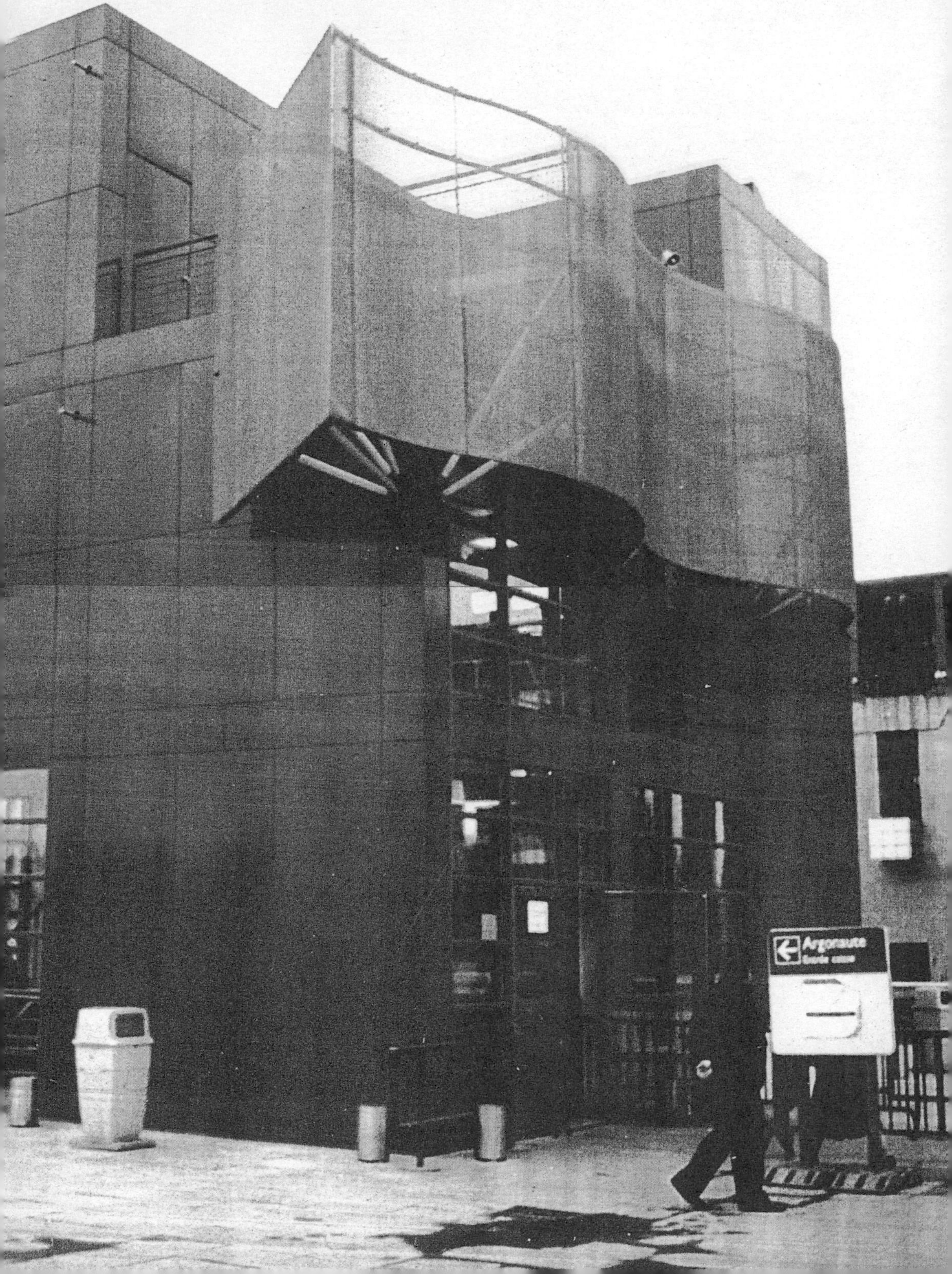
Argonaute

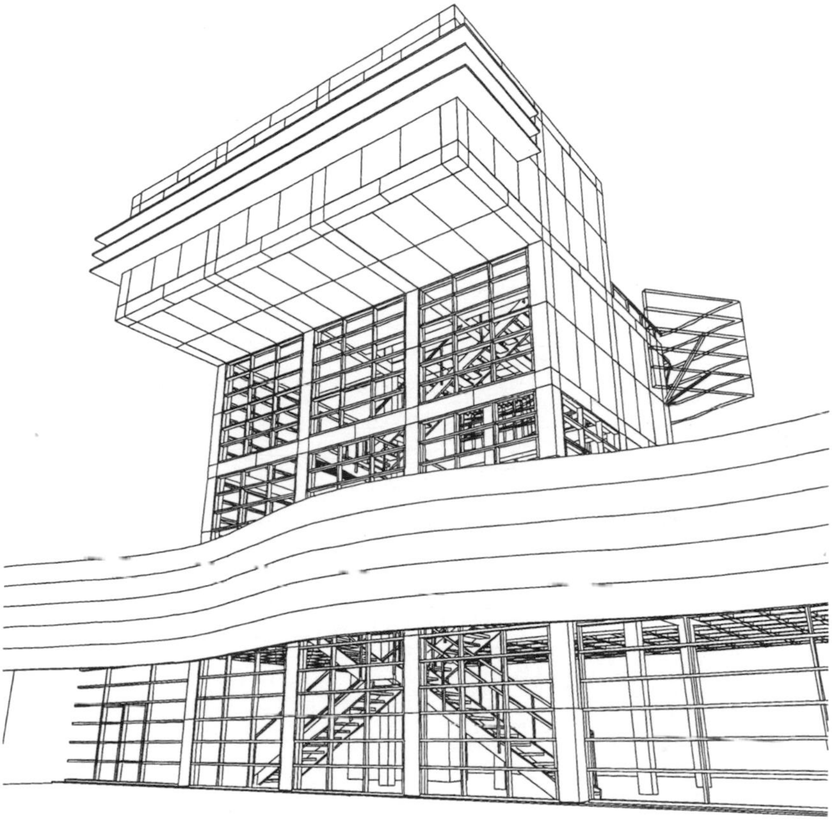

Folie P4 (Folie du Sous-Marin) Program: information and exhibition spaces on first French nuclear submarine. Lounge, entrance area, and ticket booth to submarine docked alongside the Folie

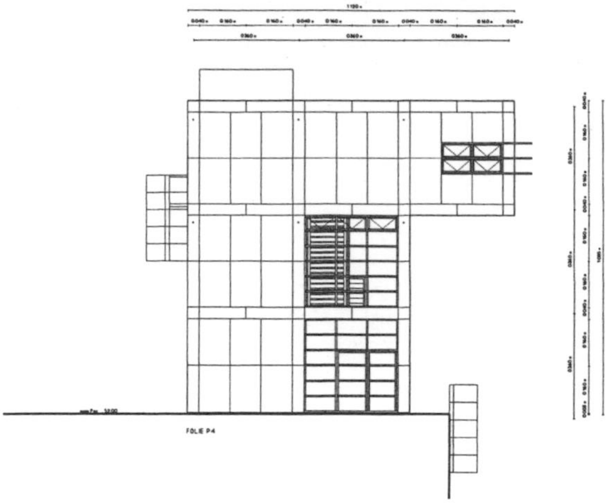
FOLIE P4

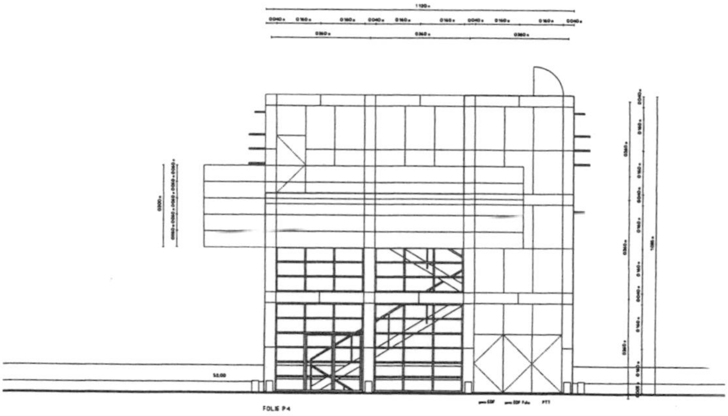
FOLIE P4

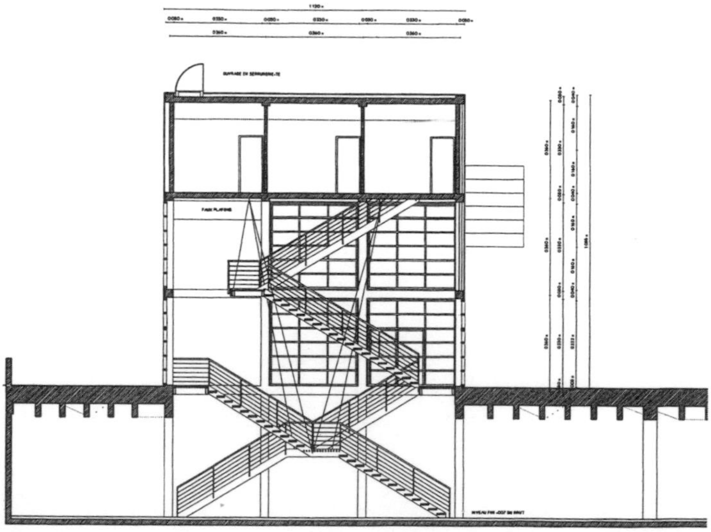

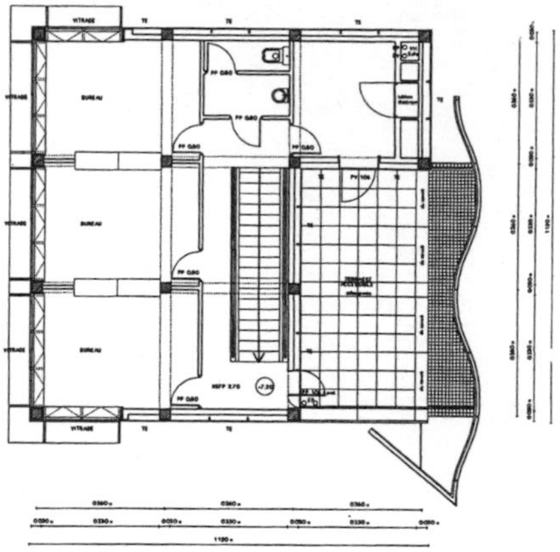

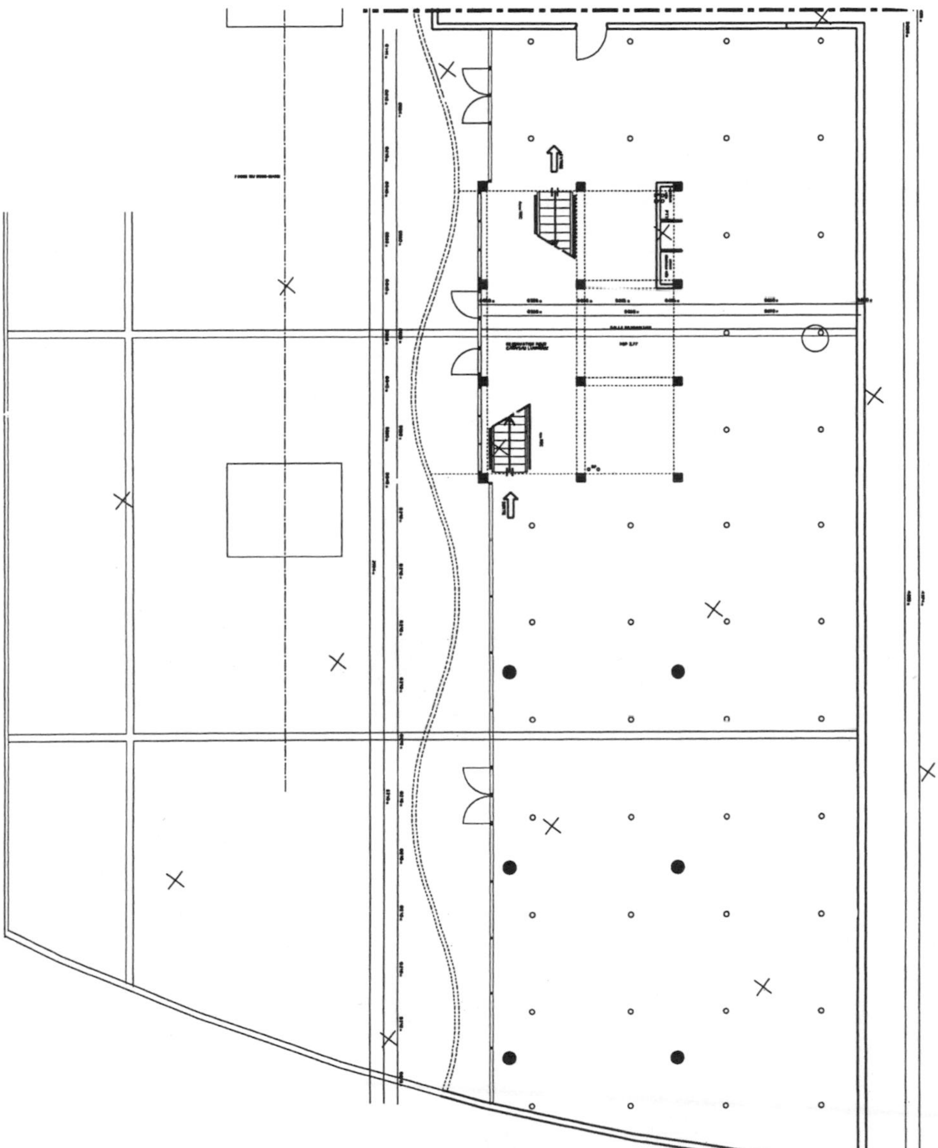

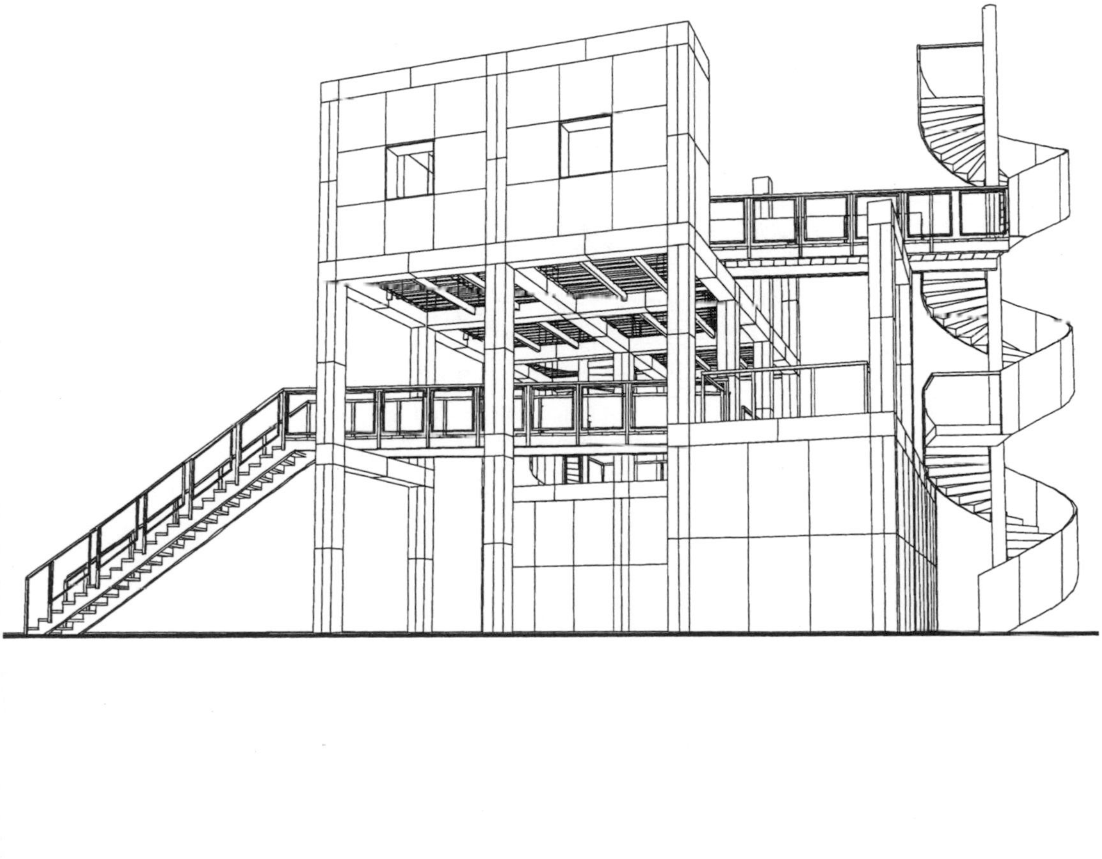

Folie N4 Program: belvedere and technical spaces for the park, storage, public bathrooms

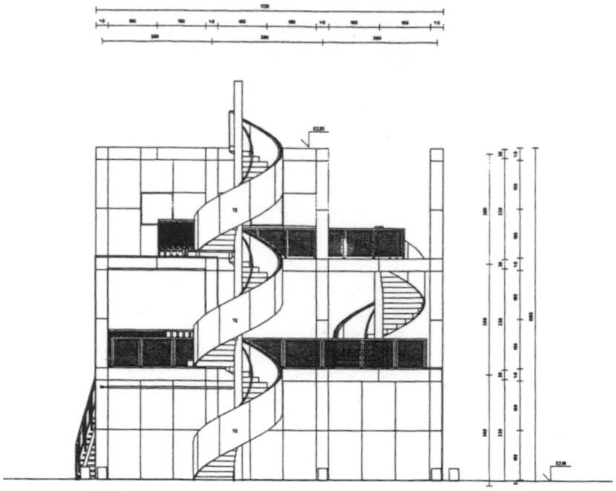

FOLIE N4

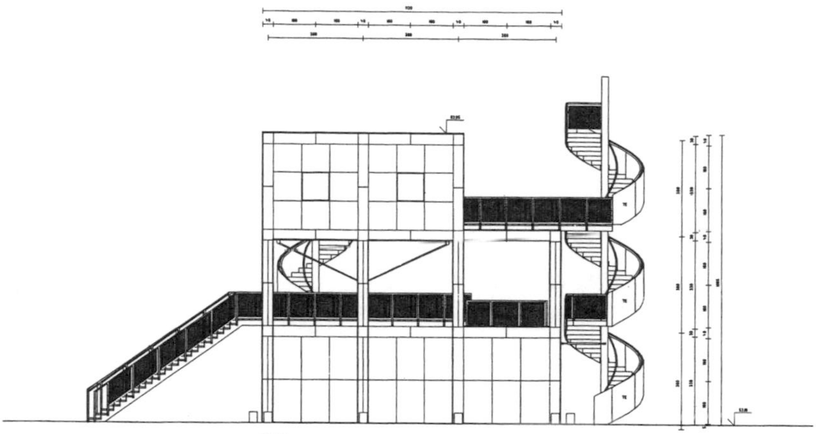

FOLIE N4

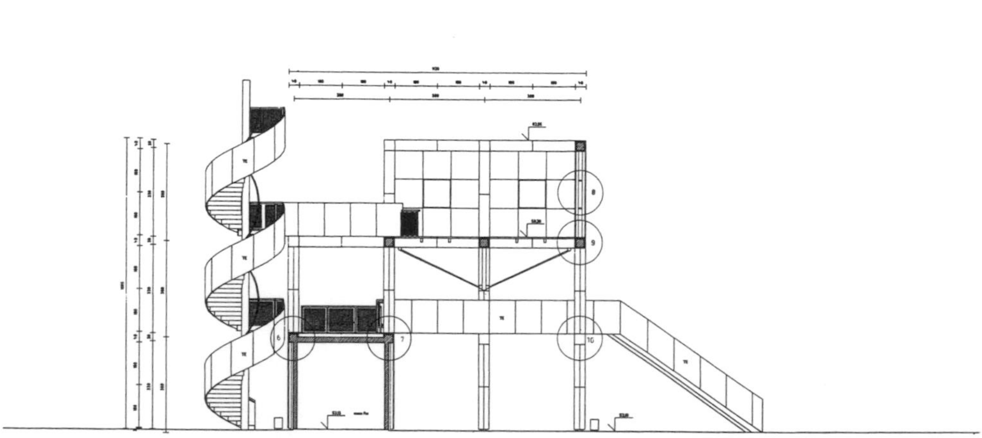

FOLIE N4

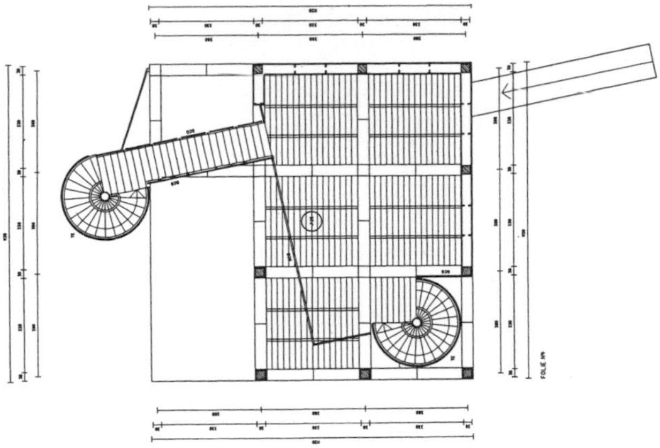

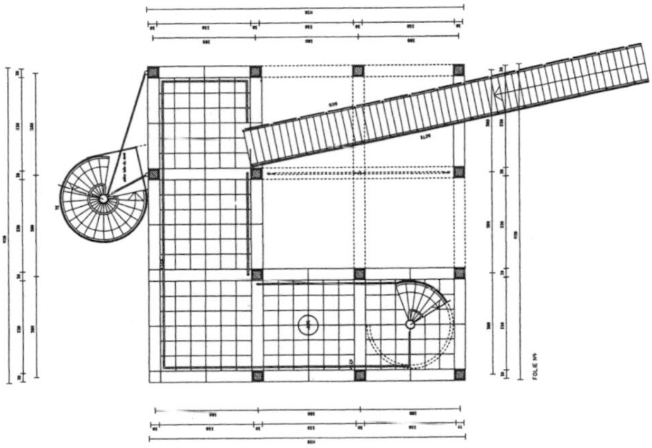

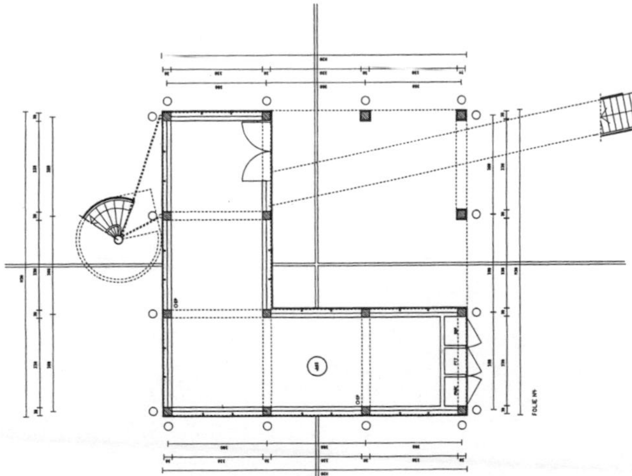

Folie L1 ("Exploded Folie") North entrance of the park, map
(as fragment located off the grid of folies)

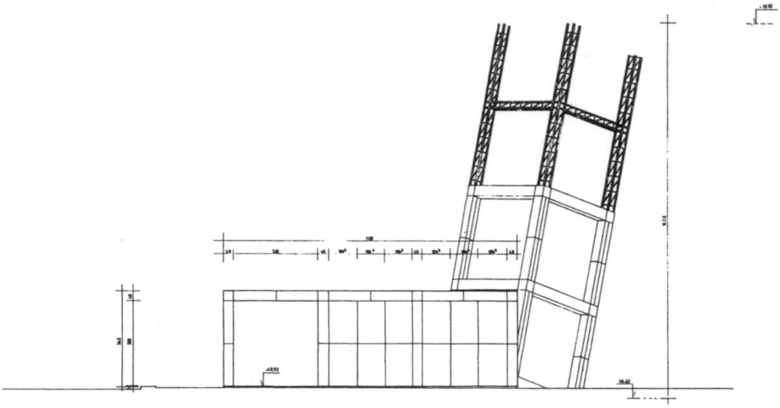

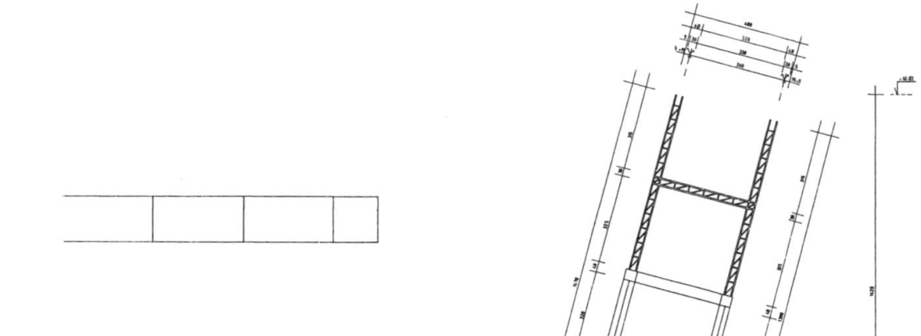

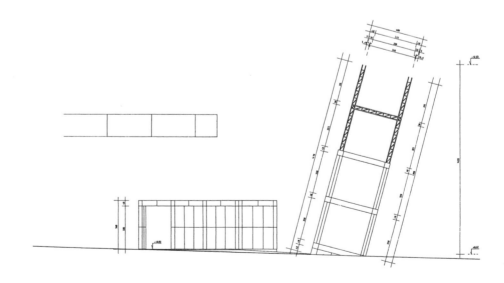

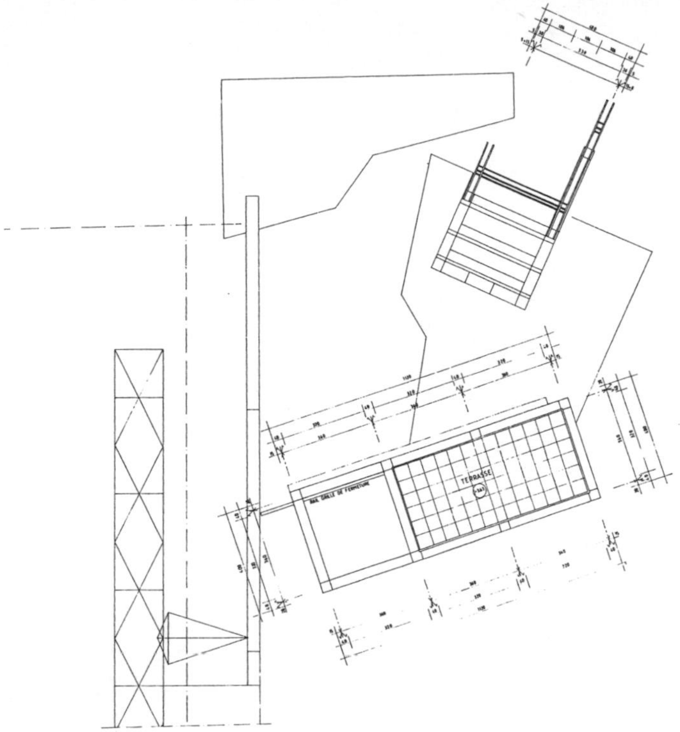
TERRASSE

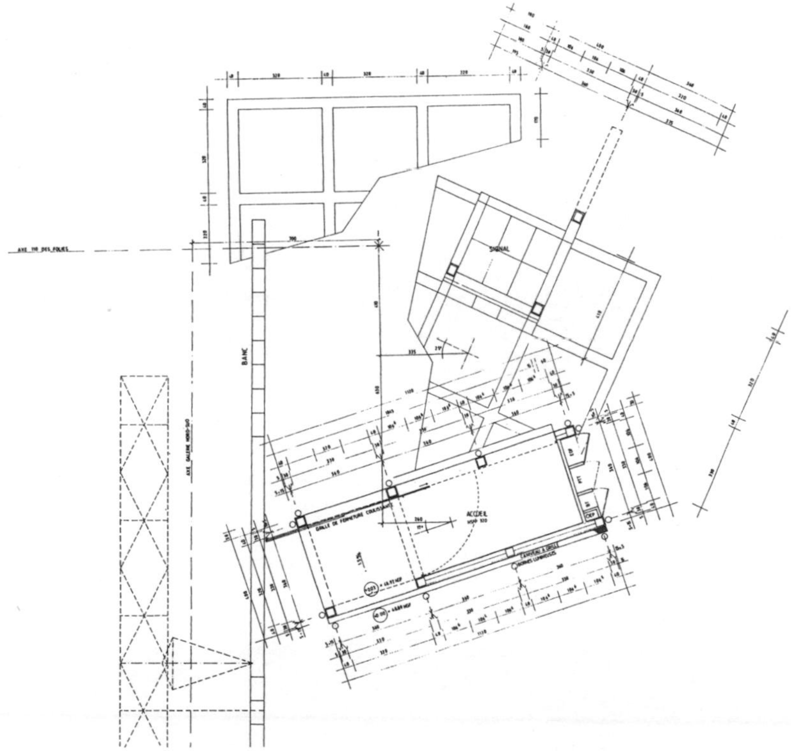
SIGNAL
ACCUEIL
BANC

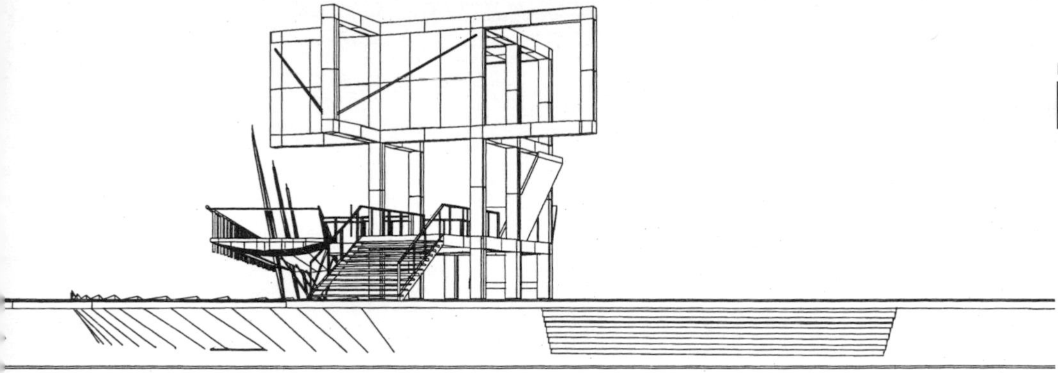

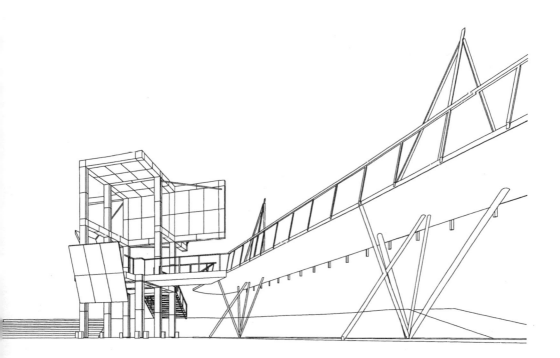

Folie J5 Program: west park entrance, access to three levels a) lower park area b) walkway along canal c) elevated walkway along canal (east-west gallery)

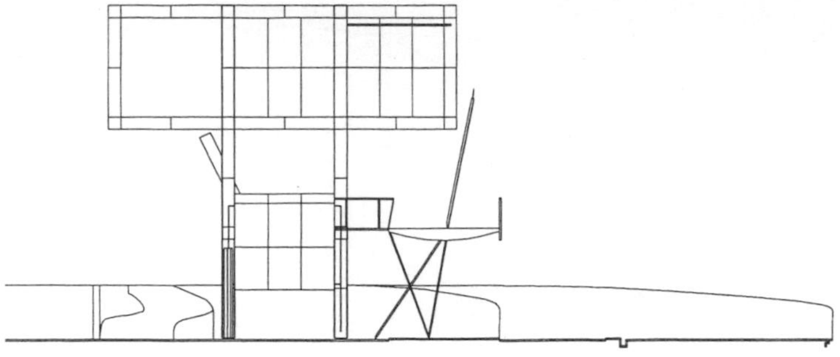

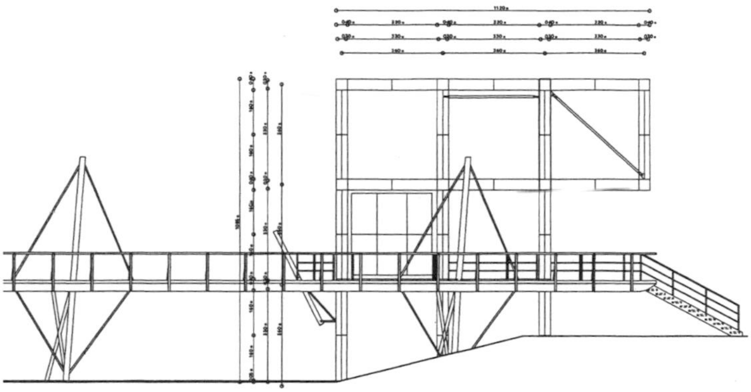

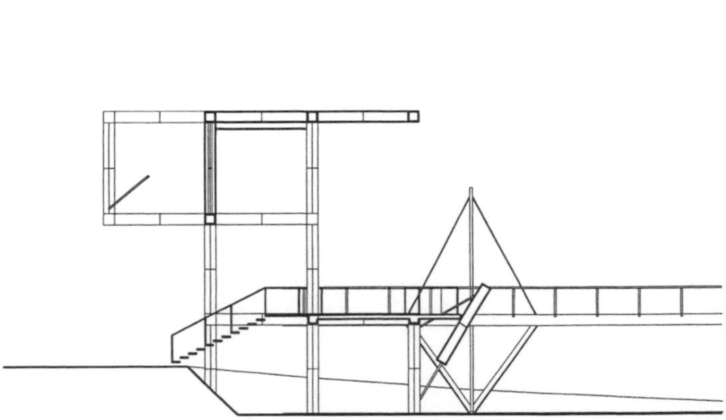

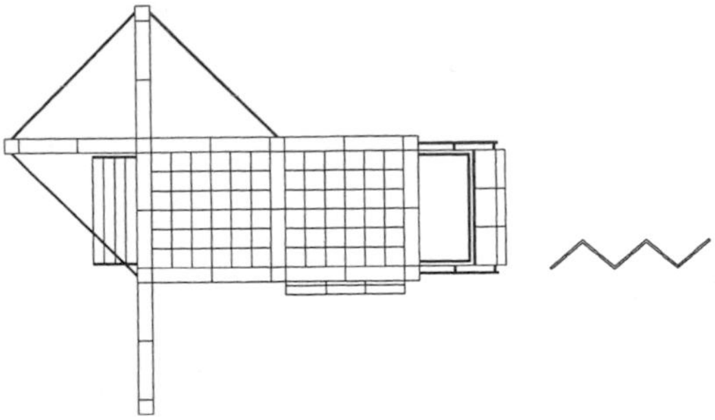

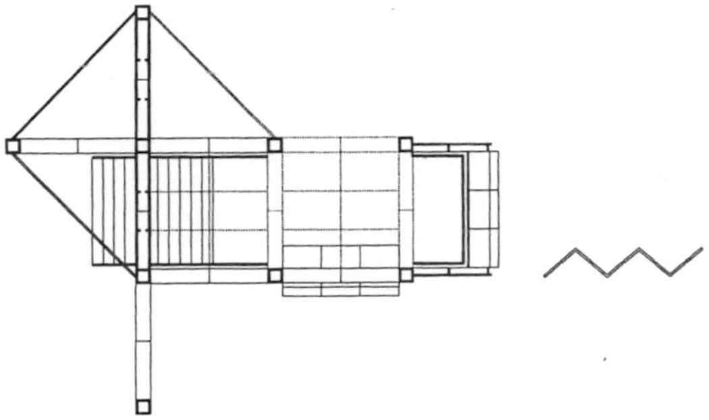

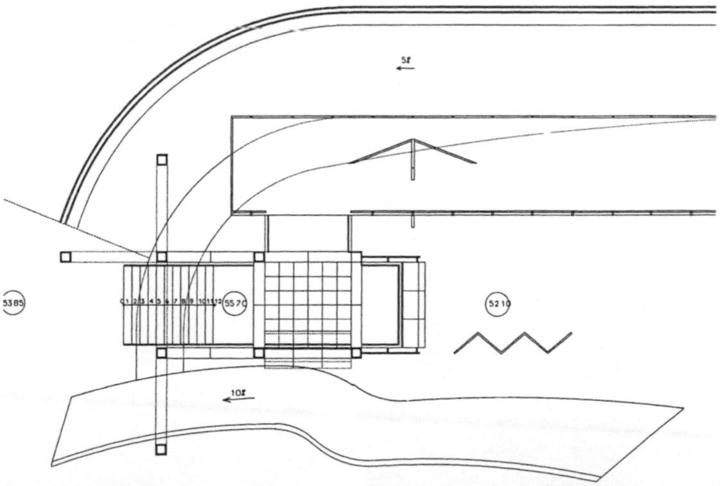
5%
5385
1 2 3 4 5 6 7 8 9 10 11 12
5570
5210
10%

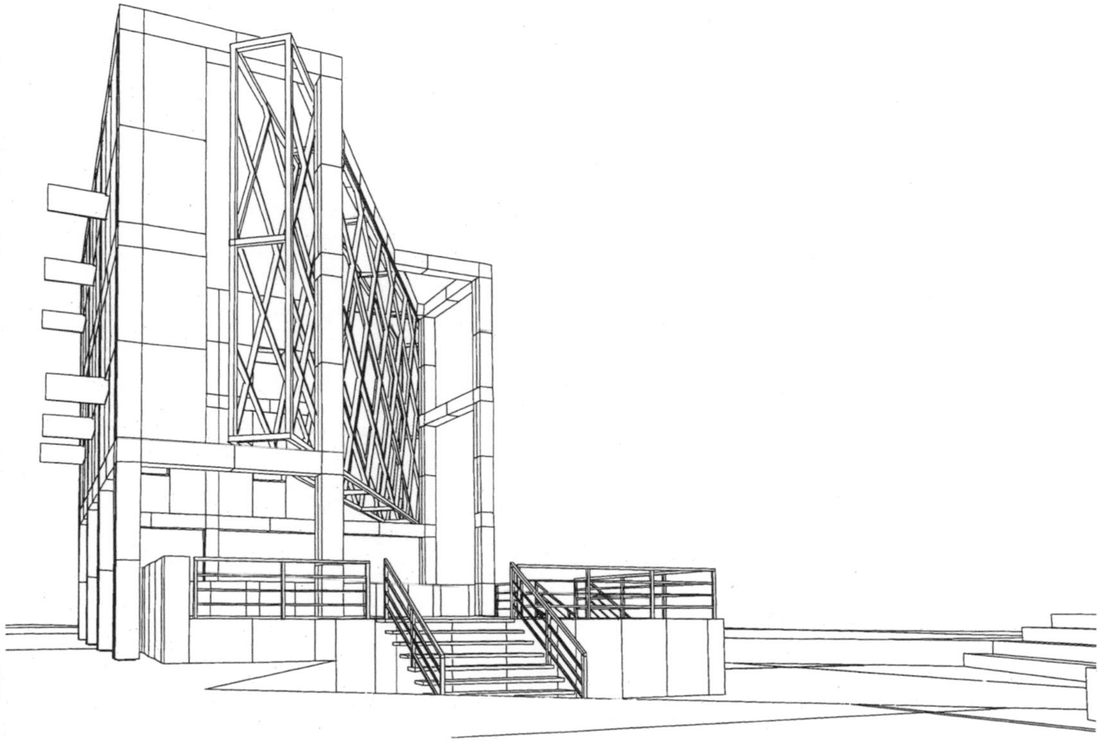

Folie L4 Program: bandstand, support structure for loudspeakers, raised stage, storage, public listening area

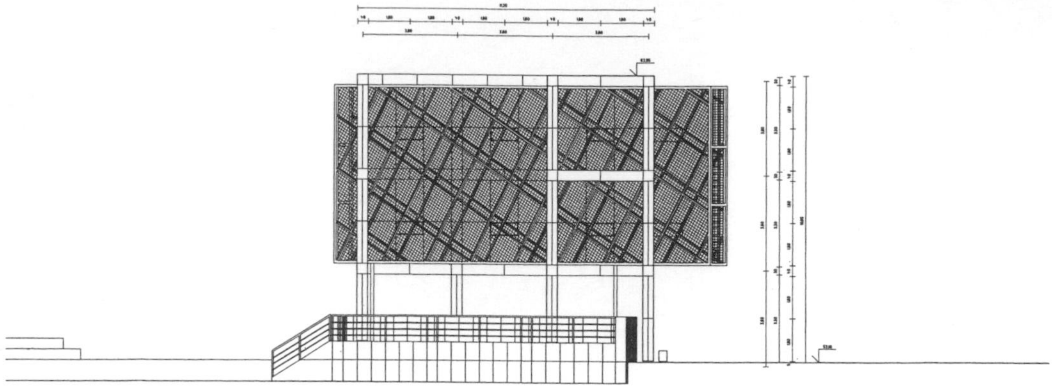

FOLIE L1

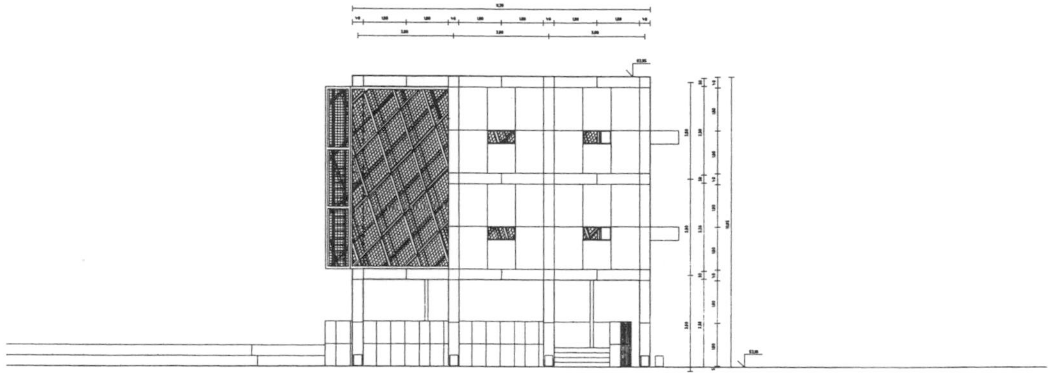

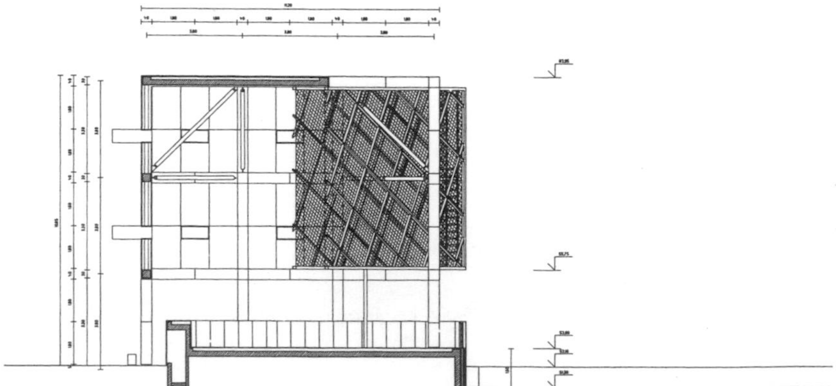

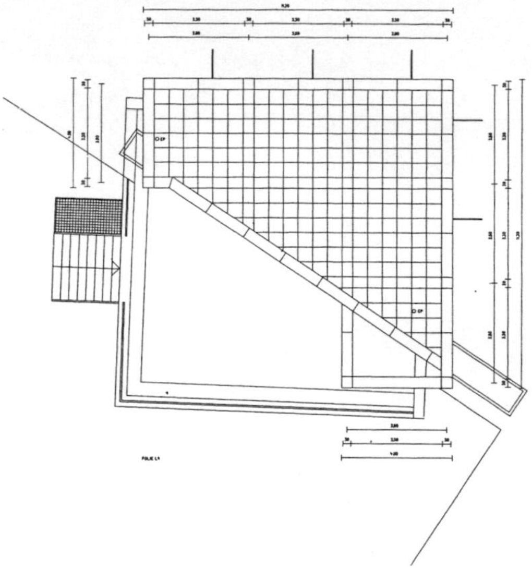

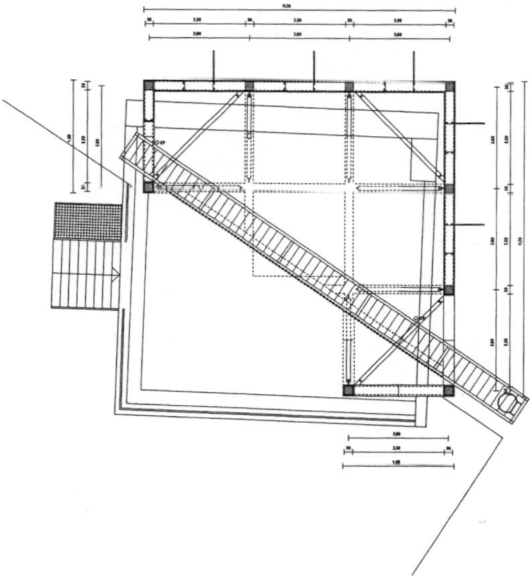

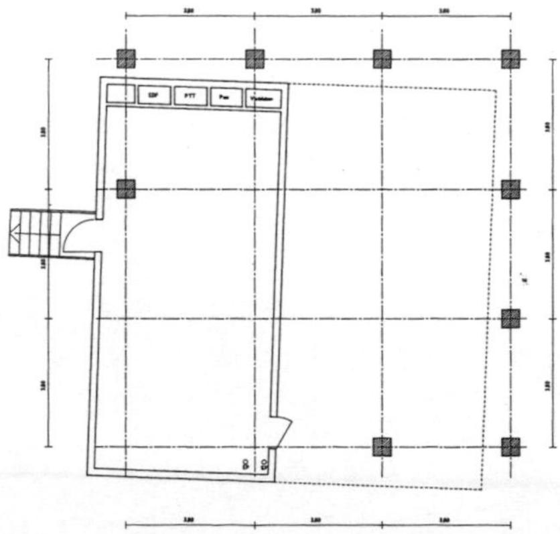
EDF
PTT

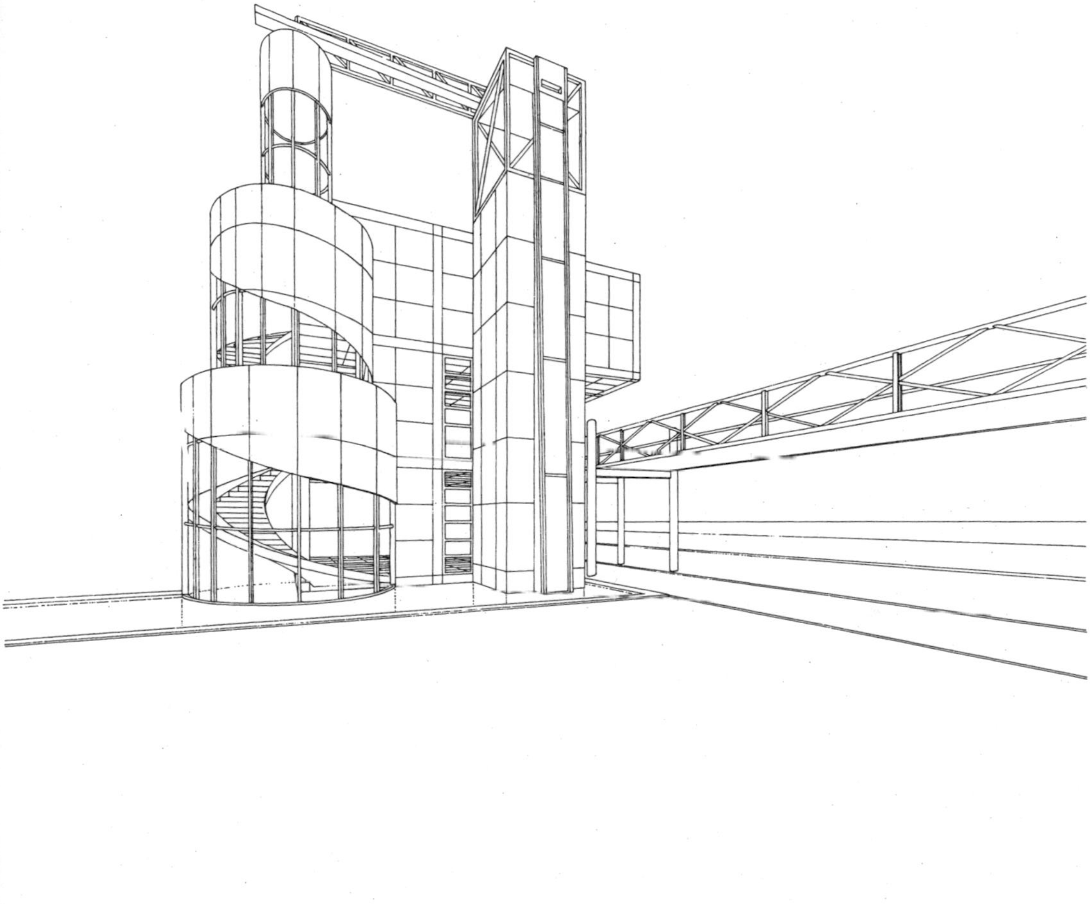

Folie N5 First program: children's playground with workshop. Second program: television studio for teenagers with recording facilities, offices

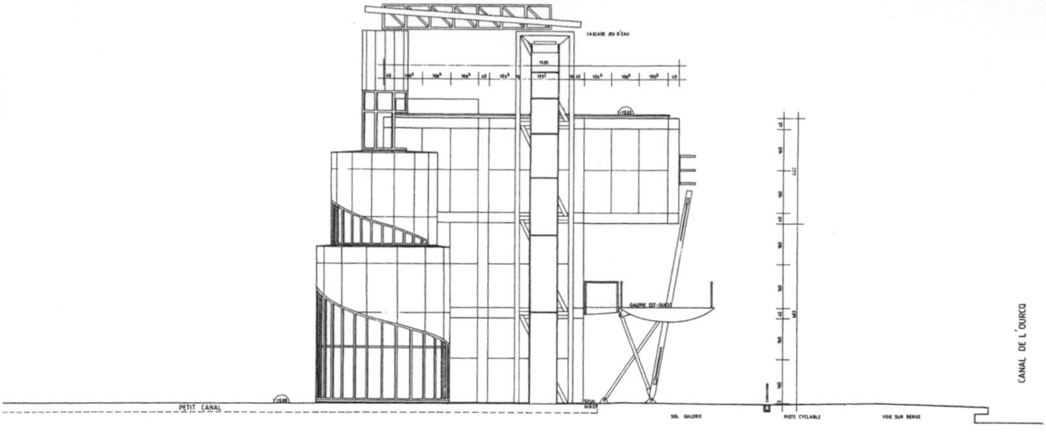
CASCADE JEU D'EAU
GALERIE EST-OUEST
PETIT CANAL
SOL GALERIE
PISTE CYCLABLE
VOIE SUR BERGE
CANAL DE L'OURCQ

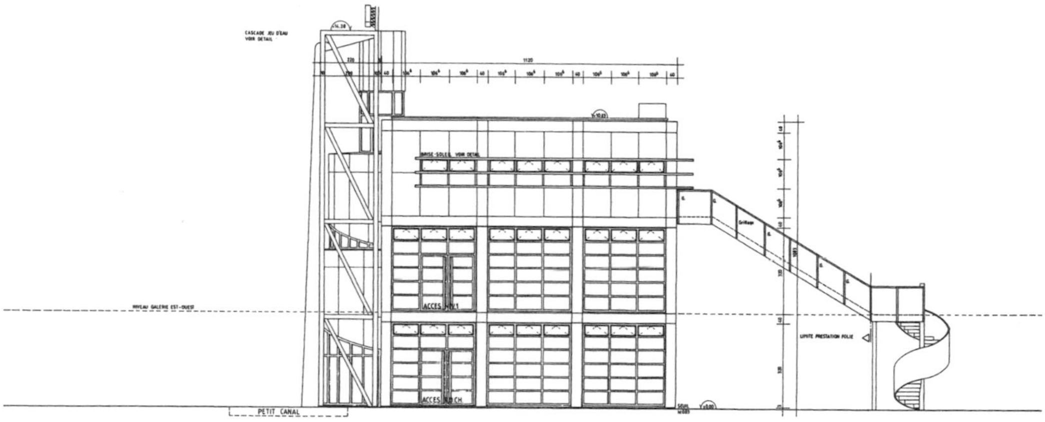
CASCADE JEU D'EAU
VOIR DETAIL
1120
BRISE-SOLEIL VOIR DETAIL
NIVEAU GALERIE EST-OUEST
LIMITE PRESTATION FOLIE
PETIT CANAL

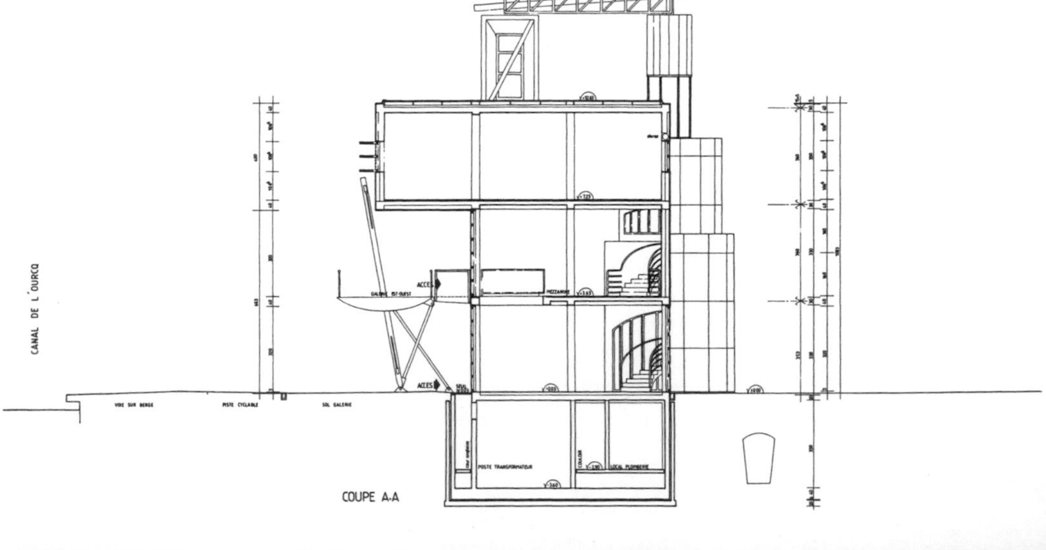
CANAL DE L'OURCQ
GALERIE EST-OUEST
ACCES
MEZZANINE
VOIE SUR BERGE
PISTE CYCLABLE
SOL GALERIE
POSTE TRANSFORMATEUR
COULOIR
LOCAL PLOMBERIE

COUPE A-A

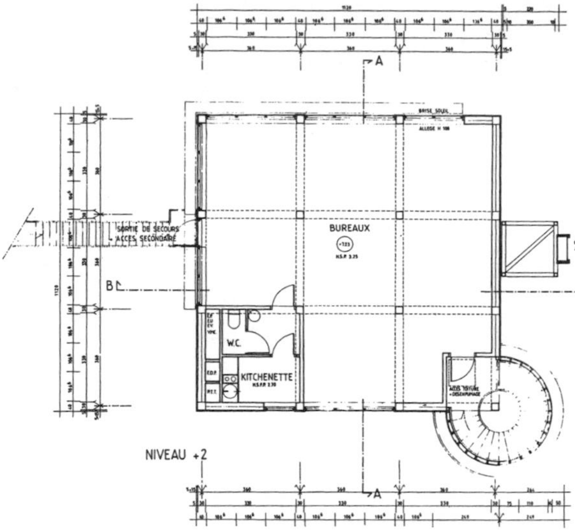

NIVEAU +2

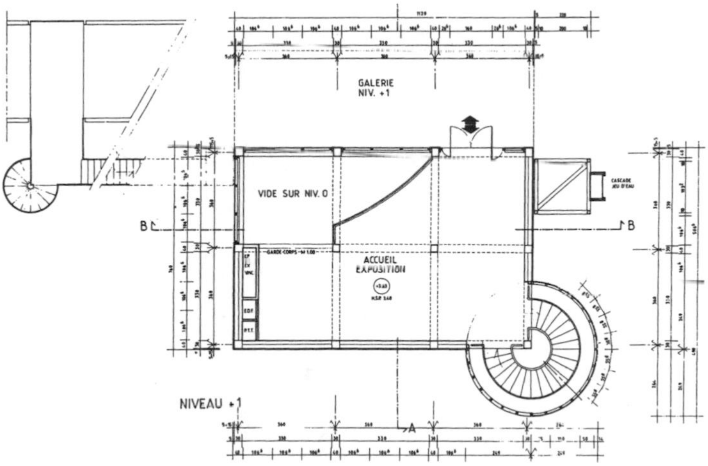

NIVEAU +1

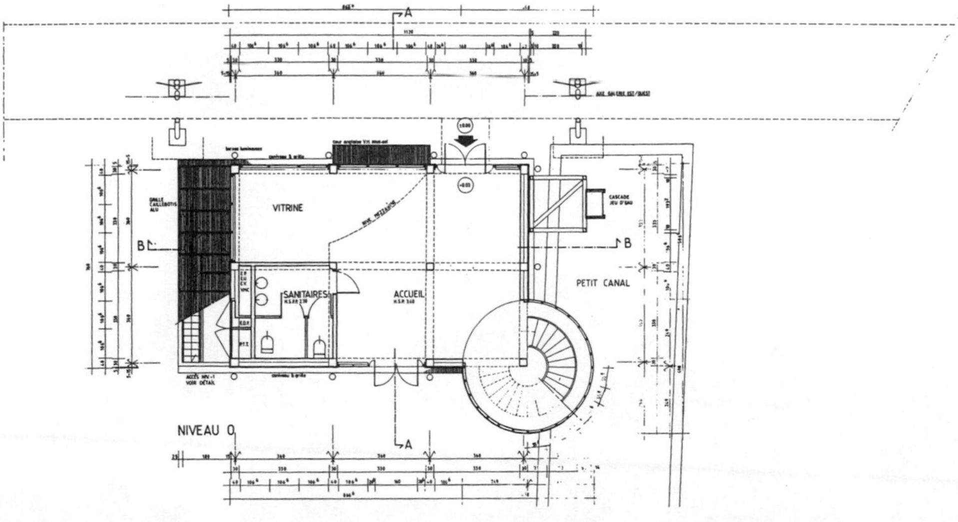

NIVEAU 0

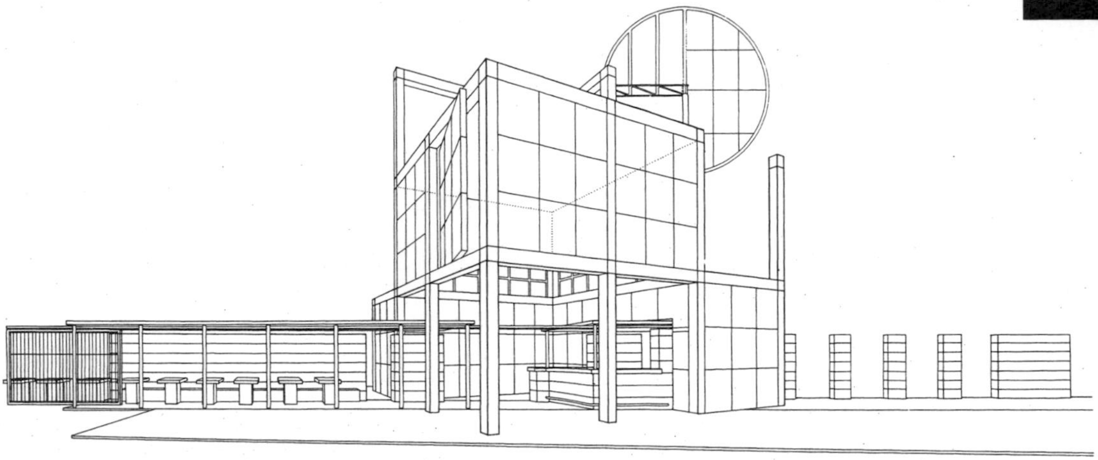

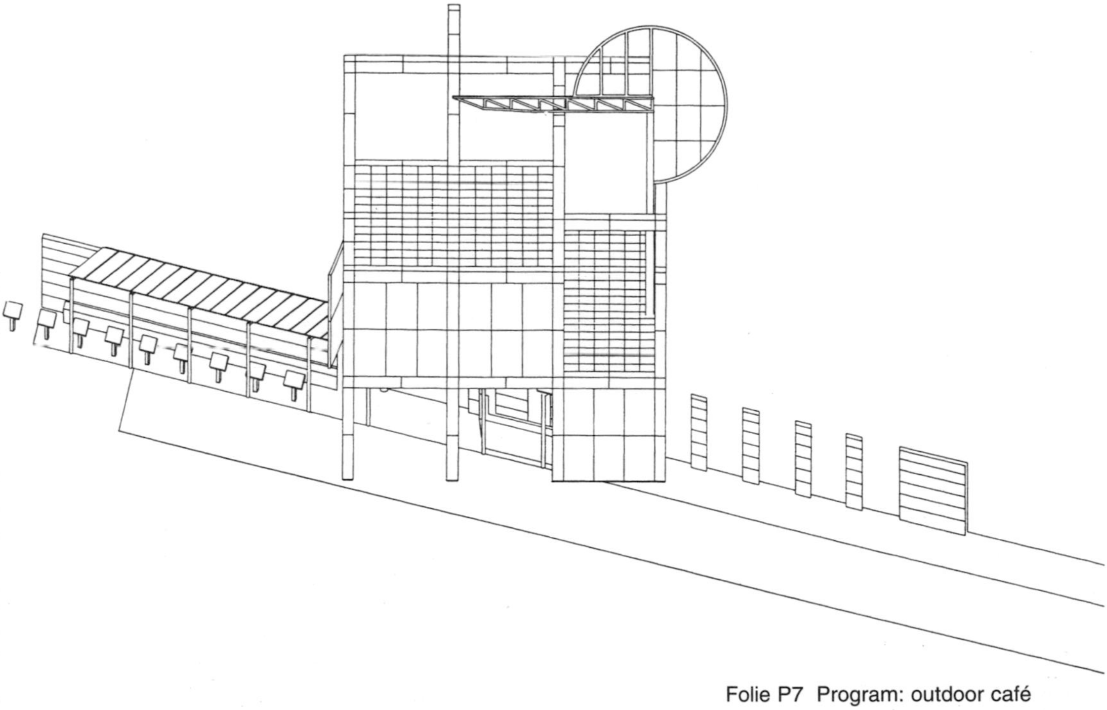

Folie P7 Program: outdoor café

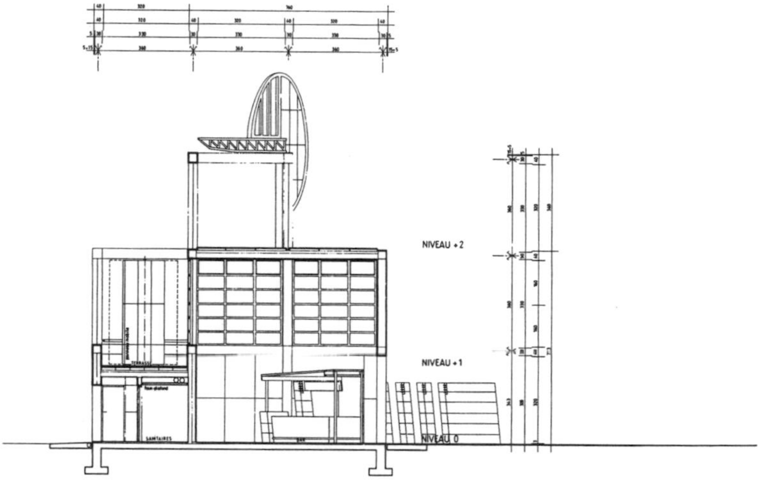
NIVEAU +2
NIVEAU +1
NIVEAU 0
TERRASSE
SANITAIRES

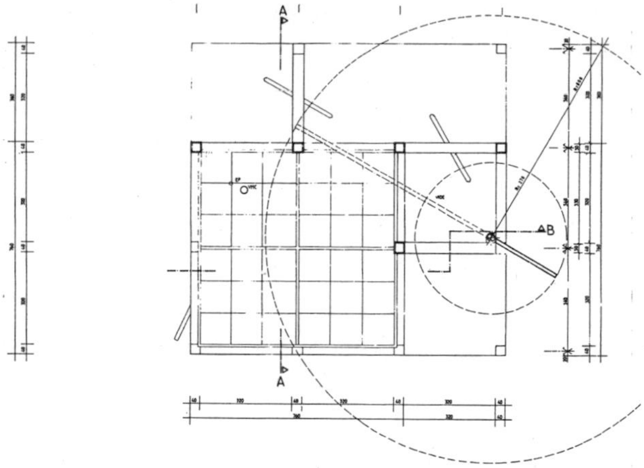

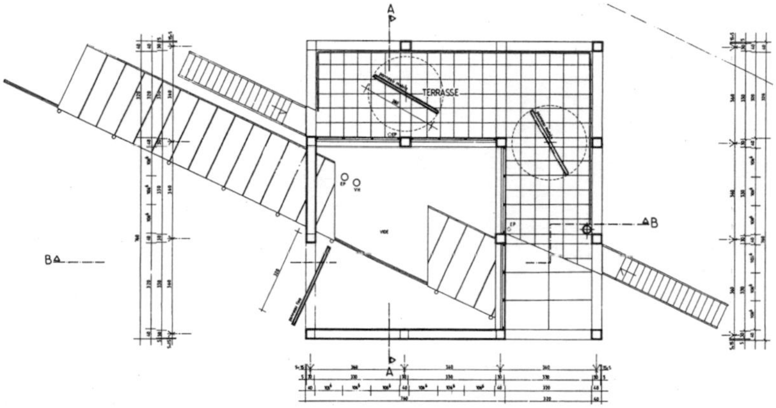
A
TERRASSE
B
A

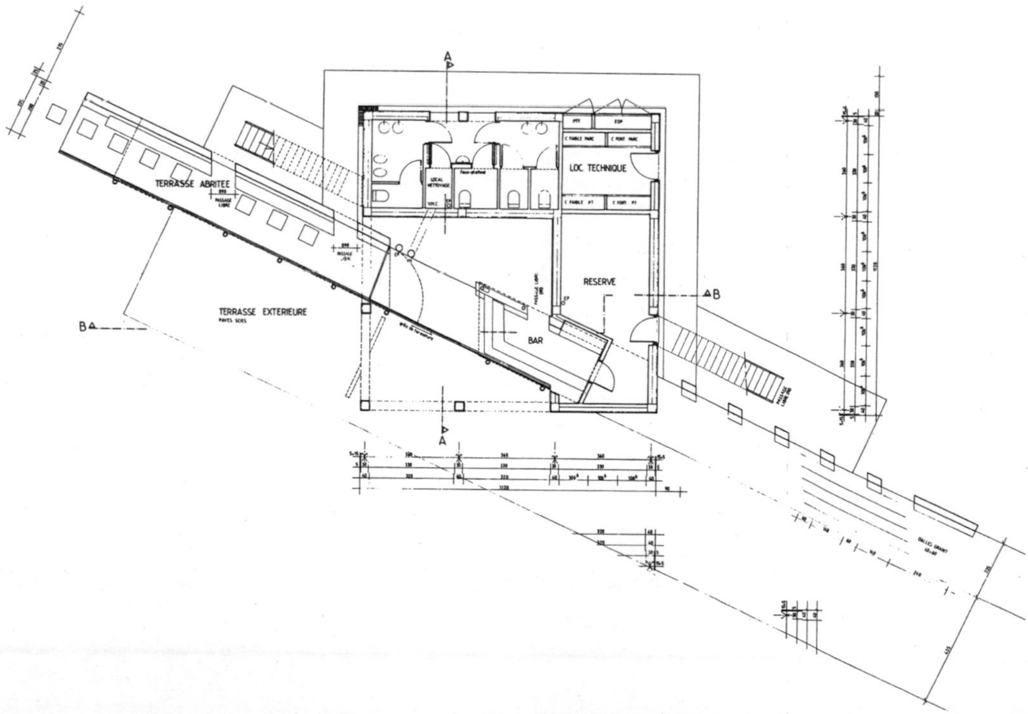
A
LOC TECHNIQUE
RESERVE
BAR
TERRASSE ABRITEE
TERRASSE EXTERIEURE
B
A

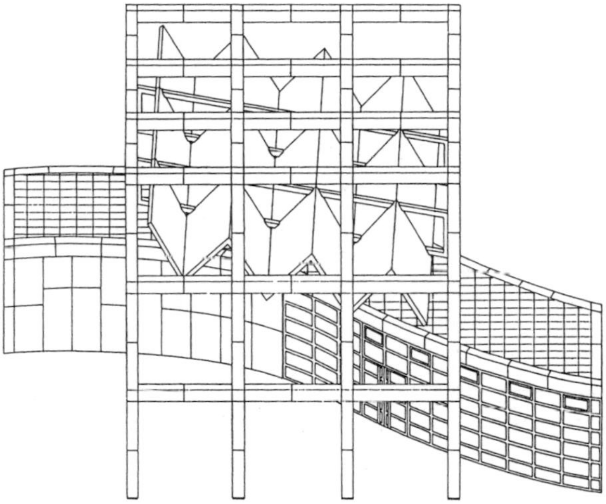

Folie L3 Program: electrical generator, staff changing rooms, storage

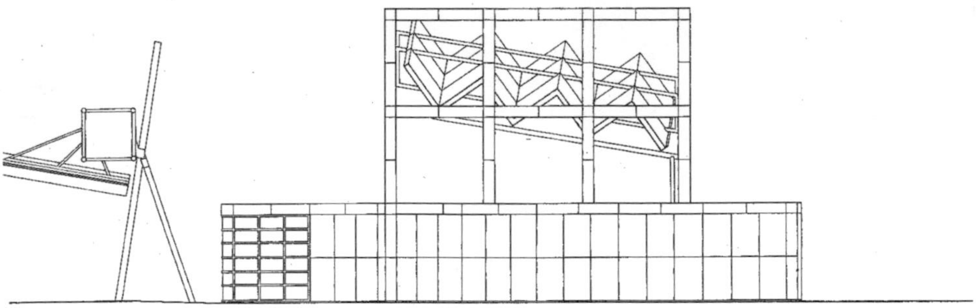

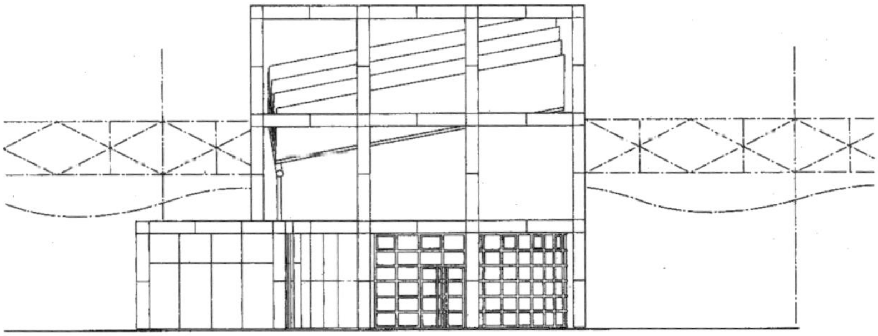

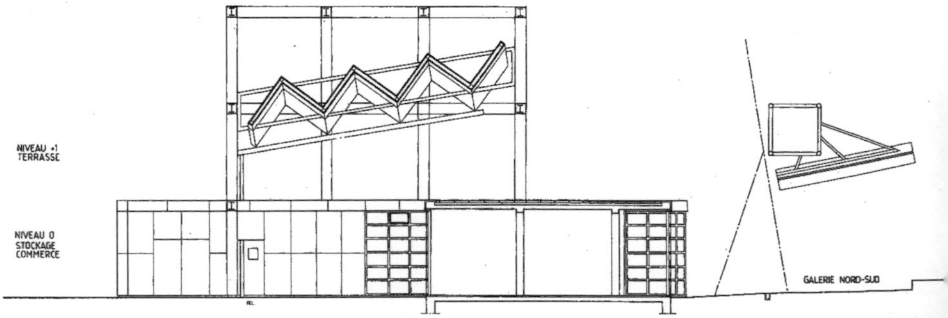
NIVEAU +1
TERRASSE
NIVEAU 0
STOCKAGE
COMMERCE
GALERIE NORD-SUD

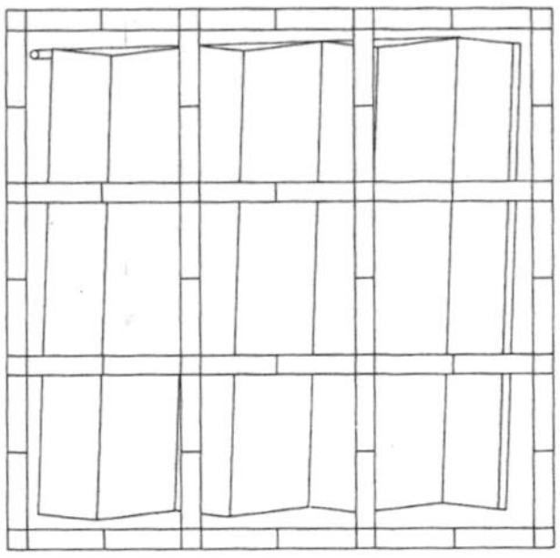

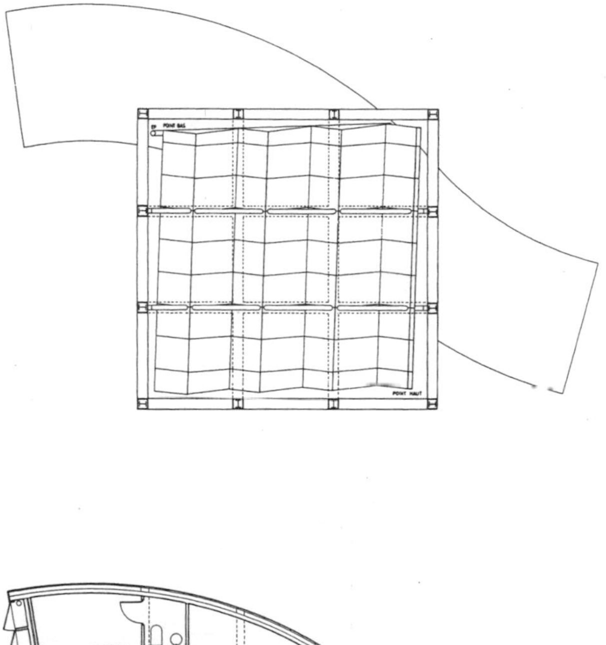
POINT BAS
POINT HAUT

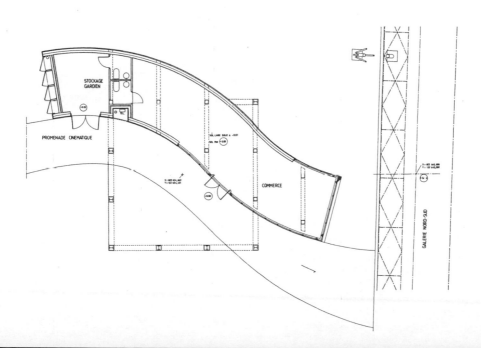

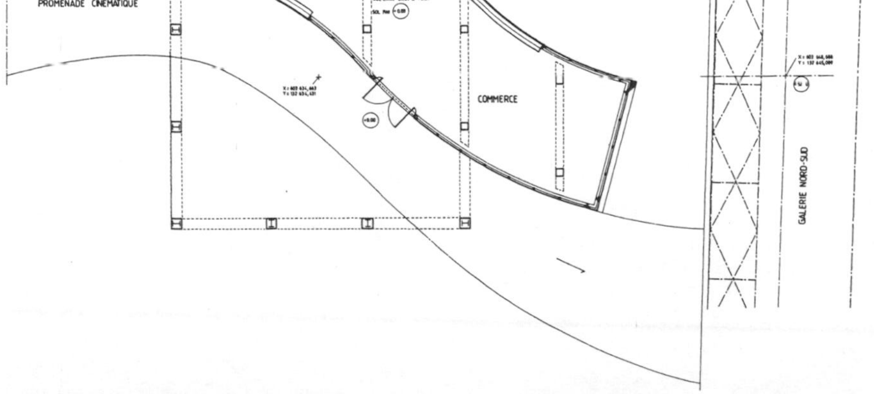
STOCKAGE
GARDIEN
TEL.
PROMENADE CINEMATIQUE
COMMERCE
GALERIE NORD-SUD

Color coding: grass is green, sky is blue, buildings are red

“Why do you always use the color red, Mr. Architect?” “Because red is not a color.”

Folie R6 Offices and ticket booths for the Zenith, a 6000-seat pop music auditorium attached to it

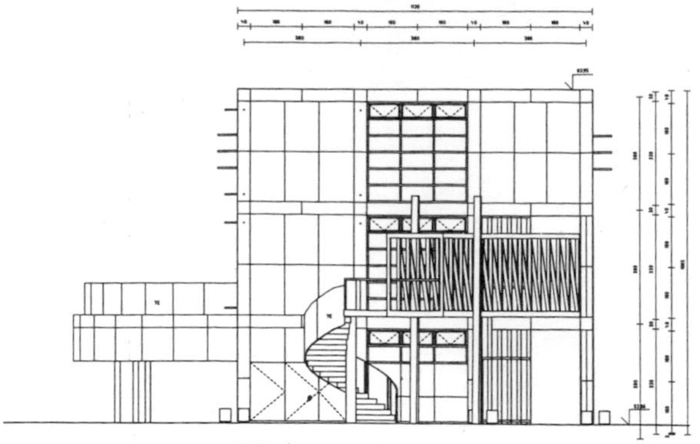

FOLIE R6

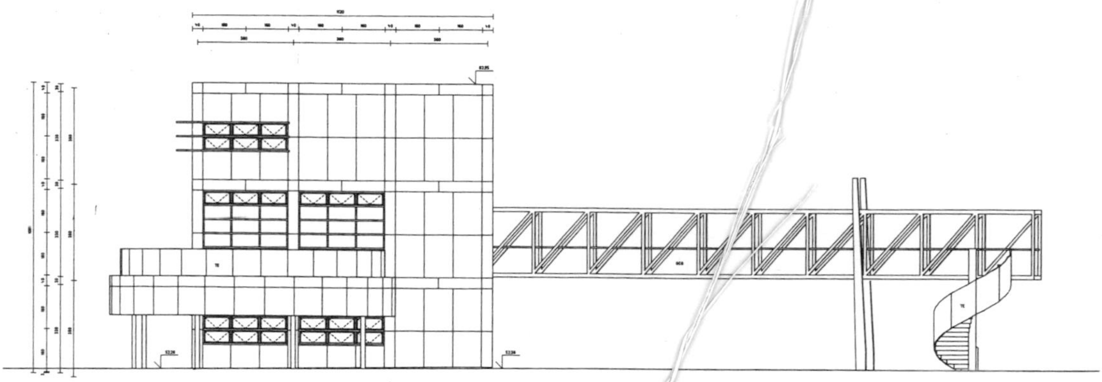

FOLIE R6

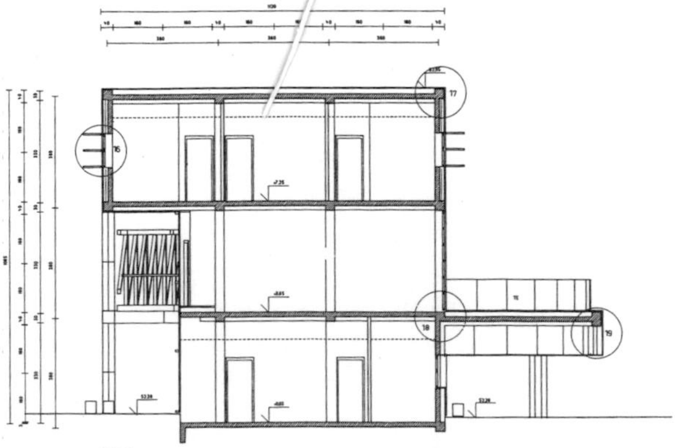

FOLIE RE

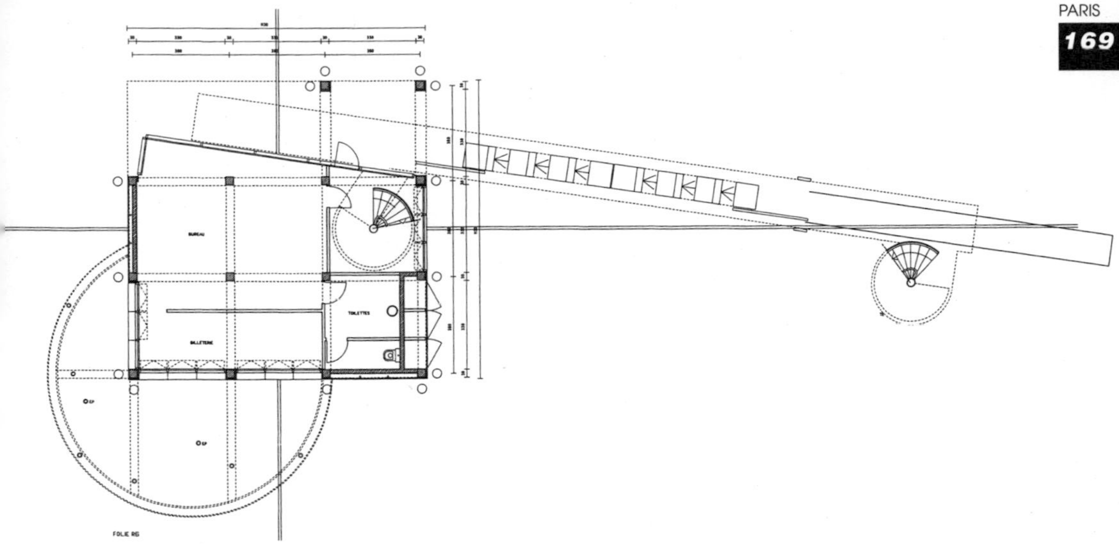

FOLIE R6

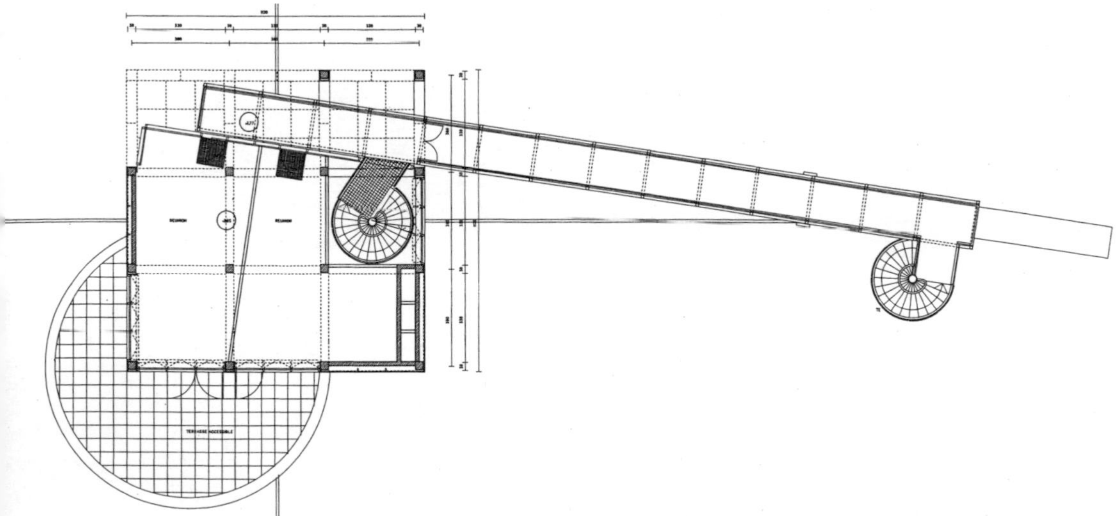

FOLIE R6

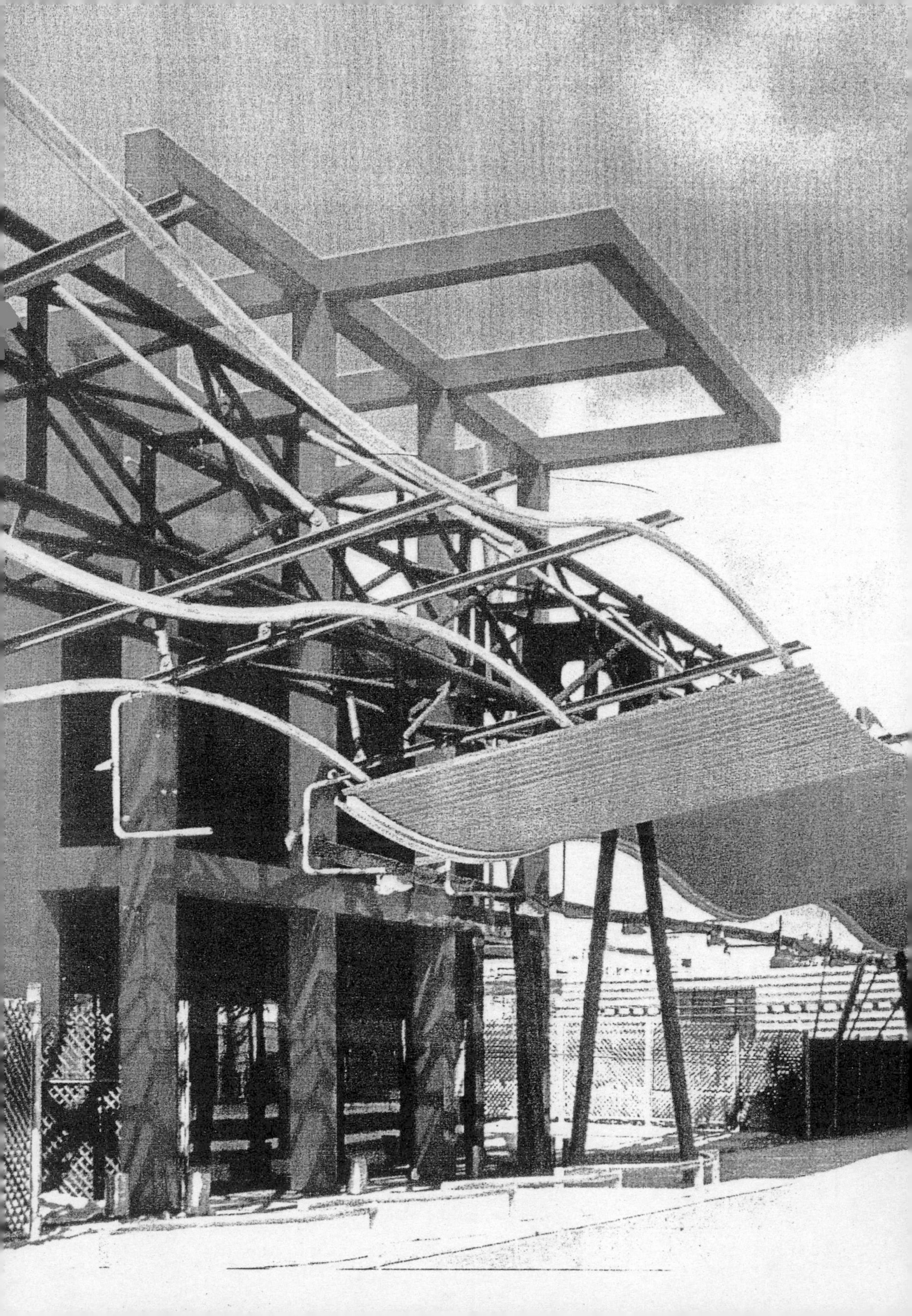

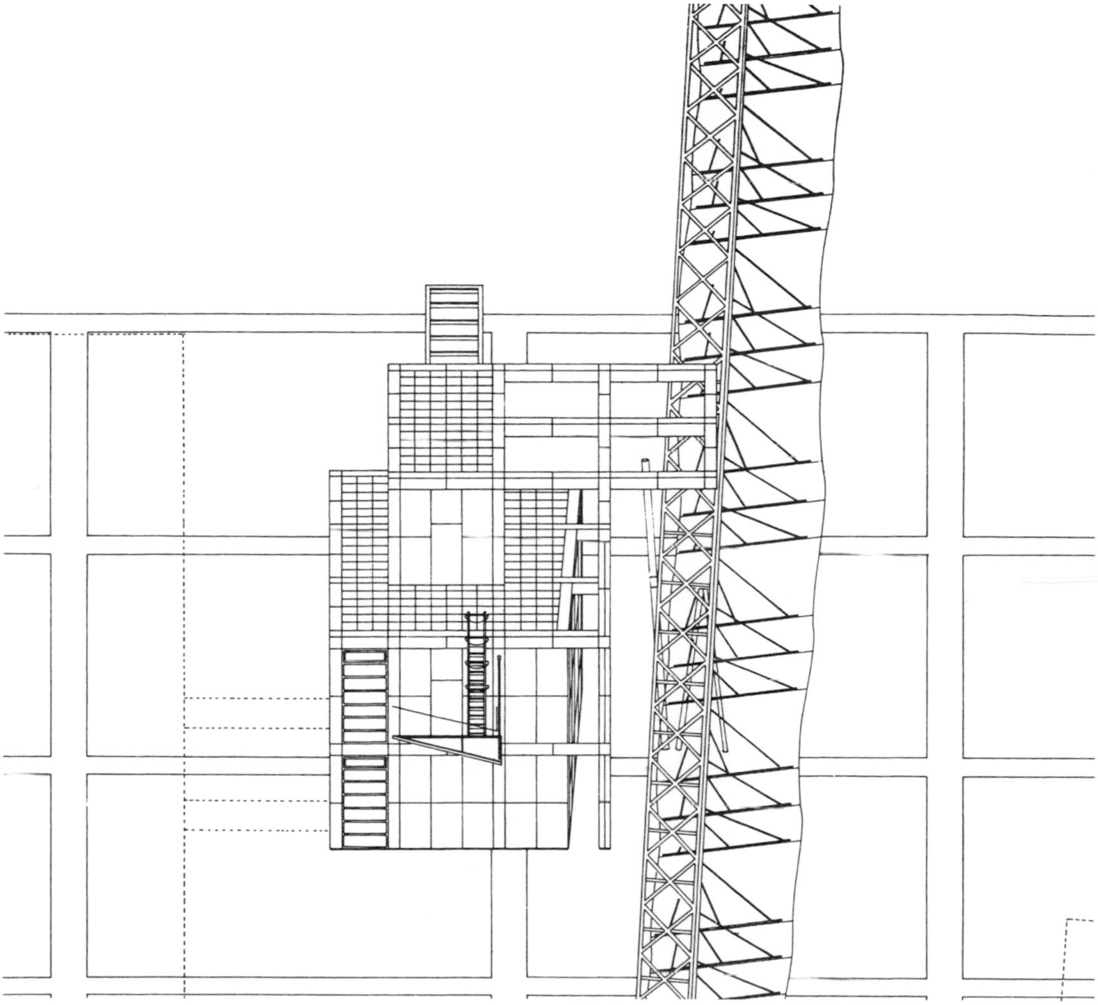

Folie L6 Entrance to children's playgrounds, lounge, bathrooms, access to slide

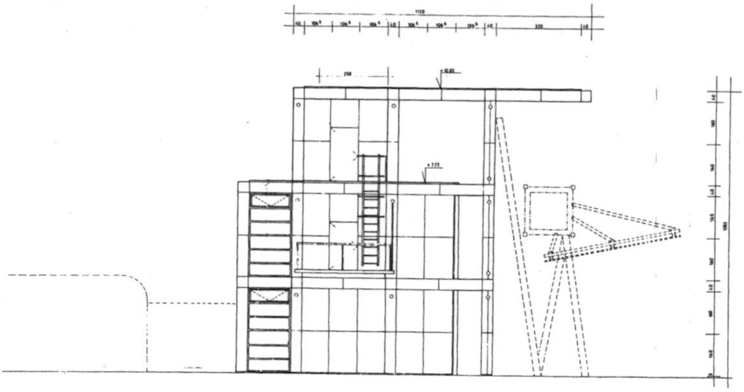

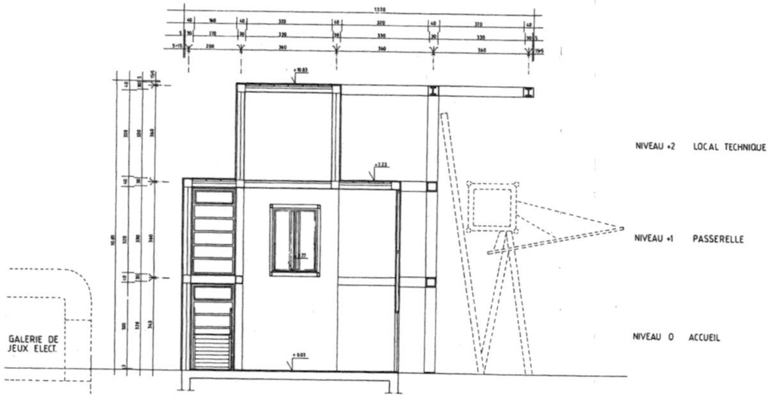
NIVEAU +2 LOCAL TECHNIQUE
NIVEAU +1 PASSERELLE
NIVEAU 0 ACCUEIL
GALERIE DE
JEUX ELECT.

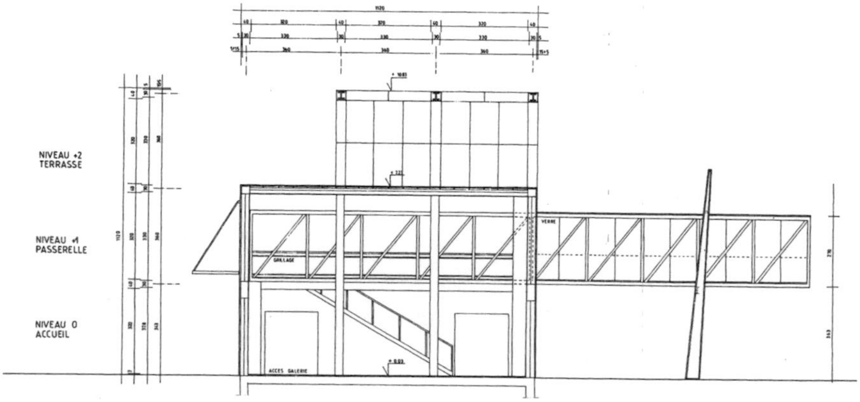
NIVEAU +2
TERRASSE
NIVEAU +1
PASSERELLE
NIVEAU 0
ACCUEIL
GRILLAGE
VERRE
ACCES GALERIE

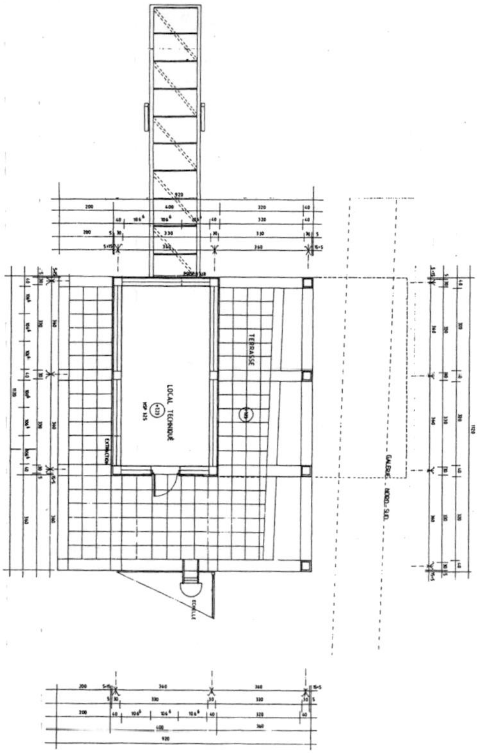
LOCAL TECHNIQUE
TERRASSE
GALERIE NORD-SUD

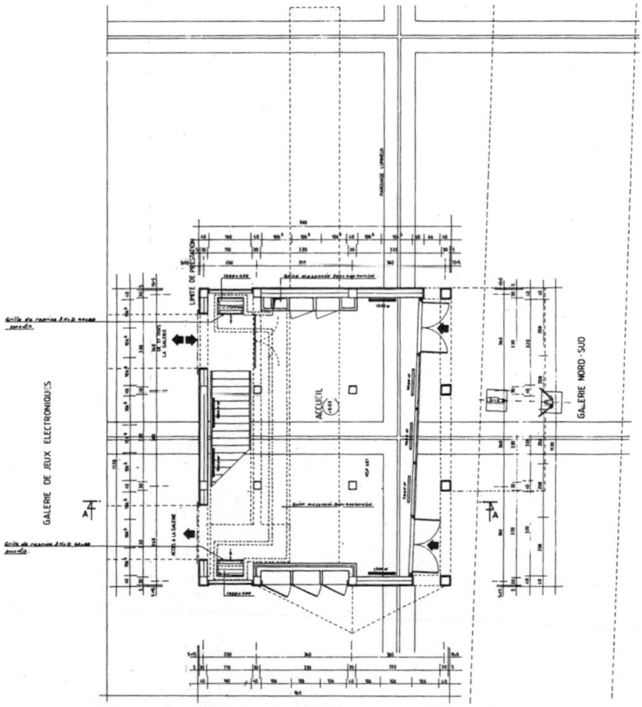
GALERIE DE JEUX ELECTRONIQUES
LIMITE DE PRESTATION
ACCUEIL
GALERIE NORD-SUD

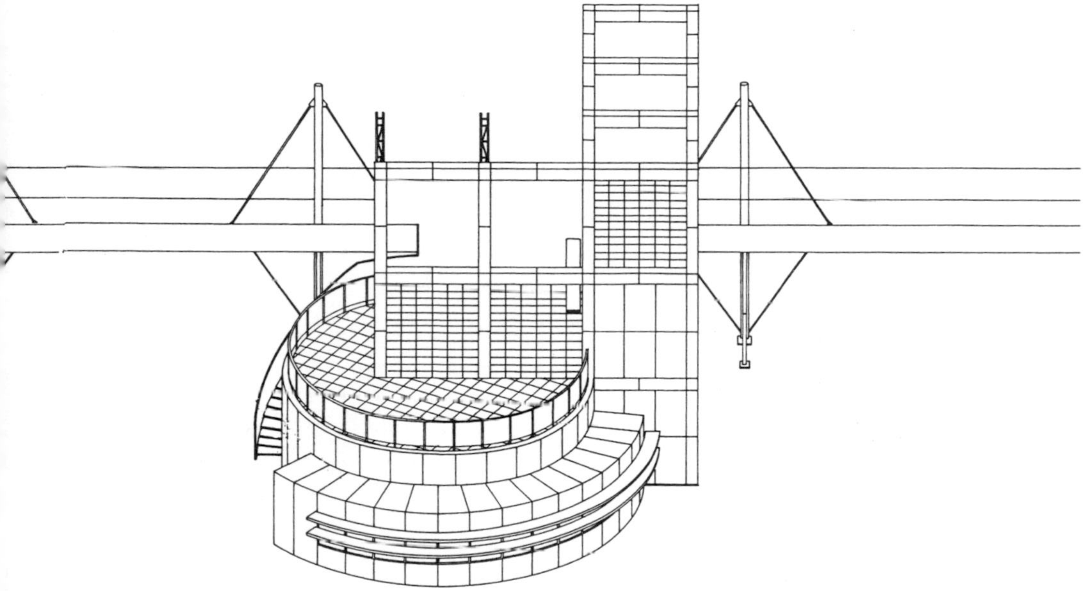

Folie P5 Program: children's workshop, storage, outdoor café, terrace

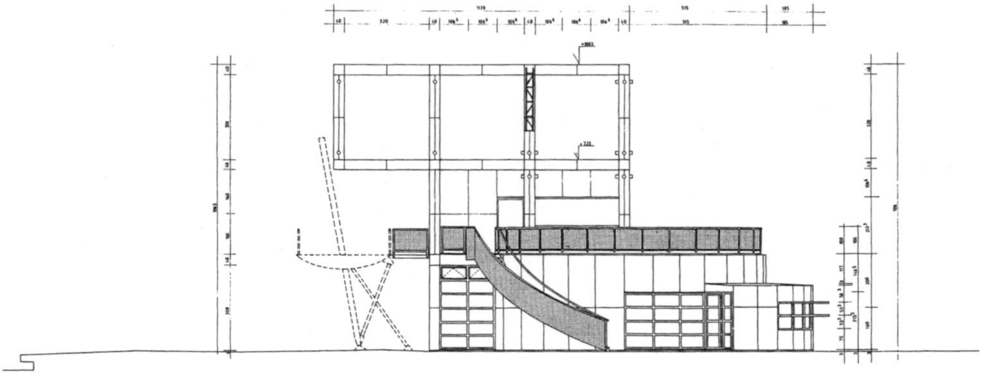

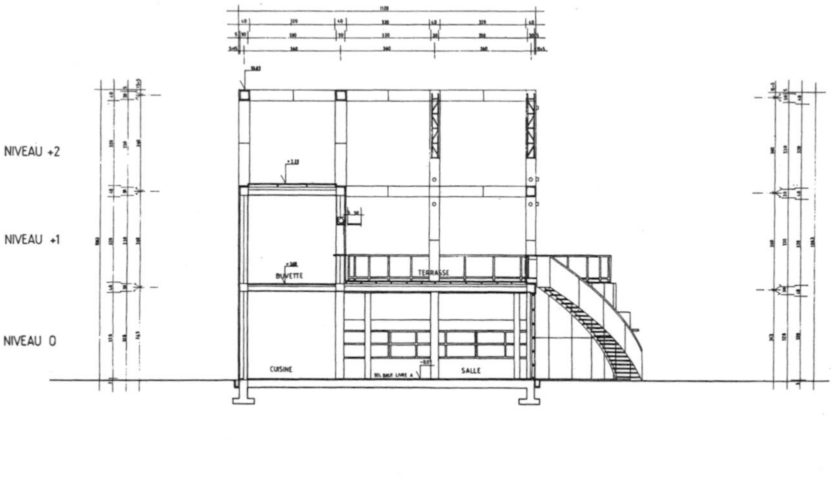
NIVEAU +2
NIVEAU +1
NIVEAU 0
BUVETTE
TERRASSE
CUISINE
SALLE

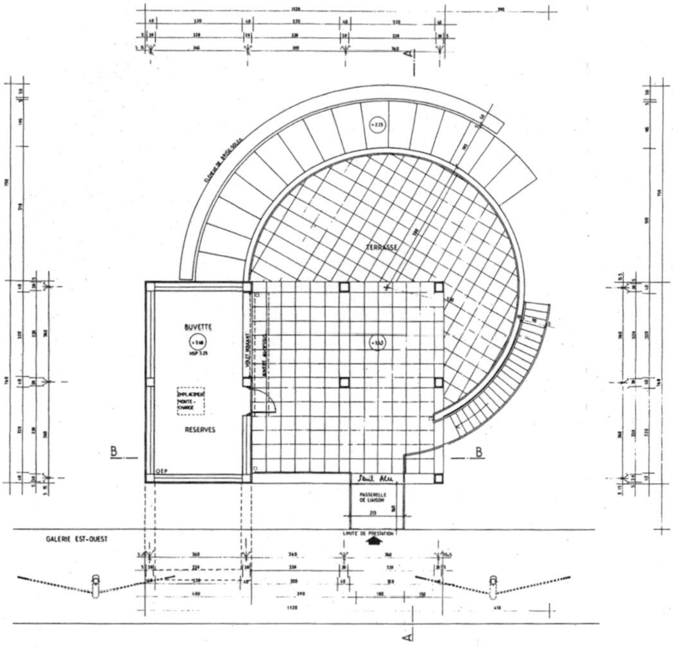
TERRASSE
BUVETTE
RESERVES
PASSERELLE DE LIAISON
GALERIE EST-OUEST
LIMITE DE PRESTATION

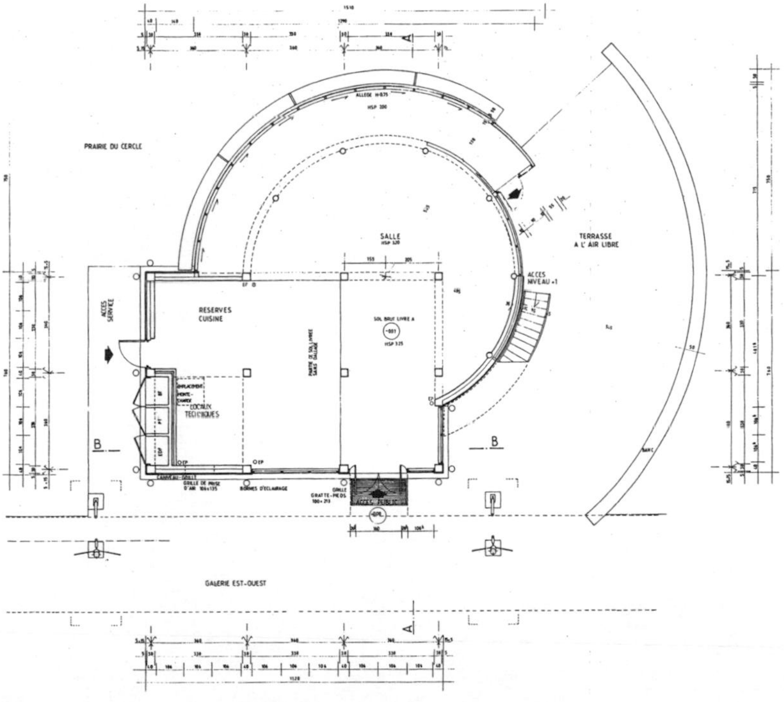
PRAIRIE DU CERCLE
SALLE
TERRASSE A L'AIR LIBRE
ACCES NIVEAU +1
RESERVES CUISINE
ACCES SERVICE
LOCAUX TECHNIQUES
GALERIE EST-OUEST

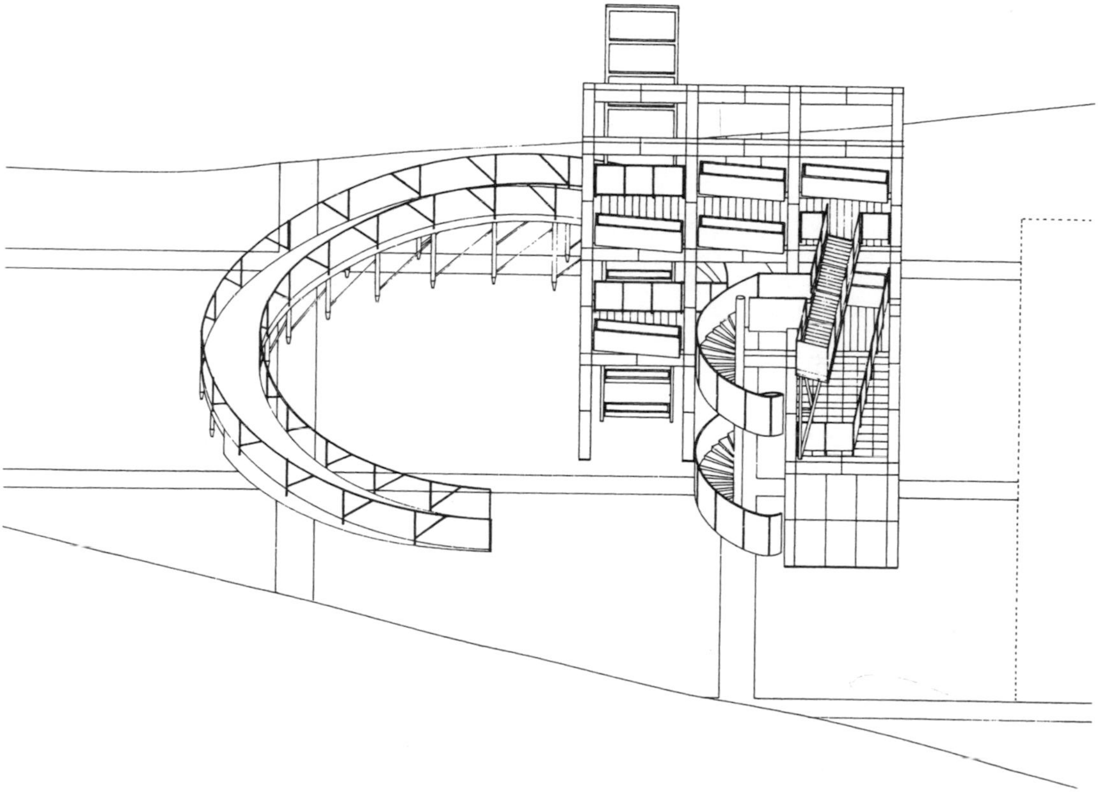

Folie P6 Prototype folie. Program: belvedere with planting over three levels

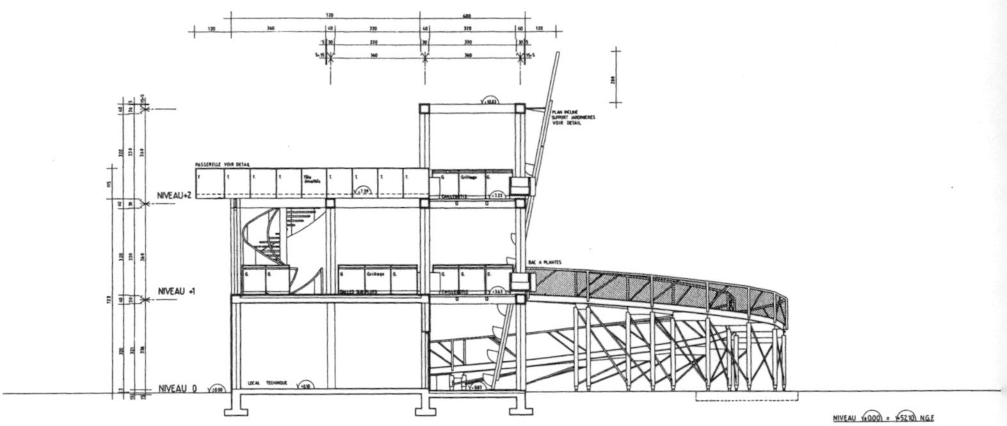
PASSERELLE VOIR DETAIL
PLAN INCLINE SUPPORT JARDINIERES VOIR DETAIL
NIVEAU +2
BAC A PLANTES
NIVEAU +1
LOCAL TECHNIQUE
NIVEAU 0

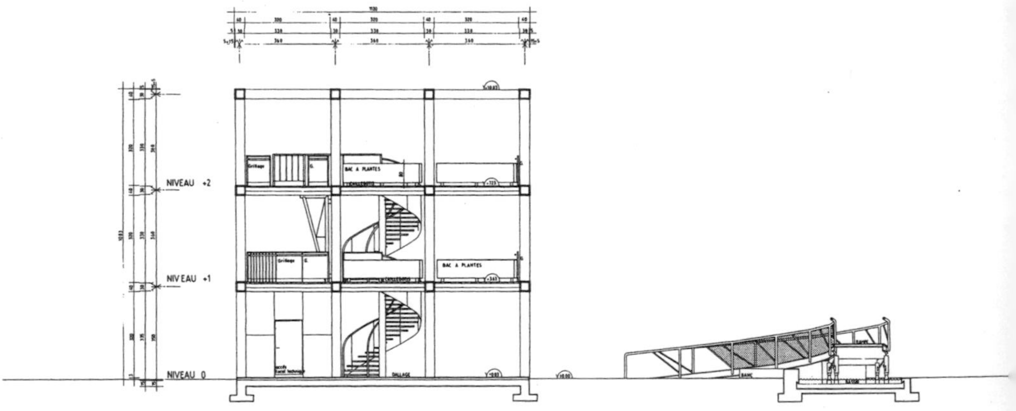
Grillage
BAC A PLANTES
NIVEAU +2
NIVEAU +1
DALLAGE
NIVEAU 0

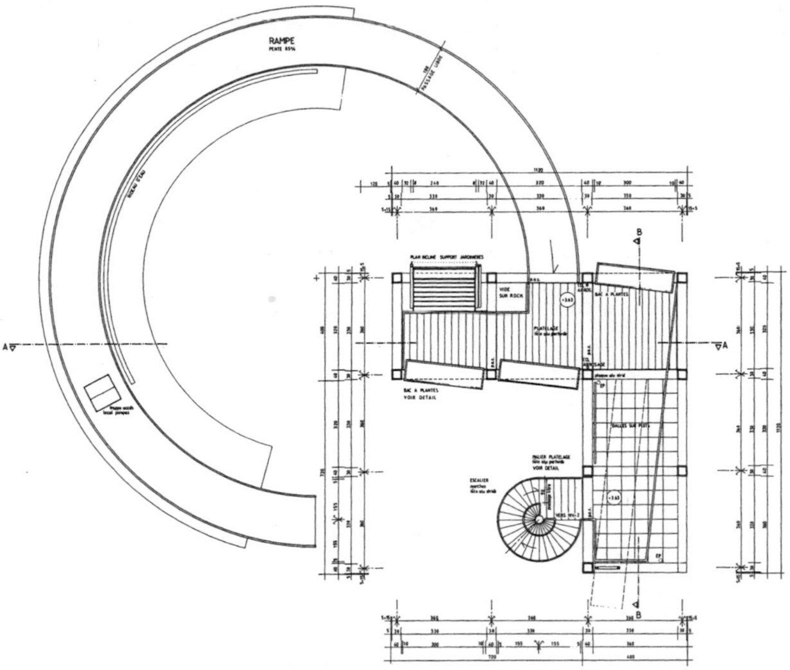
RAMPE
PENTE 8.5%
PLAN INCLINE SUPPORT JARDINIERES
VIDE SUR ROCK
BAC A PLANTES
PLATELAGE
BAC A PLANTES
VOIR DETAIL
DALLES SUR PLOTS
PALIER PLATELAGE
VOIR DETAIL
ESCALIER

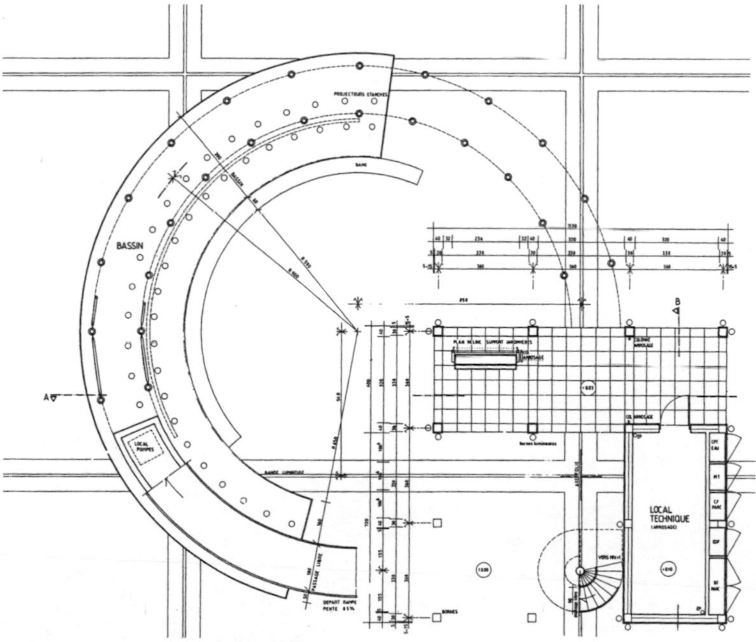
PROJECTEURS ETANCHES
BASSIN
LOCAL POMPES
PLAN INCLINE SUPPORT JARDINIERES
LOCAL TECHNIQUE
(ARROSAGE)
DEPART RAMPE
PENTE 8.5%
BORNES

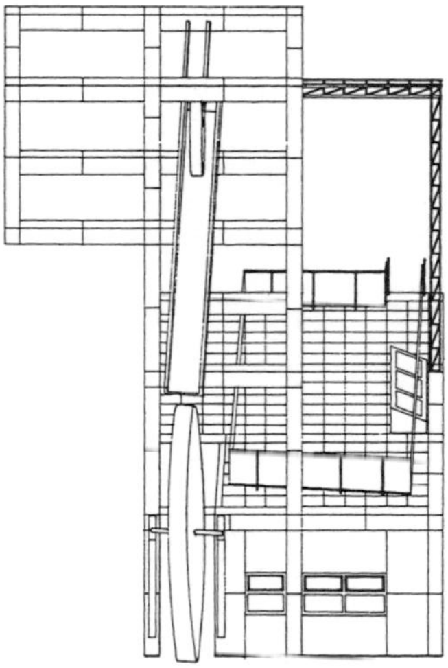

Folie N7 First aid clinic, water wheel, and raised theater stage

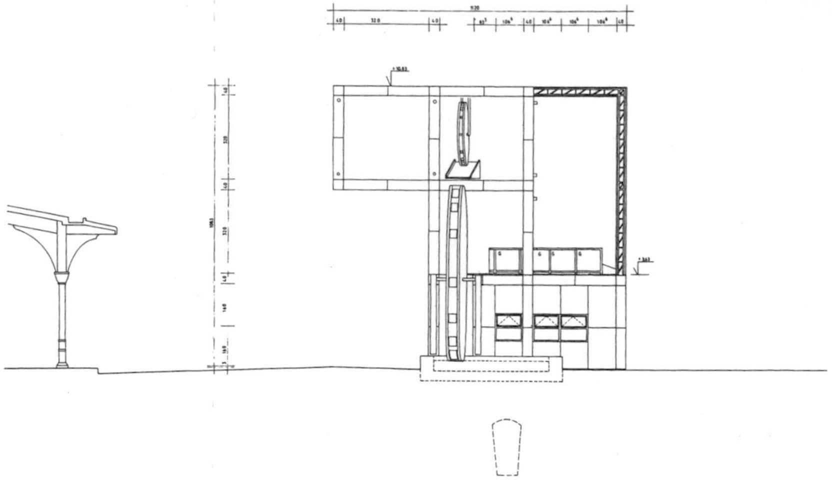

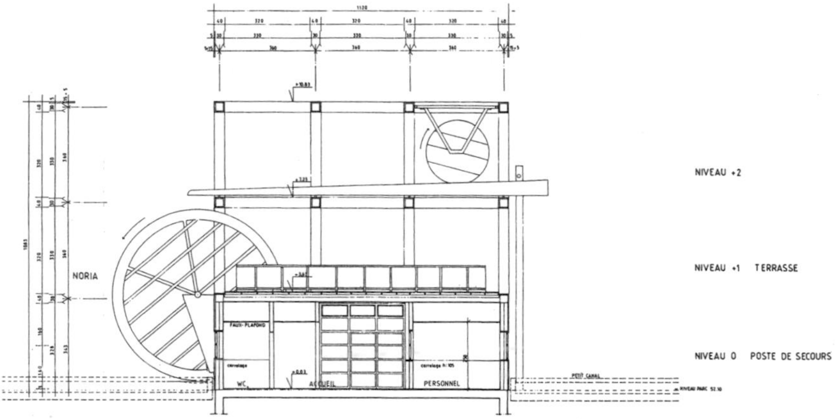
NORIA
NIVEAU +2
NIVEAU +1 TERRASSE
NIVEAU 0 POSTE DE SECOURS
FAUX-PLAFOND
WC
ACCUEIL
PERSONNEL
PETIT CANAL
NIVEAU PARC 52.10

±0.00 = 52.10 NGF

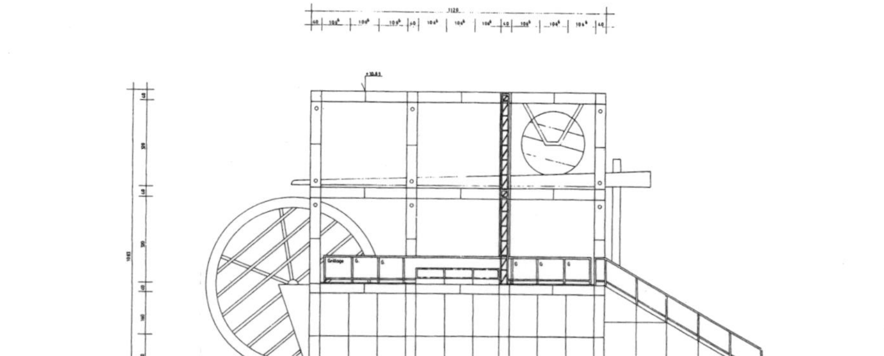

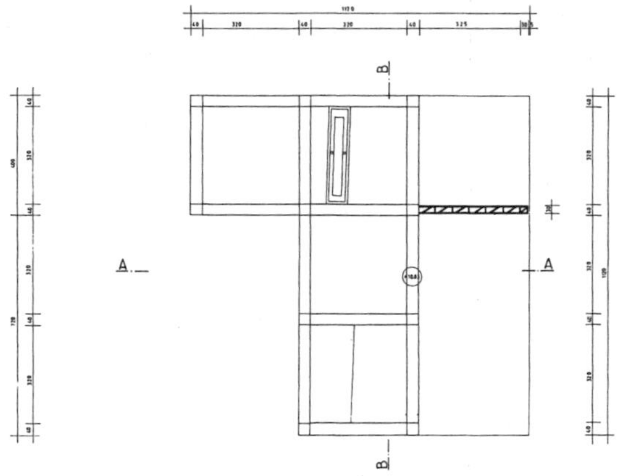
A
A
B
B

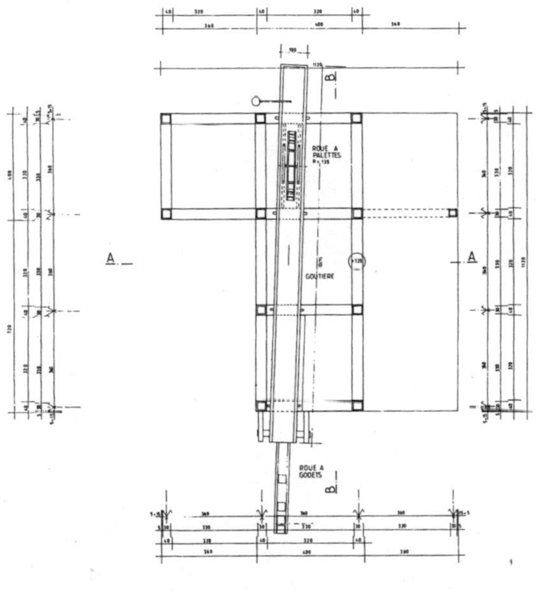
ROUE A
PALETTES
GOUTIERE
ROUE A
GODETS
A
A
B
B

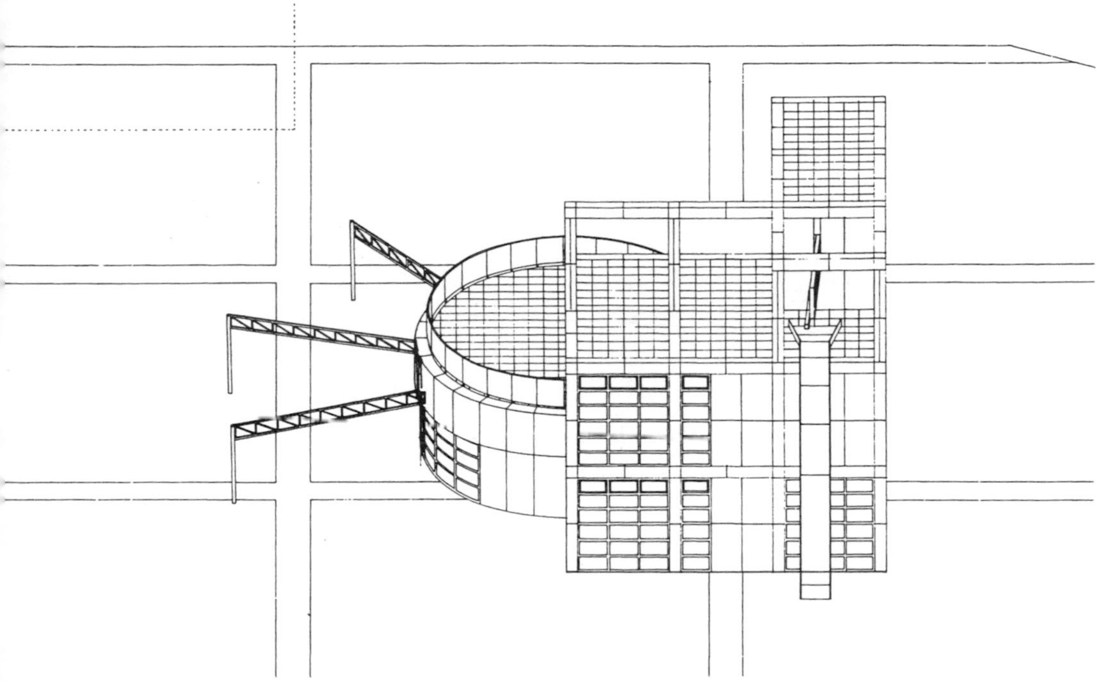

Folie N6 First program: gardening center Second program: restaurant
Third program: children's workshop
Fourth program: park buildings and grounds' departmental offices

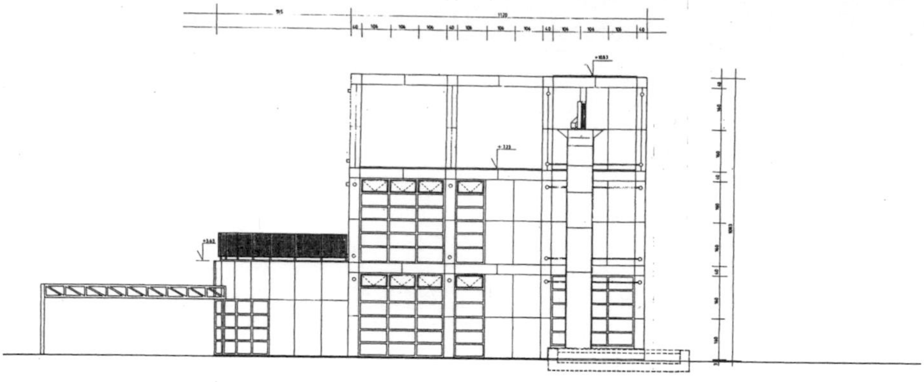

FACADE SUD

± 0.00 = 52.10 NGF

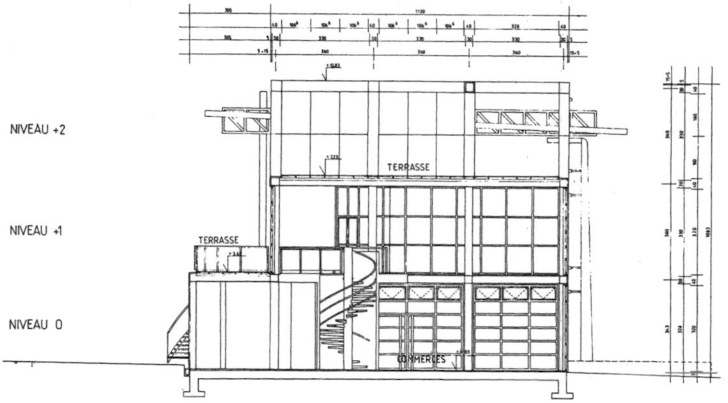

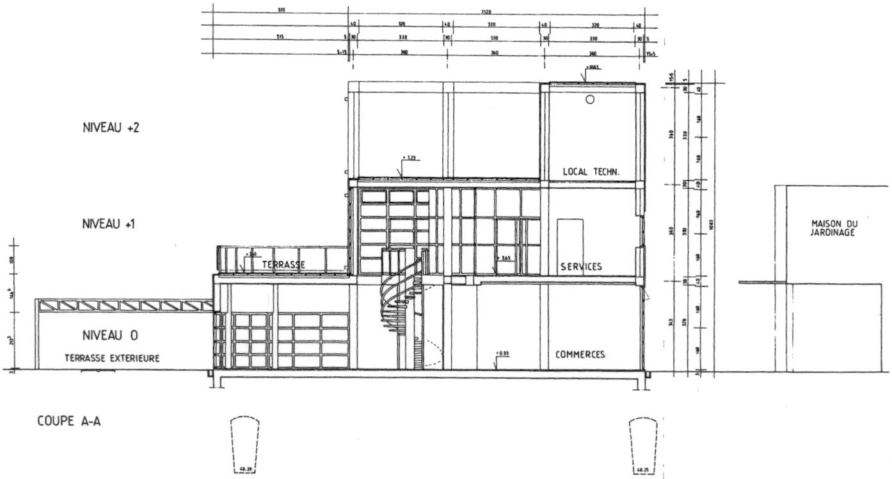

COUPE A-A

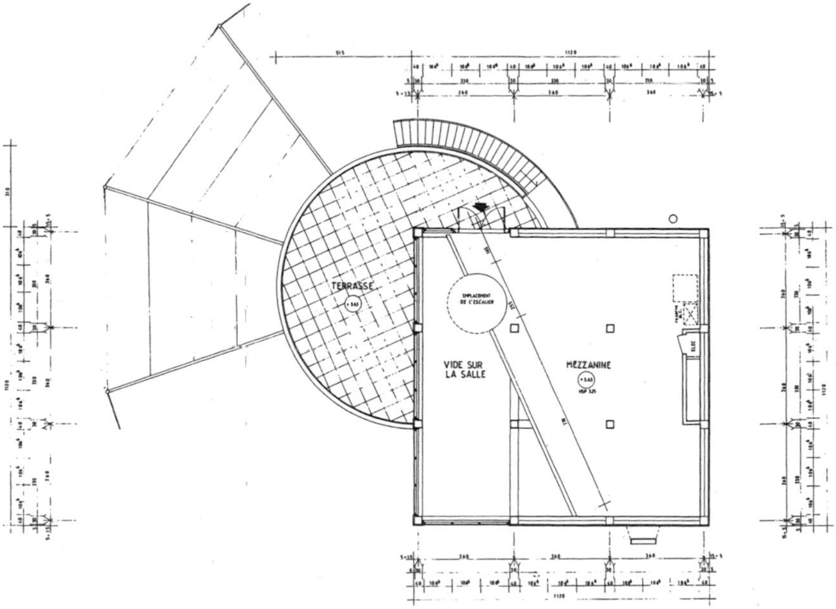
TERRASSE
EMPLACEMENT DE L'ESCALIER
VIDE SUR LA SALLE
MEZZANINE
ELEC

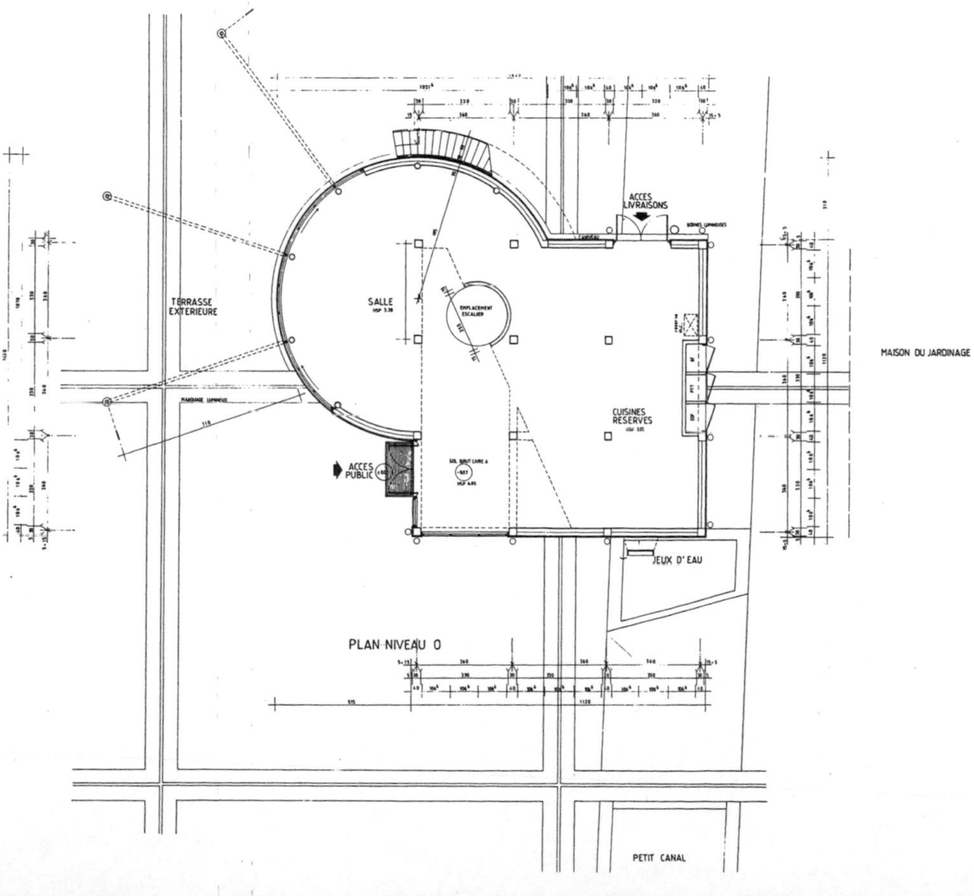
ACCES LIVRAISONS
TERRASSE EXTERIEURE
SALLE
EMPLACEMENT ESCALIER
CUISINES RESERVES
ACCES PUBLIC
MAISON DU JARDINAGE
JEUX D'EAU
PLAN NIVEAU 0
PETIT CANAL

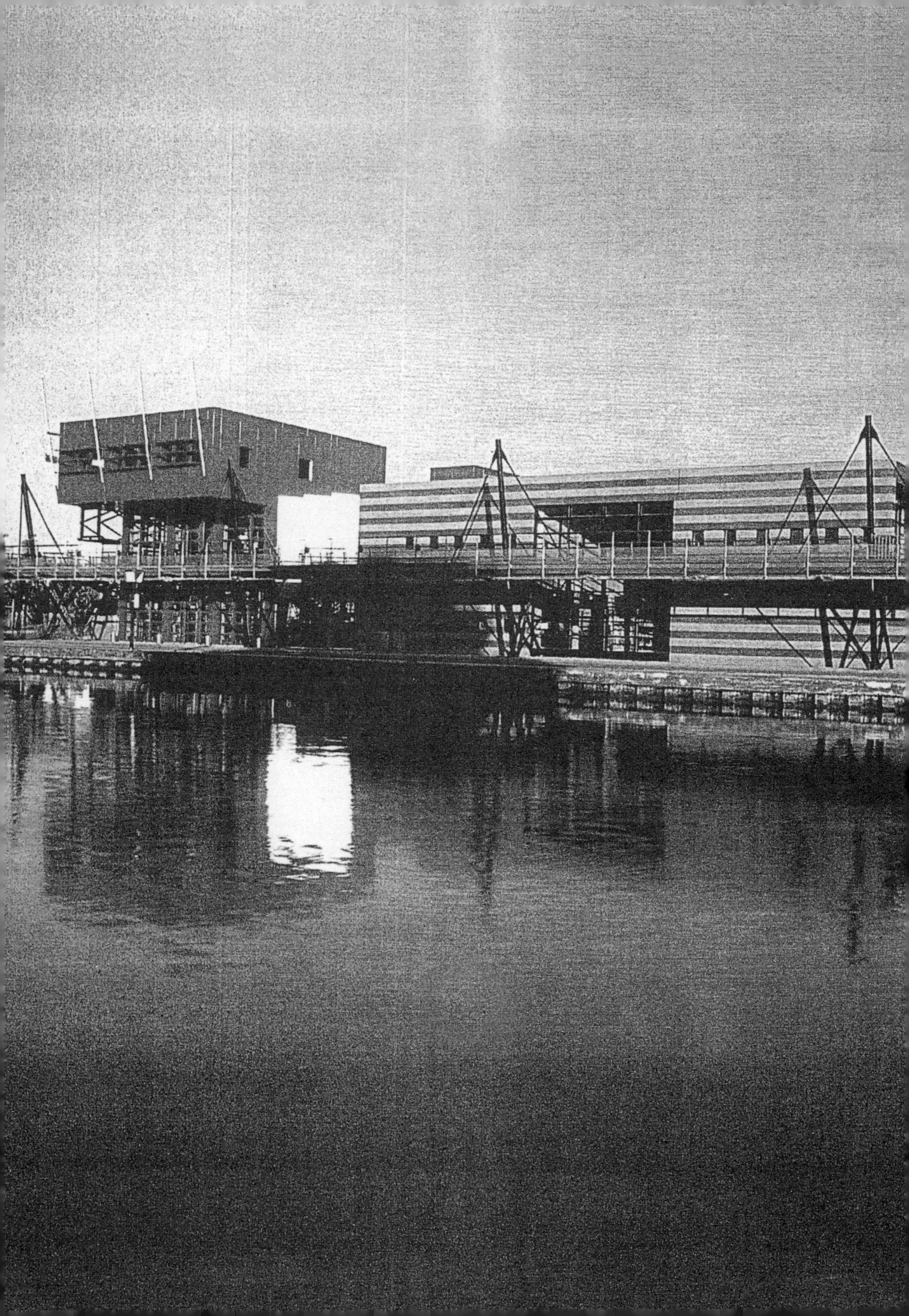

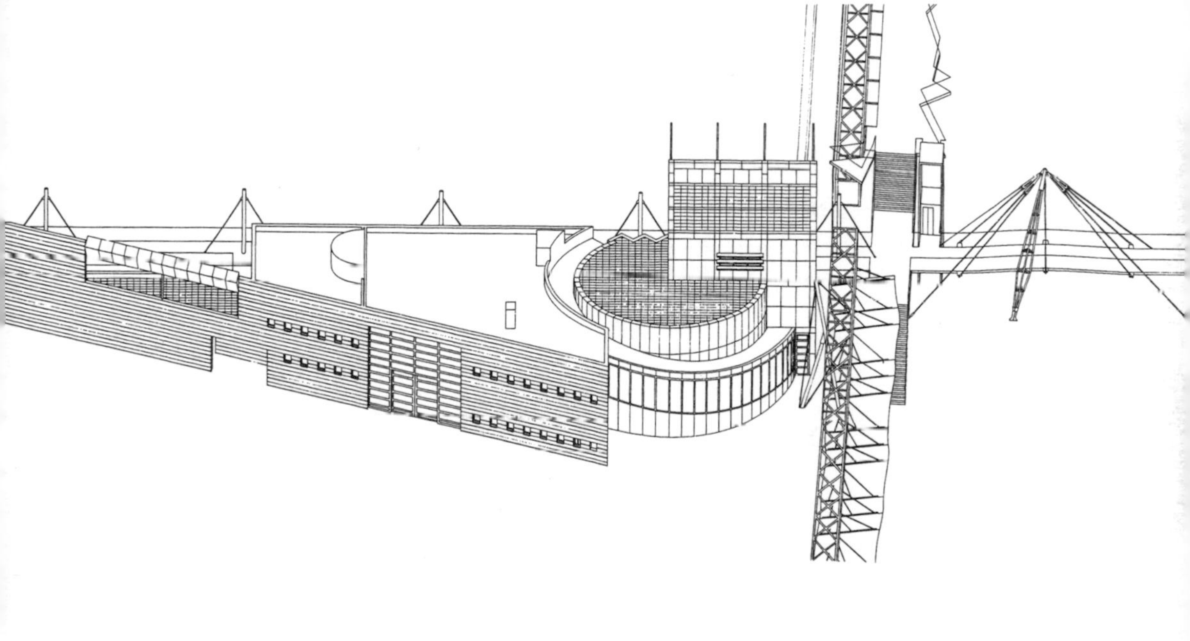

Folie L5 (at the crossing of the north-south and east-west galleries)
Group information center, small conference hall, restaurant and bar, terrace

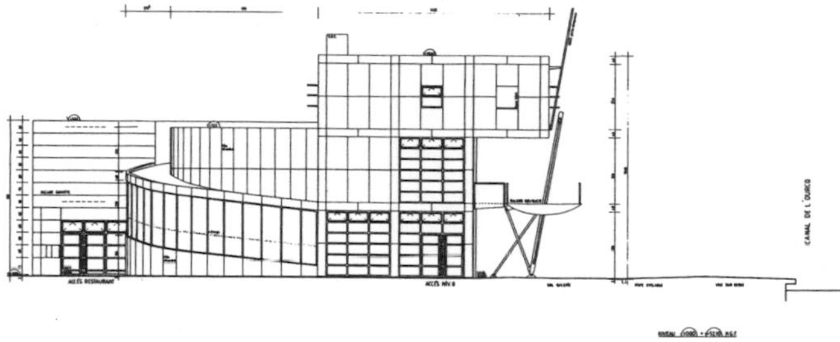
ACCÈS RESTAURANT
ACCÈS NIV 0
CANAL DE L'OURCQ

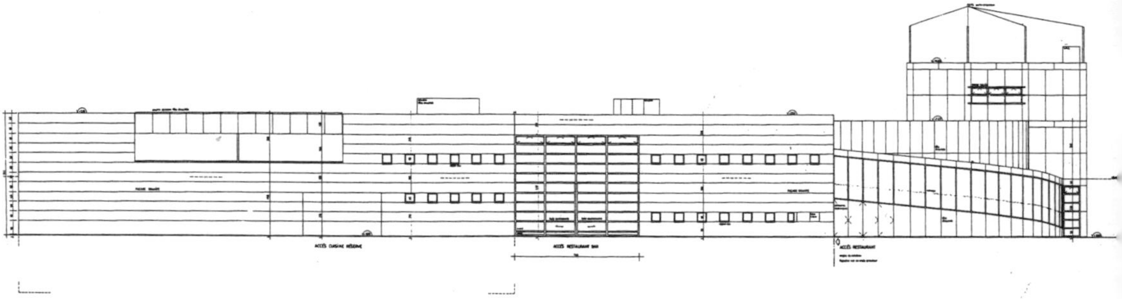
ACCÈS CUISINE RÉSERVE
ACCÈS RESTAURANT BAR
ACCÈS RESTAURANT

RAMPE
ACCUEIL GROUPES
MEZZANINE BAR
TERRASSE BAR
CARREFOUR
IMAGES/COMMUNICATION
SANITAIRES
BAR
RESTAURANT
CUISINE
PRODUCTION
SANITAIRES
LOCAL TECHNIQUE
RESERVE

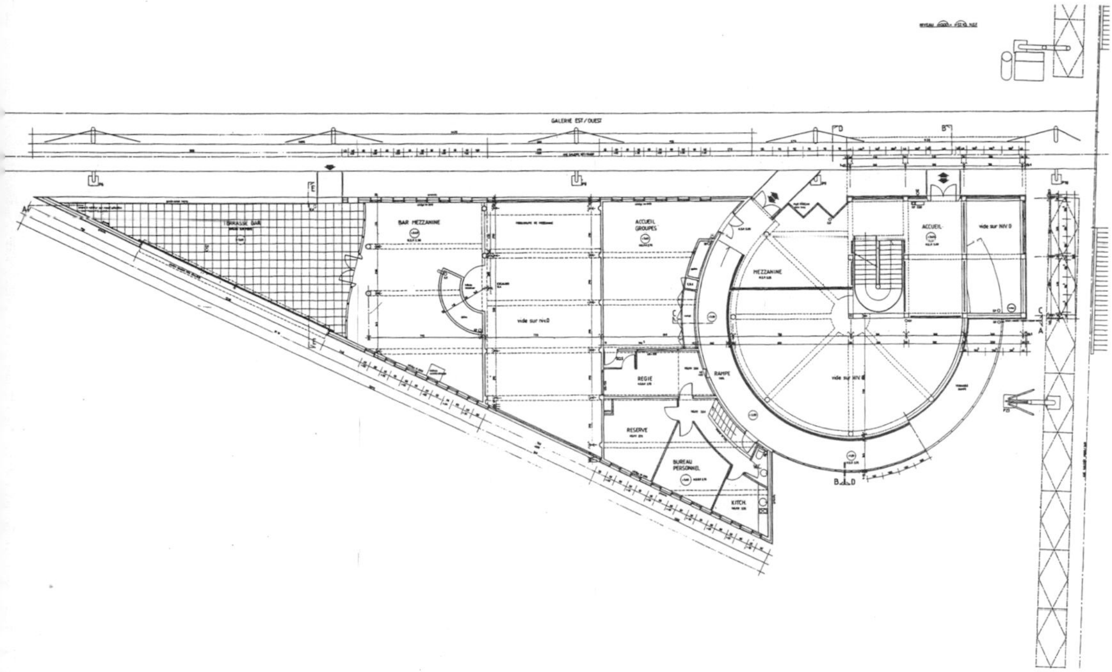
GALERIE EST/OUEST
TERRASSE BAR
BAR MEZZANINE
ACCUEIL GROUPES
vide sur niv.0
MEZZANINE
ACCUEIL
vide sur NIV 0
REGIE
RAMPE
RESERVE
BUREAU PERSONNEL
KITCH.

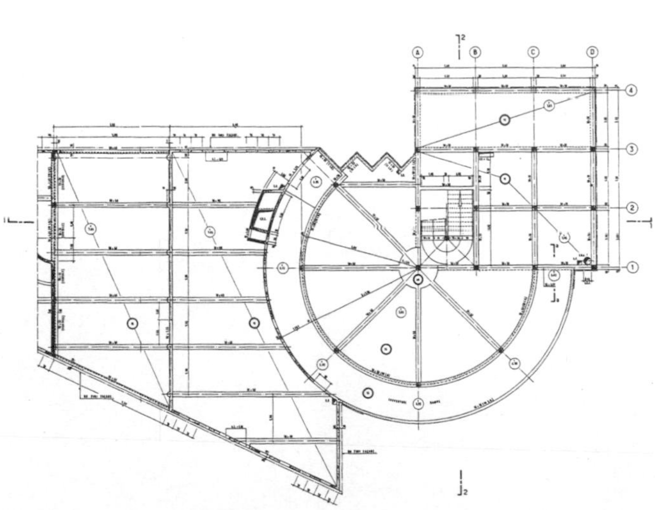

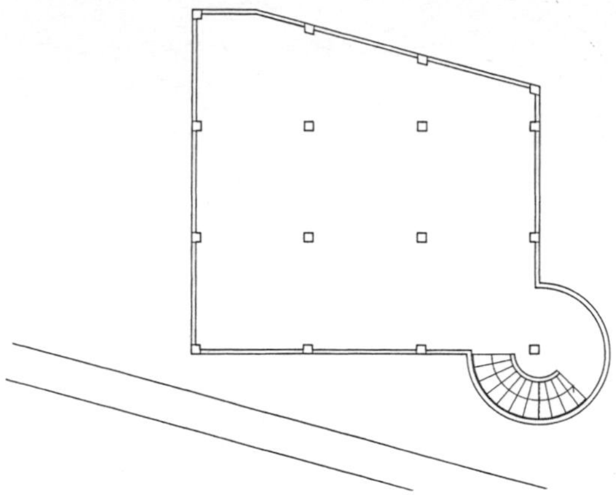

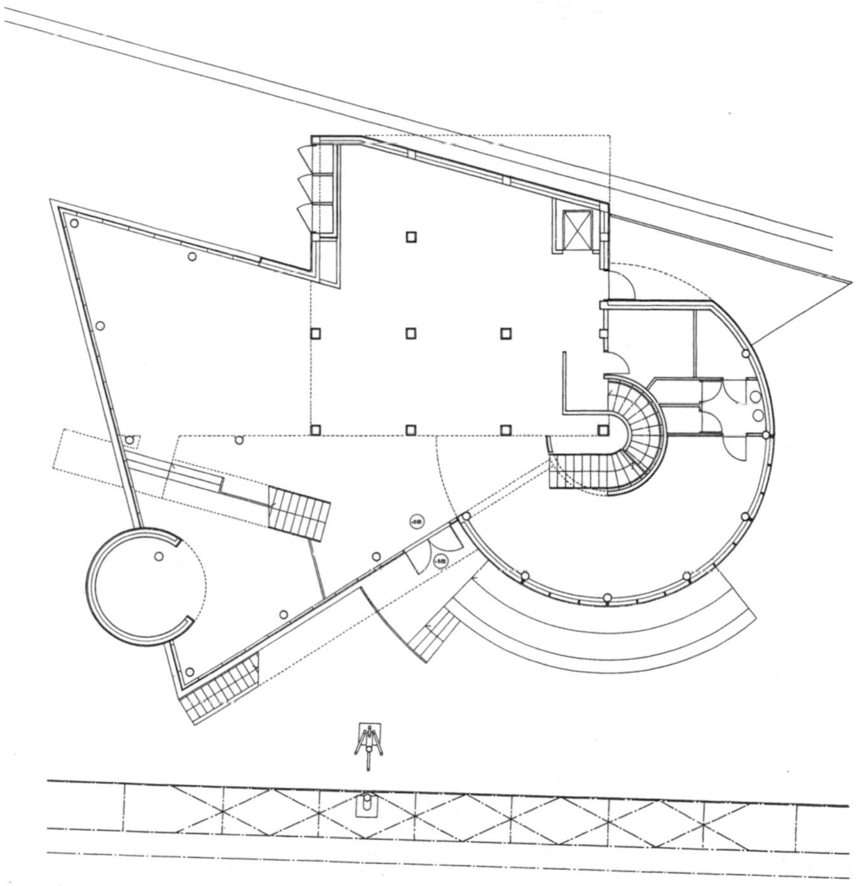

Folie L2 Program: fast food restaurant with terrace

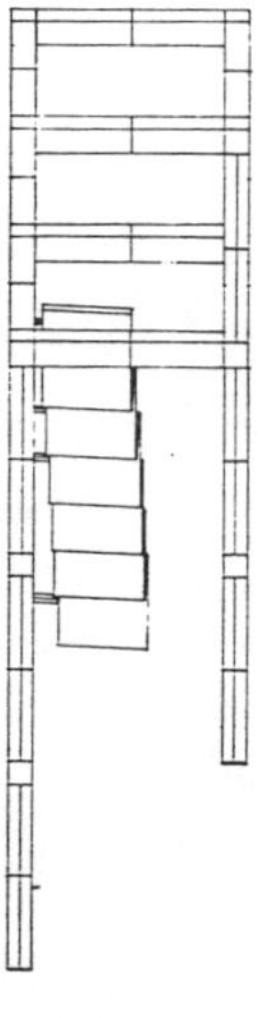

Folie N8 (no program)

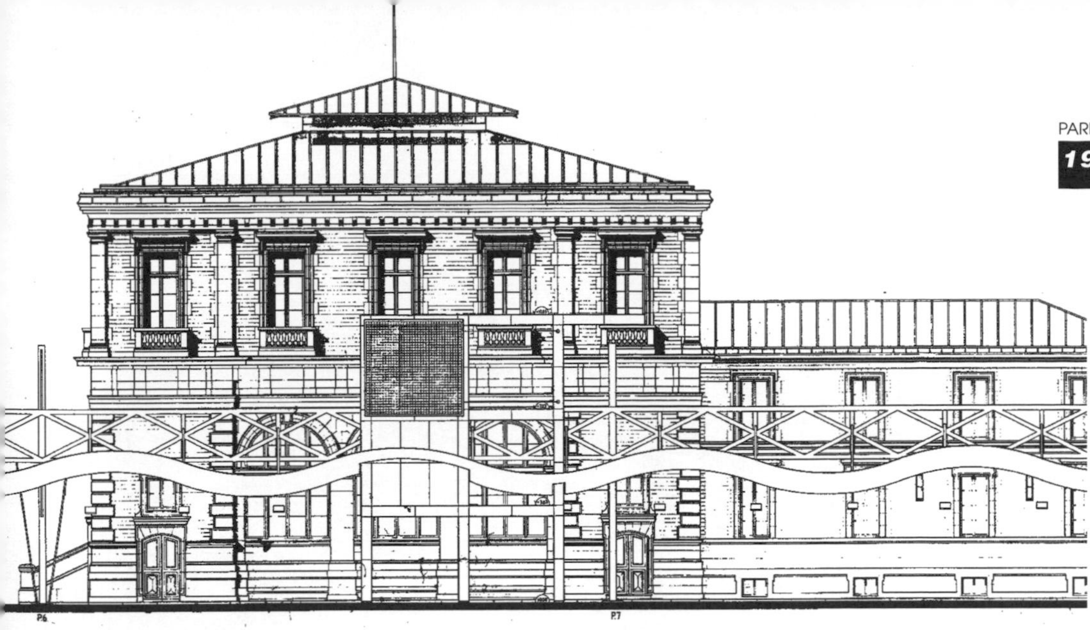

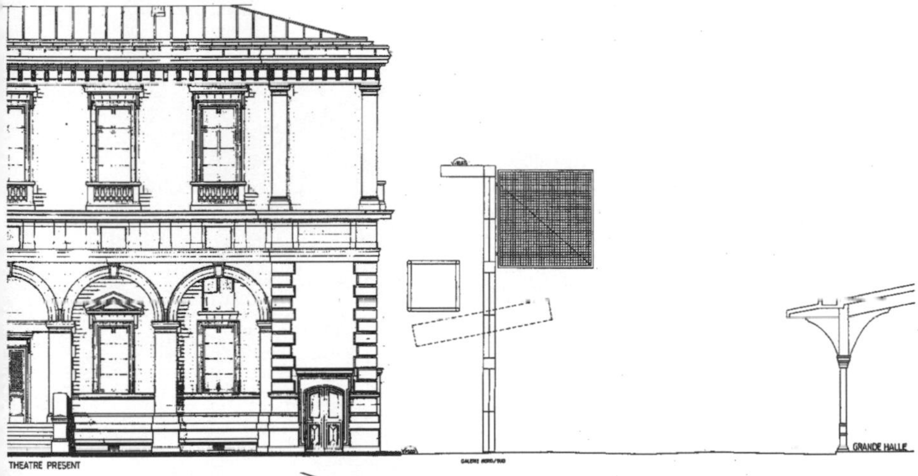

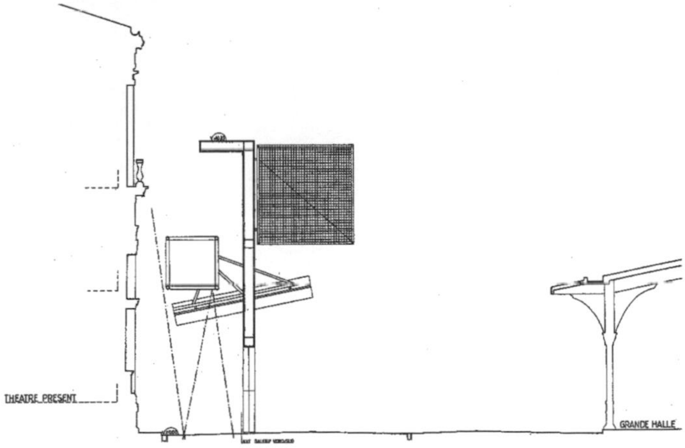

Folie L8 (no program)

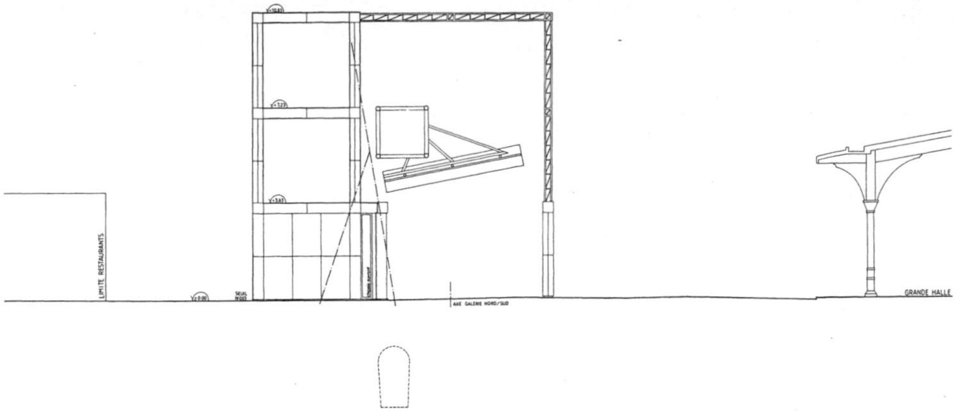

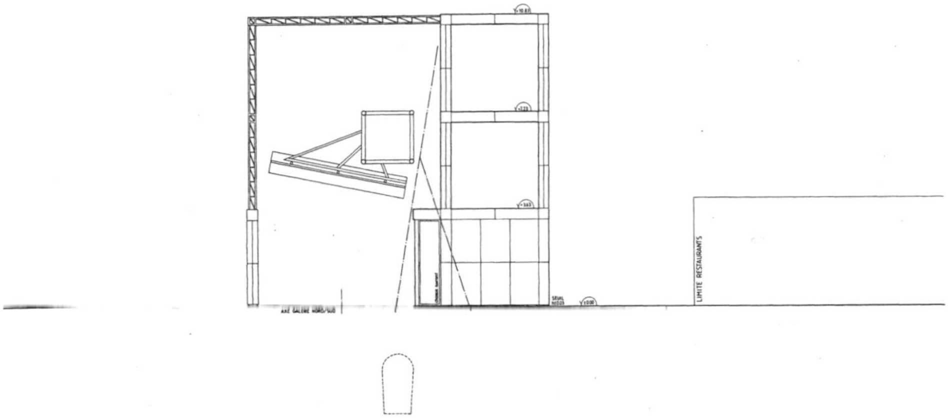

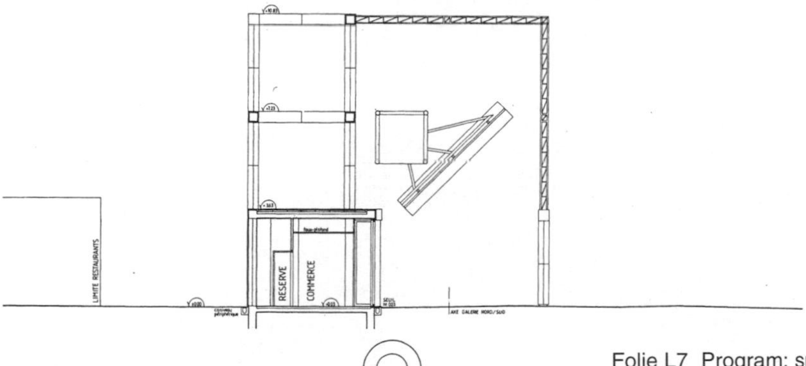

Folie L7 Program: small exhibition gallery

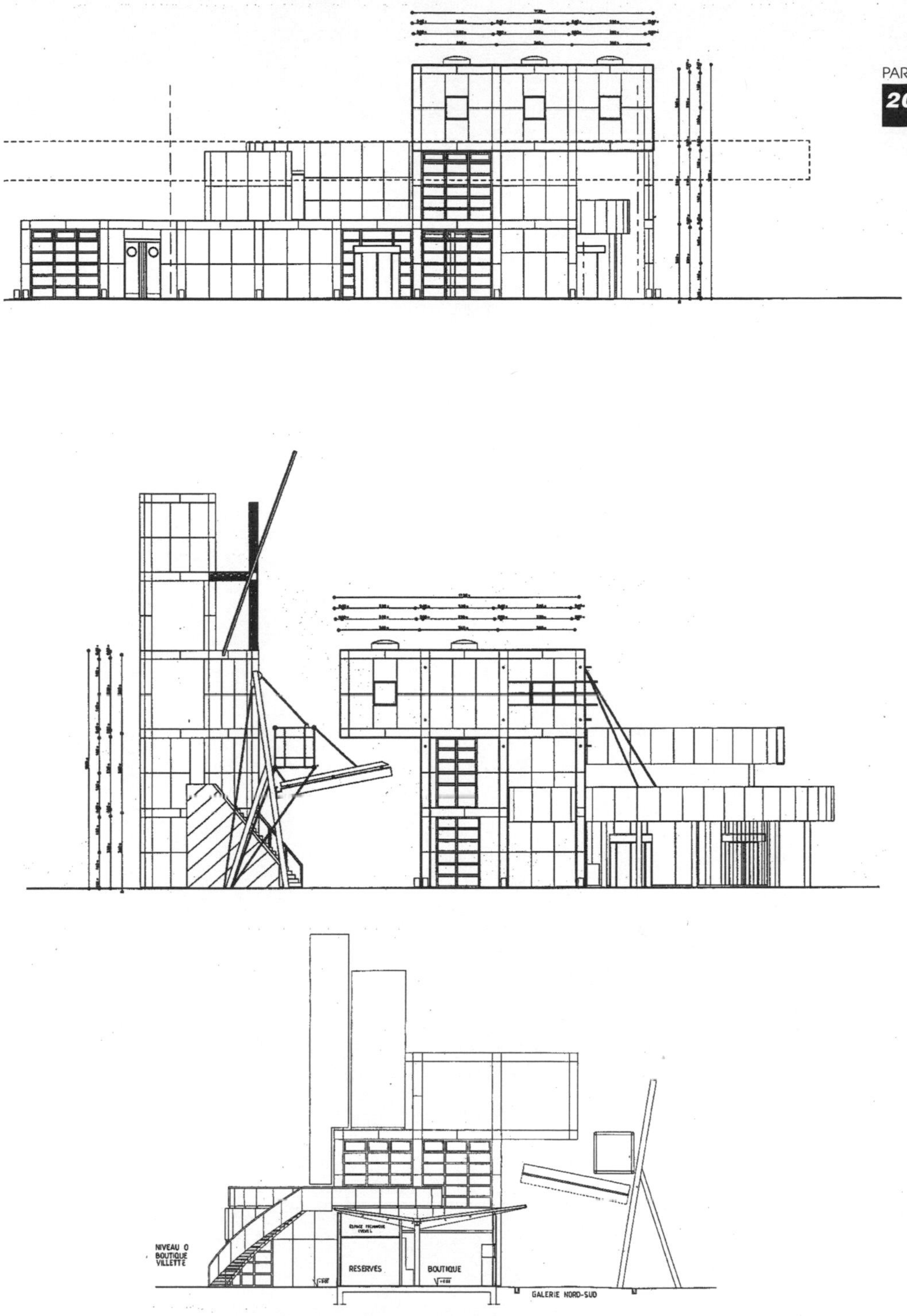

Folie L9 Program: south park entrance, information, ticket booth, large model of the park, offices, restrooms

PLANCHER HAUT REZ-DE-CHAUSSEE
Ech. 1/50

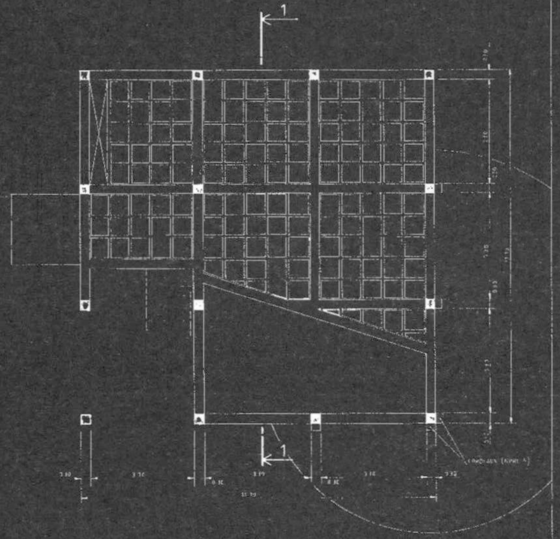

COUPE VERTICALE 1-1
Ech. 1/50

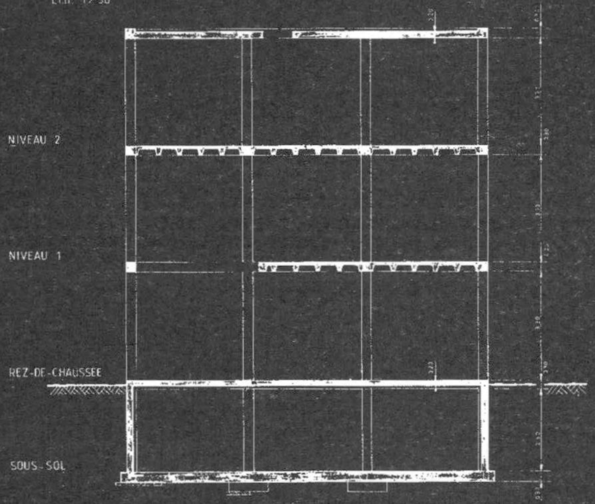

PLANCHER HAUT NIVEAU 2

Ech. 1 / 100

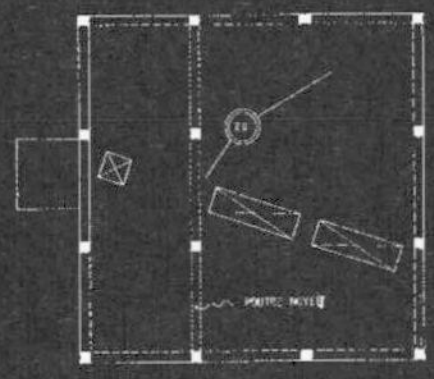

DETAILS STRUCTURE TAMBOUR

Ech. 1 / 20

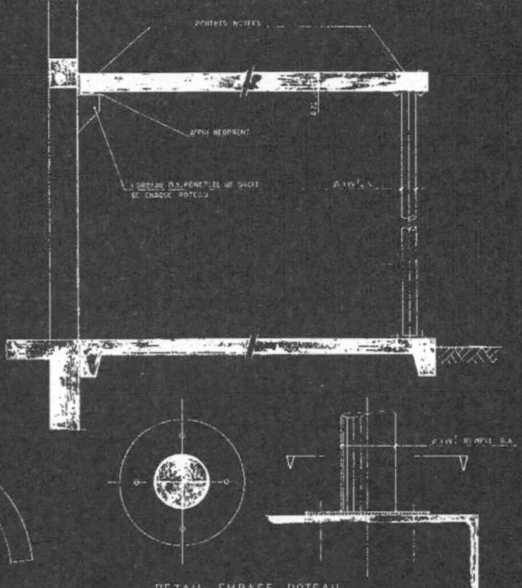

DETAIL EMBASE POTEAU

PLANCHER HAUT NIVEAU 1

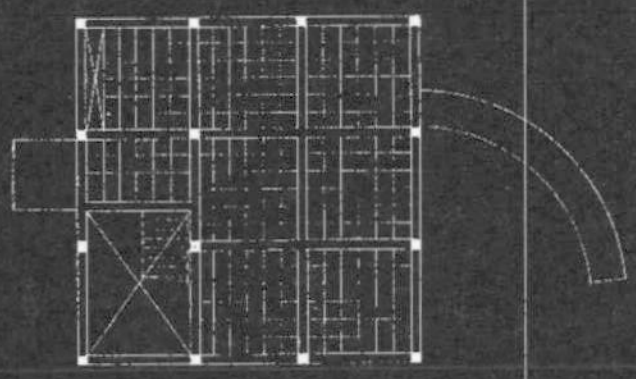

PLANCHER HAUT SOUS-SOL

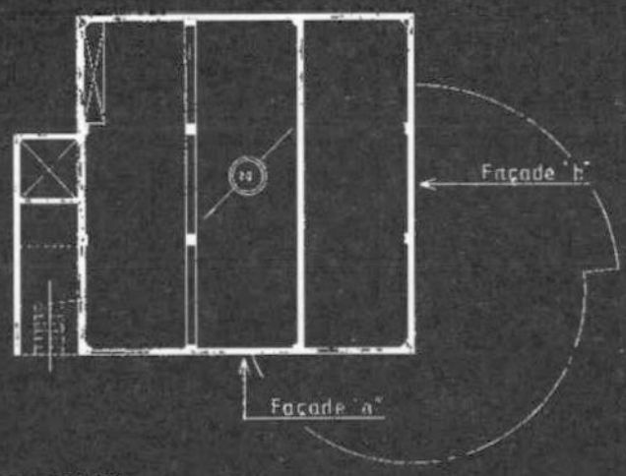

ELEVATION, FAÇADE "a"

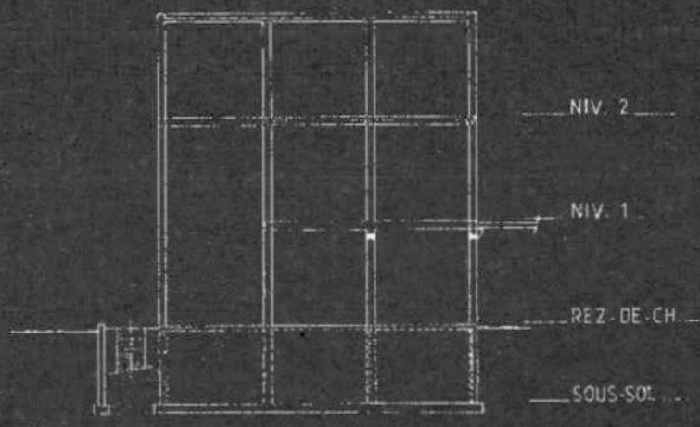

ELEVATION, FAÇADE "b"

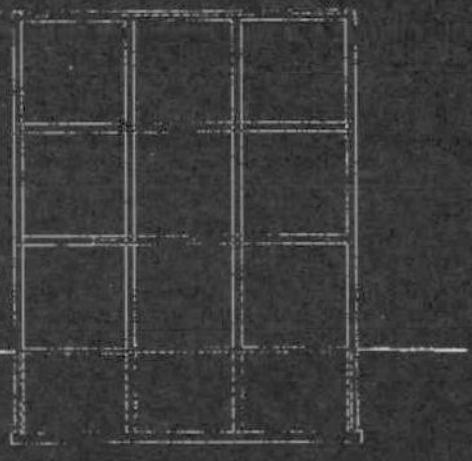

FONDATIONS

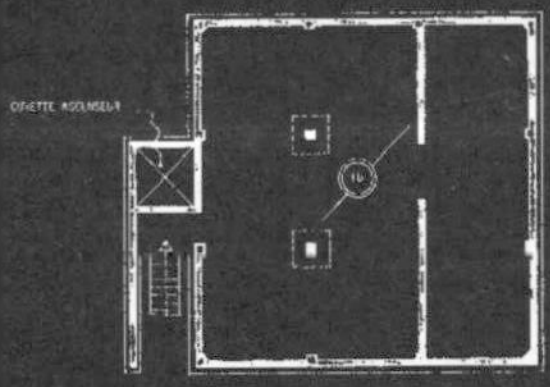

COUPE TYPE PARTIELLE, SUR PLANCHER NERVURE

Ech. 1 / 20

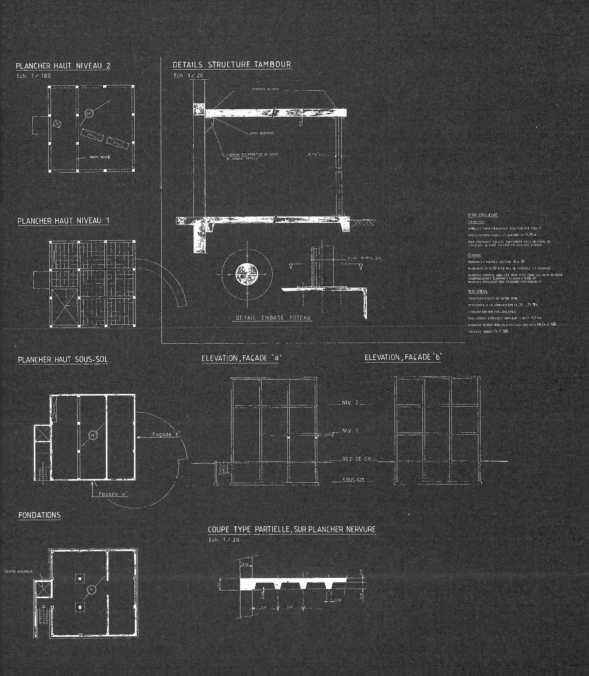

Structural System of the Galleries

If the system of points of intensity throughout the park materializes through the grid of *Folies*, the system of lines is defined by the Cinematic Promenade, the alleys of trees and, in particular, by the covered North-South and East-West Galleries which act as coordinate axes for the site. Nearly one kilometer long, linking the Porte de Pantin to the Porte de la Villette, the North-South Gallery is a brilliantly-lit public street, open 24 hours a day and connecting the urban functions of the park: the Museum of Science and Industry, Cinema-*Folies*, Restaurant-*Folies*, Video-*Folies*, the 19th-century Grand Halle, a theater, and the City of Music. The breaks in scale that can be observed on such a trajectory suggested that one could take advantage of occasional changes in ground level by keeping the main supporting beam of the Gallery rigorously horizontal, hence increasing its standard height of 5.4 meters (18 feet) to 9 meters (30 feet) near the gigantic Museum of Science and Industry. The length of the Gallery (of which no comparable example probably exists anywhere else in the world), as well as the concept of a "floating" superimposed element, suggested long 21.6 meter (65 foot) spans between vertical supports, which contrast architecturally and historically with the 8 meter (24 foot) span of the 19th-century Grand Halle. Consistent with the principle of the autonomy of the park's various conceptual systems, the construction module of the main beam differs from the grid of the undulating canopy it supports. This principle of superimposition finds its most spectacular expression in the carefully orchestrated collision between the North-South Gallery and the *Folies* that it meets on its trajectory. Parallel to the distorted parallelogram of the Grand Halle rather than to the orthogonal grid of the *Folies*, the Gallery collides four times with *Folies*, thus determining their respective architecture.

The East-West Gallery along the Canal de l'Ourcq not only extends the monumental route that leads from Ledoux's Rotunda to the suburbs, but also acts as an elevated track, a sort of balcony overlooking the park and the Museum of Science and Industry and giving second-floor access to the *Folies* located along the Canal. Again, the interpenetration of the East-West Gallery and the *Folies* that it encounters qualifies the cantilevered architecture of these *Folies*.

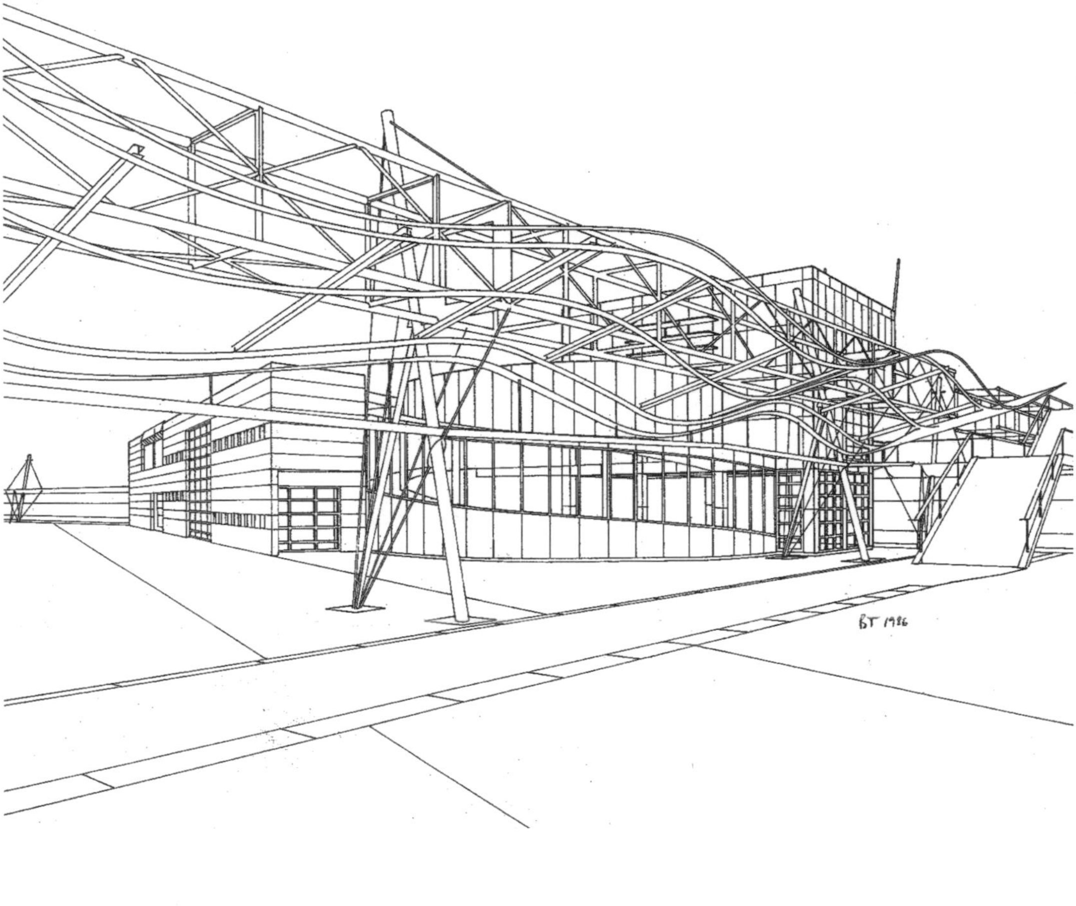

Covered galleries: motion, materialization of concept

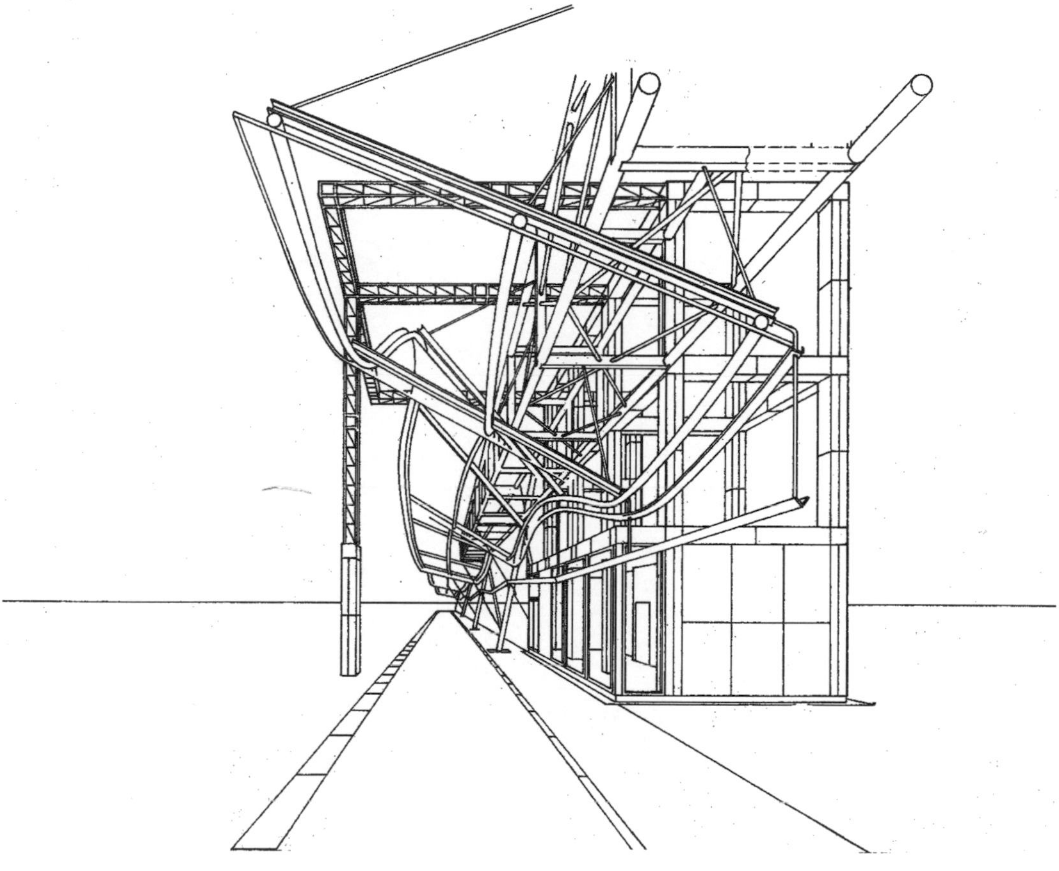

North-south gallery intersecting Folie L7

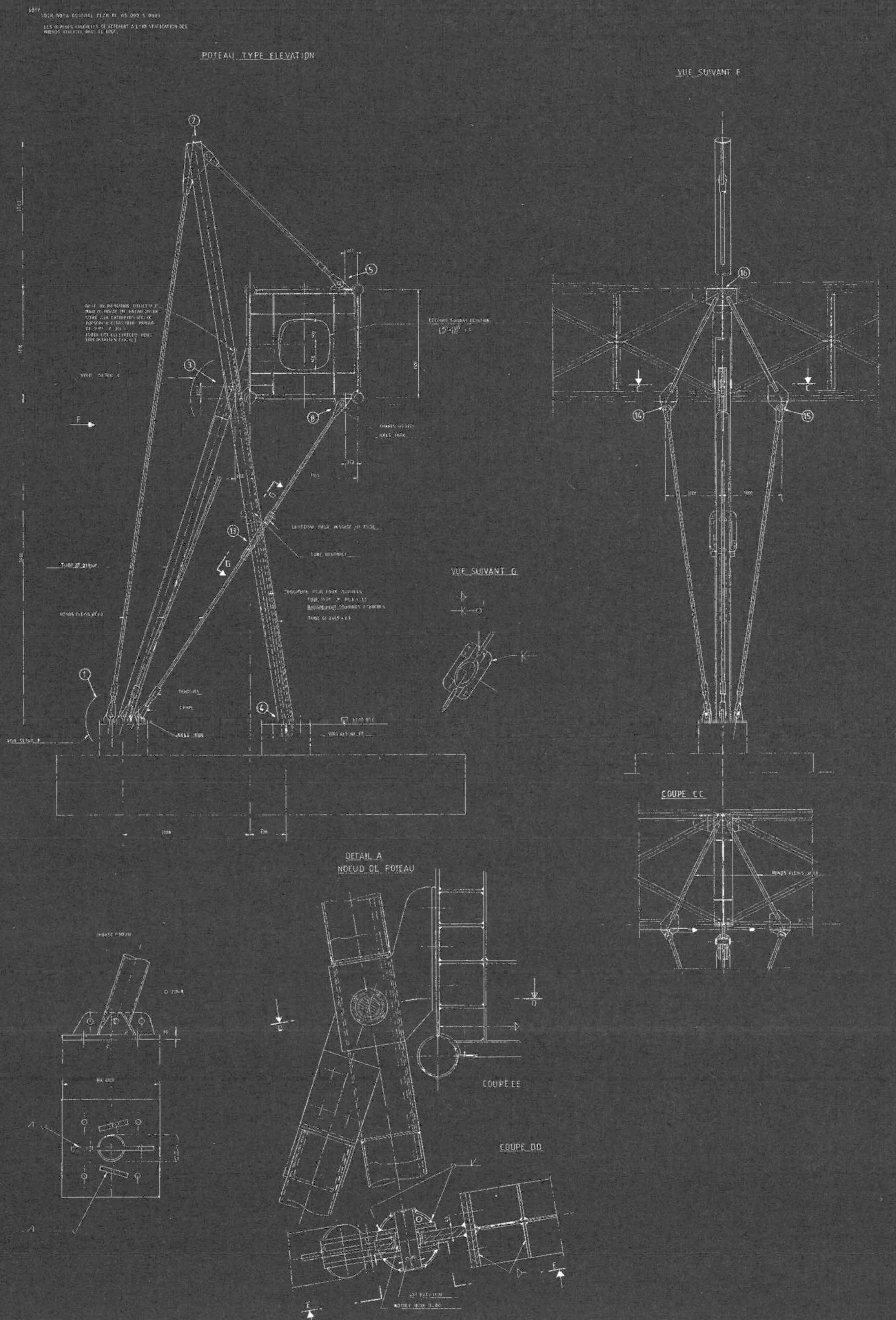
POTEAU TYPE ELEVATION
VUE SUIVANT F
VUE SUIVANT G
COUPE CC
DETAIL A
NOEUD DE POTEAU
COUPE EE
COUPE DD

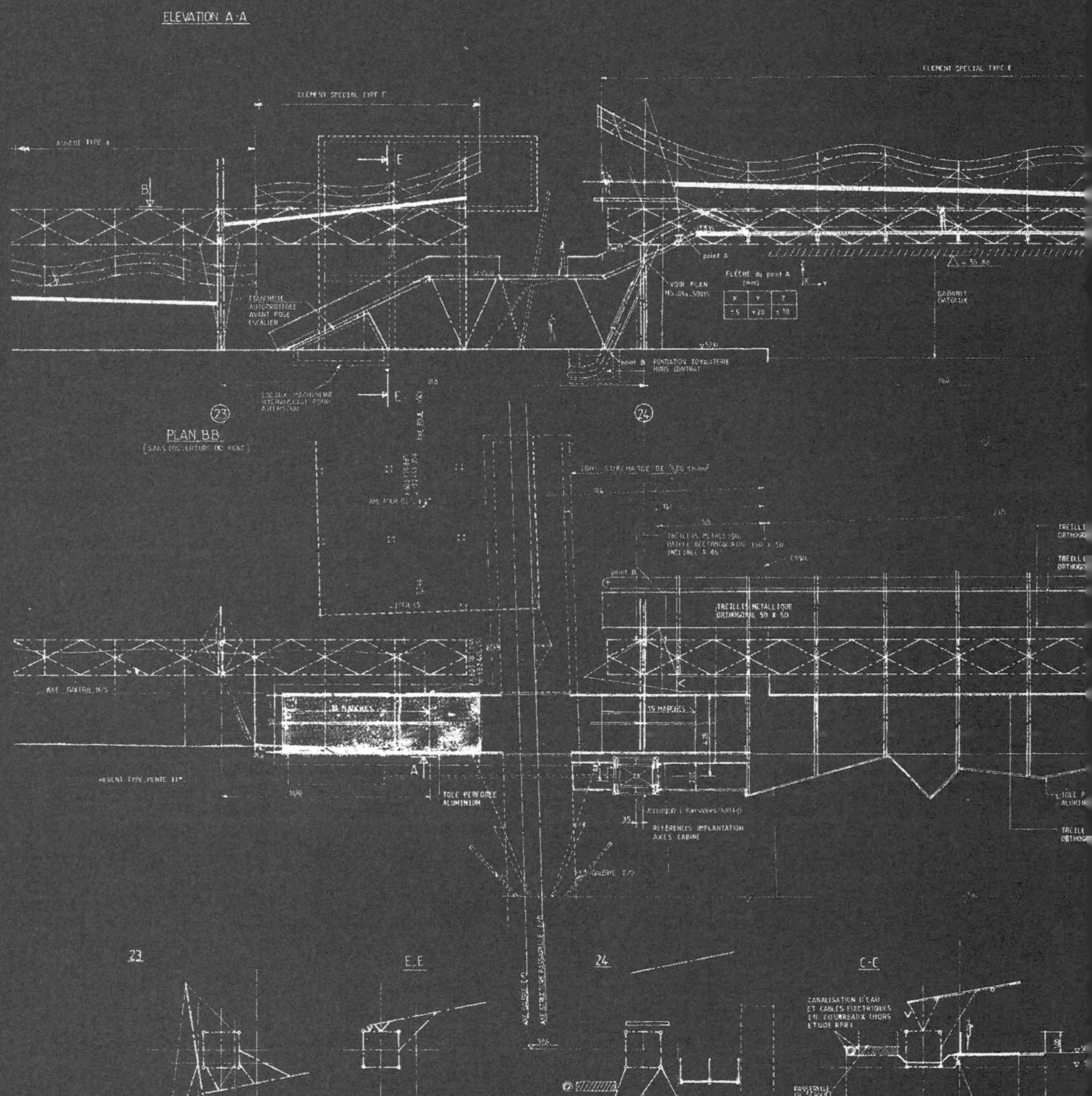
ELEVATION A-A
ELEMENT SPECIAL TYPE E
VOIR PLAN
FLECHE du point A
GABARIT
point B FONDATION TOYAUTERIE HORS CONTRAT
PLAN B.B
TREILLIS METALLIQUE ORTHOGONAL 50 X 50
15 MARCHES
TOLE PERFOREE ALUMINIUM
REFERENCES IMPLANTATION AXES CABINE
23
E.E
24
C-C
CANALISATION D'EAU ET CABLES ELECTRIQUES EN FOURREAUX (HORS ETUDE RFR)
PASSERELLE DE SERVICE
D-D

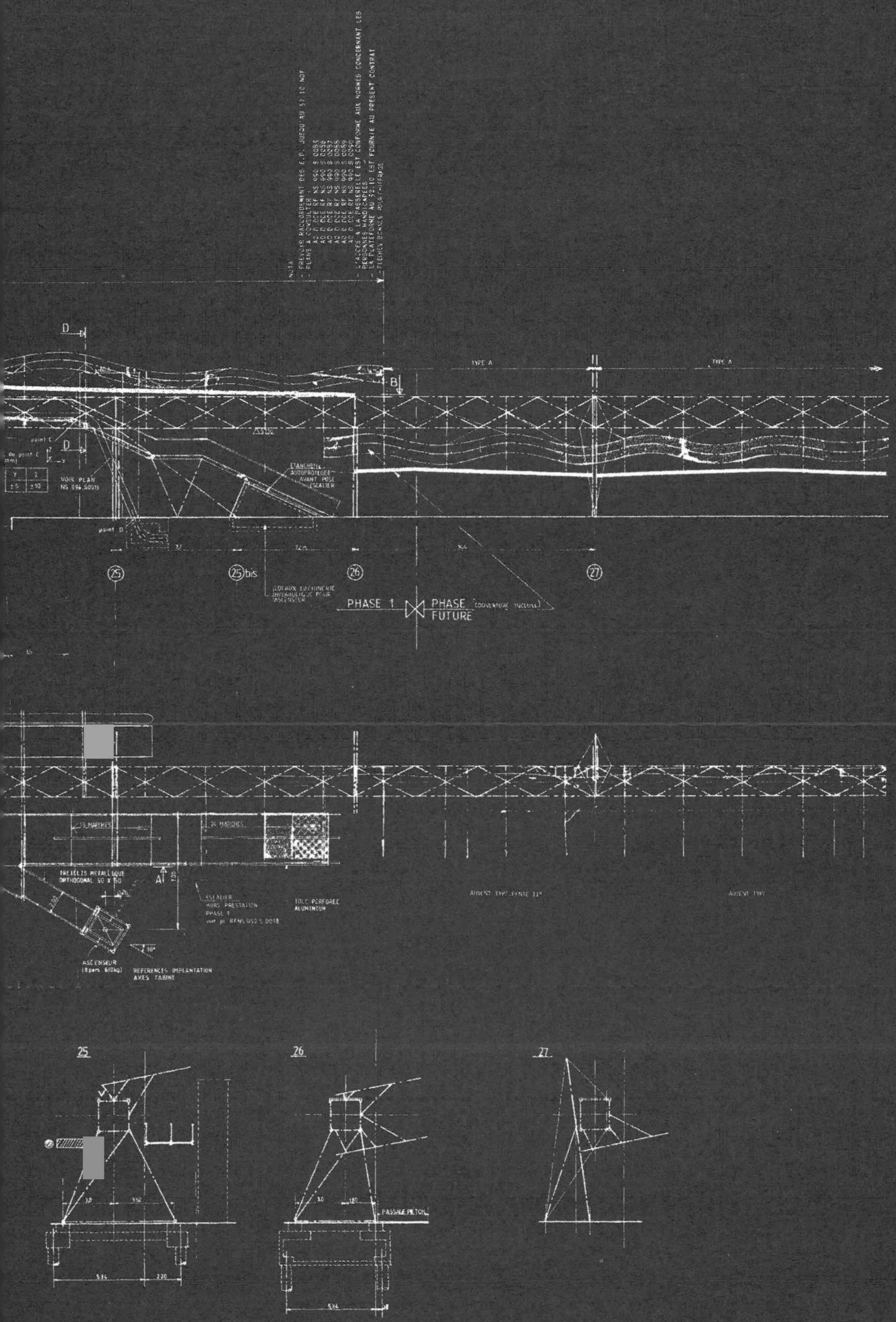

D
B
TYPE A
VOIR PLAN
ETANCHEITE
AUTOPROTEGEE
ESCALIER
25
25bis
26
27
PHASE 1
PHASE
FUTURE
19 MARCHES
TREILLIS METALLIQUE
ORTHOGONAL 50 X 50
A
ESCALIER
HORS PRESTATION
PHASE 1
TOLE PERFOREE
ALUMINIUM
30°
ASCENSEUR
REFERENCES IMPLANTATION
AXES CABINE
25
26
27
PASSAGE PIETON
534
220

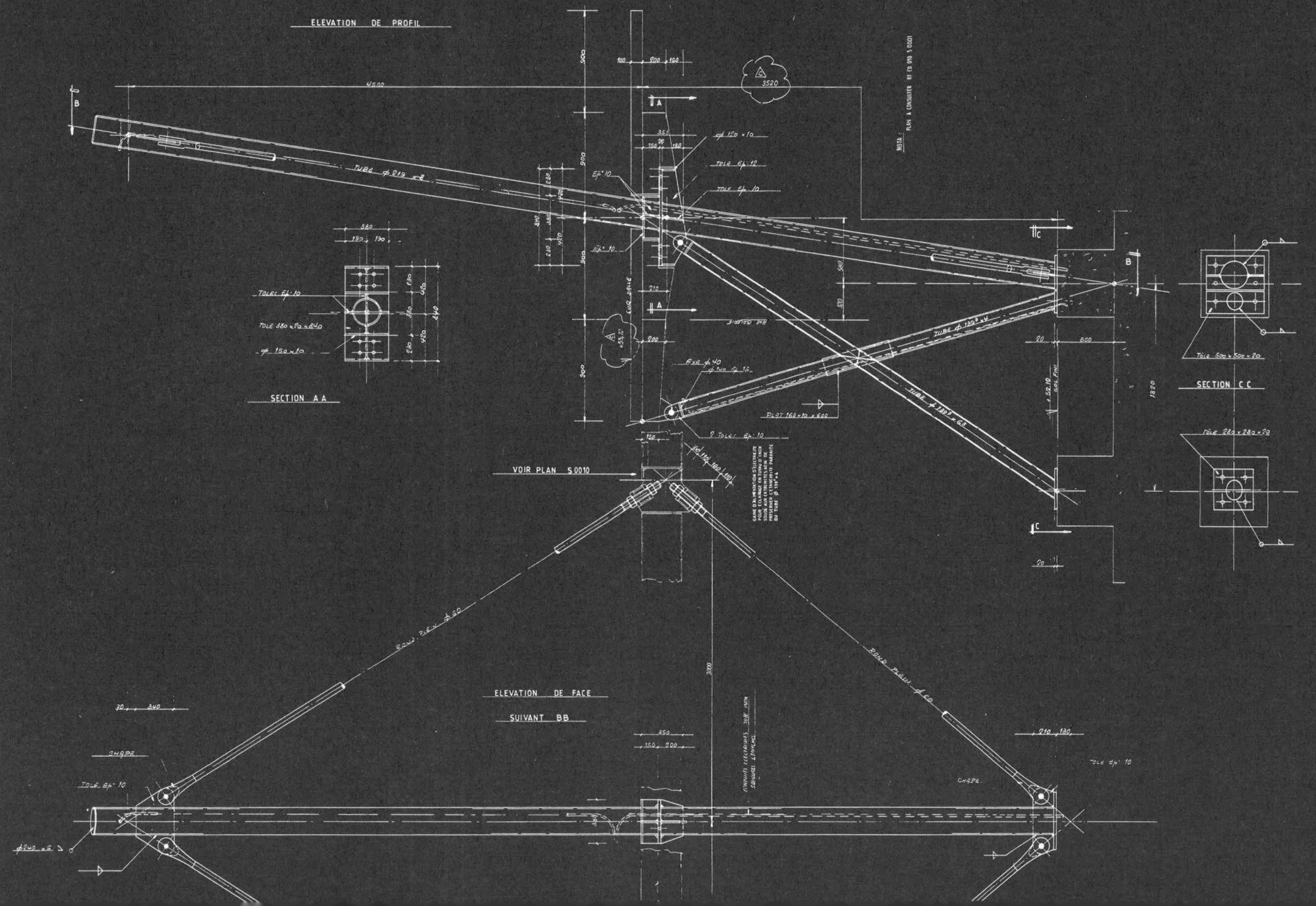

ELEVATION DE PROFIL
NOTA : PLAN À CONSULTER RF ED 010 S 0001
TUBE ϕ 219 x 8
TOLE Ep. 12
TOLE Ep. 10
SECTION A A
TOLE 380 x 80 x 840
SECTION C C
TOLE 500 x 500 x 20
TOLE 280 x 280 x 20
VOIR PLAN S 0010
ELEVATION DE FACE
SUIVANT BB
ROND PLEIN ϕ 60
CHAPE

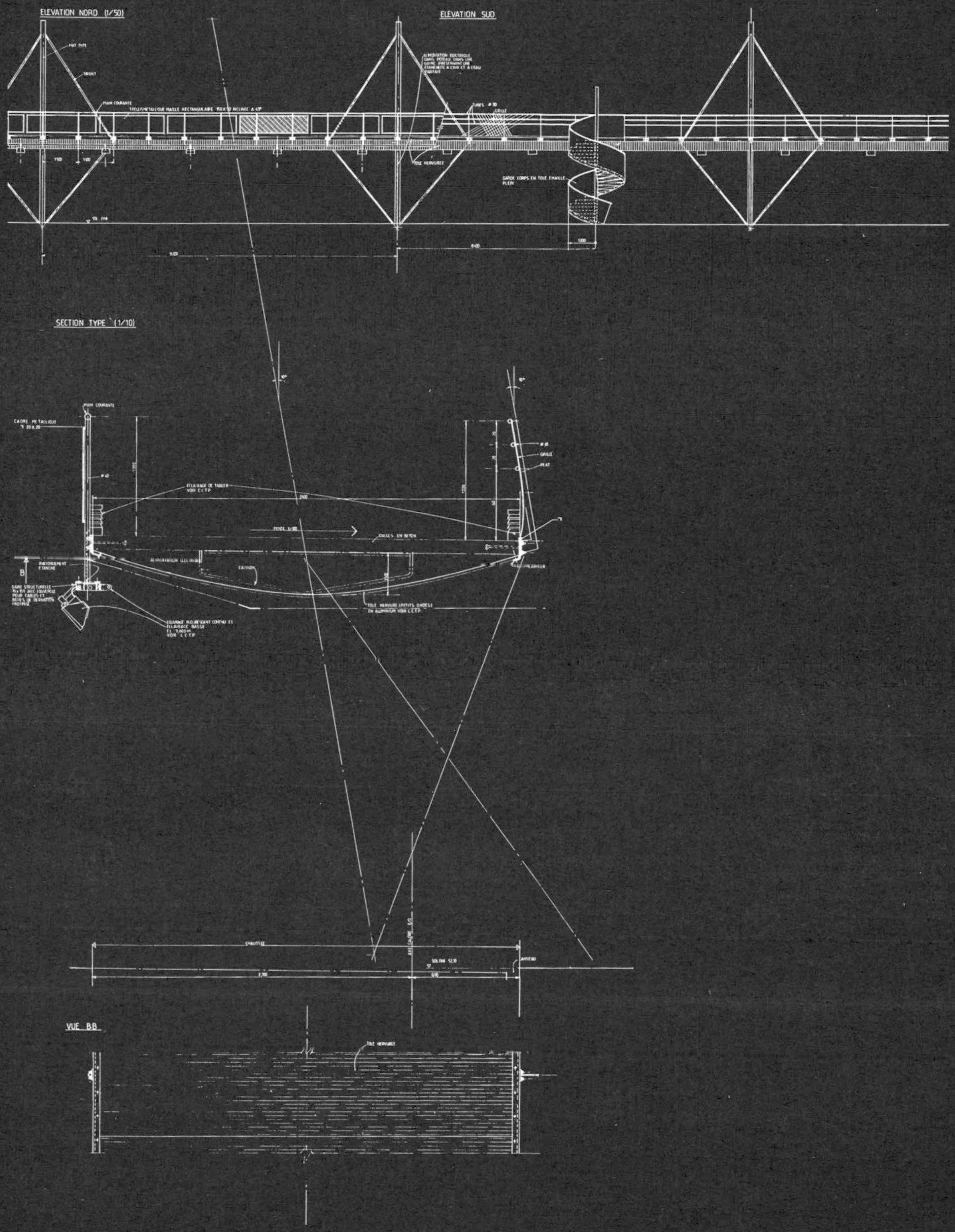
ELEVATION NORD (1/50)
ELEVATION SUD
SECTION TYPE (1/10)
VUE BB

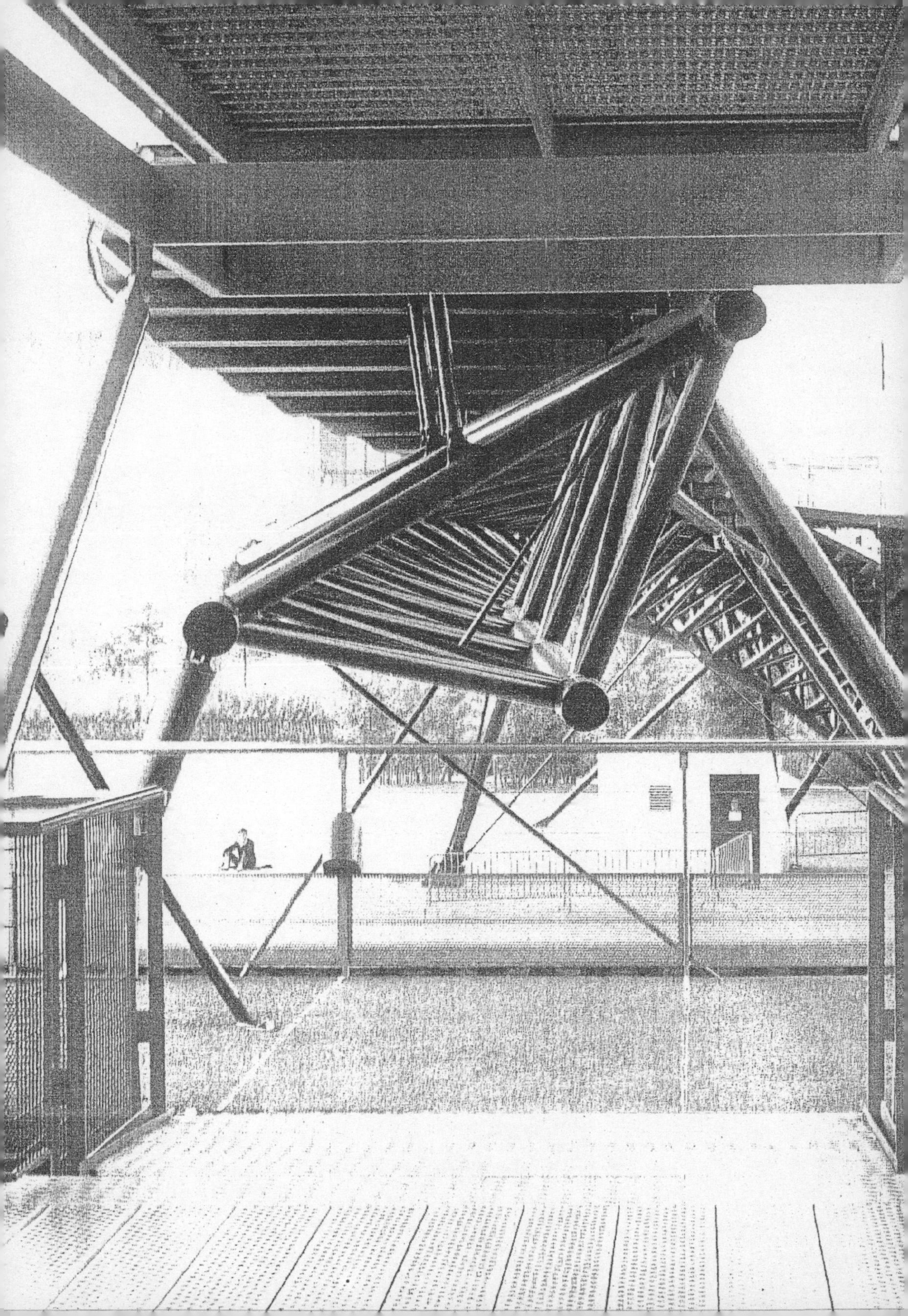

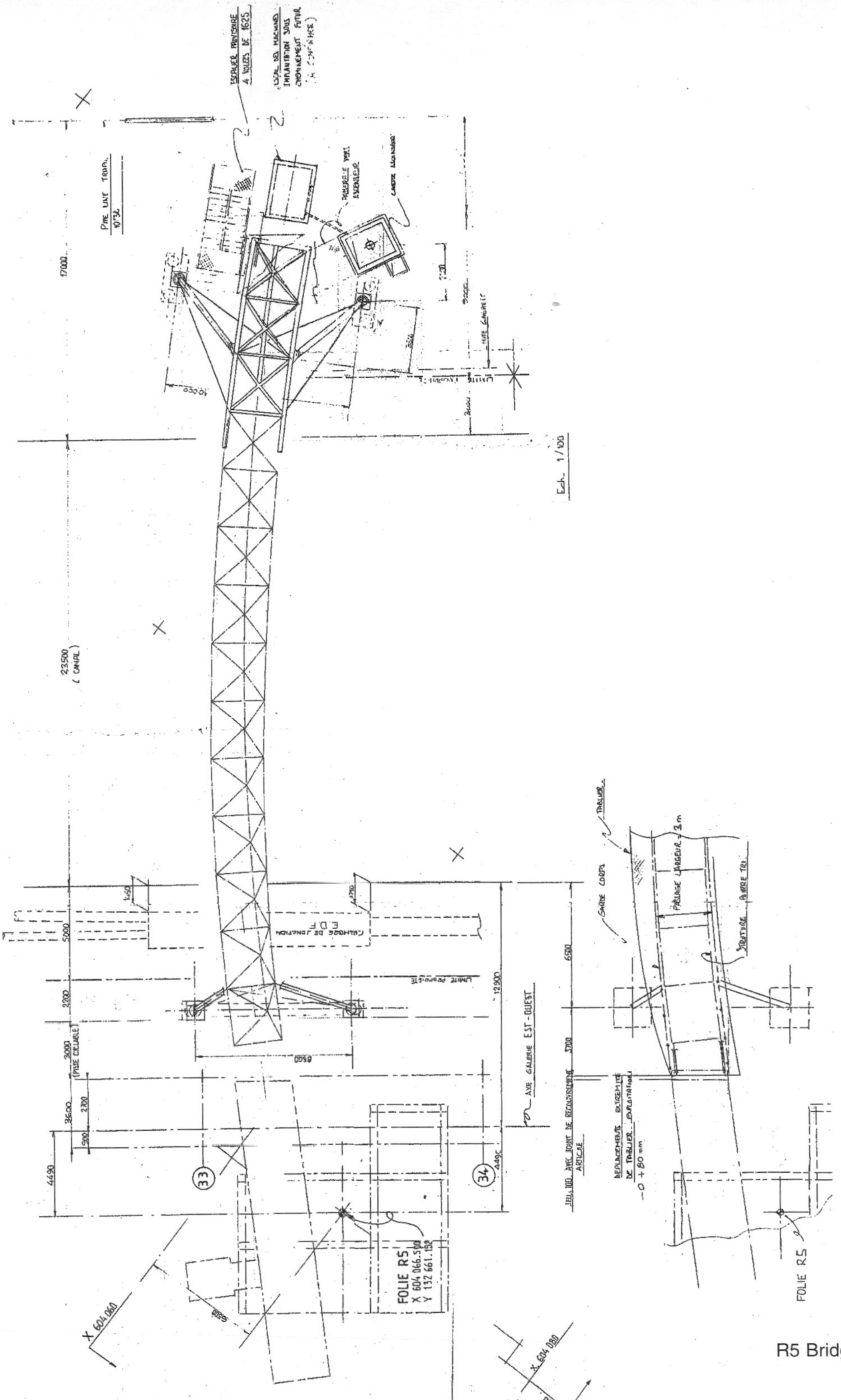
17000
23500
(CANAL)
Ech. 1/100
E.D.F
AXE GALERIE EST-OUEST
FOLIE R5
X 604 066.500
Y 132 661.132
X 604 060
X 604 080
Y 132 660
FOLIE R5

R5 Bridge

B.
Vectors

If movement is to be one of the generating factors of architecture, it will not take a single form or configuration. There is random movement, as experienced on a flat plane, free of any attraction or constriction. But there is also vectorized movement, namely, ramps, stairs, elevators, escalators, hallways, catwalks, bridges, and so on, which interact with static spaces, often activating them through the motion of the bodies that populate them. A department store, an office building, a railway station, a student center, and an art gallery in four different cities demonstrate the interaction between static or normative spaces and vectors of activity. In each case, these vectors constitute the "public" face of the buildings: they are also places of encounter, sites for the unexpected.

Zurich, K-Polis Department Store, 1995

Curved Vector through the Grid

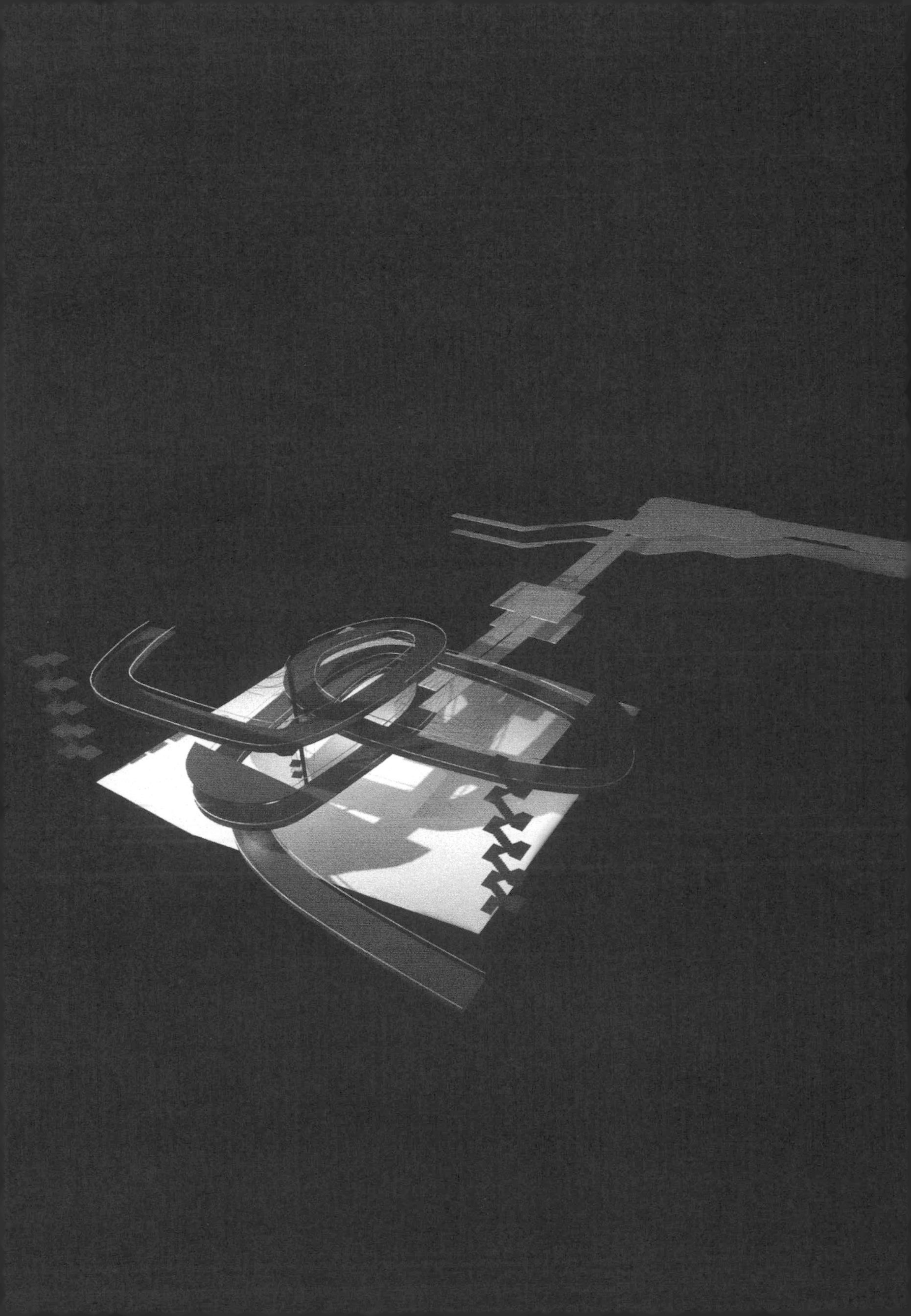

Architecture of Display—Display of Architecture

Department stores and museums have one thing in common: the need for seduction through a language of display. Each product exhibited becomes an object of desire, and walking is the preferred means to apprehend such objects of desire. A slow dance begins between two bodies—the dynamic body of the visitor/consumer and the static body of the object of consumption.

In our competition project for a new department store on the outskirts of Zurich, Switzerland, we tried to express this dance. A ramp ascends in a random manner and intersects all parts of the building. Like a long vector of movement, the ramp activates the building, defining intensity and areas of use. It is the main street of the Polis, open at late hours, and it is the route of the New. All of the new products are displayed along the ramp. Roll-down gates and sliding glass partitions can separate the night section from the day section. Major night activities are located along the ramp and at the top of the new building. The ramp is visible from inside (the large interior court) and from the outside (as it pierces through the glass skin and through the advertising screen of the building).

The ramp occasionally intersects the envelope of the building and appears as a volume on the exterior. The envelope is made out of changing electronic signage, integrated into layers of printed glass.

Duchamp's three stoppages: a random path

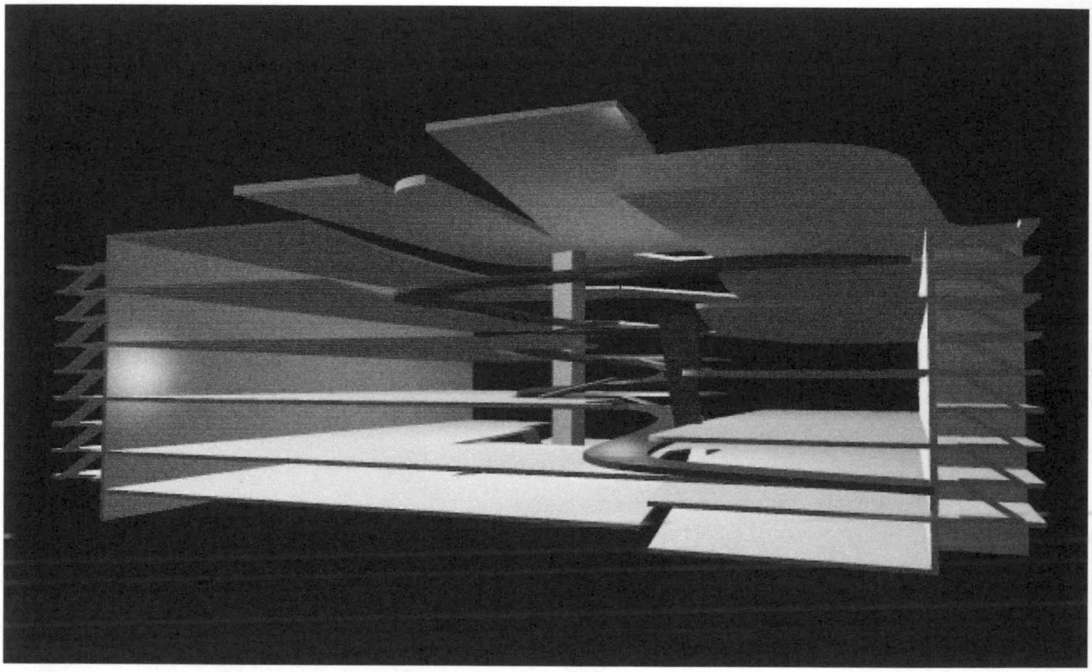

A continuous flow: intersecting and staggering floor plates

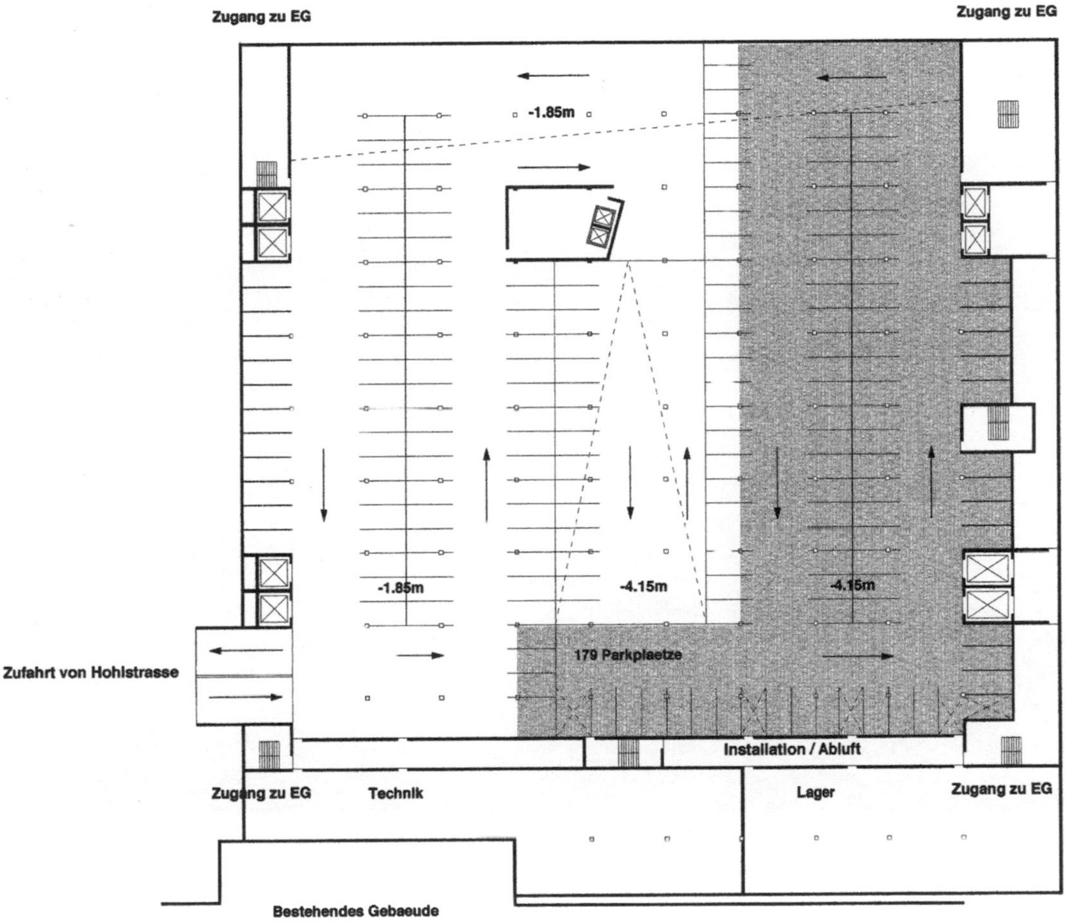
Zugang zu EG
Zugang zu EG
-1.85m
-1.85m
-4.15m
-4.15m
179 Parkplaetze
Zufahrt von Hohlstrasse
Installation / Abluft
Zugang zu EG
Technik
Lager
Zugang zu EG
Bestehendes Gebaeude

Basement

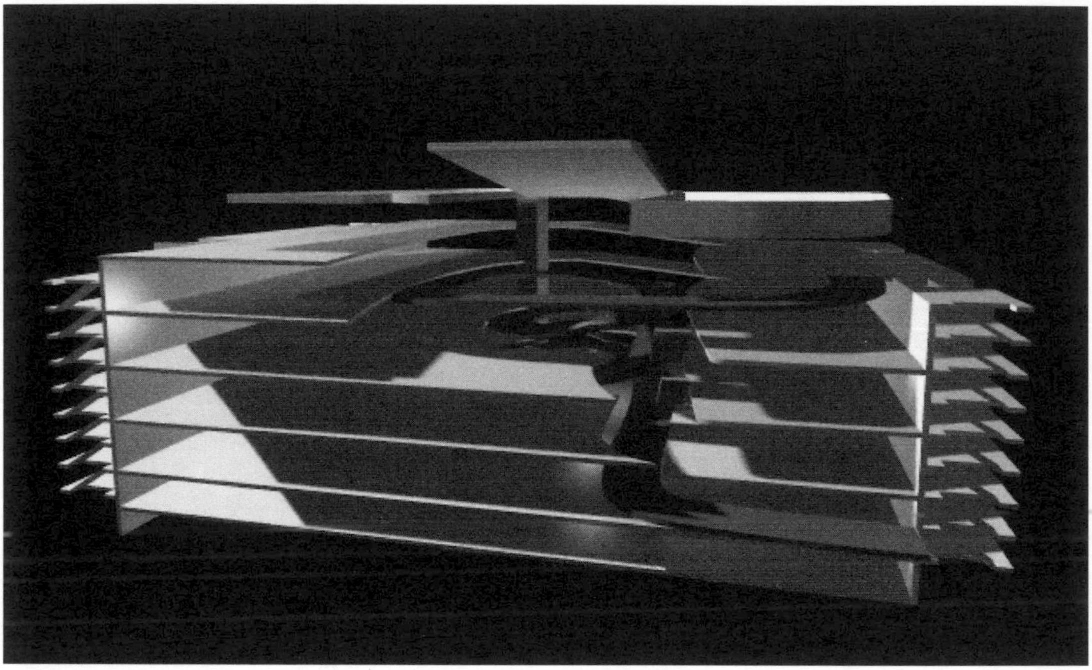

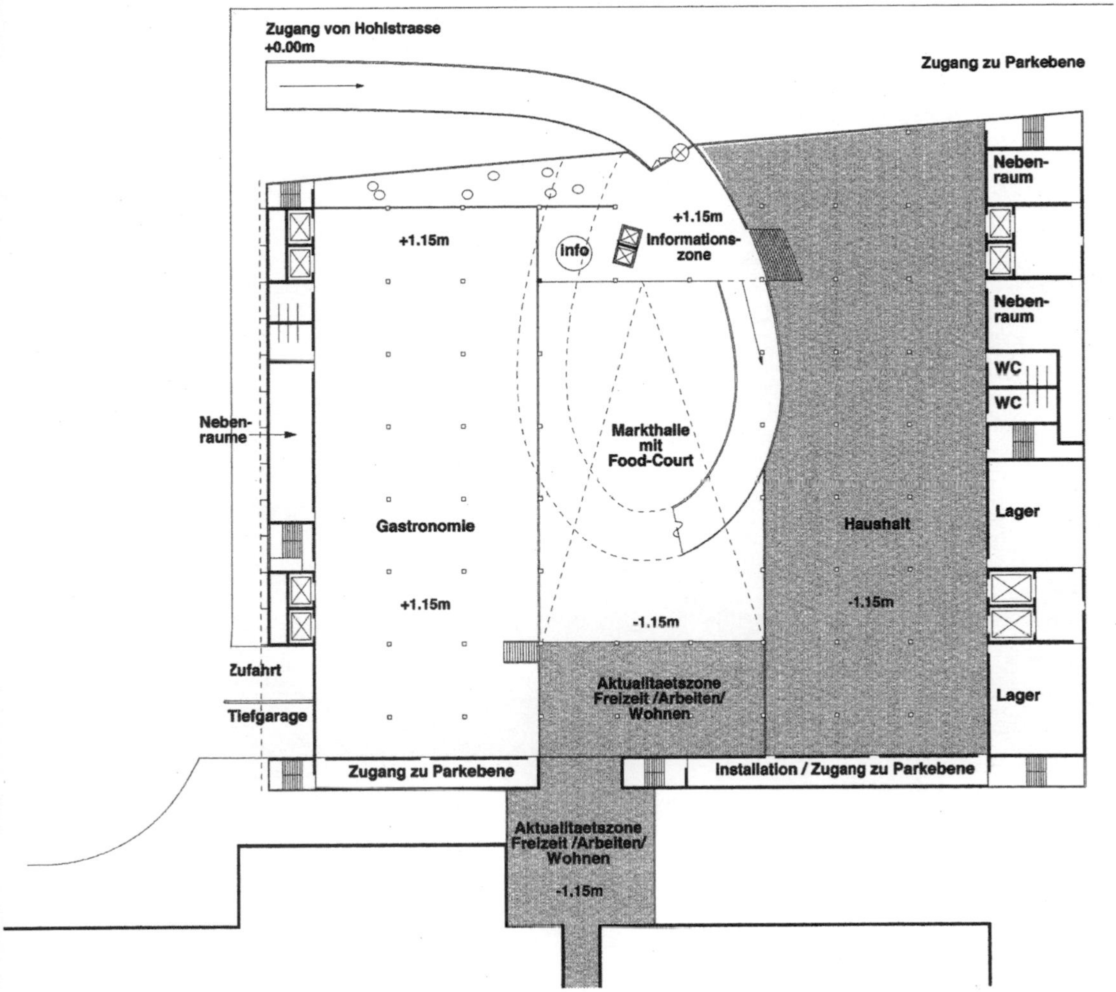
Zugang von Hohlstrasse
+0.00m
Zugang zu Parkebene
Neben-
raum
+1.15m
+1.15m
info
Informations-
zone
Neben-
raum
WC
WC
Neben-
raume
Markthalle
mit
Food-Court
Gastronomie
Haushalt
Lager
+1.15m
-1.15m
-1.15m
Lager
Zufahrt
Aktualitaetszone
Freizeit /Arbeiten/
Wohnen
Tiefgarage
Zugang zu Parkebene
Installation / Zugang zu Parkebene
Aktualitaetszone
Freizeit /Arbeiten/
Wohnen
-1.15m

First level

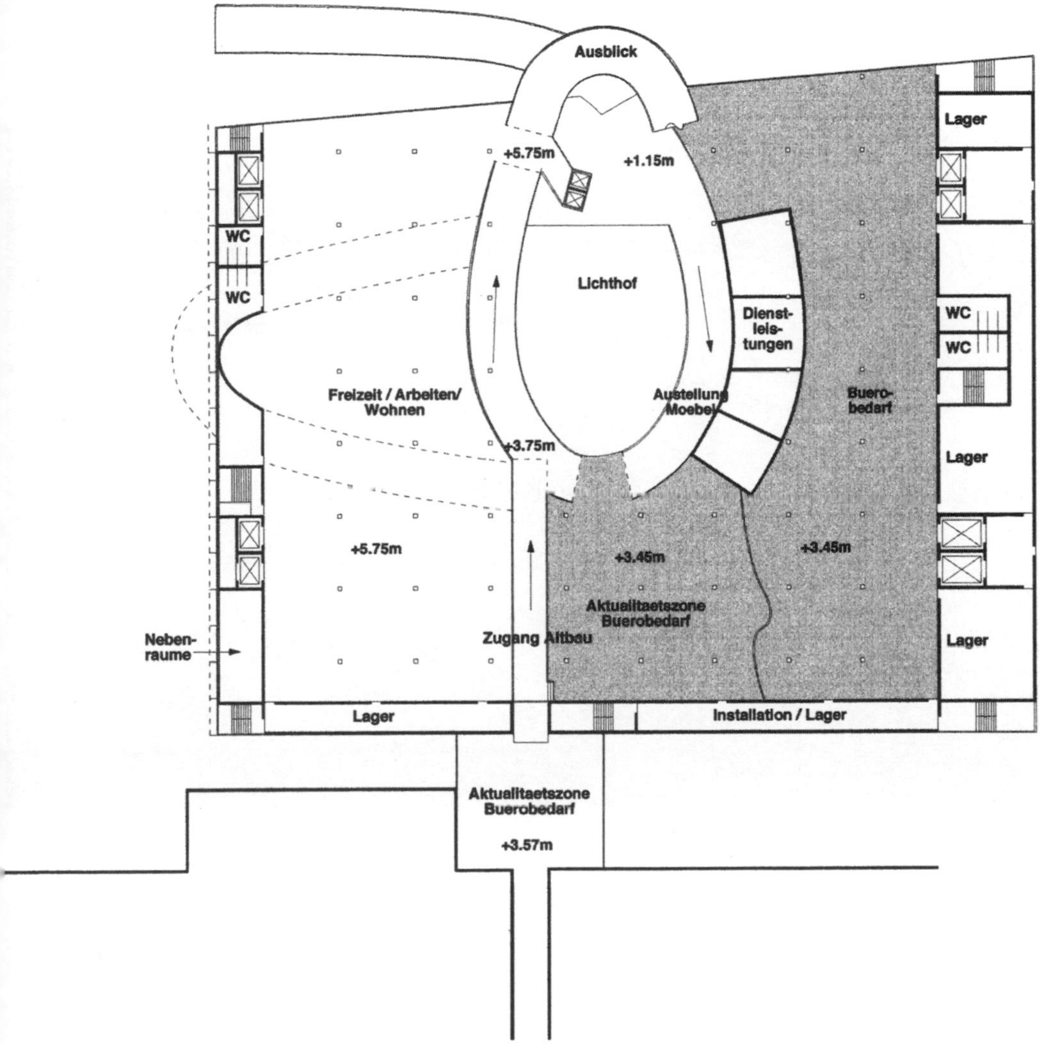

Second and third levels: random vector cuts through a regular column grid

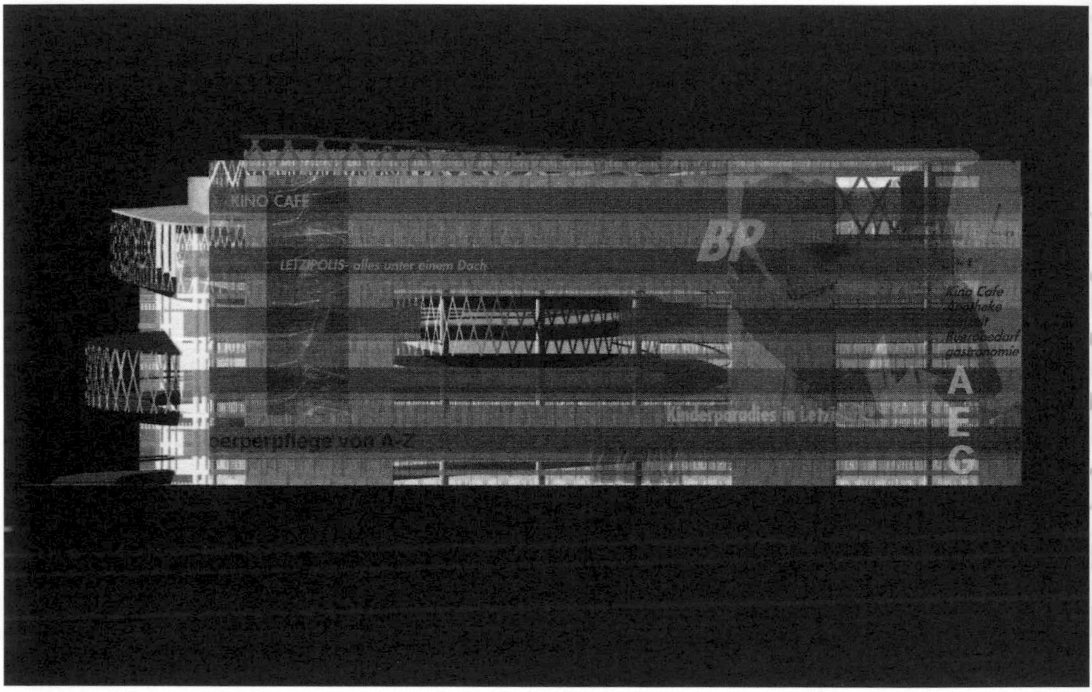

Multimedia envelope intersected by motion

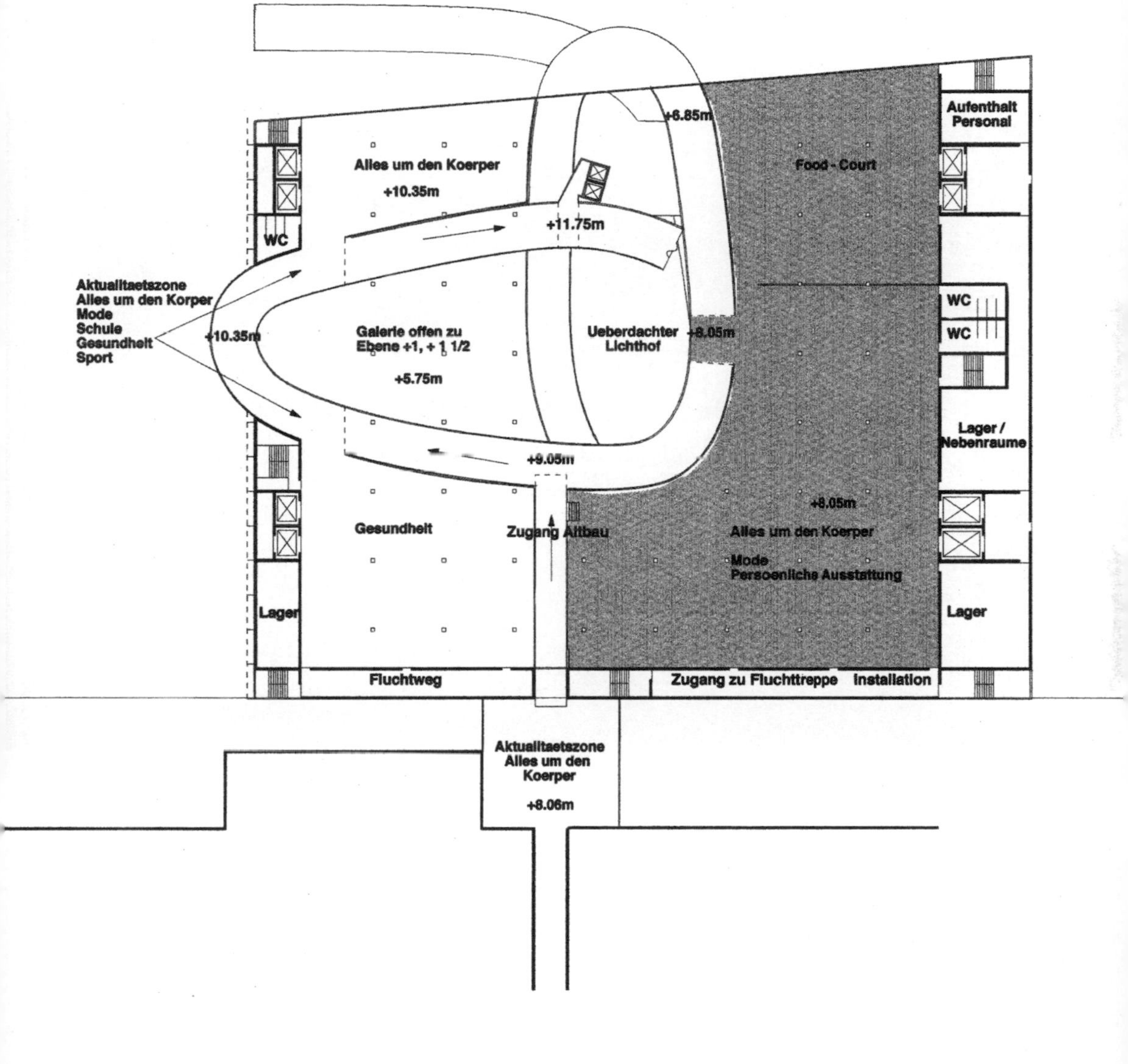

Third and fourth levels: vector path displaces floor plates, staggering them

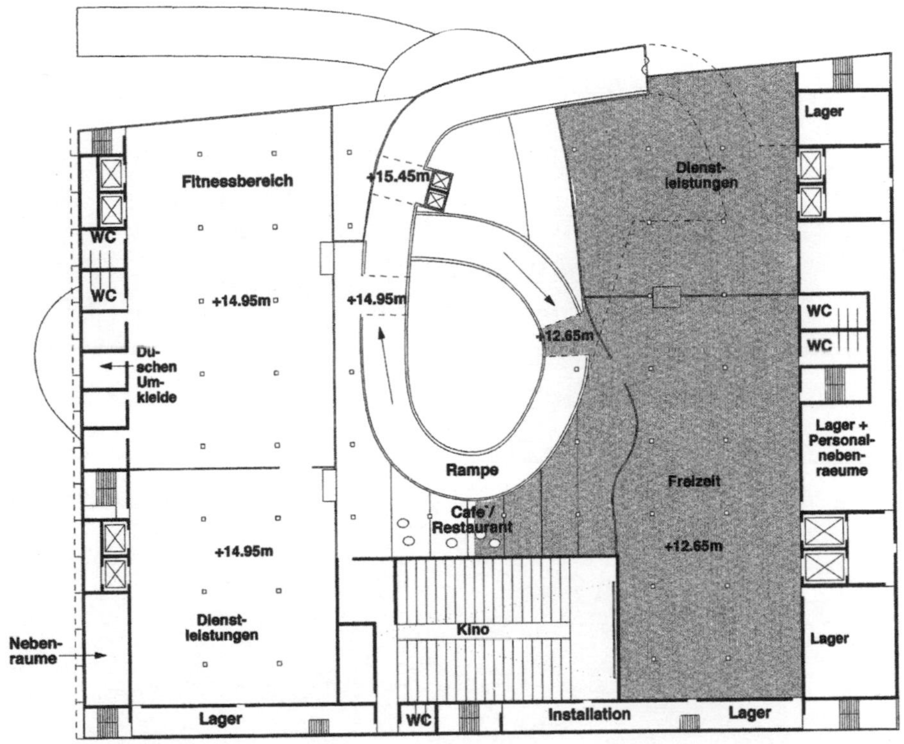

Fifth and sixth levels: from half-floor to half-floor

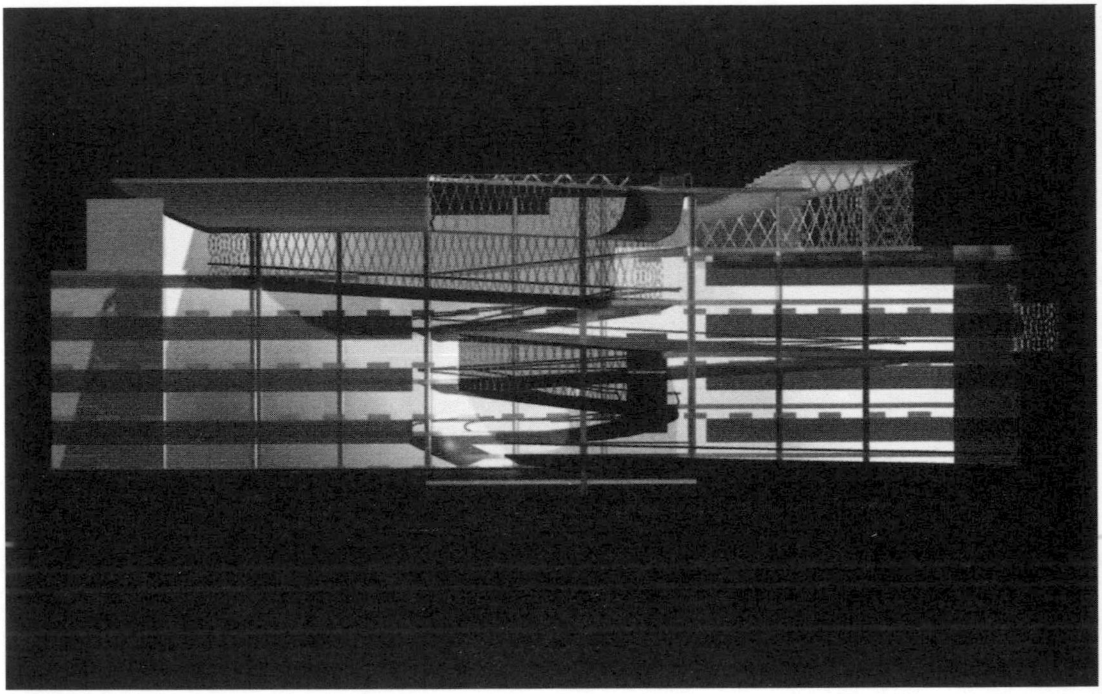

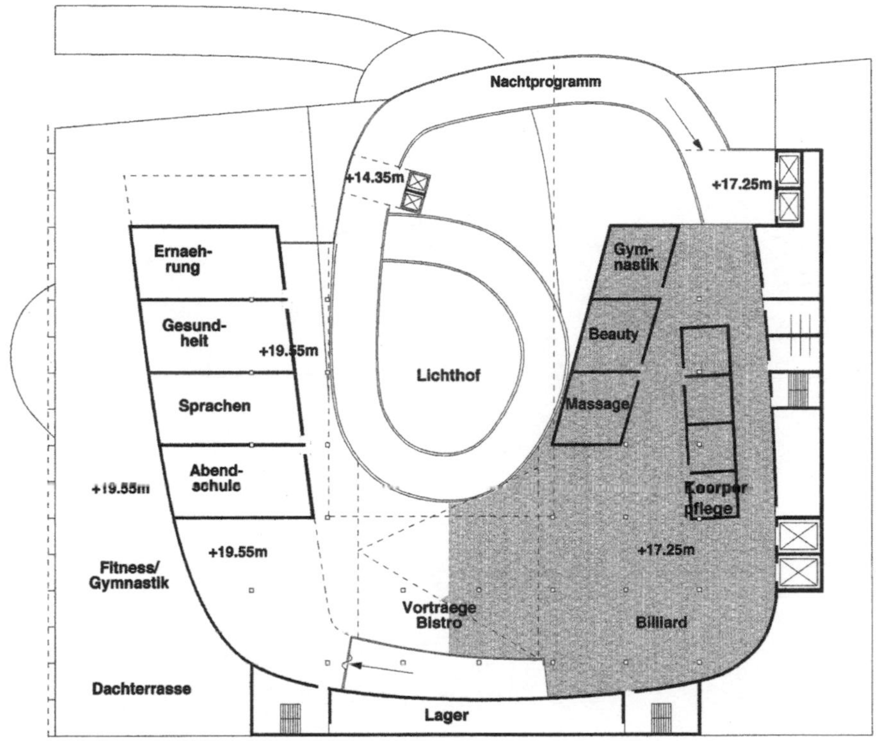

Roof levels: vector path equals spatial experience

Geneva, Organisation Mondiale Météorologique Headquarters, 1993

Vector as Landscape

Questions

The competition for the headquarters of the OMM raises the following questions:
How to build one of the facades of the city of Geneva, where the OMM headquarters will be one of the first visible modern buildings?
How to assure the proper placement of the building within the urban fabric and the neighboring parks?
How to interpret the programmatic requirements so as to insure that this administrative building is at the same time representative, functional, and innovative in its spatial organization, while offering more than just a conventional arrangement of office spaces?
How to affirm the organization's preoccupation with the protection of the environment, a climatic balance within the building, and an overall energy-efficient design?
And, finally, how to propose new working conditions that integrate the notions of social interaction and relaxation?

Concept

These questions brought us to design what could be described as a "building-landscape," a diagonal moving from the bottom to the top of the building, articulating a garden-space in an architectural promenade that links all the functional requirements of the program, joining the public spaces to the office spaces.

The building is organized in three volumes—the access volume, the linear volume, and the cylinder volume—linked by a diagonal garden. The geometry of the project resolves the intersection of two existing urban grids.

The Diagonal Garden

The diagonal garden links the entrance level to the cylindrical form at its terrace. It consists of longitudinal bands: a stair-ramp within the interior of the building's envelope, and an exterior stair-ramp along the sequence of garden spaces. Arranging plants along this slope creates the diagonal garden. It is proposed to have alternating spaces of densely planted gardens and more open terrace spaces. The essence of these spaces will be achieved by using plants of varying heights and color densities that are compatible with the sun conditions along the diagonal: *acer pennsylvanicum* (jasper maple), *daphne mezerum* (laurel), *mattencia struthiopteris* (German fern), *vinca minor* (periwinkle). The diagonal garden is a space both to inhabit and to view; it is accessible and offers small niches on the exterior where one can rest. In addition, at each level, the spaces for relaxation and social interaction are designed like open balconies on the diagonal garden. The diagonal garden is extended through a circular ramp around the cylinder where the last room—the restaurant —is designed as a winter garden.

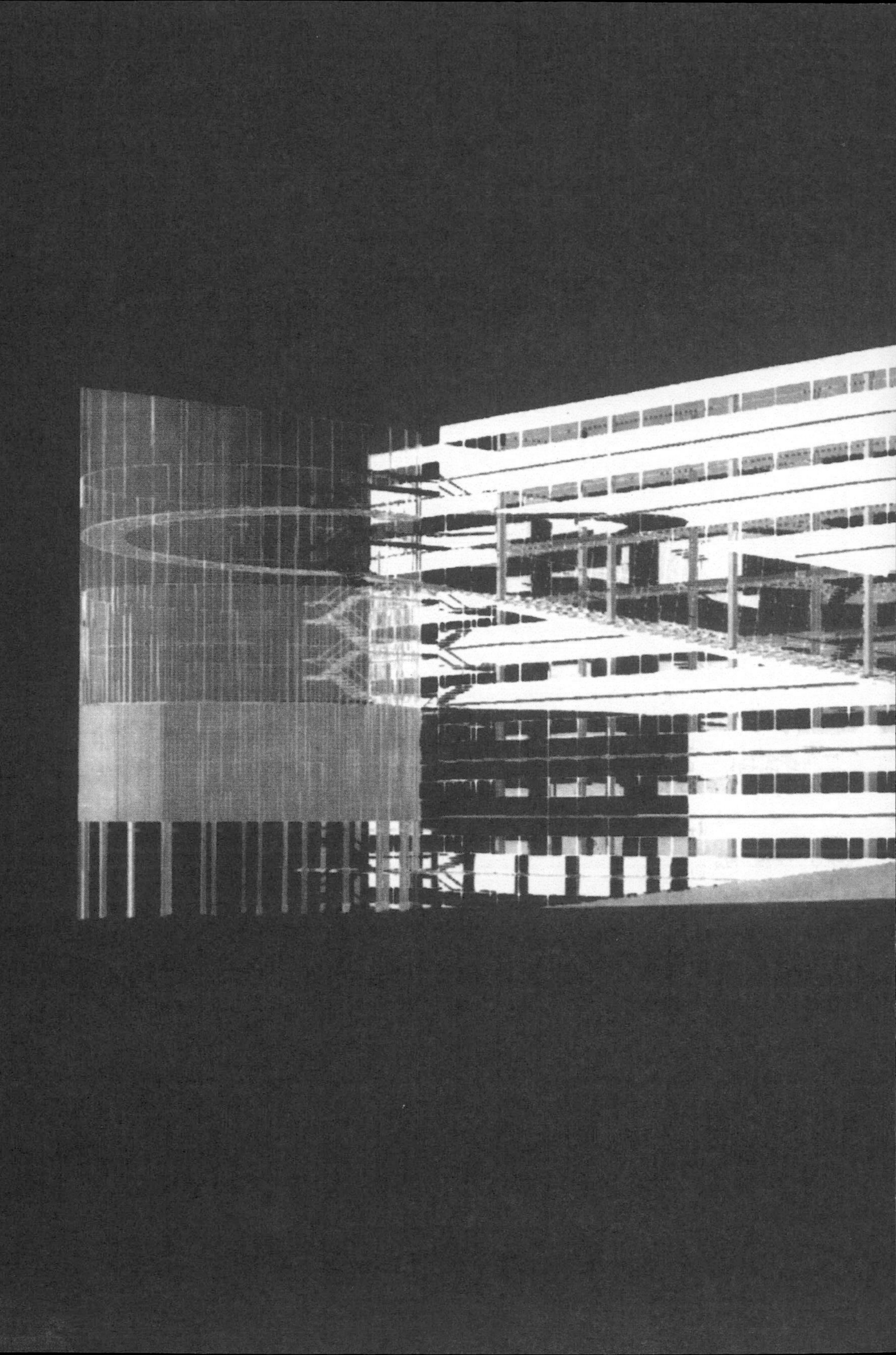

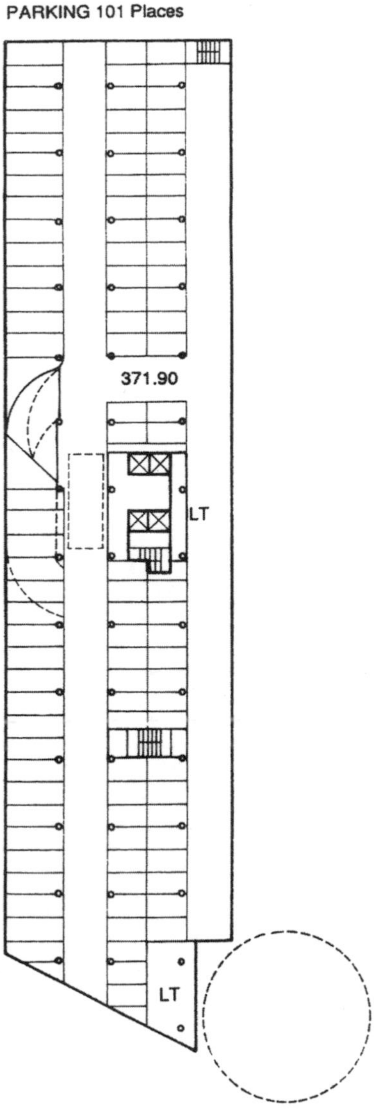

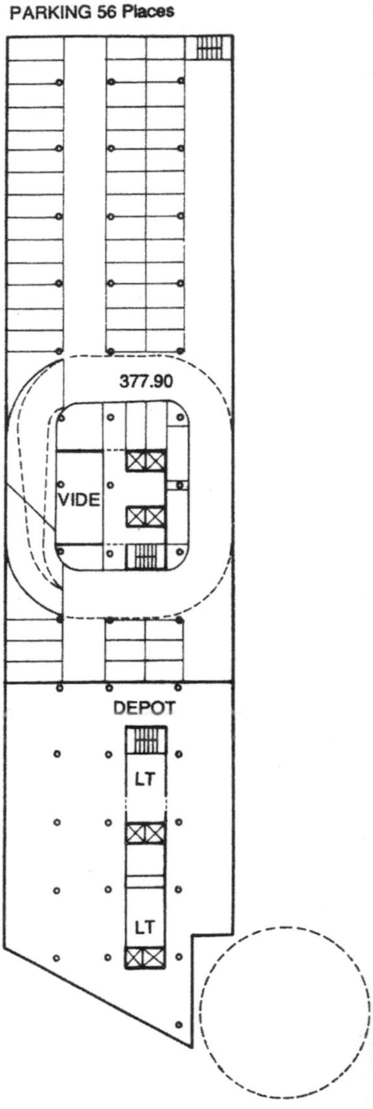

Level -5, Level -3

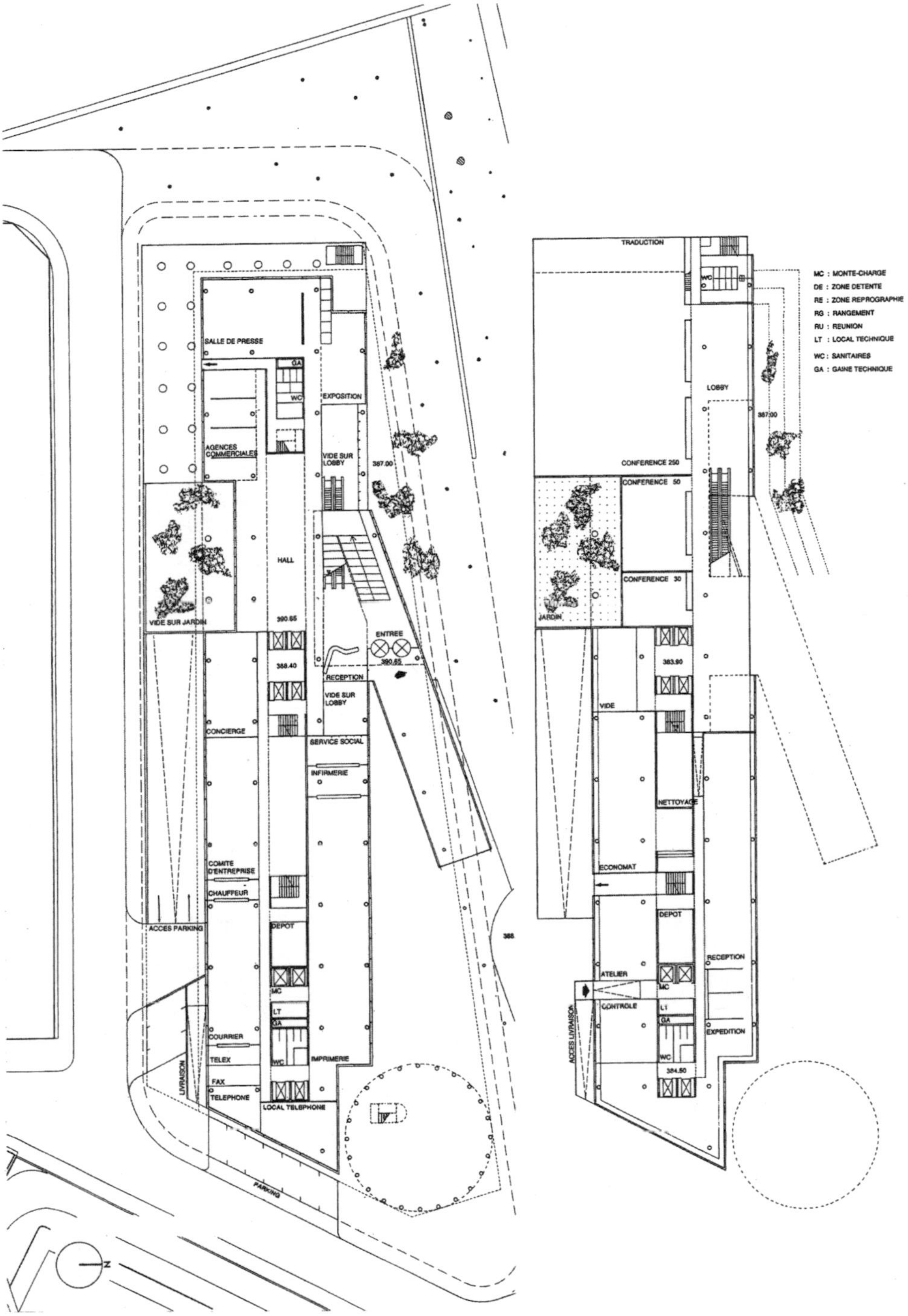

Level 0, Level -1 A generic building with a difference

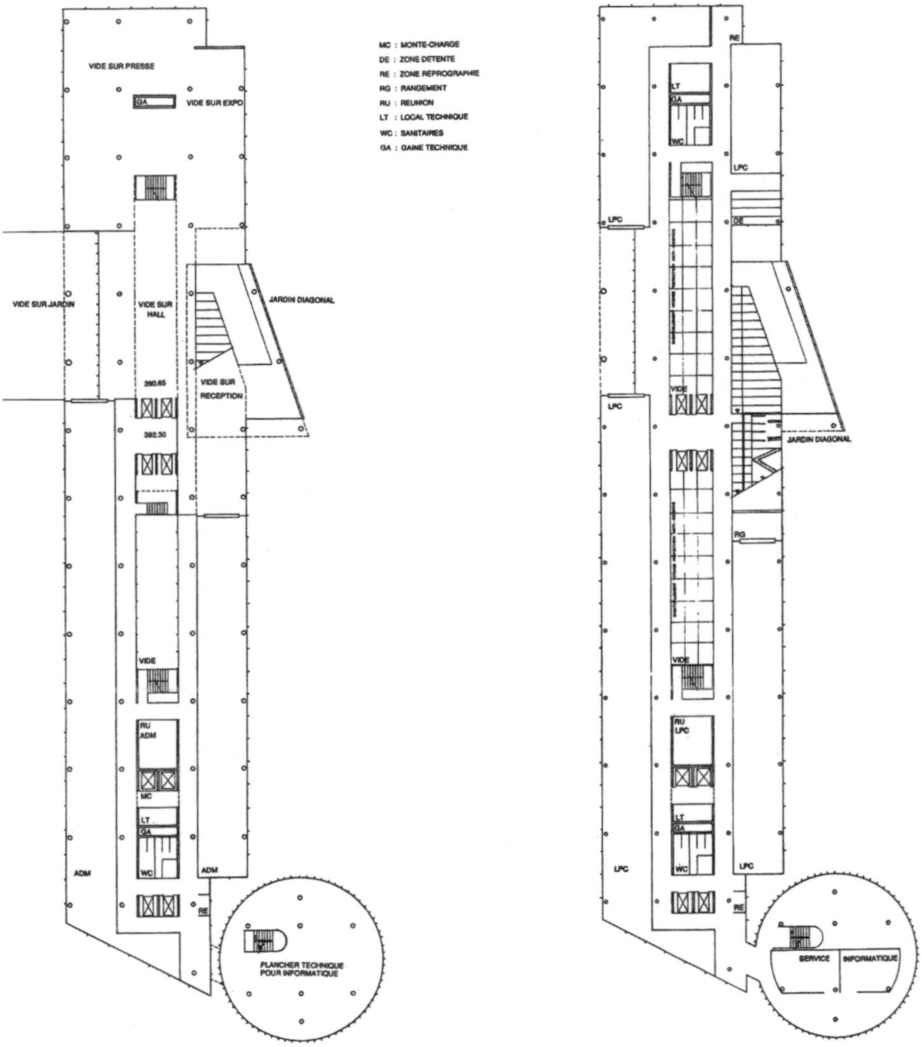

Level +1, Level +2 The oblique vector: a semi-public meeting area

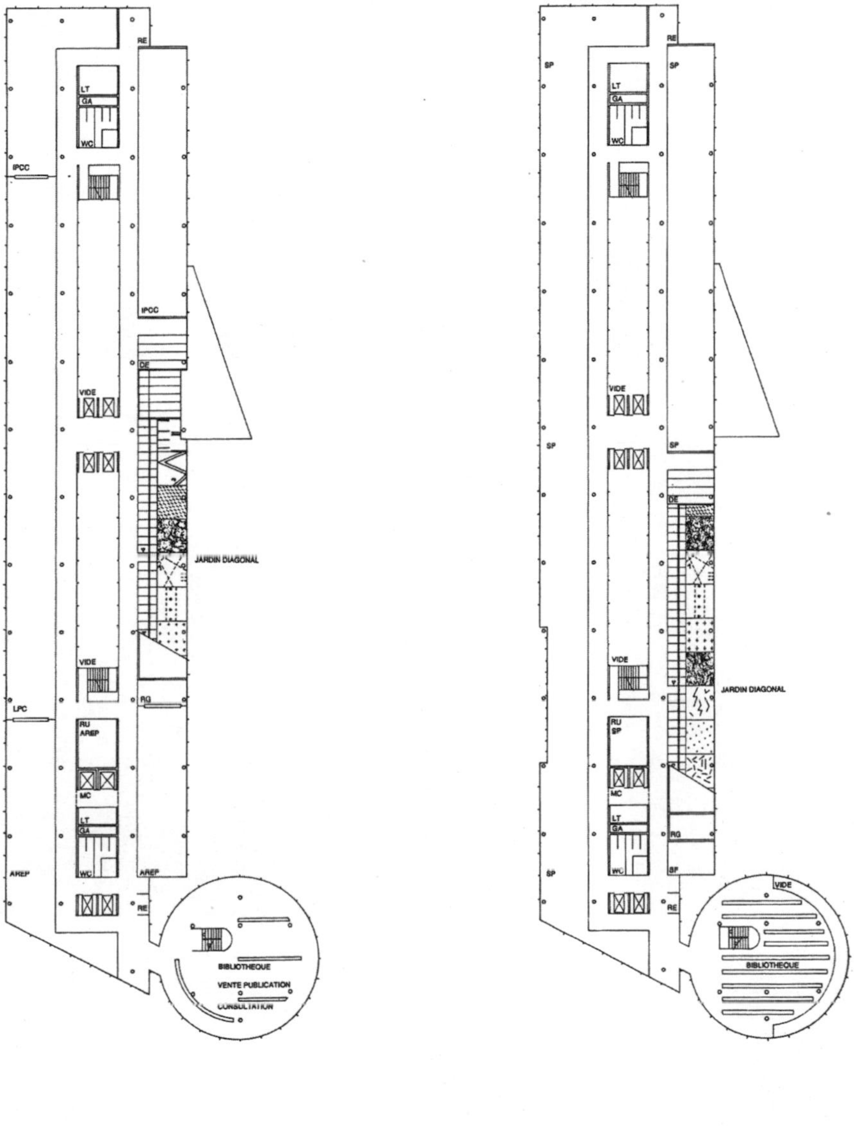

Level +3, Level +4 The oblique landscape is the project's social space

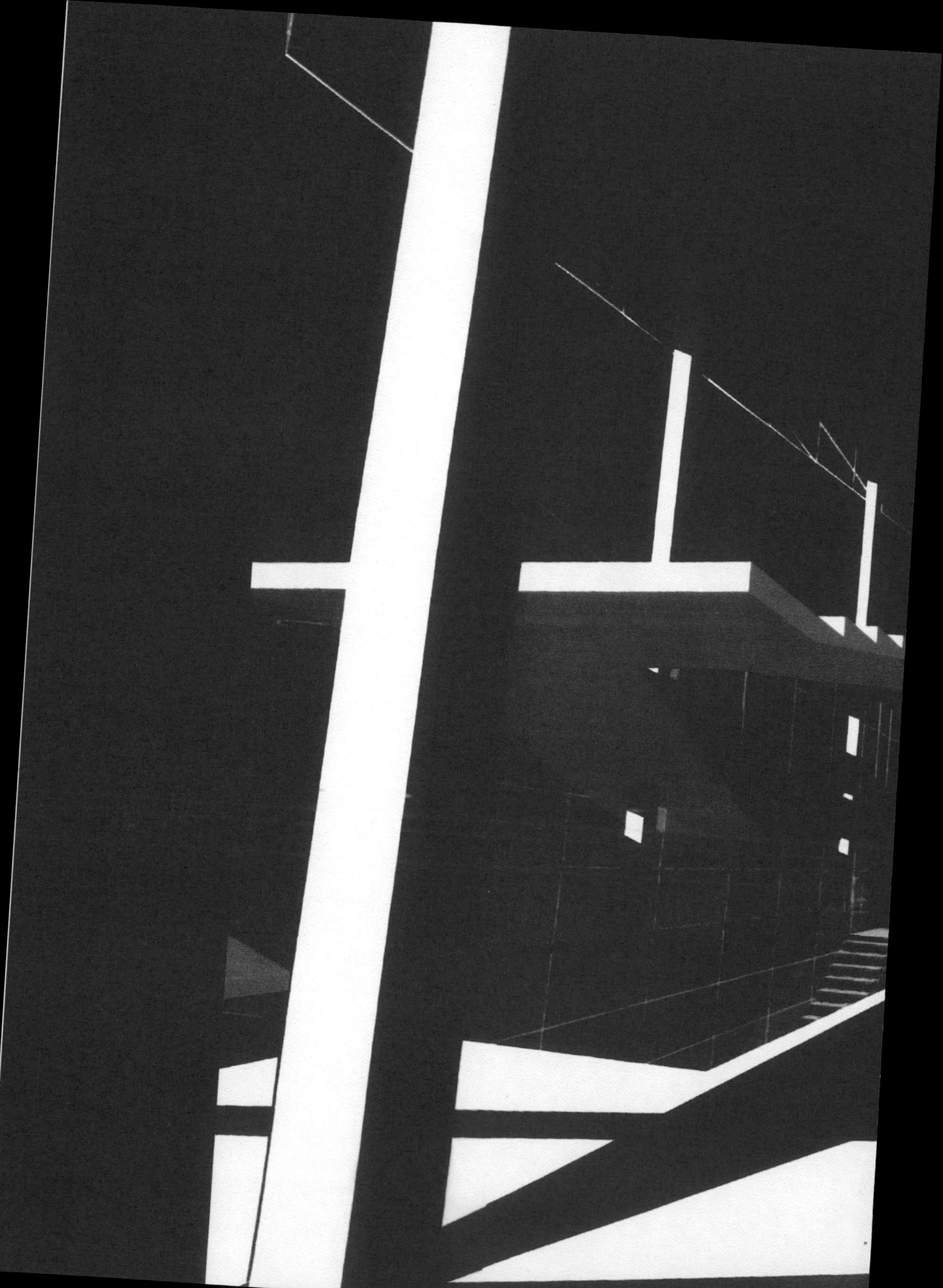

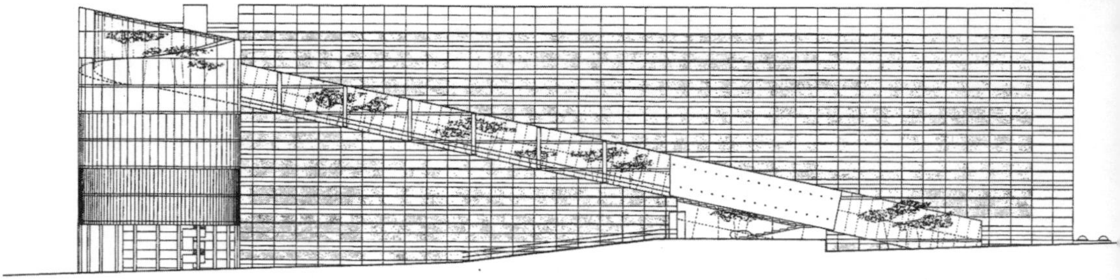

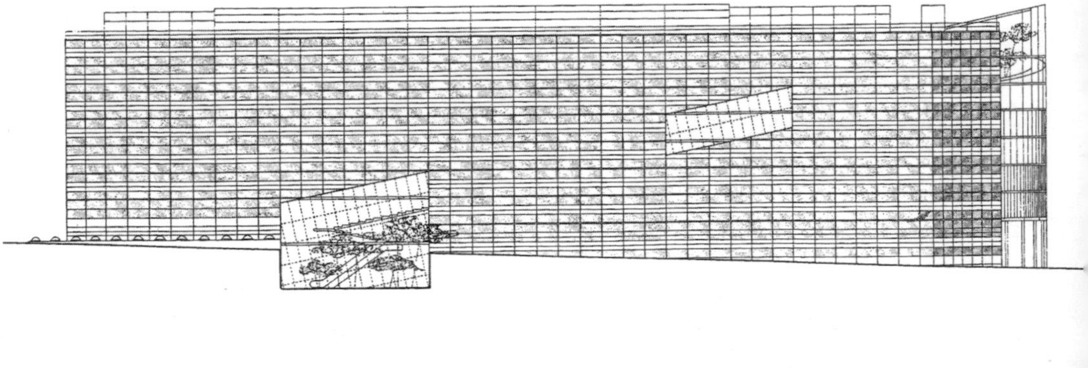

Elevations A common denominator: the oblique landscape

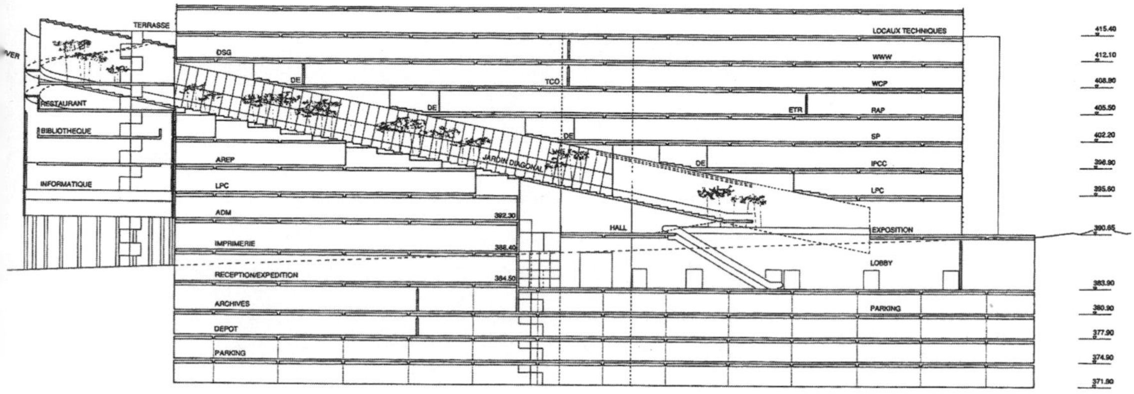

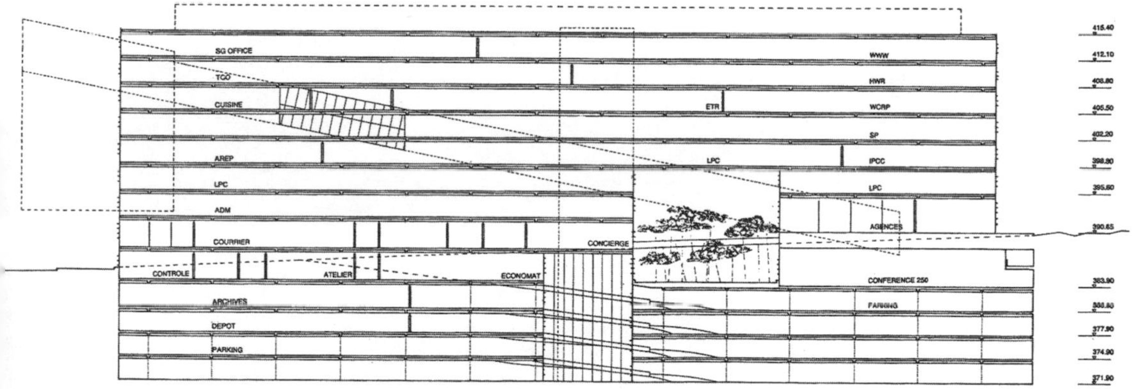

Sections Carving a path into a solid: static offices versus dynamic social space

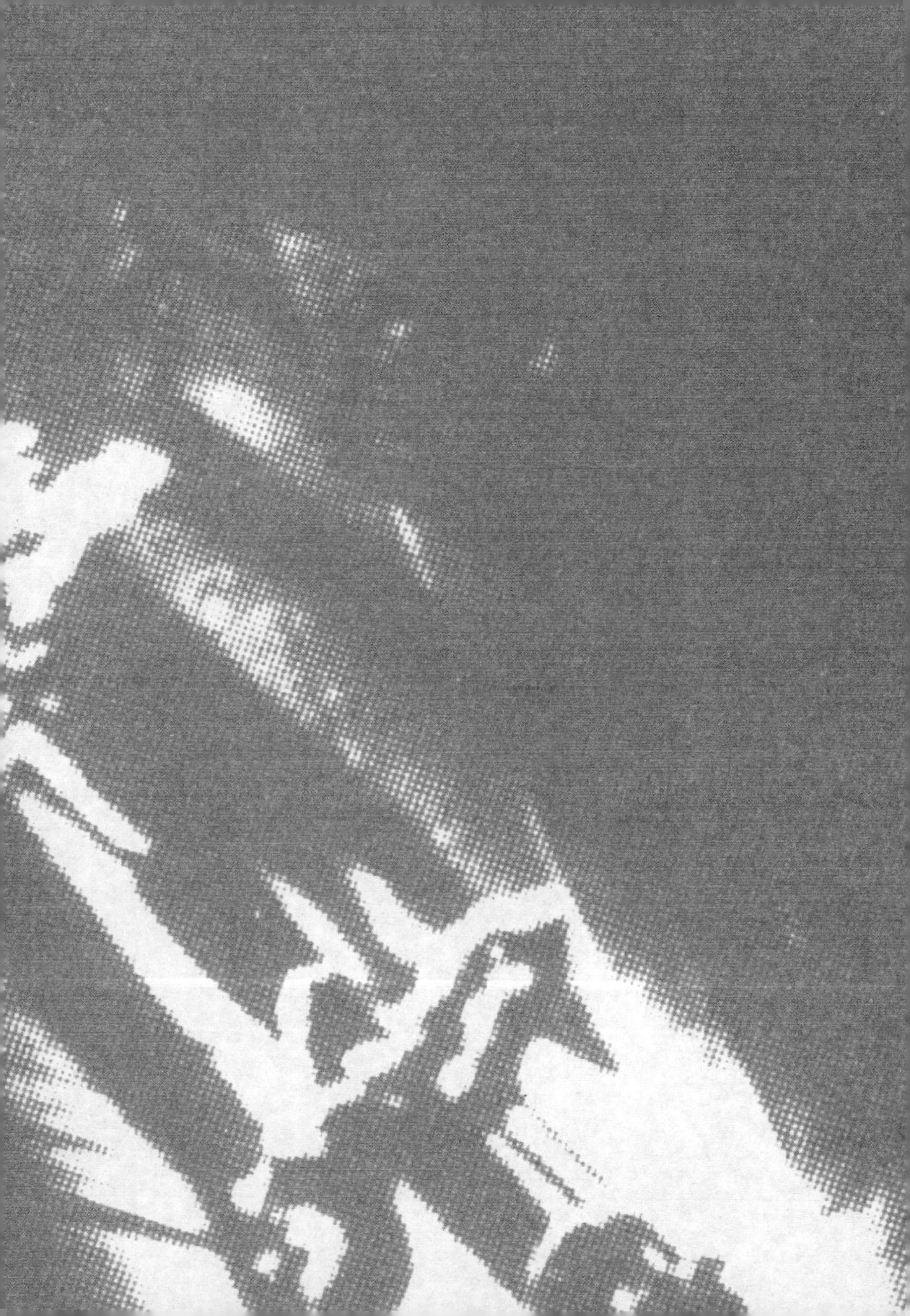

Lausanne, Interface-Flon
Bus / Railway Station, 1994-

Vector as Infrastructure

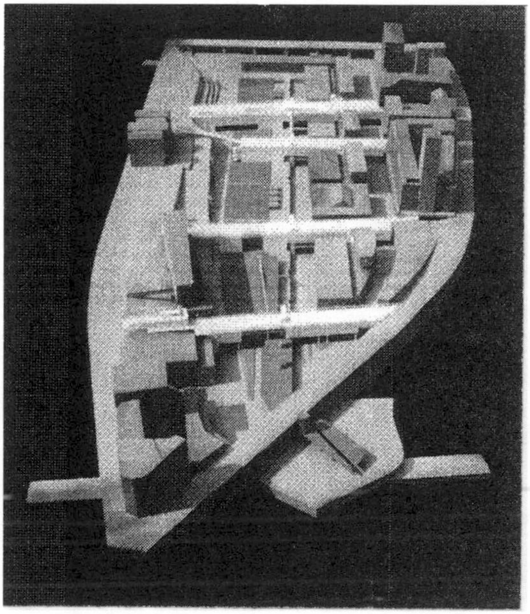

Lausanne's existing hillside topography has transformed the relation of streets to buildings, indeed the whole notion of urban space. In some parts of the city, streets are suspended and buildings buried in the ground. Rooftops act as ground floors, while the piano nobile can be found on any level. Buildings function as vertical passageways and bridges as multi-story crossings.

The practical irrelevance of a consistent datum plane has also transformed the very concept of urbanism in this city. Moreover, the no-man's-land of obsolete industry that forms a ubiquitous buffer at the periphery of the late twentieth-century city occurs, instead, at the very center of Lausanne, in the lowlands of the Flon Valley. This unusual condition allows for the implementation of the most contemporary activities in the very heart of the city.

Programmatic and spatial transformation is the basis of our intervention.[1] Instead of adopting the conservative strategy of concentrating only on the lower level of the valley (pretending to preserve the neighborhood's soul while in reality preserving only its warehouses) or of treating it as a delimited sector in need of ex nihilo rehabilitation, we took advantage of Lausanne's existing bridge typologies by radically extending them into the project area.

We proposed a number of inhabited bridges to become generators of the master plan for the area. (See *Event-Cities*, 1994.) Political changes after an election led a new and conservative city government to decide to vote "not to vote" on the new master plan (a particular provision enabled by the Swiss constitution). While this meant that three of the four inhabited bridges were postponed, we were commissioned to design and build the last one with a modified and enlarged program, this time including the underground railway station and a large-scale infrastructure design, the Interface.

The Interface

With its bridge, elevators, and escalators, the interface functions first as a new transportation interchange for the city. Located at the western end of the Flon Valley, it combines three separate terrain and subway lines on one level and two bus lines on another, with pedestrian traffic coming from four separate stories. Functioning not as an end point, but rather as a momentary pause along multiple routes, the Interface also generates new events for this part of the city. Programmatic collisions will be encouraged as mass movement intersects other functional requirements.

[1] with Luca Merlini

Interchange: a junction of horizontal levels, vertical elevators, oblique escalators

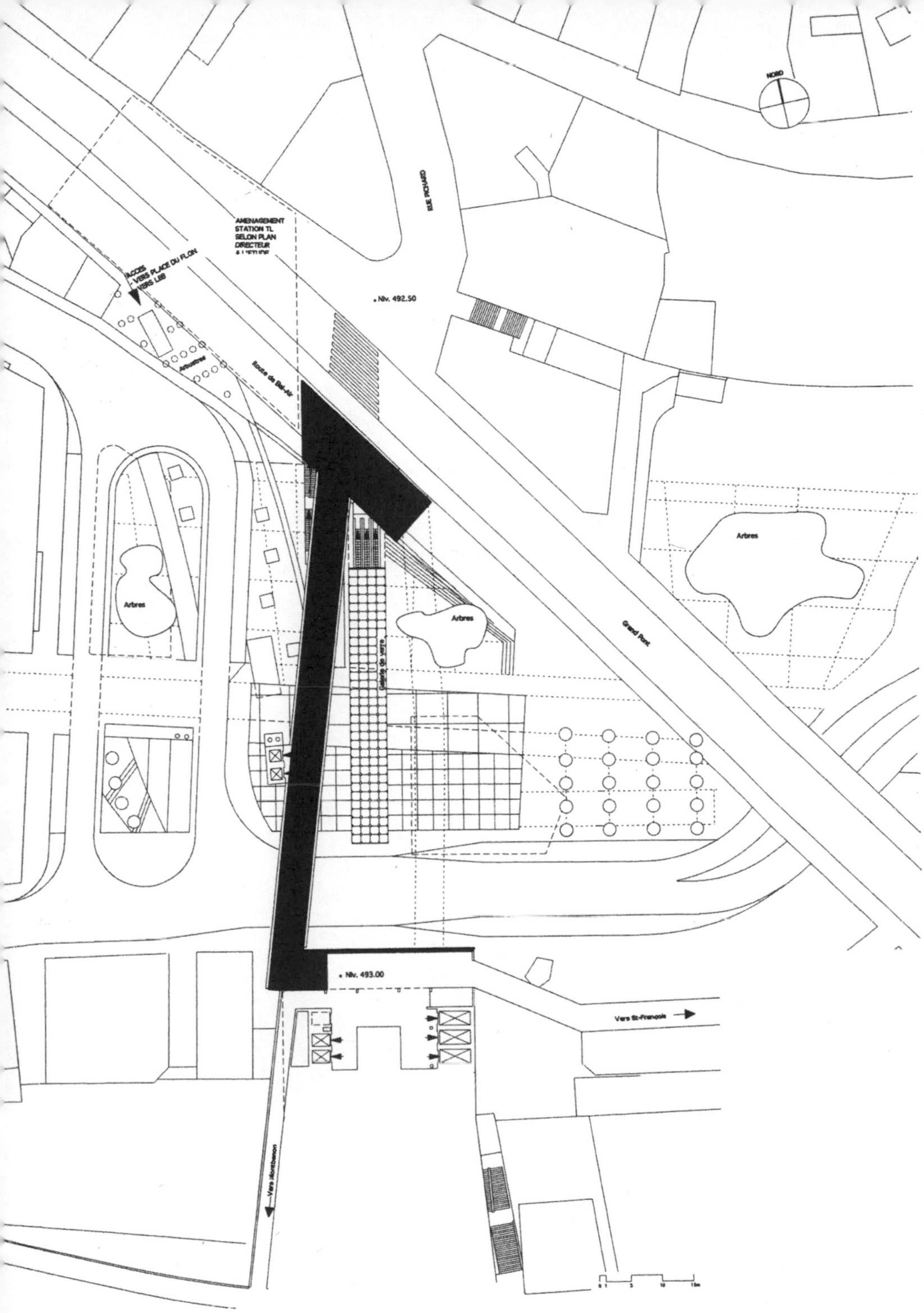

Designing a new infrastructure with program: two regional railway lines, one subway line, several bus lines, taxis, cars, pedestrians

Interface: the place where independent and often unrelated systems meet

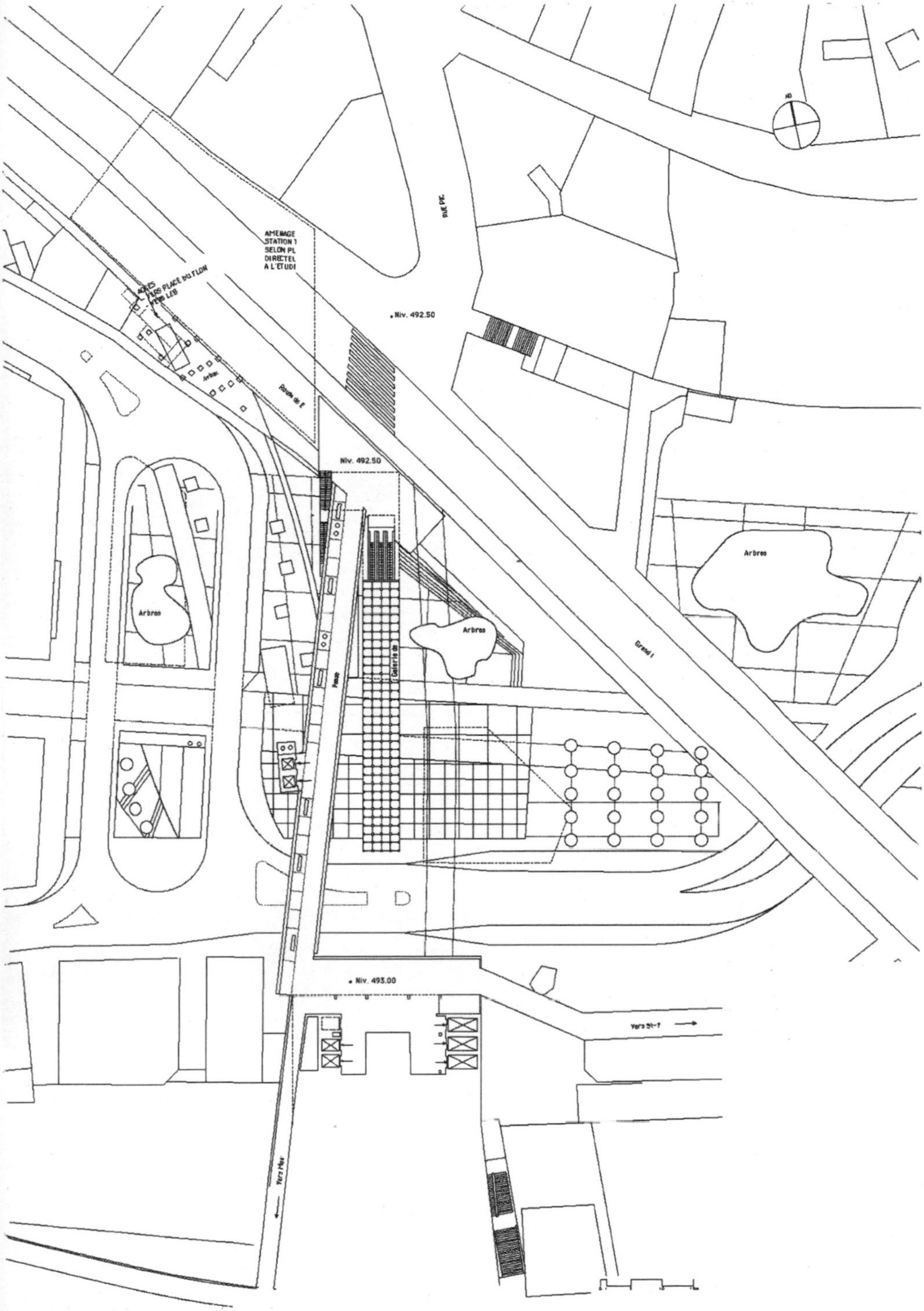

+12m Upper street level. Nothing but movement vectors

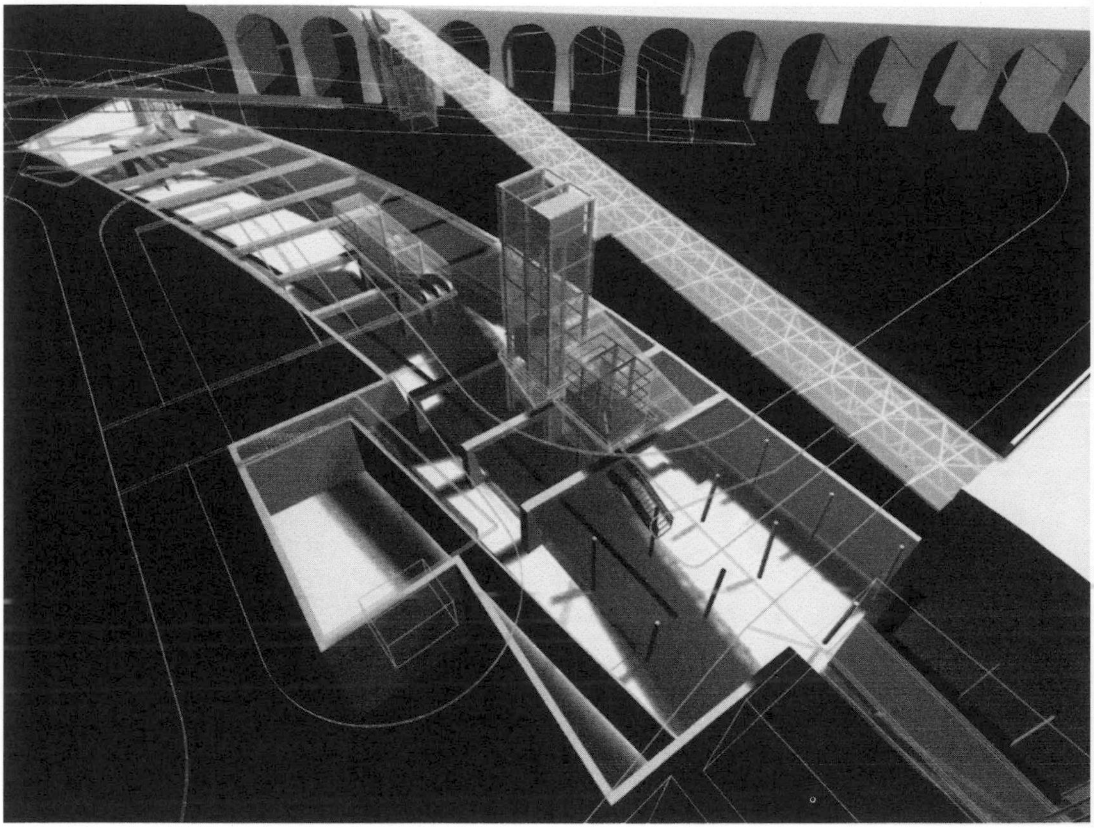

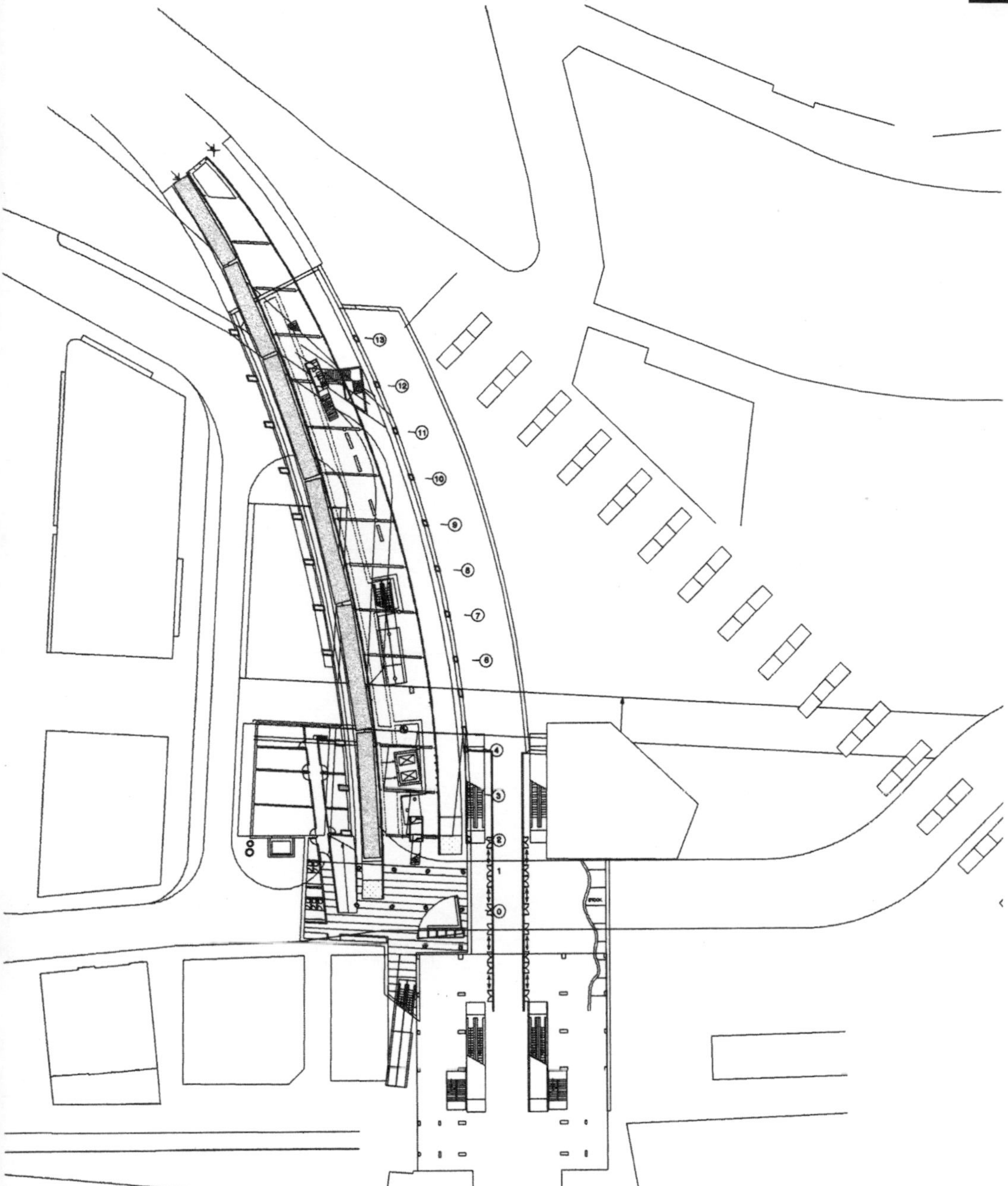

-6m Underground station (first phase) Architecture as infrastructure

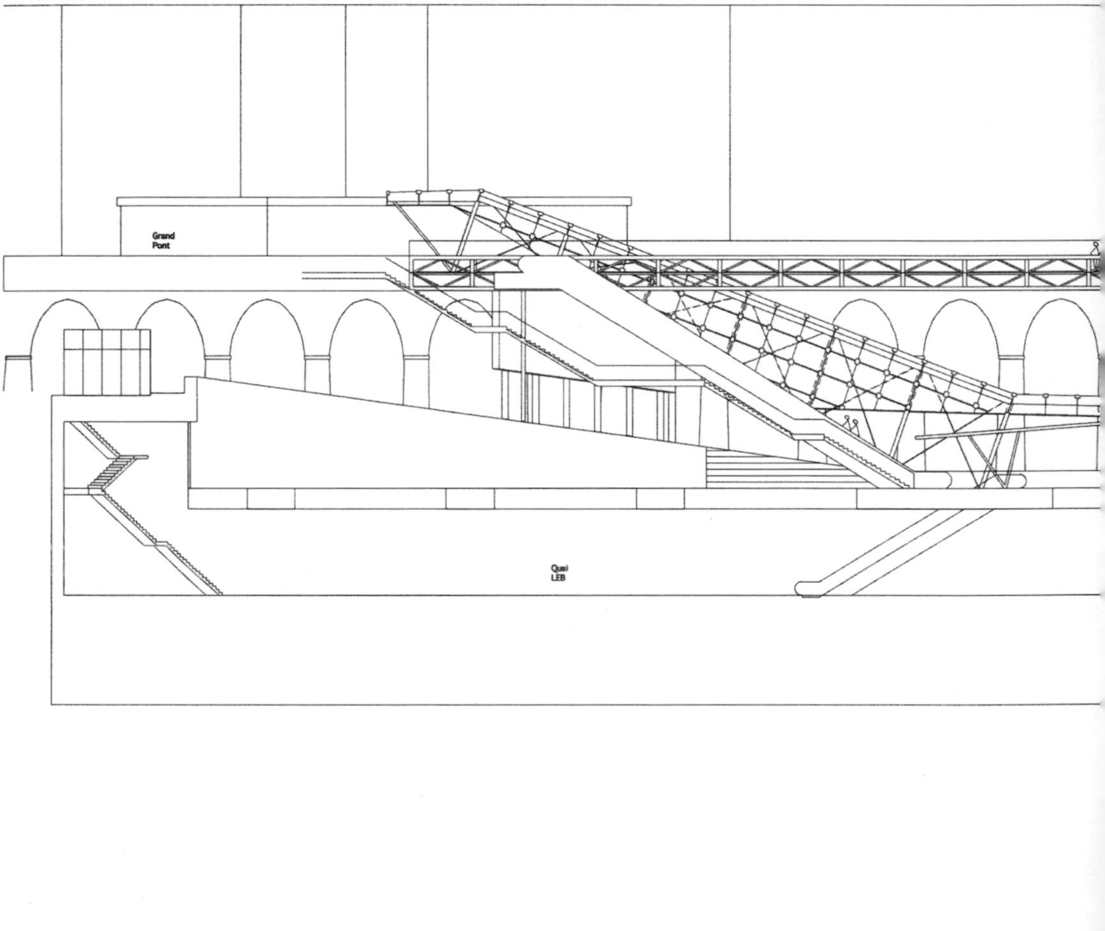

Releasing potentialities hidden in a site

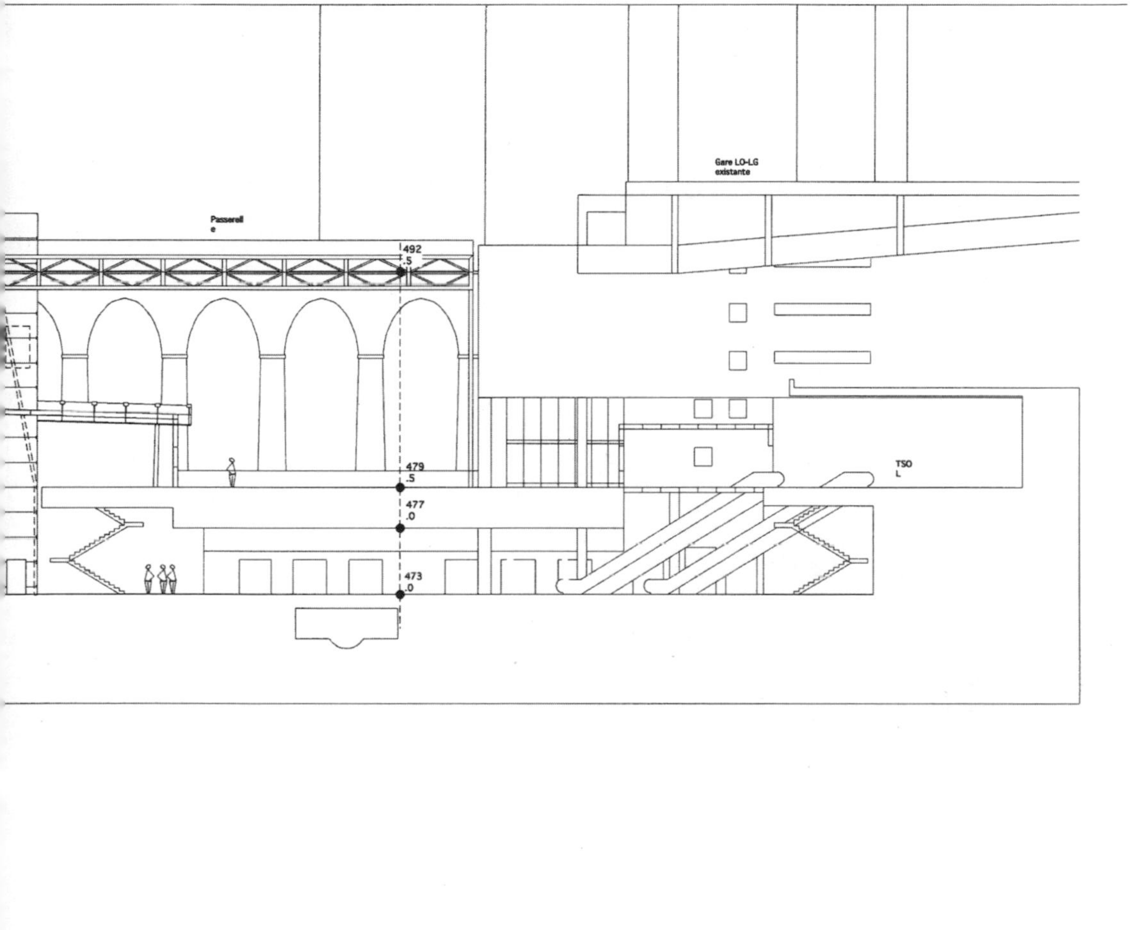

A three-dimensional city: mini-metropolis

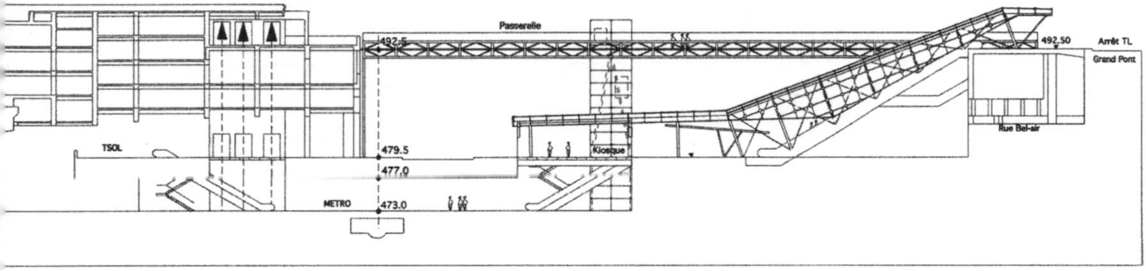

Section: from below the valley to the lower grounds, from the lower grounds to the upper levels of the valley

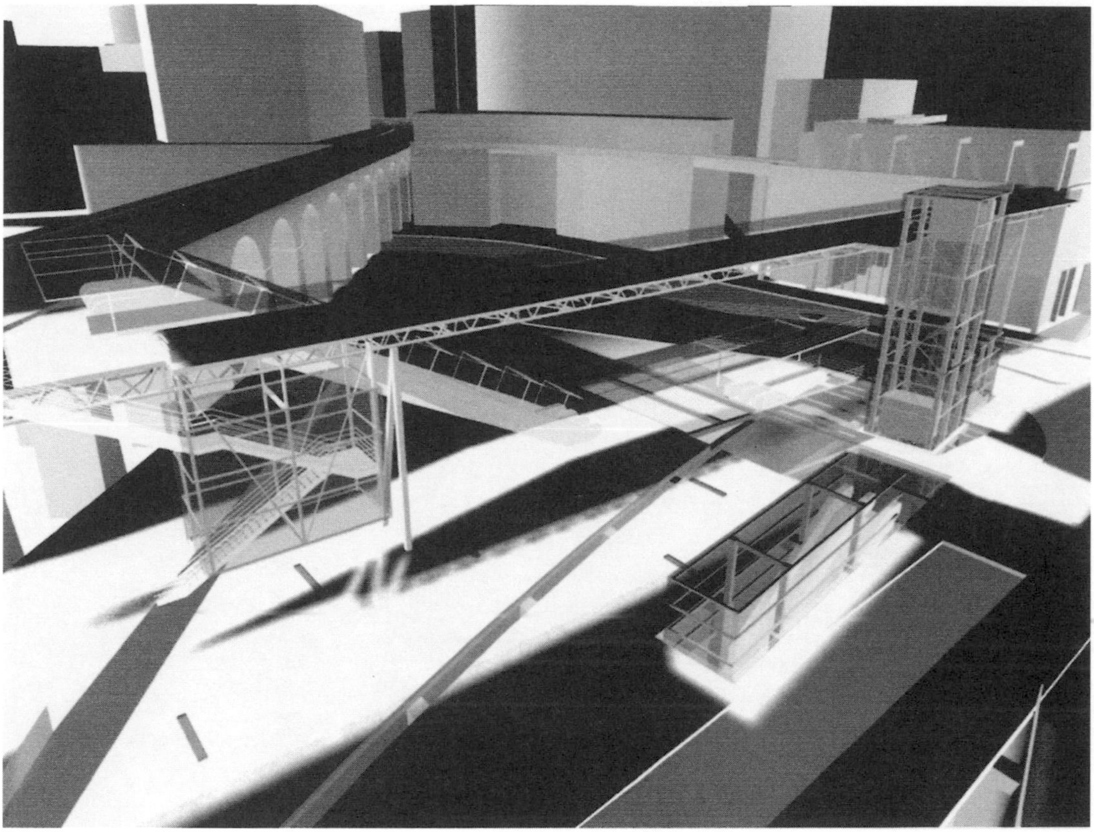

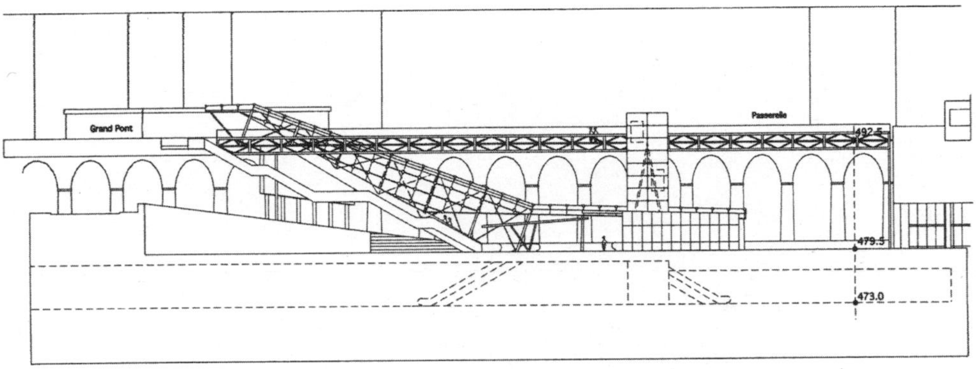

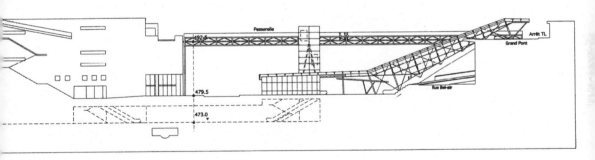

Elevation Road in x, bridge in y, elevator in z, escalator in the oblique
Next page: glass technology—materializing the movement concept
Glass is color-printed (a dot pattern with variable translucency)

290.5
266
66.5
66.5
66.5
66.5
498.08
492.83
479.97
479.95
479.00
478.00
473.00
55
175.2
2453
2508
1
5330
2
5330
3
5330

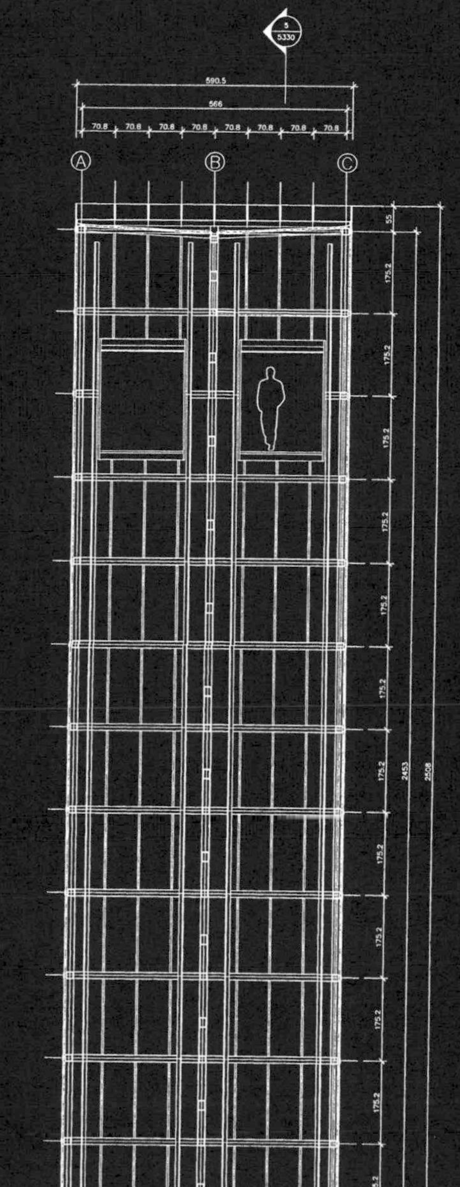
5
5330
590.5
566
70.8
A
B
C
55
175.2
2453
2508

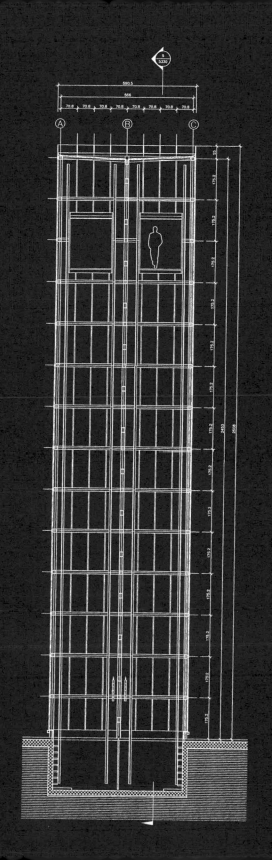

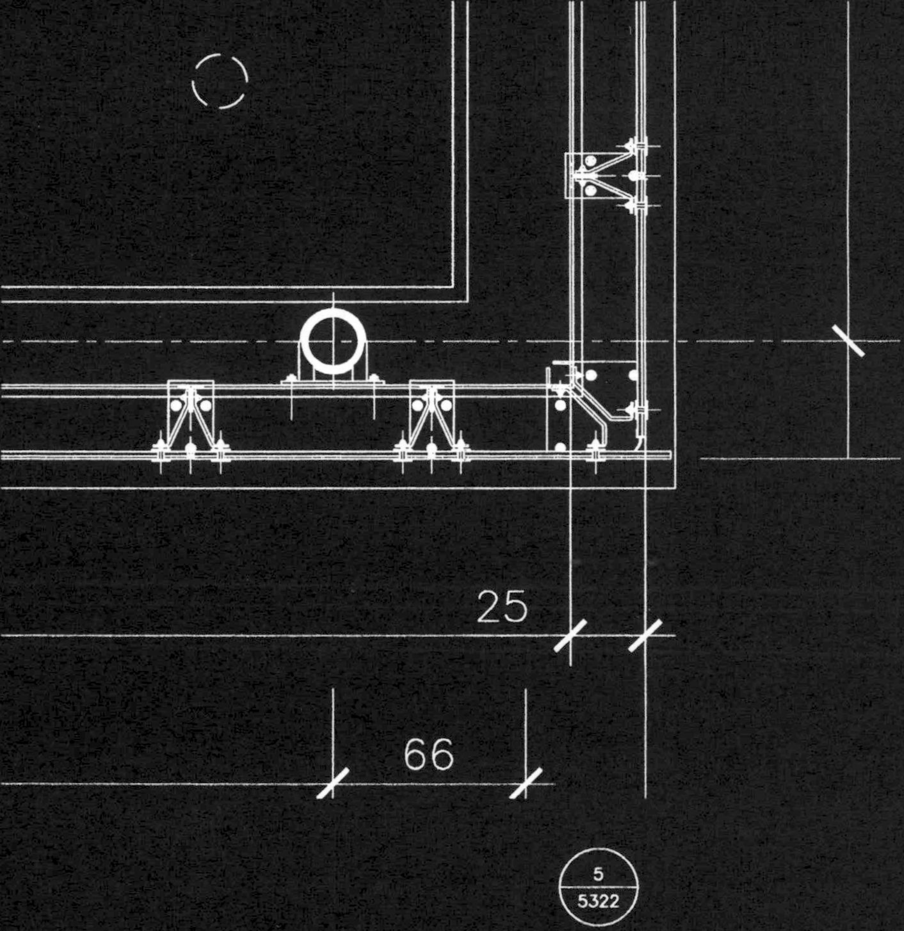
25
66
5
5322

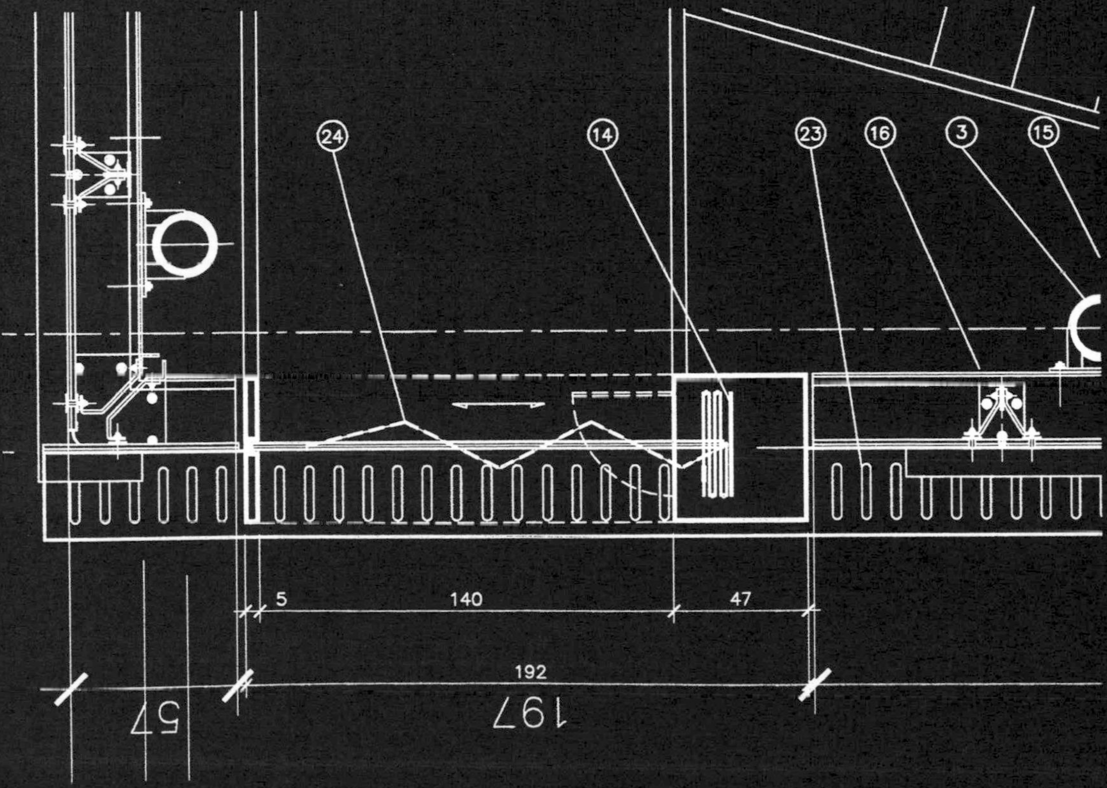
24
14
23
16
3
15
5
140
47
192
57
197

New York, Lerner Hall Student Center
Columbia University, 1994-99

Deviating from the Normative

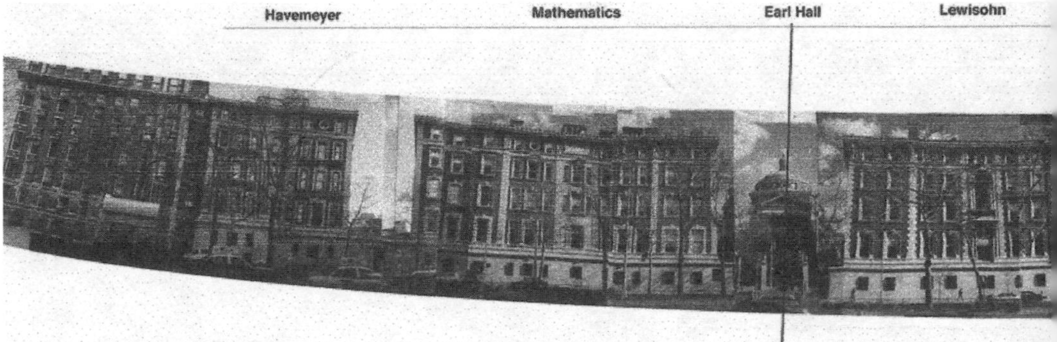
Havemeyer
Mathematics
Earl Hall
Lewisohn
117th St.

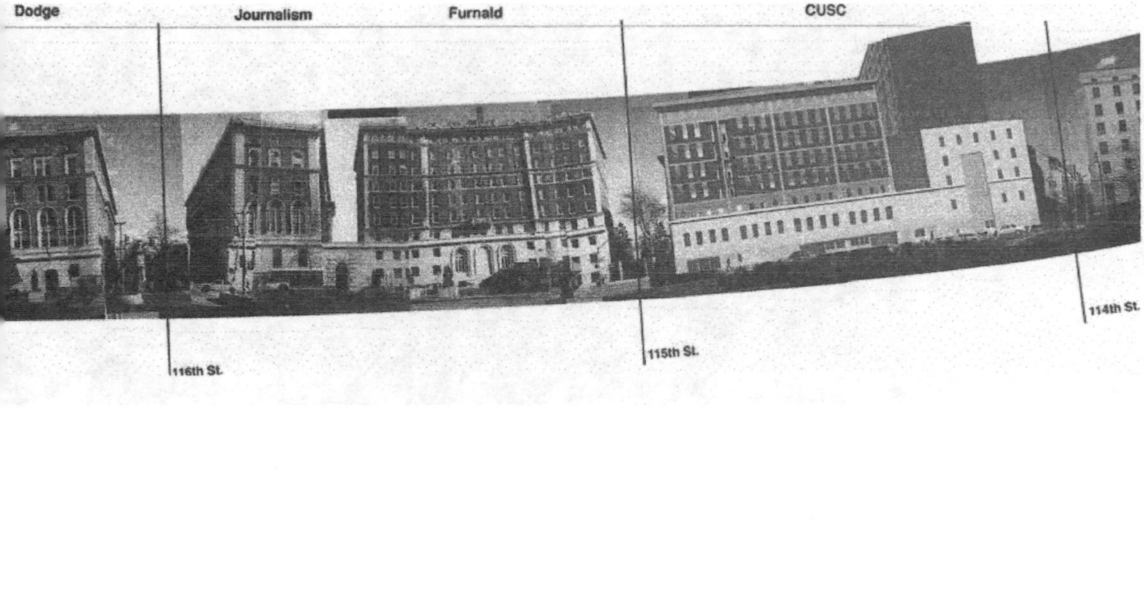
Dodge
Journalism
Furnald
CUSC
116th St.
115th St.
114th St.

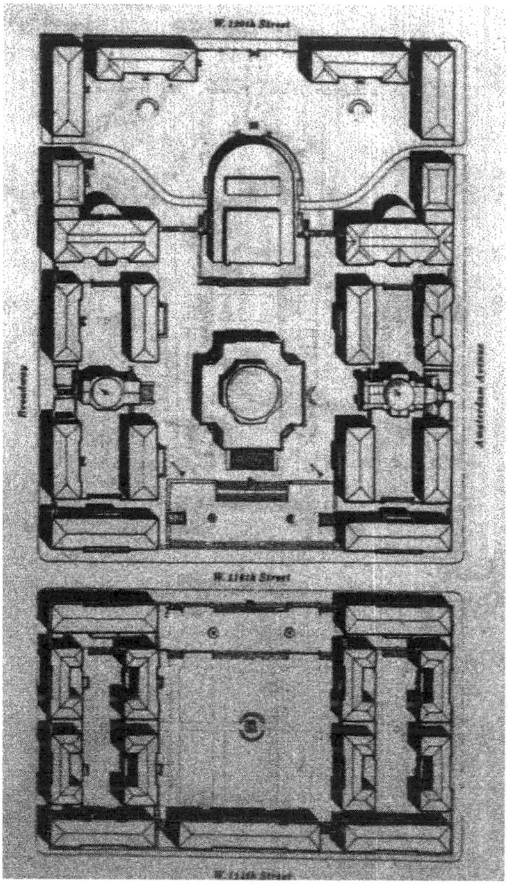
W. 120th Street
W. 116th Street
W. 114th Street

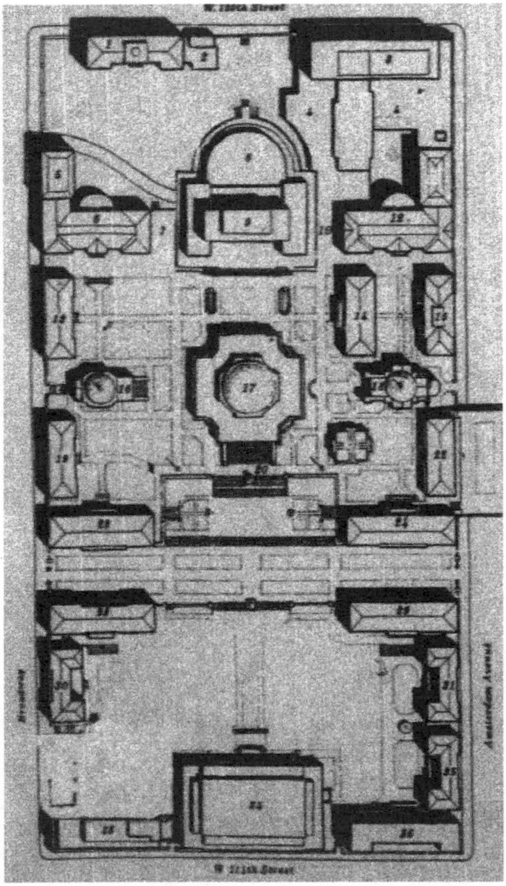

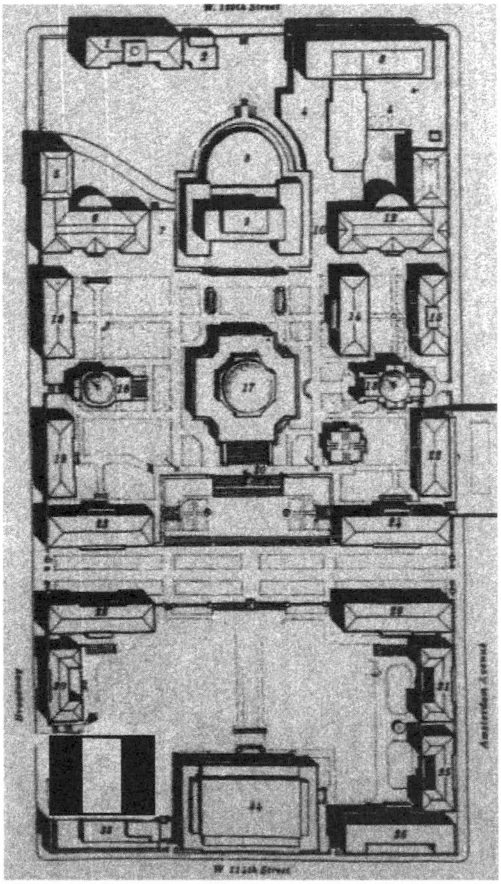

Realizing potentialities: the campus level is half a story higher than the Broadway level. Staggered floor levels allow for ramp connectors between east and west

MILLER THEATRE

The program for the 225,000 square foot new student center at Columbia University[1] in New York includes an 1100-to-1500 seat combined auditorium and assembly hall, dining facilities, lounges, meeting rooms, a bookstore, a radio station, student clubs and game rooms, administrative spaces, a black box theater, six thousand mailboxes, as well as expanded computer facilities for student use.

What did we try to achieve through a student center on the old Ferris Booth Hall site?

As it is located with one side on Broadway and the other towards McKim, Mead, and White's plan, and because it could be considered as a possible model for new buildings in the historical campus, we first looked at the student center project in terms of a general strategy.

> a) In terms of its exterior, our urban hypothesis was to return, to respect, even to reinforce the master plan of McKim, Mead, and White, i.e. the spatial and volumetric logic of the original scheme. Some of its original building materials (granite, brick, copper-like finish, glass) would also be used.
>
> b) Simultaneously, within this existing normative framework and its historical constraints, we tried to provide an innovative programmatic space that late 20th-century society can identify with—a student "city" in the "city" of Columbia in the city of New York.

This double strategy could be summarized as "a) a quiet building on the outside, b) a stimulating building on the inside."

A) The Outside (The Normative) The original master plan shows the doubling-up of the buildings parallel to Broadway and Amsterdam Avenues. Only one of these "double" buildings, Avery Hall, was ever built. The potential for this internal densification of the historical campus is as valid today as it was during the early years.

For the new student center, we suggested a strategy that works within the regulating volumetric lines of the original 1890 plan. We placed required functional rooms within the double rectangular volumes, namely, a Broadway wing and a Campus wing, while large public spaces, such as the main lobby, auditorium and black box theater, were placed between these two rectangular volumes. The two wings used the materials prevalent in the historical campus, but the space between them was intended to be as transparent as current technology allows.

The eight-story Broadway wing includes the cinema/assembly hall, the bookstore, game spaces, student administration, student clubs, WKCR, and three extra floors for potential academic or general administrative spaces. The cinema/assembly hall, seating 400, is located so that, by folding its screen, it can act as a balcony to the auditorium, bringing the auditorium capacity to 1500. In terms of its visual presence, the Broadway block extends the theme of the Columbia street front—a patterned brick facade over a granite base.

The four-story Campus wing includes the main entrance, a 24-hour area, dining, night spot (The Plex), and meeting rooms.

1 with Gruzen Samton Architects

B) The In-Between (The Exception or Deviation) If a normative "context" was our strategy for the outside, invention was our objective for the inside. The student center is a small city of sorts. It is made of public and semi-public activities that must help to define a public space.

While the old student center provided neither a breathing space nor an overview of its different uses, the new center should act as a forum, a dynamic place of exchange. Its multiple activities, from its 1500-seat combined auditorium and cinema to its meeting rooms, dining halls, game rooms, student clubs, and bookstore, are to be perceived from the series of oblique lounges that link the multiplicity of disparate functions into a new University "event." By analogy, the student center could be described as a dynamic hub that acts as a major social space.

The Hub

The Hub is the main circulatory system of the building. It concentrates lobbies and student lounges, information stands, ramps for 6000 student mailboxes, exhibitions, or student propaganda, as well as the overspill of other activities—bar, games, and so forth. Acting as the building's core, the Hub is made possible by the unusual condition of much of the Columbia campus at this location, where the campus side is half a story higher than the neighborhood, or Broadway, side. Instead of separating the building's activities into stacked full floors, we connected them into staggered half-floors. As opposed to the conventional atrium space surrounded by floors that are stacked every 12 feet and separated from one another, the floors on the campus and Broadway sides are located every 6 feet and linked by simple ramps. Hence, the building hallways can act as a continuous link connecting what would normally be discontinuous, even contradictory, activities. It is simultaneously a void (the void of McKim) and a route. During the day, light filters through the suspended glass ramps. At night, as light glows from the inside, figures in movement along this route will appear as if in a silent shadow theater.

Along the Hub, we have also located the auditorium on the Broadway level while providing easy ramp access from the Campus level. The flat-floor auditorium can alternatively be used for campus activities or turned into a special theater with direct access from Broadway, with a 1500-person capacity, that can be rented separately for a variety of purposes. Above the structure of the auditorium there is also a black box theater.

Engineered using today's cutting edge technology, the Hub glass wall and its supporting ramps provide a transparent counterpoint to the solid Campus and Broadway wings. The clearly-visible steel structure and glass surfaces contrast with the masonry-clad wings on either side; the structure spans between these two blocks, and the glass encloses the Hub void between them. The glass in the wall is used structurally, without glazing bars, and the walking surfaces on the ramps are also in glass. The articulation of the trusses and steel ramp structures directs movement in the Hub, activating the space.

Polemic

This project is about a building that was alternatively praised and attacked for the wrong reasons. For example, "conservatives" derided its large expanse of glass as heresy within the historical context, while some "progressives" said its use of "mimetic" granite, bricks, and cornice was a disgrace to the ideas of progress, newness, and creativity.

Yet this was exactly our intention from the onset: to show that you can design a building that is simultaneously normative and exceptional, generic and specific; that the whole point of the building is that it does not need to be of one style, one esthetic, one sensibility. We made this building simultaneously the norm and the exception. Columbia University had requested that we follow the Flemish bond brick pattern of the historical McKim, Mead and White buildings. We did not object to McKim's law, any more than you object to driving on the left while in England. In many ways, we considered McKim as an *object trouvé,* a Duchamp-like found object to interact with. Of course, what interested us most were the interstices in the law, the gap between the two McKim solids indicated in the master plan.

Our point was that neither the normative nor the exceptional were to be about "form." We avoided "designing" this building in the compositional sense, i.e. vertically or horizontally, fragmented or continuous, projecting or receding, sculptured or minimalist, abstract shapes or figurative ones.

Of course, you cannot not use forms as you build: everything eventually has a material form. But we see architecture as the materialization of a concept, not as the materialization of form. The materialization of the concept leads to a carefully developed technology, rather than to an imagistic assembly of shapes. Hence, the two solids follow the normative images of McKim, while the ramps use the tensile capabilities of contemporary glass and steel.

Contamination

The building is often an understatement; we tried avoiding an overstated dialectic of the normative vs. the new. Rather than a simple opposition of terms, we might talk about material contamination or hybridization.

On the campus side, the upper part of Lerner Hall (its mechanical silvery-grey sidings) acts as a neutral articulation between the new building and its background, the 1958 Carman dormitory. This upper "horizon" has another purpose, this time in relation to the building below: it purposely blurs the tripartite classical organization of the solid / void / solid principle originating from the McKim masterplan.

Also on the campus side, the passage from bricks to the glass plane can be described analogically through a filmic device: the fade-in / fade-out, the frame that results from the superposition of the last frame of the preceding sequence with the first frame of the subsequent one is a combined image—in this case, the glass blocks. Glass blocks result from the superposition of the respective images of red bricks and glass.

There are other fade-in / fade-outs, or contaminations of an image into another, throughout the building. On the Broadway facade, the place where granite meets brick is articulated, once again, through glass block: here the McKim granite bullnose is turned into a similarly-shaped assembly of glass blocks, a prefabricated feat, and acts as a transition material between granite and brick.

The last fade-in / fade-out occurs at the campus inner corner, where the bricks of the middle part of the McKim composition take over the corner edge, which normally should have been stone, according to McKim. This edge becomes a red brick column as it helps turn a highly visible corner from campus.

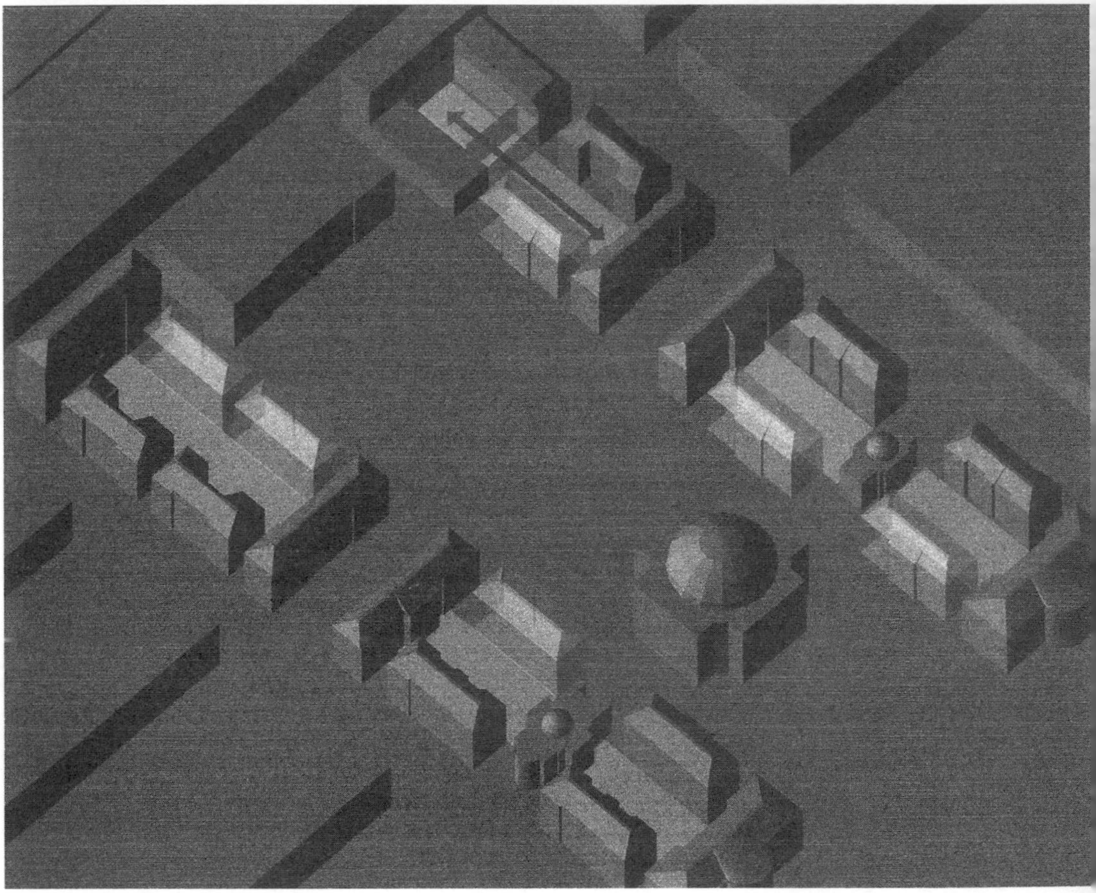

A latent condition: the fact that campus is higher than Broadway means a potential ramp system

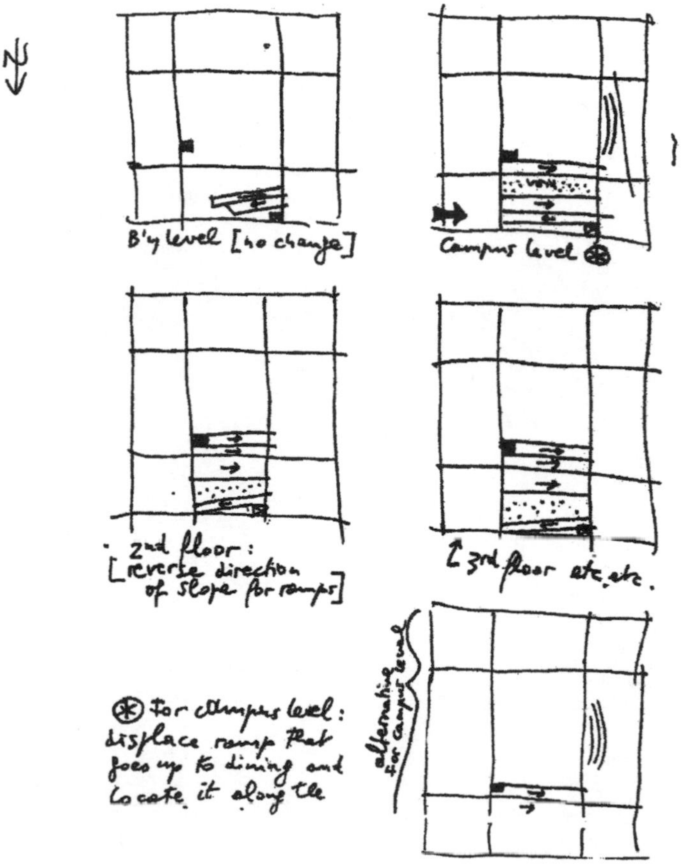

Static envelope, dynamic route: the simple circulation space of the ramps allows for a multiplicity of heterogeneous functions developing around it

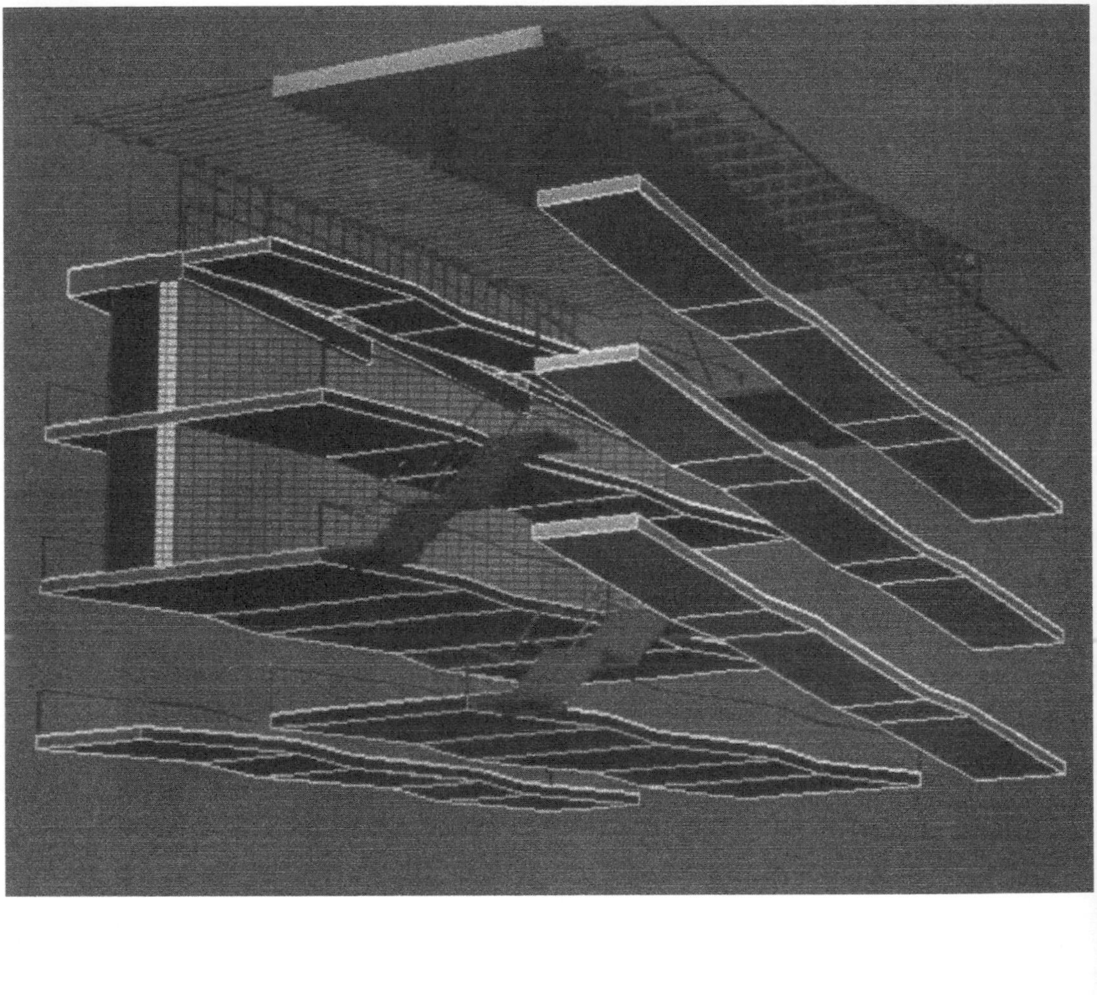

Not about forms but about forces

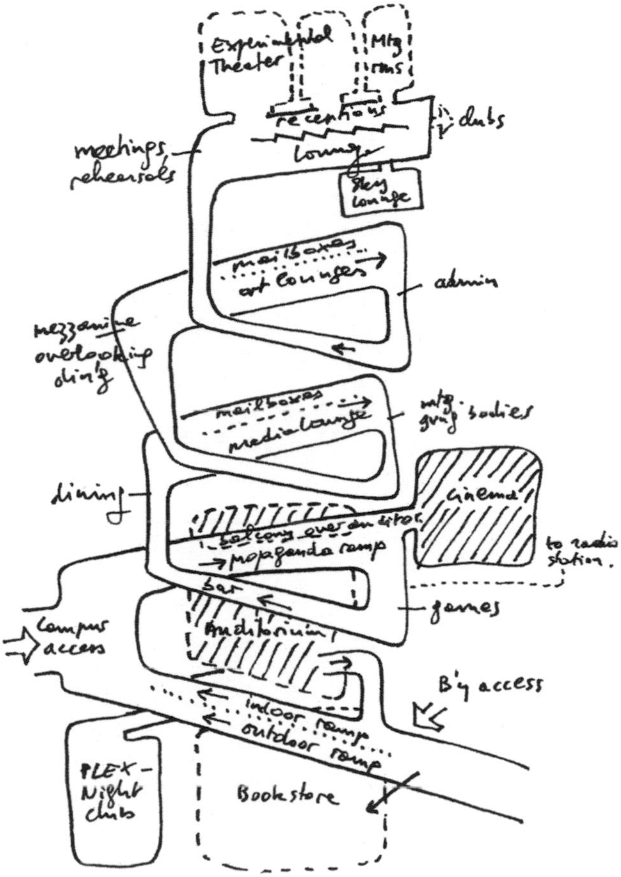

The Hub: a place of interaction

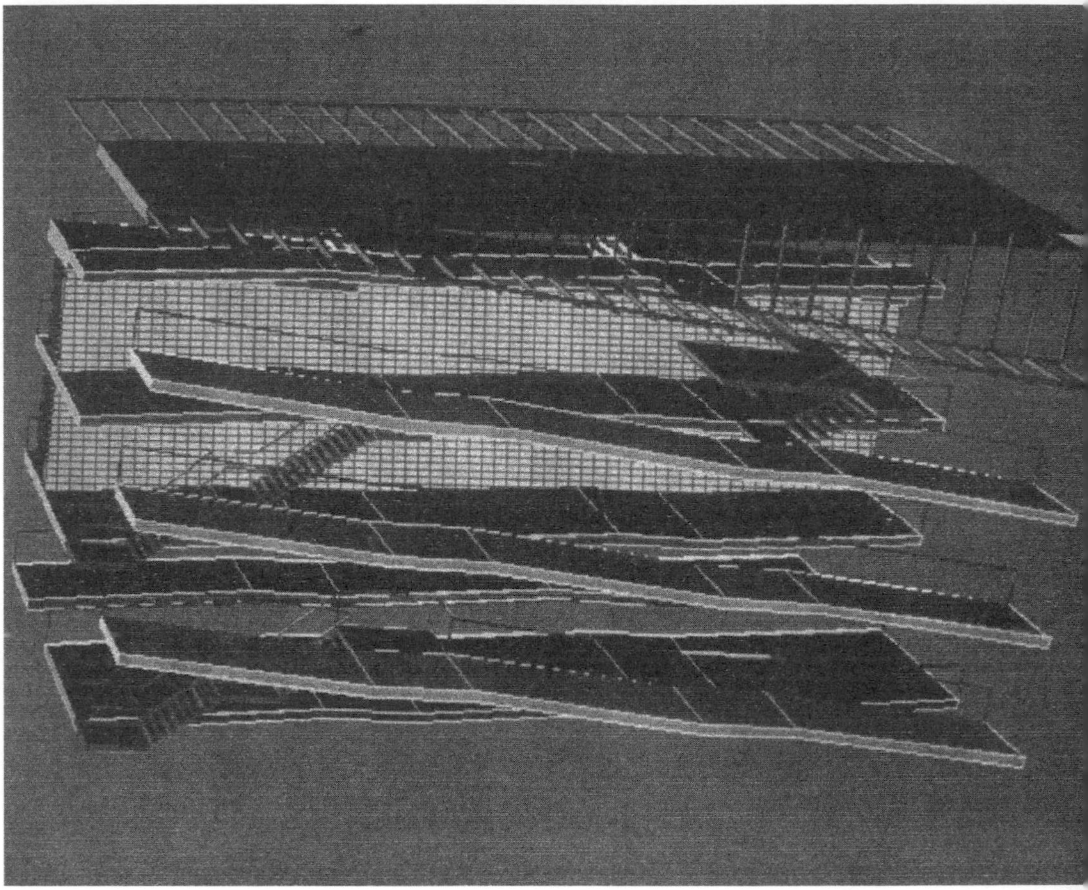

An “in-between” space activated by movement vectors

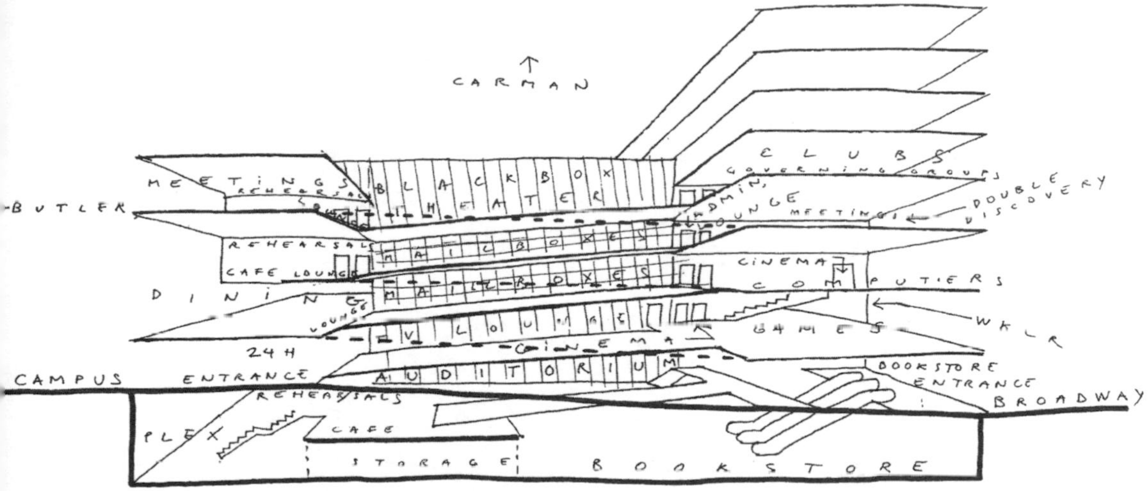

"Charging" the system: all activities face one new, unprogrammed space, the glass court or Hub

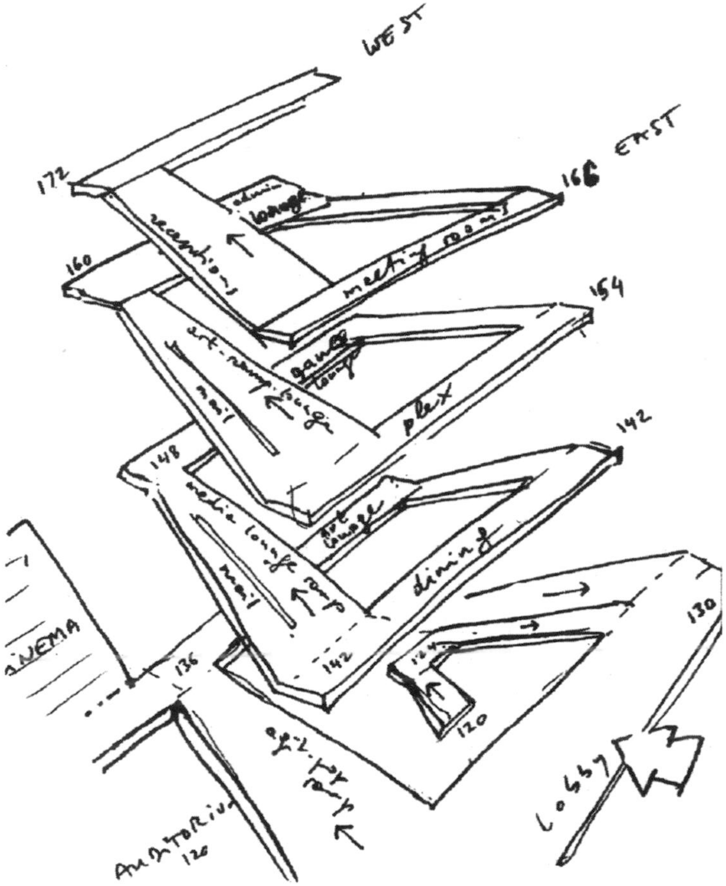

A logic of flows and vectors

It is not what a building looks like that counts, but what it does

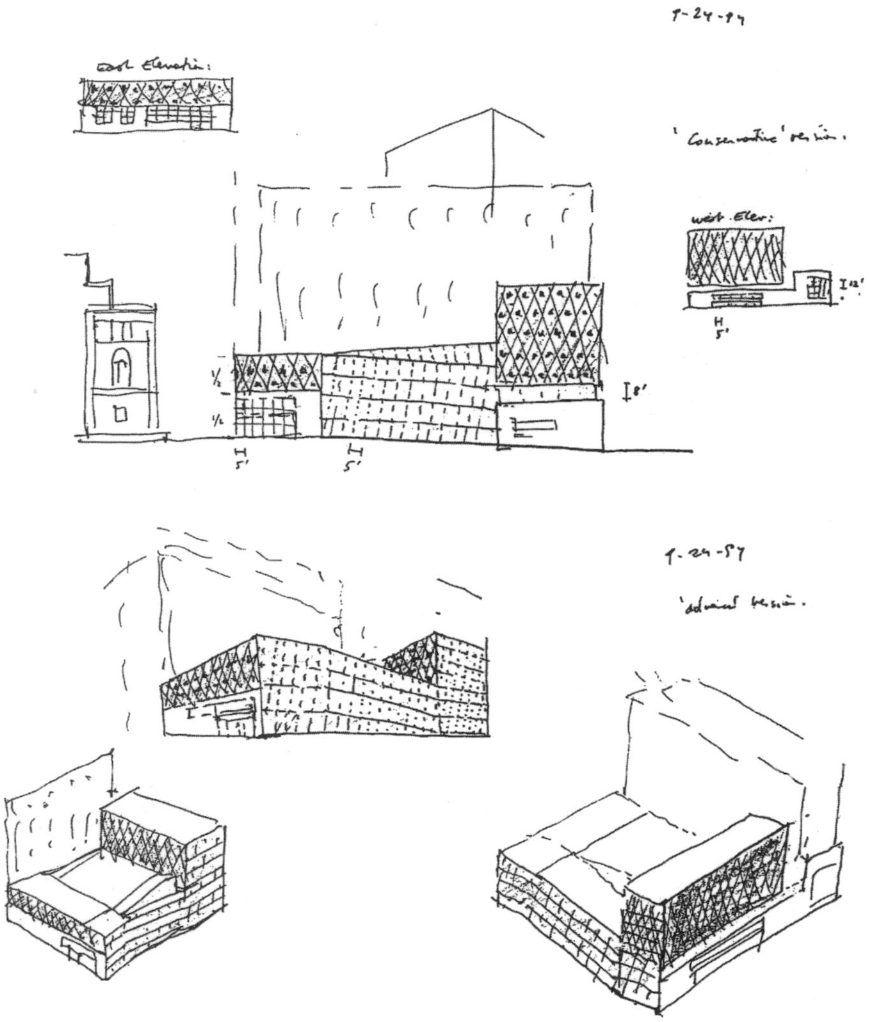

Quiet on the outside, active on the inside: early sketches

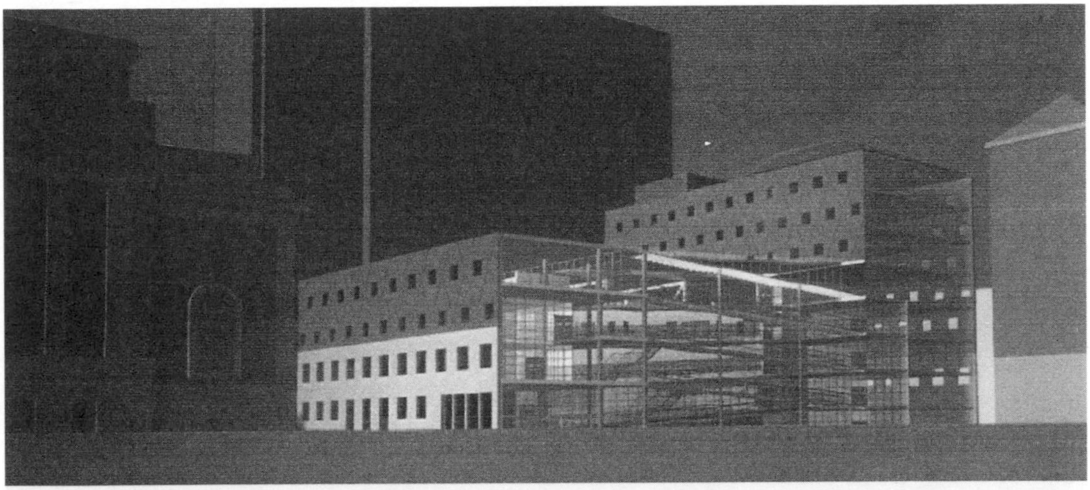

Deviation vs. the normative: the new glass technology of the ramps vs. the 19th-century neoclassicism of the wings

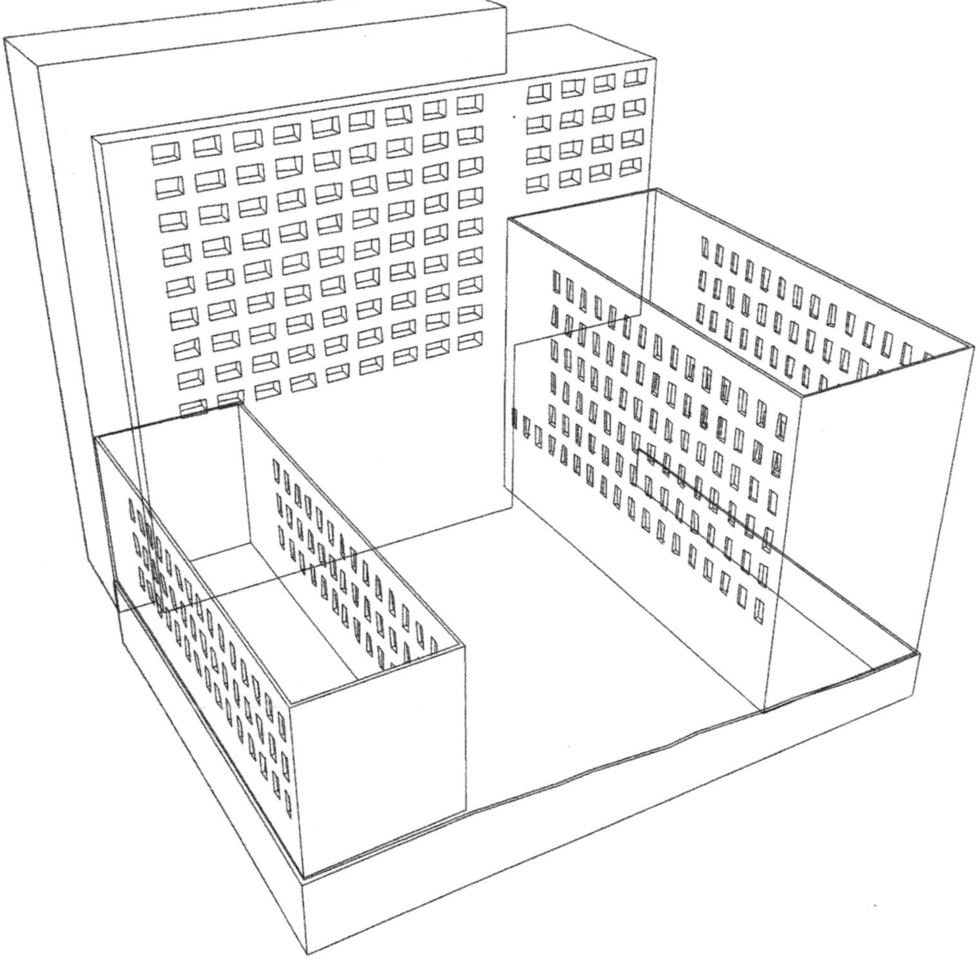

A relatively distant attitude to "context:" McKim, Mead and White as a ready-made

A given envelope with a given image

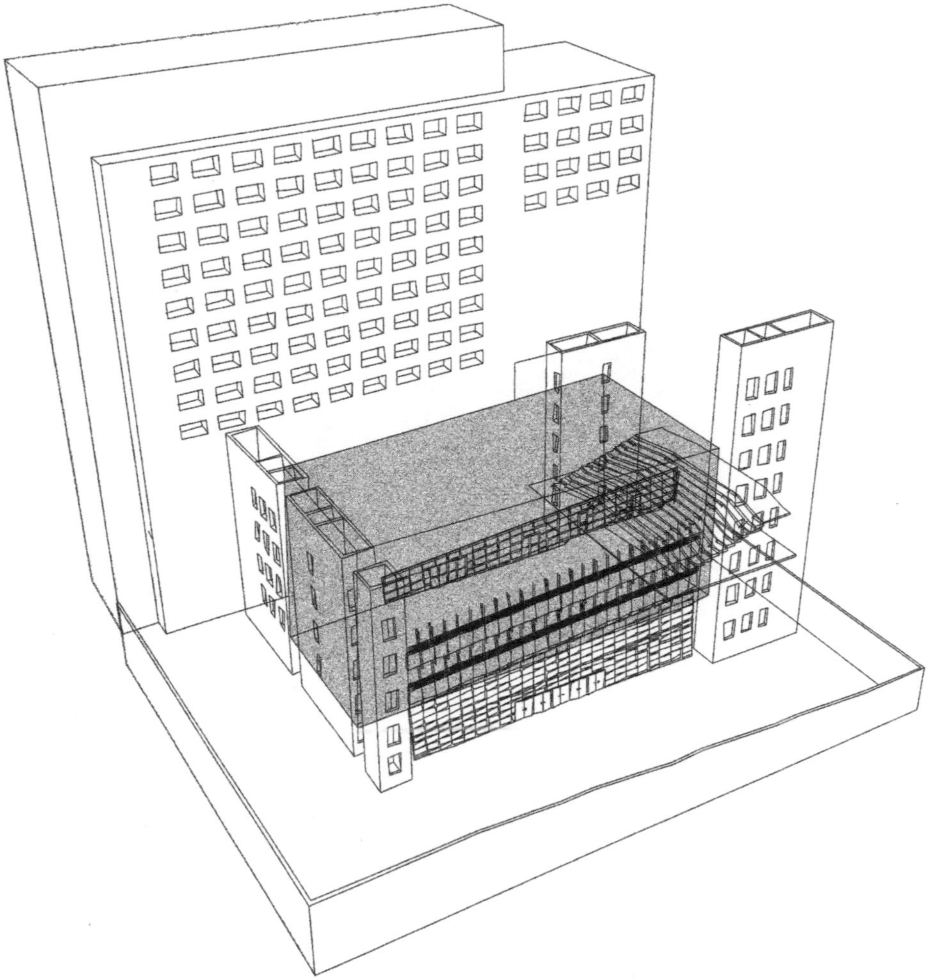

Repetition: bricks, granite, copper-like material for the wings
Difference: structural glass and stainless steel for the ramps

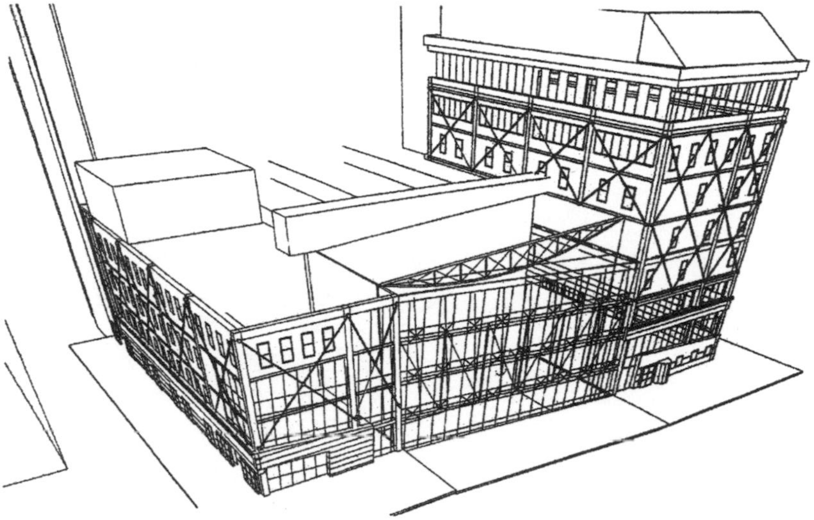

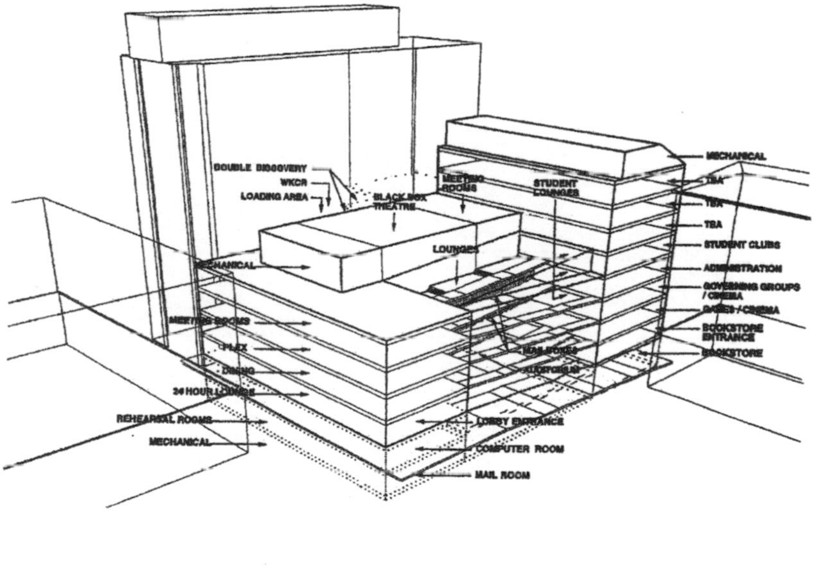

Programmatic heterogeneity: flat-floor auditorium, cinema, experimental theater, meeting rooms, dining hall, café, lounges, computer labs, pool room, radio station, 6000 mailboxes, a night club

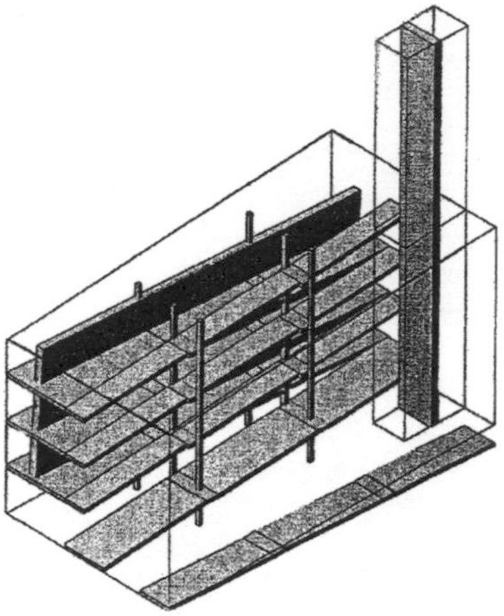

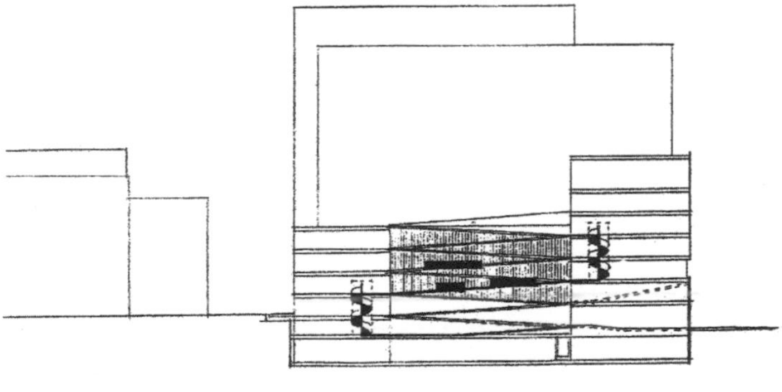

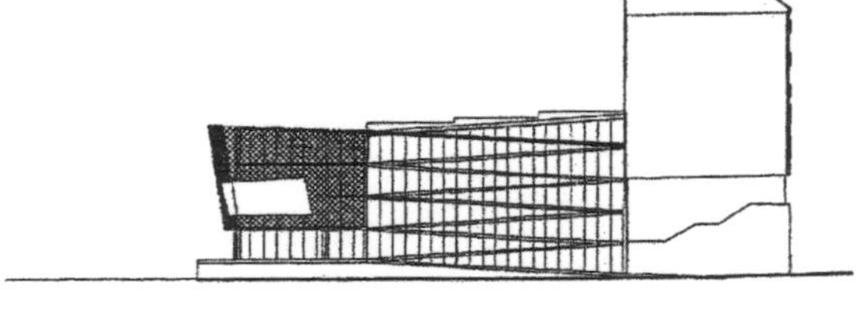

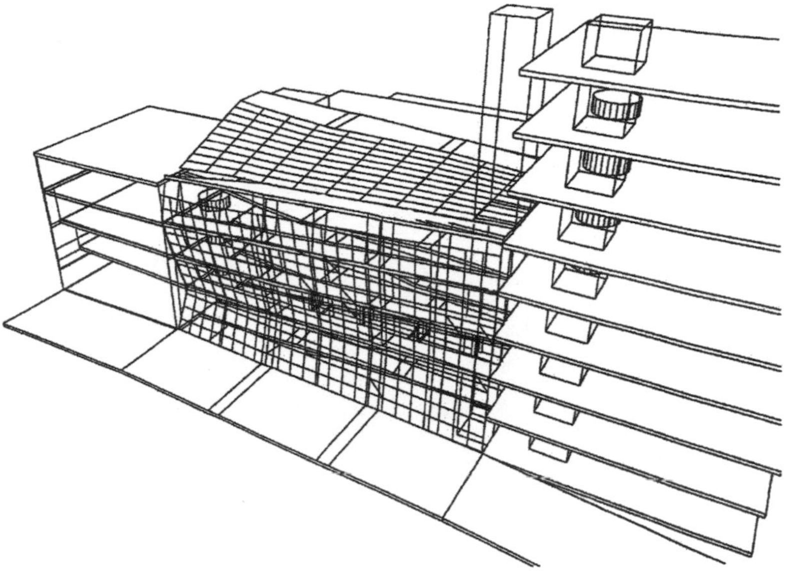

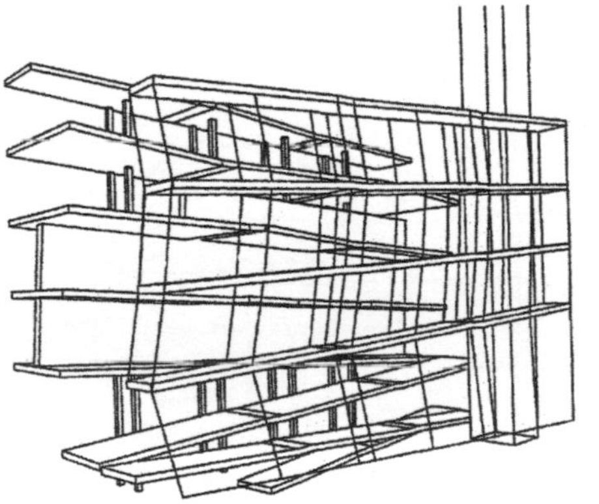

The ramps: a catalyst for contamination of activities

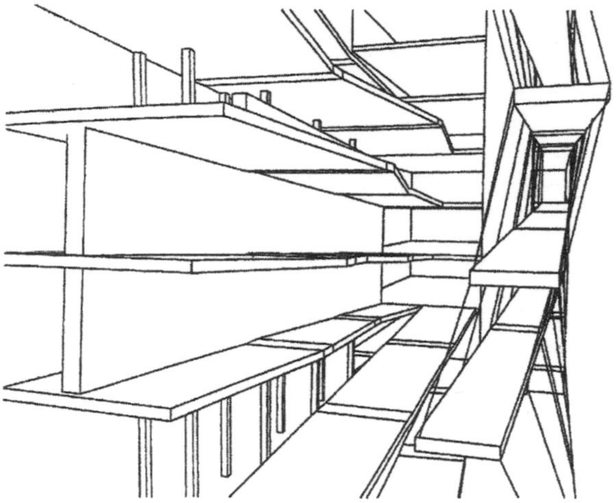

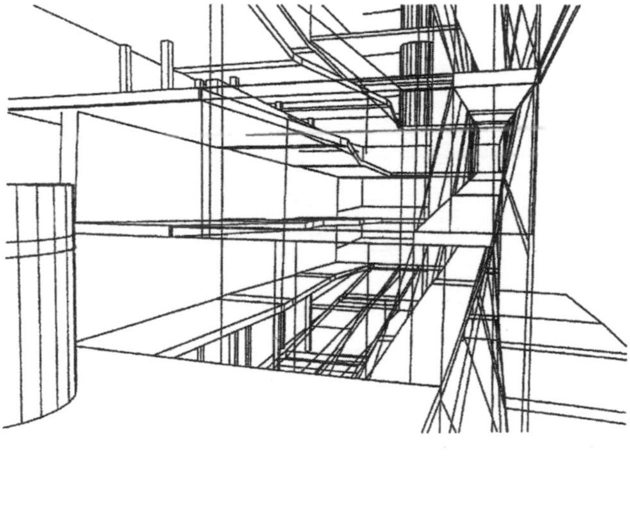

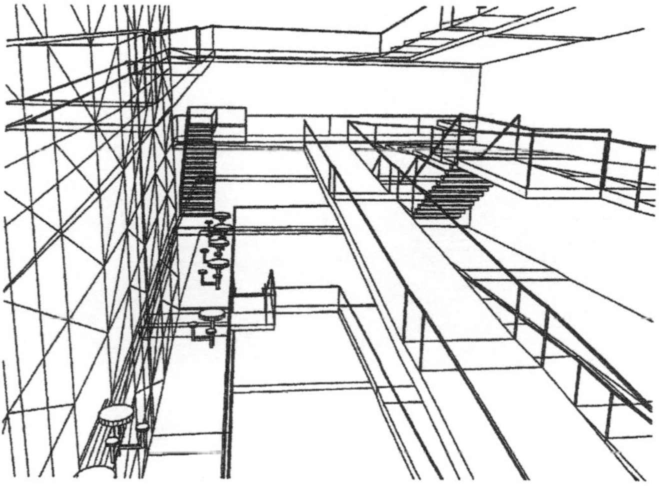

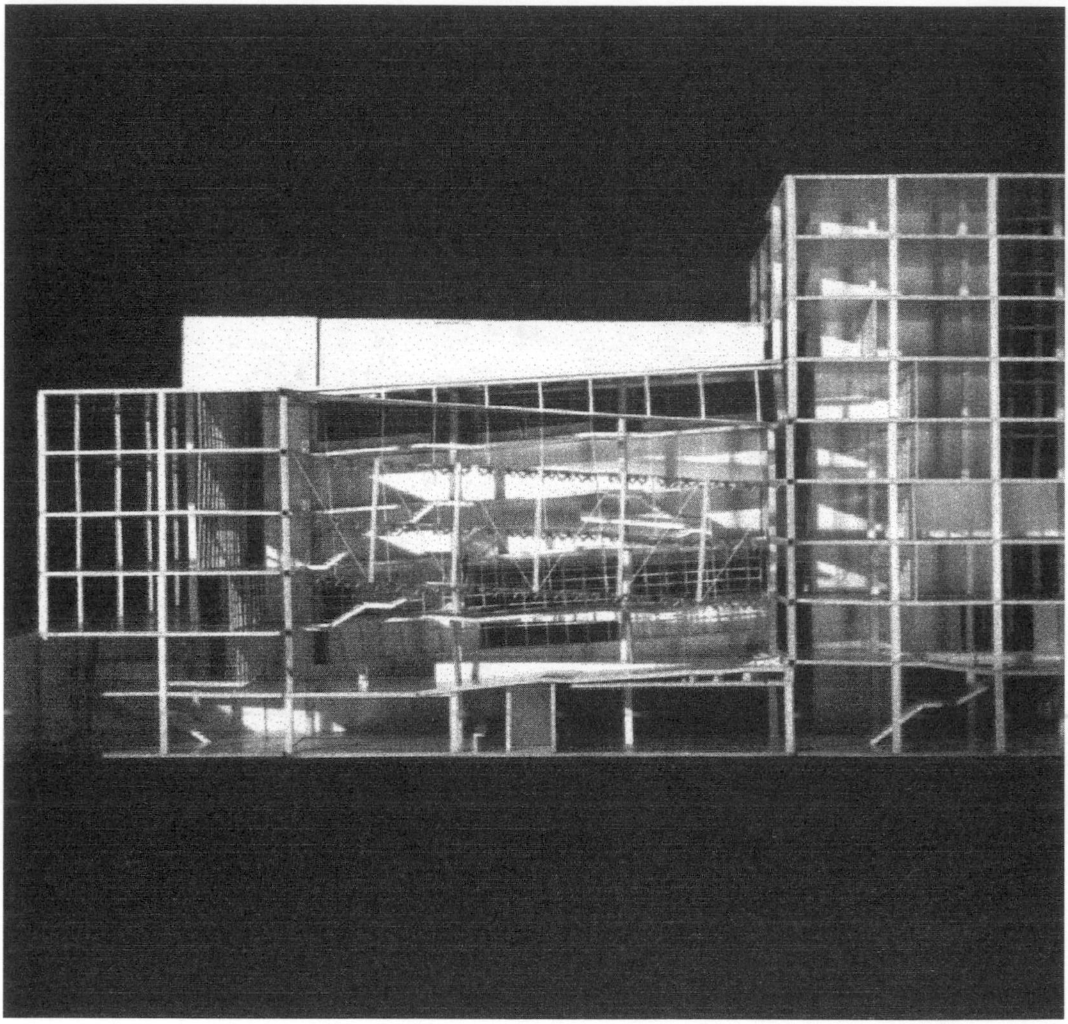

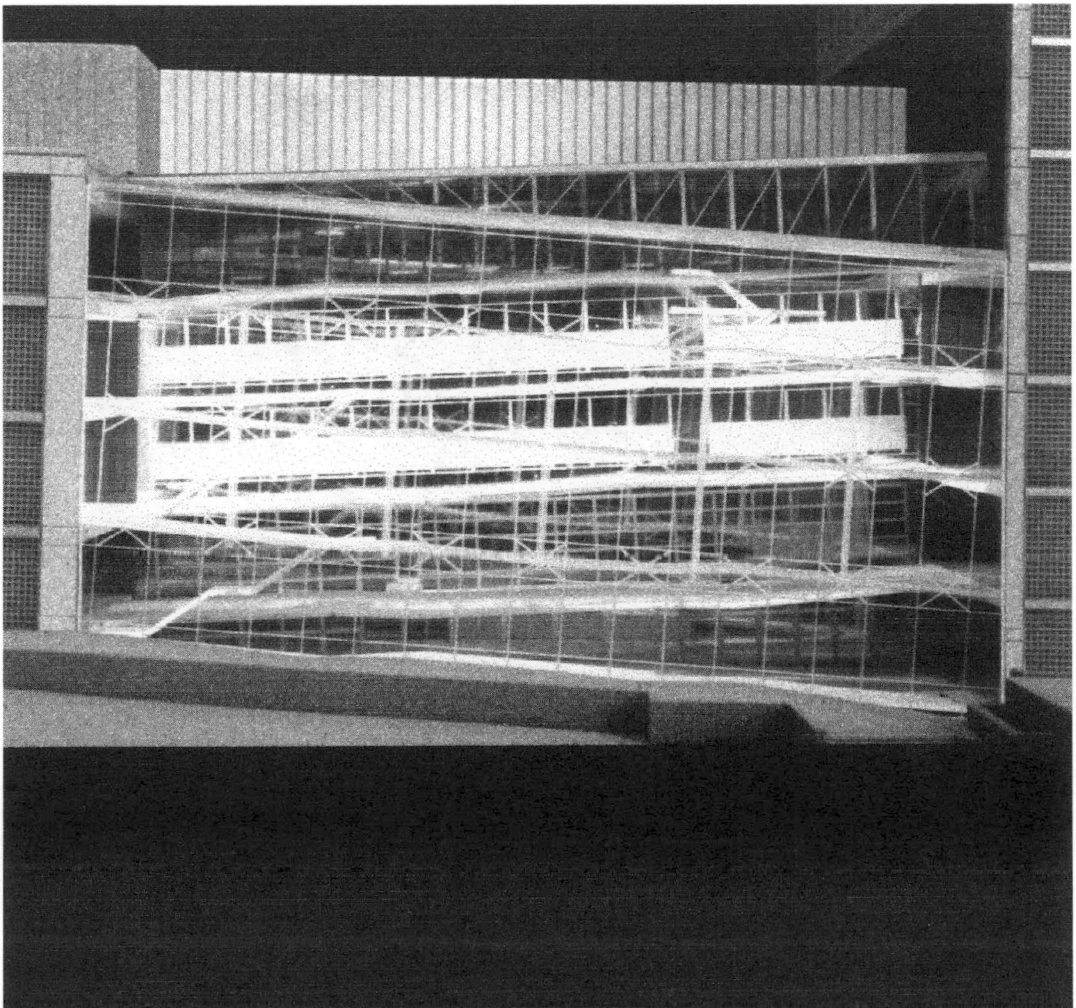

Ramps as infrastructure

Hybrid: something heterogeneous in origin and composition, a composite

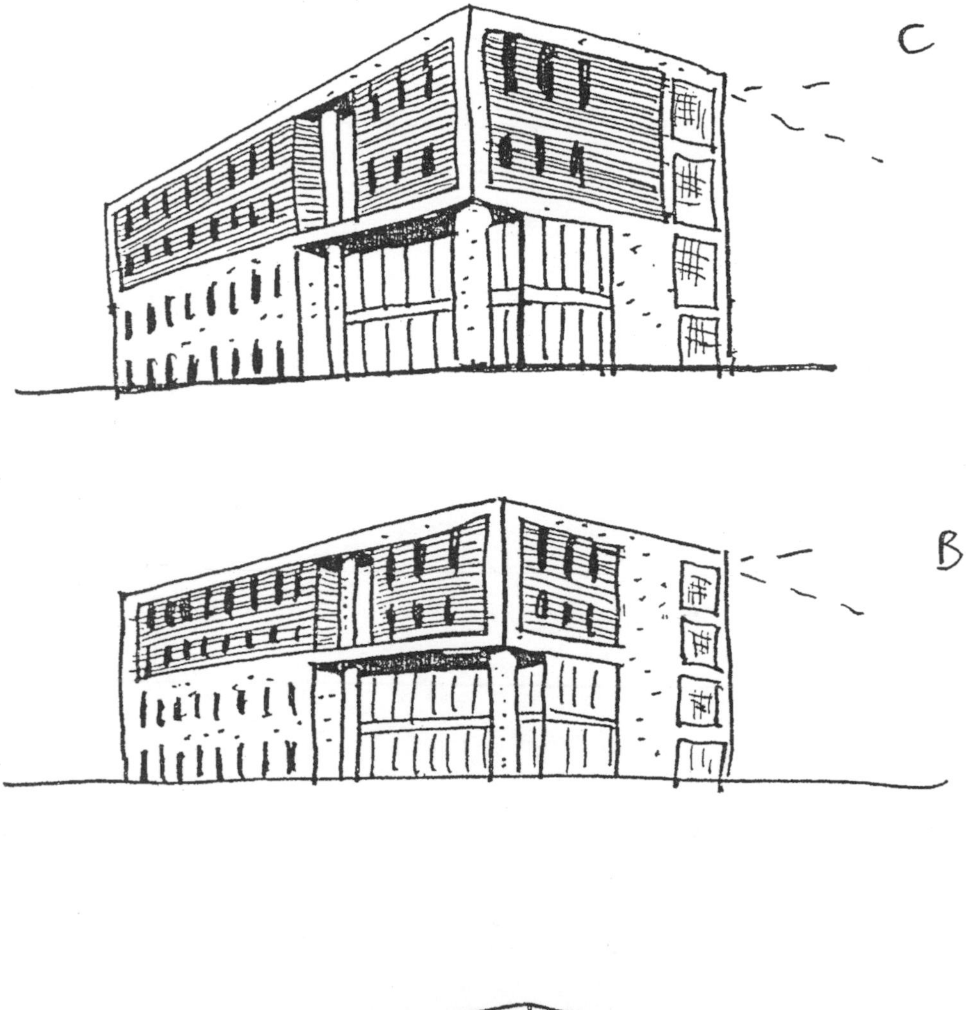

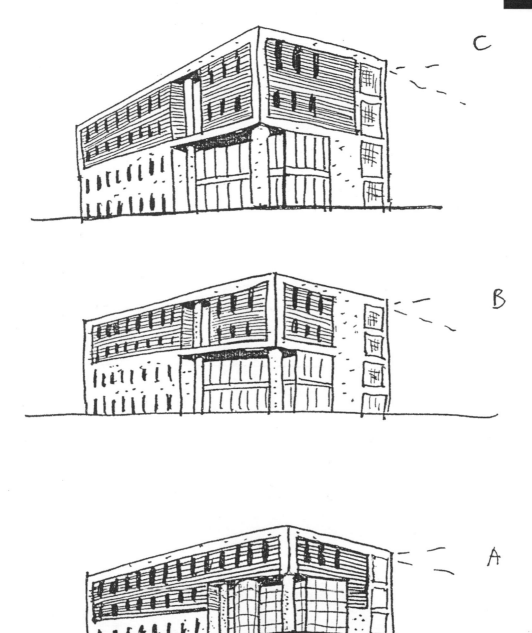

Northeast corner: interchangeability of facades (early sketches)

Identifying potentialities in a program
Program: a determinate set of expected actions
Event: an indeterminate set of unexpected outcomes

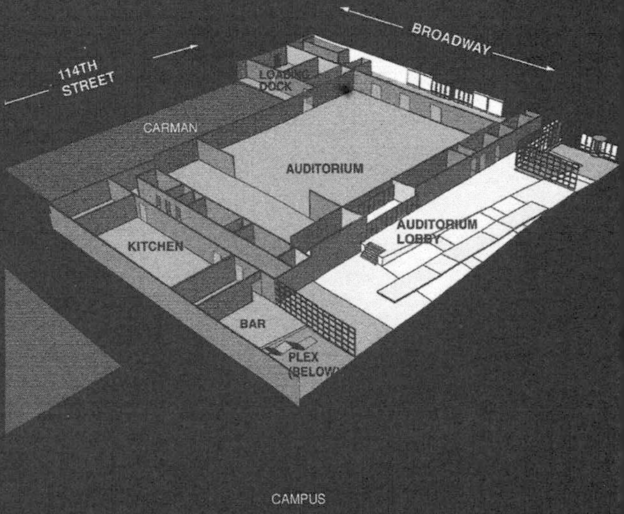
BROADWAY
114TH
STREET
LOADING
DOCK
CARMAN
AUDITORIUM
AUDITORIUM
LOBBY
KITCHEN
BAR
PLEX
(BELOW)
CAMPUS

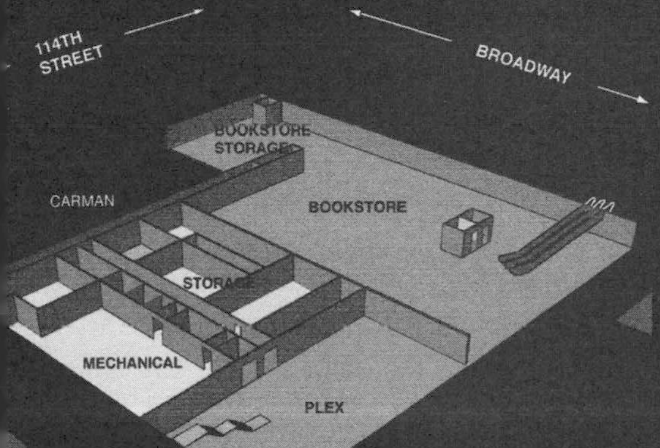
114TH
STREET
BROADWAY
BOOKSTORE
STORAGE
CARMAN
BOOKSTORE
STORAGE
MECHANICAL
PLEX

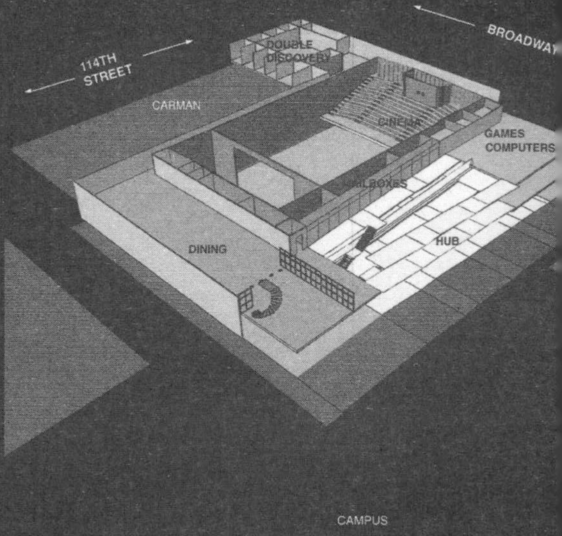

114TH
STREET
BROADWAY
DOUBLE
DISCOVERY
CARMAN
GAMES
COMPUTERS
DINING
HUB
CAMPUS

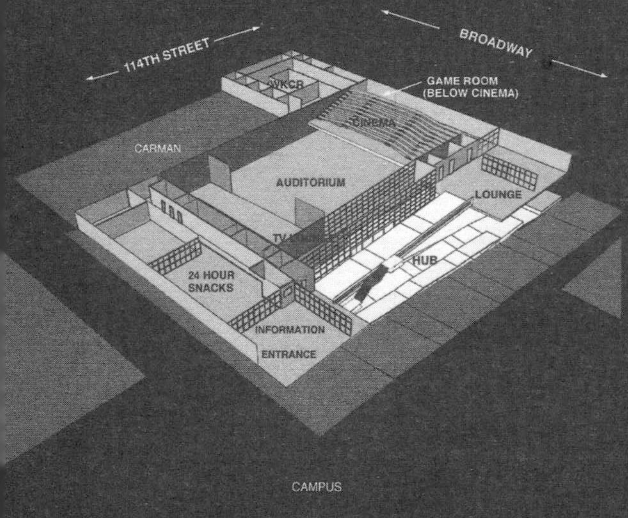

114TH STREET
BROADWAY
WKCR
GAME ROOM
(BELOW CINEMA)
CINEMA
CARMAN
AUDITORIUM
LOUNGE
HUB
24 HOUR
SNACKS
INFORMATION
ENTRANCE
CAMPUS

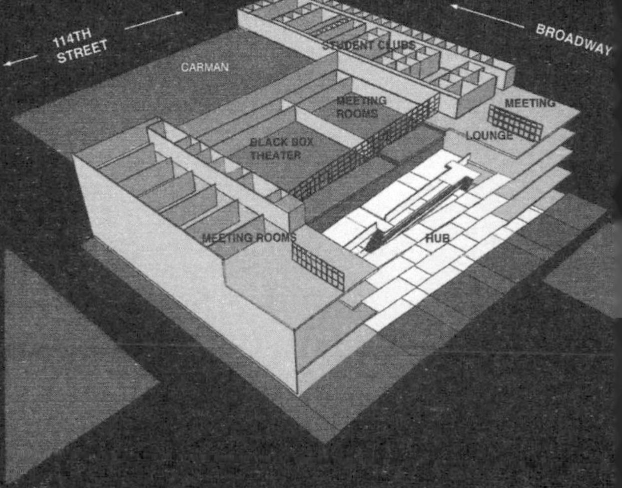
114TH STREET
BROADWAY
CARMAN
STUDENT CLUBS
MEETING ROOMS
MEETING
LOUNGE
BLACK BOX THEATER
MEETING ROOMS
HUB

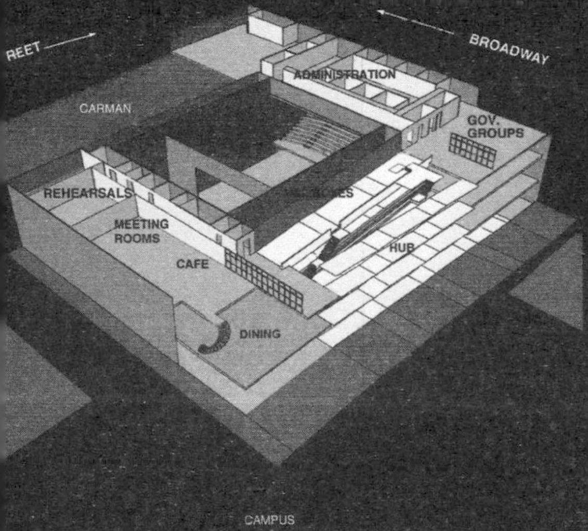
REET
BROADWAY
ADMINISTRATION
CARMAN
GOV. GROUPS
REHEARSALS
MEETING ROOMS
CAFE
HUB
DINING
CAMPUS

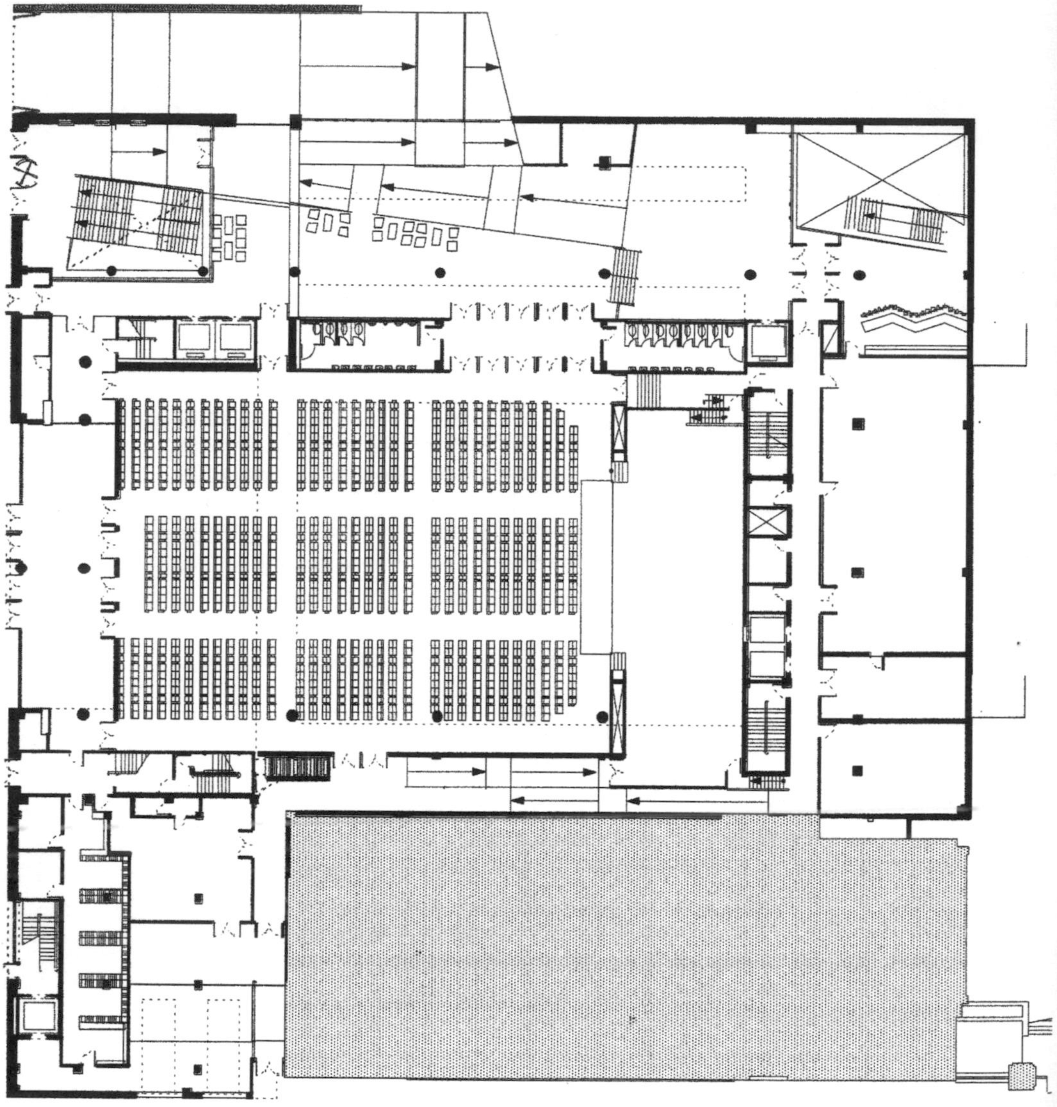

Broadway level: 1100-seat, flat-floor, multipurpose auditorium with stage, main lobby towards campus, special events' lobby towards Broadway. Main kitchen facilities, postal sorting office, and access to bookstore are also from Broadway

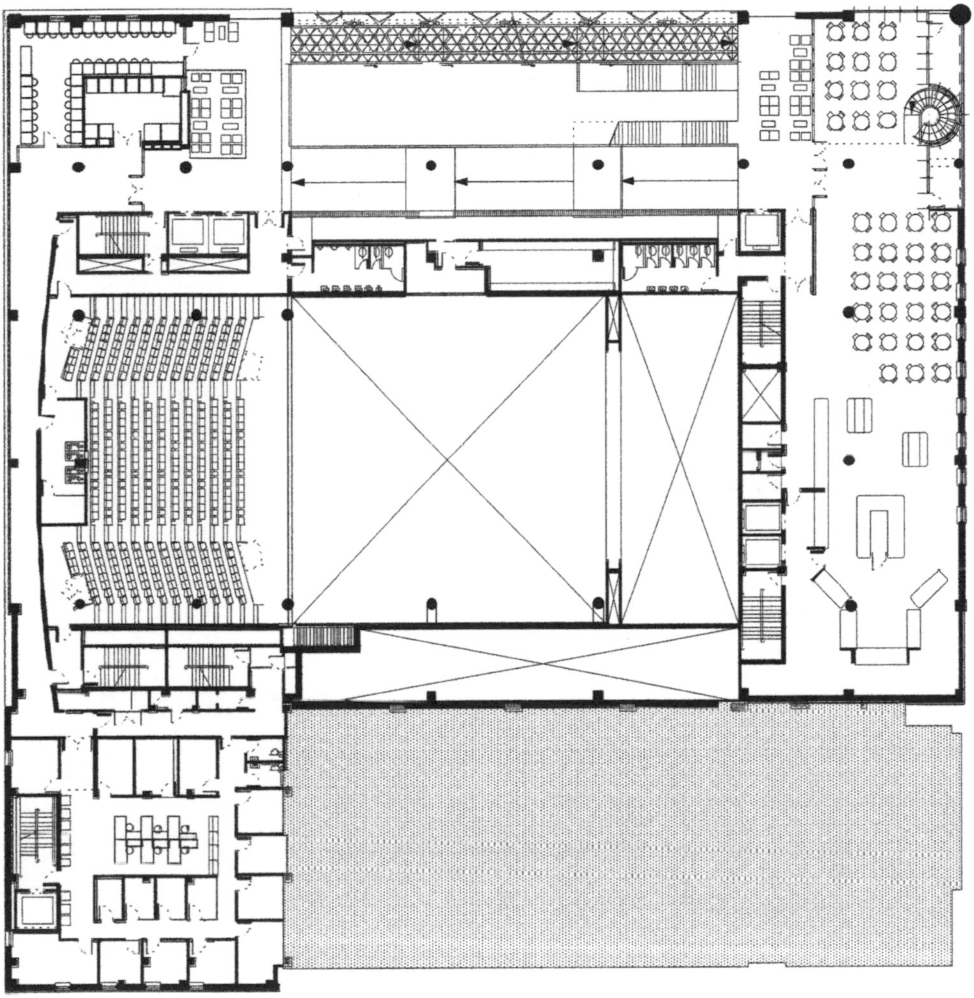

Third floor: 400-seat cinema, computer room, lounges, half of 6000 mailboxes on ramp, dining facilities

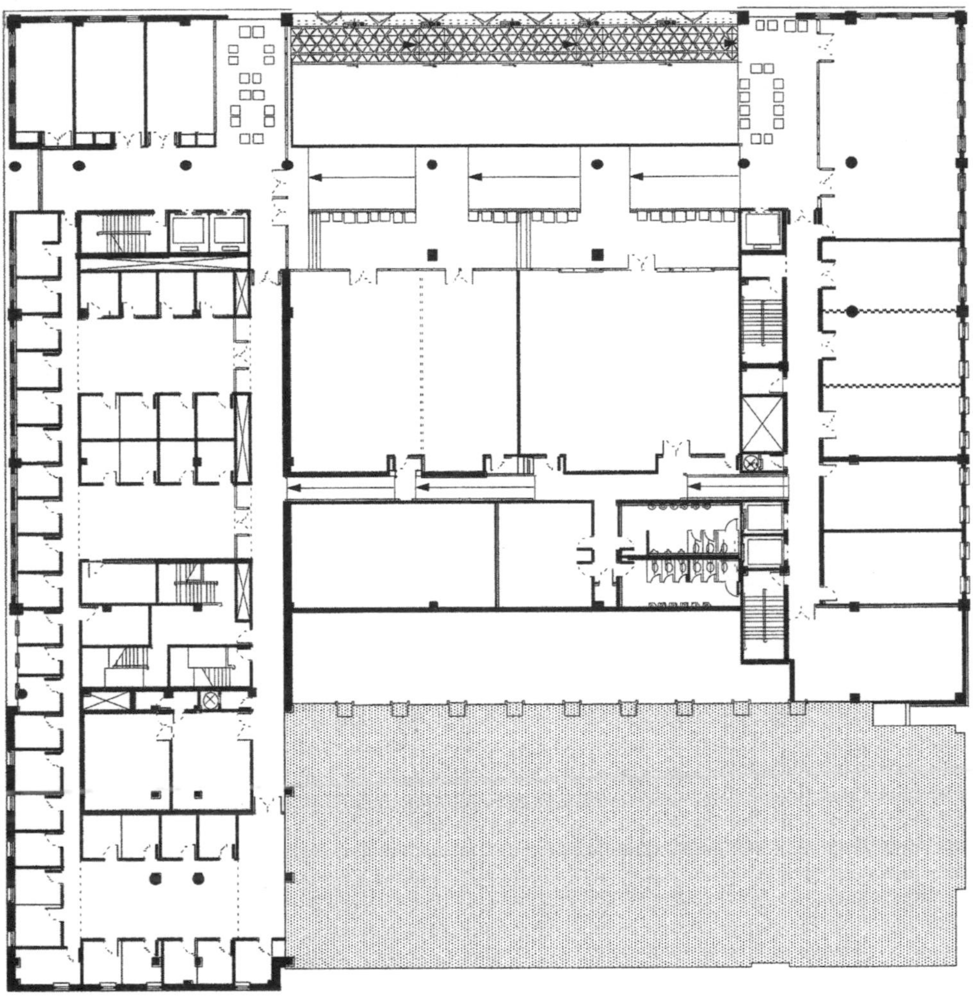

Fifth floor: student clubs, orchestra room, black box theater, meeting rooms, rehearsal rooms

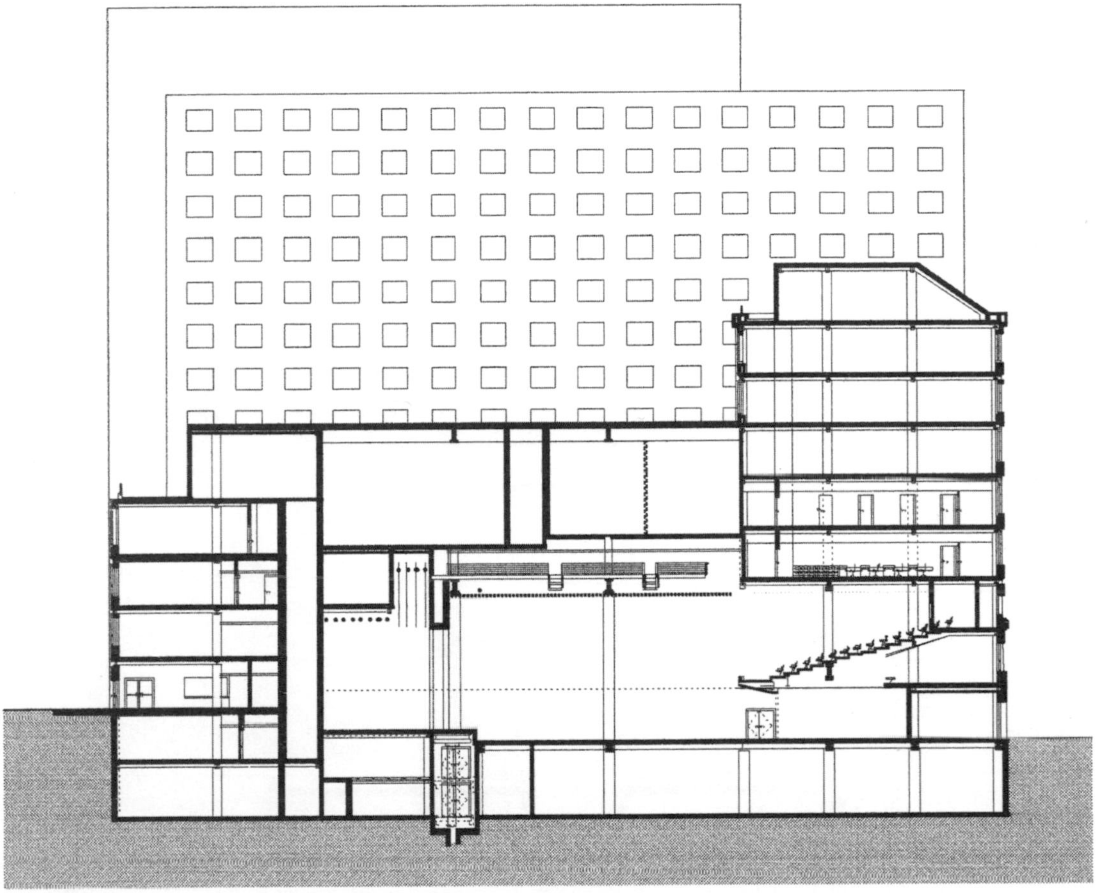

When the screen of the raked cinema lifts up, the cinema becomes the balcony of the multipurpose auditorium below. Above: an experimental theater and an orchestra room

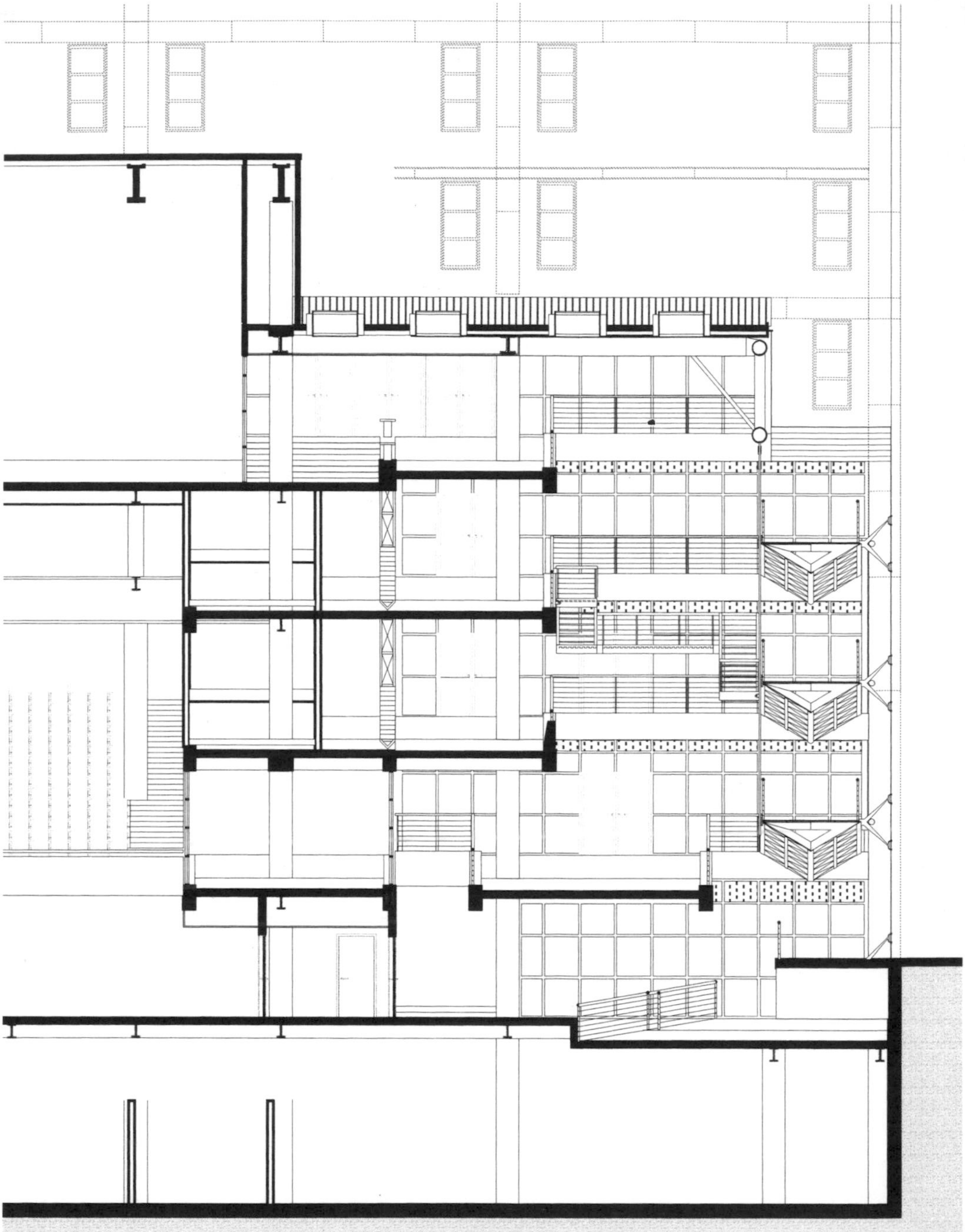

Partial section through auditorium, lounges, mailboxes and ramps, looking towards the cinema

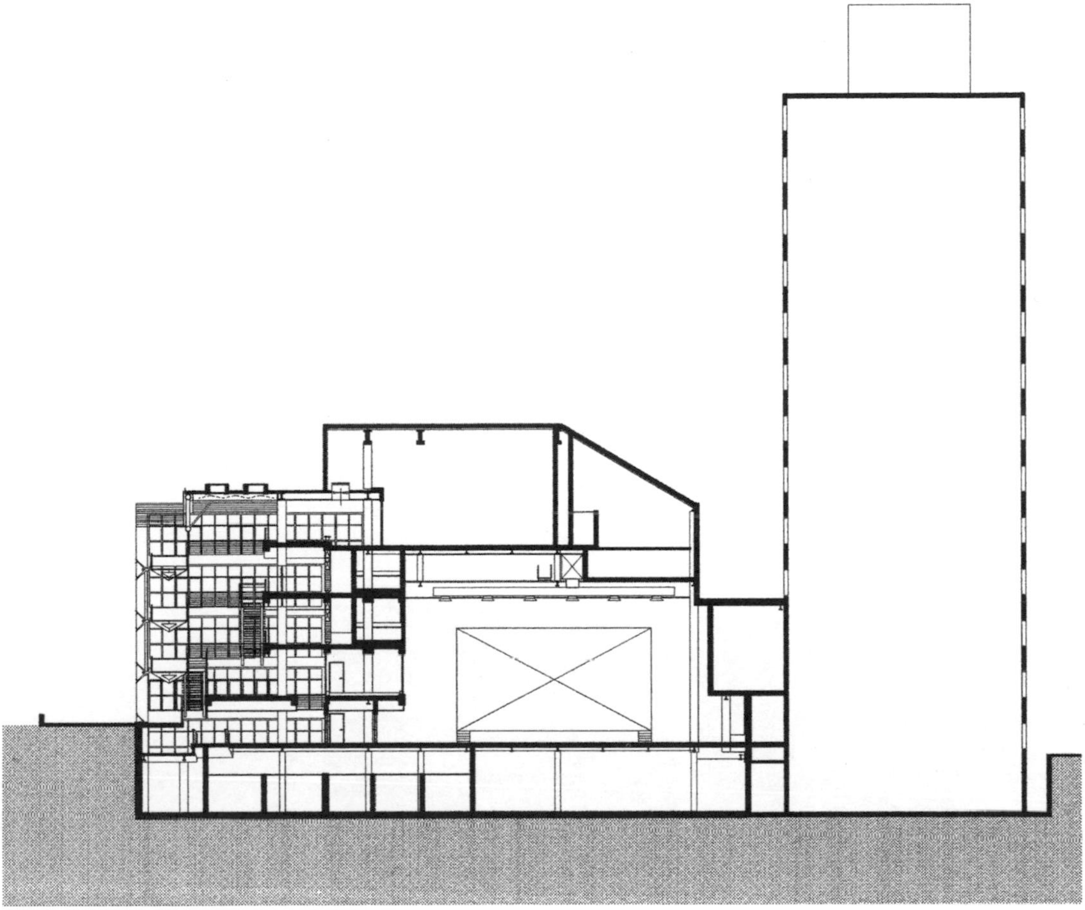

Located between the ramps and the multipurpose auditorium are some of the lounges. A large picture window allows views of activities between the ramps, the lounges, and the auditorium
Above: the black box theater

FRAME 20

FRAME 30

FRAME 60

FRAME 70

Walk-through animation sequence, moving from the entrance up the ramps

FRAME 100

FRAME 110

FRAME 120

FRAME 140

FRAME 150

FRAME 160

Continuity: an uninterrupted connection, with short-cuts

FRAME 10

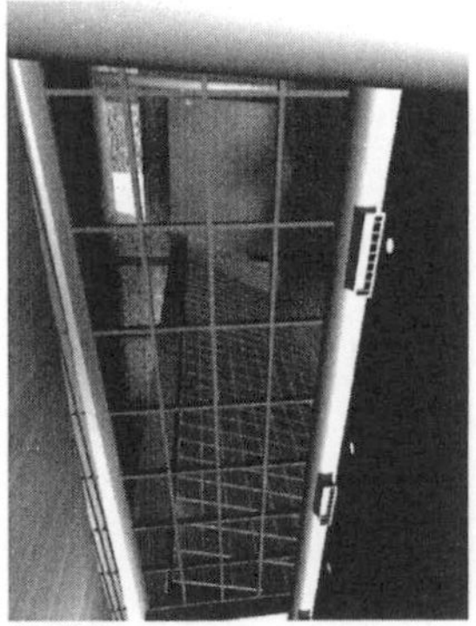
FRAME 20

FRAME 50

FRAME 60

FRAME 100

FRAME 110

FRAME 120

FRAME 140

FRAME 150

FRAME 160

Before the flow of crowds

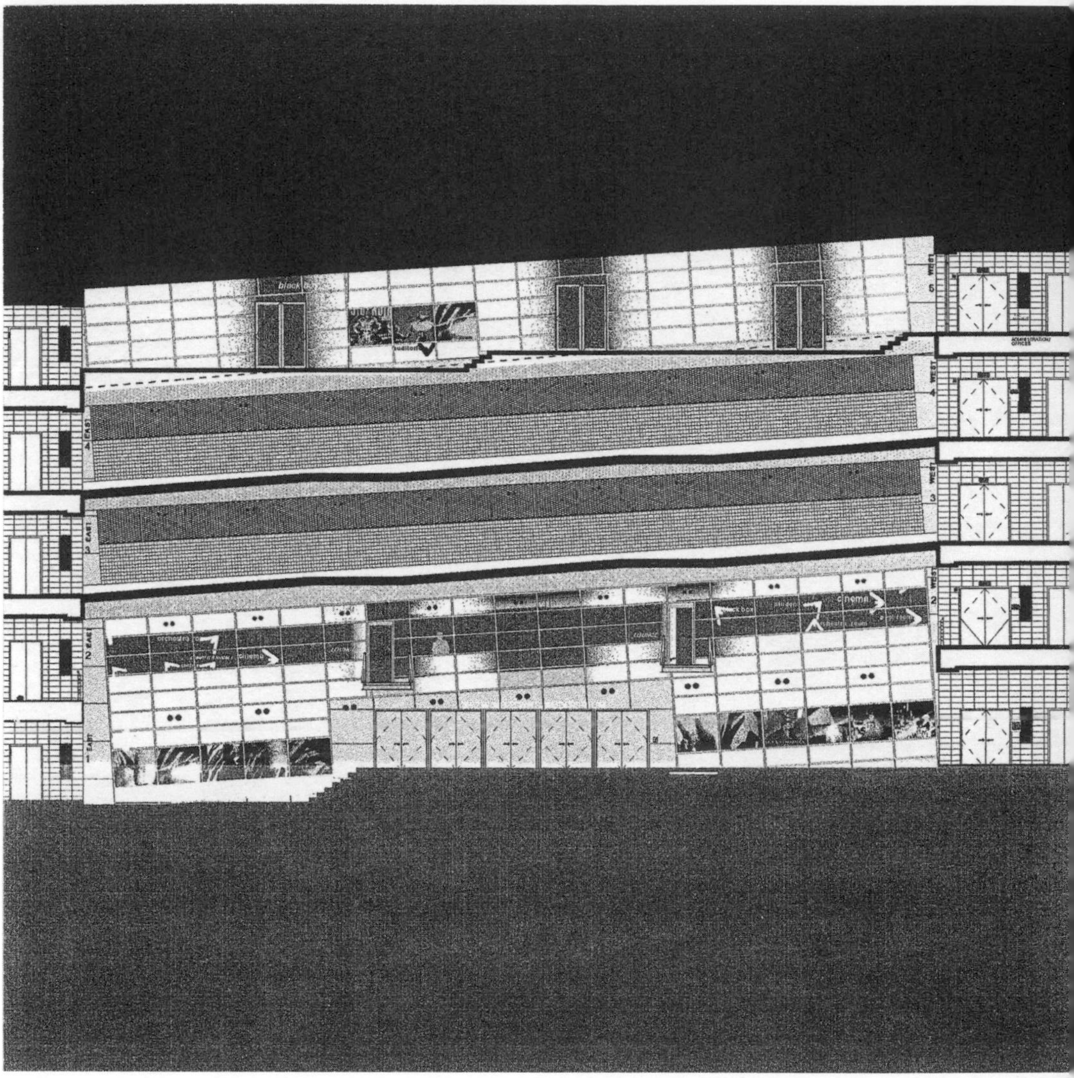

Interior elevation from top to bottom: printed glass in front of experimental theater and orchestra room, mailboxes with linear acoustical spounges above, computer room and student lounges, auditorium lobby

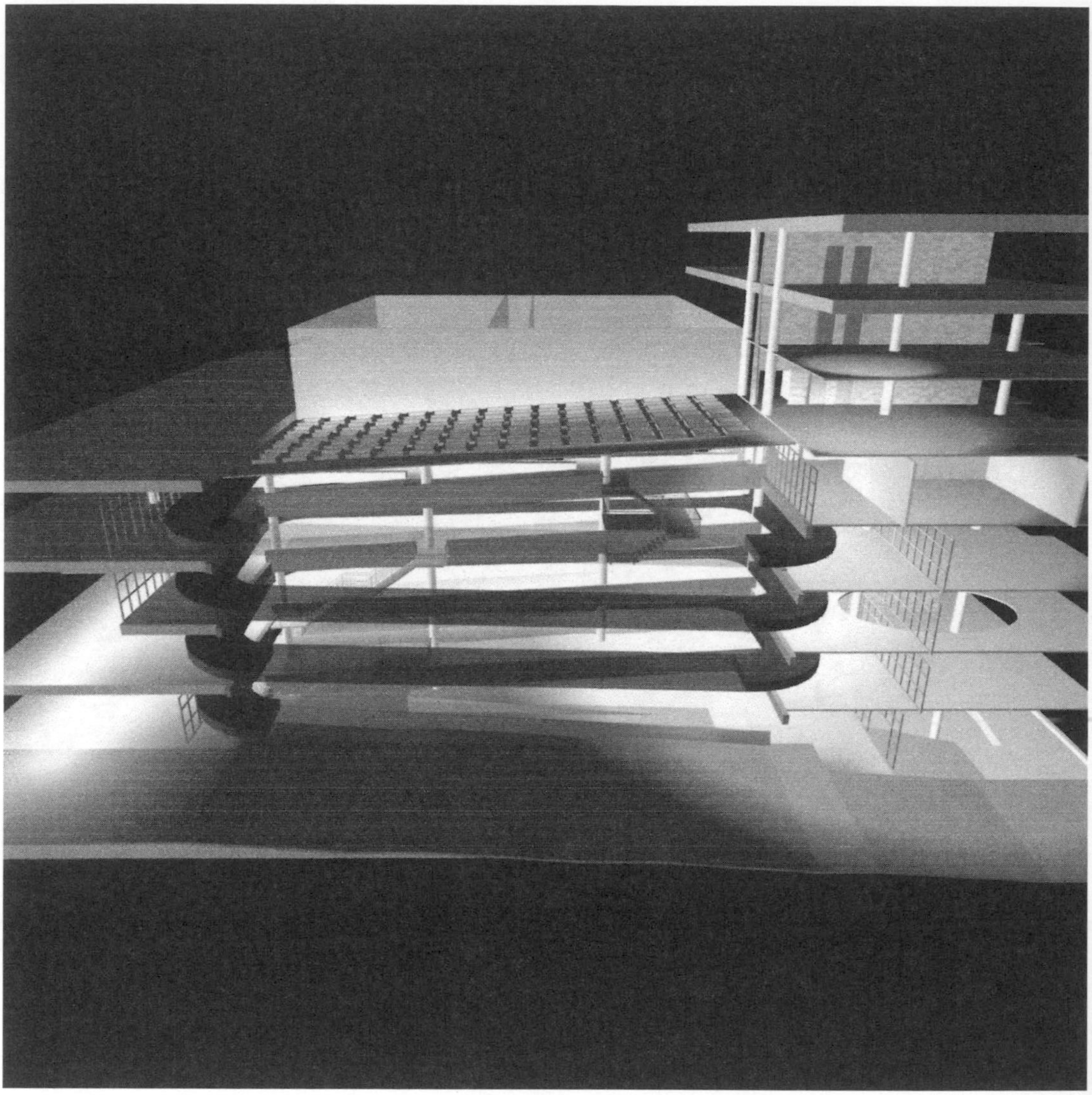

Continuous vector throughout the building

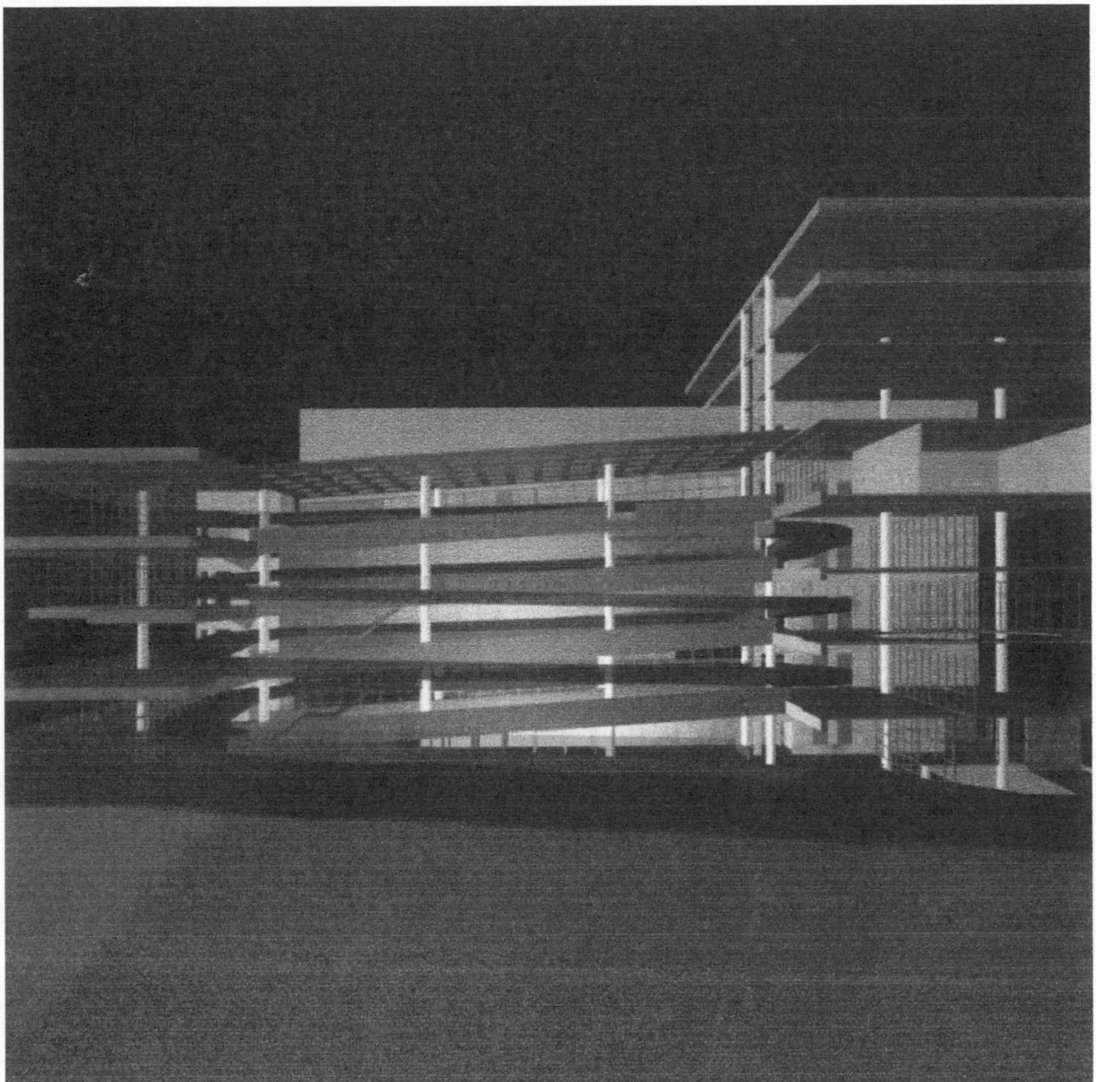

Glass wall / glass ramps: a principle

View from ramps towards cinema, through lounges

View towards lounges

Hub: a multiplicity of potential occurences

View towards a computer room

Lower-level party space

Dining hall

Cinema, used here as a balcony for the auditorium, with bay window looking towards campus

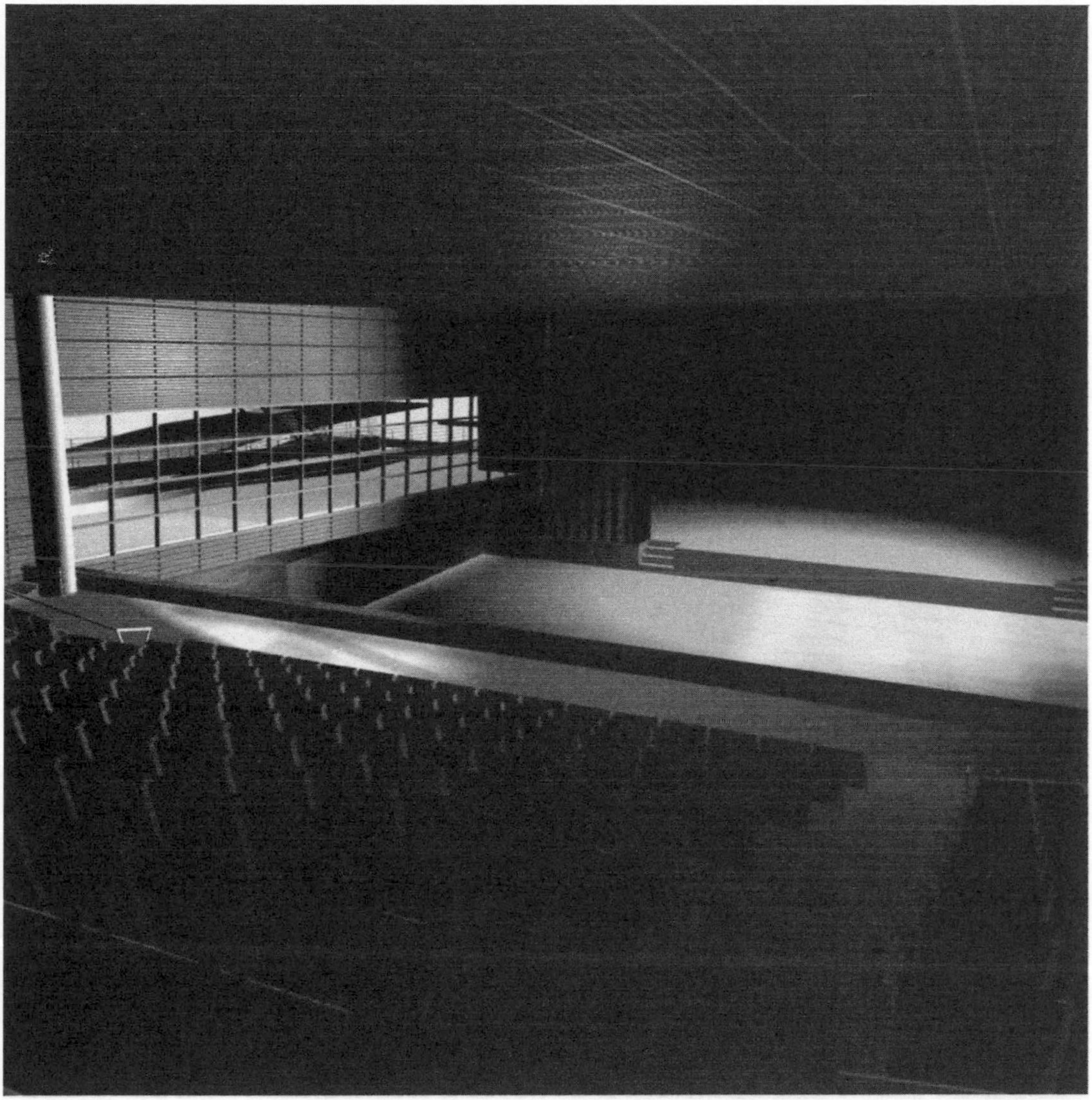

Cinema, auditorium, experimental theater, radio station, etc.: programmed activities that charge an otherwise unprogrammed space—the ramps or "in-between"

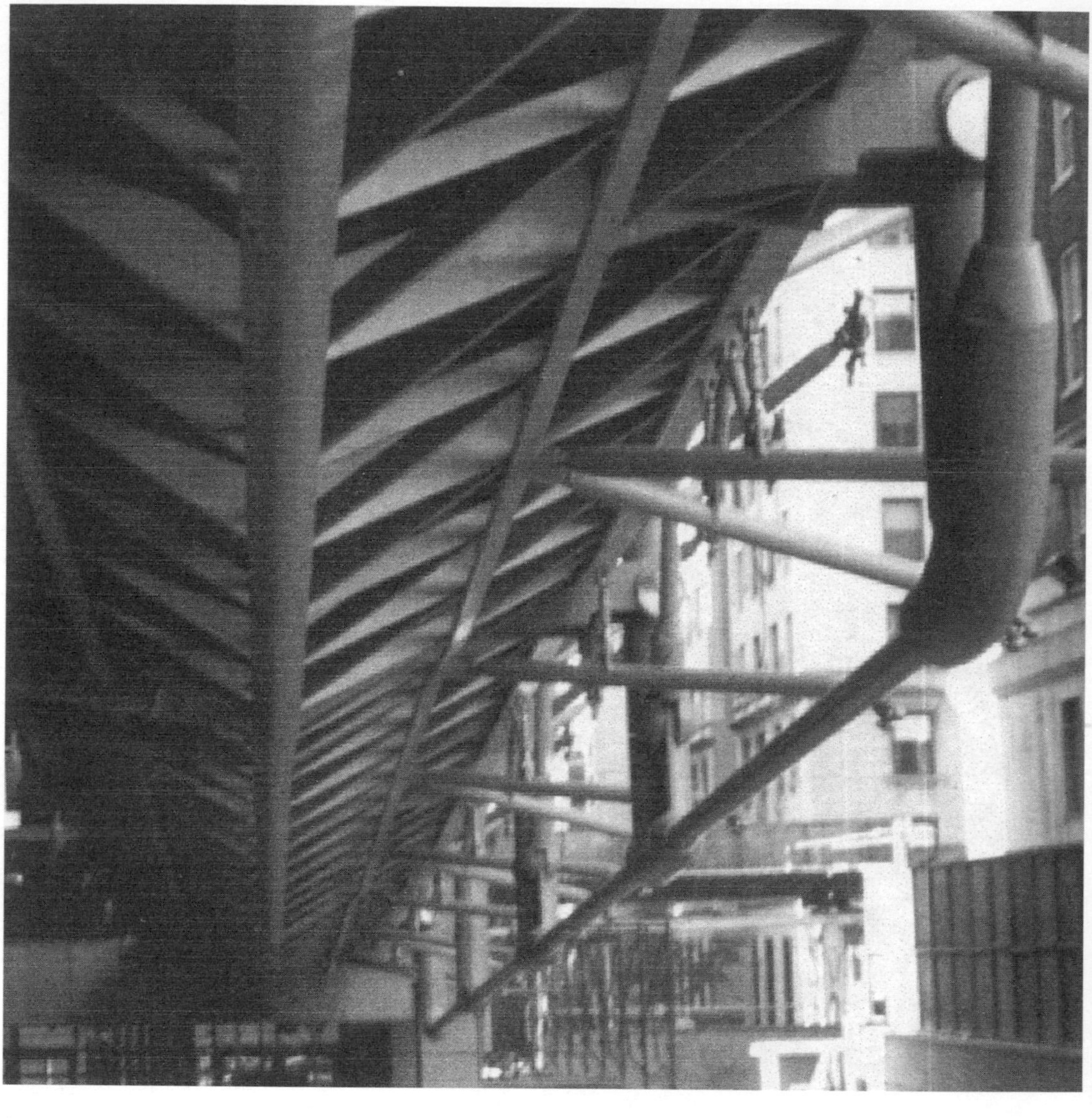

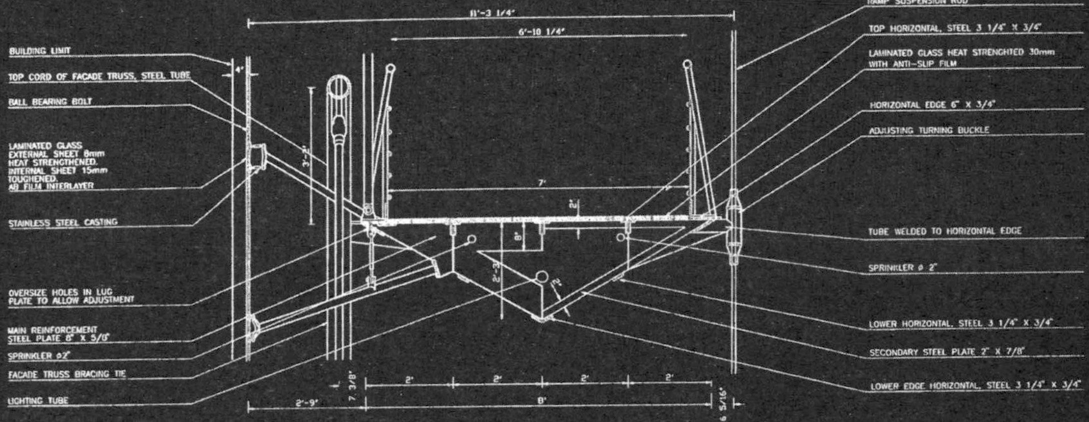
11'-3 1/4"
6'-10 1/4"
BUILDING LIMIT
TOP CORD OF FACADE TRUSS, STEEL TUBE
BALL BEARING BOLT
LAMINATED GLASS
EXTERNAL SHEET 8mm
HEAT STRENGTHENED.
INTERNAL SHEET 15mm
TOUGHENED.
AB FILM INTERLAYER
STAINLESS STEEL CASTING
OVERSIZE HOLES IN LUG
PLATE TO ALLOW ADJUSTMENT
MAIN REINFORCEMENT
STEEL PLATE 8" X 5/8"
SPRINKLER ø2"
FACADE TRUSS BRACING TIE
LIGHTING TUBE
RAMP SUSPENSION ROD
TOP HORIZONTAL, STEEL 3 1/4" X 3/4"
LAMINATED GLASS HEAT STRENGHTED 30mm
WITH ANTI-SLIP FILM
HORIZONTAL EDGE 6" X 3/4"
ADJUSTING TURNING BUCKLE
TUBE WELDED TO HORIZONTAL EDGE
SPRINKLER ø 2"
LOWER HORIZONTAL, STEEL 3 1/4" X 3/4"
SECONDARY STEEL PLATE 2" X 7/8"
LOWER EDGE HORIZONTAL, STEEL 3 1/4" X 3/4"
2'-9"
8'
2'
2'
2'
2'
7 3/8"
6 5/16"

SECTION A–A – ARM CONNECTION TO RAMP

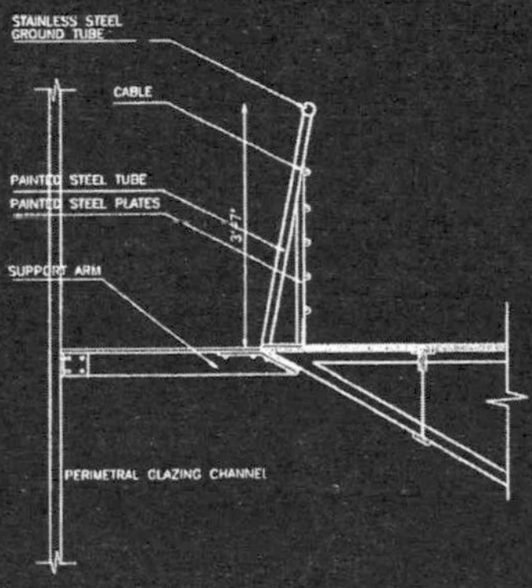
STAINLESS STEEL
GROUND TUBE
CABLE
PAINTED STEEL TUBE
PAINTED STEEL PLATES
SUPPORT ARM
PERIMETRAL GLAZING CHANNEL

SECTION B–B RAMP SLIDING END

1' 2'

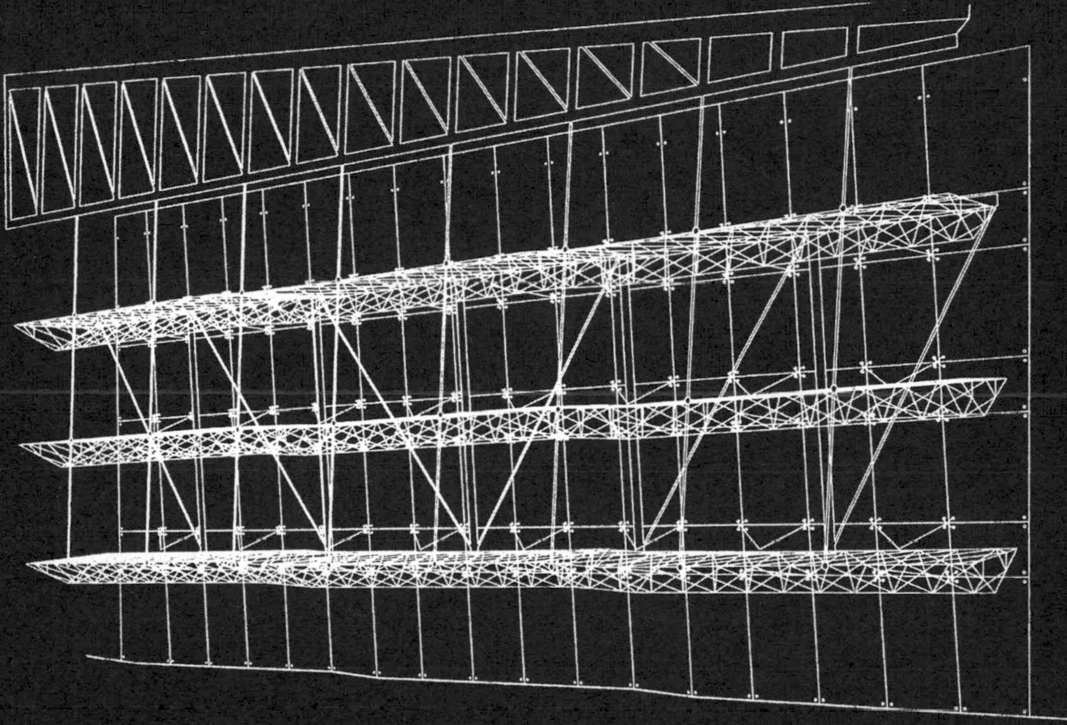

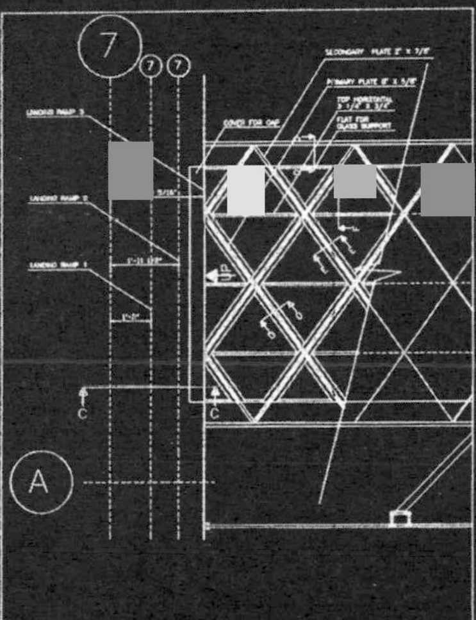

CASE A – RAMP END

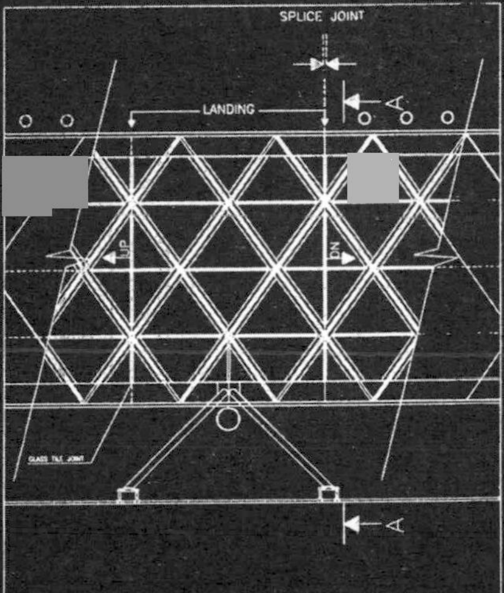

CASE B – RAMP TYPICAL LANDING

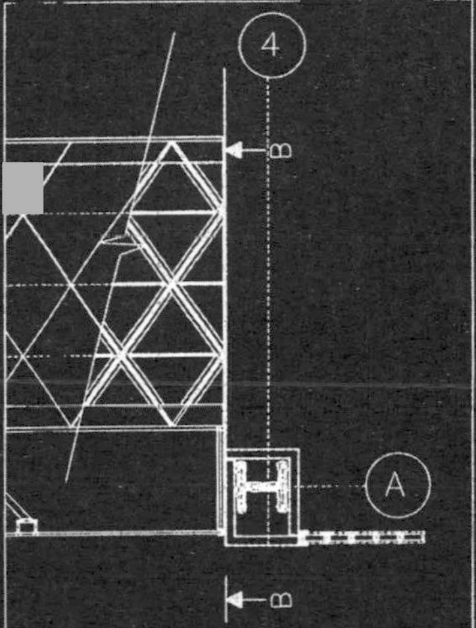

CASE C – RAMP SLIDING END

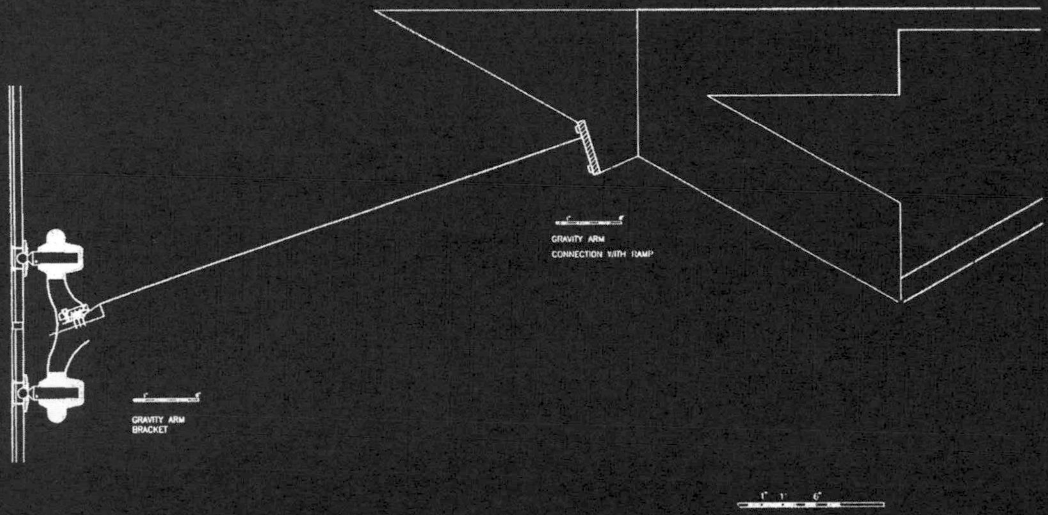
GRAVITY ARM
CONNECTION WITH RAMP
GRAVITY ARM
BRACKET

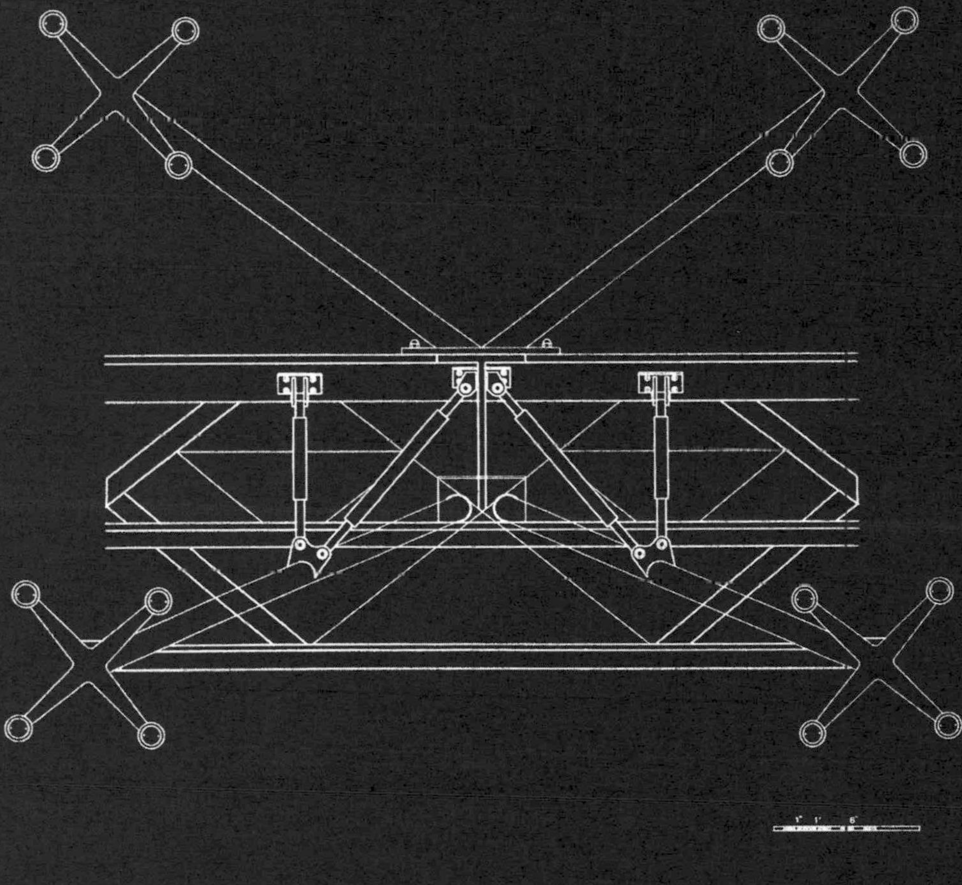

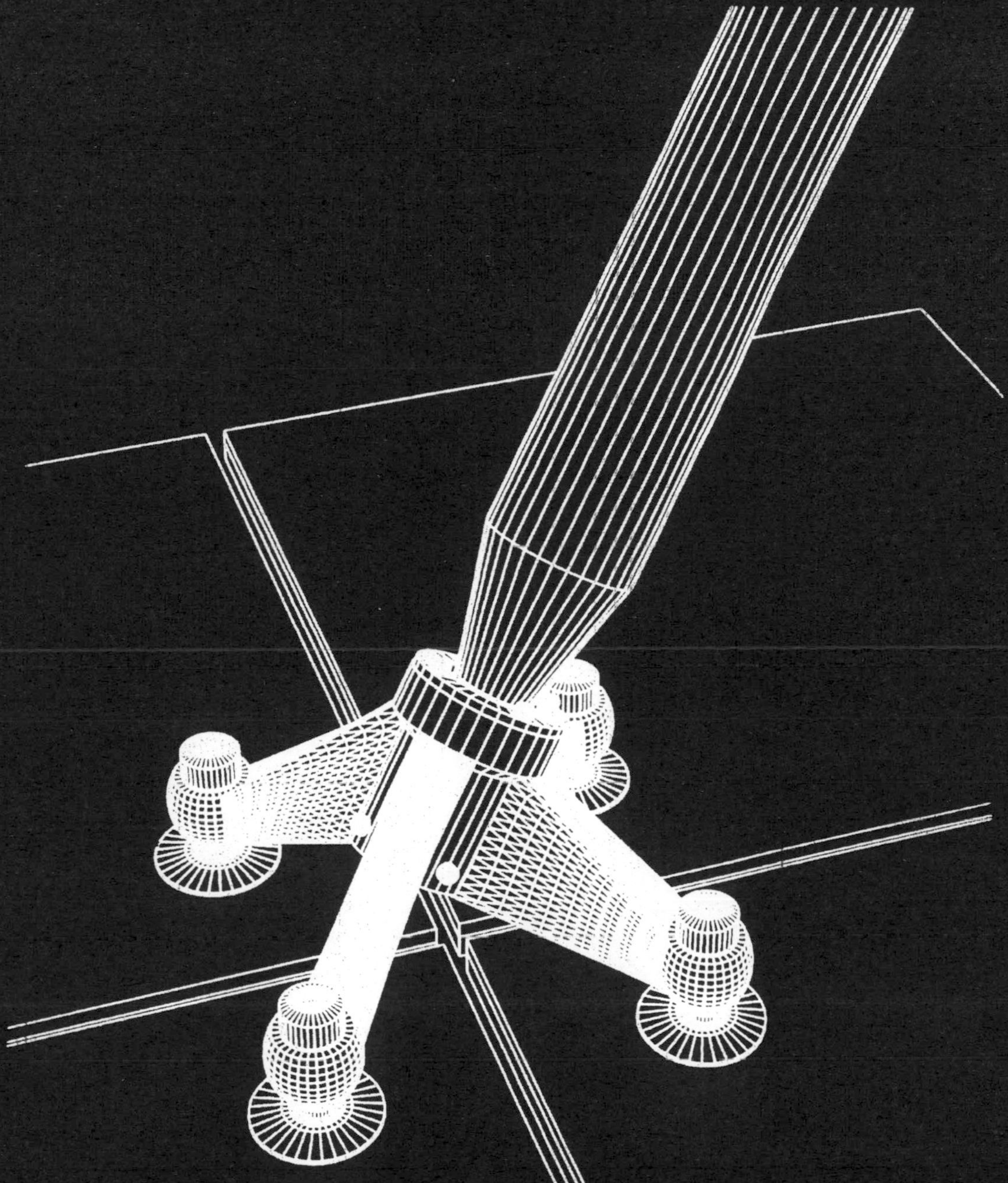

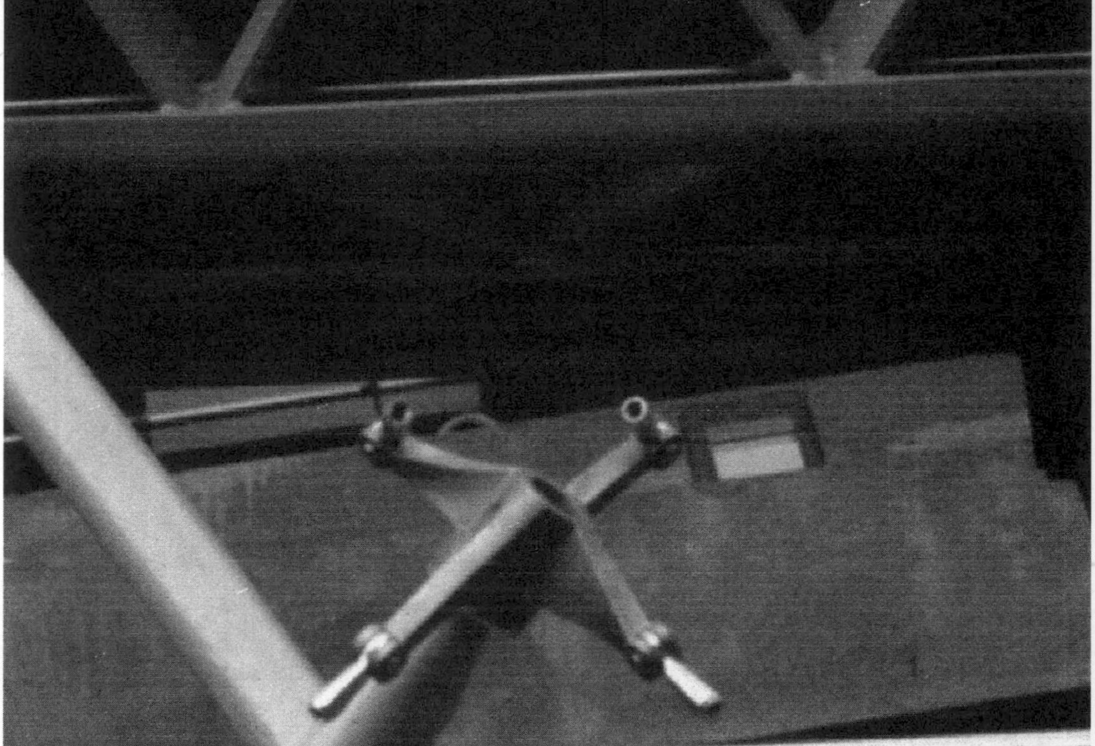

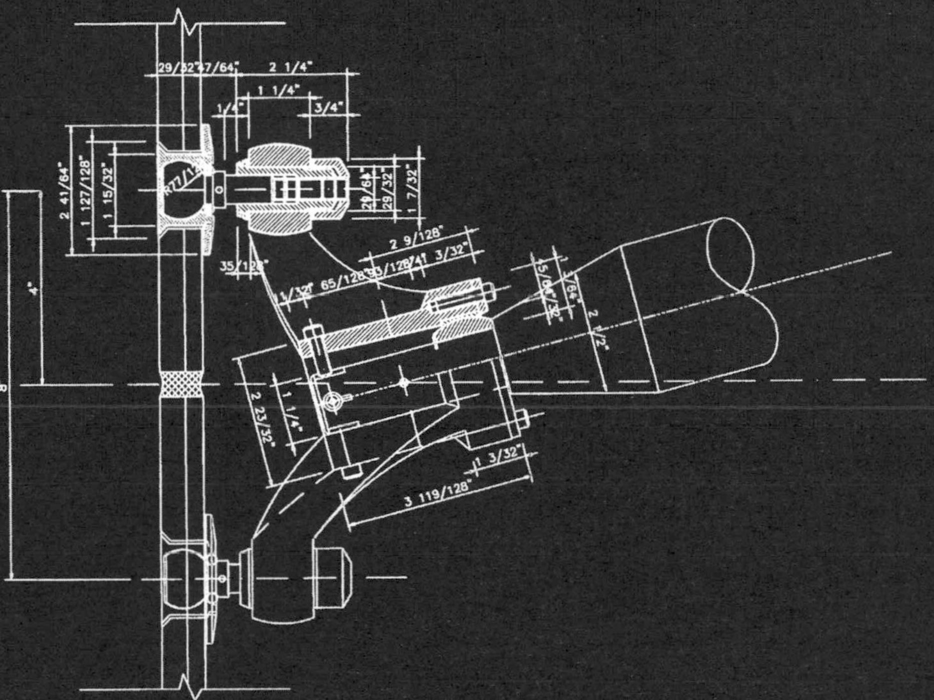

29/32"
47/64"
2 1/4"
1 1/4"
1/4"
3/4"
2 41/64"
1 127/128"
1 15/32"
29/64"
29/32"
1 7/32"
35/128"
2 9/128"
65/128"
4"
8"
2 23/32"
1 1/4"
1 3/32"
3 119/128"

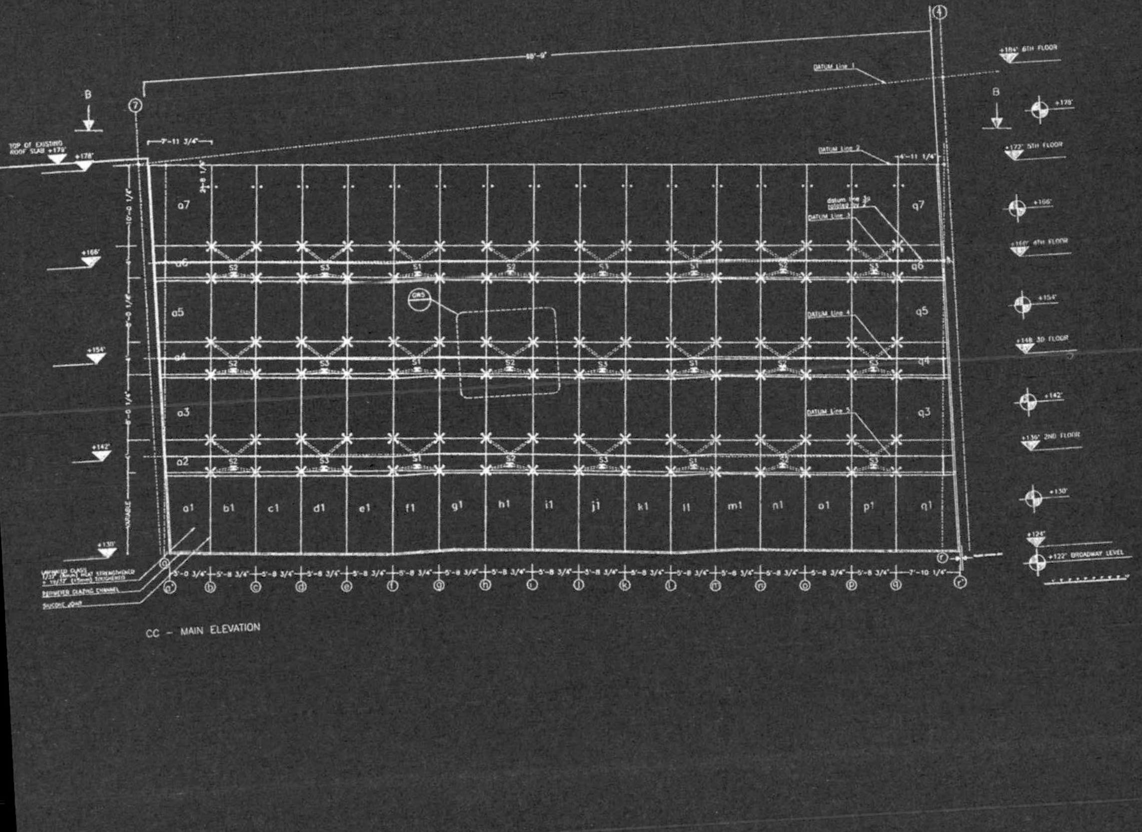

CC – MAIN ELEVATION

New York, Franklin Furnace Gallery, 1994-95

Carving through the Normative

In 1994 the Franklin Furnace Archive, a performance art and exhibition gallery in New York, asked us to design a new space on three levels of an existing loft building in the Tribeca region of the city.

After completing the schematic design phase, we agreed with the director of the gallery that the new artistic developments the organization was promoting, such as art on the Internet and virtual reality schemes, did not require a real space, and that only the gallery's virtual presence on the Internet was necessary to its mission. In 1995 we therefore designed an interactive and virtual space, organizing the exhibitions and events on a web-site that is accessible by millions of people almost simultaneously.

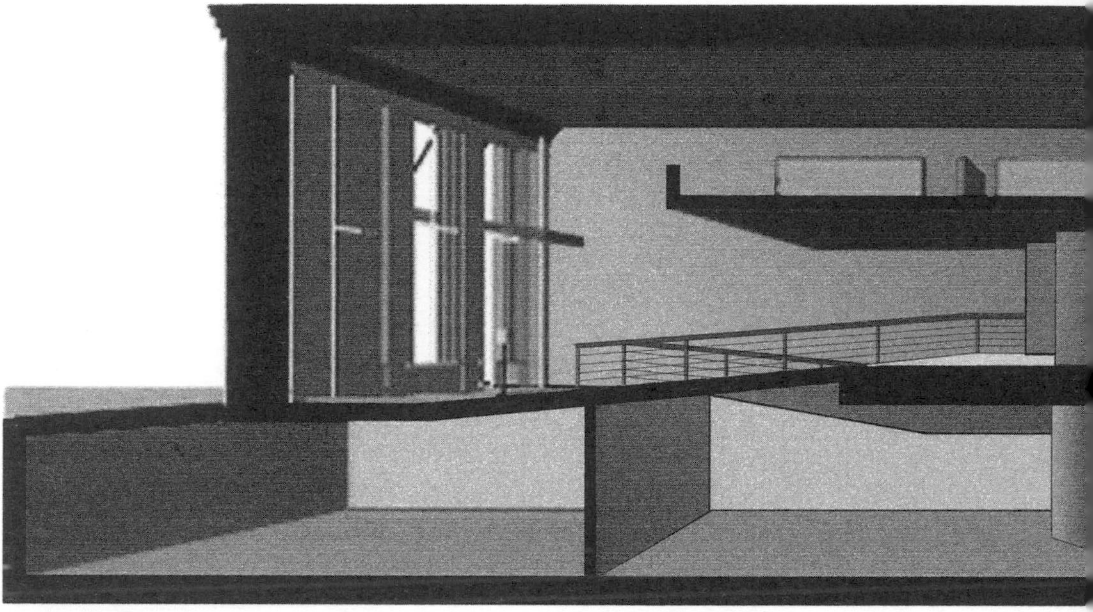

Interior is partly hollowed out in order to allow for ramp connectors

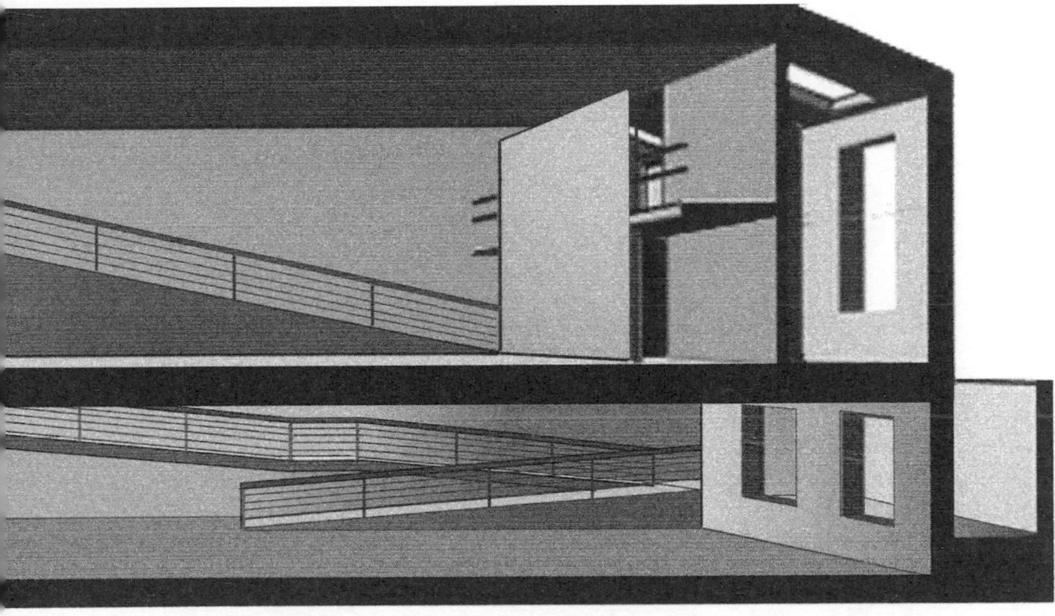

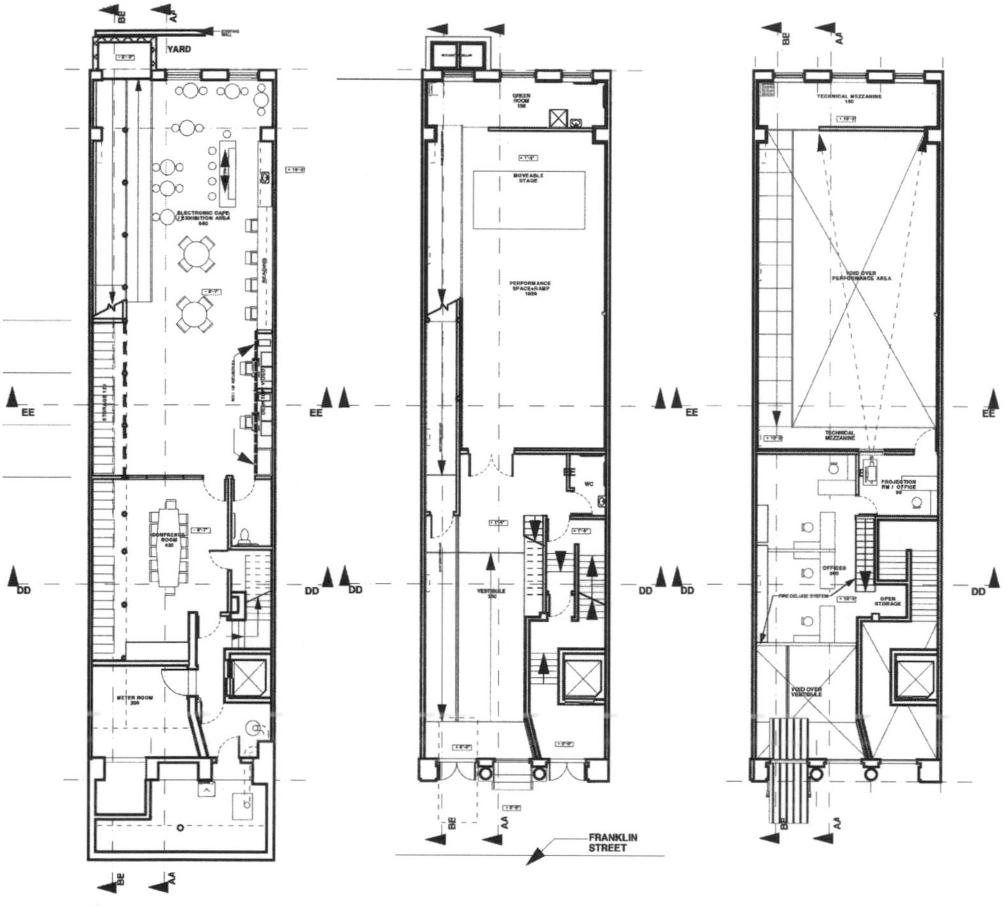

Program: a gallery for performance artists, with a public assembly or performance space for 75 people, an art gallery, a cyber-café, some administrative space and a meeting room

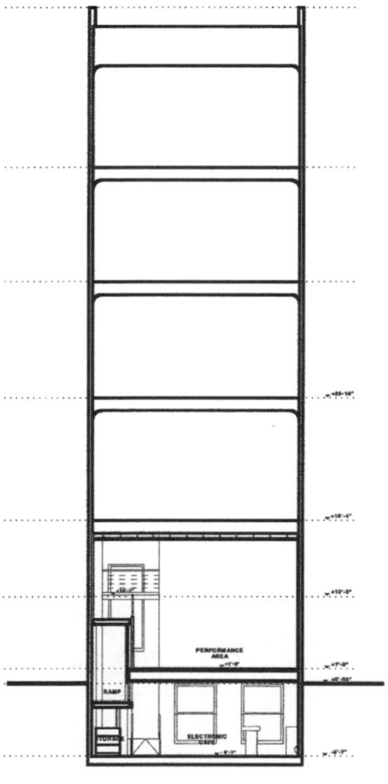

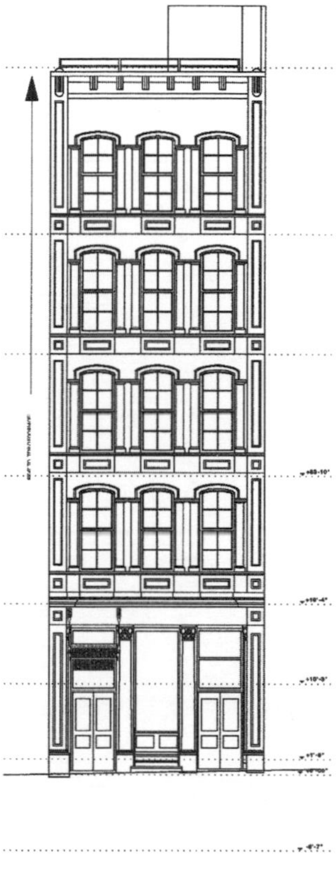

No exterior intervention except for awning and signage: the historical cast-iron facade is retained

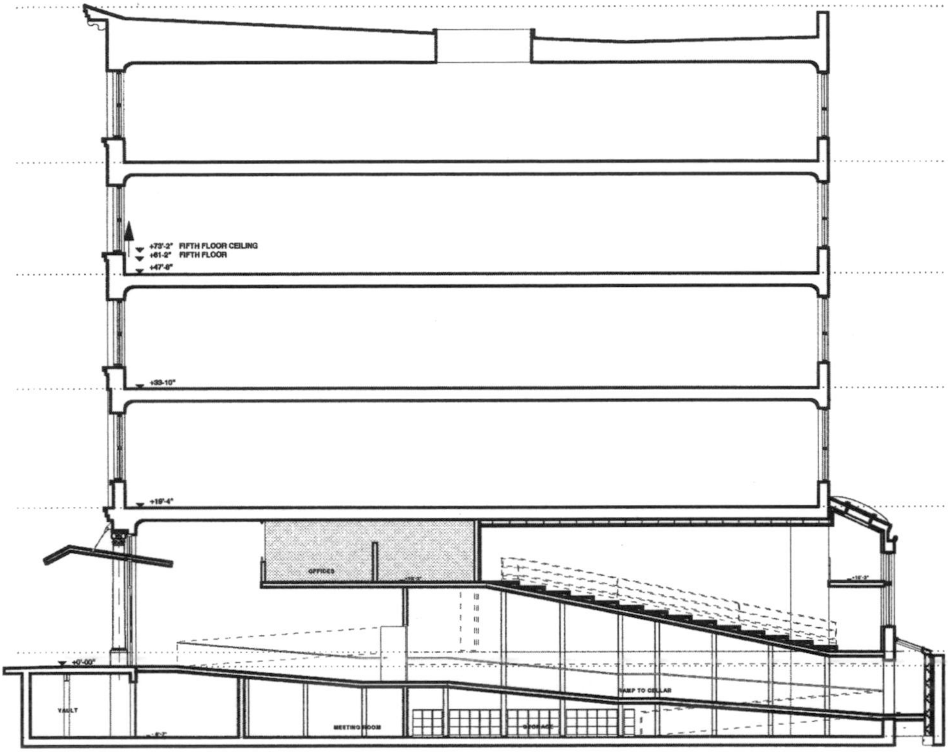

Potential for a continuous circuit: a loop

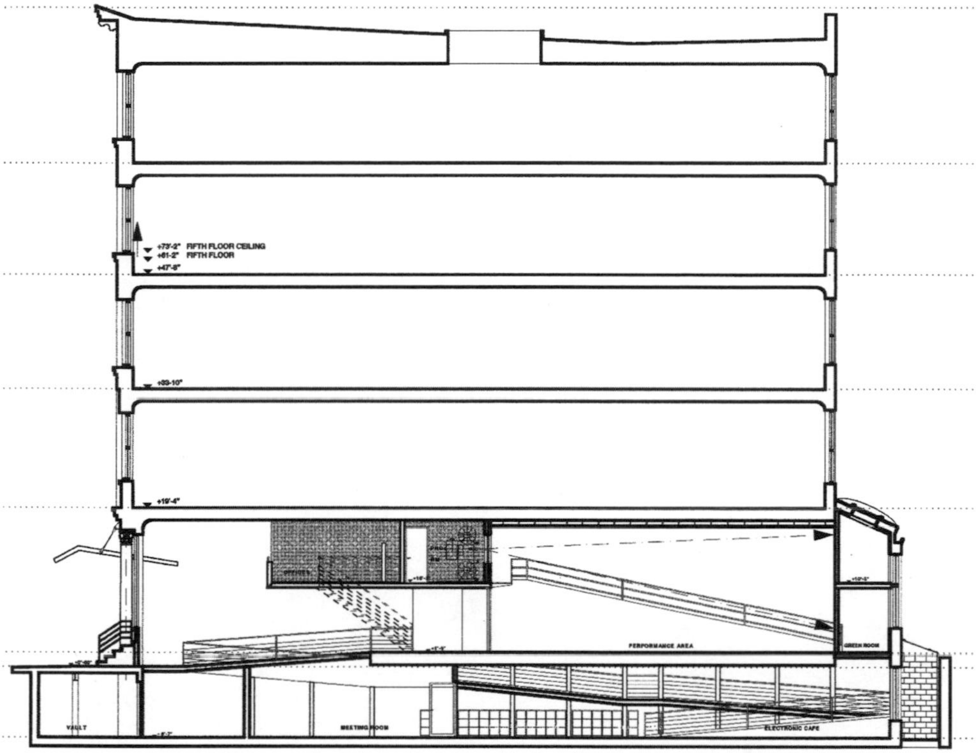

But do art and architecture need a real space to exist?

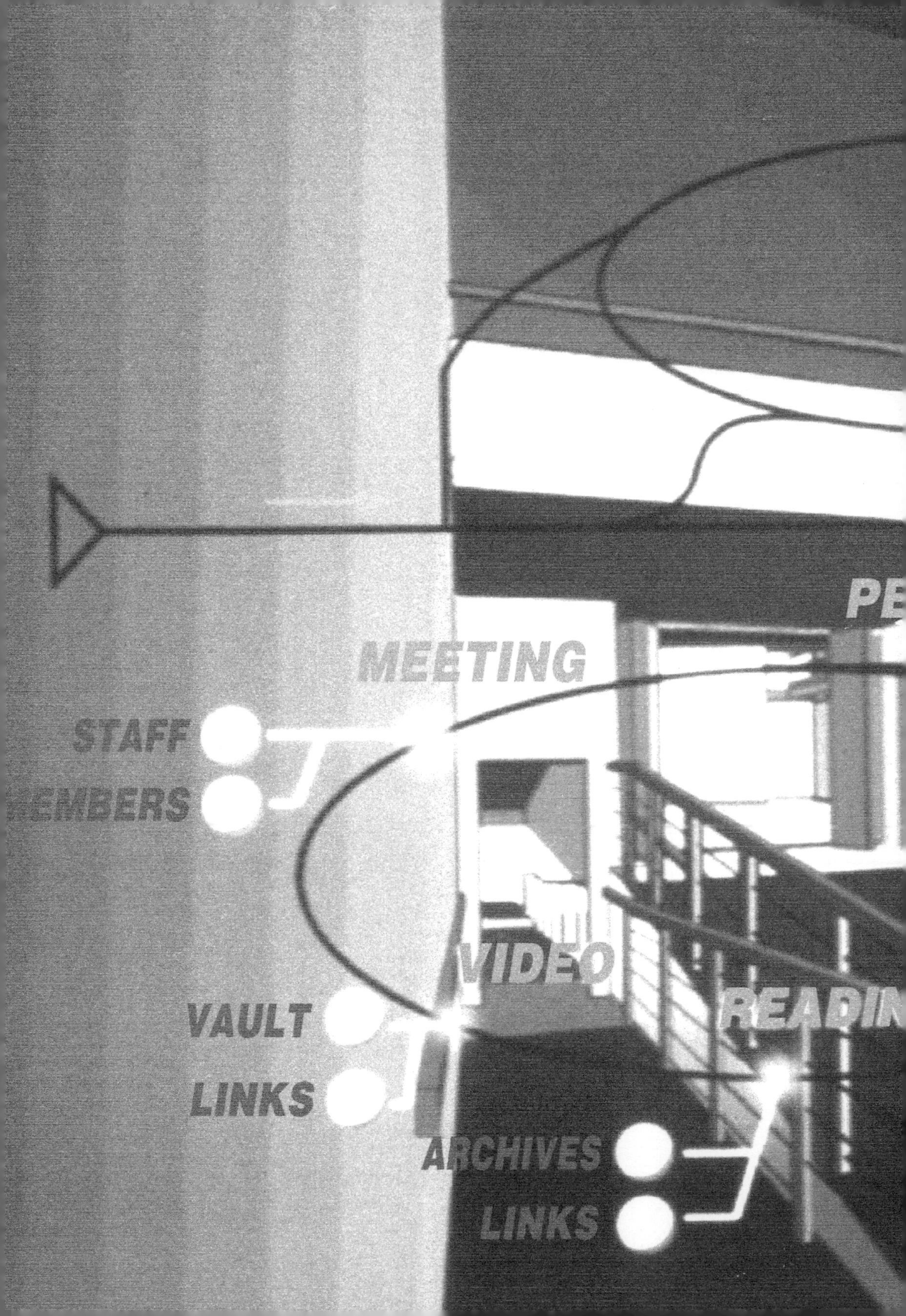
PE
MEETING
STAFF
MEMBERS
VIDEO
READIN
VAULT
LINKS
ARCHIVES
LINKS

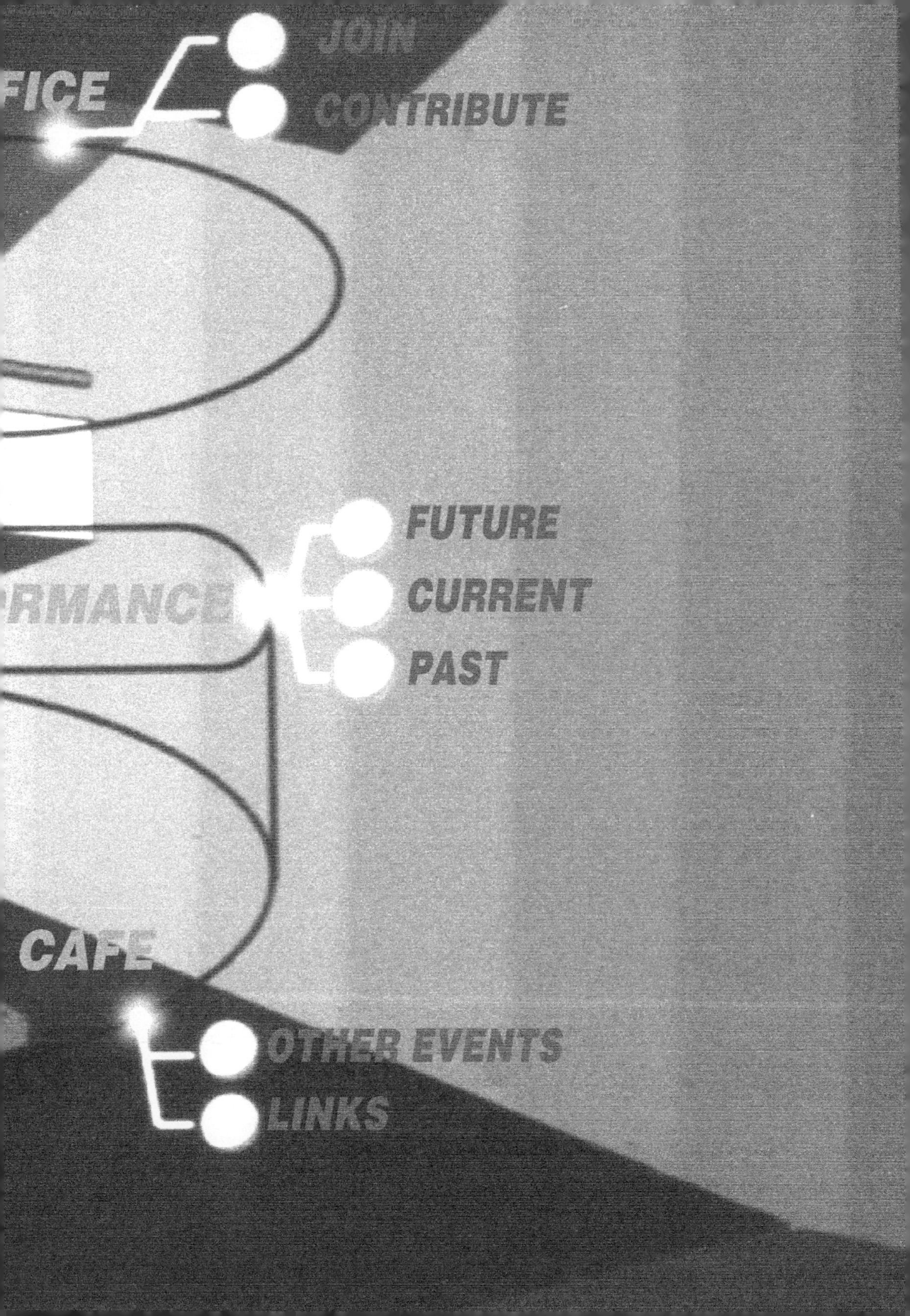
FICE
JOIN
CONTRIBUTE
RMANCE
FUTURE
CURRENT
PAST
CAFE
OTHER EVENTS
LINKS

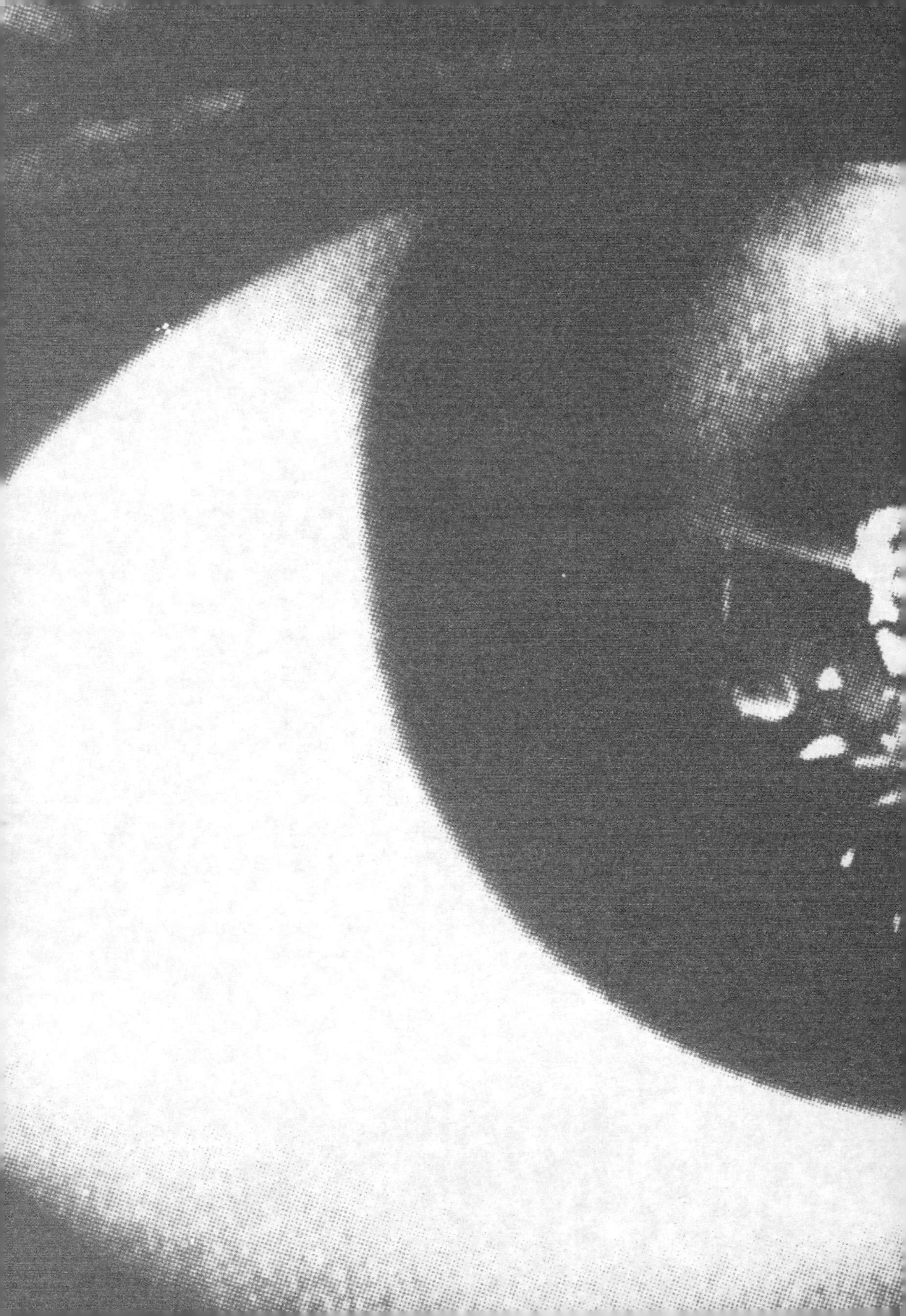

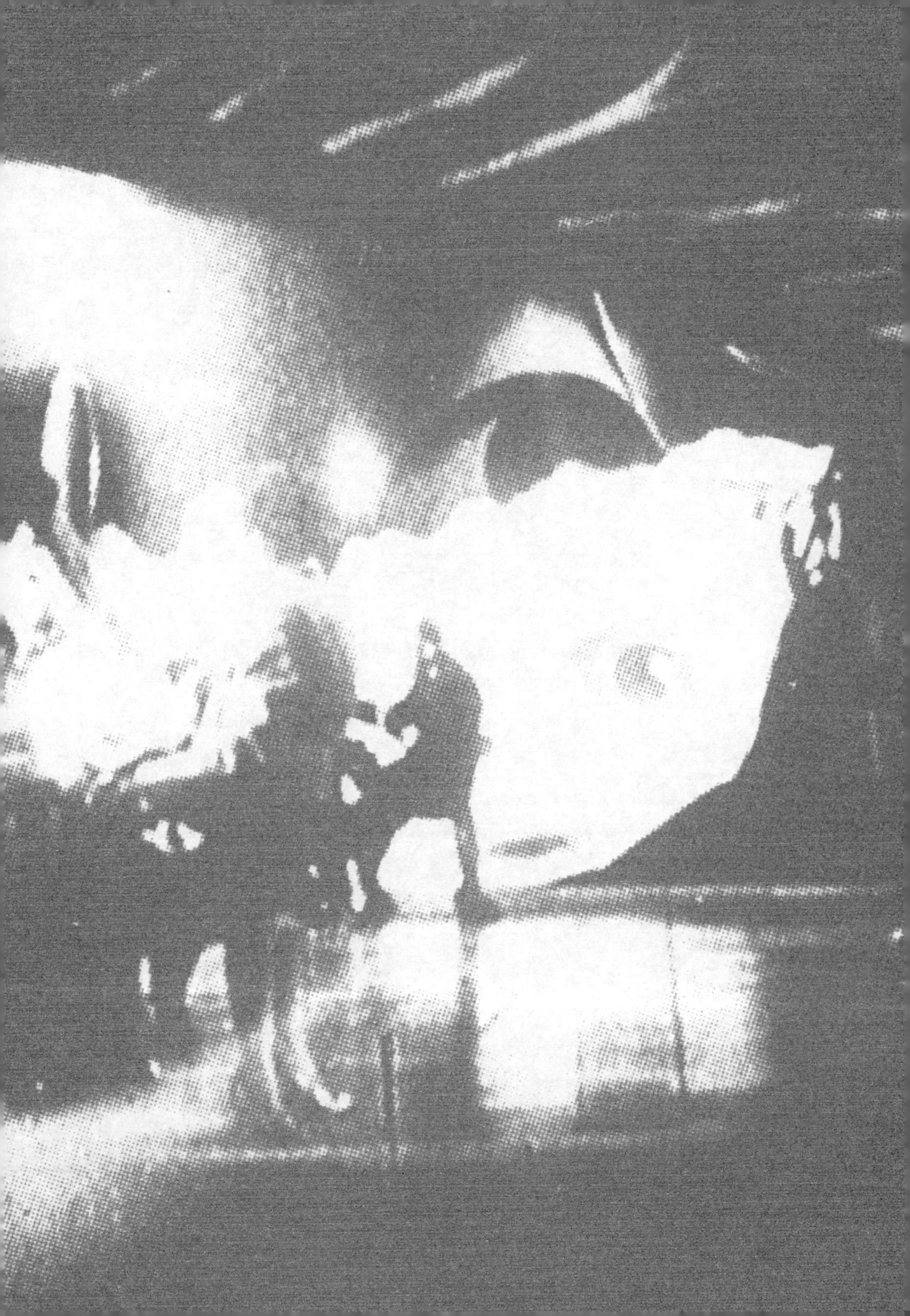

C.
Voids and Solids

Historically, carving voids out of a solid or organizing solid matter around a preconceived void has been a major device for making architecture. Typologically, there are courts or courtyards, with regular configurations. Topologically, there are voids or "holes" susceptible to any deformation. In an art gallery in a small town in Brittany, a major museum in New York City, and an educational and research institution in Lausanne, voids or courts are either carved into solids or simply defined through perimeter walls. Within institutions, these voids are public places of sorts, where space is "unprogrammed" and, therefore, open to appropriation: the place of events?

Nantes, FRAC Art Center, 1997

Zero Degree Architecture I

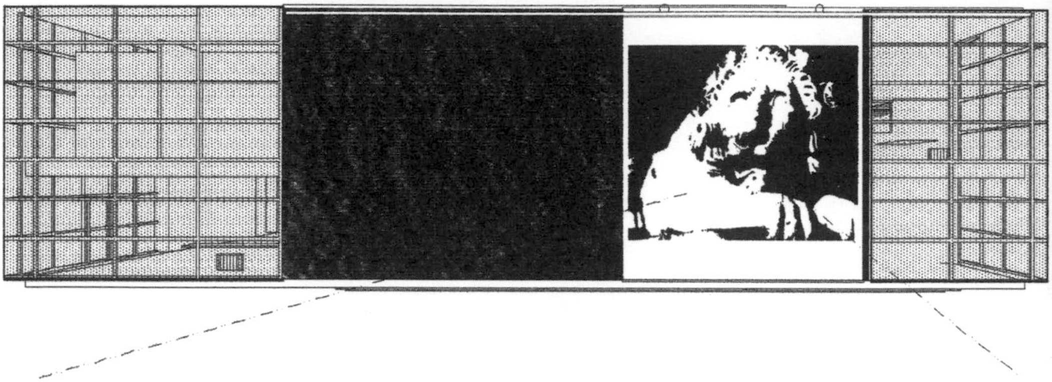

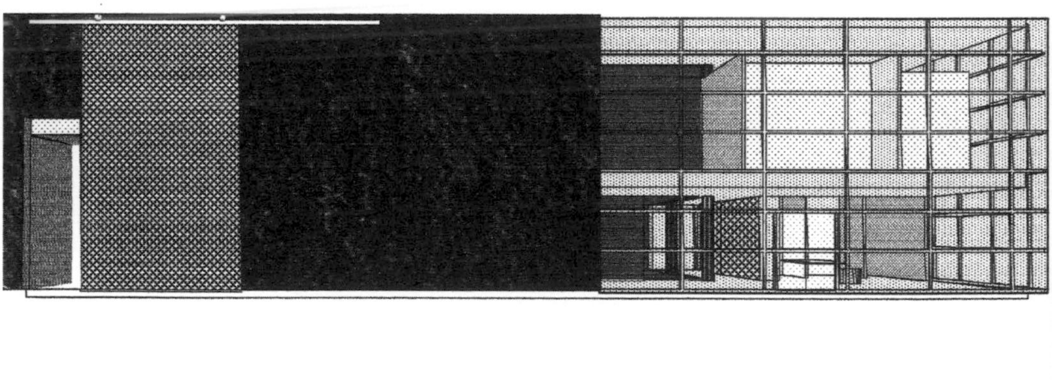

Facades: mobile screens, including the screen of the outdoor cinema

FRAC: a small experimental art center in a wooded area on the outskirts of the city of Nantes, France. Program: a regional collection of contemporary art, open to the public, and participating in the development and diffusion of all contemporary modes of creation.

With a tight budget but with the desire to create an exemplary building, a new model for regional collections is created. Contrary to many of its predecessors, this FRAC will be located in a building designed specifically for it, rather than in rehabilitated existing buildings.

The Device

Interior: First, one is to design the simplest and most performative device possible, in which the 1400-square-meter area responds precisely to all programmatic and budgetary demands, while simultaneously adding a "plus"—through generosity, simplicity, and dignity of space, offering a new potential.

All activities—the conference rooms, library, and administrative offices—are organized around a large gallery. The lobby is the pivot of the building. The large gallery is illuminated evenly by diffused natural light along its walls.

Exterior: The walls are made of slate, like the roofs throughout the region. The windows manifest large simple surfaces with exterior structural sealant glazing. The specific elements are three full-height sliding screens.

Screen 1: Expanded metal in front of the delivery access

Screen 2: Large operable rubber strips to block, to a certain extent, the light entering the gallery

Screen 3: A white Teflon canvas screen that can be used for projecting films in the open air

There is no gratuitous formal effect, nor a monumental gesture. The FRAC will be a simple tool for work.

The Site

The working device would have been only a pure organizational concept if it did not have a specific relationship to its site. Actually, the location intersects a major axis given by the master plan of the surrounding region, and is expressed in the building itself: with a subtle level change, a slightly perceptible obliquity, the generic building is anchored to the site.

On the exterior, towards the southwest, a paved terrace hosts public events or exhibitions. Towards the northeast, taking advantage of the slope and the view of the neighboring castle, is a screen for open-air film projections.

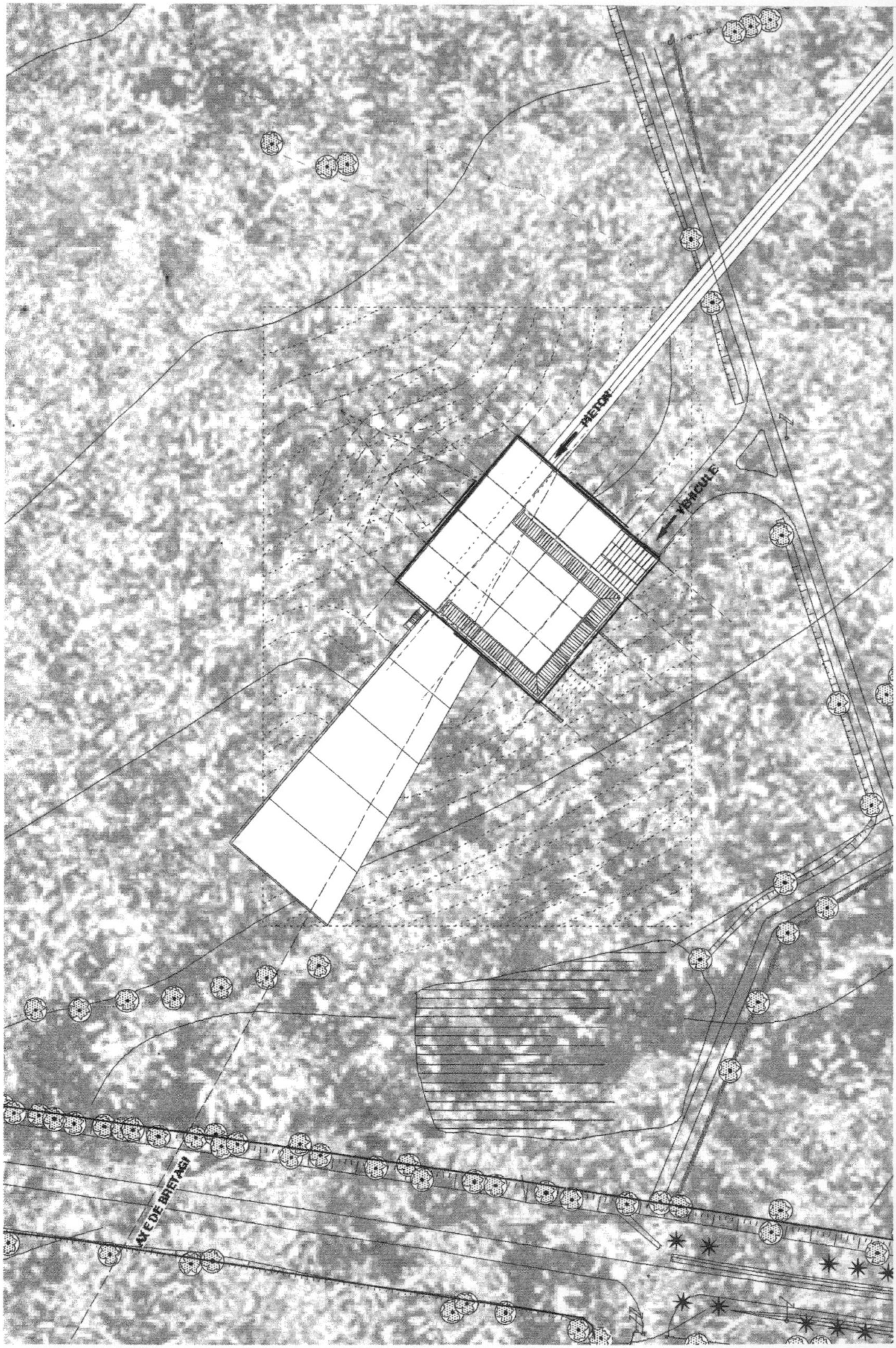
PIETON
VEHICULE

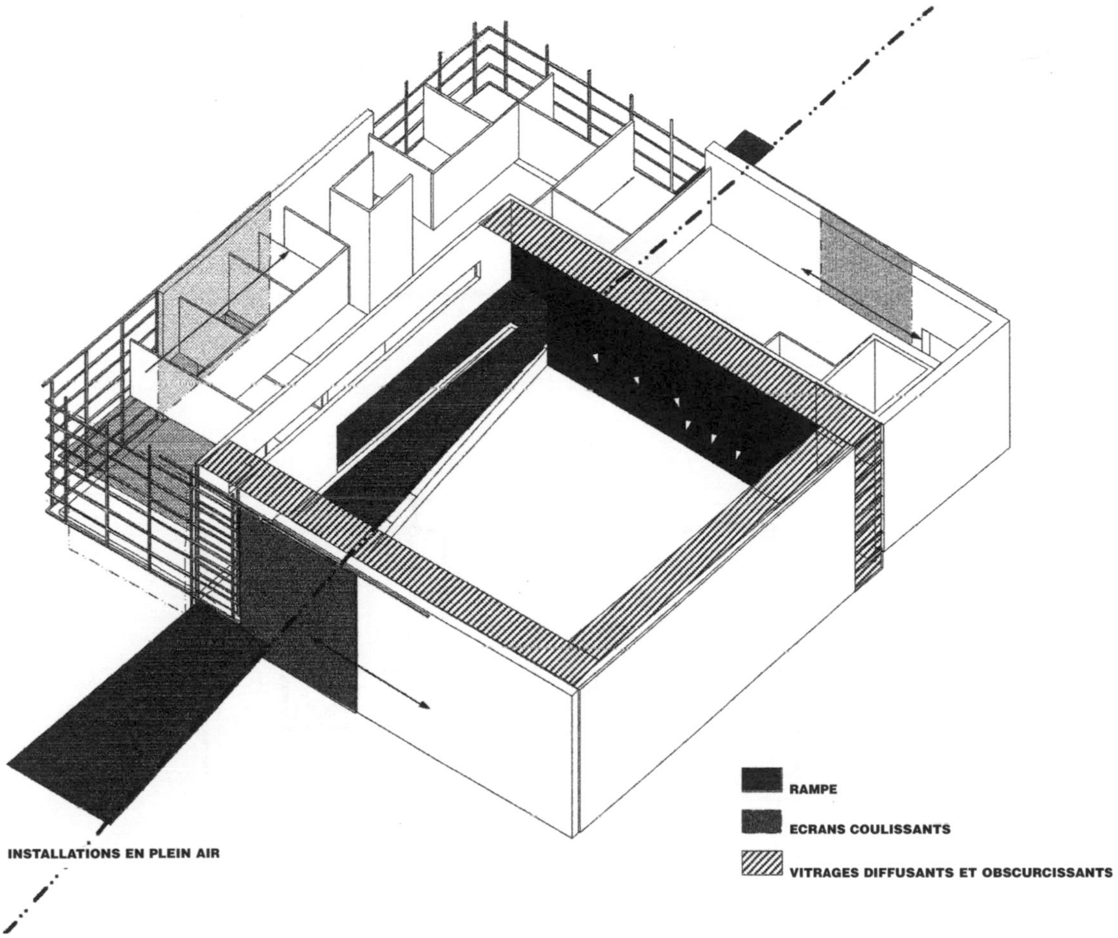

A two-story building around a double-height gallery / performance space:
a ramp engages the site, intersecting the gallery

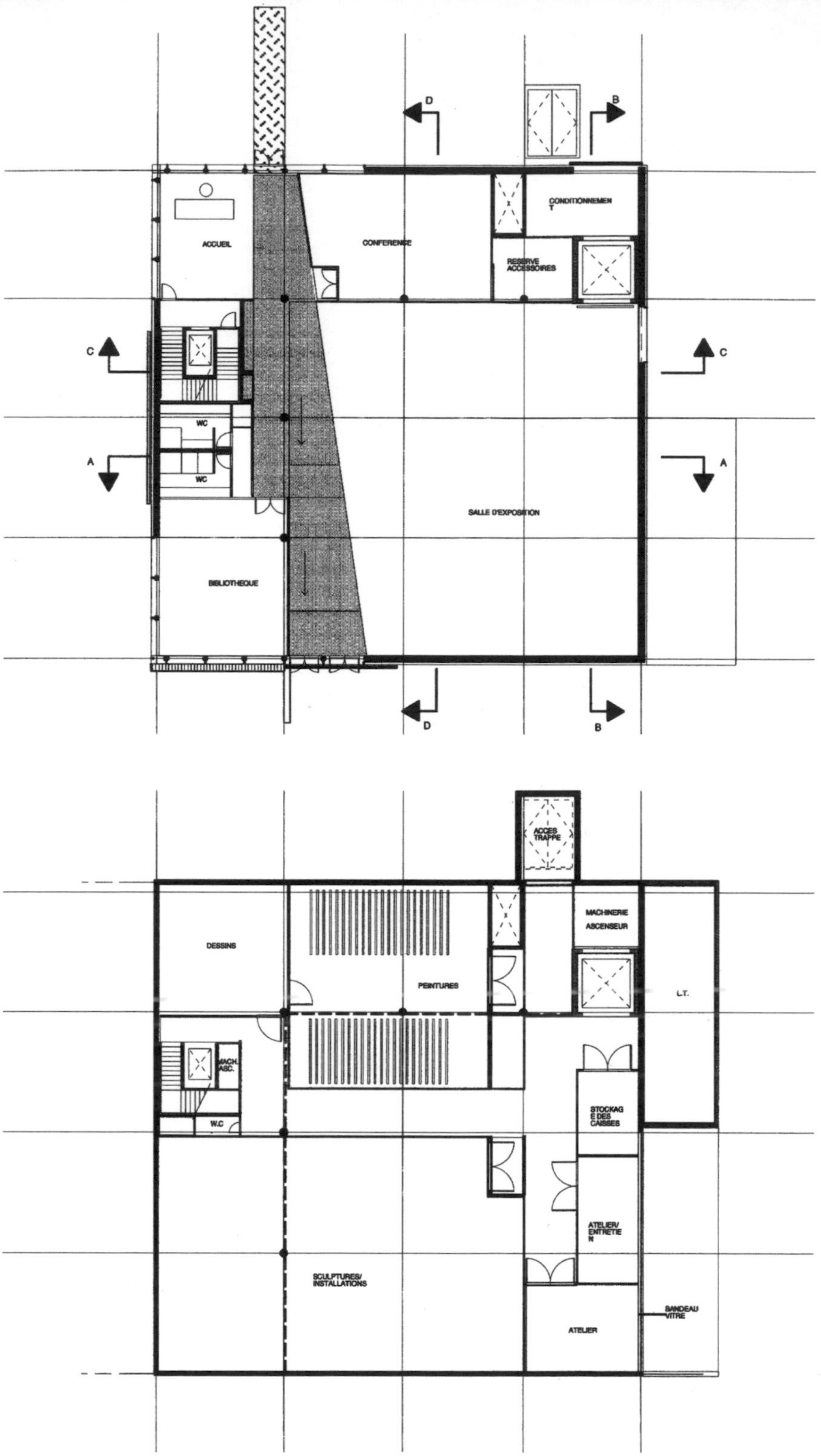

Ground floor plan, basement plan: a simple rectilinear envelope activated by a ramp intersecting it

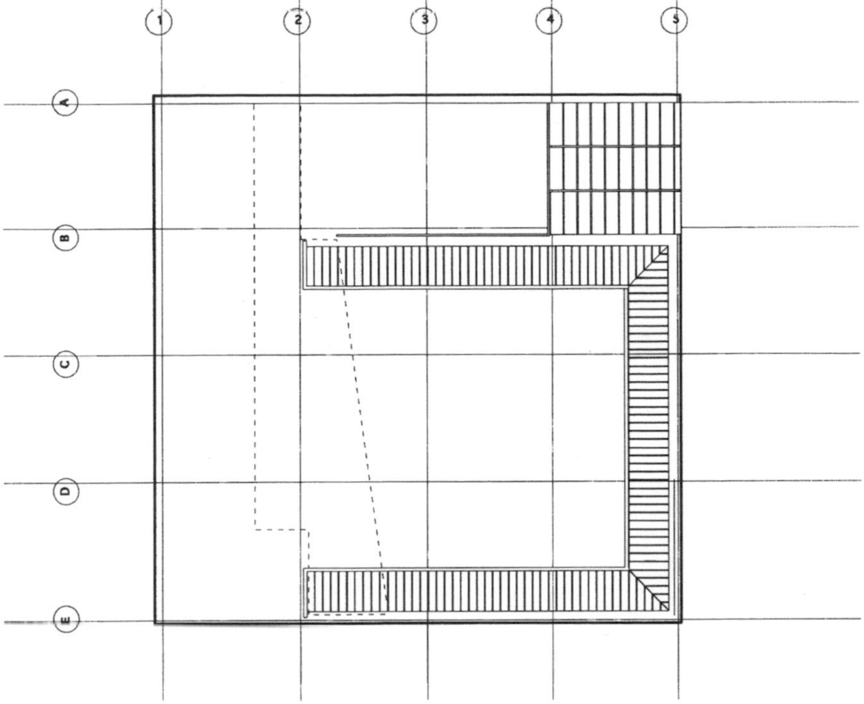

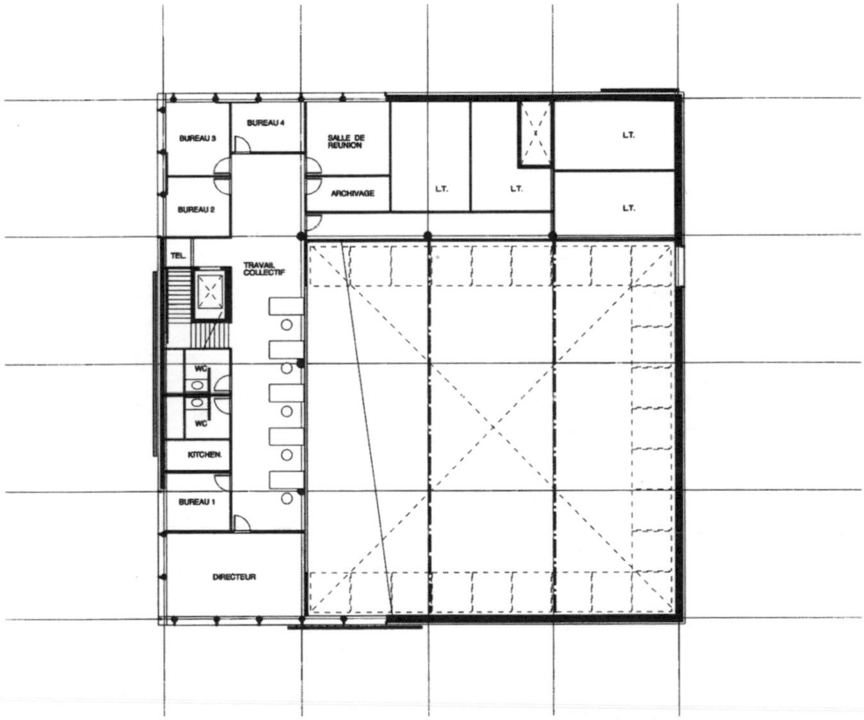

Roof plan, upper level: a simple, large, sky-lit space: no incongruous architectural form here

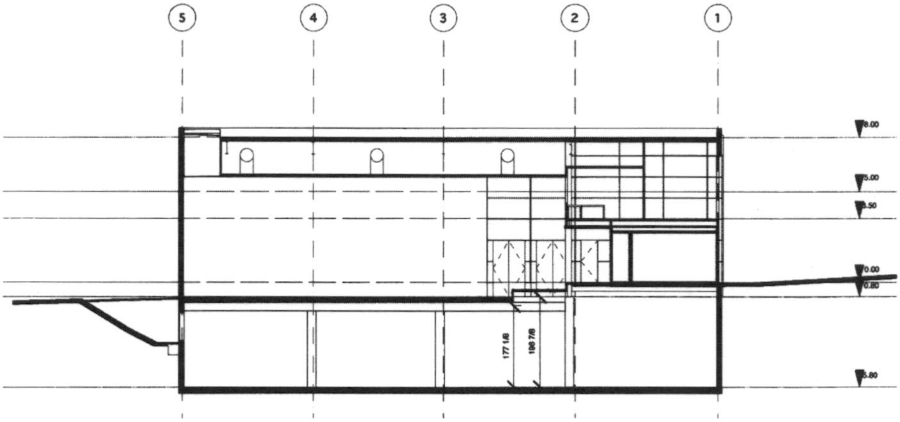

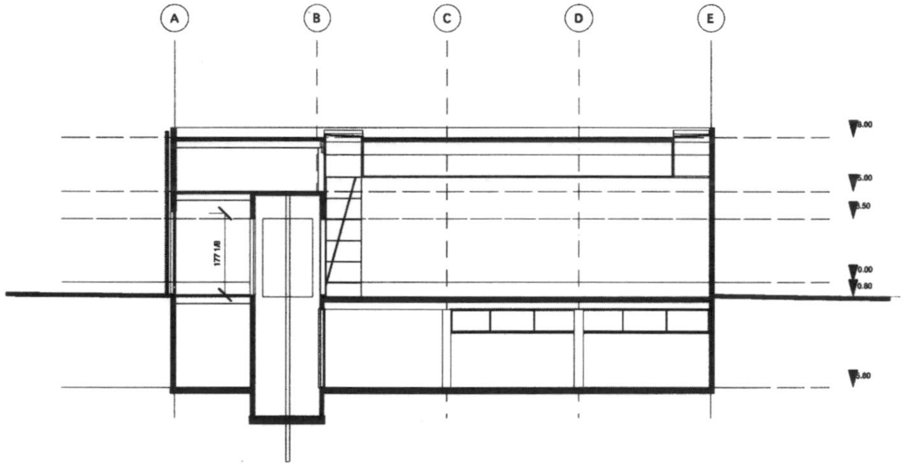

Sections: gallery on main level, administration on mezzanine, storage below ground

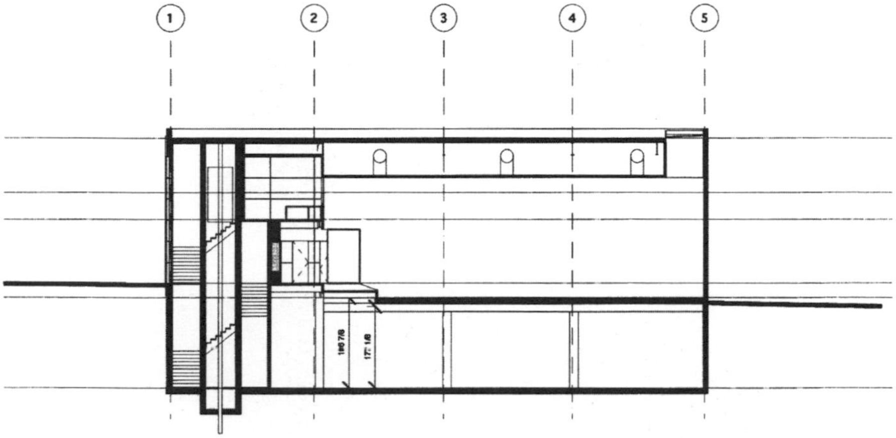
1
2
3
4
5

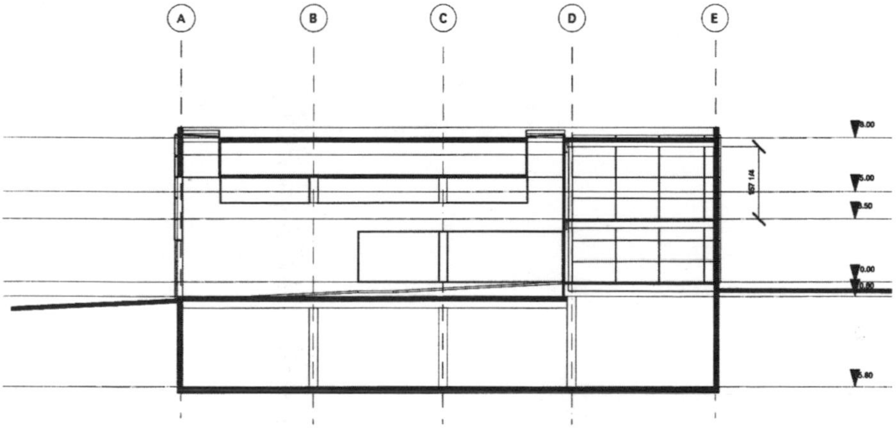
A
B
C
D
E

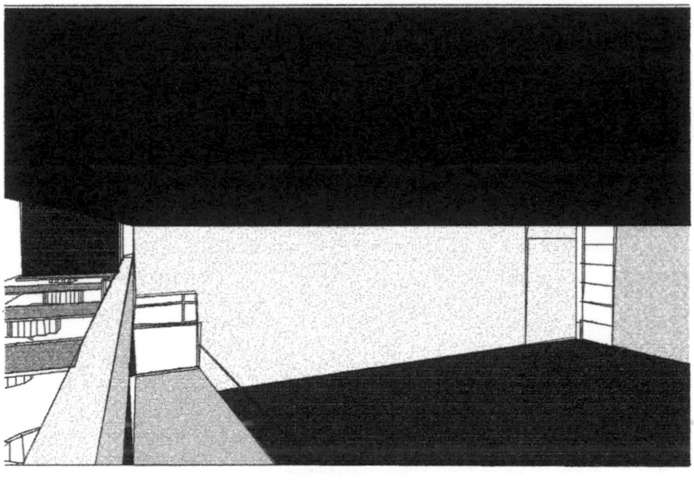

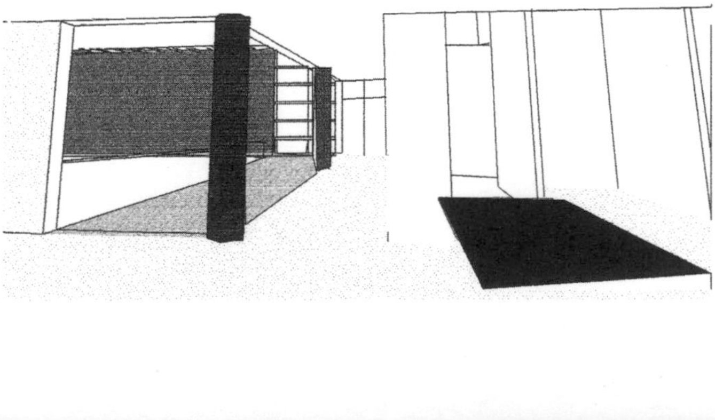

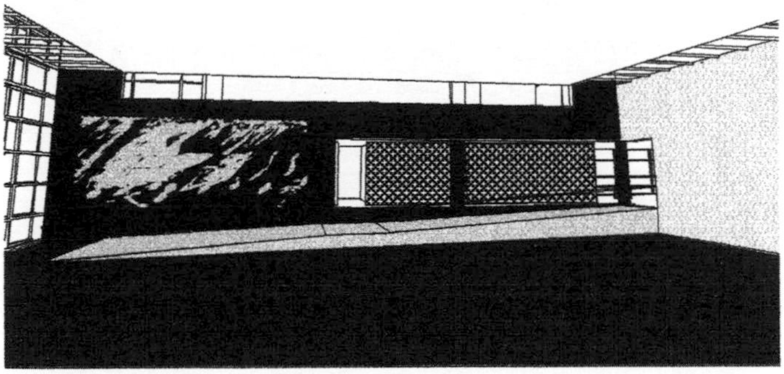

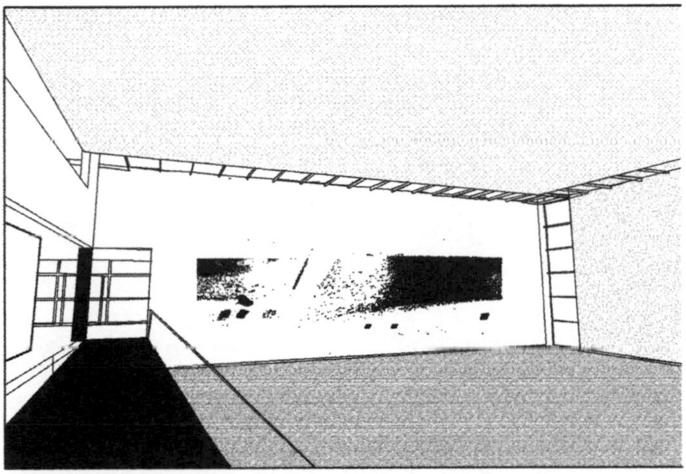

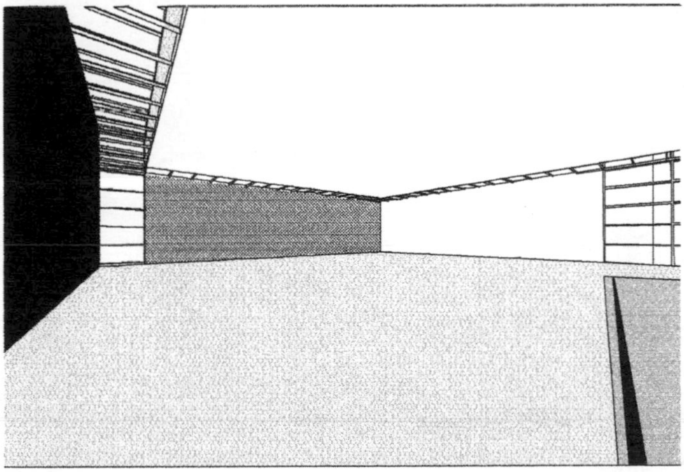

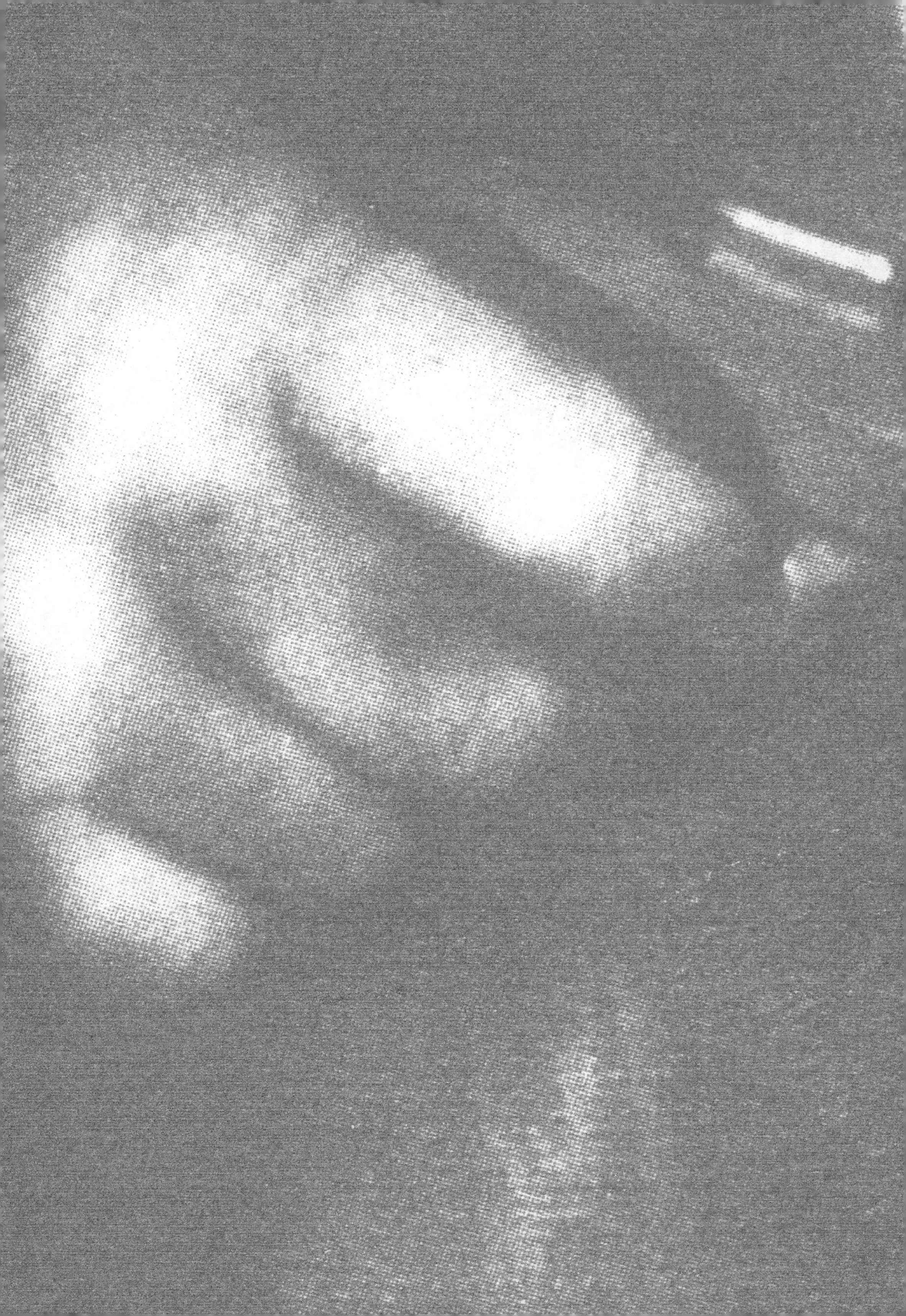

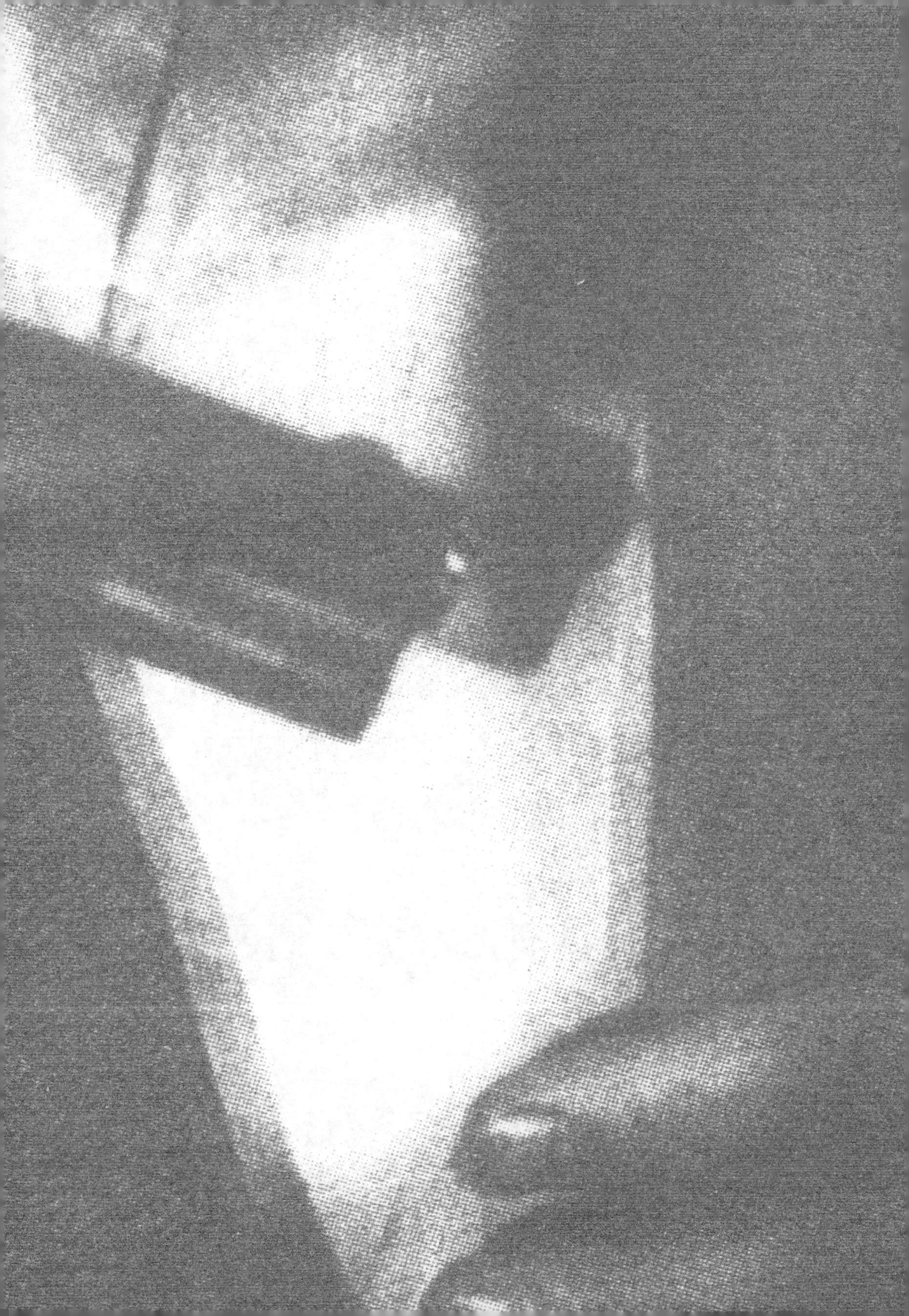

New York, Expansion of The Museum of Modern Art, 1997

Sequence of Voids

A Museum Manifesto (Extracts from the Charrette Phase Submission)

The site of The Museum of Modern Art reproduces a characteristic situation of the world today, in which older metropolises are overbuilt, filled with architectural treasures or buildings of sufficient historical significance not to be demolished. The museum site contains buildings such as the 1939 Goodwin-Stone original building (sentimentally too precious to be demolished); the Museum Tower (economically too valuable to be tampered with); and two Johnson additions of 1954 and 1964, which are historically significant enough to be retained. A beloved garden in their midst further complicates the situation. Moreover, the general massing of new construction on adjacent sites is mostly predetermined by the restrictive zoning regulations in this part of New York City.

This situation necessitates a different approach, a strategy that accounts for existing constraints as well as for new museum needs. This means that at no moment can the expansion be conceived of as a self-sufficient totality, but that each part will function fully only in conjunction with another, older or newer part, and will be slightly off-balance alone. Moreover, the existing site conditions rule against starting from the outside—from platonic or ideal volumes (cube, prism, cylinder, etc.)—and in favor of starting from the inside, carving a series of interior spaces that would be somewhat like an outside, but inside. In this interior city, the elevations would reveal the logic of the interior route rather than following esthetic compositional rules.

A crucial dimension is the concept of carving spaces into a solid. The solid would be made out of the existing buildings and notional envelopes defined by zoning regulations. The carved spaces would trace an urban route with "streets" and "squares" or "plazas" linking the exhibition spaces and functions, describing one or multiple paths through the museum. The building would be somewhat like a city carved into a mass of solid matter, with careful filtering and distribution of light into the core.

This strategy of carving interior spaces into the mass of the existing and of the zoning envelope puts pressure on the exterior envelope of the new museum and its appearance. Thus, the facades must express the underlying logic of the museum while simultaneously presenting those aspects of the older structure that are foundational for the newly-defined complex. The elevations, therefore, provide an overall reading of the museum as well as a specific reading of its architectural history, providing a distinctive image of the new in the museum's impact on the urban fabric and on artistic practice.

The spatial organization of the new MoMA reflects our view that architectural considerations are never independent of urban circumstances, and that the internal logic of a building must respond to its external conditions. In order to reflect its own "historicity"—the unique texture of time and culture that distinguishes its period and needs from others—the new MoMA may have to introduce a new form of museum by reversing conventional a priori. We therefore propose three reversals that, together, constitute an operative concept rather than an arrangement of arbitrary forms:

First reversal: The museum is not conceived as a sculptural object, but as an interior city or route. Its exterior form must be derived from and expressive of its interior dimensions. Moreover, the route is not a linear sequence with a fixed beginning, middle, and end, but a multiple sequence that can be accessed or departed from at many points.

Second reversal: The new Museum of Modern Art is not a unitary totality, but a heterotopia. It combines three distinct types on its site: a received type, the 25-foot-square column grid and double bay of the historical MoMA, for its departments; a borrowed type, the columnless factory type, for its temporary exhibitions; a new type, our proposal for fixed spaces, variable spaces, and interspaces, for the permanent collection.

Third reversal: The third reversal is strategic rather than constructed. It is about architecture as strategy as much as architecture about form. The constraints of the site, program, and zoning regulations are such that imposing a simple external model onto it would be a losing proposition. A different strategy is necessary, akin to Judo, in which the forces of the opponent are used to one's advantage. The site conditions, historical and artistic heterogeneity of the museum, and the demands of new art are productive forces, requiring a reversal of architectural conventions.

Together, these three reversals introduce a new model for, and approach to, the urban museum in the 21st century.

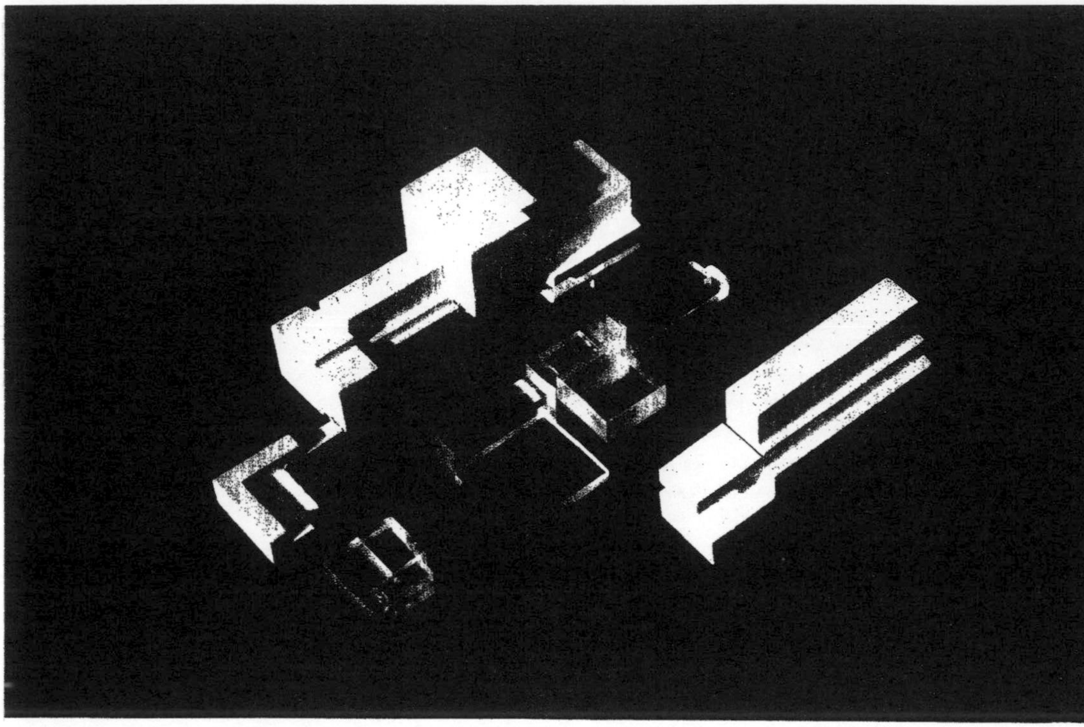

Museum Sequences. The Garden and the Courts
Interlocking solids & voids, old & new.

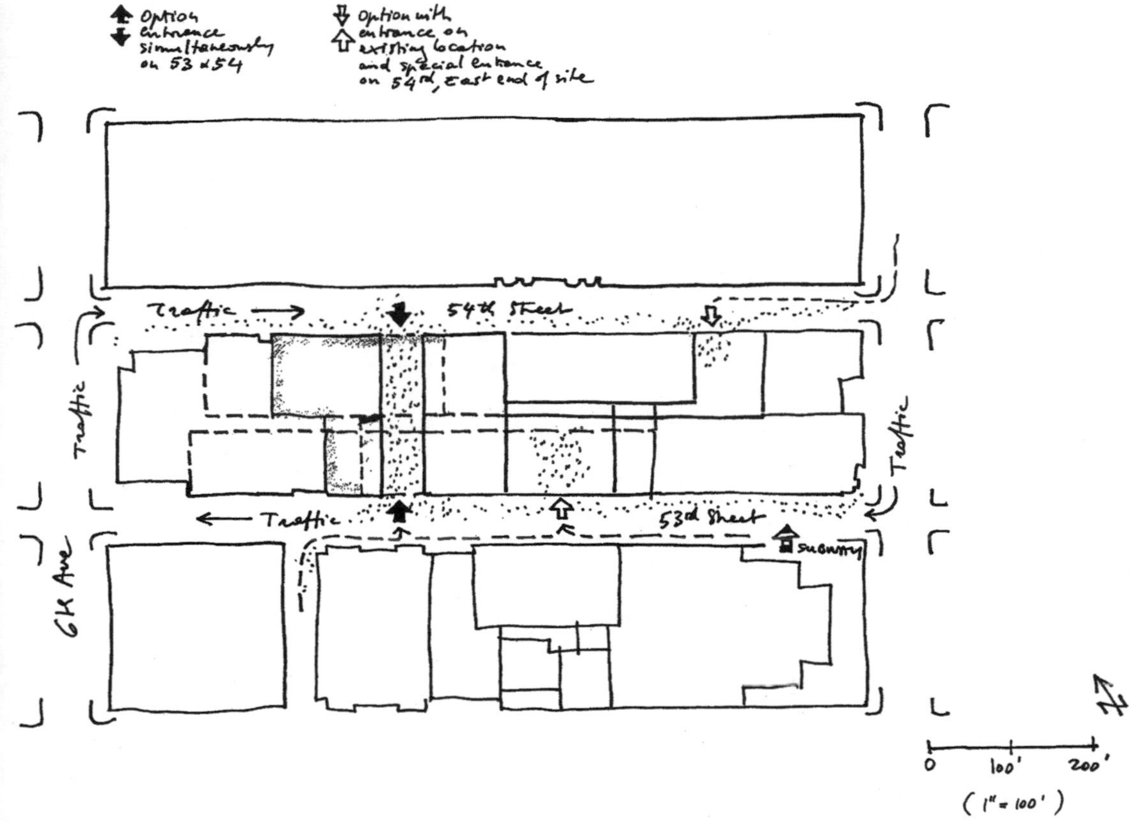
Option entrance simultaneously on 53 & 54
Option with entrance on existing location and special entrance on 54th, East end of site
Traffic
54th Street
Traffic
Traffic
Traffic
53rd Street
subway
6th Ave
0
100'
200'
(1" = 100')

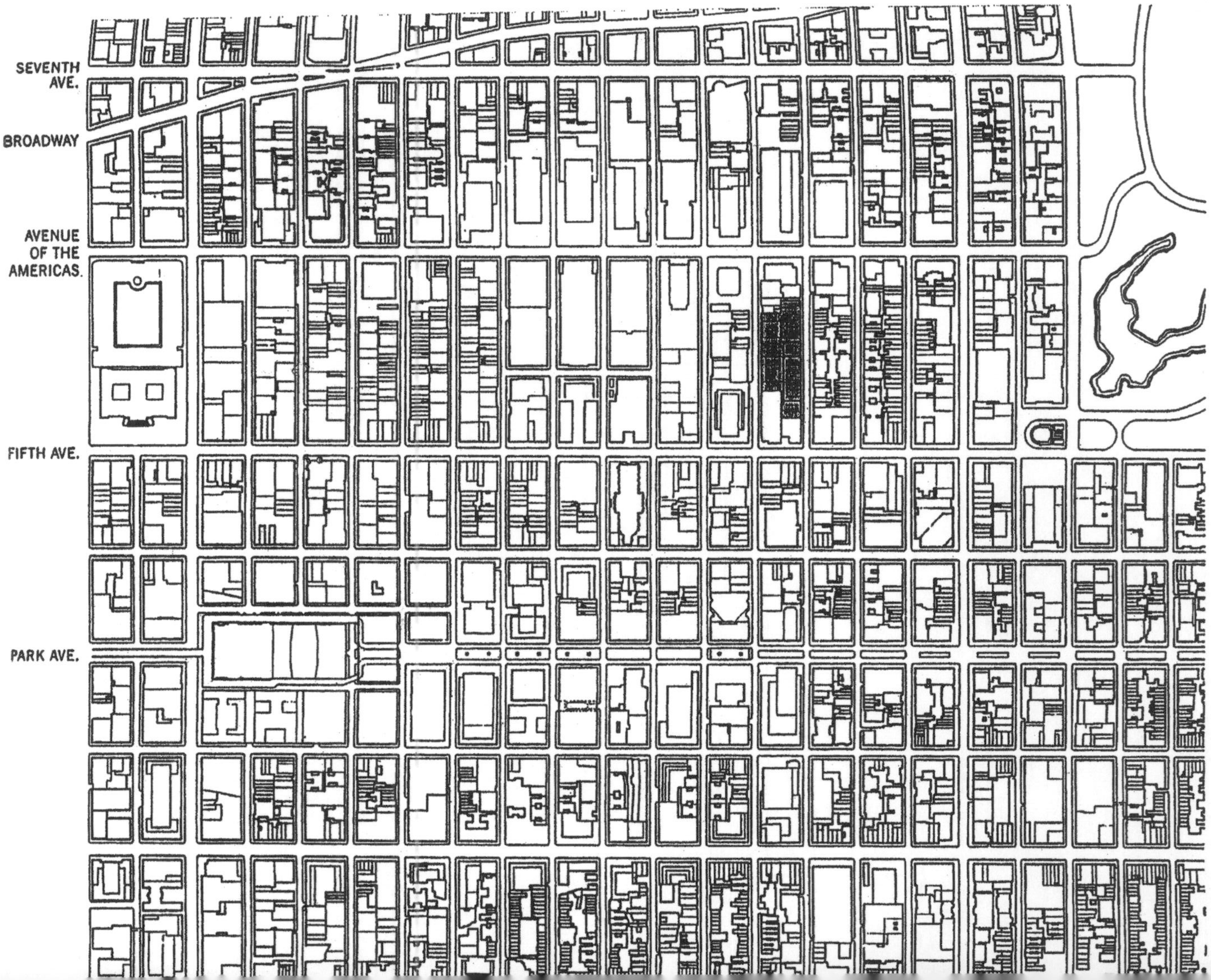
SEVENTH AVE.
BROADWAY
AVENUE OF THE AMERICAS.
FIFTH AVE.
PARK AVE.

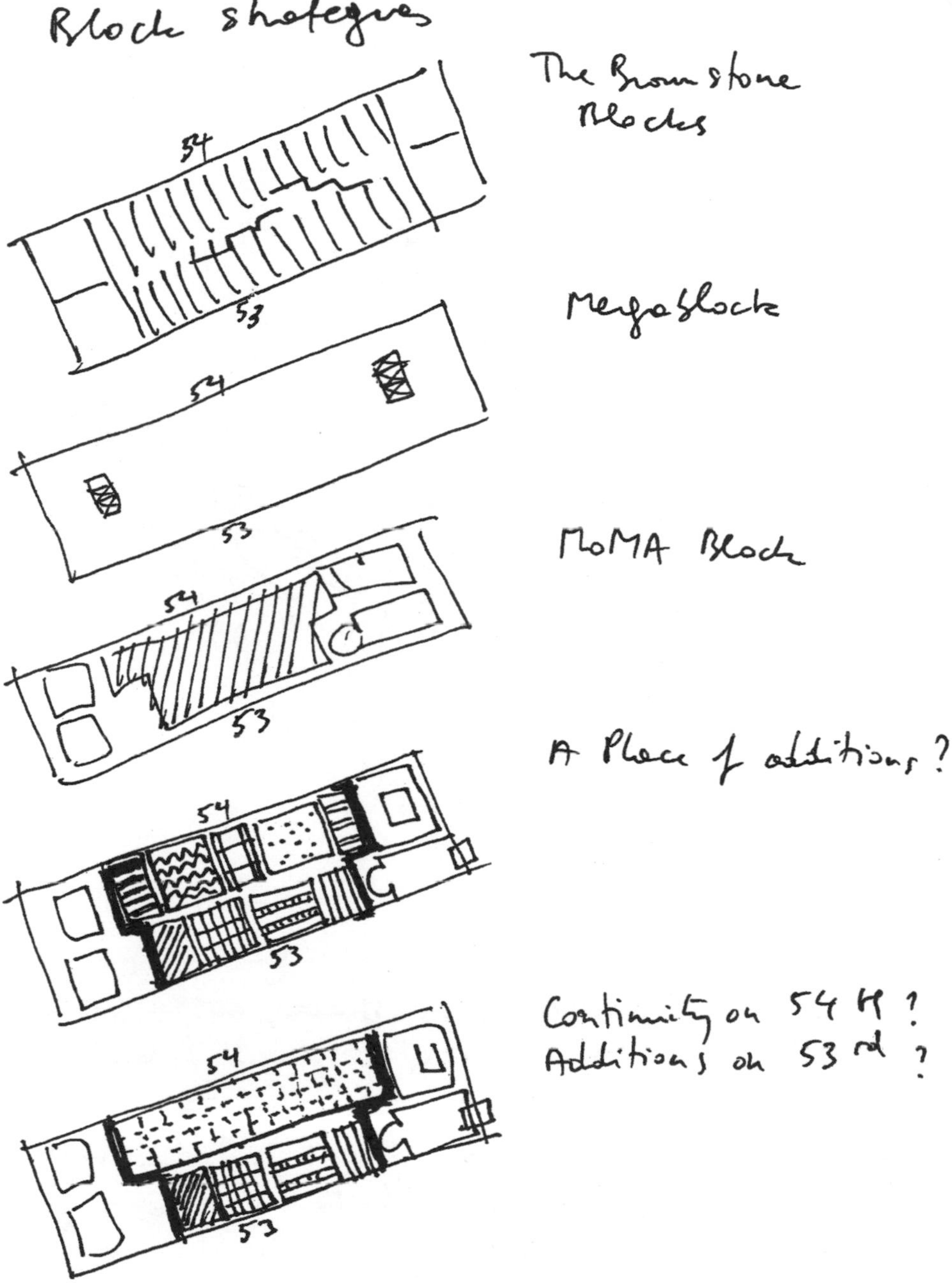
Block strategies
The Brownstone Blocks
54
53
Megablock
54
53
MoMA Block
54
53
A Place of additions?
54
53
Continuity on 54 st?
Additions on 53rd?
54
53

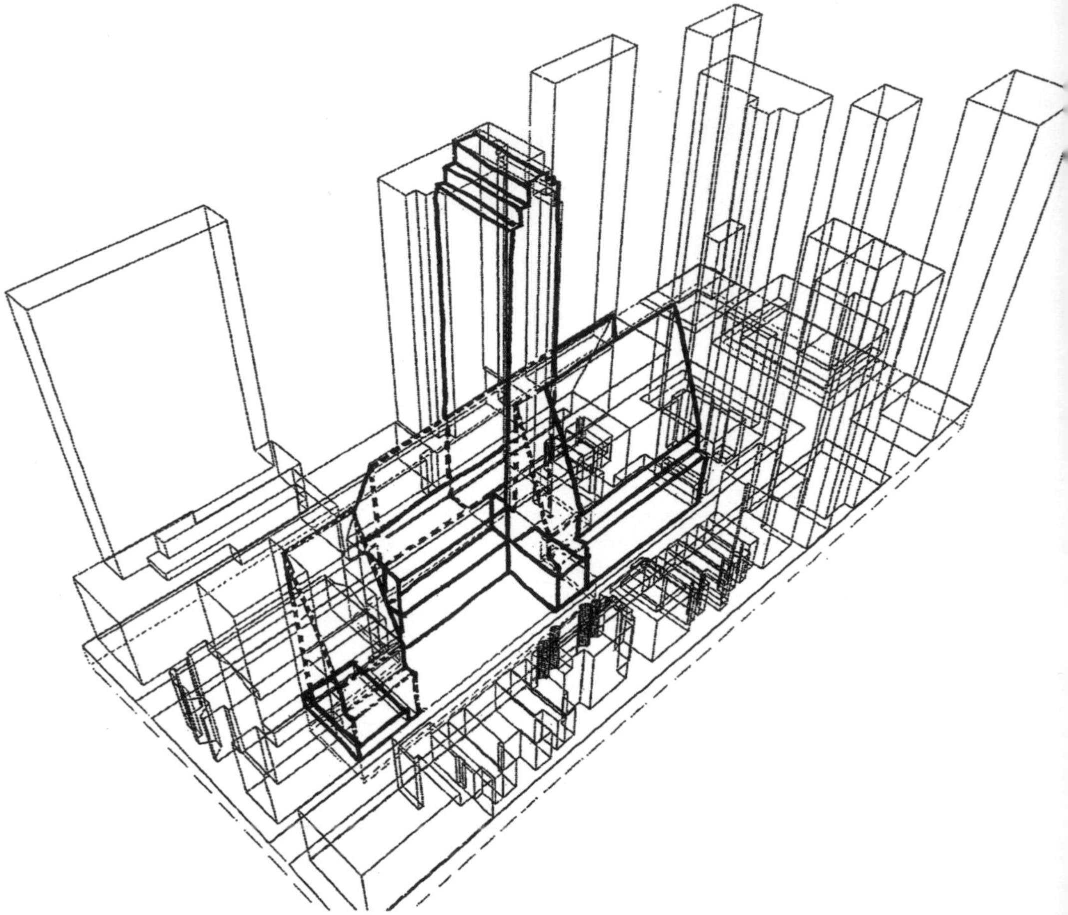

A paradox: intimacy of art spaces, as in brownstones - yet MoMA's growth inevitably displaces brownstones, and that particular definition of intimacy
Another paradox: planning the ideal museum, within the vagaries of historical precedents and erratic zoning envelopes.

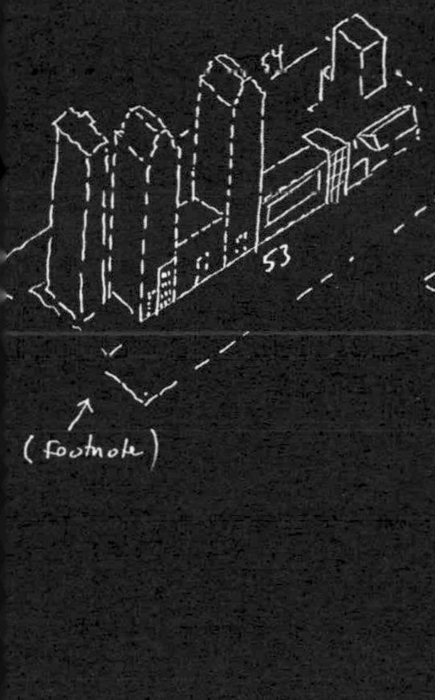

(footnote)

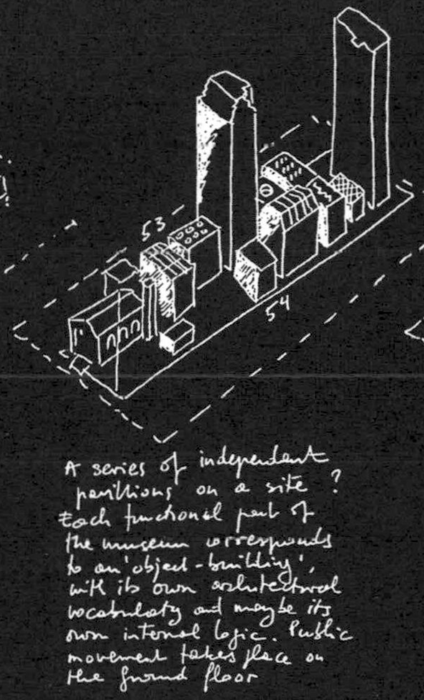

A series of independent pavilions on a site? Each functional part of the museum corresponds to an 'object-building', with its own architectural vocabulary and maybe its own internal logic. Public movement takes place on the ground floor

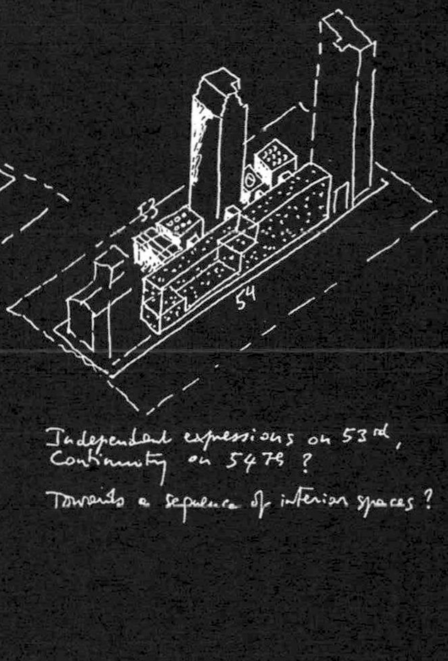

Independent expressions on 53rd, Continuity on 54th?

Towards a sequence of interior spaces?

2/11

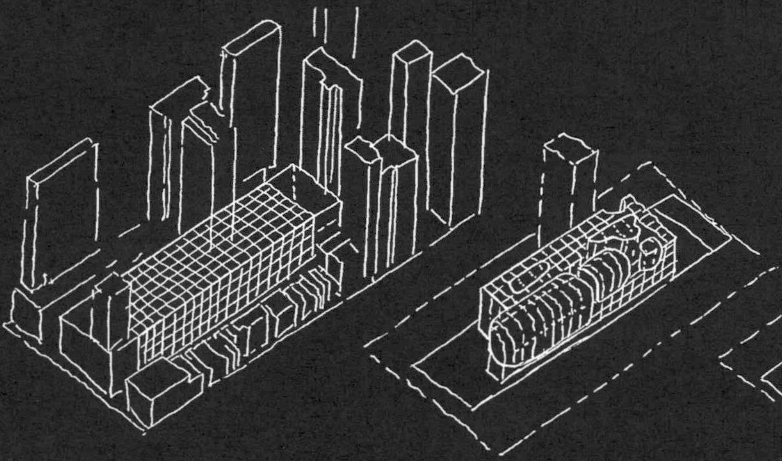

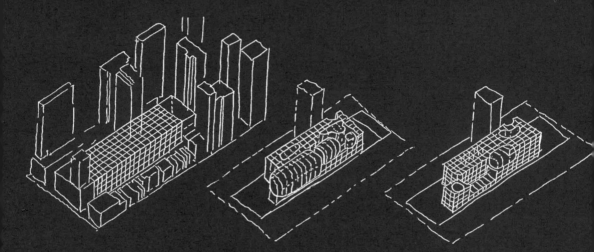

City of voids: within a solid mass made of undifferentiated floors, a number of voids are cut and become major indoor or outdoor spaces.

2/11

Spaces and flows:

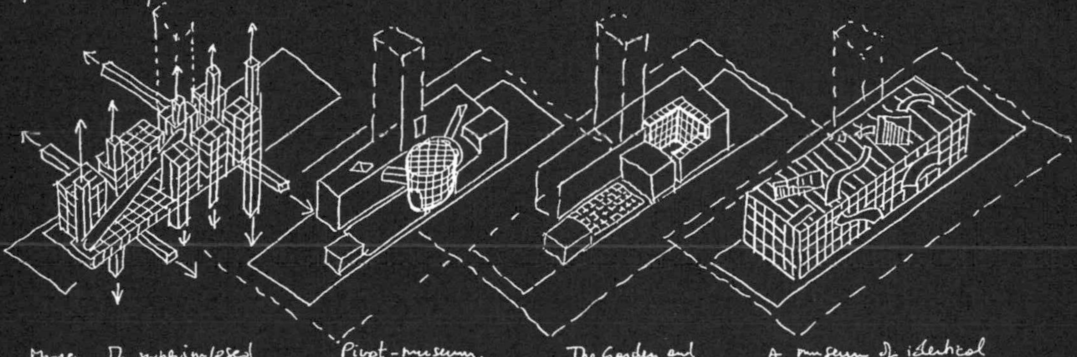

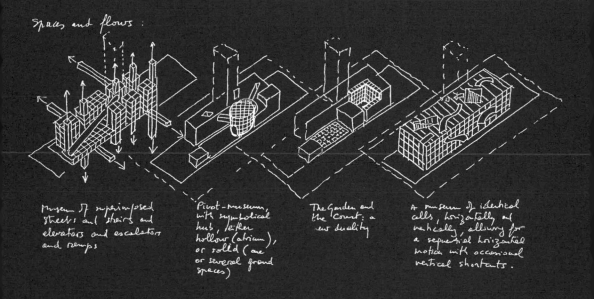

Museum of superimposed streets and stairs and elevators and escalators and ramps

Pivot-museum, with symbolical hub, either hollow (atrium), or solid (one or several grand spaces)

The Garden and the Court: a new duality

A museum of identical cells, horizontally and vertically, allowing for a sequential horizontal motion with occasional vertical shortcuts.

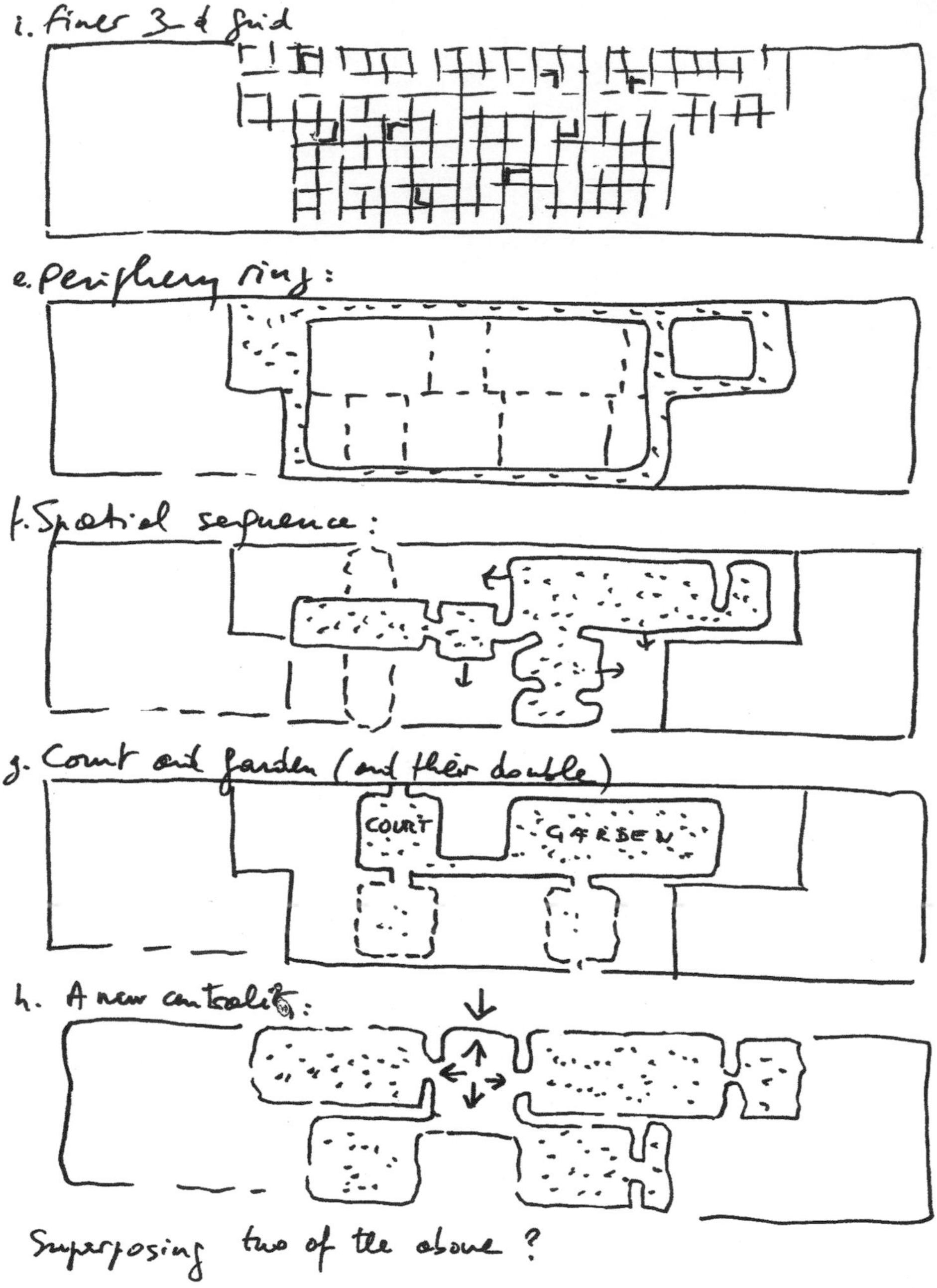

Local zoning constraints must be taken advantage of: practically all architectural interventions will be internal, carving into the mass

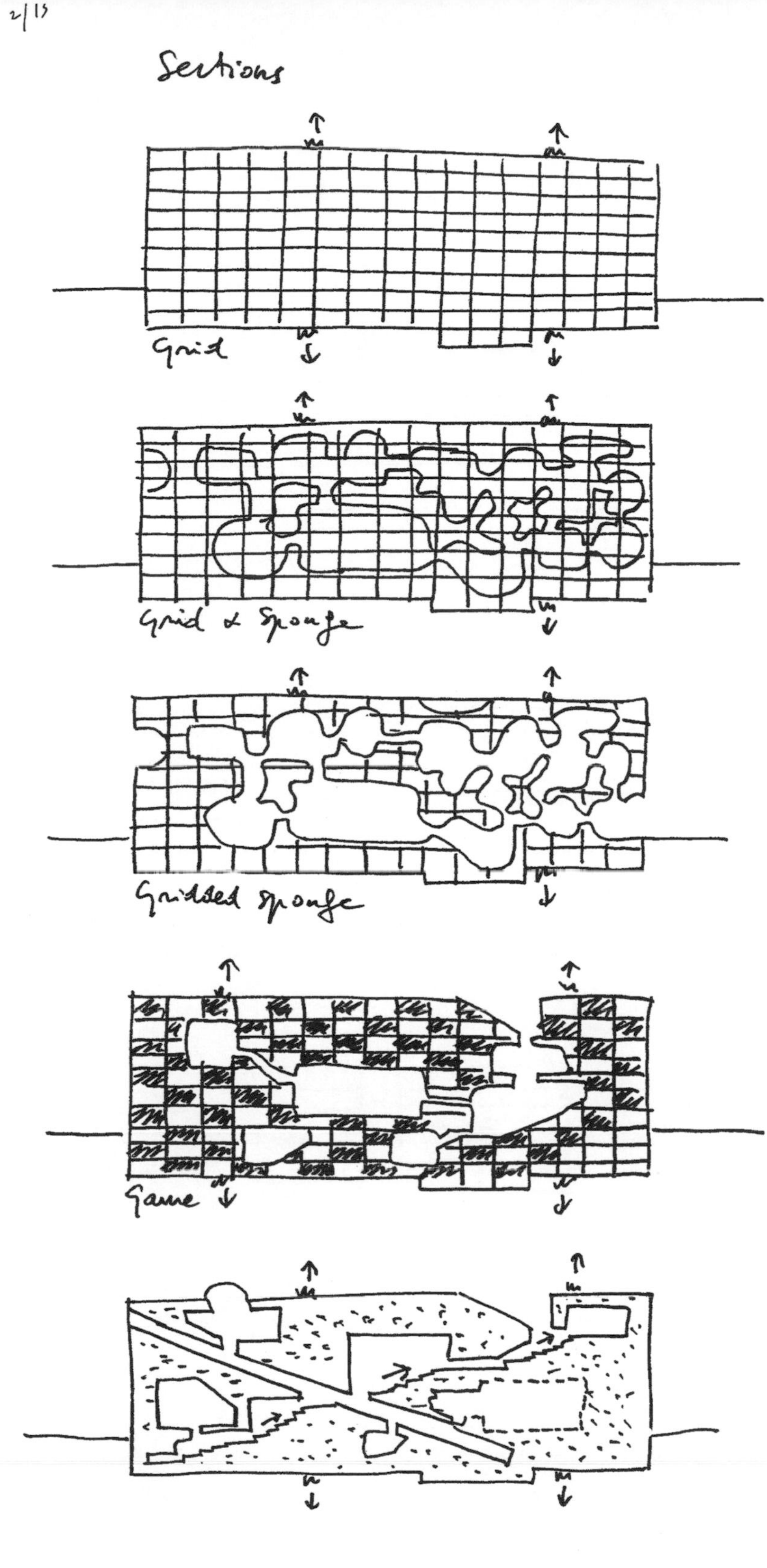
2/15
Sections
Grid
Grid & Sponge
Gridded Sponge
Game

v|13

Layers

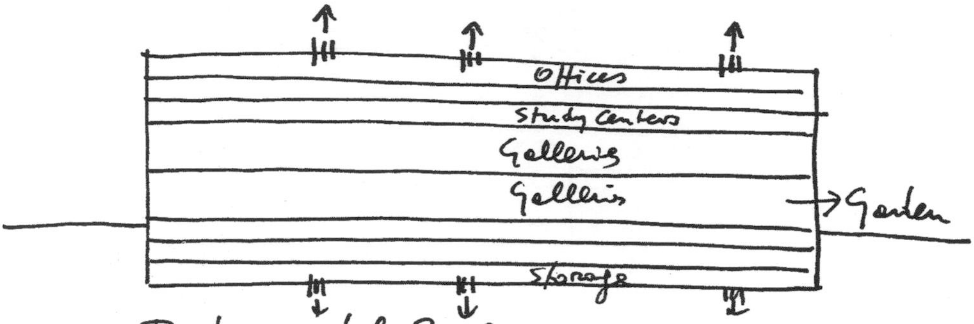

The Horizontal Museum

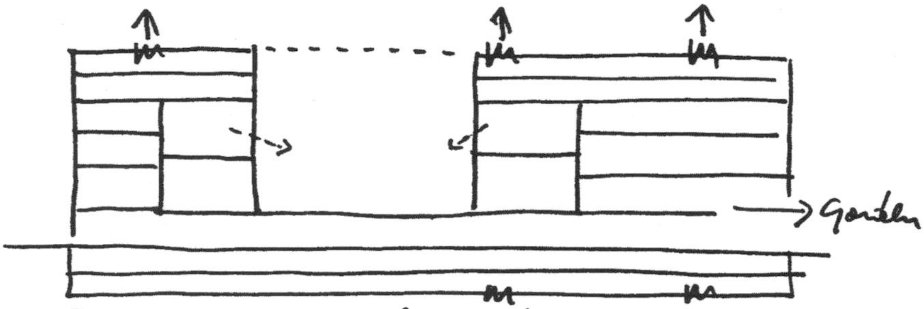

The Atrium or Single Court Museum

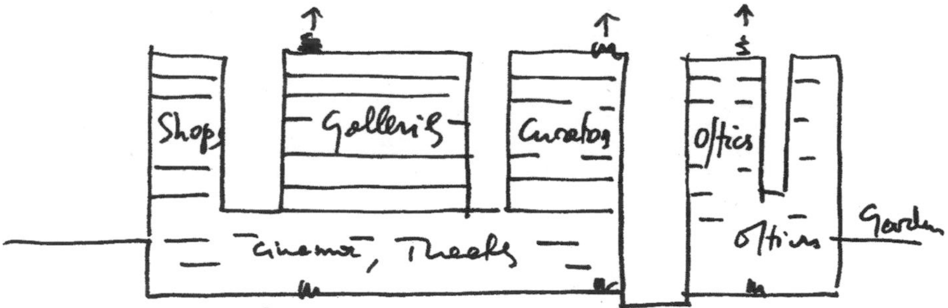

The vertical (and segregated) Museum

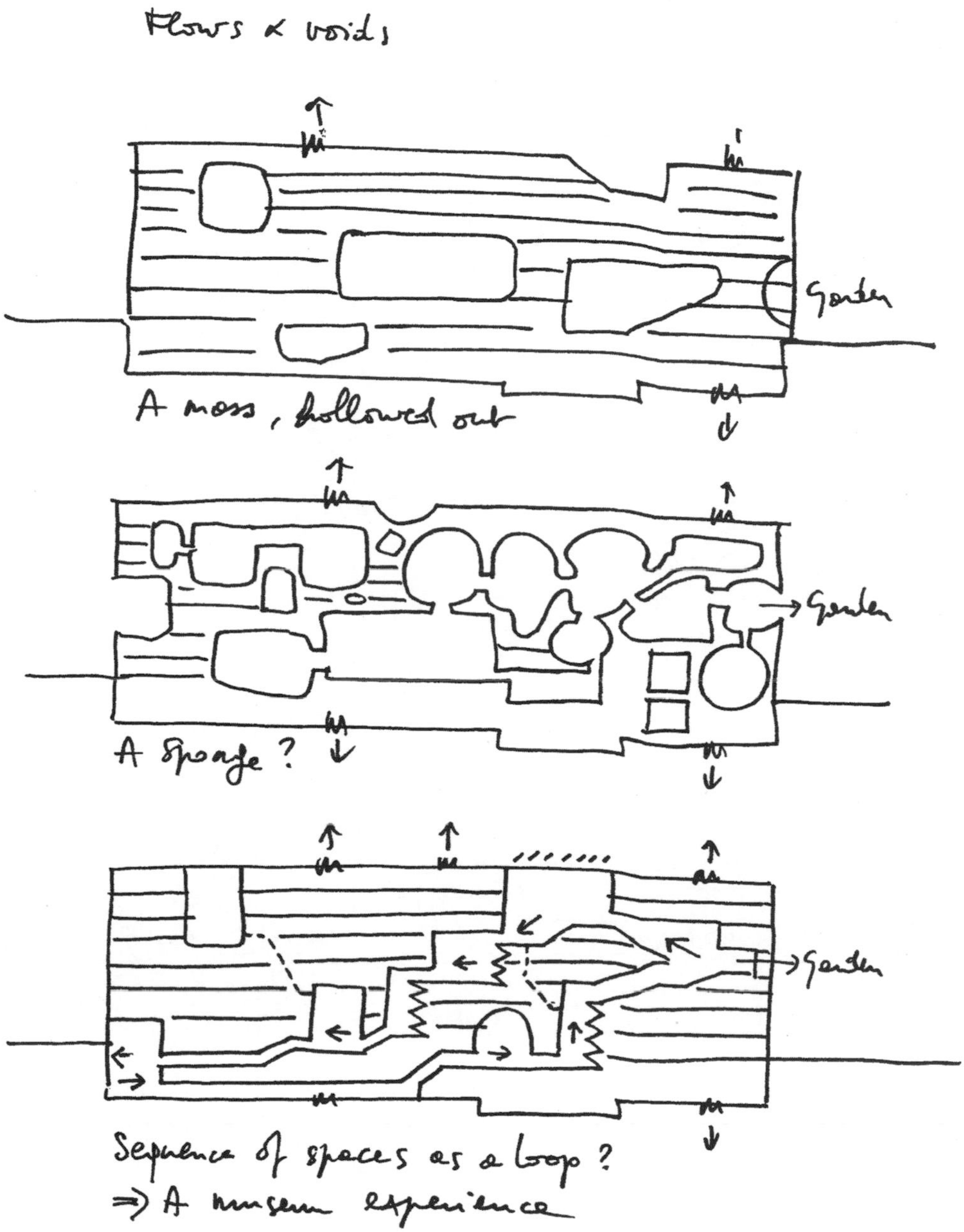
Flows & voids
Garden
A mass, hollowed out
Garden
A sponge?
Garden
Sequence of spaces as a loop?
⇒ A museum experience

2/25

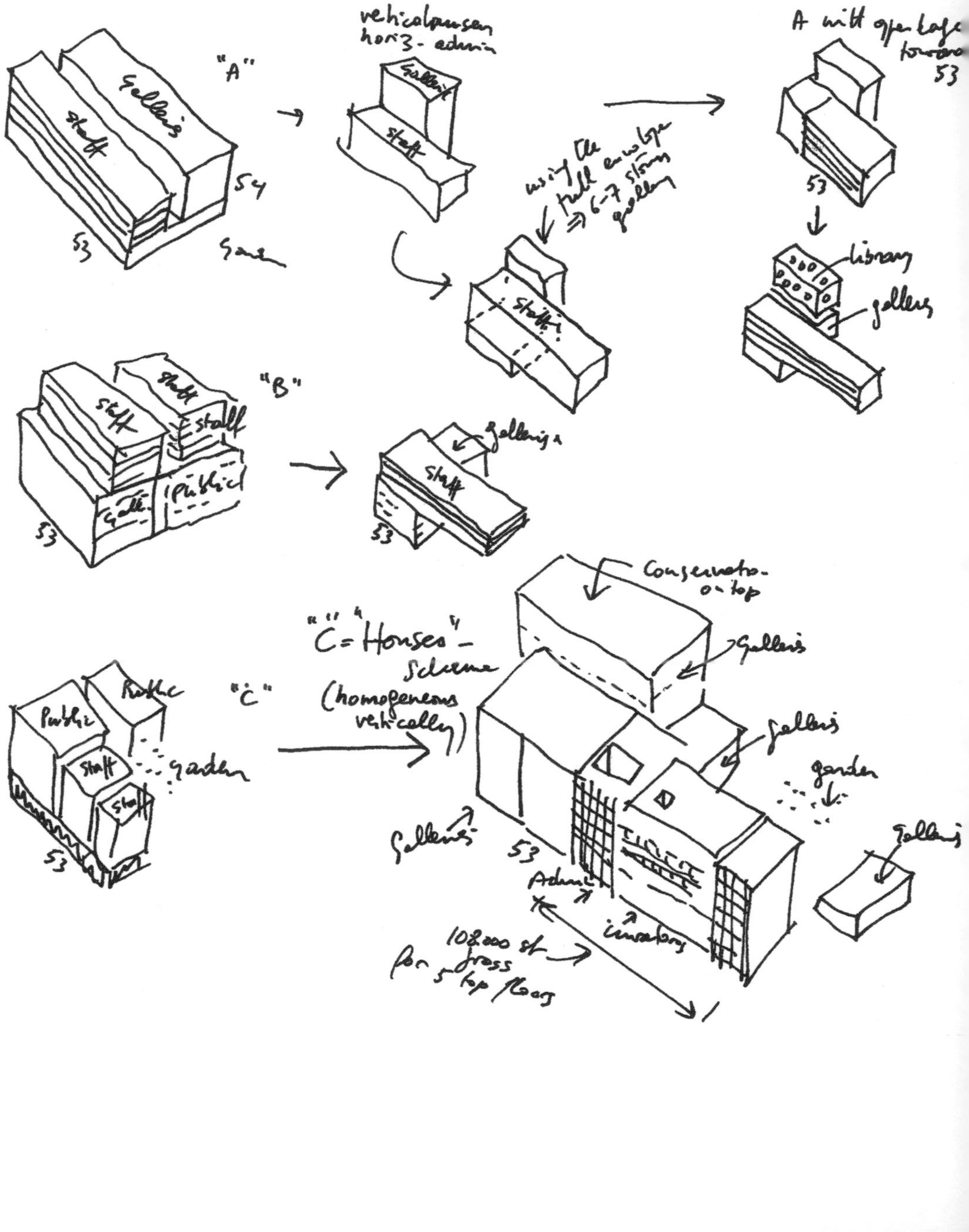
"A"
Staff
54
53
"B"
staff
Public
53
library
gallery
"C"
Public
Staff
garden
Conservator on top
Galleries
Admin
elevators
108,000 sf gross for 5 top floors

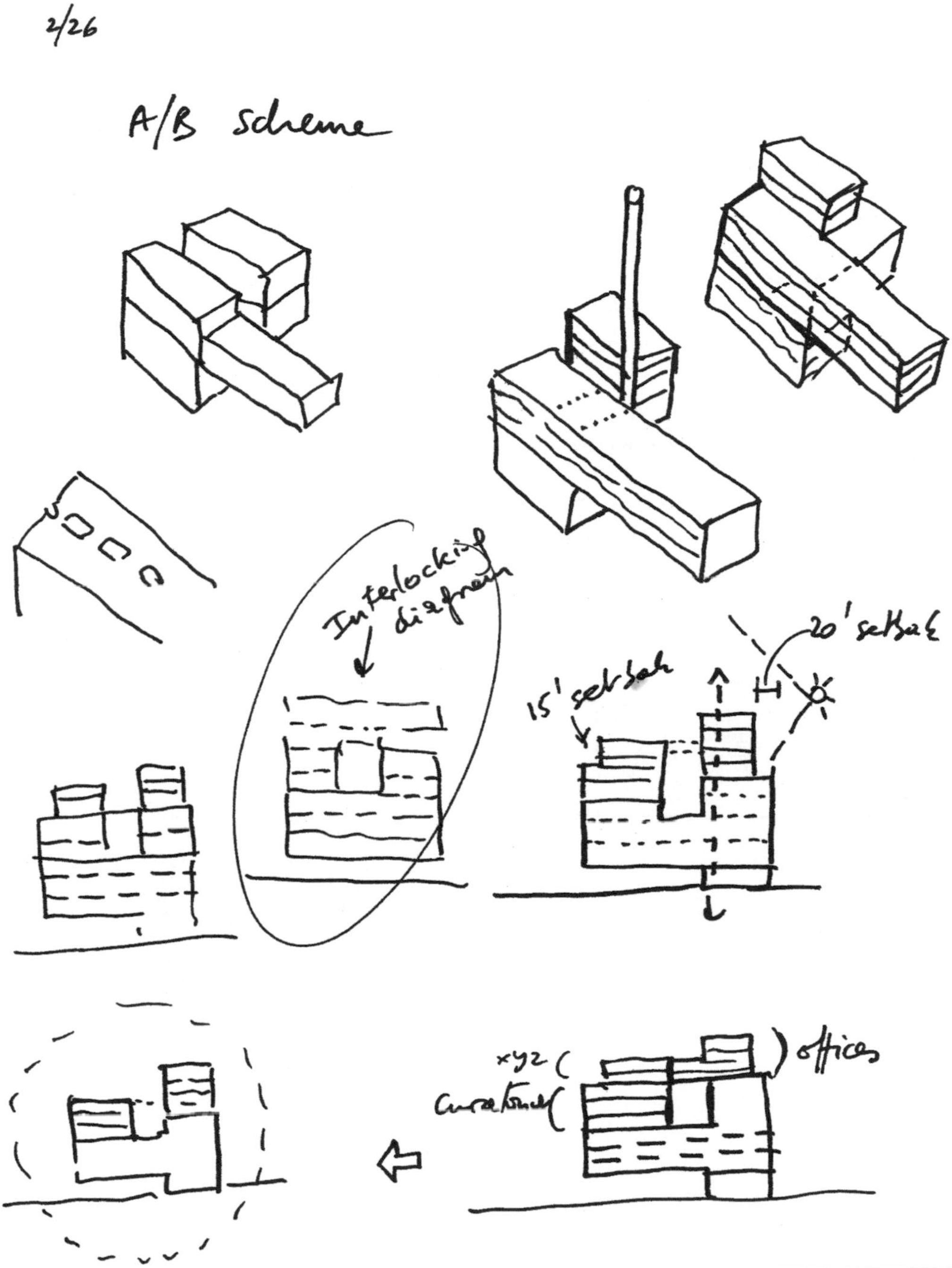
2/26
A/B scheme
Interlocking diagram
15' setback
20' setback
xyz (
Curator
) offices

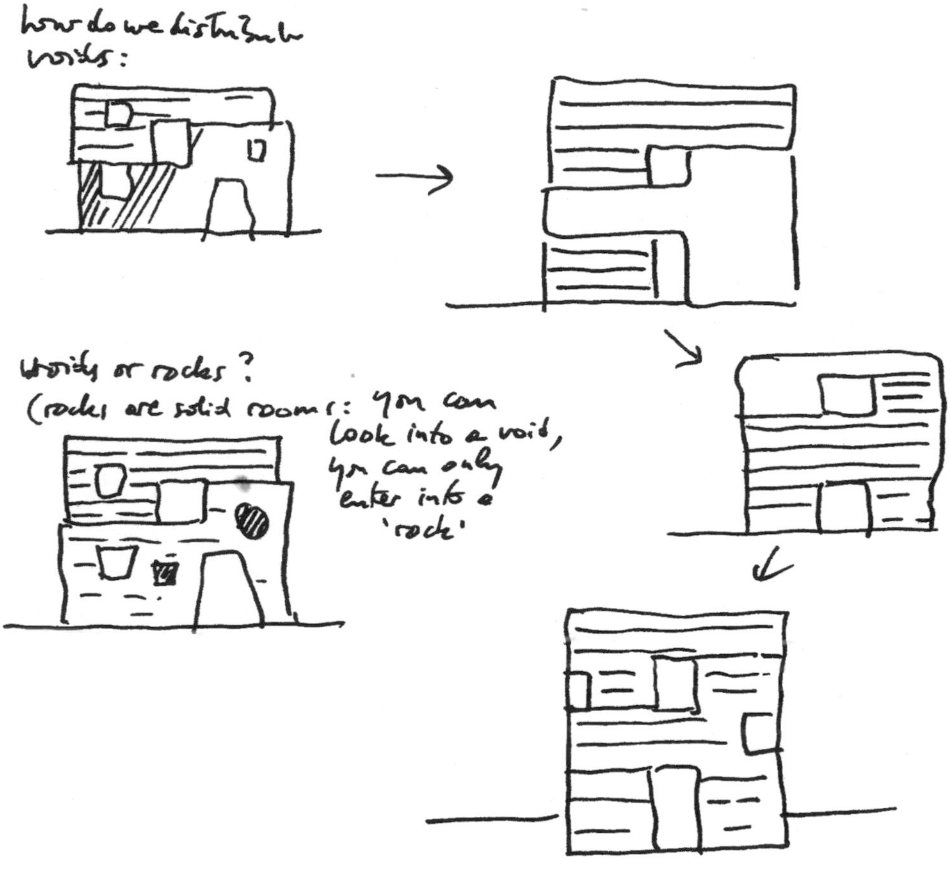
how do we distribute
voids:
voids or rocks ?
(rocks are solid rooms: you can
look into a void,
you can only
enter into a
'rock'

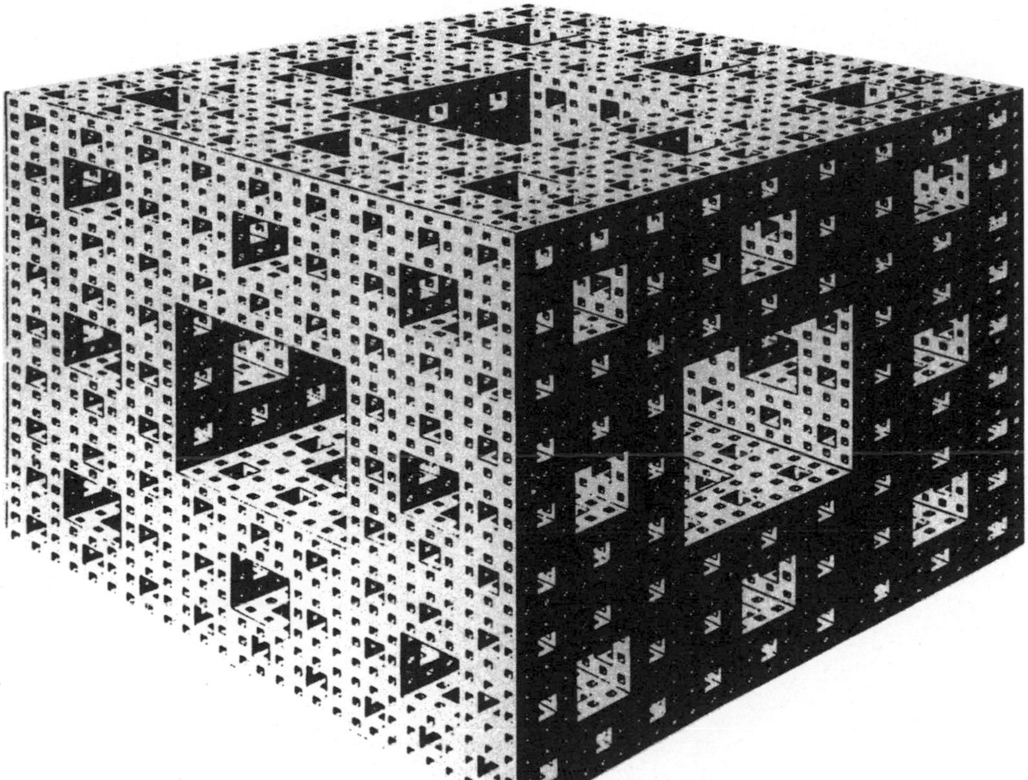

Menger sponge (Sierpensky's sponge): the spatial organization of the museum should not be a spine, but rather a sponge

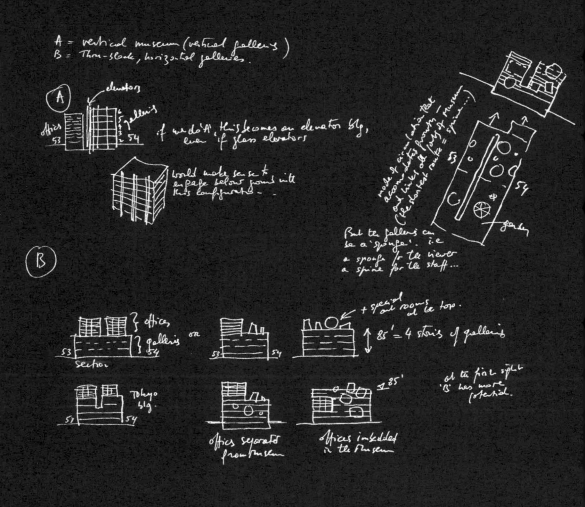

A = vertical museum (vertical galleries)
B = Three-stack, horizontal galleries.

if we do 'A', this becomes an elevator blg, even if glass elevators

would make sense to engage below ground with this configuration – –

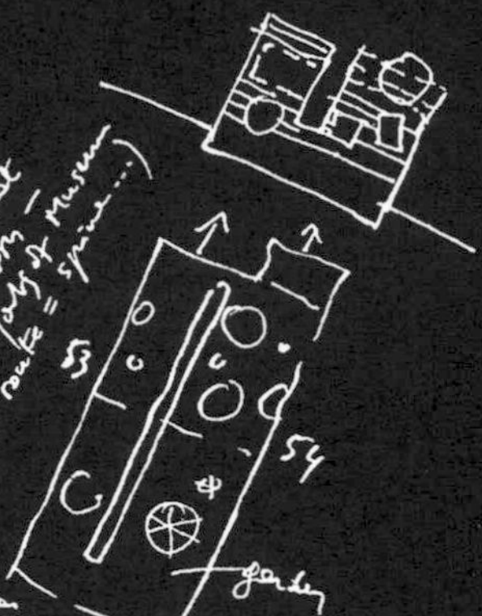

mode of circulation that accommodates growth — and links all parts of museum (the shortest route = spine ...)

But the galleries can be a 'sponge'. i.e
a sponge for the viewer
a spine for the staff ...

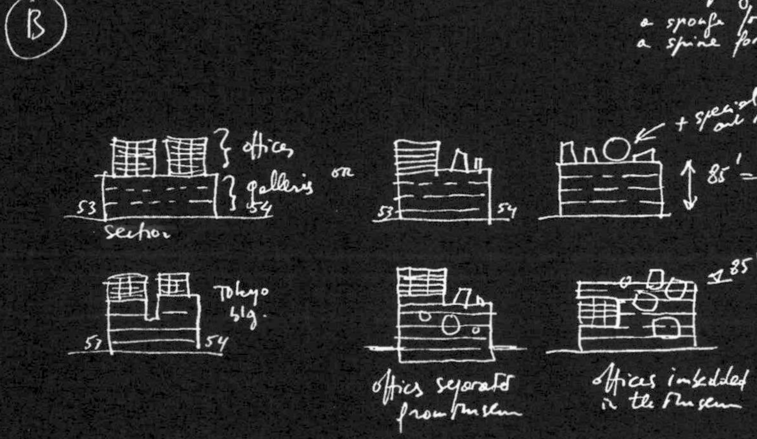

at the first sight 'B' has more potential.

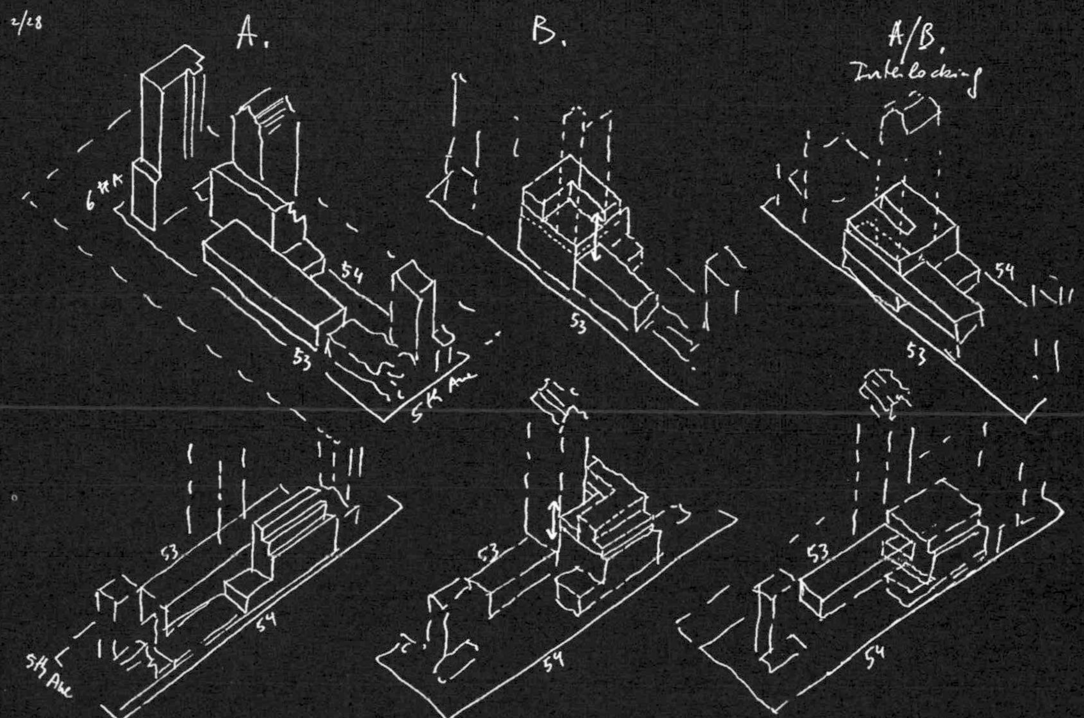
2/28
A.
B.
A/B.
Interlocking
6th A
54
53
5th Ave
53
54
53
54
53
54
53
54
5th Ave

2/28

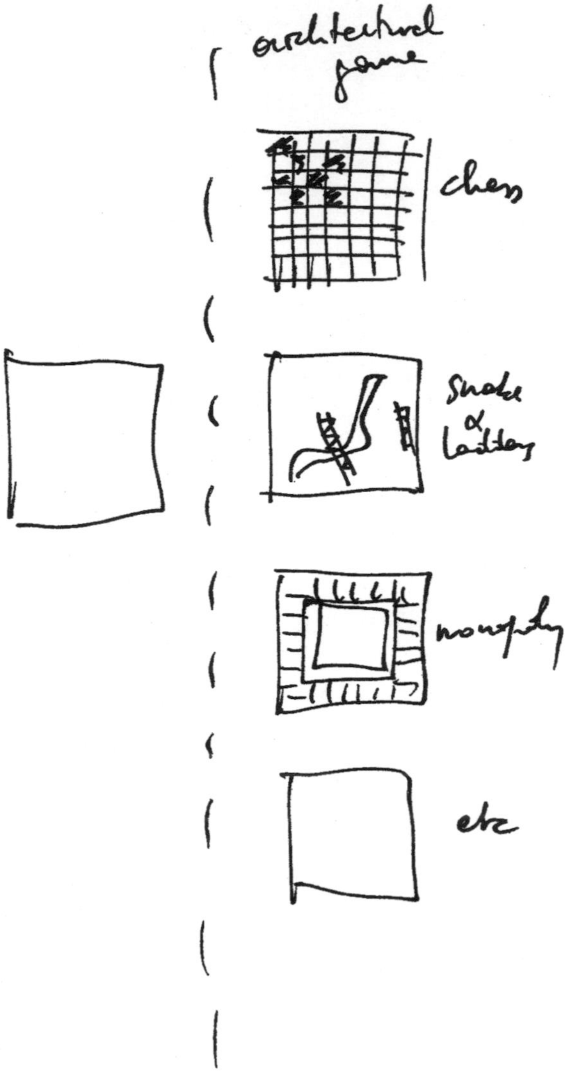

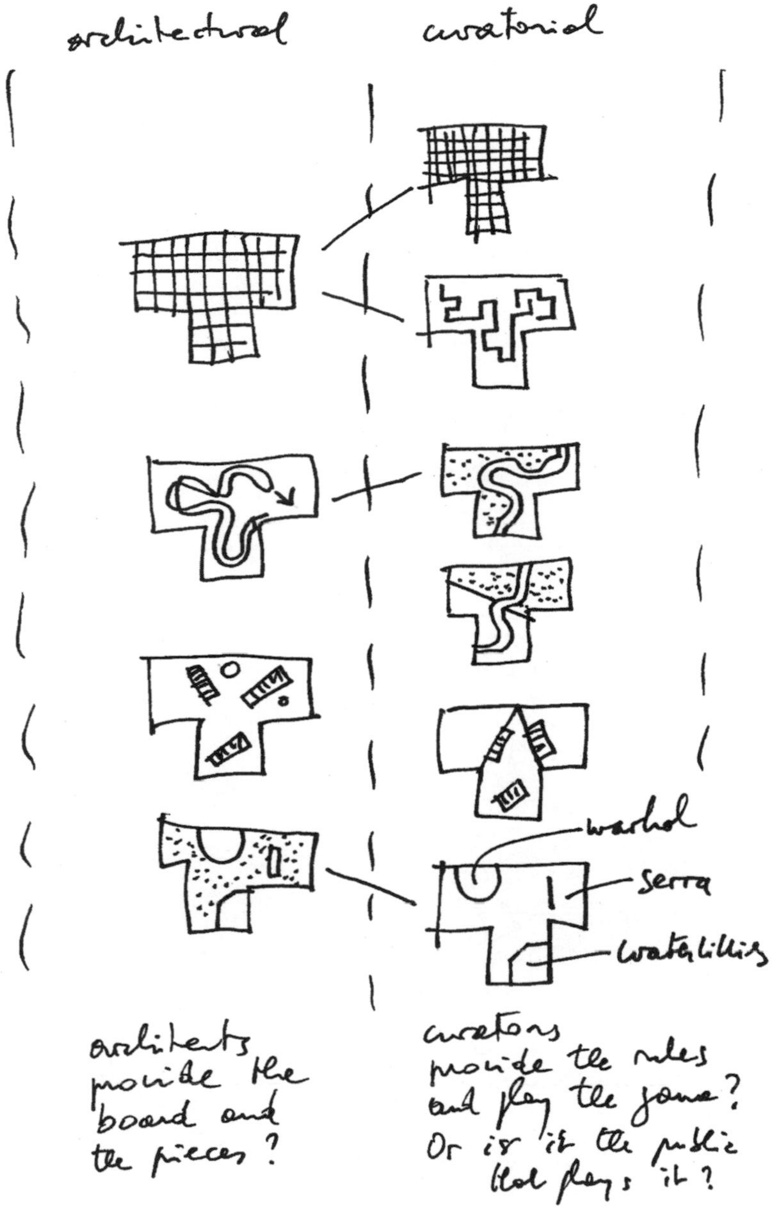
architectural
curatorial
warhol
serra
waterlilies
architects provide the board and the pieces?
curators provide the rules and play the game? Or is it the public that plays it?

5 Mar[illegible]

<u>Voids</u> can be located structurally or randomly

Structurally, according to the characteristics of the site, its massing, its volumetric distribution

Randomly: according to a random pattern, independent from the site — even against it

<u>Flows</u> can be traced structurally or randomly

A random flow is equivalent to the Situationist "drift" walking "au hasard" in the city

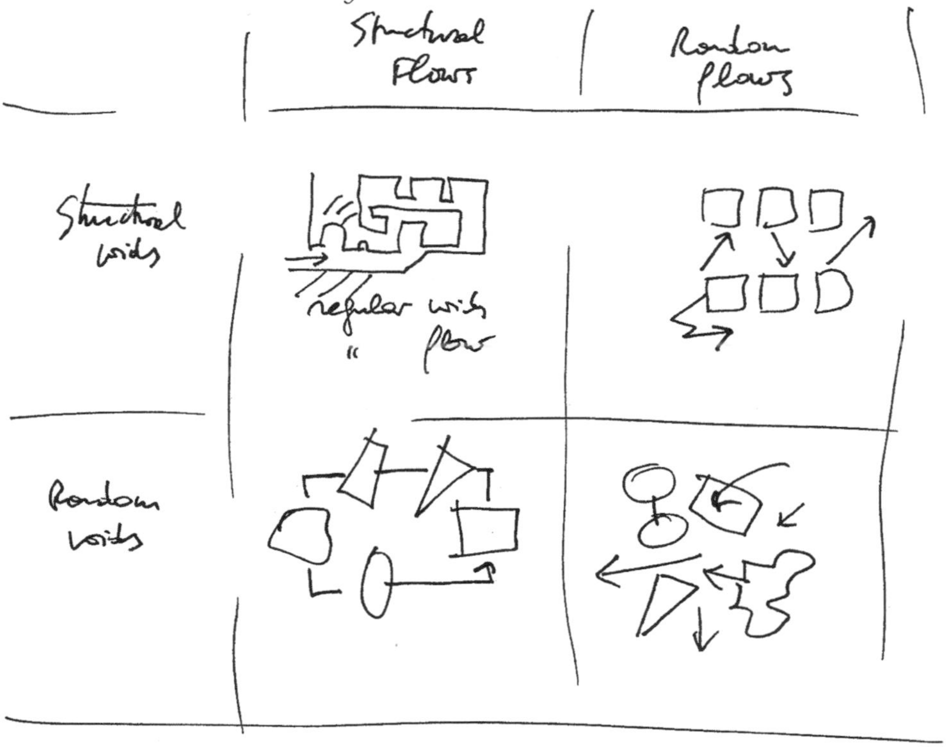

Hypothesis: if rooms/spaces (voids) are ordered and repetitive, flows should be eventful and unpredictable. If rooms/voids are randomly placed and unpredictable, flows must be ordered and predictable

Core & Satellite
The Strategy

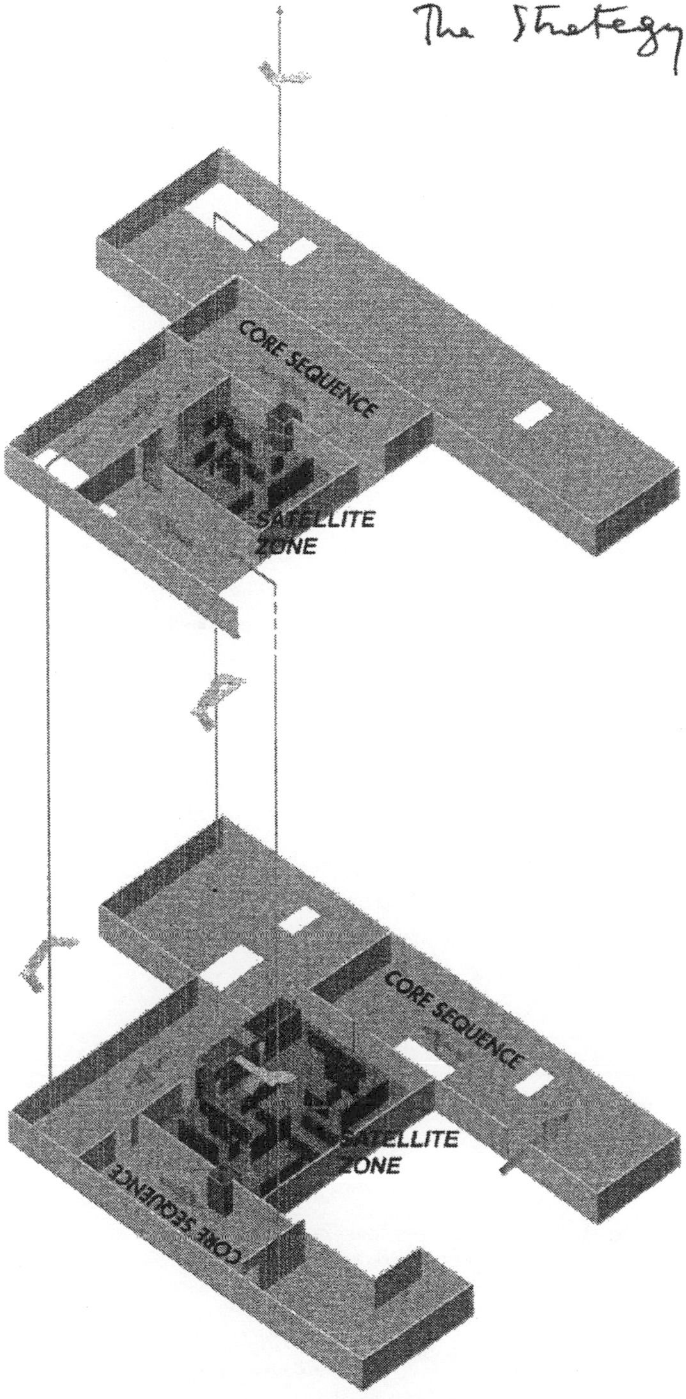

We reverse expectations, placing “satellite galleries” required by the museum at the core, and “core galleries” at the periphery, hence securing the best light and the maximum flexibility

CONCEPTUAL FOOTNOTES
(4 pages)

Implosion or inversion!

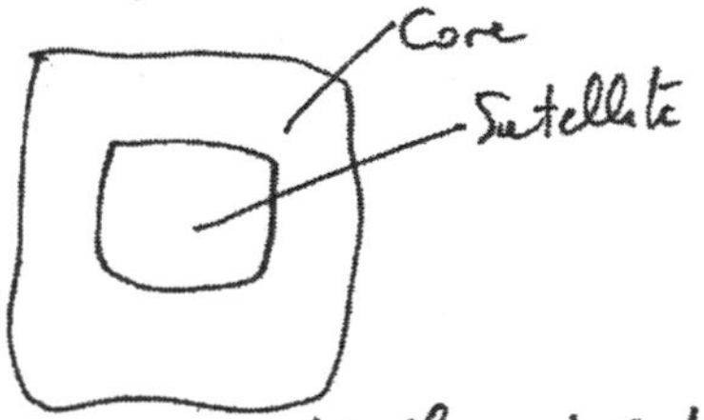
Core
Satellite

(Turning the glove inside out)

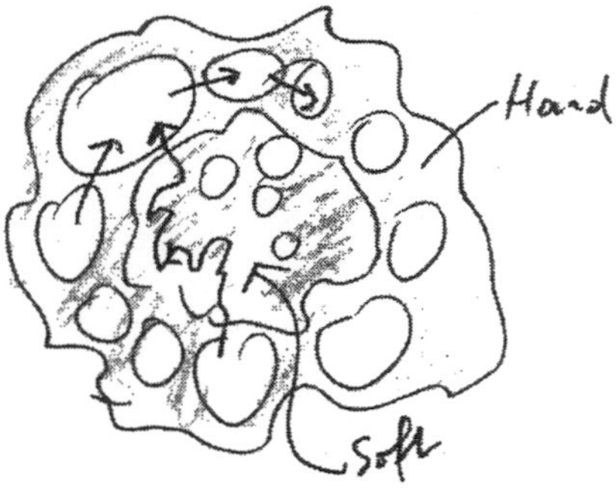
Hard
Soft

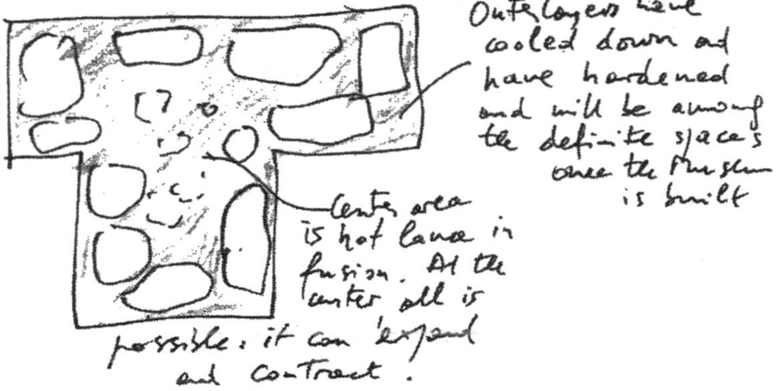
Outerlayers have cooled down and have hardened and will be among the definite spaces once the Museum is built
Center area is hot lava in fusion. At the center all is possible: it can expand and contract.

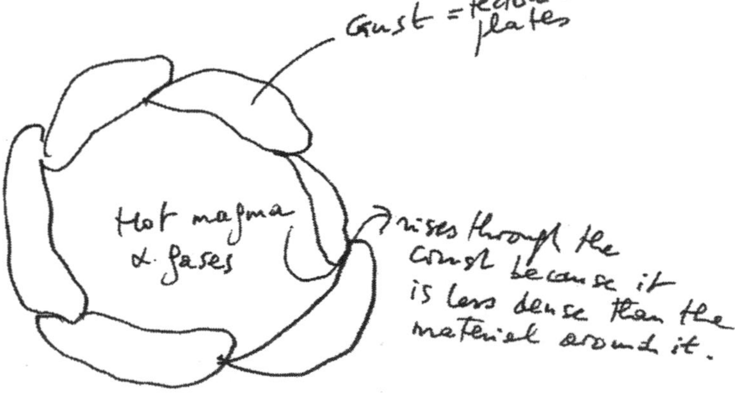
Crust = tectonic plates
Hot magma & gases
rises through the crust because it is less dense than the material around it.

1/4

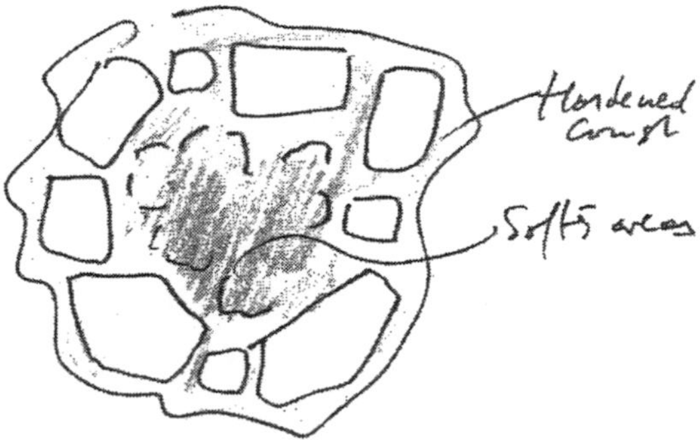
Hardened crust
Soft areas

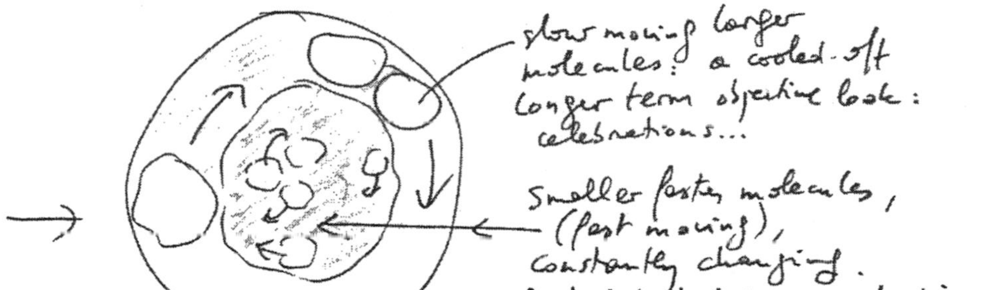
slow moving larger molecules: a cooled-off longer term objective look: celebrations...
Smaller faster molecules, (fast moving), constantly changing.
A hot bed of experimentation.
(The heart of the Museum, the place of questioning, debate, risks, controversy)

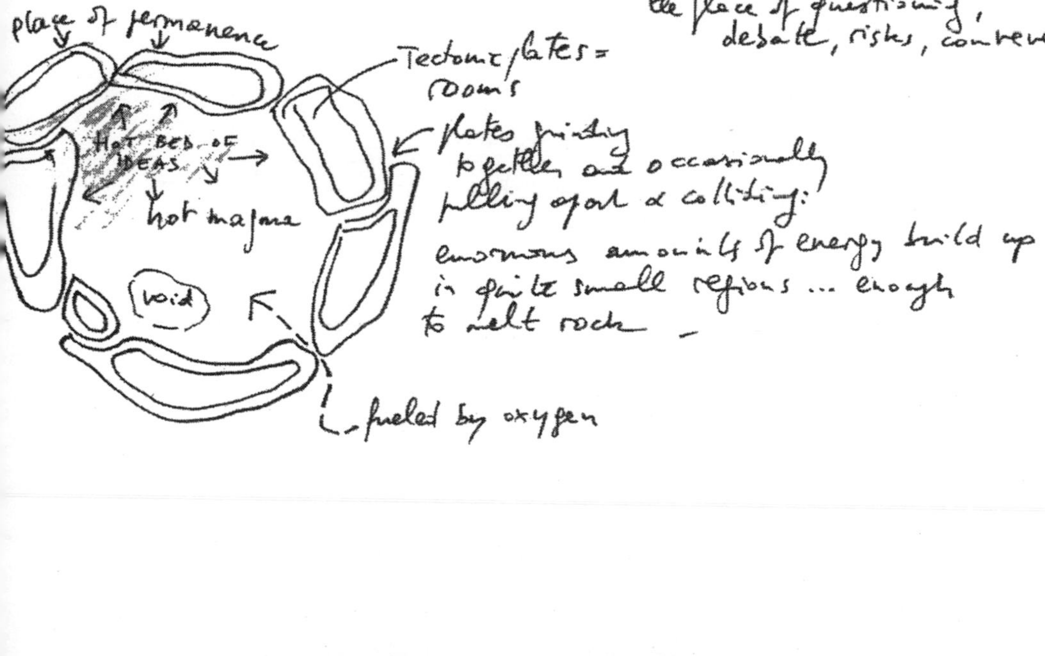
place of permanence
Tectonic plates = rooms
HOT BED OF IDEAS
hot magma
void
plates grinding together and occasionally pulling apart & colliding:
enormous amounts of energy build up in quite small regions ... enough to melt rock
fueled by oxygen

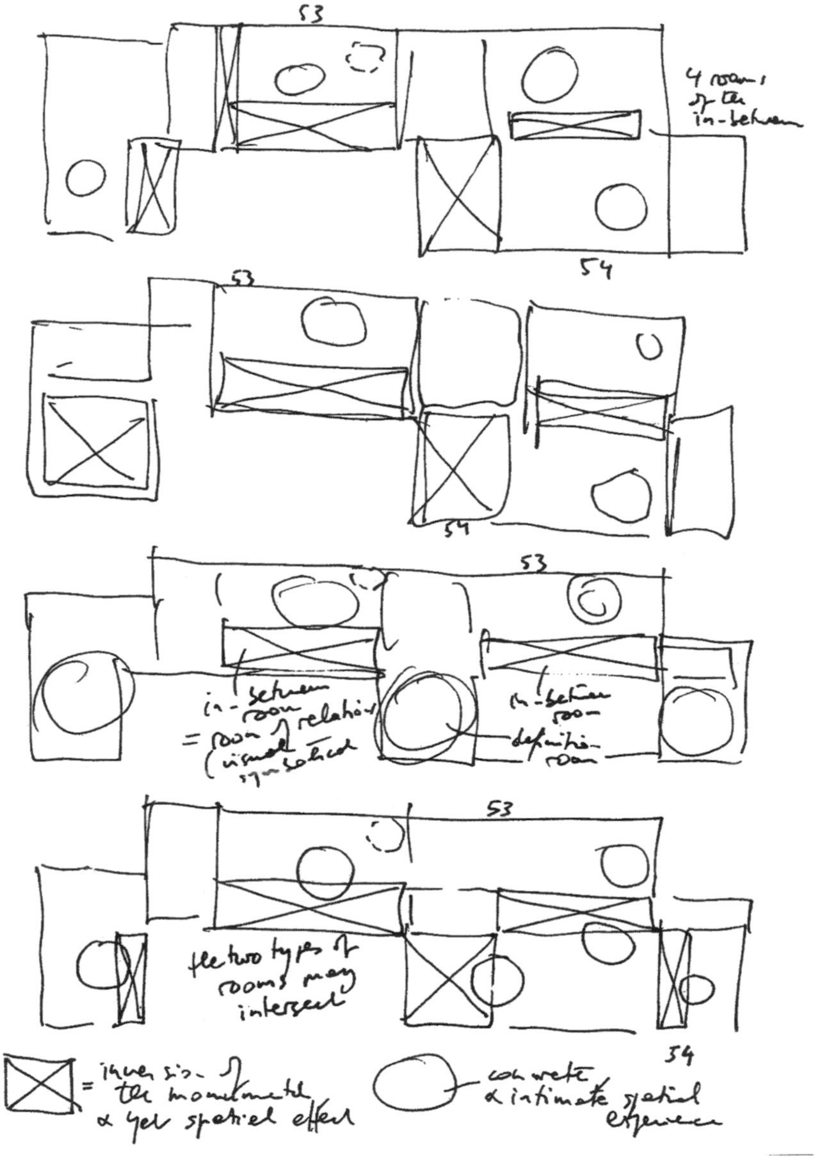
53
4 rooms of the in-between
54
53
54
53
in-between room
= room of relation (visual symbolical)
in-between room
definition room
53
the two types of rooms may intersect
54
= inversion of the monumental & yet spatial effect
concrete & intimate spatial experience

3-16

Rooms of the in-between
generally include circulation areas

Rooms of the intimate provide occasional
visual links

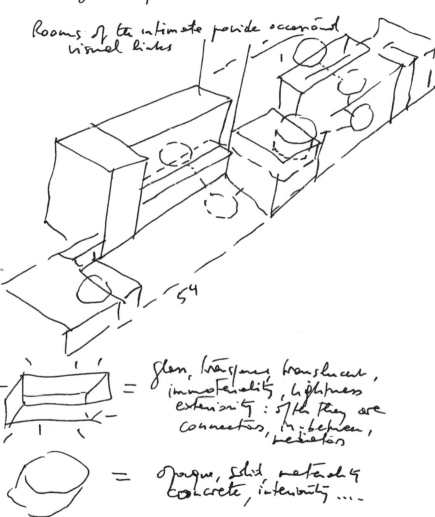

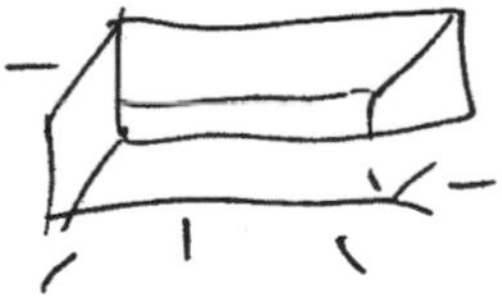
= glass, transparency translucent,
immateriality, lightness
extensivity: often they are
connectors, in-between,
mediators

= opaque, solid materiality
concrete, intensity ....

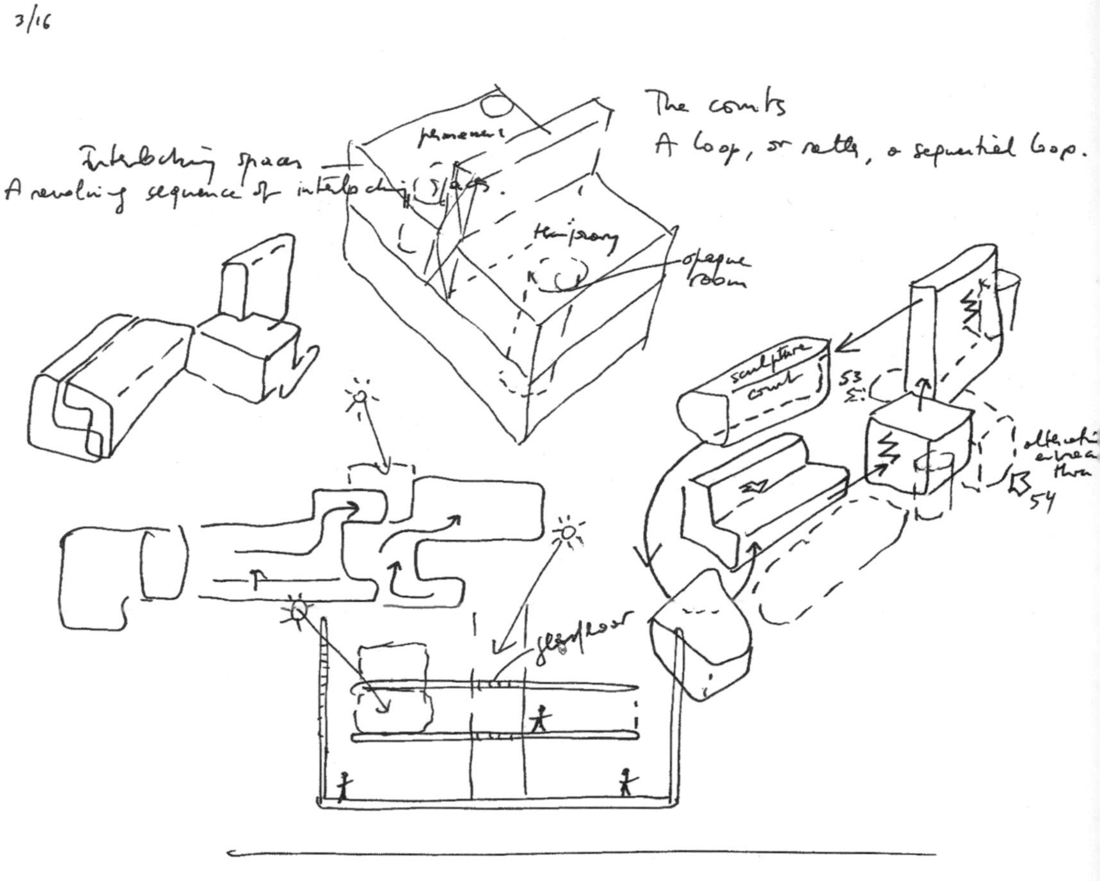

Engaging the whole site over several levels, through a carefully-studied movement sequence

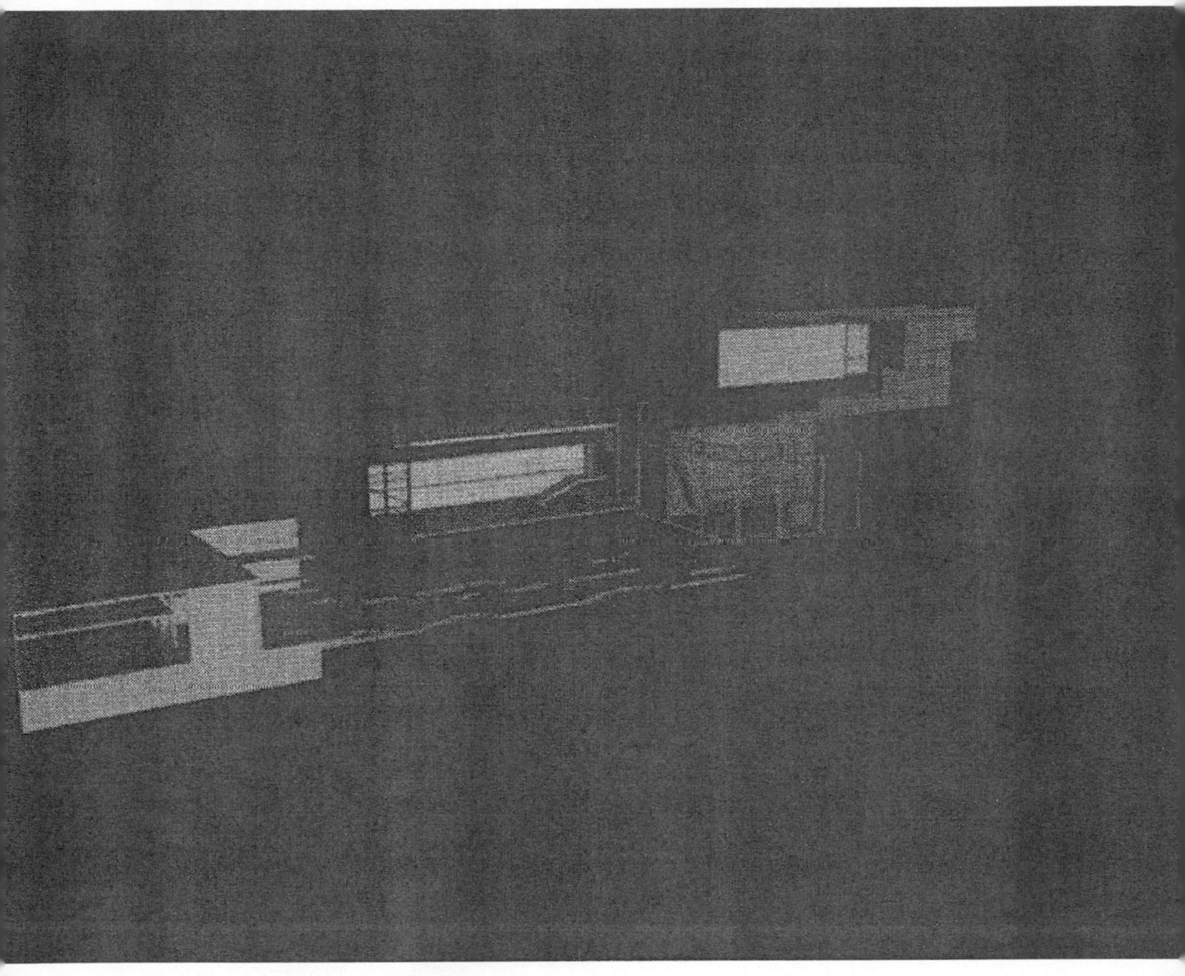

Interlocking spaces: a revolving sequence of interconnected courts

3/11 void space, final

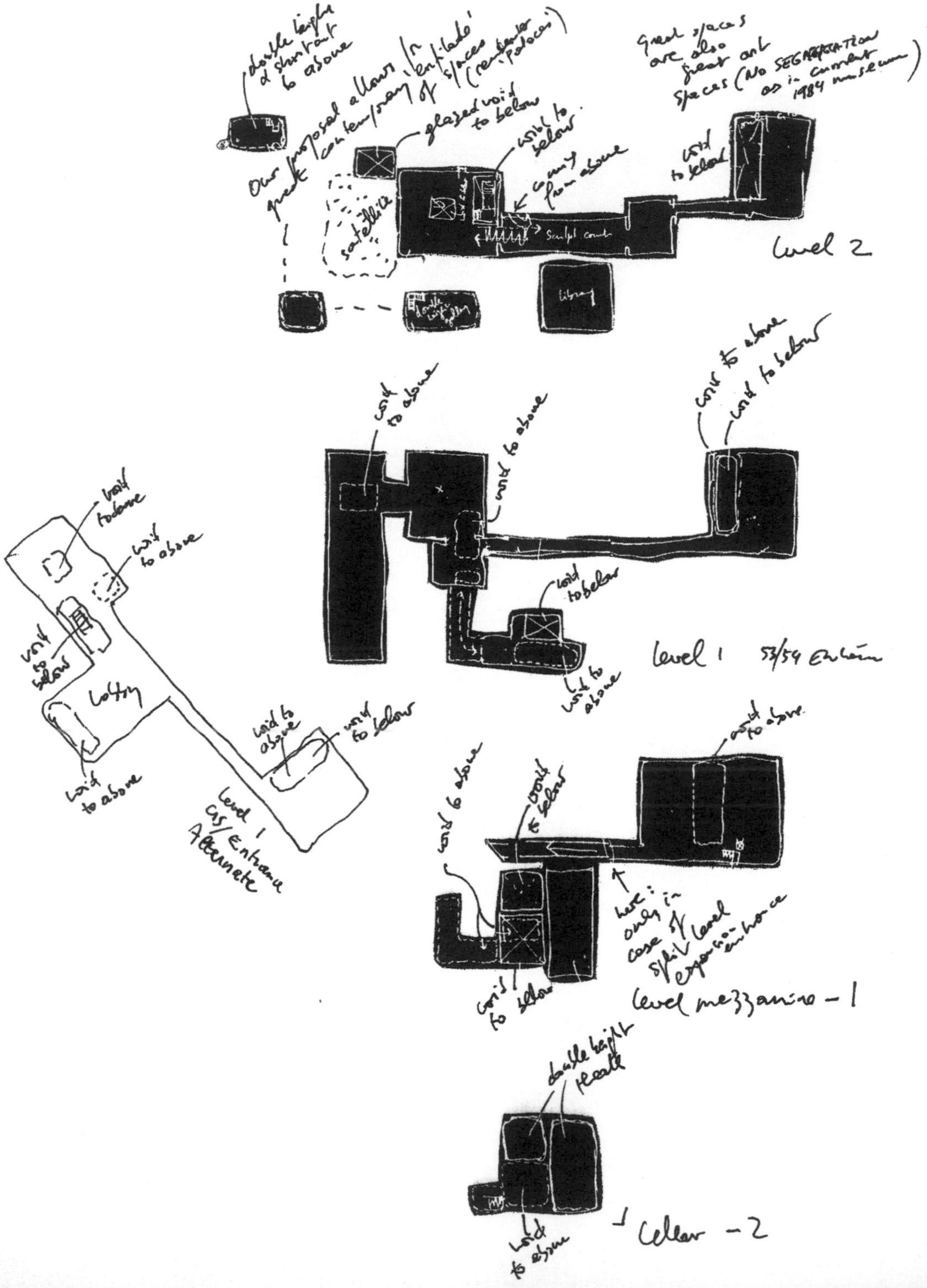

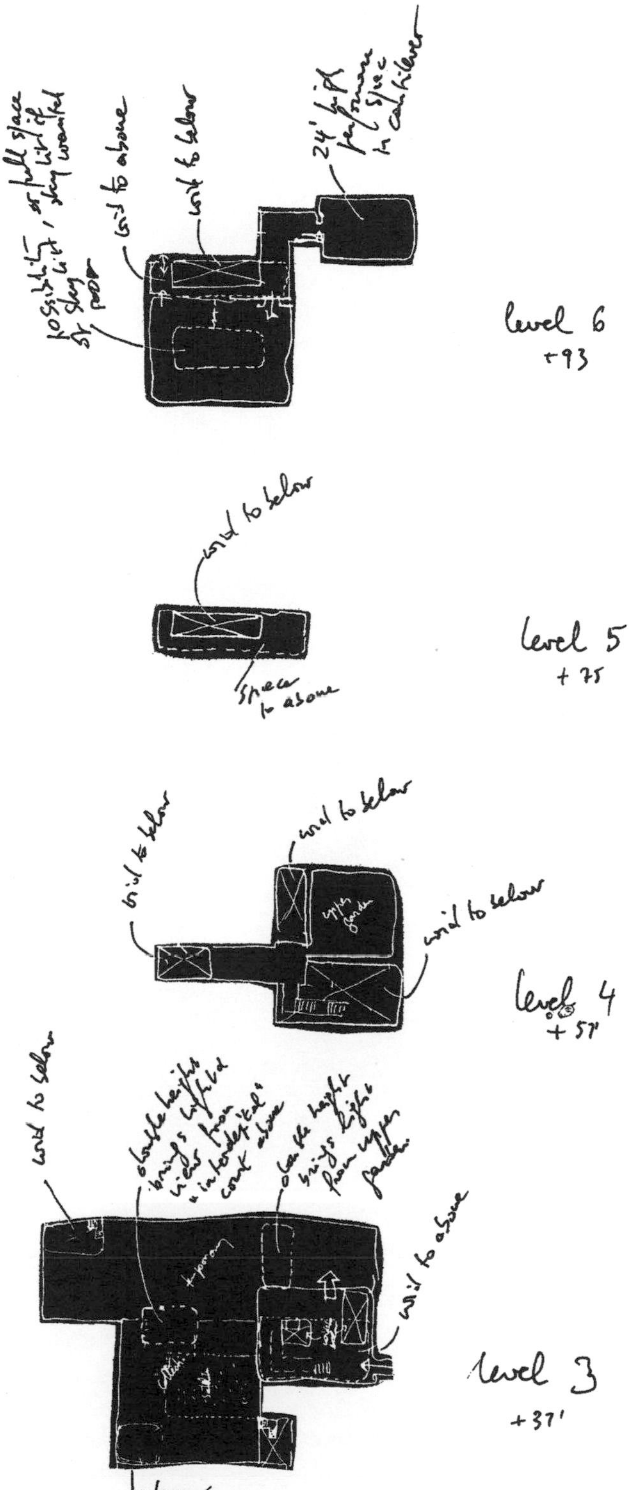
void to above
void to below
24' high performance space in cantilever
level 6
+93
void to below
space to above
level 5
+75
void to below
void to below
void to below
level 4
+57'
void to below
void to above
level 3
+37'
void to below

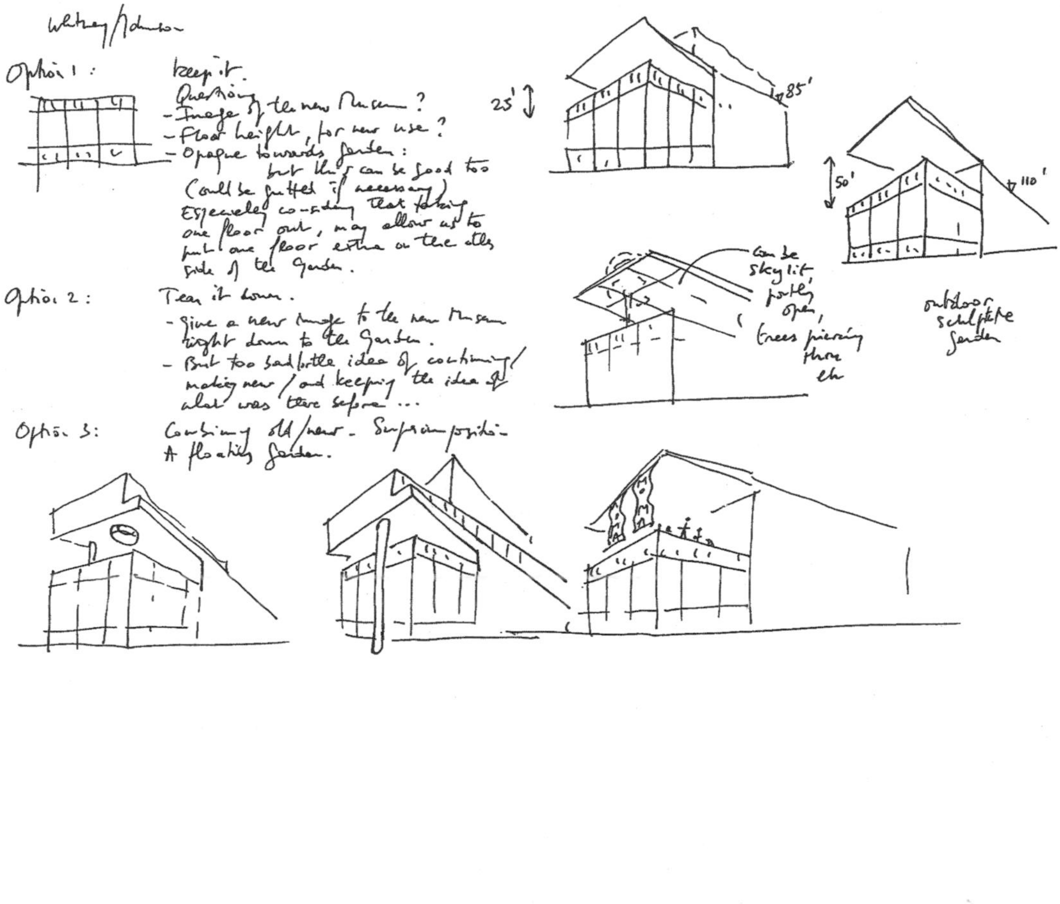

One single exterior architectural move: the cantilevered contemporary galleries over the 1954 addition becomes a sign for the new MoMA

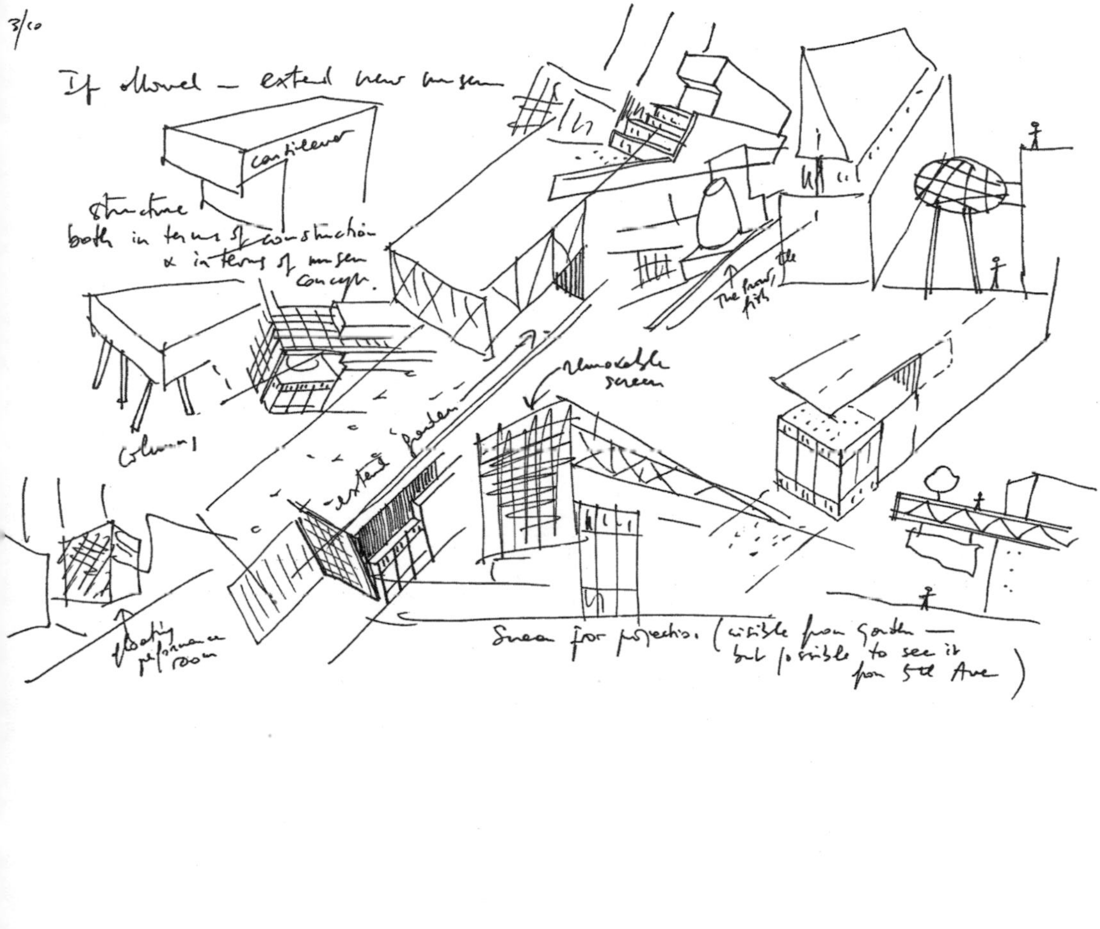
If allowed — extend new museum
cantilever
structure
both in terms of construction
& in terms of museum concept.
columns
removable screen
extend garden
floating performance room
Screen for projection (visible from garden — but possible to see it from 5th Ave)

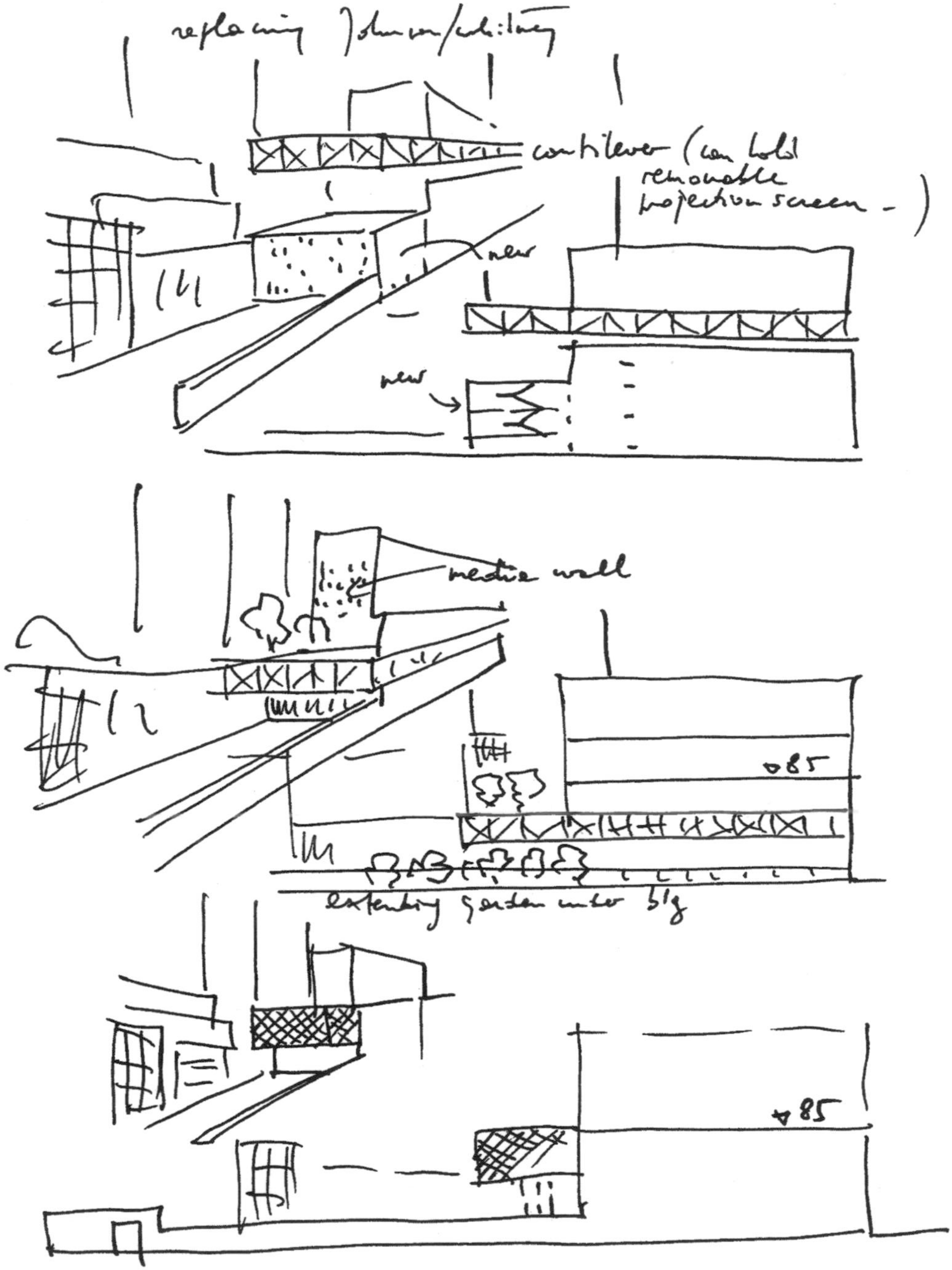
replacing
cantilever (can hold
removable
projection screen –)
new
new
media wall
85
85

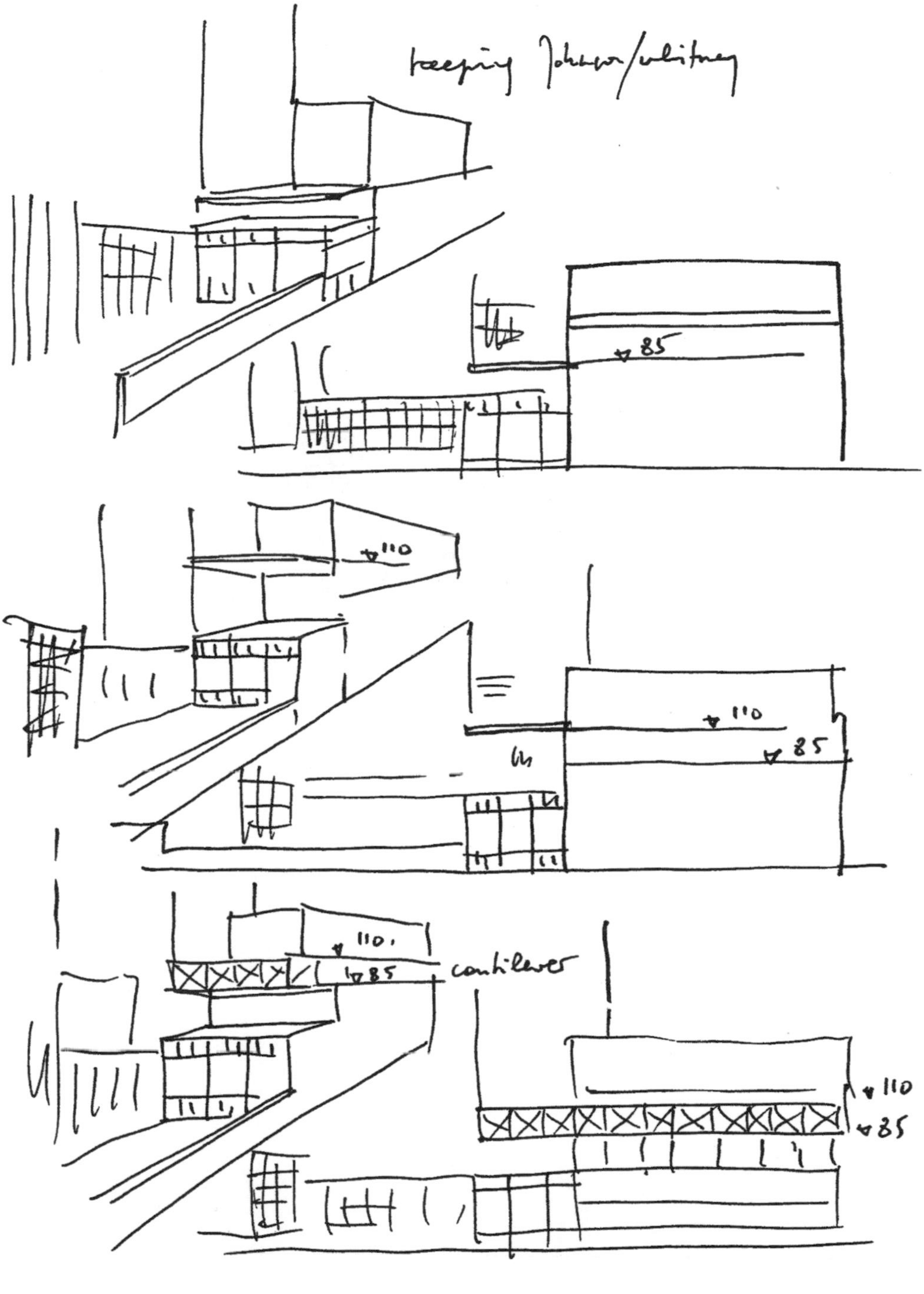
▽85
▽110
▽110
▽85
▽110
▽85
cantilever
▽110
▽85

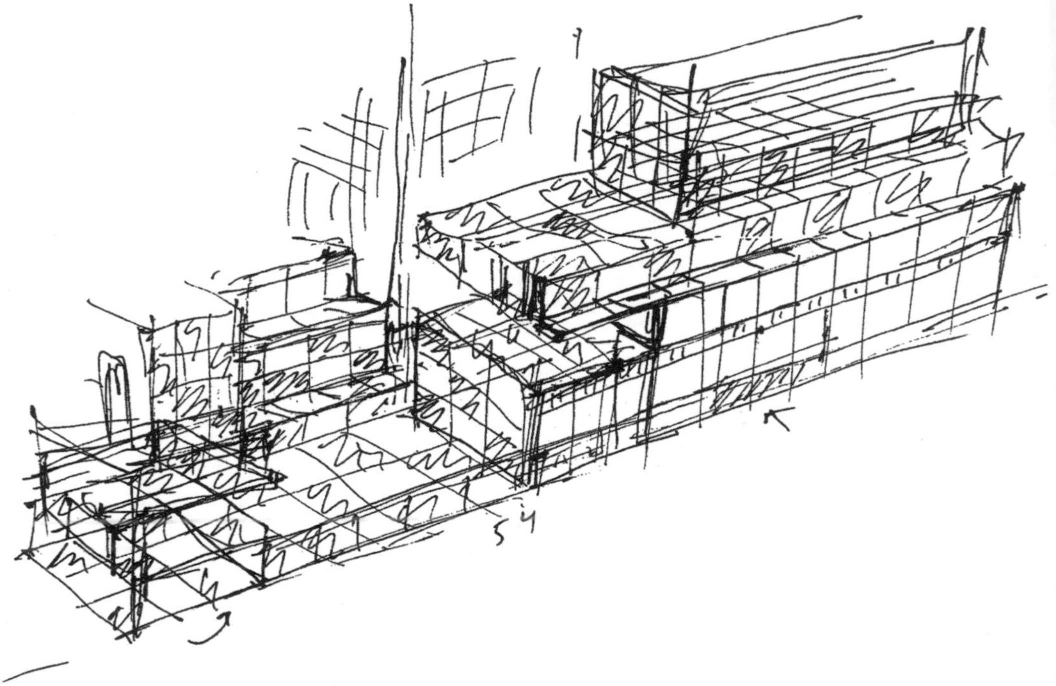

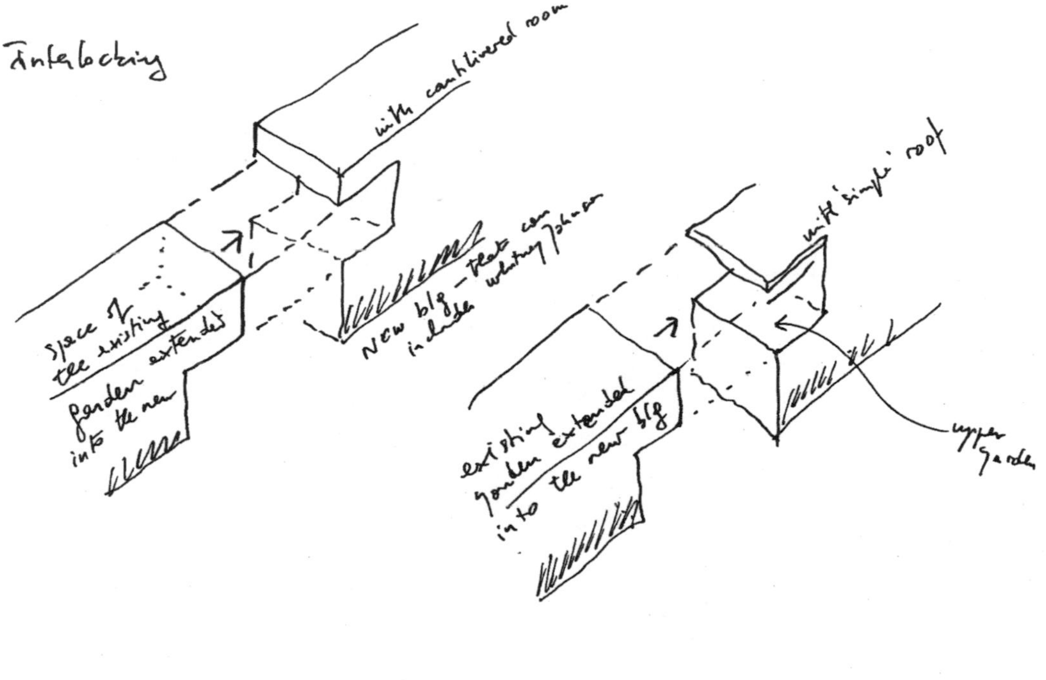
Interlocking
with cantilevered room
space of the existing
garden extended
into the new
with 'simple' roof
existing
garden extended
into the new blg
upper
garden

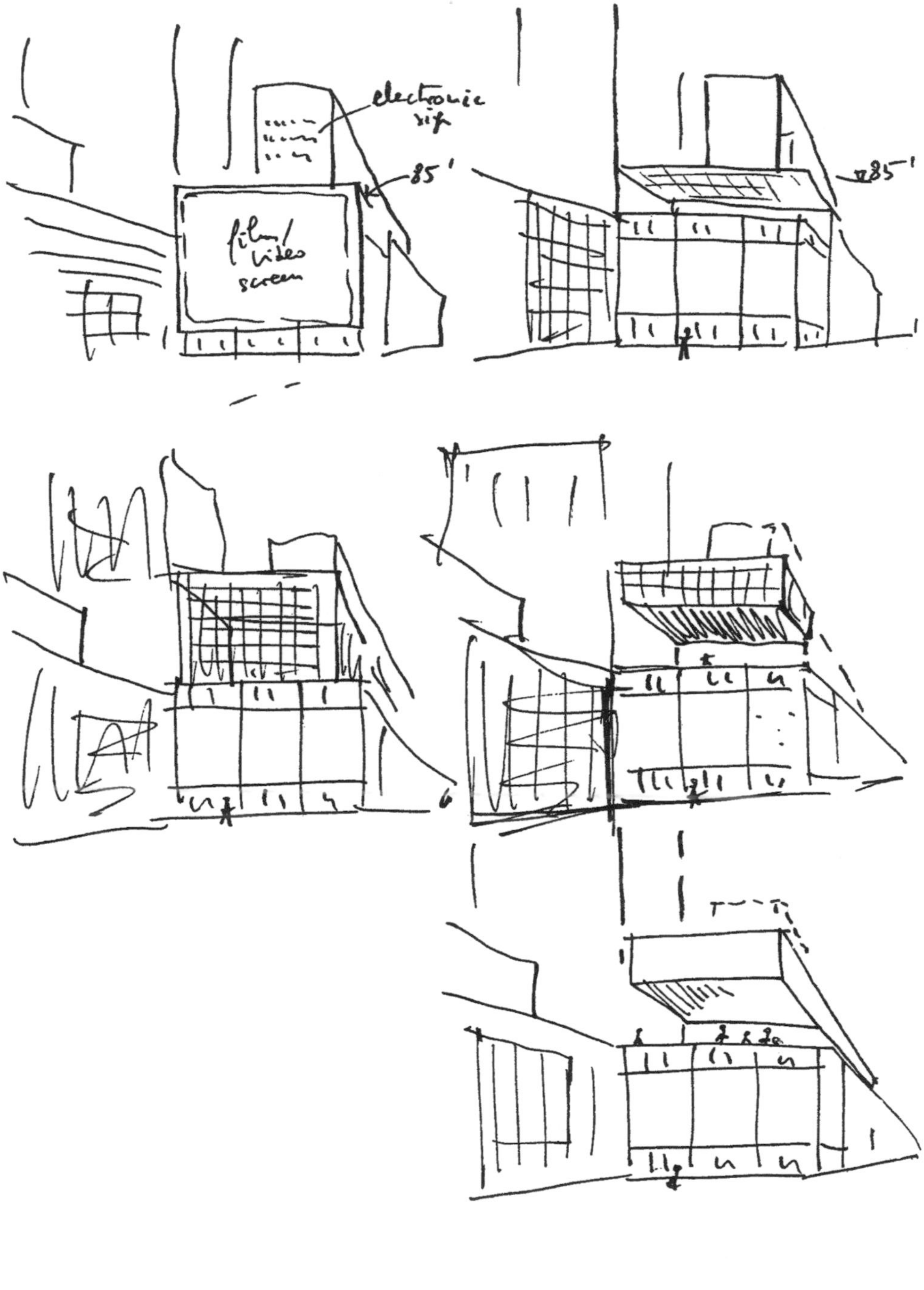
electronic
85'
film/
video
screen
85'

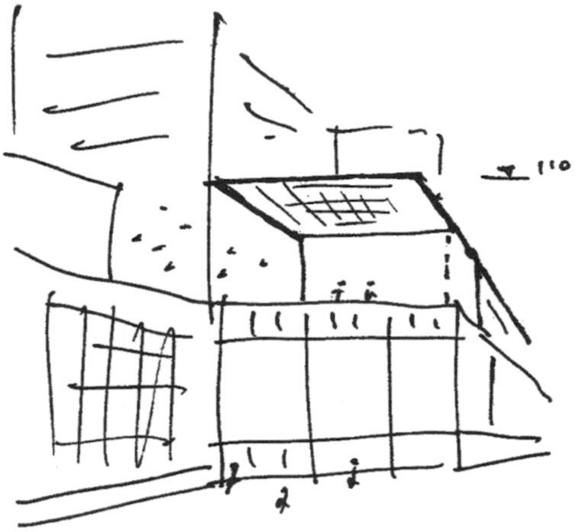

SCREEN

MoMA

View from 54th & Fifth – High roof over upper garden.

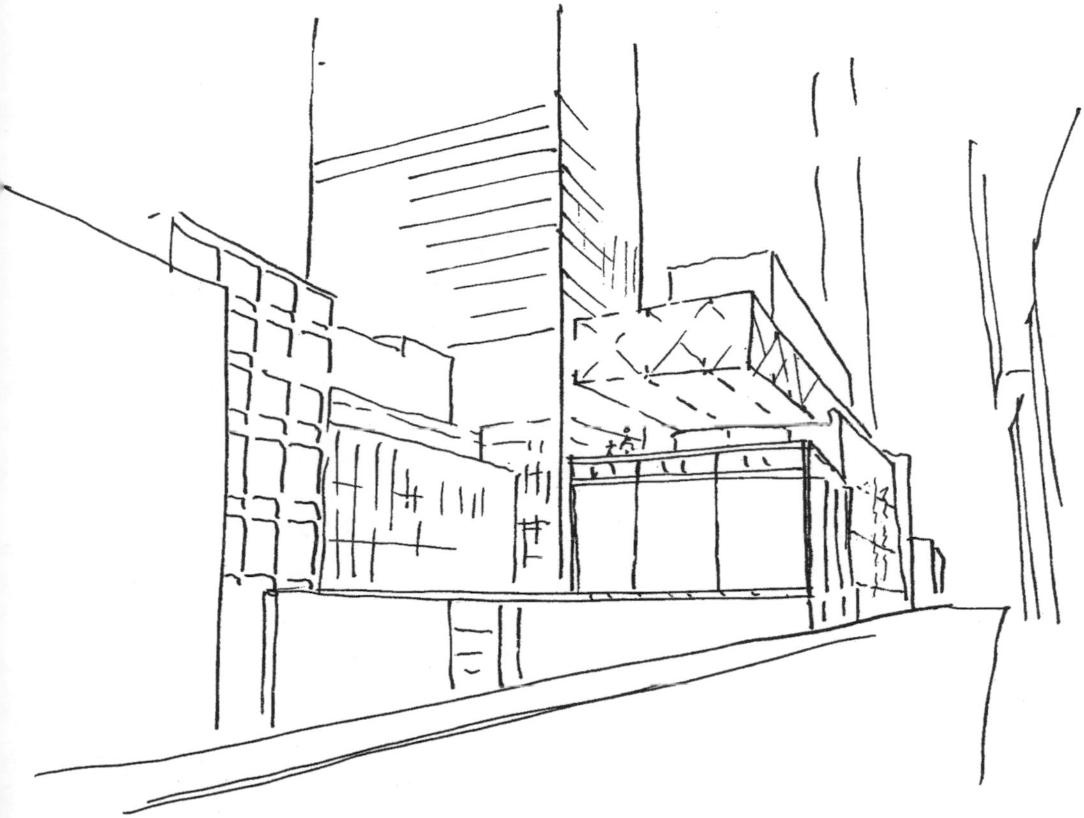

View from 54th & Fifth. Cantilever roof over upper garden.

Competition Phase

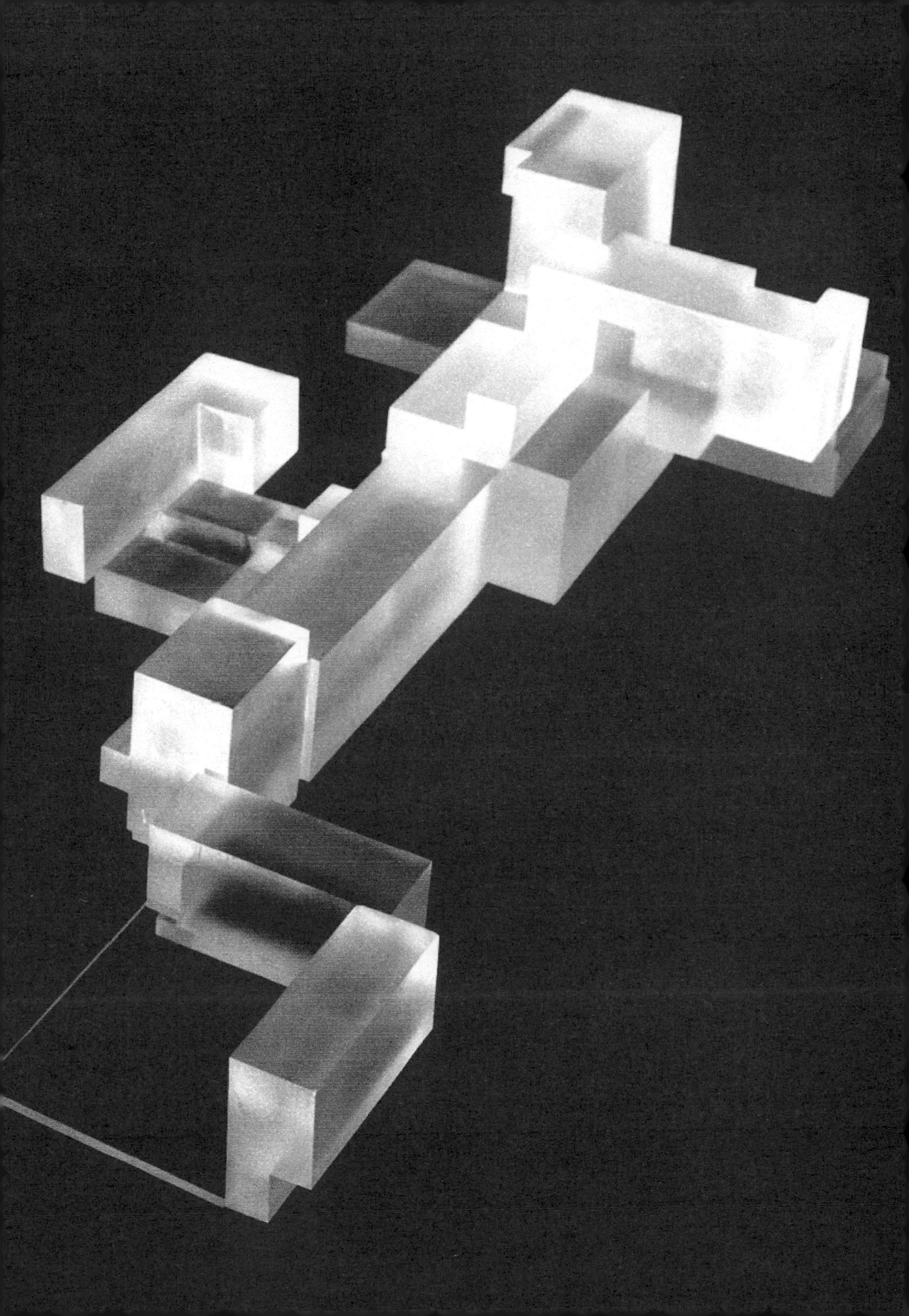

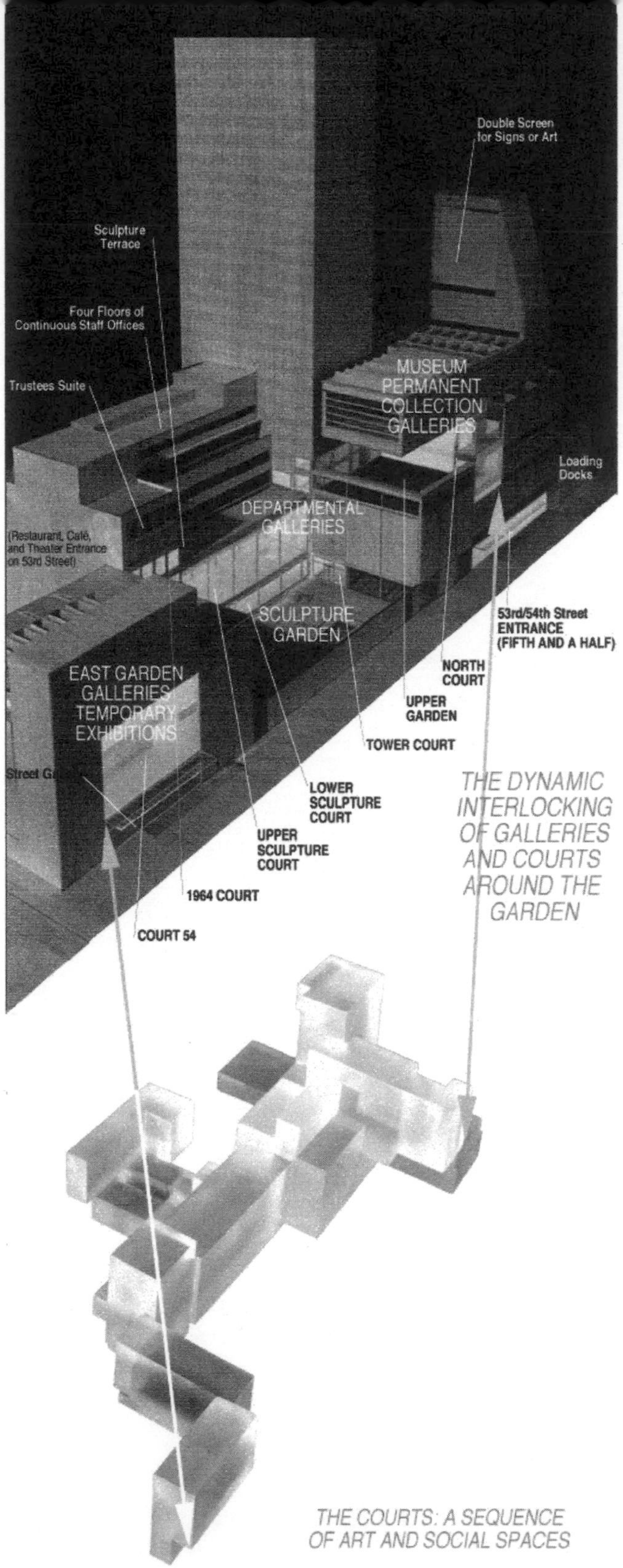

the galleries: a private experience

the courts: a public experience

Extracts from the Competition Phase Submission

How to turn a disparate and additive series of buildings constructed over a period of sixty years into a coherent whole, without losing the heterogeneity that marks the Museum's identity?

How to conceptualize retroactively what was first defined through an aggregate of additive parts and a bureaucratic zoning envelope?

How to mediate between art, education, scholarship, and entertainment in an original or unprecedented way?

These questions introduced our charette submission in early 1997, as we laid down basic principles governing a major expansion of The Museum of Modern Art. In view of the complex interrelations among urbanistic, architectural, and esthetic strategies required by the expansion, we stayed away from the imagistic approaches often favored by architects.

Rather than using an existing typology or trying to invent a new one that would create havoc with the existing past of the museum or ignore it altogether, we determined "to actualize potentialities," to analyze the programmatic logic of MoMA and map it against the nature of the site and its existing buildings. Our aim was to arrive at a new operative concept, a conceptual armature in which the museum could develop. This is the concept of Garden and Courts, interlocking the old and the new.

In this new phase we developed this structure further. However, we felt the need to interject an additional question that was implicit in our early proposal but not explicitly expressed:

How to provide exhibition spaces that will offer paradigms for contemporary art practice, informing and inspiring the work of contemporary artists?

The museum architecture must create spaces in which artists not only wish to exhibit because of the sensuous particularities of the galleries, but also, and importantly, take those spaces, in their esthetic, social, and public implications, to the heart of their creative production. Indeed, the modern museum inherits a legacy that obliges it to reconsider its historical role both as a repository for its collections and as an influential context for the art of its time. Today, that art requires new conditions of public content and address. No museum to date has accounted for the reality of the public in the arts themselves as well as in the museum's relations to its expanding and diverse visitors. No current museum has attended to the underlying mandate of the modern museum to be at once comprehensive and polemical, historical and actual.

We wished, then, to interlock the old and the new, the existing and the emerging, by stressing the ongoing nature of modernity. Our strategy for presenting the vitality of the museum as a generative concept for art takes its cue from the social and programmatic capacities of the Garden, which are extended through the museum in a sequence of Courts—Courts that mediate between art space and social space, affording public exhibition contexts and gathering spaces juxtaposed to the more private and individual galleries.

Increasingly, the multiple facets that define the new museum require that it not be a singular, "simple," monolithic, even a kind of all-embracing container for a range of activities; instead, the museum must be relational and multiple, interlocking its different aspects in a dynamic relationship.

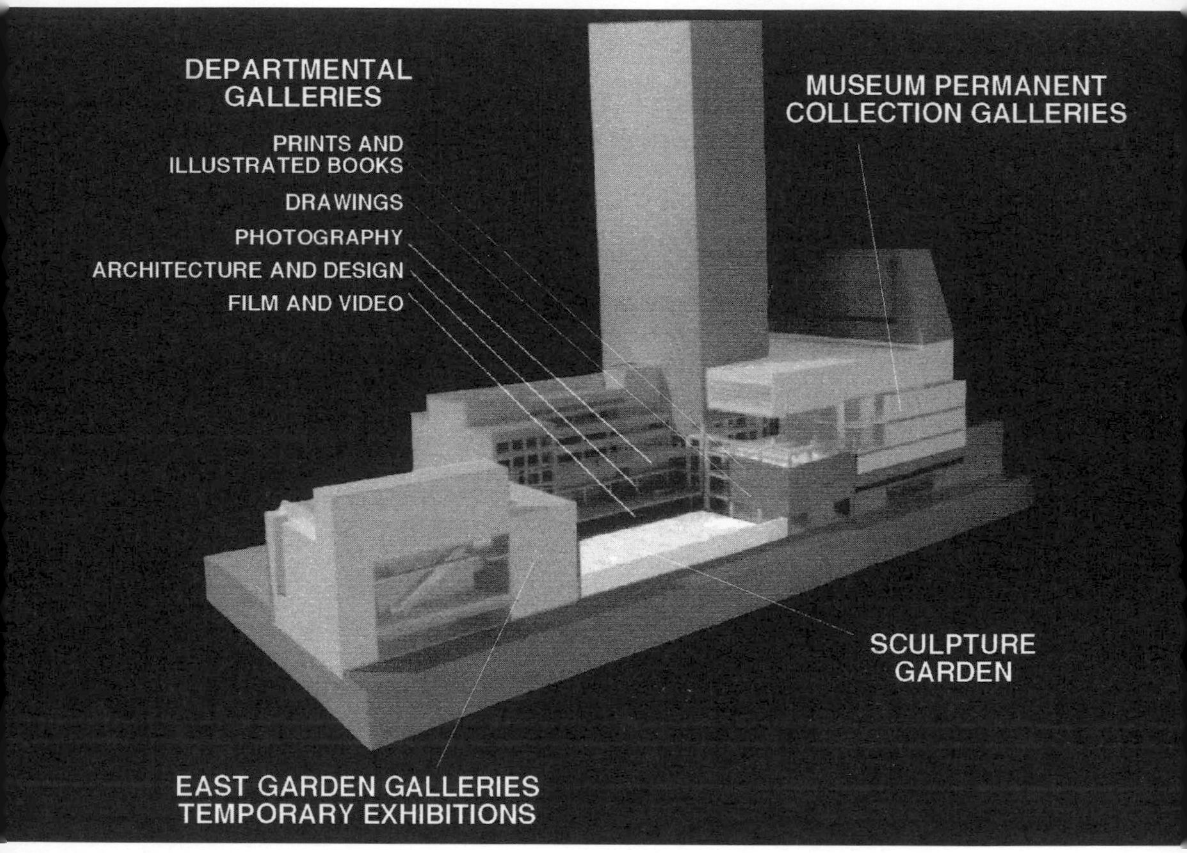

A precise relationship between four major parts, each with its own critical mass, structures the museum: the permanent collection to the west, the temporary exhibition galleries to the east, the departmental galleries and the new Sculpture Court in the existing buildings to the south (and also northwest), and the Garden to the north. The Museum Tower could be described as a fifth and vertical part. The four programmatic elements of the museum hence correspond to the four volumetric elements of the complex. This physical arrangement of galleries avoids privileging media or disciplines while encouraging viewers to frequent different parts of the museum; for example, the departmental galleries are located along the axial link or route between the eastern and the western structural elements. The Garden provides a center or core, regularly visible along the visitor's path within the museum and serving as a point of reference; the temporary and permanent collection wings are each visible, the one from the other, across the space articulated by the Garden.

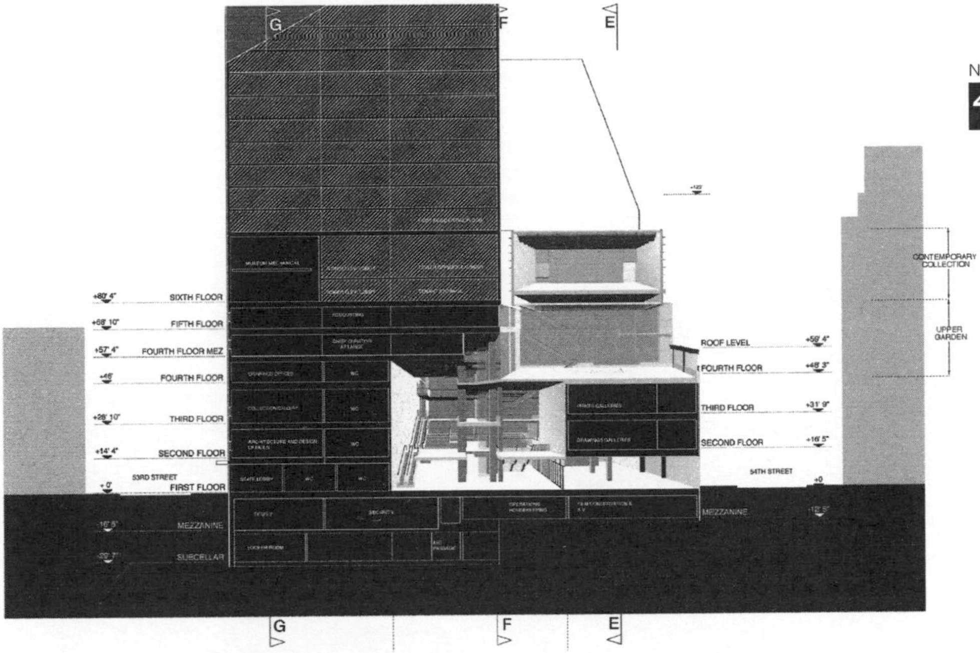

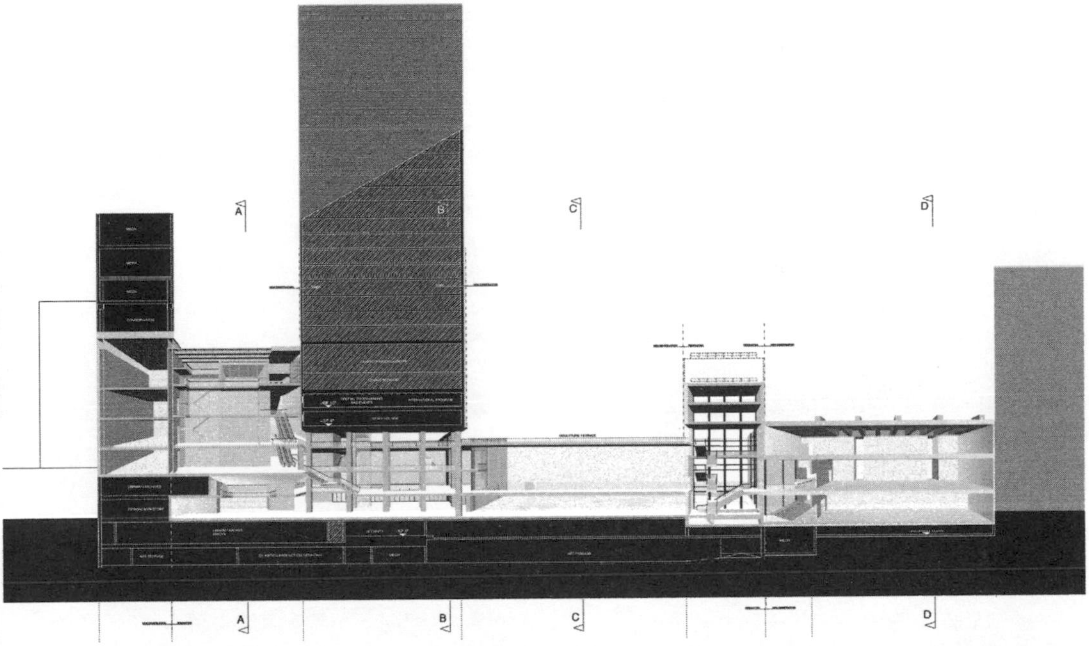

A sequence of major interior spaces or "courts" that extend the museum's urban scale throughout the building, offering a spatially varied experience that alternates between art and social space. While providing a clear structure, the courts permit a number of routes through the building rather than a single, linear pathway. Some of the spaces are destined to show art, while others are primarily social; some can be used for special museum events.

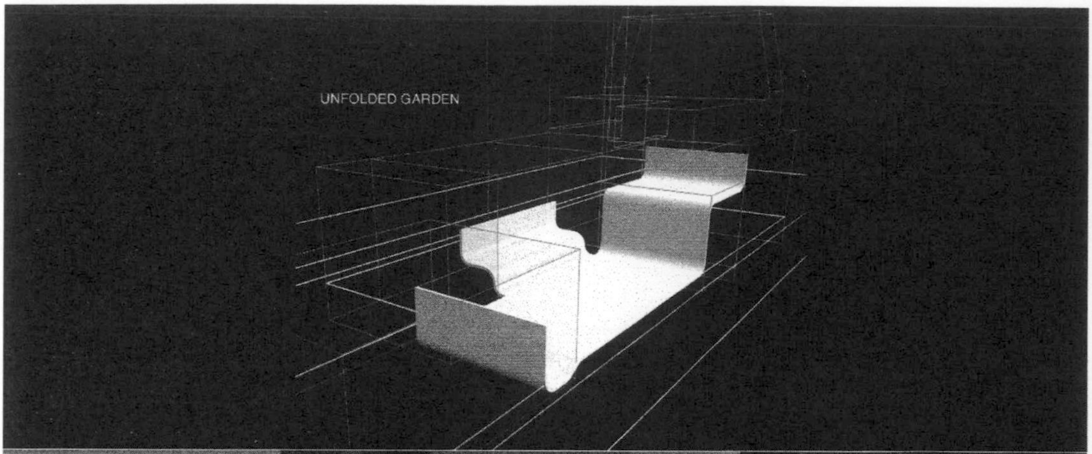
UNFOLDED GARDEN

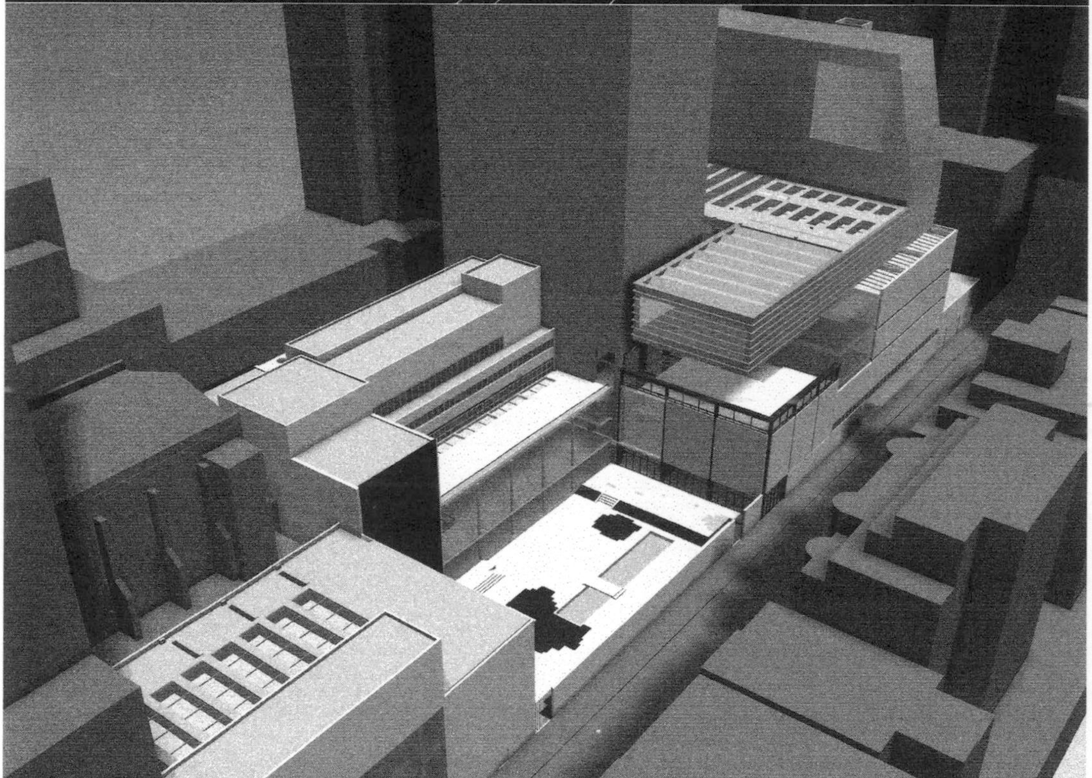

An urban museum: Our project proposes a dual-street museum that takes advantage of its mid-block site and the unique conditions of both 53rd and 54th Streets. Heterogeneity on 53rd Street, calm and continuity on 54th Street is our hypothesis. We express this architecturally through a variety of facades on 53rd Street and a single material theme (the beige glazed brick of the Garden wall) on 54th Street, as well as programmatically; book and design store, cafe, restaurant, staff and film theater access are all located on 53rd Street. Along 54th Street, a new street gallery, located in the temporary exhibitions wing, and glimpses of the Garden are visible. We offer two main museum entrance options: a new dual-entrance court ("Fifth-and-a-Half Avenue"), linking the two streets together, and the historical entrance is also proposed as an additional, separate entry for large-scale temporary or blockbuster exhibitions.

In addition to defining the atmosphere of the street, the elevations provide extended vistas from the avenues. A new presence will be visible from Fifth Avenue at 54th Street in a quiet but spectacular architectural event located above the north wing—a new covered upper garden, in three-dimensional interaction with the city. The possibility of a dual-avenue museum is suggested in a double screen, located 140 feet above the street on the West Penthouse and visible from Fifth and Sixth Avenues, for the display of large-scale temporary signs, either prepared by the museum for information purposes or by artists as temporary installations. The visibility of the screen to the east and west dynamically extends the museum "site."

The garden is extended into the museum: The upper part of the existing Garden and the building literally interlock. A stunning new Upper Garden is created under a cantilevered space hovering high above the North Wing and containing a major gallery or performance space, unencumbered by columns and lit by natural light as well as by nighttime artificial illumination. In a sense, one could say that this roof garden expands the experience of the existing Garden to the west at a higher level. The Sculpture Court and Sculpture Terrace, which rise above the current Garden Hall, also provide venues for indoor and outdoor sculpture overlooking the Garden, as well as for large-scale social events.

Interlocking is the name of the game throughout the scheme. Each of the major interior spaces is the place of interlocking: between the old and the new; between the permanent and the temporary; between the Painting and Sculpture collections and other departments; between public areas and the curatorial offices or education areas; between galleries and film theatre spaces; and so on. This interlocking is both structural—a spatial diagram—and conceptual. The interlocking between say, the old and the new, is a way to avoid being caught in simplistic polarities between linearity (spine) and centrality (atrium), history and contemporary practice.

The Garden is the symbolic key to this interlocking. The Garden is usually viewed as an oasis of nature within the urban culture of New York. While acknowledging this important perspective, we also call attention to the Garden's other, less acknowledged attribute as a space of remarkable range and flexibility that equally accommodates a variety of artforms and performances (Summergarden) and social events of both a private and public nature. We feel that this quality of programmatic flexibility and social space provides places for activities and for artforms that are not easily contained within conventional exhibition galleries. Our concept extends this quality throughout the museum in the form of multiple courts. The inherently public nature of the courts offers not only opportunities for contemporary art practices and performances but also, in proximity to the permanent collections, serves to dynamize and revitalize readings of art's ongoing history.

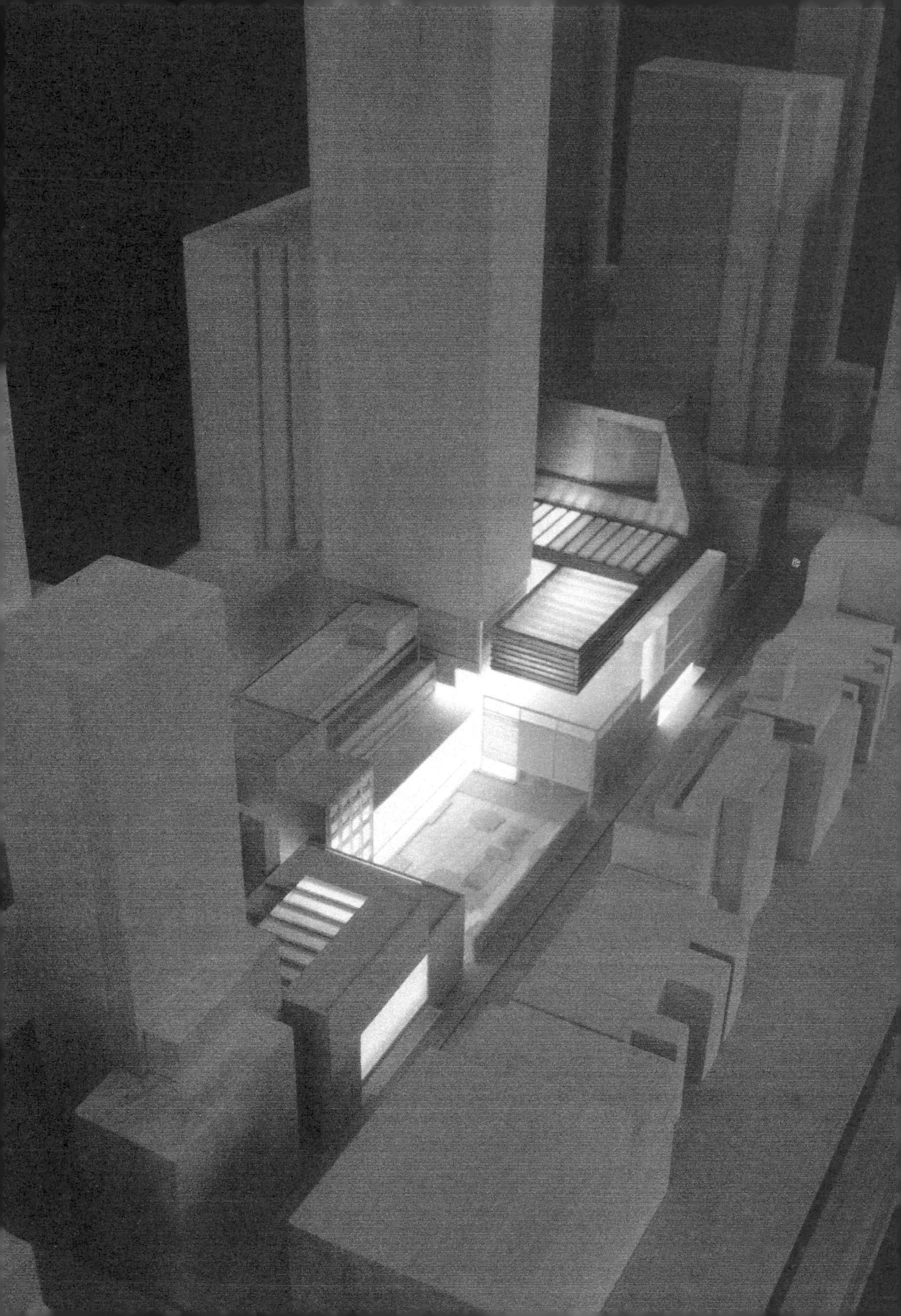

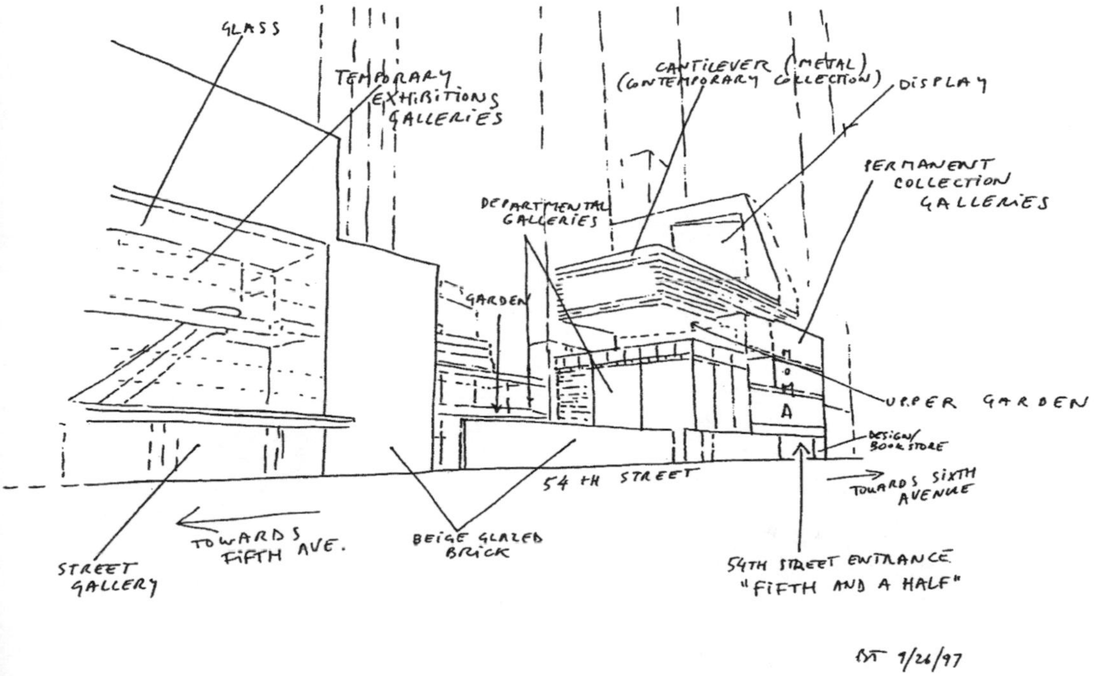

An urban museum: all major interior spaces (the "courts") are visible from the street. The museum engages the city

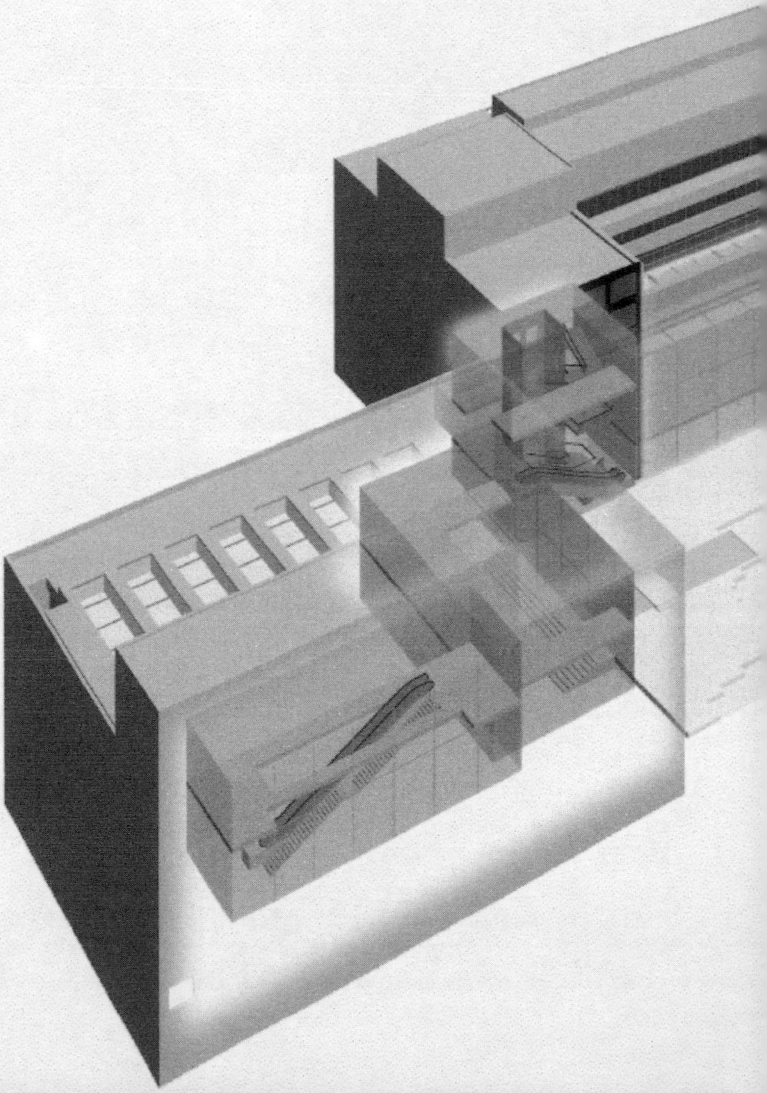

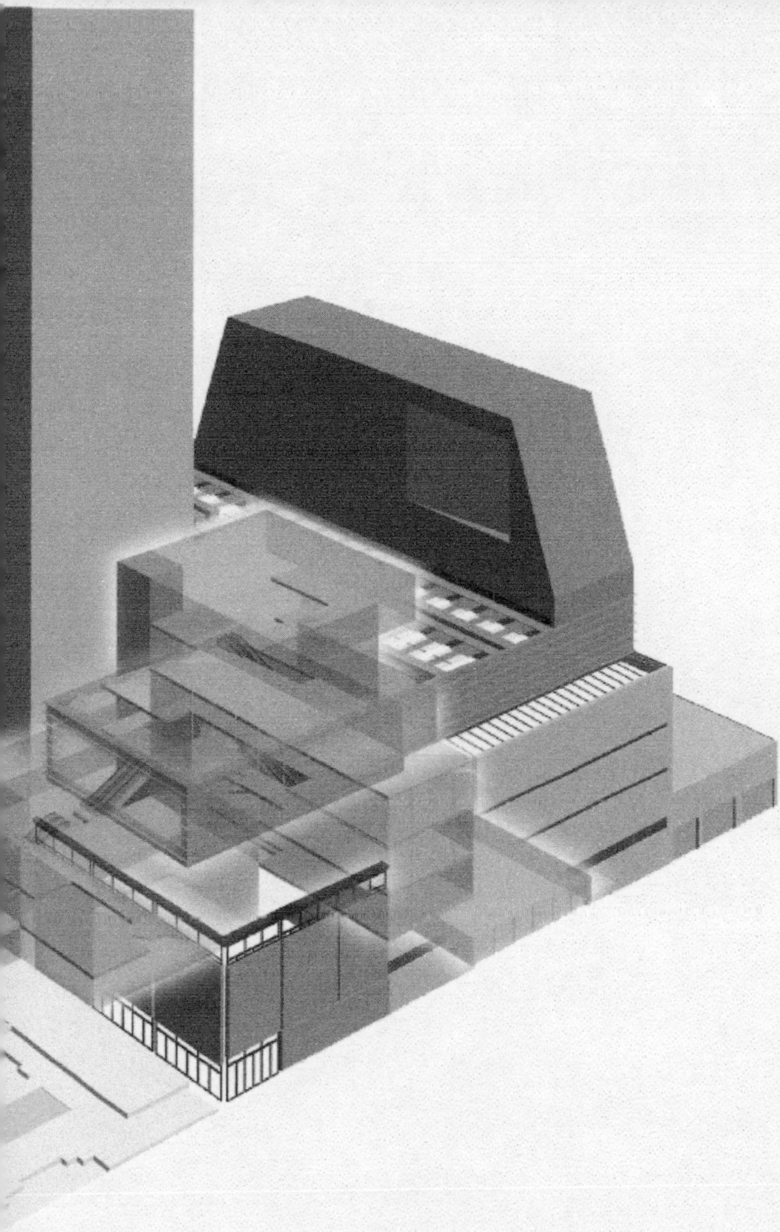

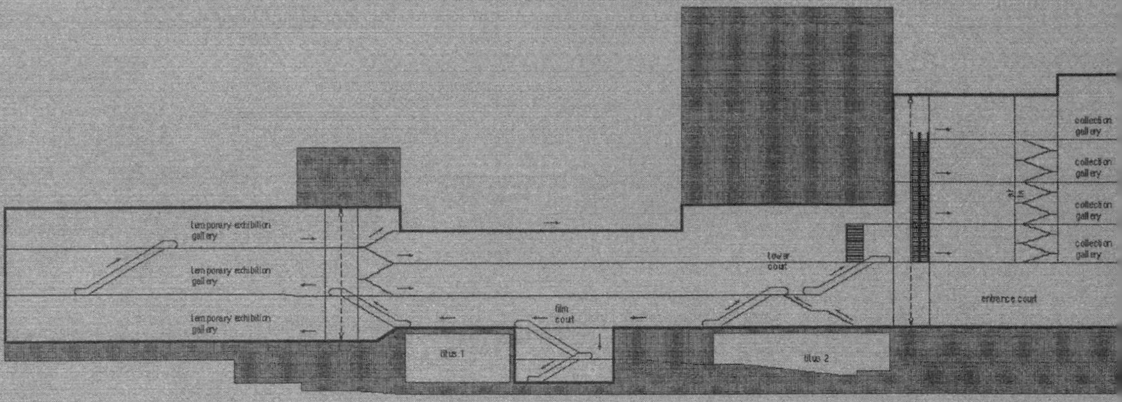

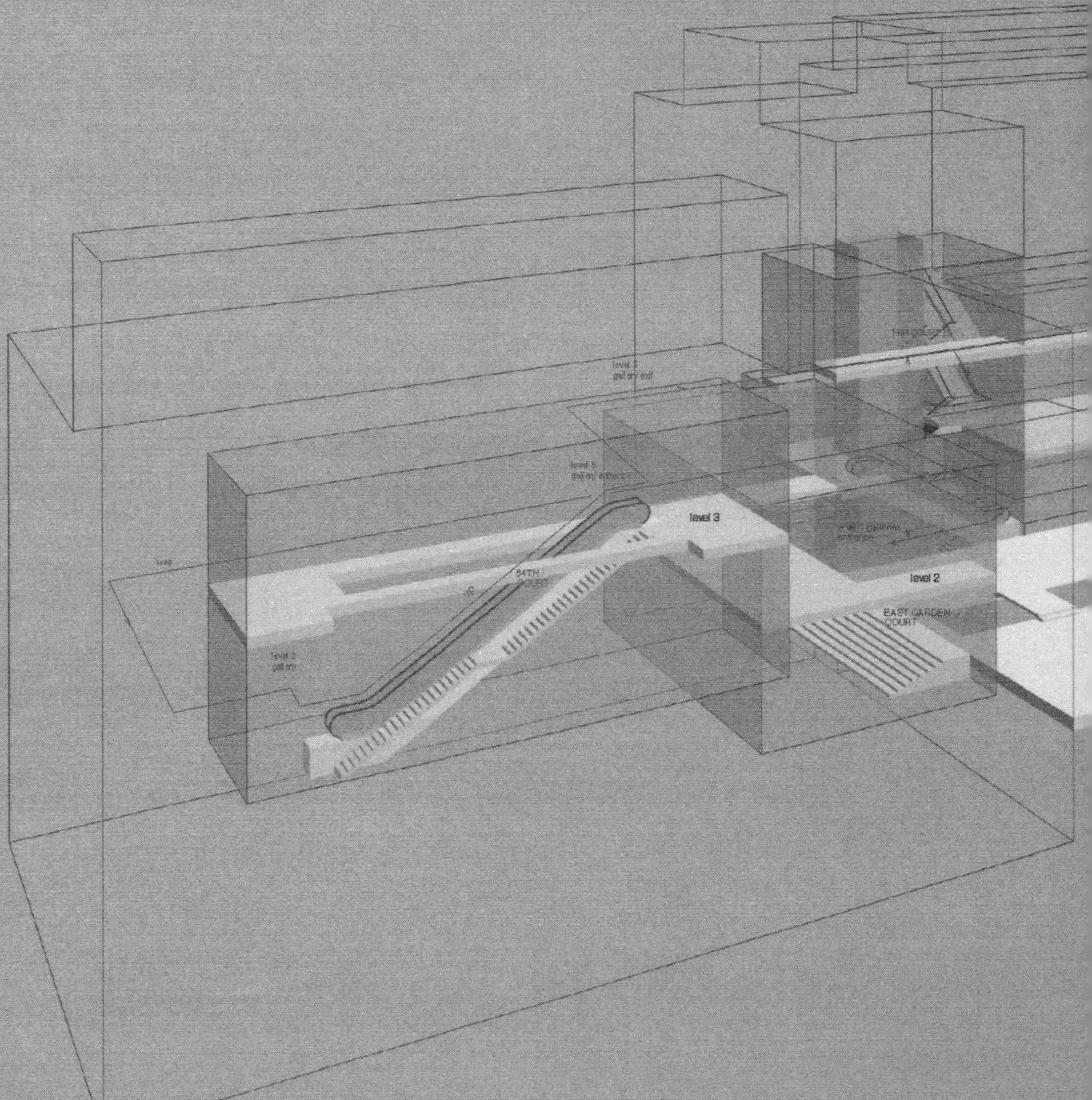

Spaces and Flows:
To our sequence of spaces (the Courts) corresponds a sequence of movements: Loops at different levels allow a multiplicity of circuits throughout the museum while retaining a clarity of orientation.

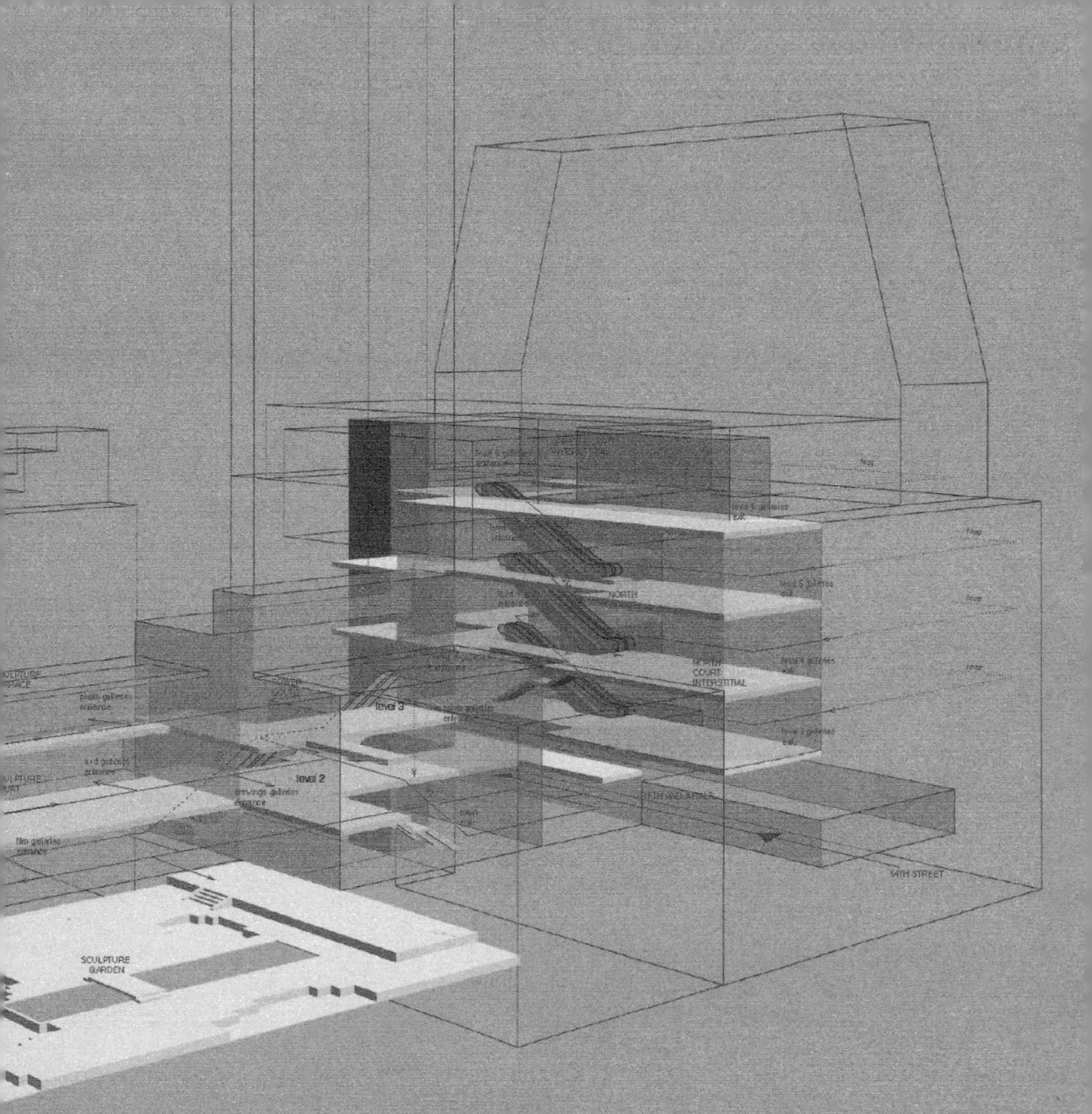

photo galleries entrance
level 3
level 2
drawings galleries entrance
film galleries entrance
NORTH
NORTH COURT INTERSTITIAL
54TH STREET
SCULPTURE GARDEN

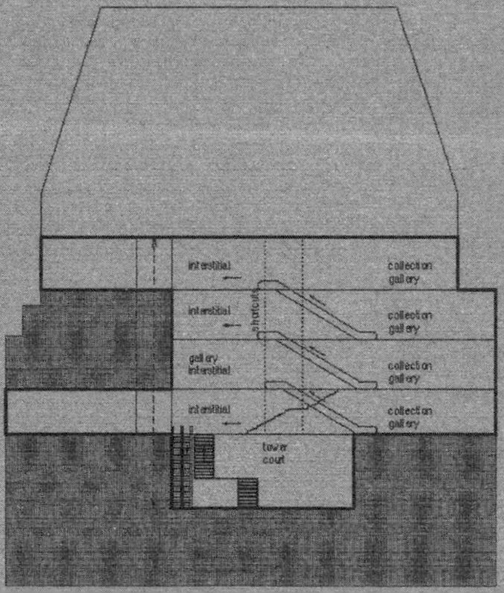

interstitial
collection gallery
interstitial
shortcuts
collection gallery
gallery interstitial
collection gallery
interstitial
collection gallery
tower court

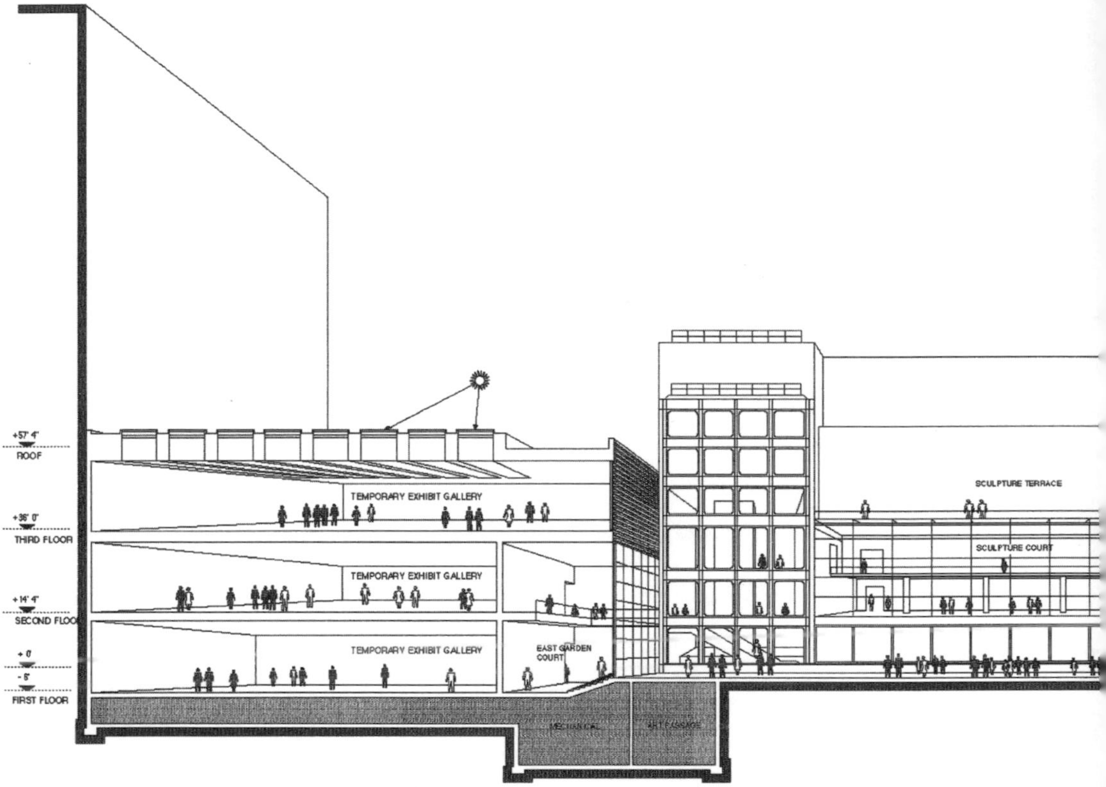
+57' 4"
ROOF
+36' 0"
THIRD FLOOR
+14' 4"
SECOND FLOO
+ 0'
- 6'
FIRST FLOOR
TEMPORARY EXHIBIT GALLERY
TEMPORARY EXHIBIT GALLERY
TEMPORARY EXHIBIT GALLERY
EAST GARDEN COURT
MECHANICAL
ART PASSAGE
SCULPTURE TERRACE
SCULPTURE COURT

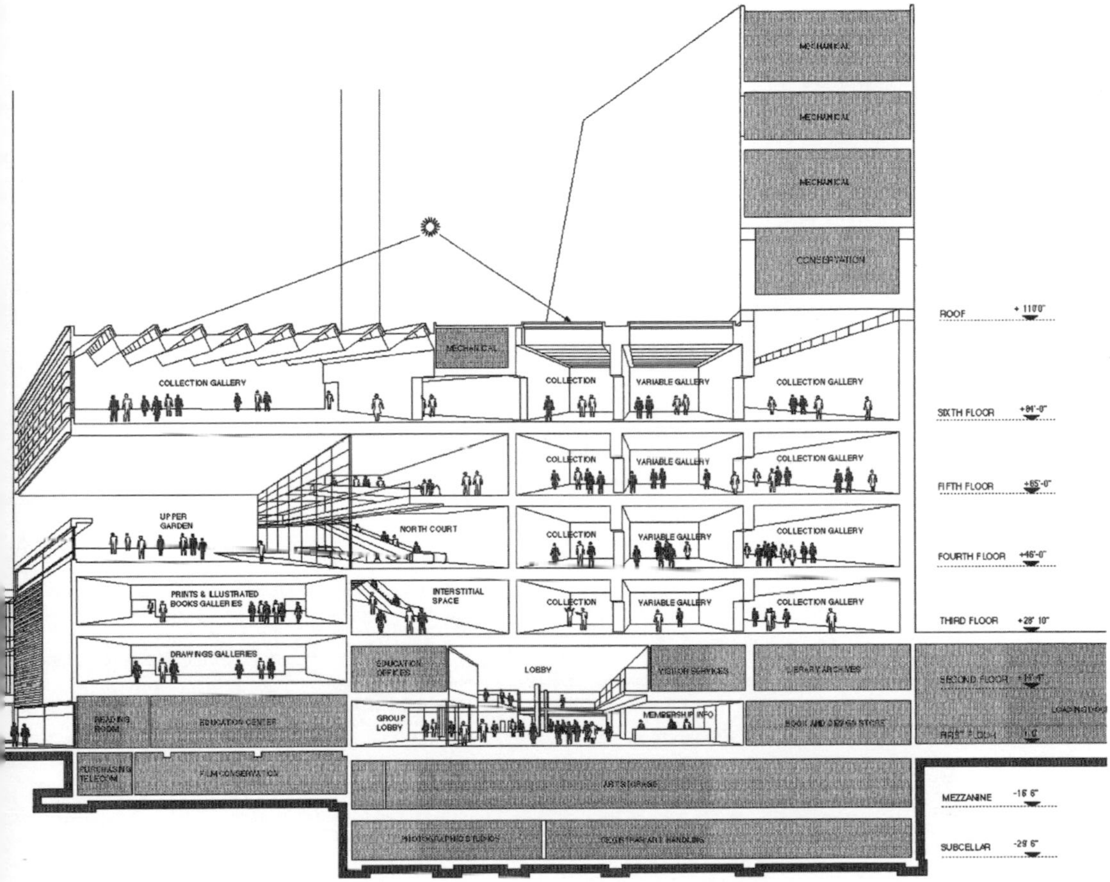
MECHANICAL
MECHANICAL
MECHANICAL
CONSERVATION
ROOF +110'0"
MECHANICAL
COLLECTION GALLERY
COLLECTION
VARIABLE GALLERY
COLLECTION GALLERY
SIXTH FLOOR +84'-0"
COLLECTION
VARIABLE GALLERY
COLLECTION GALLERY
FIFTH FLOOR +65'-0"
UPPER GARDEN
NORTH COURT
COLLECTION
VARIABLE GALLERY
COLLECTION GALLERY
FOURTH FLOOR +46'-0"
PRINTS & ILLUSTRATED BOOKS GALLERIES
INTERSTITIAL SPACE
COLLECTION
VARIABLE GALLERY
COLLECTION GALLERY
THIRD FLOOR +28' 10"
DRAWINGS GALLERIES
EDUCATION OFFICES
LOBBY
VISITOR SERVICES
LIBRARY ARCHIVES
SECOND FLOOR
READING ROOM
EDUCATION CENTER
GROUP LOBBY
MEMBERSHIP INFO
PURCHASING TELECOM
FILM CONSERVATION
ART STORAGE
MEZZANINE -16' 6"
SUBCELLAR -29' 6"

EAST

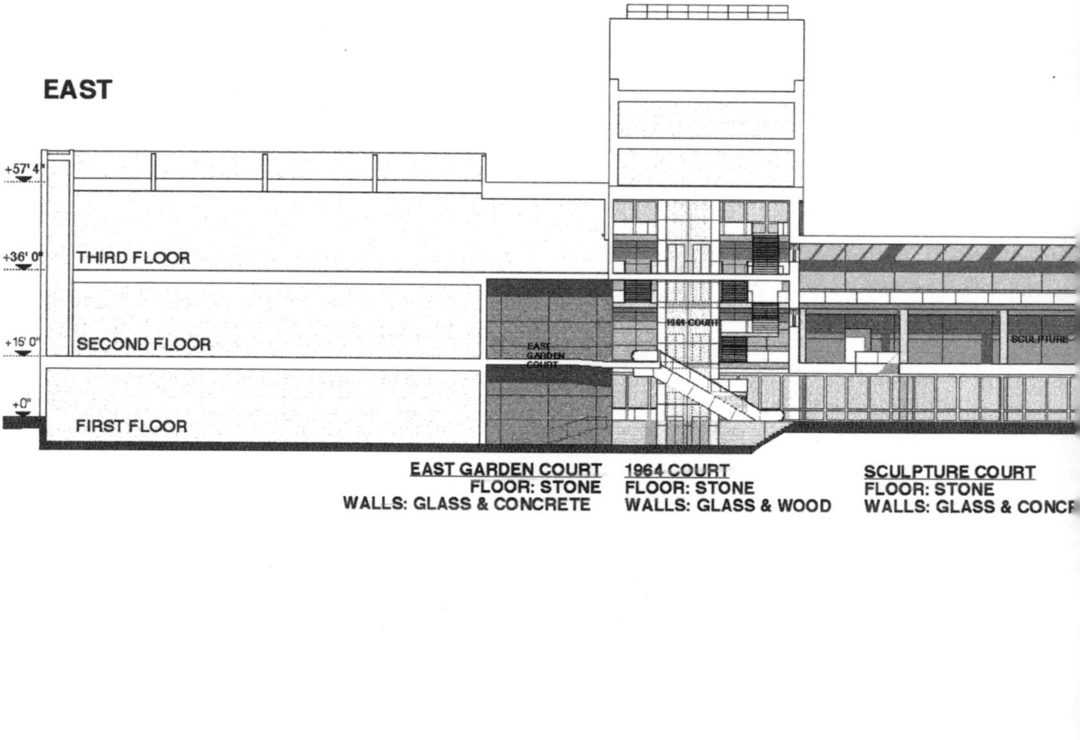
+57' 4"
+36' 0"
THIRD FLOOR
+15' 0"
SECOND FLOOR
+0"
FIRST FLOOR
EAST GARDEN COURT
1964 COURT
SCULPTURE
EAST GARDEN COURT
FLOOR: STONE
WALLS: GLASS & CONCRETE
1964 COURT
FLOOR: STONE
WALLS: GLASS & WOOD
SCULPTURE COURT
FLOOR: STONE
WALLS: GLASS & CONC

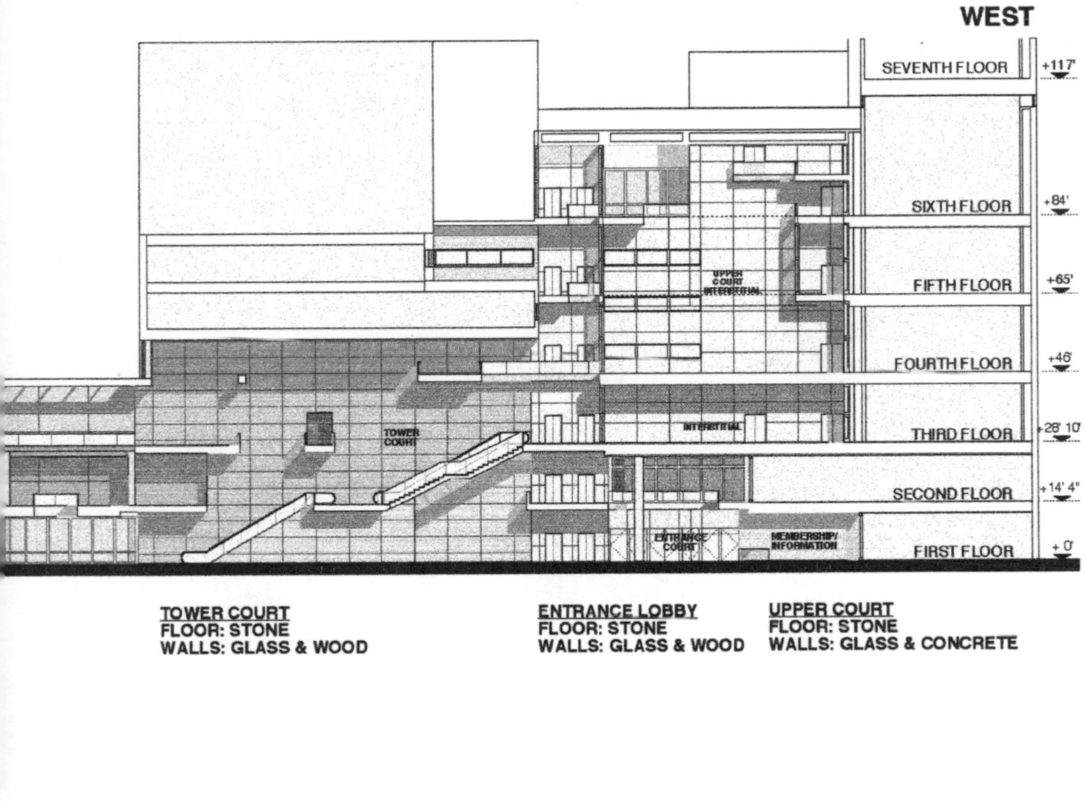

TOWER COURT
FLOOR: STONE
WALLS: GLASS & WOOD

ENTRANCE LOBBY
FLOOR: STONE
WALLS: GLASS & WOOD

UPPER COURT
FLOOR: STONE
WALLS: GLASS & CONCRETE

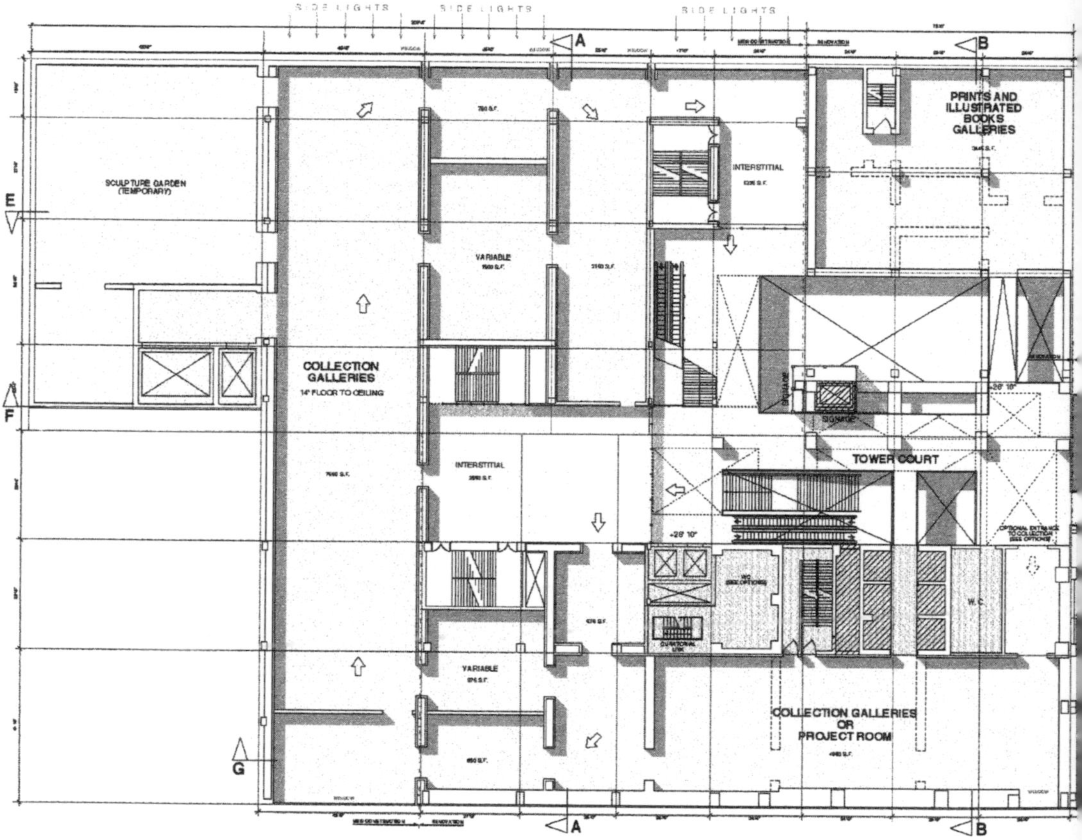
SIDE LIGHTS
SIDE LIGHTS
SIDE LIGHTS
A
B
PRINTS AND ILLUSTRATED BOOKS GALLERIES
INTERSTITIAL
SCULPTURE GARDEN (TEMPORARY)
E
F
G
VARIABLE
COLLECTION GALLERIES
14' FLOOR TO CEILING
INTERSTITIAL
SIGNAGE
TOWER COURT
+28' 10"
OPTIONAL ENTRANCE TO COLLECTION (SEE OPTIONS)
W.C. (SEE OPTIONS)
W.C.
VARIABLE
COLLECTION GALLERIES OR PROJECT ROOM

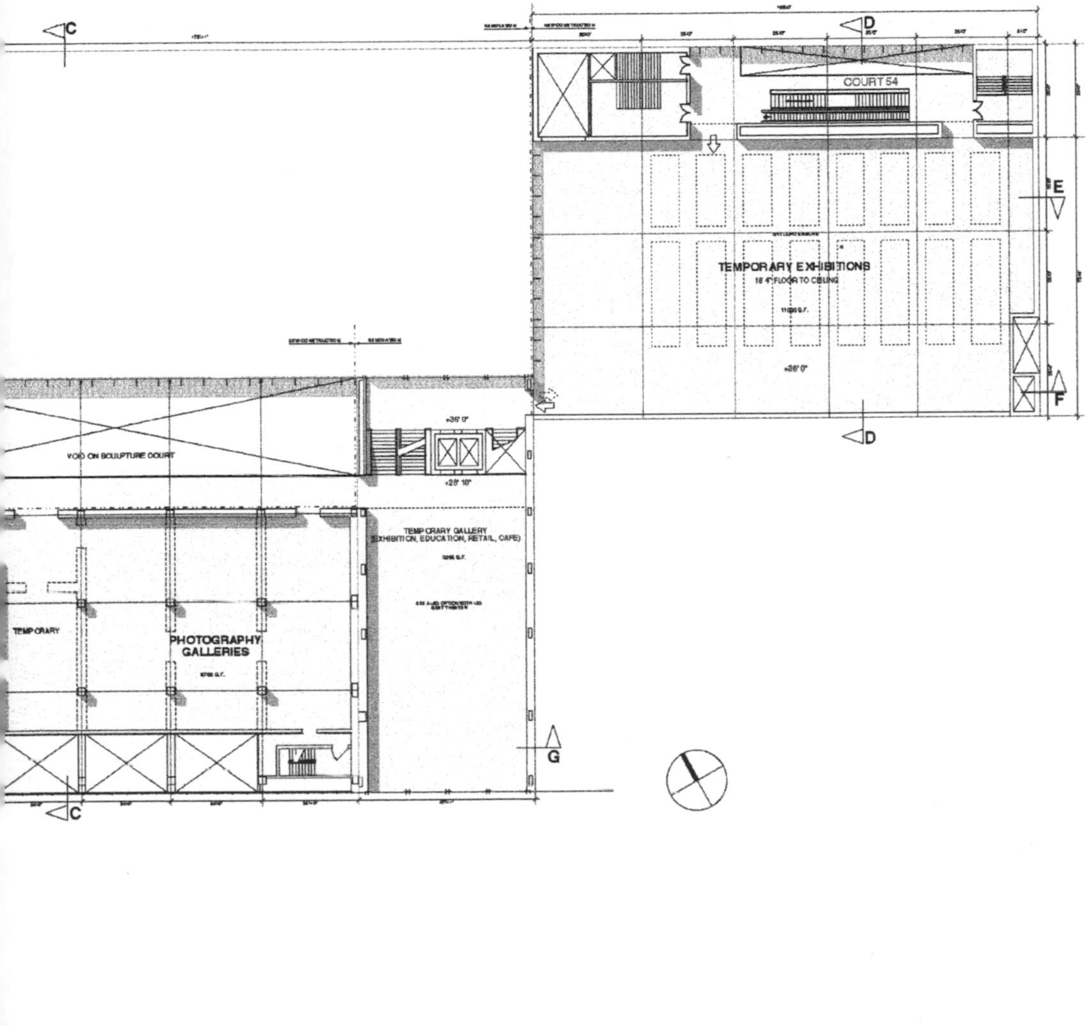
C
D
COURT 54
E
TEMPORARY EXHIBITIONS
F
D
VOID ON SCULPTURE COURT
TEMPORARY GALLERY
(EXHIBITION, EDUCATION, RETAIL, CAFE)
TEMPORARY
PHOTOGRAPHY
GALLERIES
G
C

Third floor

The Courts

The qualities of programmatic flexibility and social space that characterize the Garden are pulled through the museum in the form of multiple interior courts. Diagramming the main circulation spaces within the museum, they serve as public conduits and provide places for activities and artforms that are not easily contained within conventional exhibition galleries, or that require public or social means of address. Several, such as the large Sculpture Court and Upper Garden, can be used for special museum events or performances. The courts need not be used for exhibition—they can serve as simple circulation or voids—but should answer the need for public content as is it arises, providing an important resource for the exhibition of current and emerging art.

Designed with largely glass surfaces, the courts set themselves off from the major galleries and into a more urban, multifaceted, public space. Easily fitted with benches or seating arrangements, they can accommodate video or interactive art as well as electronic installations. Moreover, the location of the courts in proximity to the Permanent Collections and Departmental galleries serves to dynamize readings of art's ongoing history.

The location of specific courts gives visibility to specific media that have not fared well within traditional exhibition contexts. For example, video and related installations can be viewed comfortably in the centrally-located Film Court on the ground-floor level. The very large Sculpture Court, placed on the axis linking Collection to Temporary Exhibition galleries and connecting the Departmental galleries, is a double-height gallery accommodating all foreseeable dimensions of artwork. It permits works to be arranged "synchronically," outside the chronological focus of the Collection galleries, allowing curators to elaborate individual perspectives within different periods or movements of art. Installations and performances as well as large museum events are intended for this highly flexible space that mediates exhibition and social functions. The double-height of the East Garden Court, which serves as a common area linking the different spaces of the Temporary Exhibitions Wing, can make use of vistas across the Garden in conjunction with special exhibitions of the electronically-oriented Barbara Krugers of the future.

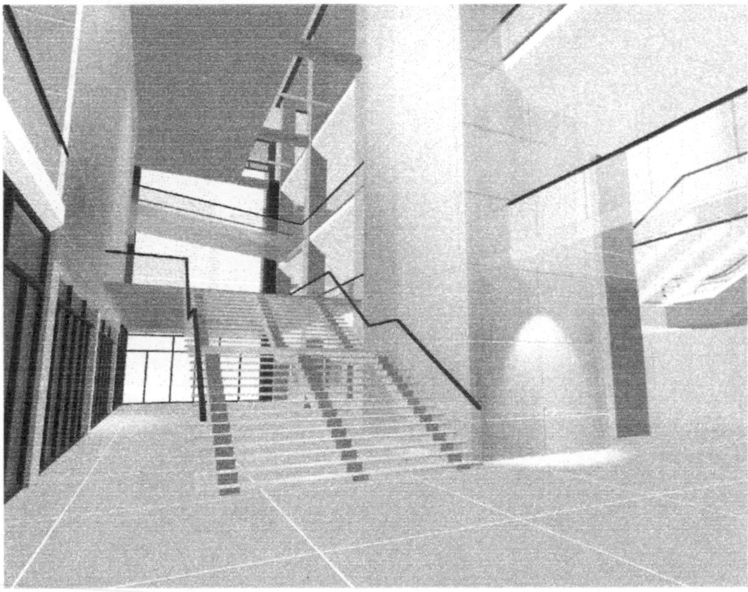

COLLECTION
GALLERIES

COLLECTION
GALLERIES

The Collection Gallery Sequence

As opposed to the dynamic spaces of the courts, the galleries are largely conceived as static spaces. Their starting point is simplicity and sobriety, with details that do not call attention to themselves. Pure space and diffused light are regarded as the optimal conditions for viewing art.

The structure of fixed and variable galleries allows for asides, for presenting works differing in style or approach but related in period; for exhibiting works from other disciplines or media—architecture, drawings, prints, photographs—so as to enrich the field of perception of the work on view. Extraneous historical or biographical material can also be integrated in this manner. The "gameboard" principle allows for curatorial intervention in the configuration of individual galleries.

The ceiling of the 6th-floor cantilever gallery contains controlling systems that can filter or obscure light, allowing video or projected art to be exhibited. A "black box" gallery, divisible into independent spaces, also occupies this floor.

"GAMES"

ALTERNATIVE 1:
ENFILADES OF INTERMEDIATE SIZED GALLERIES OF DIFFERENT PROPORTIONS

EXTENDED VISUAL AXES CONNECT A CLEARLY ORDERED SEQUENCE OF GALLERIES.

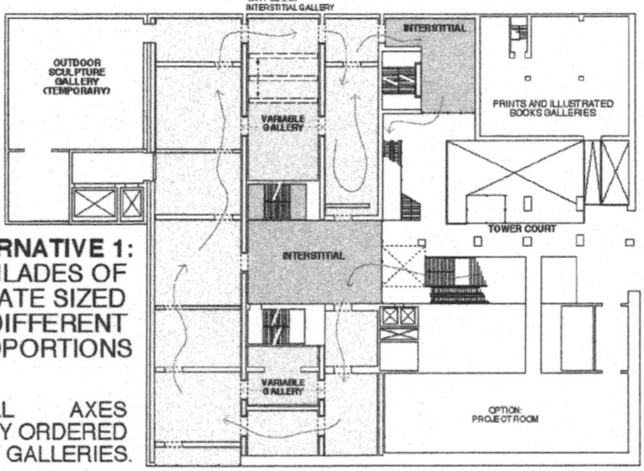

ALTERNATIVE 2:
INTIMATE GALLERIES WITH MULTIPLE RELATIONSHIPS TO THE PRIMARY SEQUENCE

THE GALLERIES ARE SUBDIVIDED INTO A GREATER NUMBER OF SMALLER ROOMS. ALL ROOMS DO NOT HAVE TO BE TRAVERSED TO COMPLETE THE THIRD FLOOR SUB-SEQUENCE; SOME GALLERIES ARE "SIDE GALLERIES" (1) AND OTHERS ARE "PARALLEL GALLERIES" (2).

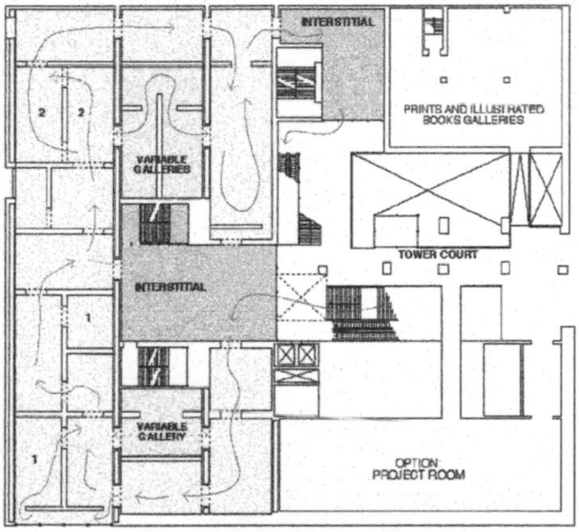

ALTERNATIVE 3:
AN EXPANDED COLLECTION SEQUENCE WITH ENTRANCE ADJACENT TO SCULPTURE COURT

THE PROJECT ROOM IS REPLACED BY THE FIRST SEVERAL GALLERIES OF THE COLLECTION SEQUENCE; THE REST OF THE COLLECTION SEQUENCE REMAINS THE SAME. THE STAIRS AND ESCALATORS FROM THE GROUND FLOOR LOBBY ARE REVERSED TO ARRIVE IN FRONT OF THIS NEW COLLECTION ENTRANCE.

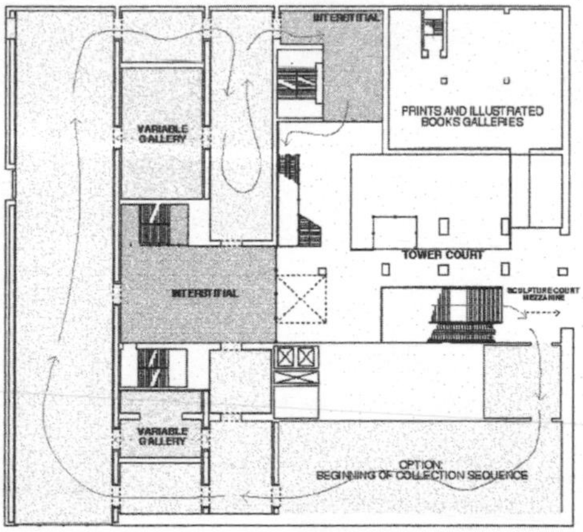

EXIT

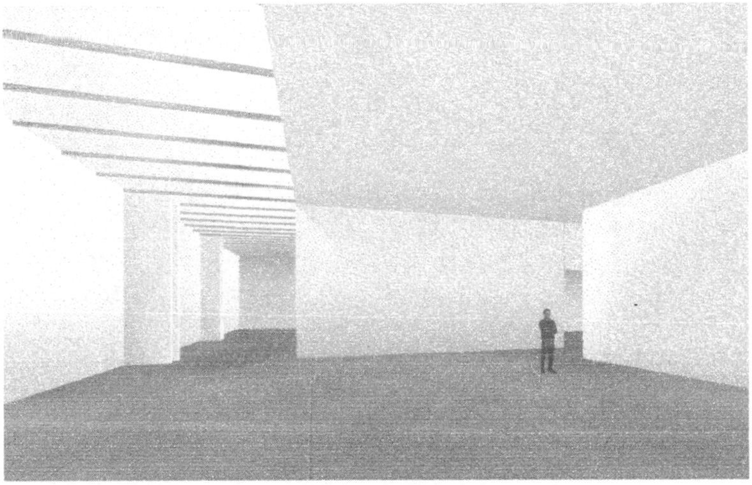

Lausanne, EPFL Extension, 1993

Solids and Voids: Reversal

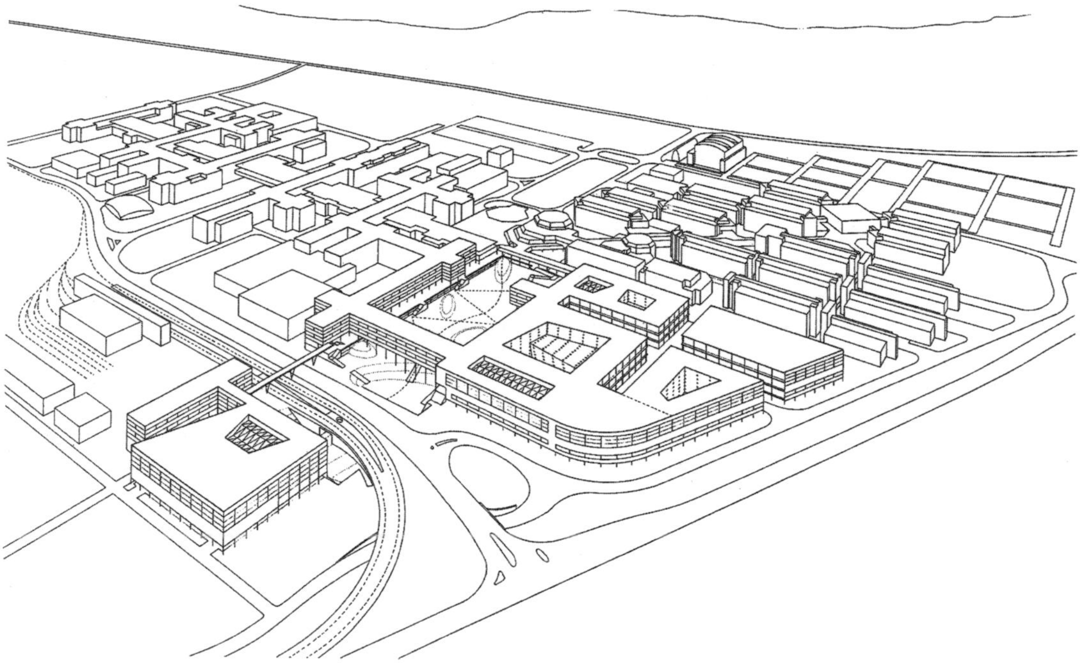

Reversal (Inversion)

A competition was organized for the extension of the Federal Institute of Technology in Lausanne (EPFL), requesting space for a new school of architecture, a biophysics institute, and a large auditorium. One question raised was the relation between the new buildings and the existing master plan.

To continue the grid system of bands of building blocks of the two first stages of EPFL would have repeated the current problems of the ensemble—an often rigid circulation system and an architecture of residual spaces. At the same time, it would have been just as inappropriate to replace these bands totally with a monumental object, creating a rupture with the existing buildings.

On the contrary, we tried to rehabilitate spaces that maintain a certain quality: the urban spaces, the "patios," the "green spaces." Using a play on words in the French language, these are "les cours"—both "le cours" and "la cour"—since the plural "les cours" can also be used in the singular, suggesting both a long, rectangular, and often tree-lined plaza ("le cours") and a courtyard ("la cour").

In the balancing of solids and voids, we proposed a concept that brings a vision of a whole to the two preceding phases, and retroactively gives them meaning. We wanted this new phase to be perceived as a point of departure for EPFL, so that the first phases seem to follow the same logic as the last phase.

This manifests a fundamental process of reversal:
What was solid has become void.
What was void has become solid.

What was built has become open space.
What was open space has become built.

What was "figure" has become "ground."
What was "ground" has become "figure."

We began by employing the hypothesis of a terrain totally occupied by a dense, continuous, built mass that is 16 meters high (the average height of the first-phase buildings). The bands of the 86.4-meter-square built grid of the first phase are used, but emptied, so that they emerge as open space. Other spaces are added, following the programmatic and architectural demands of this new phase.

The Voids

In short, our project was to instill the creation of spaces rather than the creation of forms. Each of these spaces, these "cours," possesses its own specific character in its own particular facade type.

The Solids

We did not want to privilege the voids at the expense of the solids in the program. Hence, we sought clarity and a precise typology for each different department so both to permit a clear reading of the buildings, and to allow for simple and flexible organization and phasing.

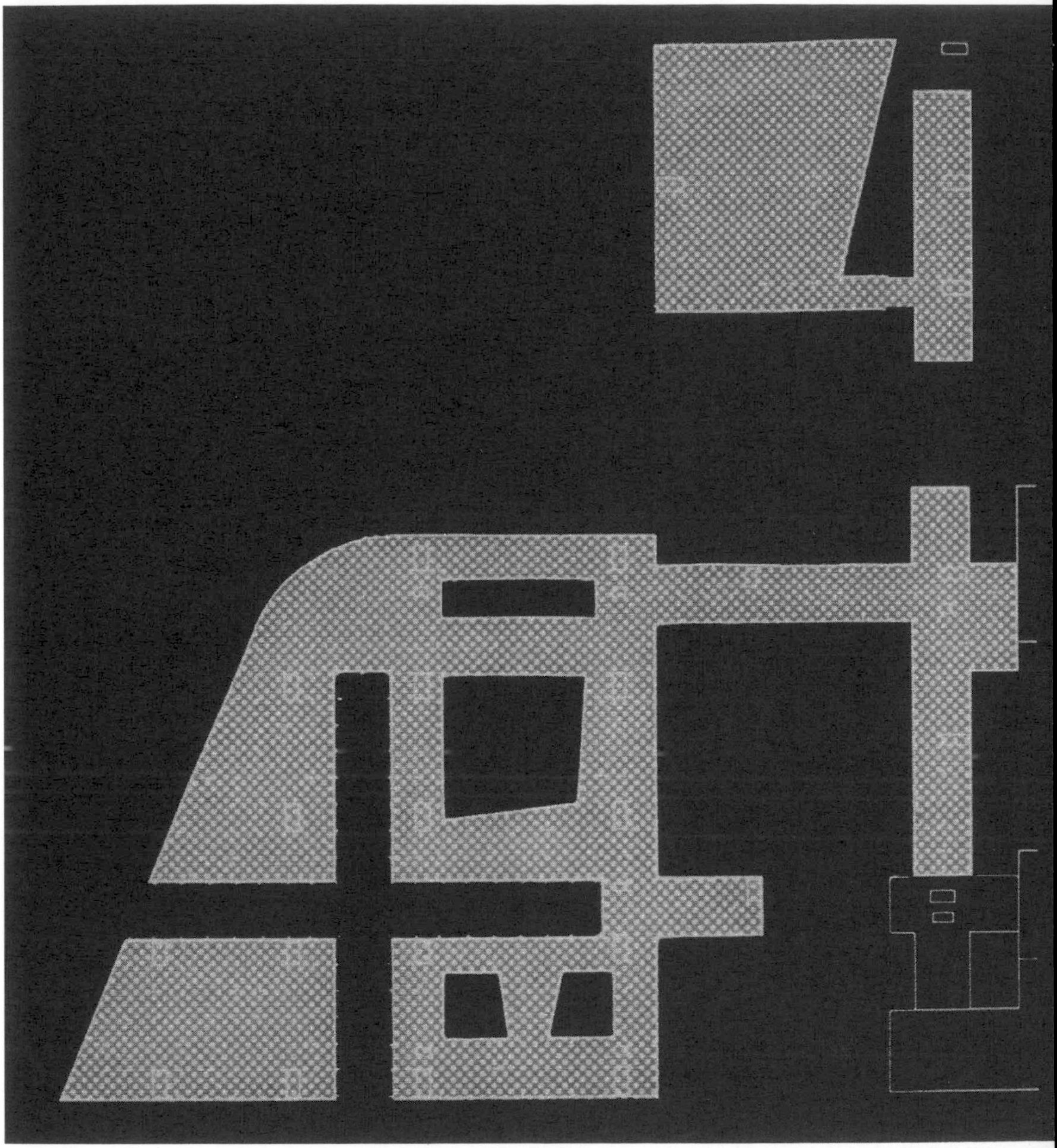

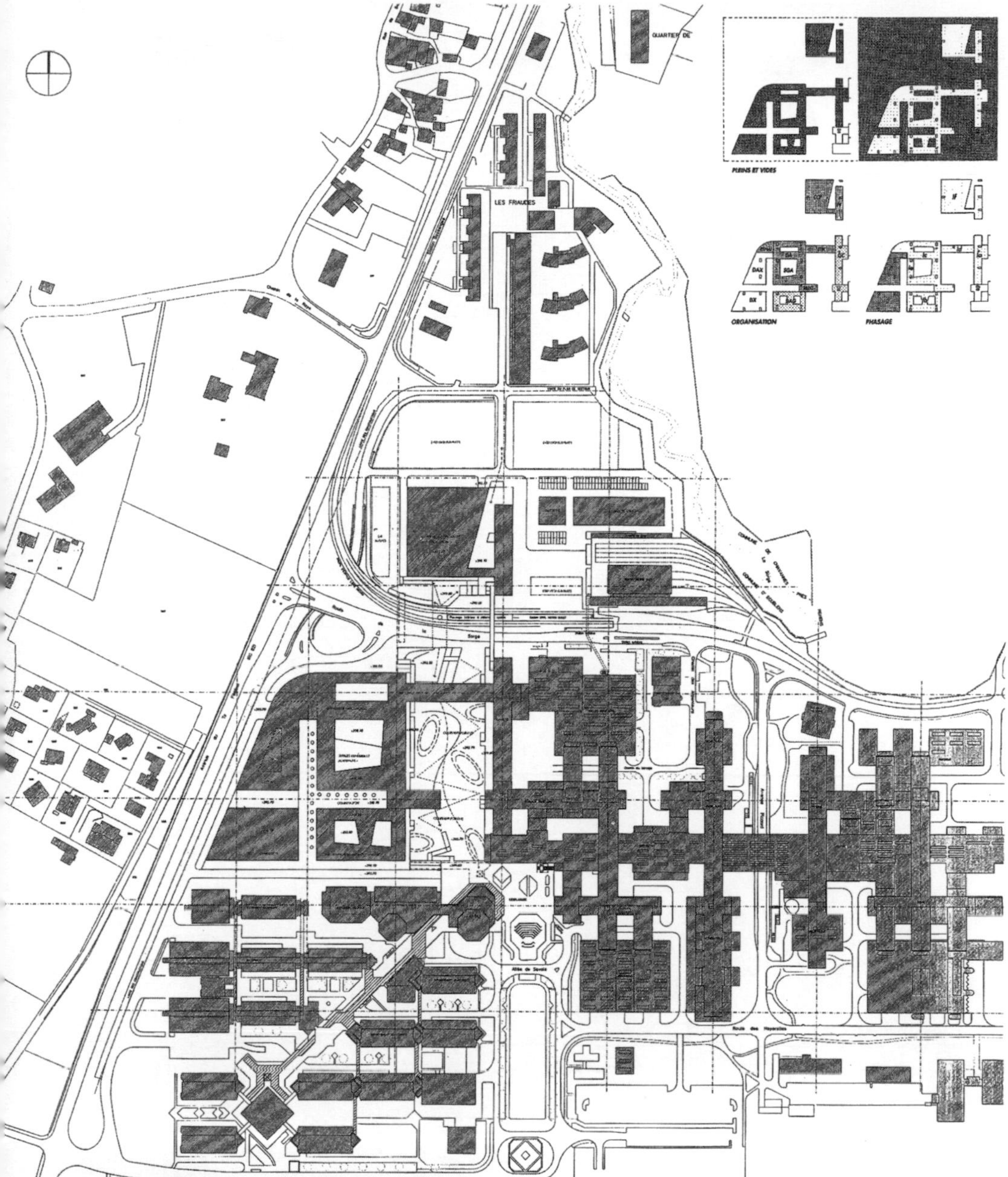

Site plan: our proposition (upper-middle left, with a curved wall) reverses the logic of the original master plan (middle right of plan above). Solids become voids, voids become solids

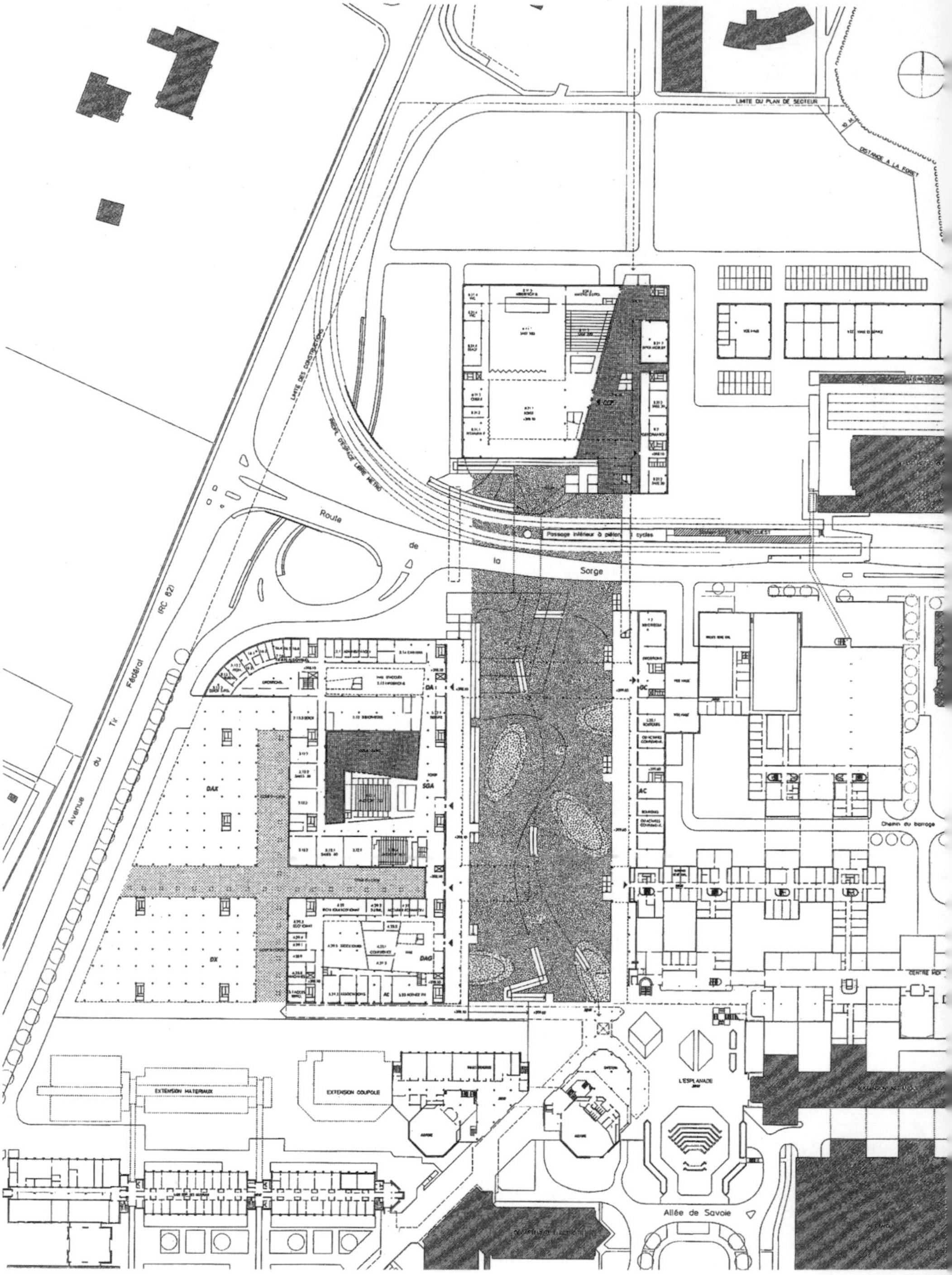

Ground floor plan

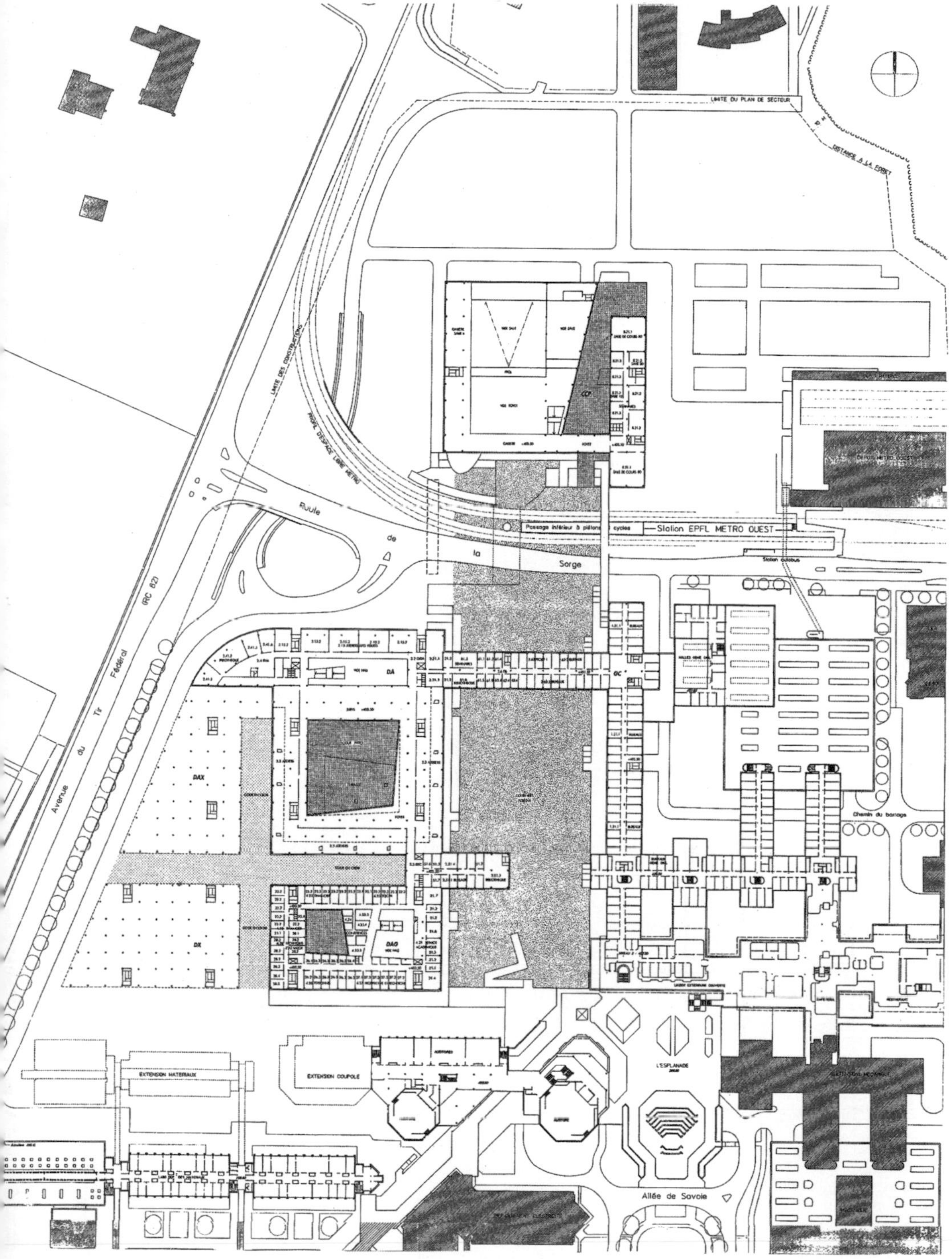

First floor plan

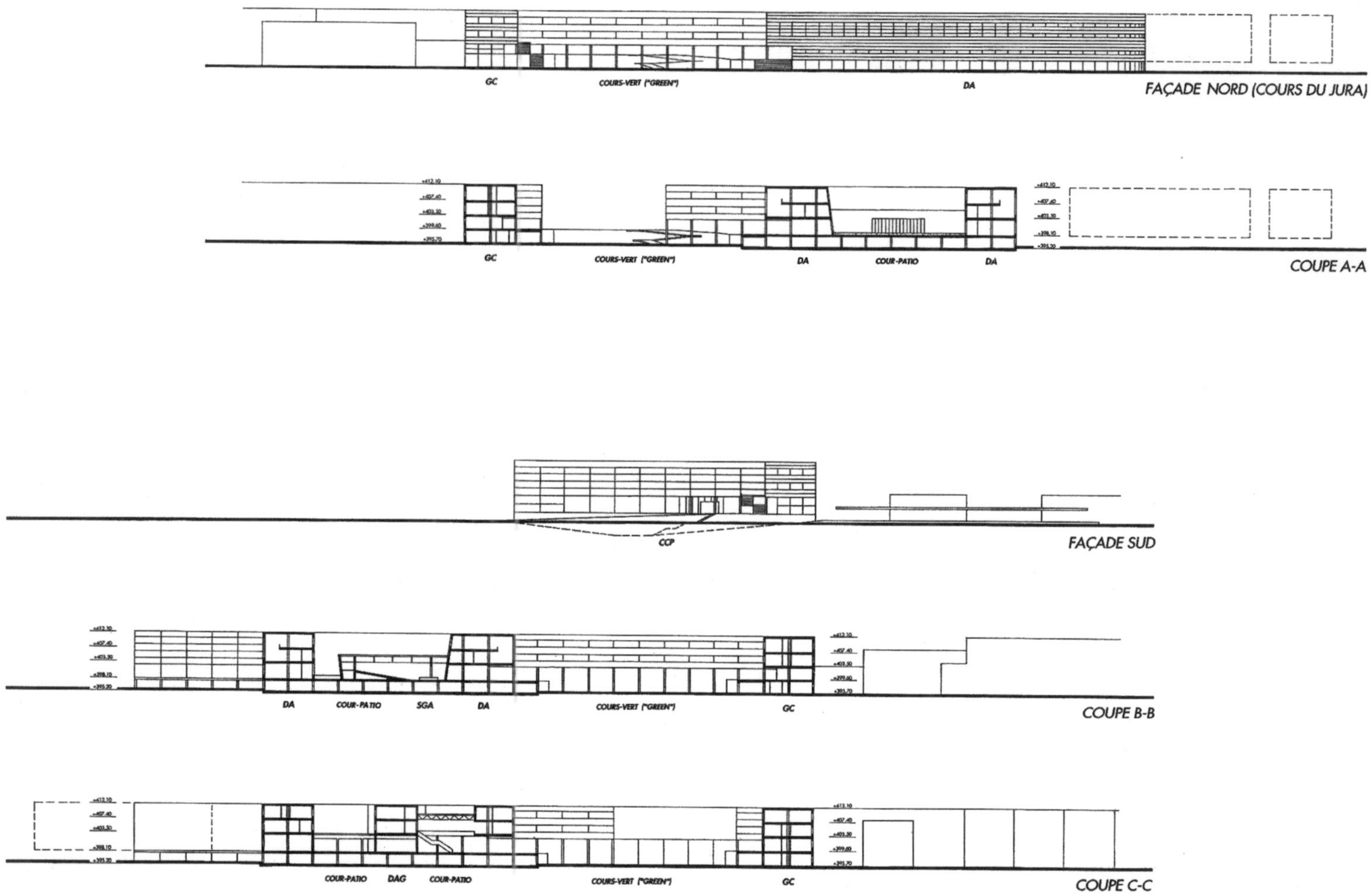
GC
COURS-VERT ("GREEN")
DA
FAÇADE NORD (COURS DU JURA)
GC
COURS-VERT ("GREEN")
DA
COUR-PATIO
DA
COUPE A-A
CCP
FAÇADE SUD
DA
COUR-PATIO
SGA
DA
COURS-VERT ("GREEN")
GC
COUPE B-B
COUR-PATIO
DAG
COUR-PATIO
COURS-VERT ("GREEN")
GC
COUPE C-C

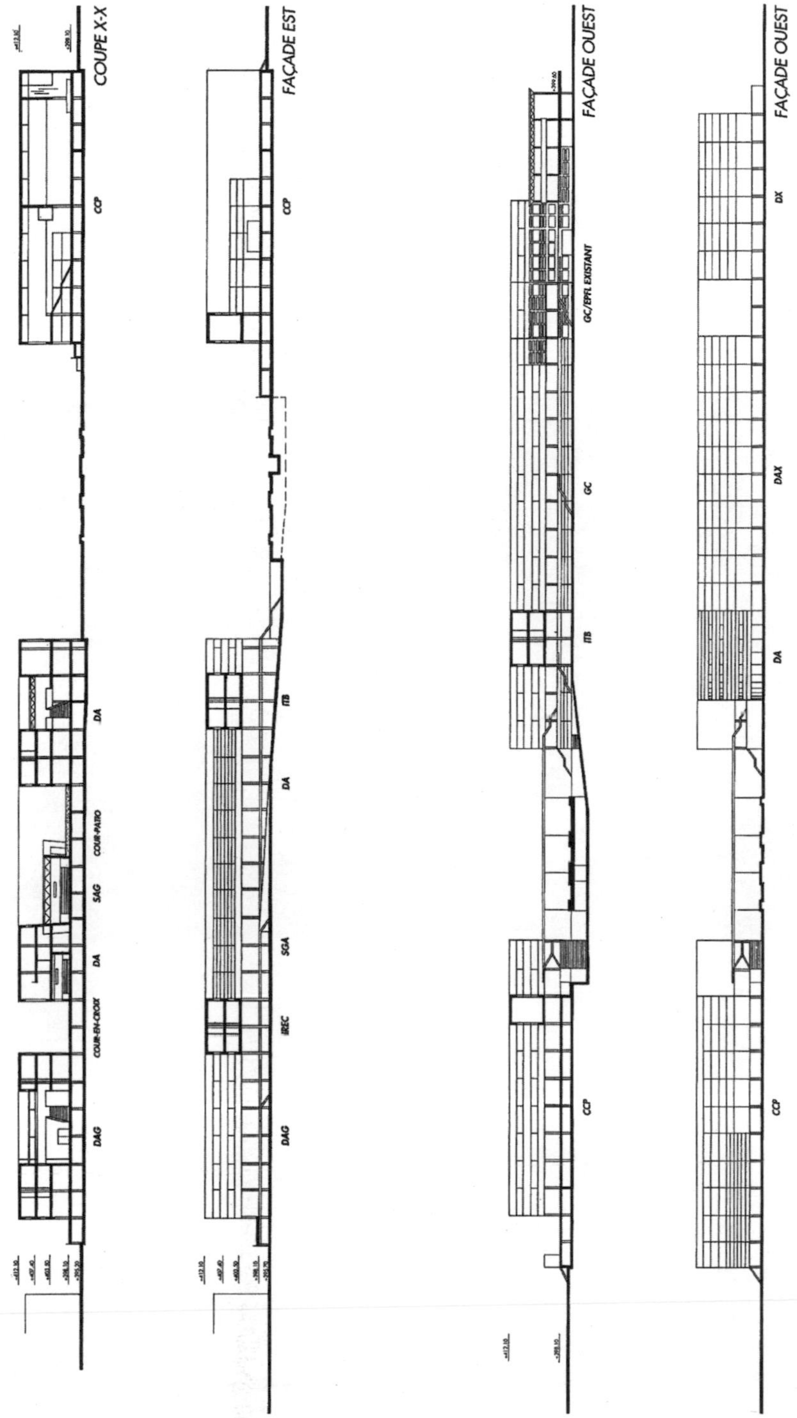
COUPE X-X
CCP
DA
COUR-PATIO
SAG
DA
COUR-EN-CROIX
DAG
FAÇADE EST
CCP
ITB
DA
SGA
IREC
DAG
FAÇADE OUEST
GC/EPFL EXISTANT
GC
ITB
CCP
FAÇADE OUEST
DX
DAX
DA
CCP

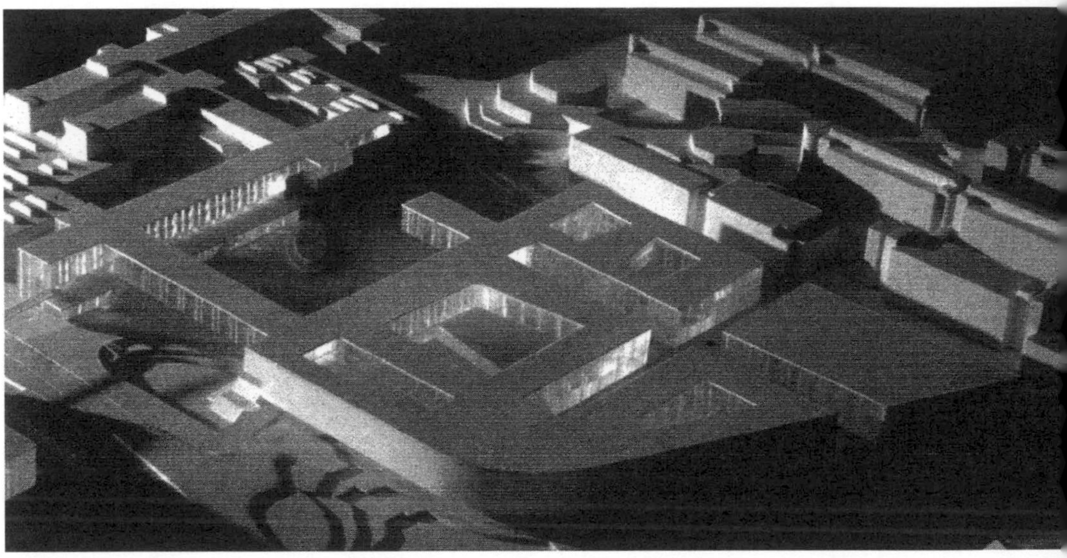

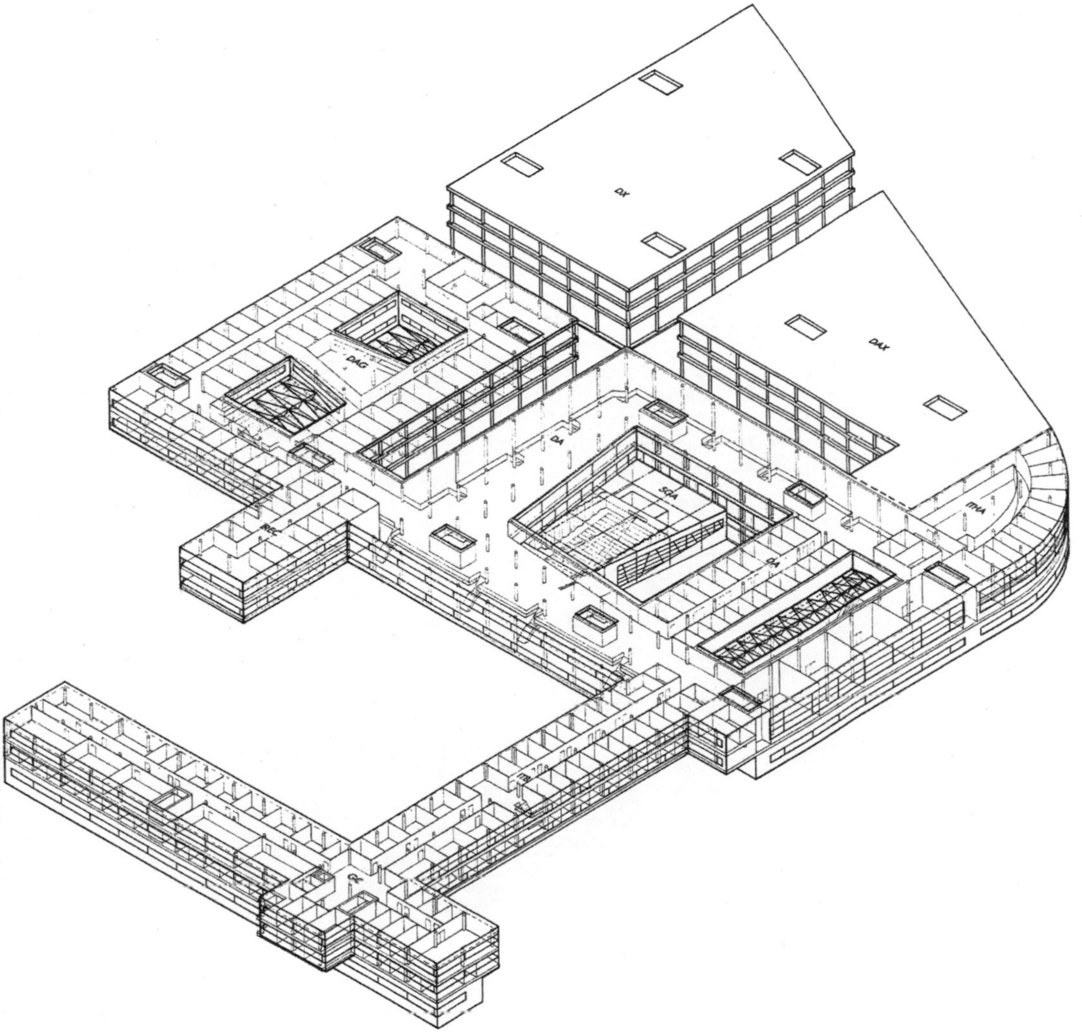
DX
DAX
DAG
DA
SGA
ITHA
REC
DA

C.G.T.

RENAULT
C.G.T.
AUGMENTATION IMMÉDIATE
SALAIRES
Pour le

Paris, Renault Ile Seguin
Master Plan, 1995

Linear Solids

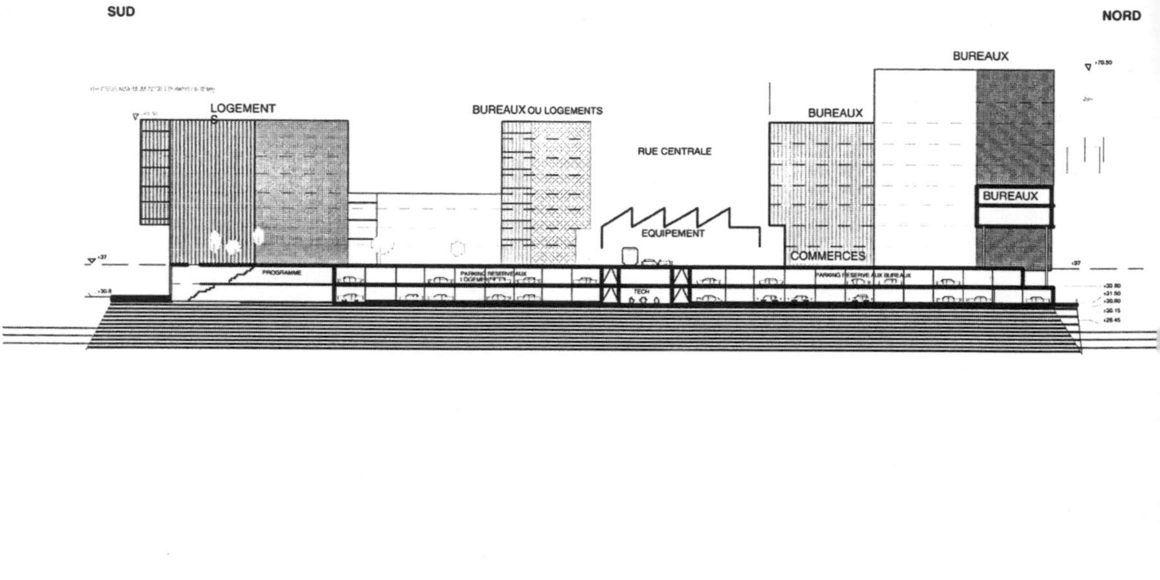

Cross section

After the Renault car factory on the Ile Seguin on the outskirts of Paris moved to other locations, an important part of the social and industrial history of the early 20th-century was left vacant. (The striking ship-like image of a factory floating on the River Seine is part of the French collective imagination). Renault decided, against all sentimentality, to demolish the decayed industrial remnants in order to build a major program of housing, offices, and a Museum of the Automobile. As opposed to Fiat's Lingotto in Turin, the pre-World War II construction of the Renault factory took place incrementally, and is made of often-improvised additions which are now severely rusting and difficult, if not impossible, to restore or re-use.

We proposed to demolish the existing buildings but retain the assembly-like spirit as well as ship-like fortress appearance of the original building. To achieve this, we kept the idea of a relentless organizing grid, and defined programmatic territories in a linear manner. The solid bulk of the ship-like mass has found its counterpart in the articulation of linear solids along the longitudinal direction of the island. Offices and housing are implemented according to the required programmatic density, while the museum is located at the tip of the island, at its most symbolic location. The linear solids define linear voids for circulation and unprogrammed activities.

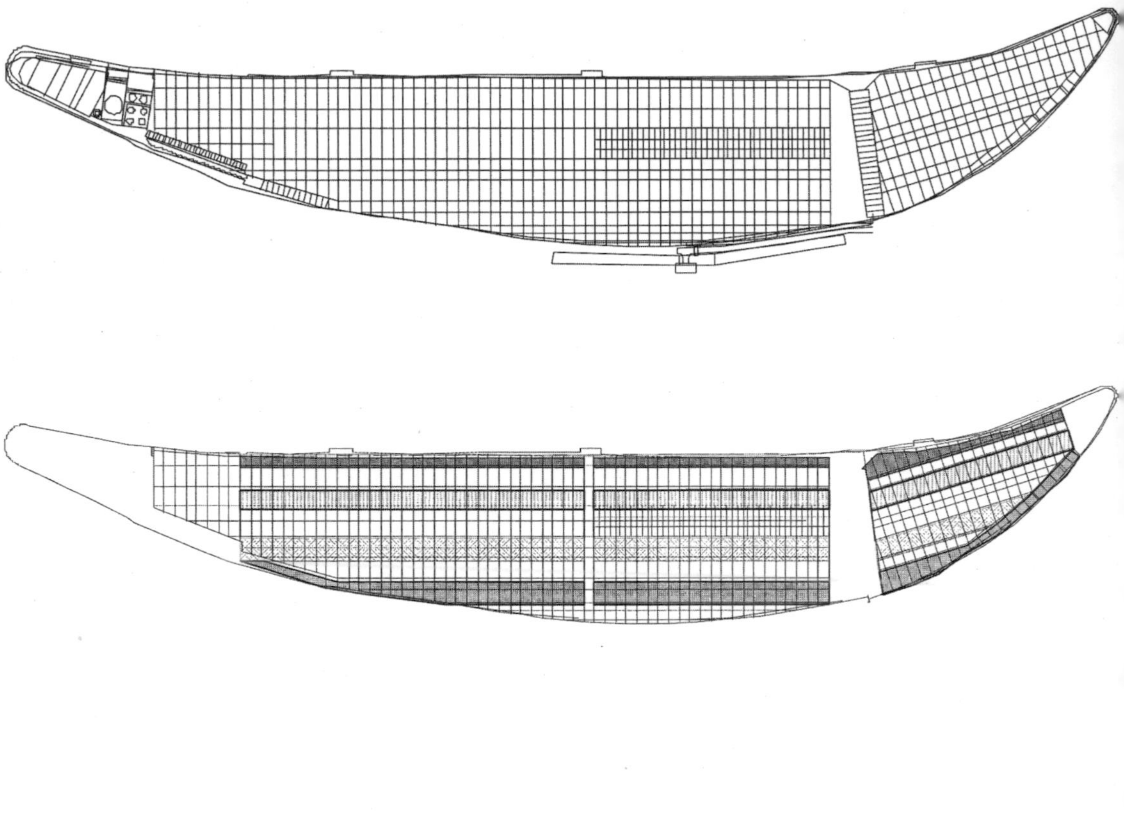

Existing grid and grid of island

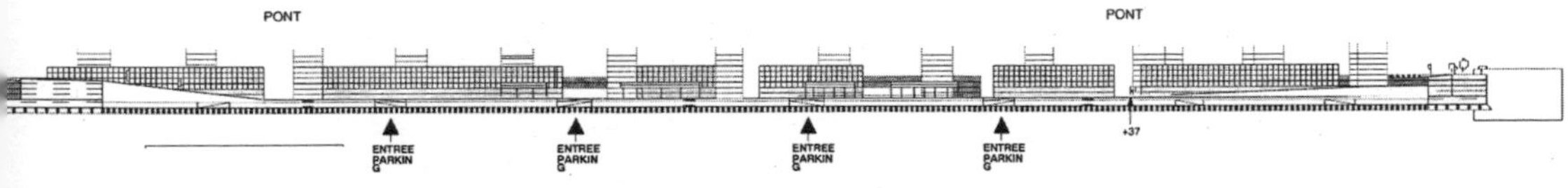

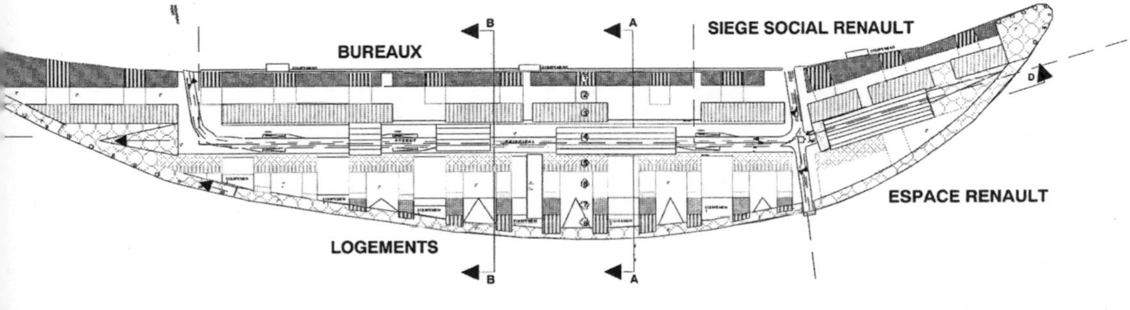

Longitudinal section and plan: offices, housing, Renault headquarters, Museum of the Automobile

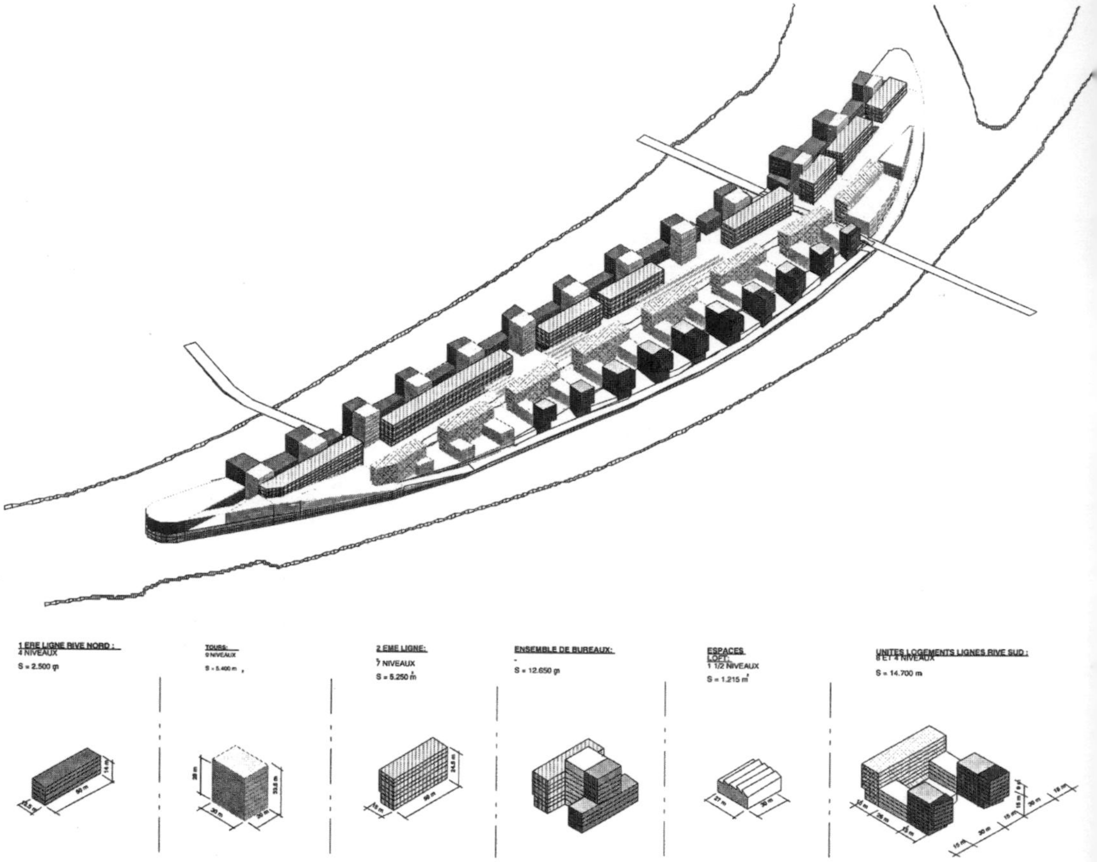

A typology of solids and voids

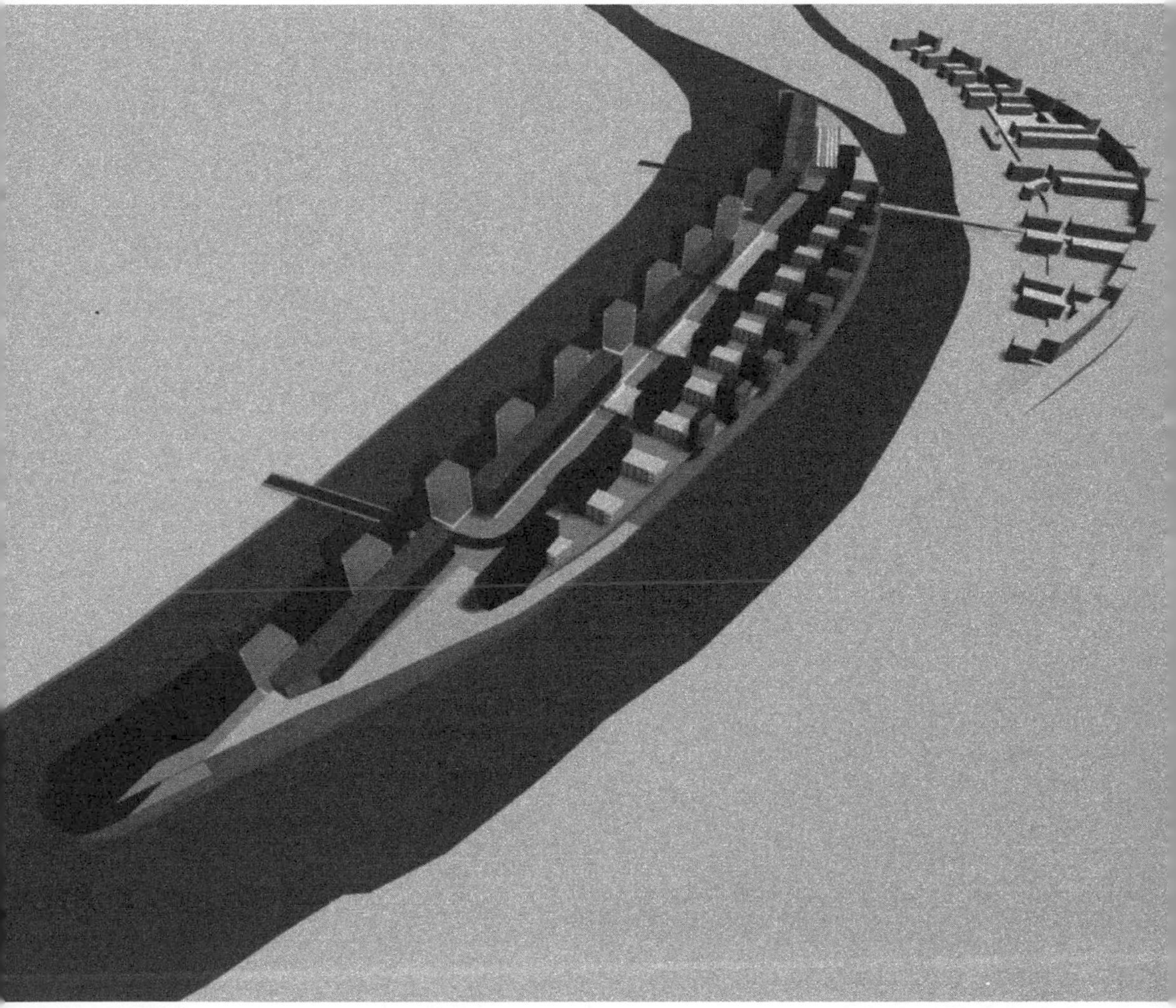

D.
Activators

Two schools of architecture, one on the outskirts of Paris, the other on the edges of Miami, Florida, are similarily organized. Two generic wings—one for studios, the other for offices—define a central unprogrammed space, activated by "generators" containing the more public functions of the program (auditorium, reading room, art gallery, café, etc.). All circulation occurs along and within the open space and through the generators, so that the movement vectors activate the main public space of the building. Here, too, the unprogrammed space is the place for appropriation, the potential place of the occasional event.

Marne-la-Vallée, School of Architecture, 1994–

Zero Degree Architecture 2

cite

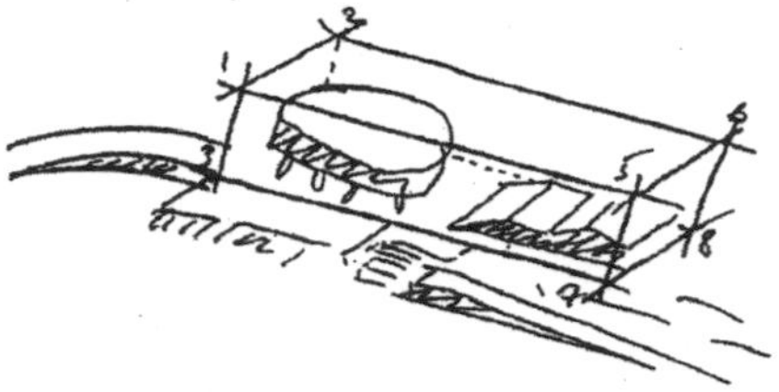

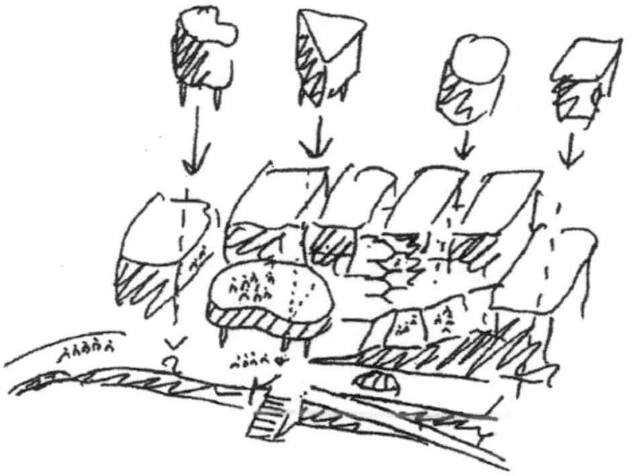

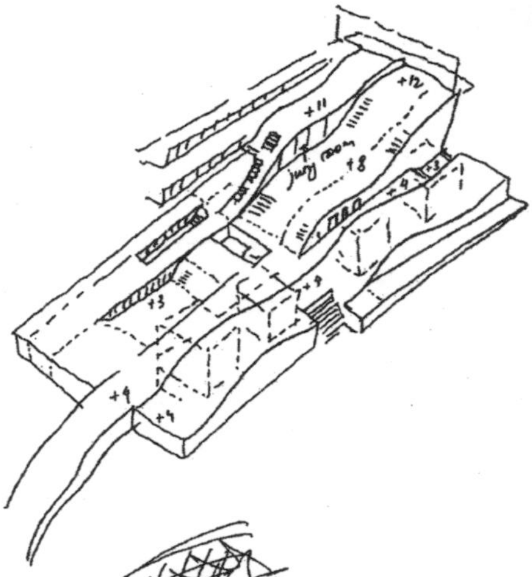
+11
+12
jury room
+8
+4

Urbanism

1.1 Conceiving of a new school of architecture located 30 minutes outside Paris raises two questions. The first has to do with the direction that architectural education will take in the next decades. The second has to do with the attraction that a school situated on the edge, the periphery, the margin of the social, economic, and cultural density of an urban center can have.

1.2 Today, a triple revolution—informational, interdisciplinary, and ideological—is in the making. At Marne-la-Vallée, located a short distance from the heart of Paris, one is at the same electronic distance from London, Berlin, Tokyo, New York, or Delhi. Now there is global architectural culture and information; the conditions alone are local.

1.3 Historically, people headed towards the centers in order to learn, teach, and debate. Here, at Marne, one does the opposite: one decenters, "marginalizes" oneself in some way. However, what could appear as a considerable handicap can be transformed into a valuable advantage. Located away from habits of thought related to the conservation of historical centers, the site, set amidst a new 20,000-student technological complex, can be seen as a starting point for a new model.

1.4 For this new school we aimed at designing a space conceived for the age of the modem and mobility, a new type of architecture school that does not look for inspiration to the old Ecole des Beaux Arts, the Bauhaus, the American universities, or elsewhere.

1.5 Our project starts from the following thesis: there are building-generators of events. They are often condensers of the city. As much through their programs as through their spatial potential, they accelerate a cultural or social transformation that is already in progress.

Architecture

2.1 What we call the City of Architecture rearranges all the rigorously programmed activities around an unprogrammed, event-oriented, large central space (25 by 100 meters), activated by the density of what surrounds it, which, in the most unexpected way, becomes a space for celebrations and balls, encounters and debates, projections and artists' installations, the most serious symposia and avant-garde exhibitions. A social and cultural space, the central hall gathers together all of the circulation in the school. Whatever the level of attendance on any given day, one sees the constant movement of students, giving the hall liveliness and dynamism.

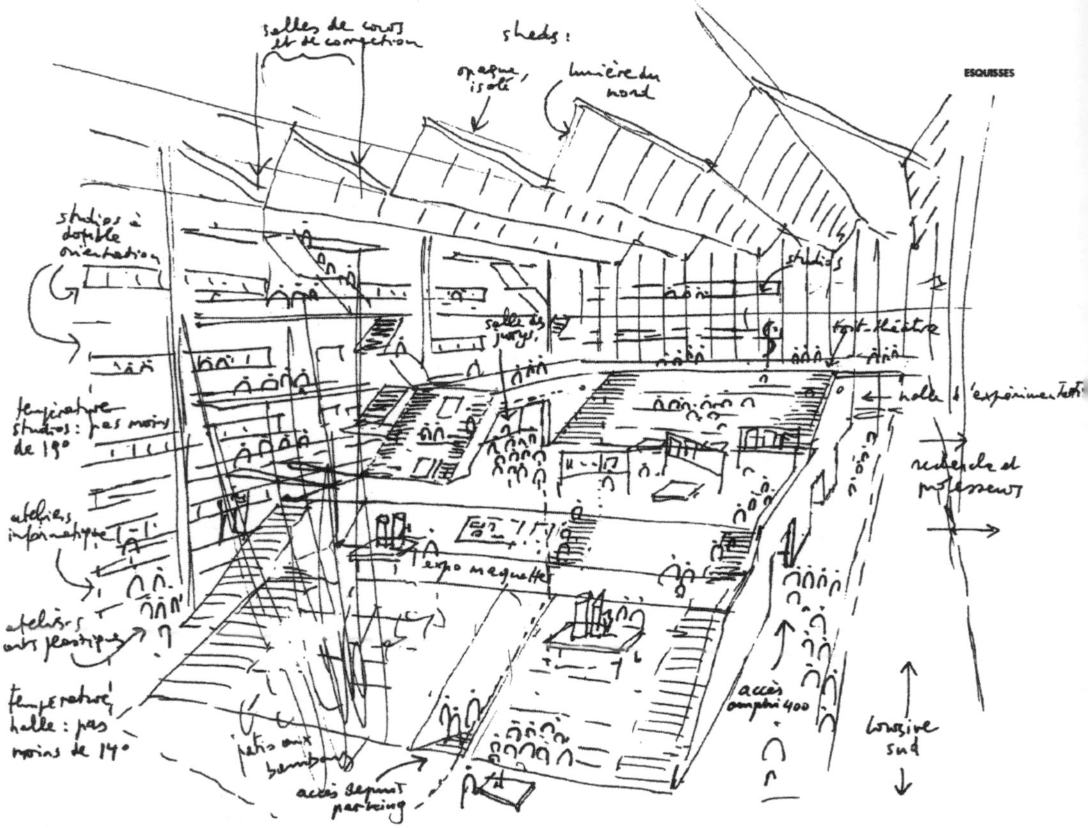
salles de cours et de correction
sheds :
opaque, isolé
lumière du nord
studios à double orientation
studios
salle des jurys
température studios : pas moins de 19°
recherche et professeurs
ateliers informatique
expo maquettes
ateliers arts plastiques
température halle : pas moins de 14°
patio aux bambous
accès depuis parking
accès amphi 400
coursive sud

2.2 All the functional and programmatic parts of the school open onto the large interior rectangle: the studios, the ateliers, the computer spaces, the médiathèque, the faculty offices, the administration and research areas surround and define this cultural, communal, and event-seeking space.

2.3 The building is also a large promenade which, as in a city, can have several points of departure. The two main ones are from the staircase towards the south in the continuation of the Descartes axis and from the ramp to the west. From the main entry (south), one arrives at the reception area, the exhibition spaces and the bar / restaurant. Walking in an oblique direction, one then climbs at an oblique angle over the 400-seat ampitheater and reaches the jury spaces and studios. One could also take the "short-cut" provided by the staircase towards the research areas, the administration, or the studios. Other short-cuts (from the roofs of the auditoriums) allow direct passage from the walkways of the administration or faculty offices to the studios.

2.4 As in many institutions, access to the site is often by car through an interior parking area. In the City of Architecture, this arrival is made through a patio in the middle of the hall.

2.5 From the central hall it is possible to see activity in the studios. The production of projects is part of the image of the school: students and teachers see what is happening—information, communication, discussion. The double orientation of the studios gives them a south side (towards the large hall) and a north side with the stable light necessary for the new extensive use of computers in architectural design.

2.6 The general level for the reception and circulation is at +3.50 meters in order to allow a better relation with the studios and the staircases. The interior landscape slopes up to level +10.50 meters, passing through the jury and student-work exhibition spaces and above the amphitheaters seating 400 and, alternatively, 135 or 90 people. Exchange is the heart of the school.

2.7 The studio spaces and the ateliers are based on the same loft-space envelope that allows maximum flexibility for groups of 25, 50, or 75 students. The seminar and jury / pin-up rooms are interchangeable, inserted between studios so as to encourage debate between design projects and history / theory.

2.8 The small blocks of the south facade permit a supple organization of faculty offices, research facilities, and administrative spaces. Their "carving" tries to avoid framing and any monolithic or bureaucratic effect.

2.9 Equally an urban environment and an electronic machine, the City of Architecture is wary of aesthetic tendencies as well as of humanist theories directed towards formal morality. It is, instead, through the rigorous amplification of its programmatic logic that the school develops the conditions required for inquiry into the new century's architectural conditions.

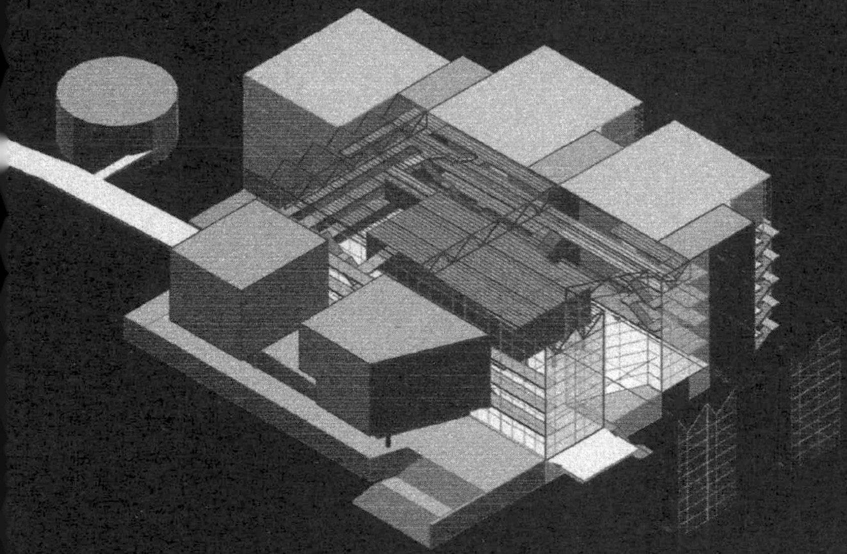

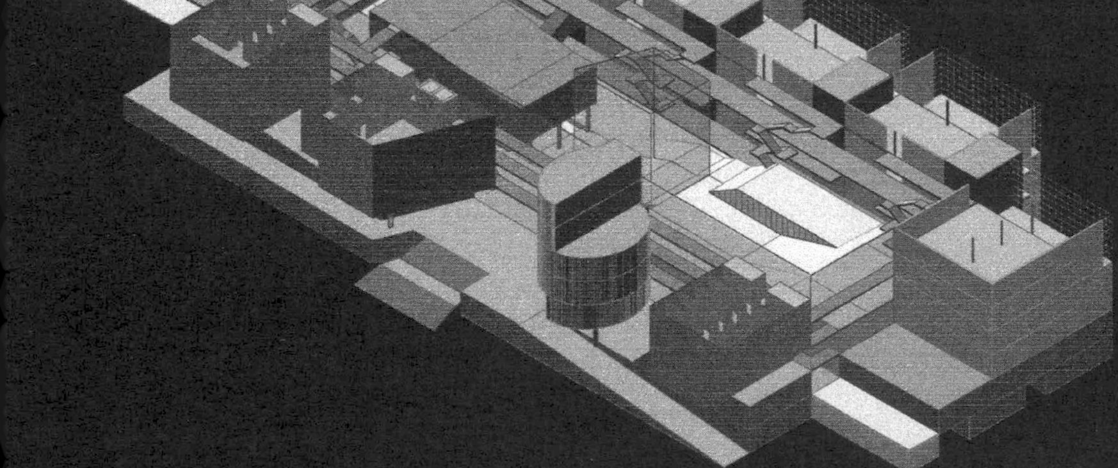

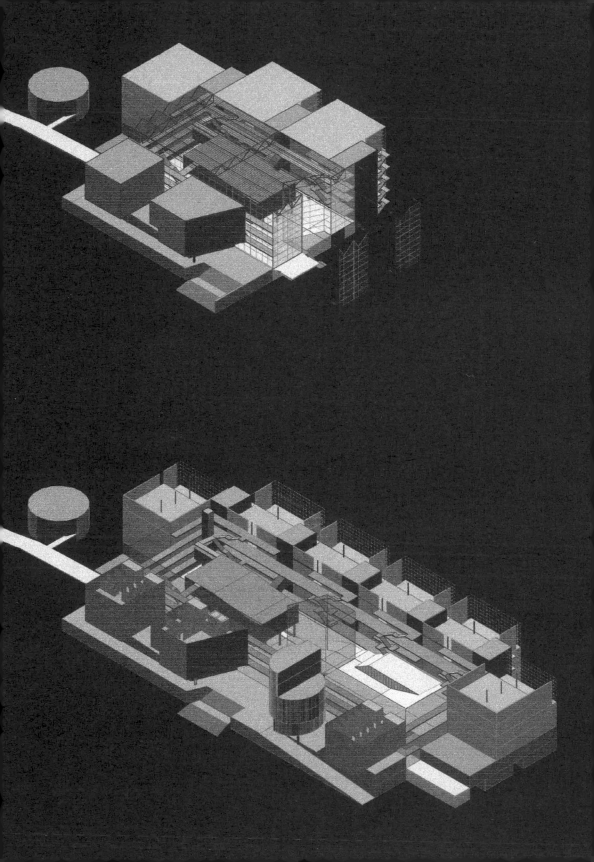

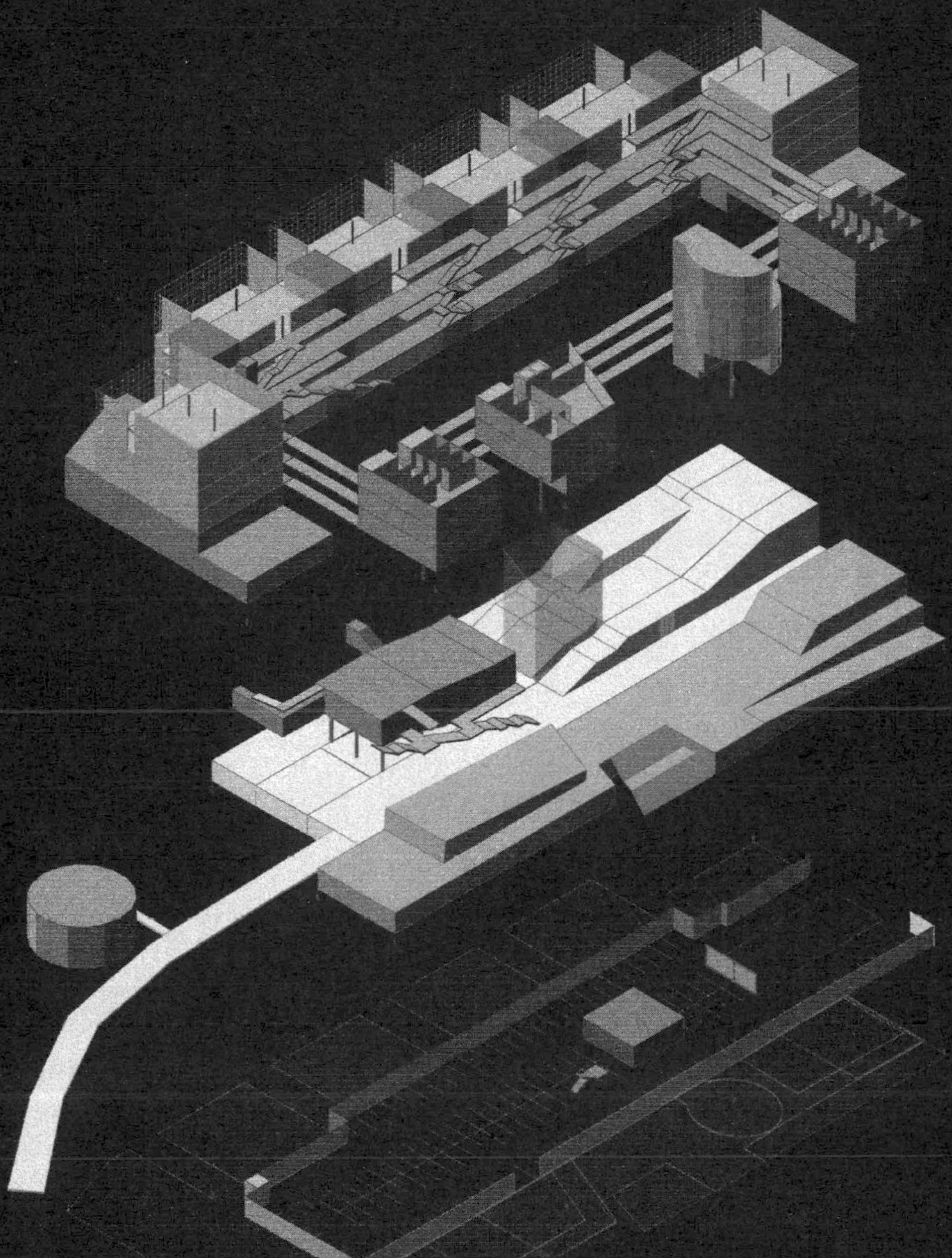

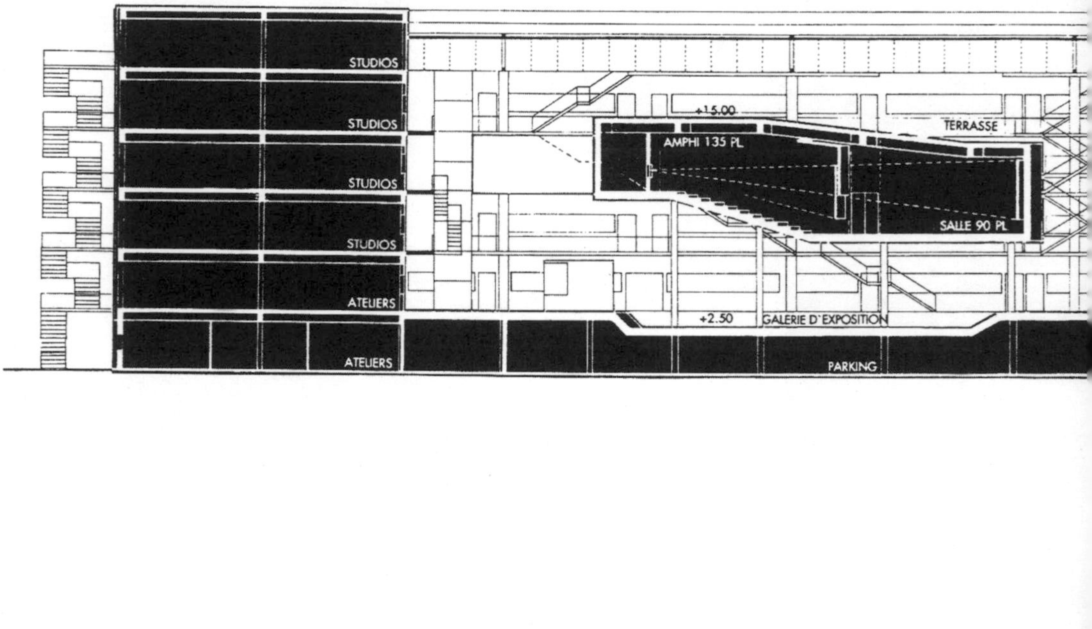

Designing conditions rather than conditioning design

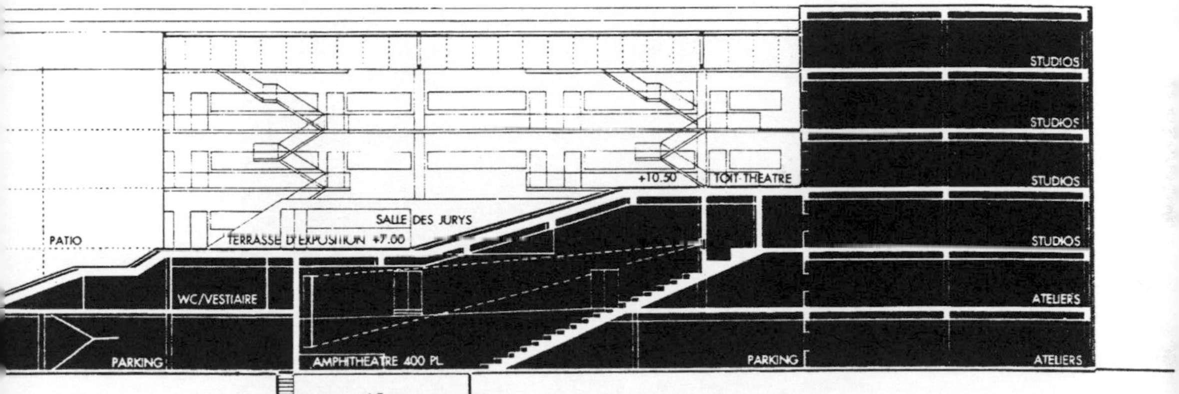

Section (competition phase)

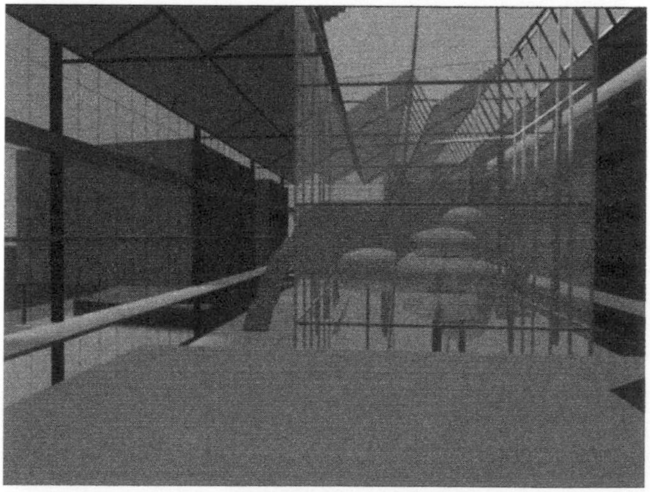

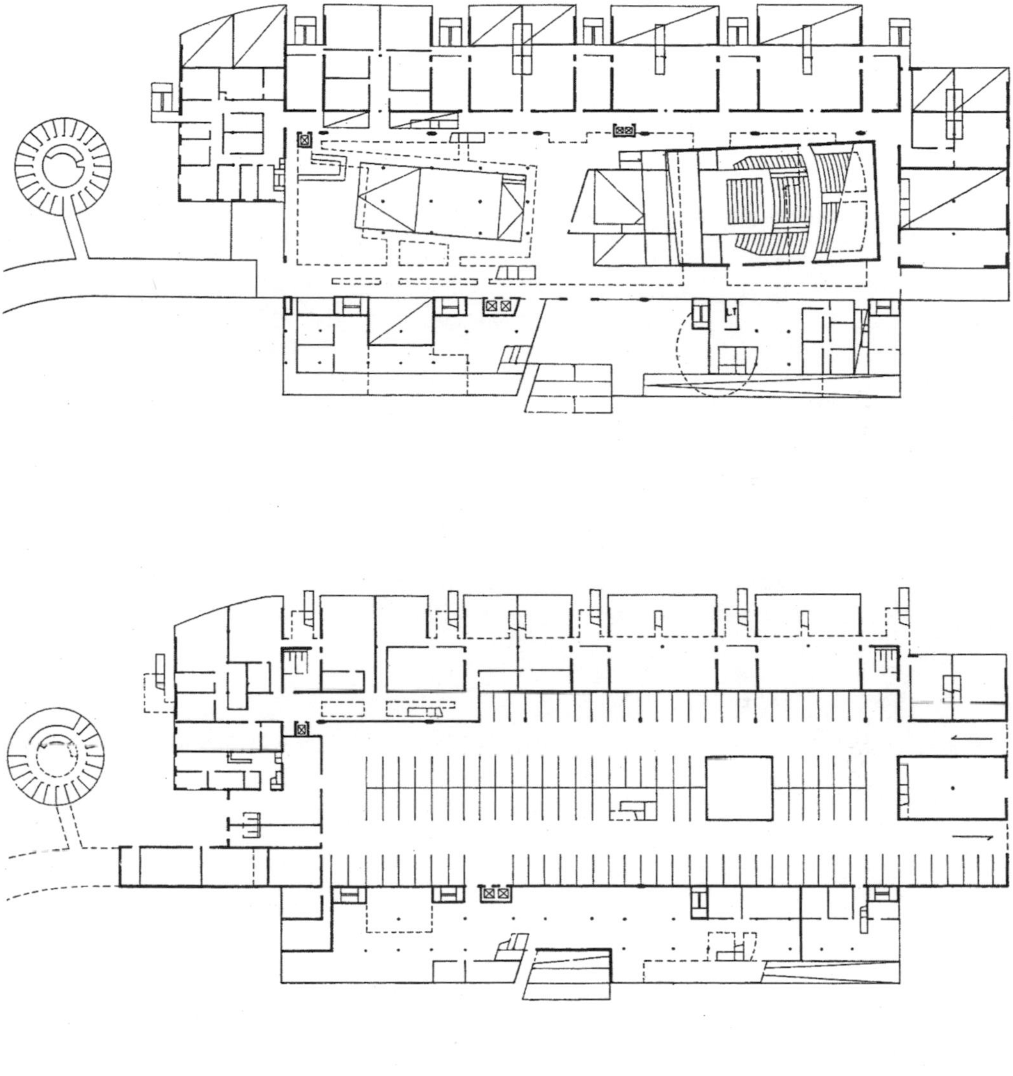

Plans (competition phase) Levels +0 meters, +3.5 meters

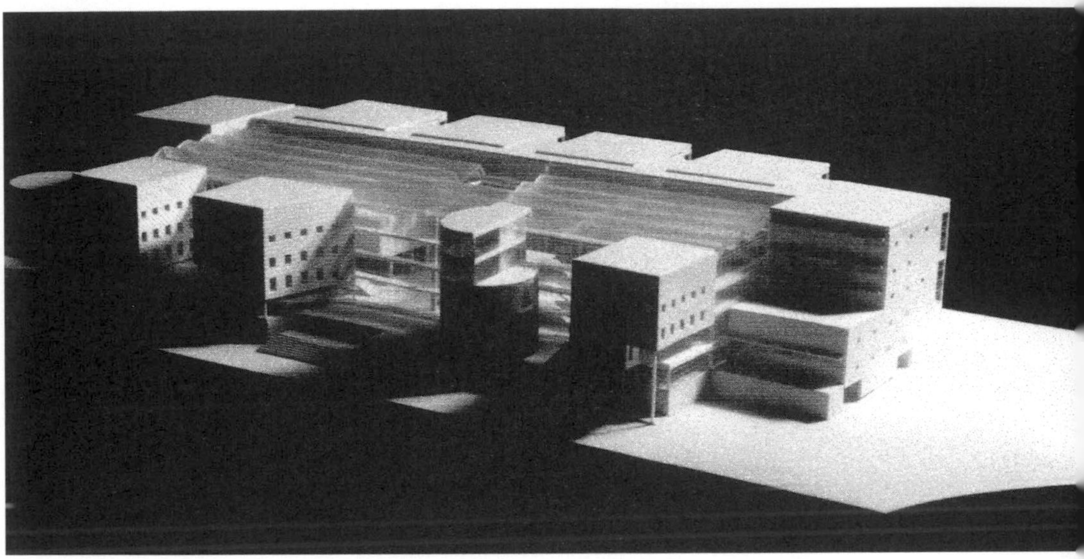

Aggregate: to collect or gather into a whole

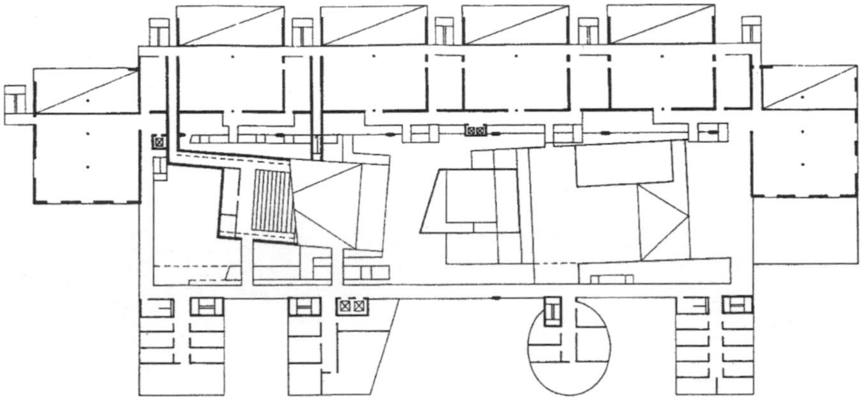

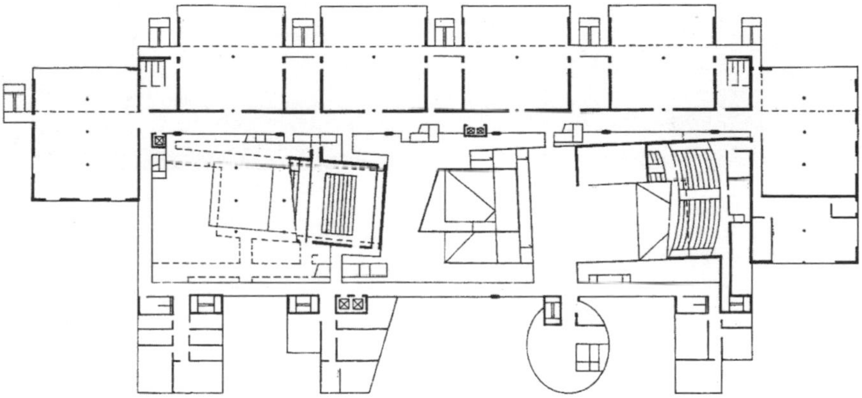

Plans (competition phase) Levels +7 meters, +10.5 meters

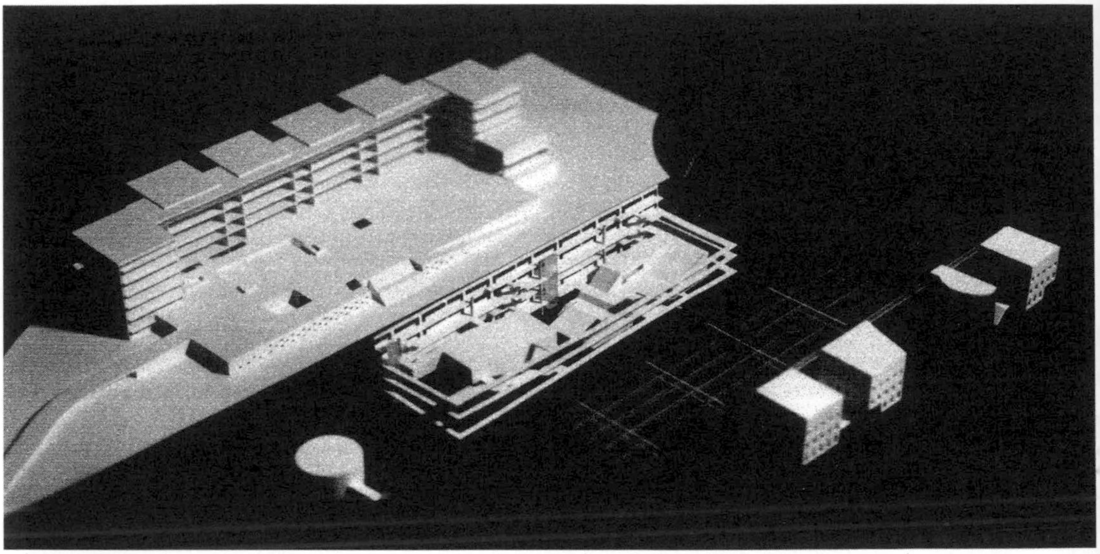

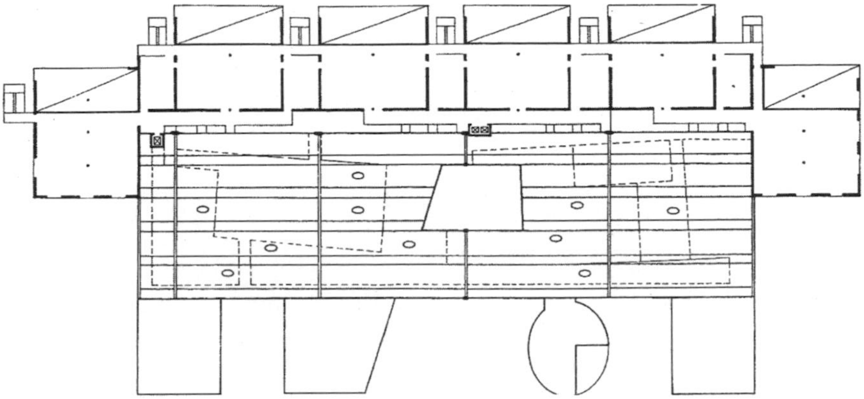

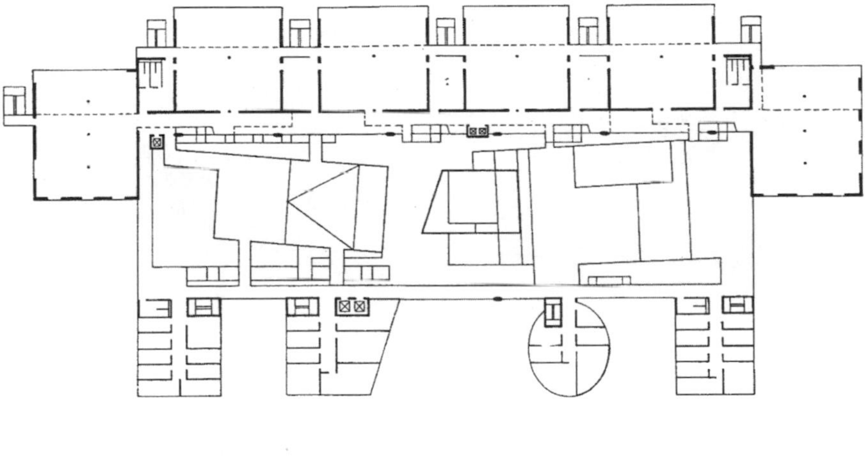

Plans (competition phase) Levels +14 meters, +17.5 meters

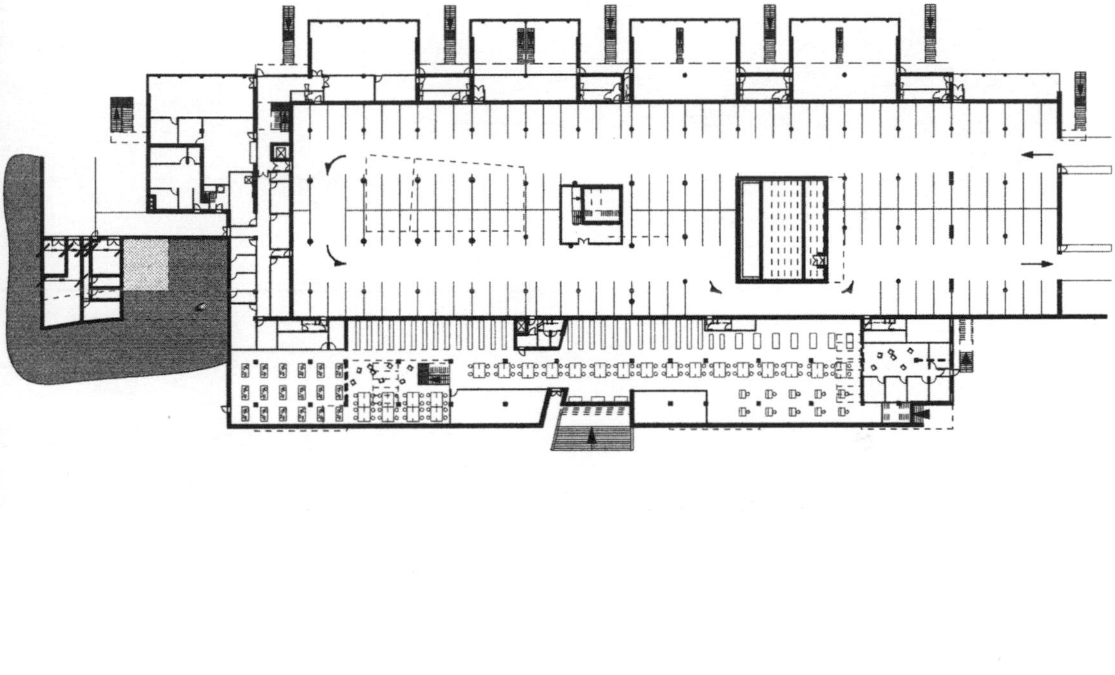

Plan (construction documents): ground level The competition rules indicated that program and building, but not educational content, should be designed

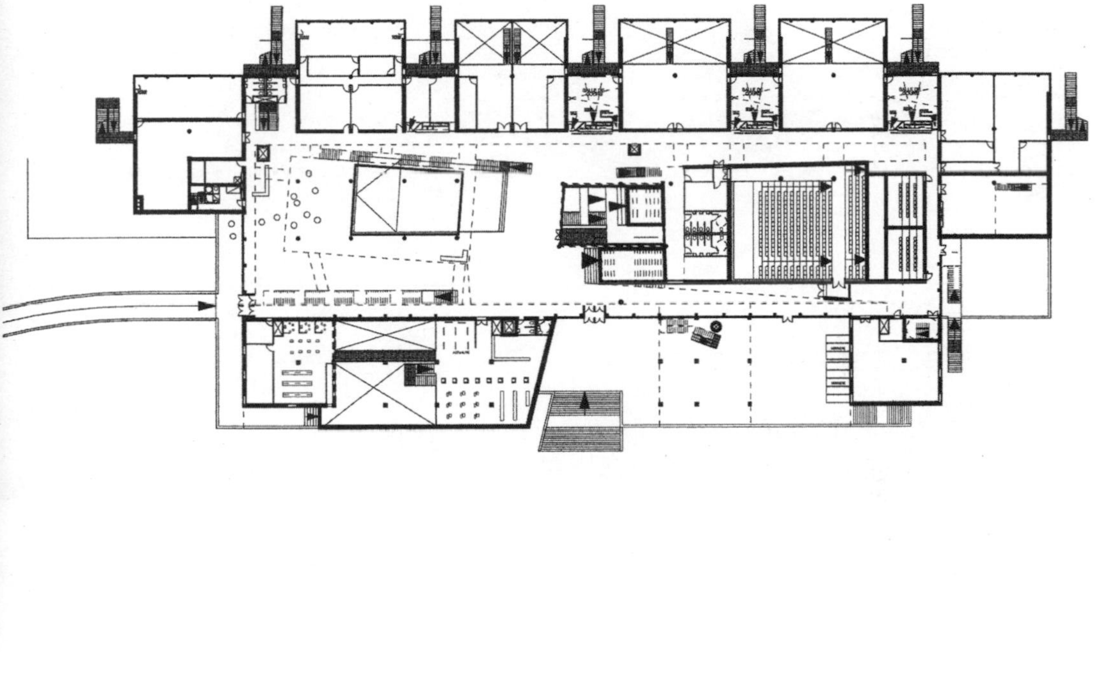

Plan (construction documents): +3.5 meters
Should an architectural organization dictate a future pedagogy?

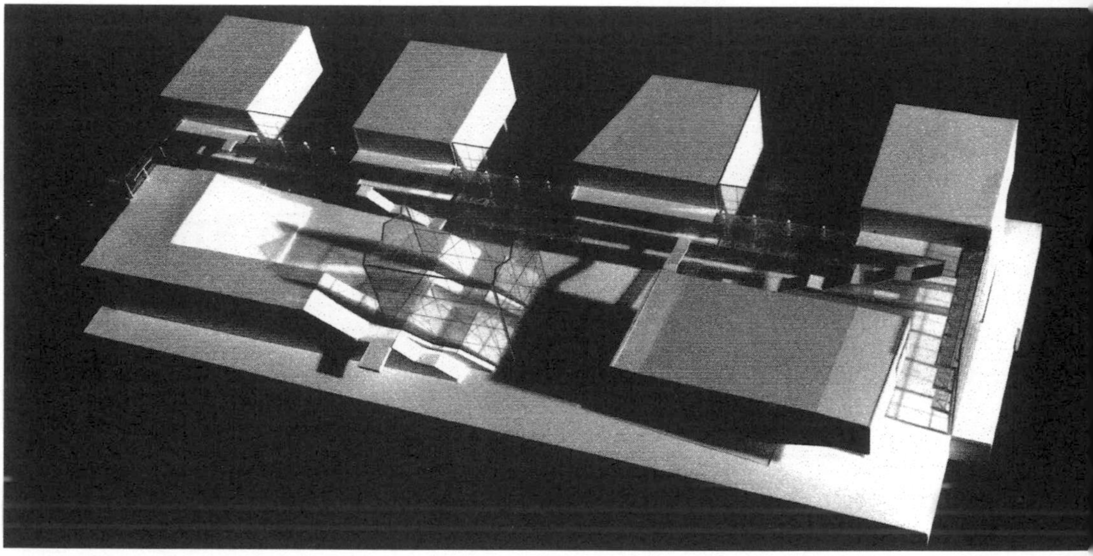

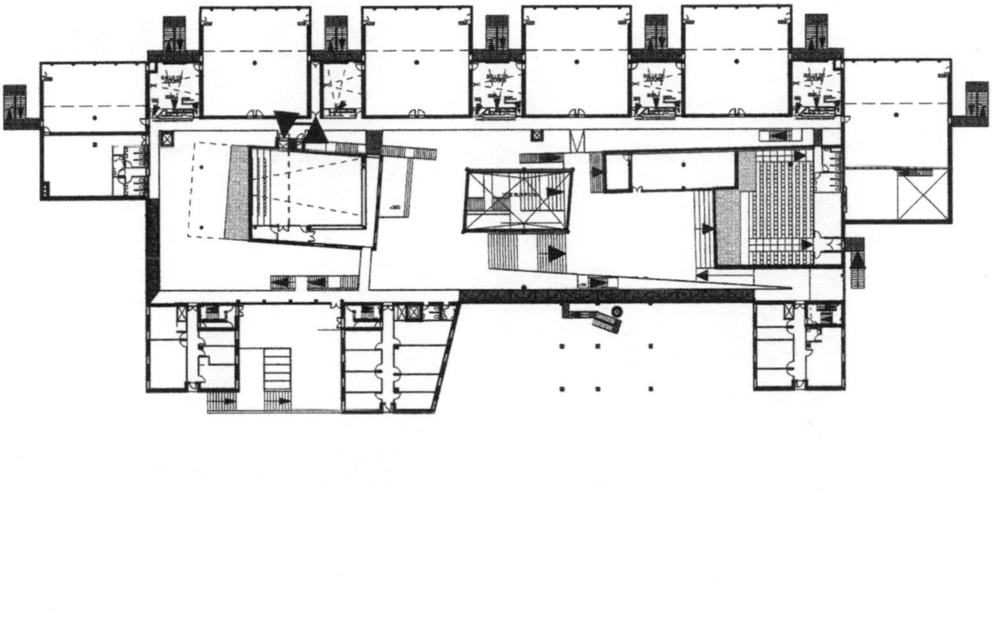

Plan: +7 meters We decided to encourage maximum interaction through architecture, offering spaces for appropriation and the intermingling of functions

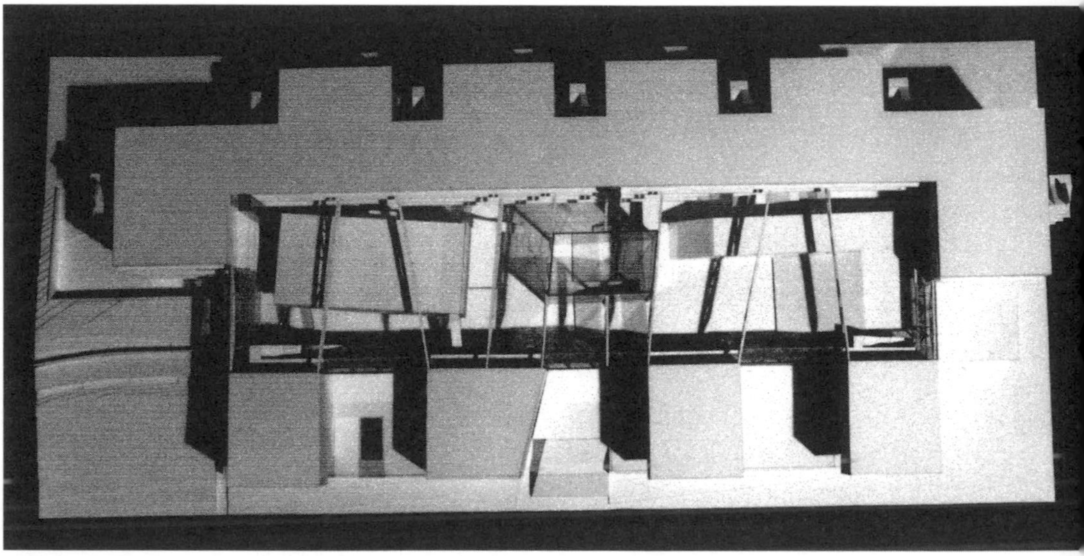

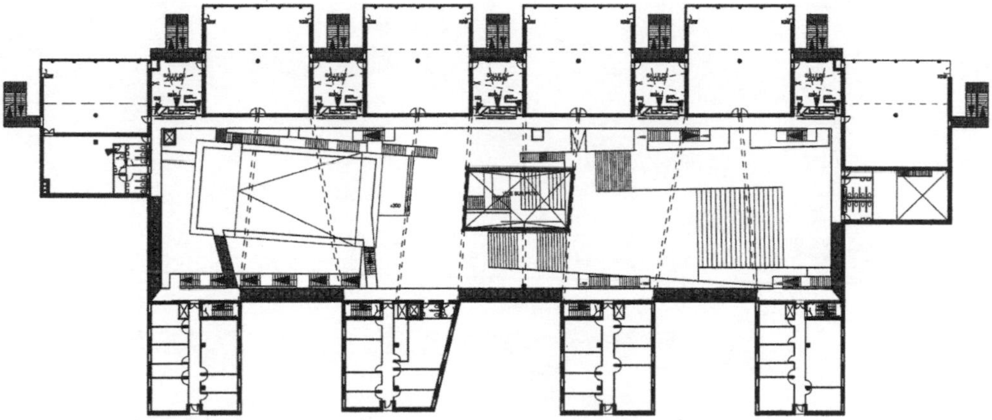

Plan (construction documents): +10.5 meters Zero-degree architecture: each decision results from a social or programmatic move, never from an aesthetic one

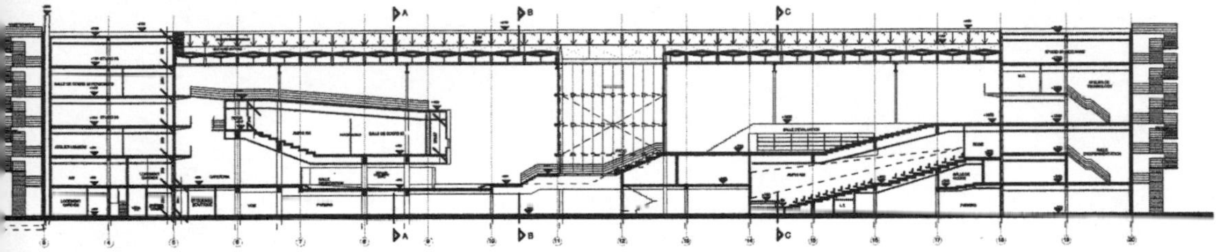

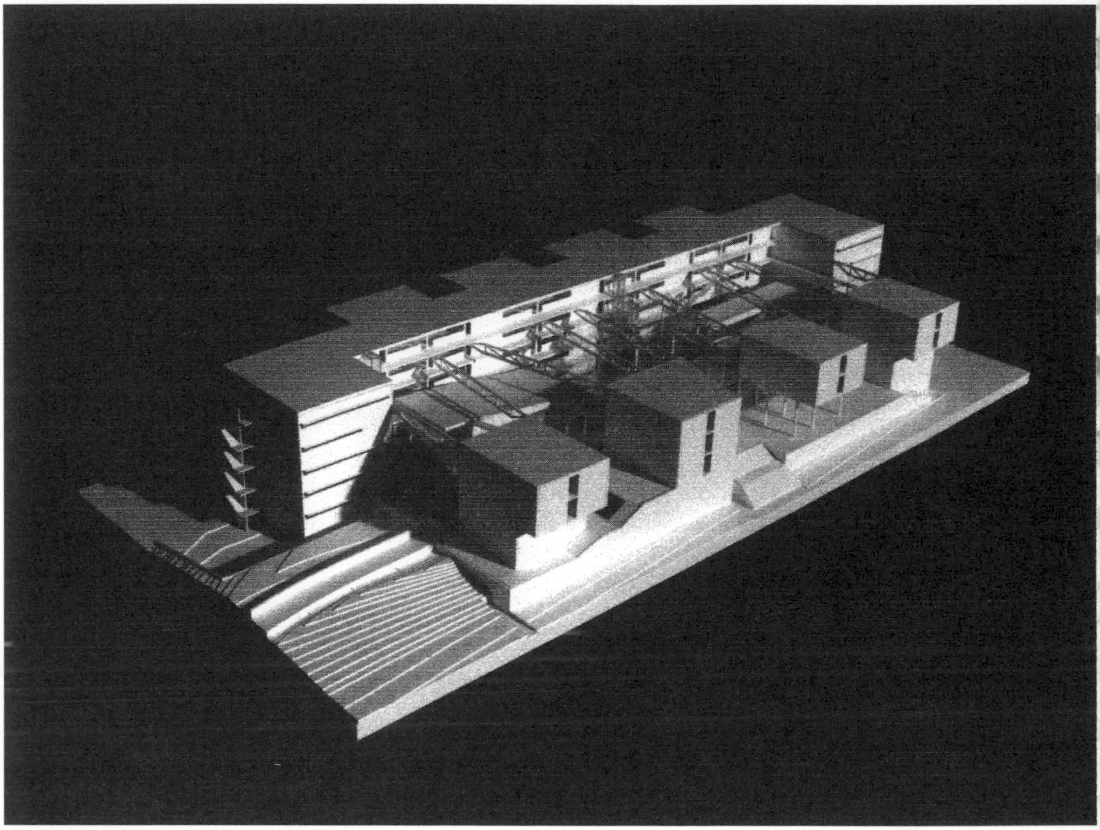

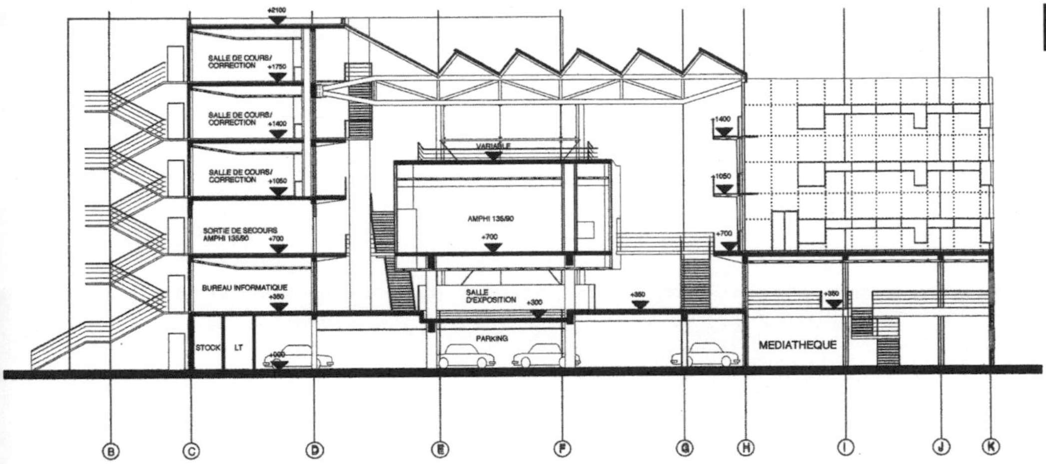
+2100
SALLE DE COURS/ CORRECTION +1750
SALLE DE COURS/ CORRECTION +1400
SALLE DE COURS/ CORRECTION +1050
SORTIE DE SECOURS AMPHI 135/90 +700
BUREAU INFORMATIQUE +350
STOCK
LT
+000
VARIABLE
AMPHI 135/90
+700
SALLE D'EXPOSITION +300
+350
PARKING
+1400
+1050
+700
+350
MEDIATHEQUE
B
C
D
E
F
G
H
I
J
K

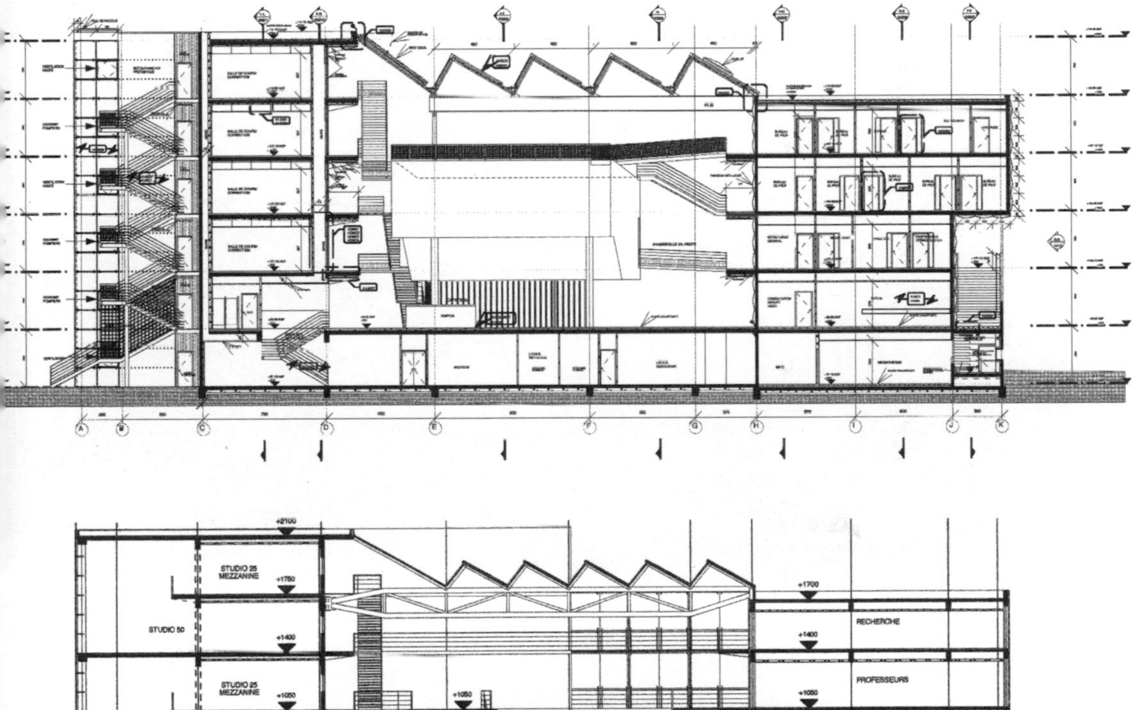

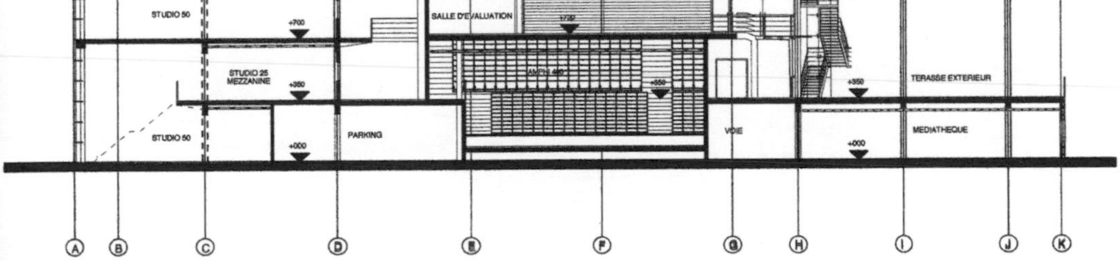
+2100
STUDIO 25 MEZZANINE +1750
STUDIO 50
+1400
STUDIO 25 MEZZANINE +1050
STUDIO 50
+700
STUDIO 25 MEZZANINE +350
STUDIO 50
+000
PARKING
+1050
SALLE D'EVALUATION
AMPHI 460
+350
VOIE
+1700
RECHERCHE
+1400
PROFESSEURS
+1050
+350
TERASSE EXTERIEUR
MEDIATHEQUE
+000
A
B
C
D
E
F
G
H
I
J
K

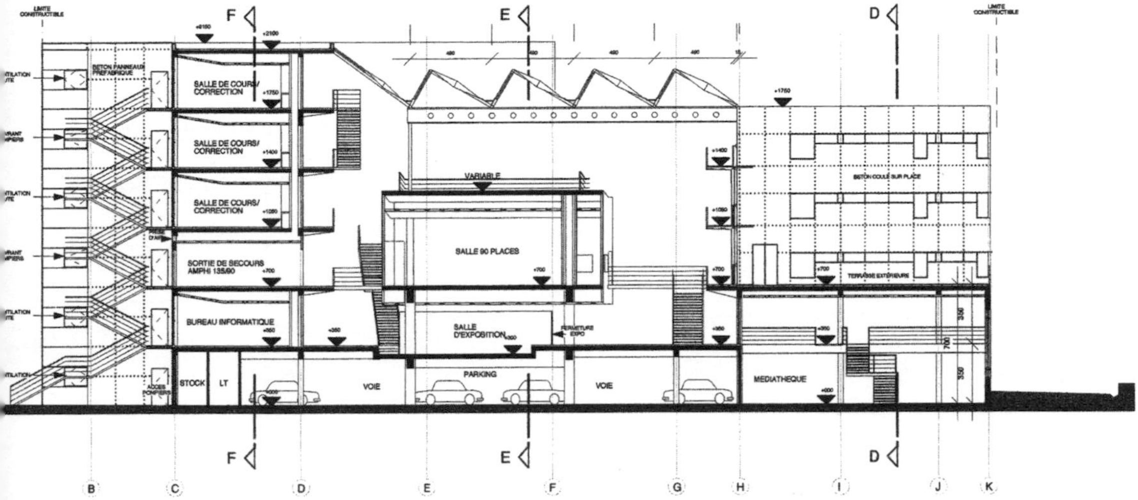
SALLE DE COURS/ CORRECTION
SALLE DE COURS/ CORRECTION
SALLE DE COURS/ CORRECTION
SORTIE DE SECOURS AMPHI 135/90
BUREAU INFORMATIQUE
STOCK
LT
VOIE
PARKING
VOIE
VARIABLE
SALLE 90 PLACES
SALLE D'EXPOSITION
MEDIATHEQUE
BETON COULE SUR PLACE
F
E
D
B
C
D
E
F
G
H
I
J
K

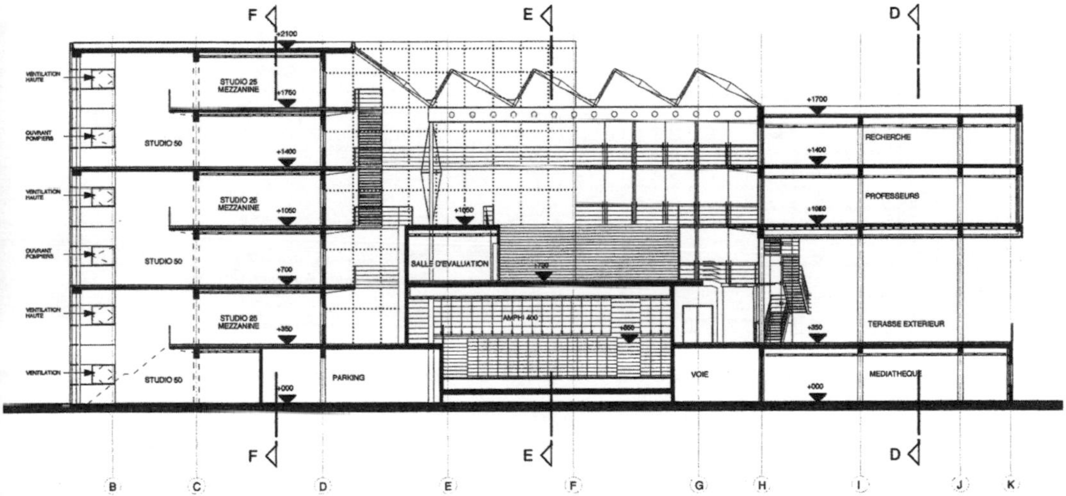
VENTILATION HAUTE
OUVRANT POMPIERS
VENTILATION HAUTE
OUVRANT POMPIERS
VENTILATION HAUTE
VENTILATION
STUDIO 25 MEZZANINE
STUDIO 50
STUDIO 25 MEZZANINE
STUDIO 50
STUDIO 25 MEZZANINE
STUDIO 50
PARKING
SALLE D'EVALUATION
AMPHI 400
VOIE
RECHERCHE
PROFESSEURS
TERASSE EXTERIEUR
MEDIATHEQUE
+2100
+1750
+1400
+1050
+700
+350
+000
+1700
F
E
D
B
C
D
E
F
G
H
I
J
K

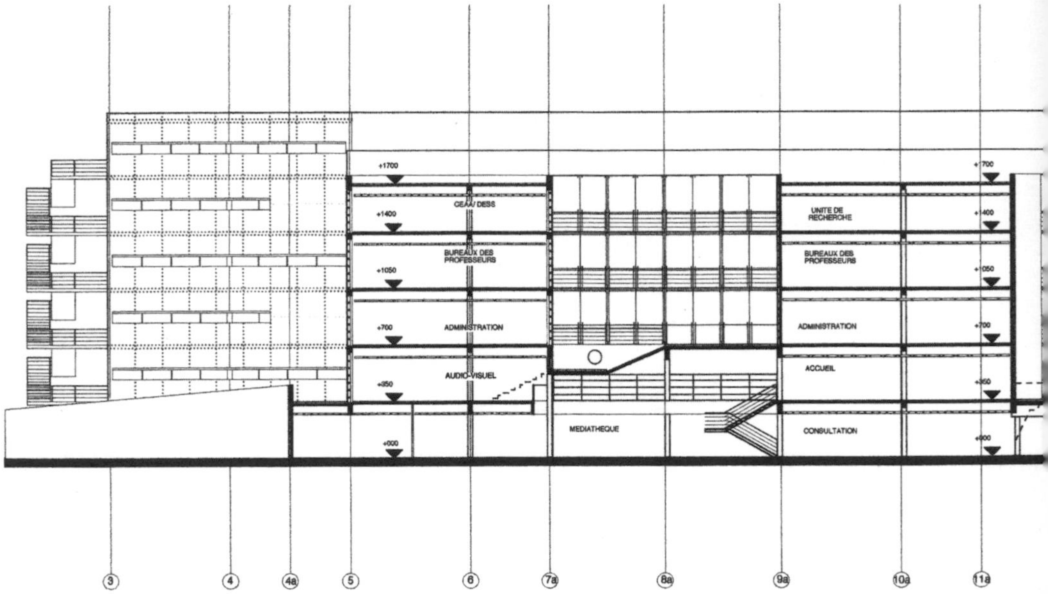
+1700
CEAA/DESS
+1400
BUREAUX DES PROFESSEURS
+1050
ADMINISTRATION
+700
AUDIO-VISUEL
+350
+000
MEDIATHEQUE
UNITE DE RECHERCHE
BUREAUX DES PROFESSEURS
ADMINISTRATION
ACCUEIL
CONSULTATION
3
4
4a
5
6
7a
8a
9a
10a
11a

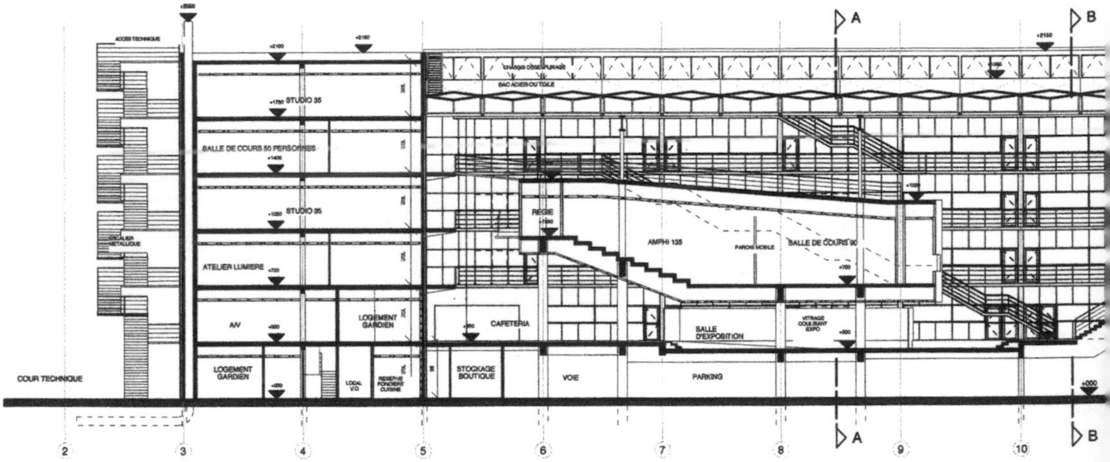
A
B
STUDIO 35
SALLE DE COURS 50 PERSONNES
STUDIO 35
ATELIER LUMIERE
A/V
LOGEMENT GARDIEN
LOGEMENT GARDIEN
COUR TECHNIQUE
STOCKAGE BOUTIQUE
CAFETERIA
REGIE
AMPHI 135
SALLE DE COURS 90
SALLE D'EXPOSITION
VOIE
PARKING
2
3
4
5
6
7
8
9
10

+1700
UNITE DE RECHERCHE
+1400
BUREAUX DES PROFESSEURS
+1050
+350
+350
+000
CONSULTATION
+1700
CEAA/DESS
+1400
BUREAUX DES PROFESSEURS
+1050
ADMINISTRATION
+700
MATERIATHEQUE
+350
MEDIATHEQUE
+000
12a
13a
14a
15a
16a
17a
18
19
20

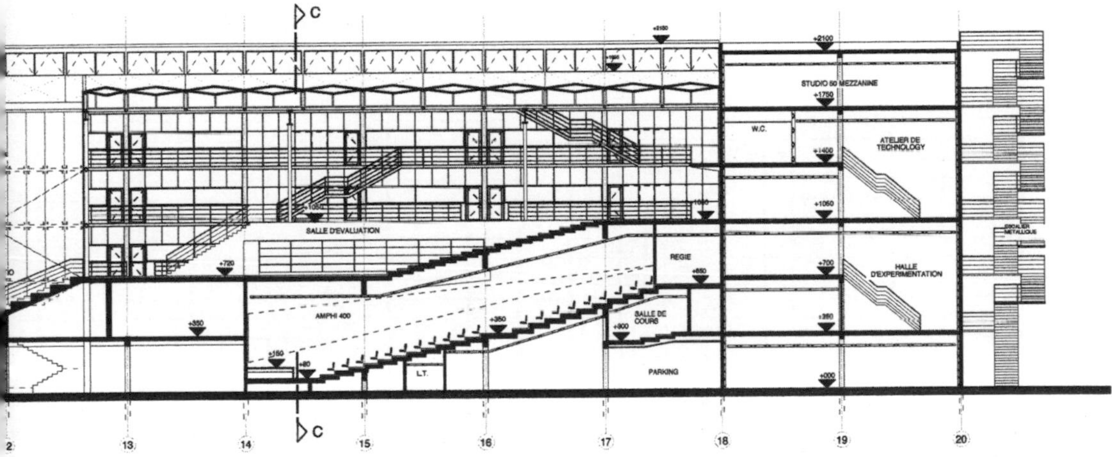
C
+2150
+2100
STUDIO 50 MEZZANINE
+1750
W.C.
+1400
ATELIER DE TECHNOLOGY
+1050
+1050
SALLE D'EVALUATION
+720
REGIE
+650
+700
HALLE D'EXPERIMENTATION
+350
AMPHI 400
+350
SALLE DE COURS
+900
+350
+150
+80
L.T.
PARKING
+000
ESCALIER METALLIQUE
C
13
14
15
16
17
18
19
20

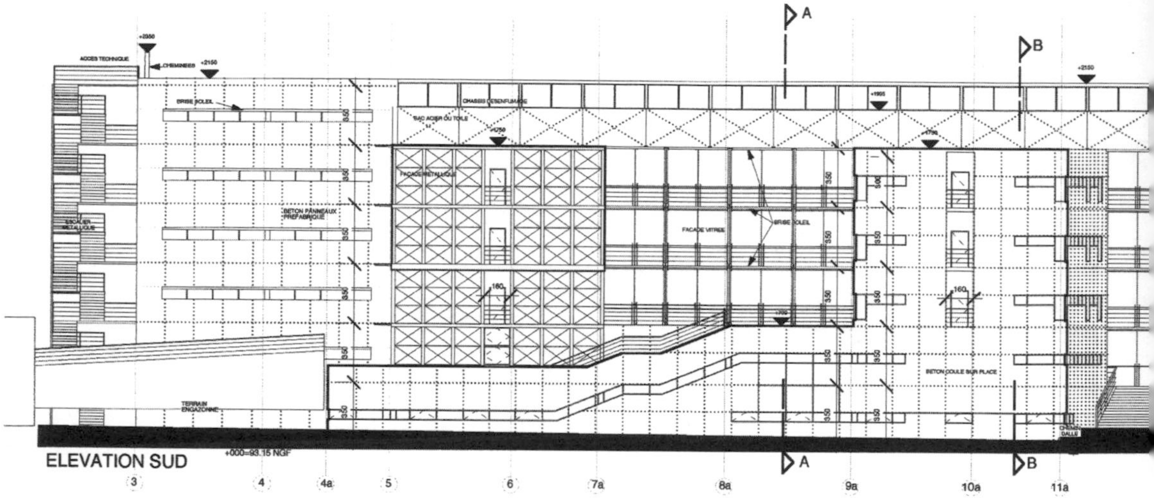
A
B
+2350
ACCES TECHNIQUE
CHEMINEES
+2150
BRISE SOLEIL
CHASSIS DESENFUMAGE
BAC ACIER OU TOILE
FACADE METALLIQUE
ESCALIER METALLIQUE
BETON PANNEAUX PREFABRIQUE
FACADE VITREE
BRISE SOLEIL
BETON COULE SUR PLACE
TERRAIN ENGAZONNE
+000=93.15 NGF
ELEVATION SUD
3
4
4a
5
6
7a
8a
9a
10a
11a

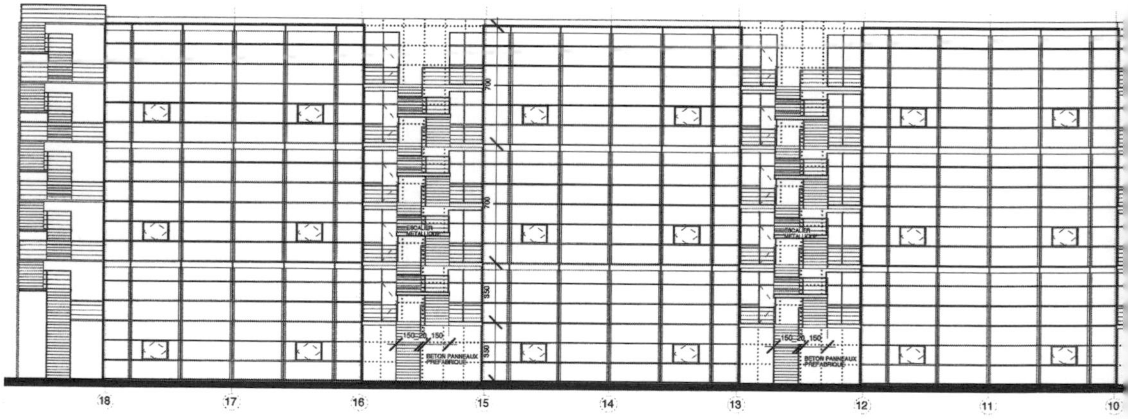
ESCALIER METALLIQUE
BETON PANNEAUX PREFABRIQUE
18
17
16
15
14
13
12
11
10

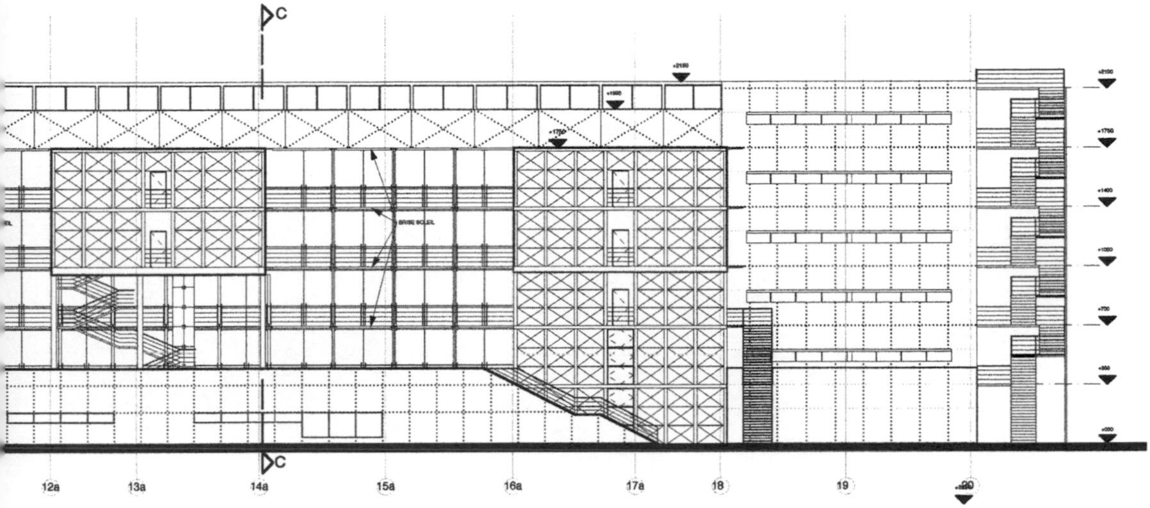
C
BRISE SOLEIL
C
12a
13a
14a
15a
16a
17a
18
19
20

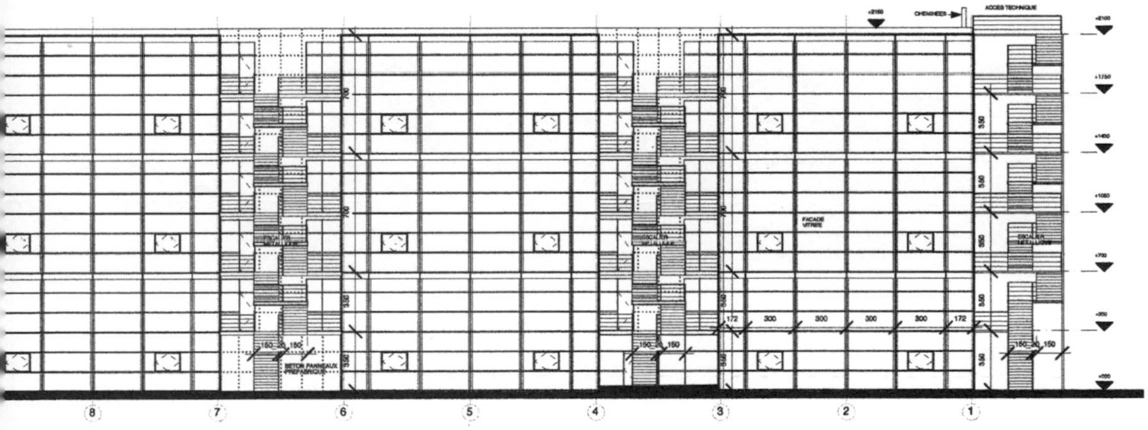
CHEMINEES
ACCES TECHNIQUE
FACADE VITREE
BETON PANNEAUX PREFABRIQUE
+2100
+1750
+1400
+1050
+700
+350
172
300
300
300
300
172
150 20 150
8
7
6
5
4
3
2
1

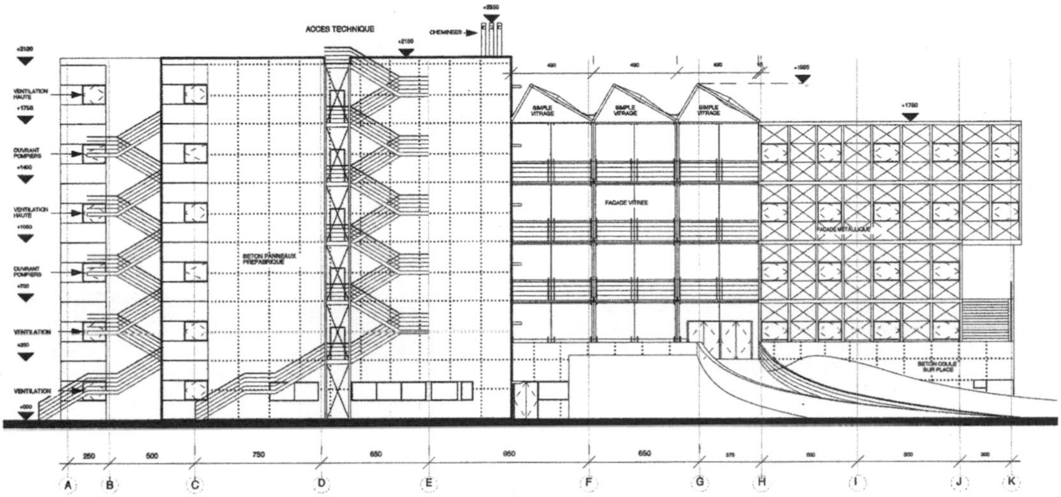
ACCES TECHNIQUE
CHEMINEES
SIMPLE VITRAGE
FACADE VITREE
FACADE METALLIQUE
BETON PANNEAUX PREFABRIQUE
BETON COULE SUR PLACE
VENTILATION HAUTE
OUVRANT POMPIERS
VENTILATION
250
500
750
650
950
650
A
B
C
D
E
F
G
H
I
J
K

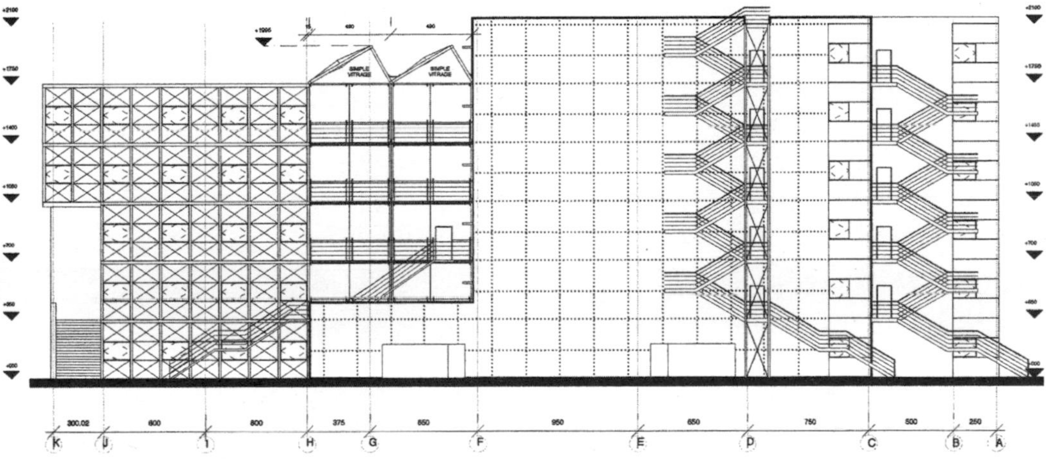
SIMPLE VITRAGE
300.02
800
800
375
650
950
650
750
500
250
K
J
I
H
G
F
E
D
C
B
A

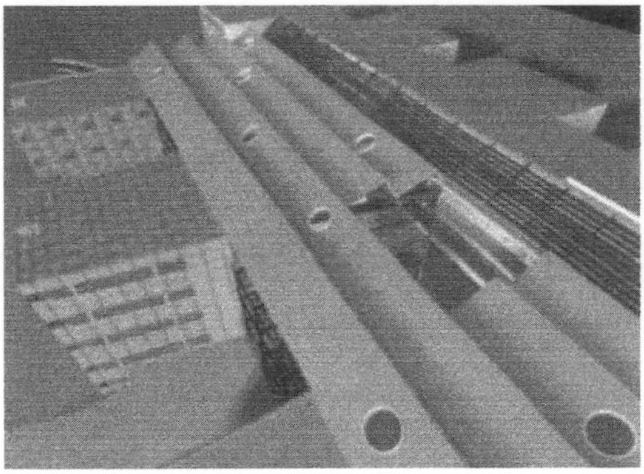

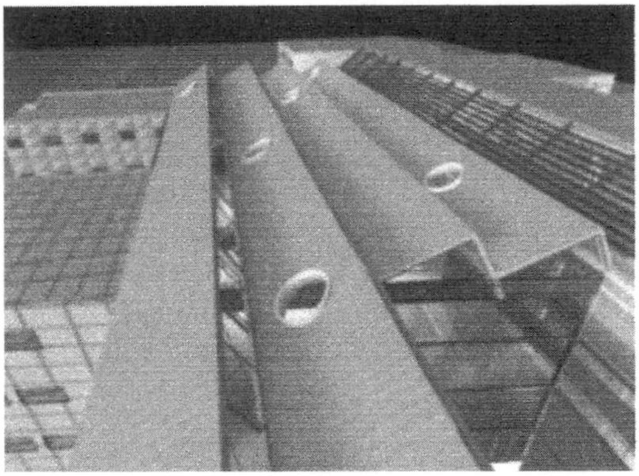

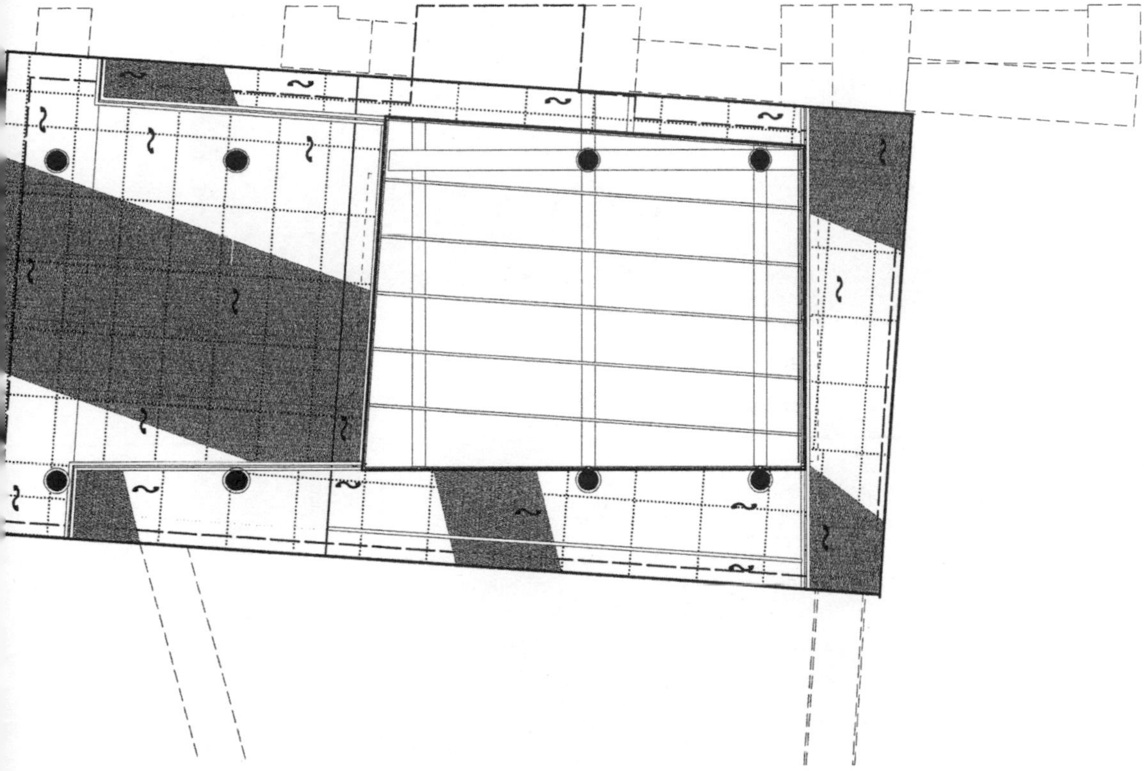

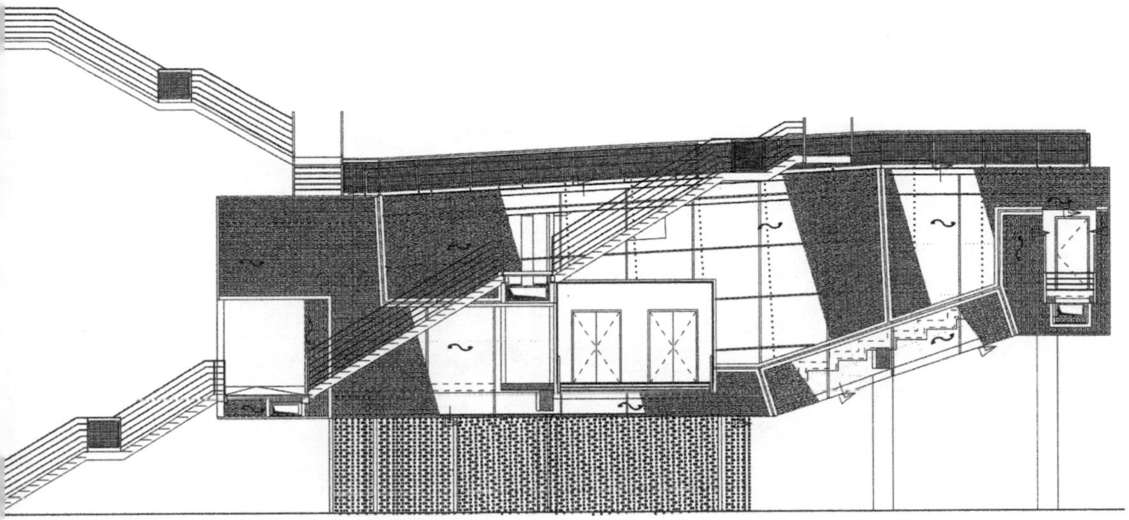

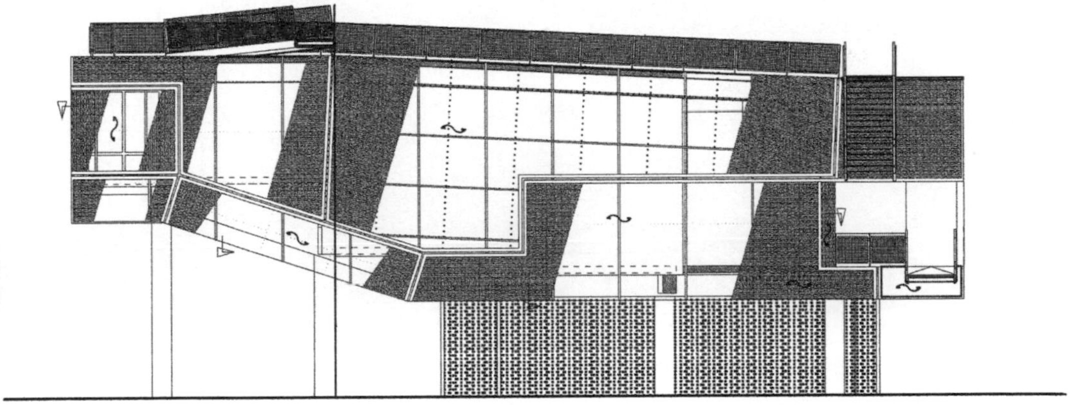

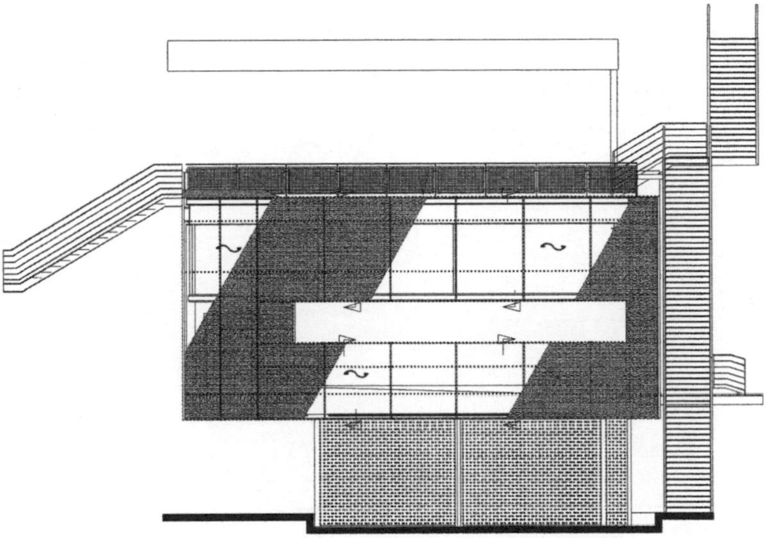

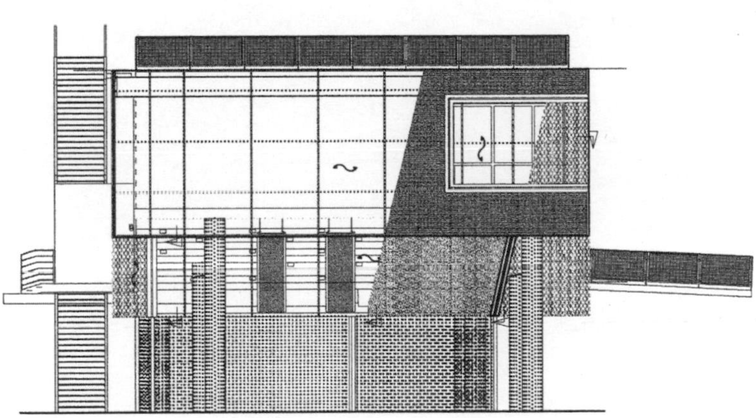

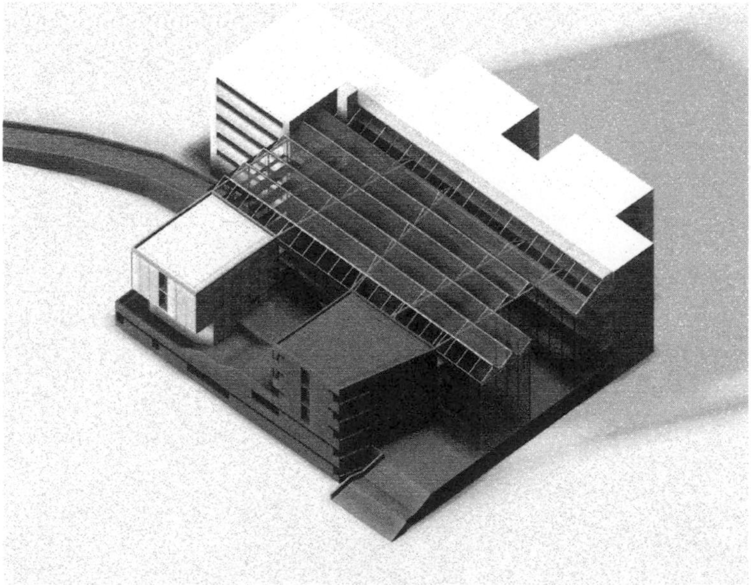

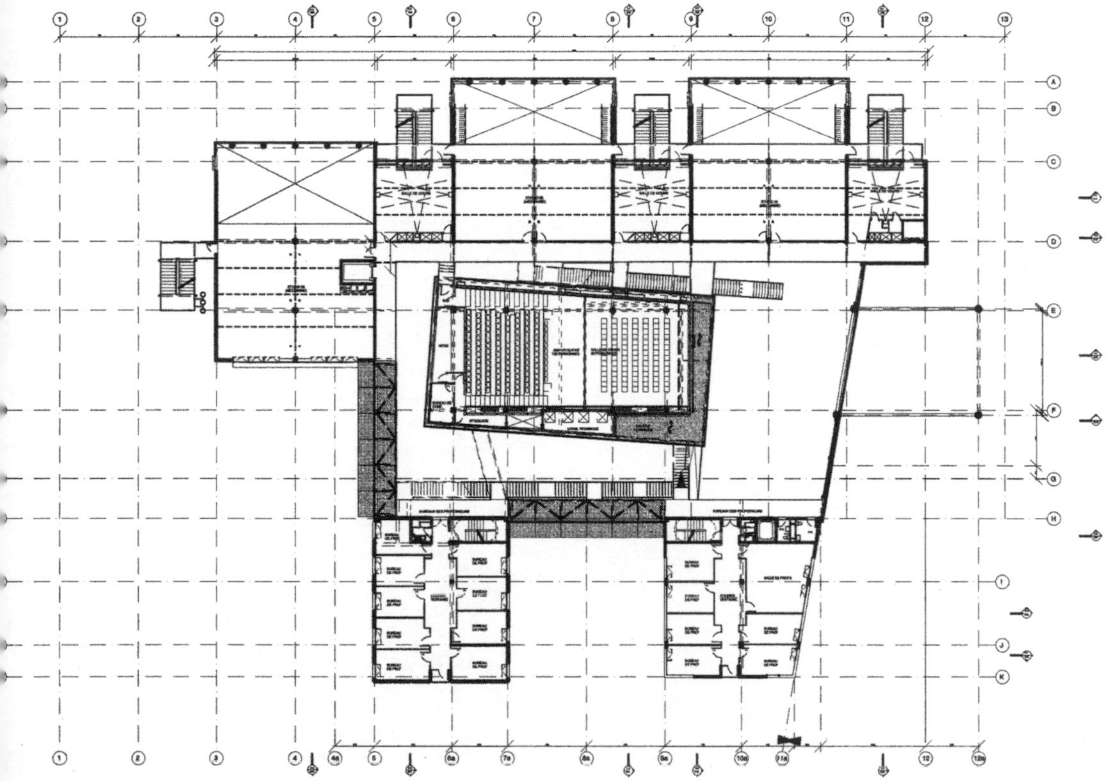

A project in two phases. (First phase, above) The second phase, when built, will give full impact to the large interior space of interaction

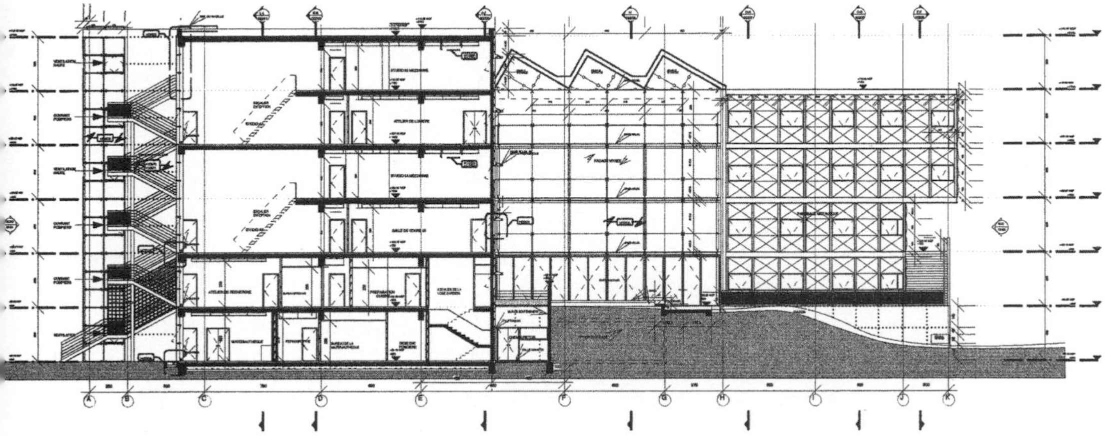

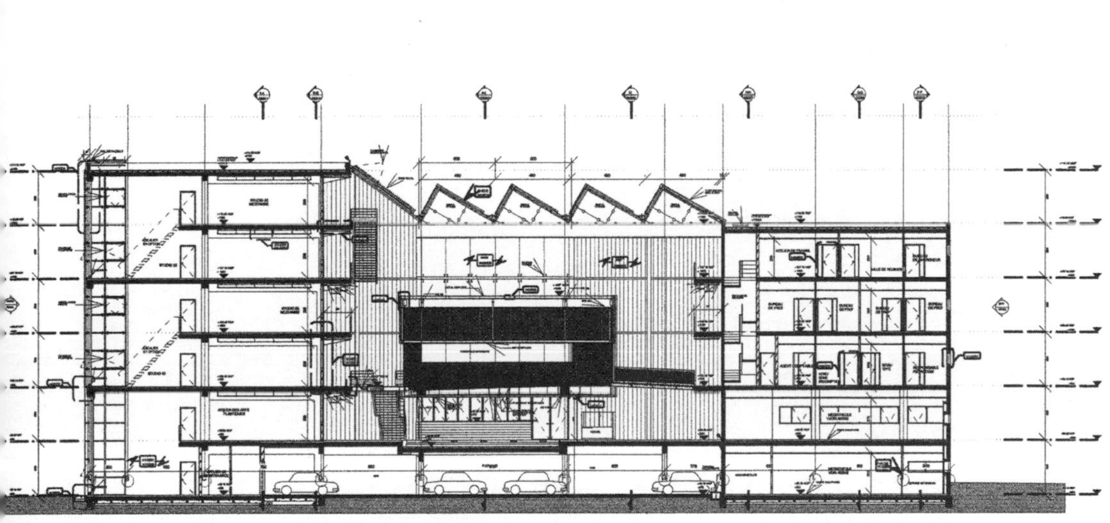

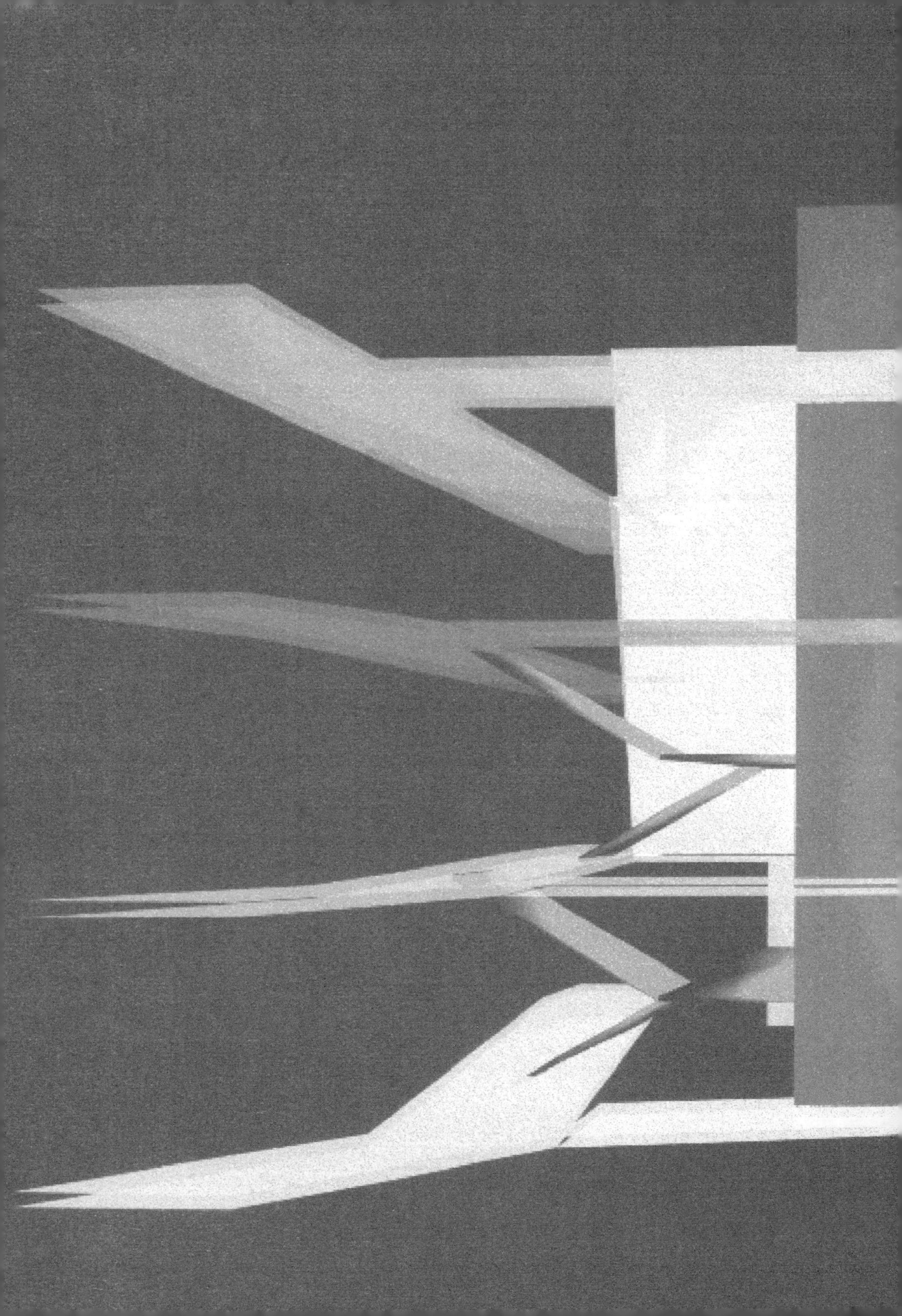

Miami, FIU School of Architecture, 1999–

Warped Solids

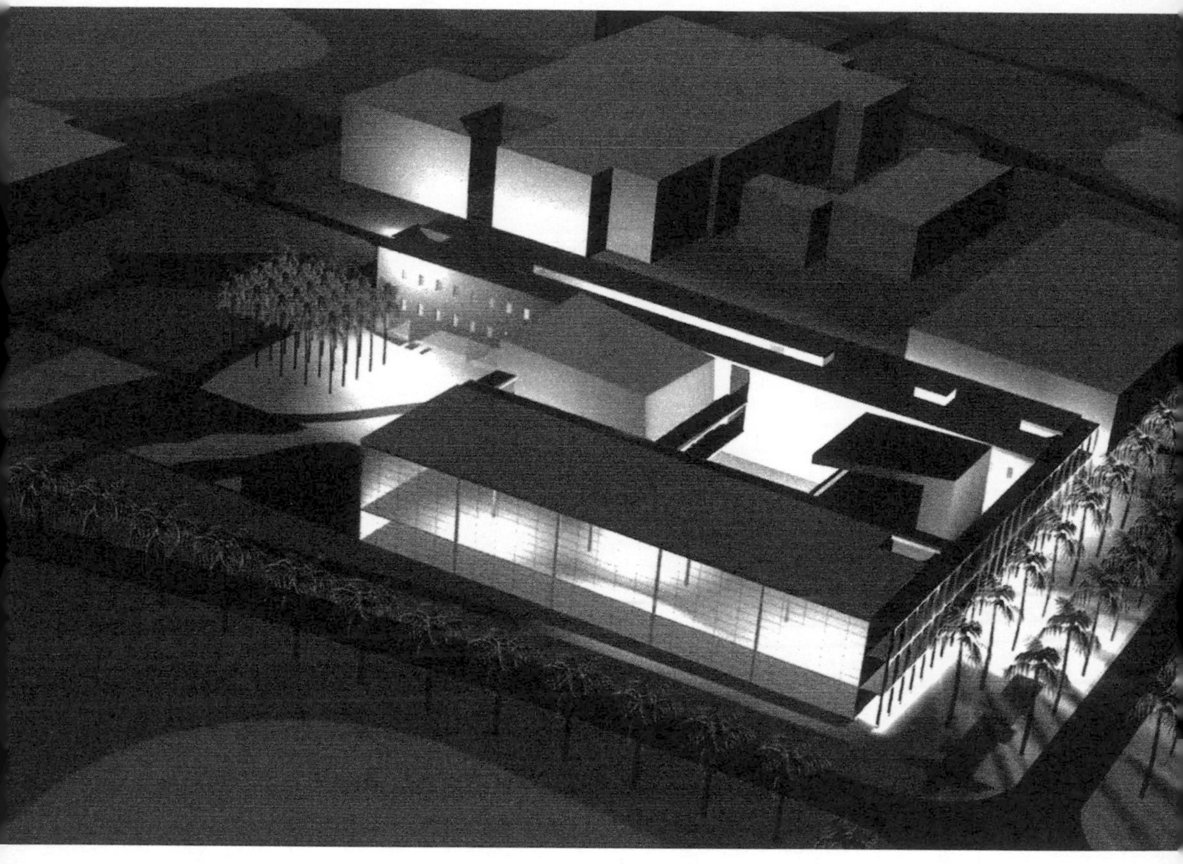

A New Identity

Key for a new school of architecture is an ability to set a stage, a scene, a culture and to be identified with it. Its new building must contribute to making that scene and that identity. Here, what the building *does* becomes as important as what it *looks like*. The building must act as a generator, activating spaces as well as defining them.

A Hub of Cultures

Florida International University is located in the largest and fastest-growing metropolis in the southeast United States, combining glamour with commerce and situated at the epicenter of a zone of influence that extends into South America and the Carribean. A major new building that succeeds socially, educationally, and culturally will benefit the University as a whole: its School of Architecture and College of Urban and Public Affairs have the potential to become a hub of ideas between two major cultures.

Social Exchange or Computers?

The young School of Architecture at F.I.U. has been described as a "commuter" school, in which students divide their time among an office where they earn a living, the school where they study, and the home where they often oversee family responsibilities. Often considered an impediment, this situation can be turned into an advantage. In this project we argue that computer technology has freed designers from the fixity of the drafting table. Disks and files can be e-mailed instantly anywhere, and the location of actual work becomes secondary. What is primary, however, is the social exchange, the discussion, debate, and clash of ideas between friends, colleagues, and teachers. This can happen only at the school. Between computers and social interaction, the school at F.I.U. could introduce a new type of strategy, suggesting a new educational model.

The Three Generators: Sobriety and Exuberance

Our project starts from the following thesis: There are buildings that are generators of events and interaction. As much through their programs as through their spatial organization, they can intensify a social or cultural interface.

Our project can be described as the sobriety of two wings defining a space activated by the exuberance of three colorful generators. The sober wings are made of precise yet user-friendly pre-cast concrete; the three generators of, respectively, varied yellow ceramic tiles, varied red ceramic tiles (remember Gaudi), and nature (the Royal Palm trees).

Movement in the Courtyard

The new building arranges all requested programmed activities around an event-oriented central courtyard (60 by 90 feet), activated by two generators on either side, one containing a lecture hall, the other, an art gallery / reading room. Review rooms and a demonstration room also look over the courtyard so that it can become a large space for encounters and debates, celebrations and balls, end-of-year exhibitions, serious symposia, and avant-garde exhibitions. Gathering together all of the school circulation and major social and cultural spaces, the central generators shade the courtyard during the morning and late afternoon hours. Whatever the level of attendance on any given day, one sees a constant movement of students on the shaded steps, periphery, and unprogrammed space above the lecture hall, which gives the court liveliness and dynamism. Studios, classrooms, faculty offices, and administration open onto this large communal, multipurpose, event-seeking courtyard.

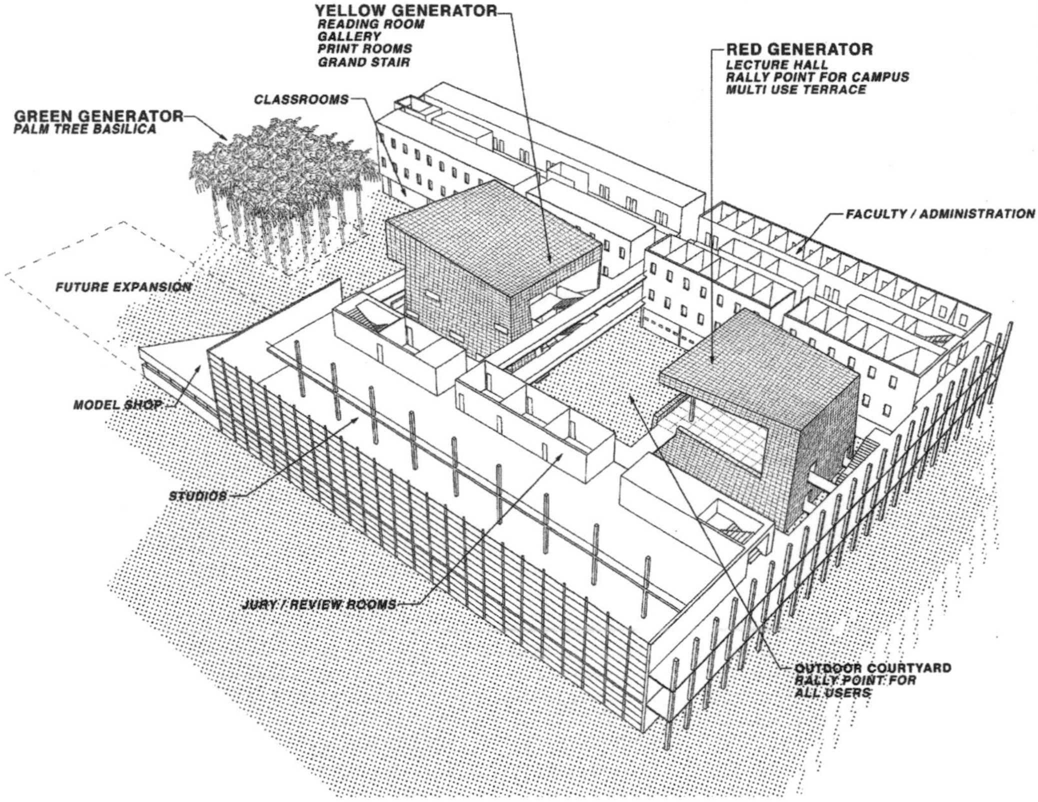

Architecture as the materialization of a concept: two generic wings define a linear space activated by three specific "generators," which define two active courtyards

The Gallery, The Reading Room, The Student Lounge (The Yellow Generator)

Users of the architecture school will enter through the yellow generator, taking either the elevator or the grand stairs, and walk into the reception area or, alternatively, cross over the courtyard to the studios. On the ground floor is the gallery, acting as a focus for the university as a whole. The reading room is located above it as an obligatory passage-point for all destinations in the building.

The Lecture Hall and Covered Terrace (The Red Generator)

Those wishing to go to the university-wide lecture hall can enter directly from the Mall or from the courtyard. Above the lecture hall is an important social space, an outdoor, unprogrammed space usable for parties, discussions, construction exercises, or simply for appropriation by students for their own uses. It could eventually provide a swing space should the school urgently need to expand.

The Palm Columns by the Water (The Green Generator)

Arranged in a square plan, twenty-five Royal Palm trees by the water provide a shaded "basilica." Here, architecture and landscape become one.

The Studio Wing

From the courtyard it is possible to see the activity in the review rooms. The production of projects is part of the school's image; students and teachers can see information, communication, debate. The double orientation of the review rooms gives them a south side facing the courtyard, and a north side with the stable light necessary for the extensive use of computers in contemporary architectural design.

Studio spaces are based on a loft-space envelope that allows maximum flexibility for groups of fifteen, thirty, or more. At any time, drywall partitions can be installed perpendicular to the glass wall to provide intimacy. The jury / pin-up rooms are inserted between the studios and the walkways to encourage debate and visibility. Private lockers allow students to leave material comfortably in proximity to the studios.

The Office Wing

The south wing permits a supple organization of the faculty offices and administrative spaces. Their indoor, double-height court avoids the bureaucratic effect of corridors.

Architecture is the Materialization of a Concept

If sobriety defines studios and offices, the red, yellow, and green "generators" of activities are places of exuberant invention. In contrast to the linear rigor of the wings, these three volumes challenge the poetry of the right angle. Here, movement has informed form. The forces of bodies moving in space and of the wind deflected so as to cool the ground have provided our means of defining the geometry of the envelopes of the red and yellow generators. These will be places for the unexpected.

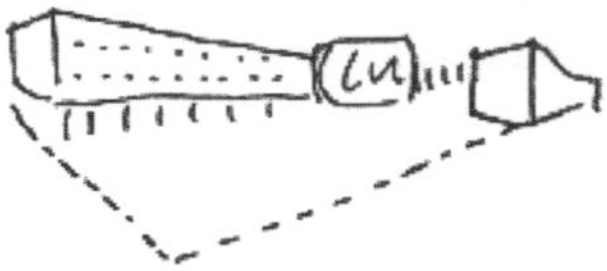

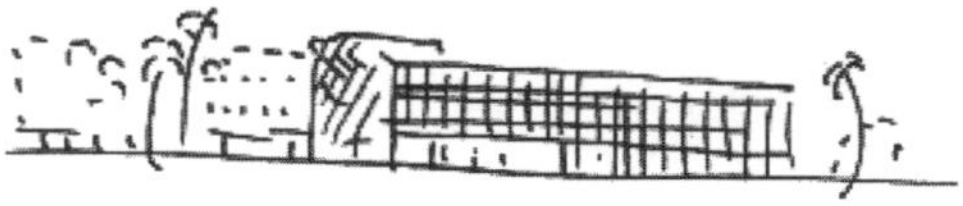

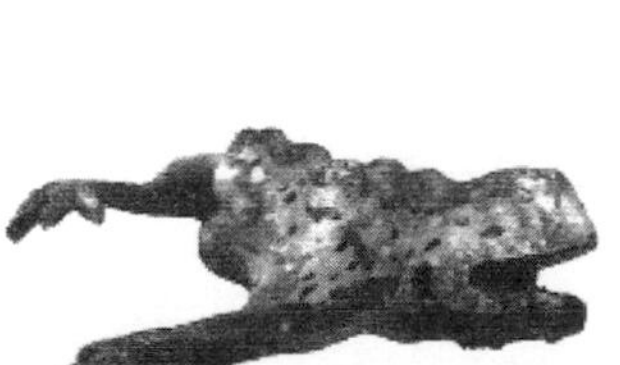

MOVEMENT GENERATOR
inform
form

ACTIVATOR
GENERATOR

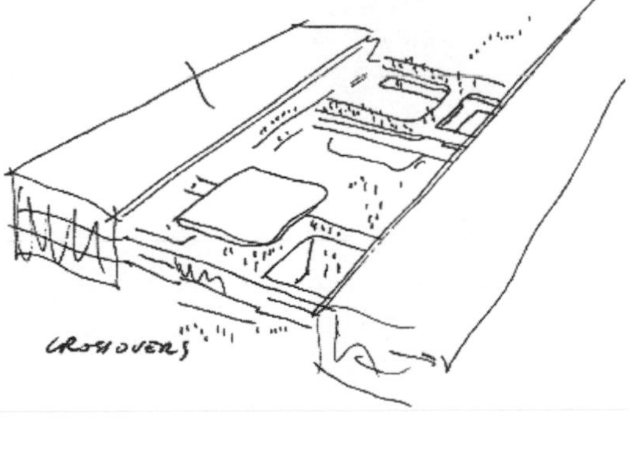
CROSSOVERS

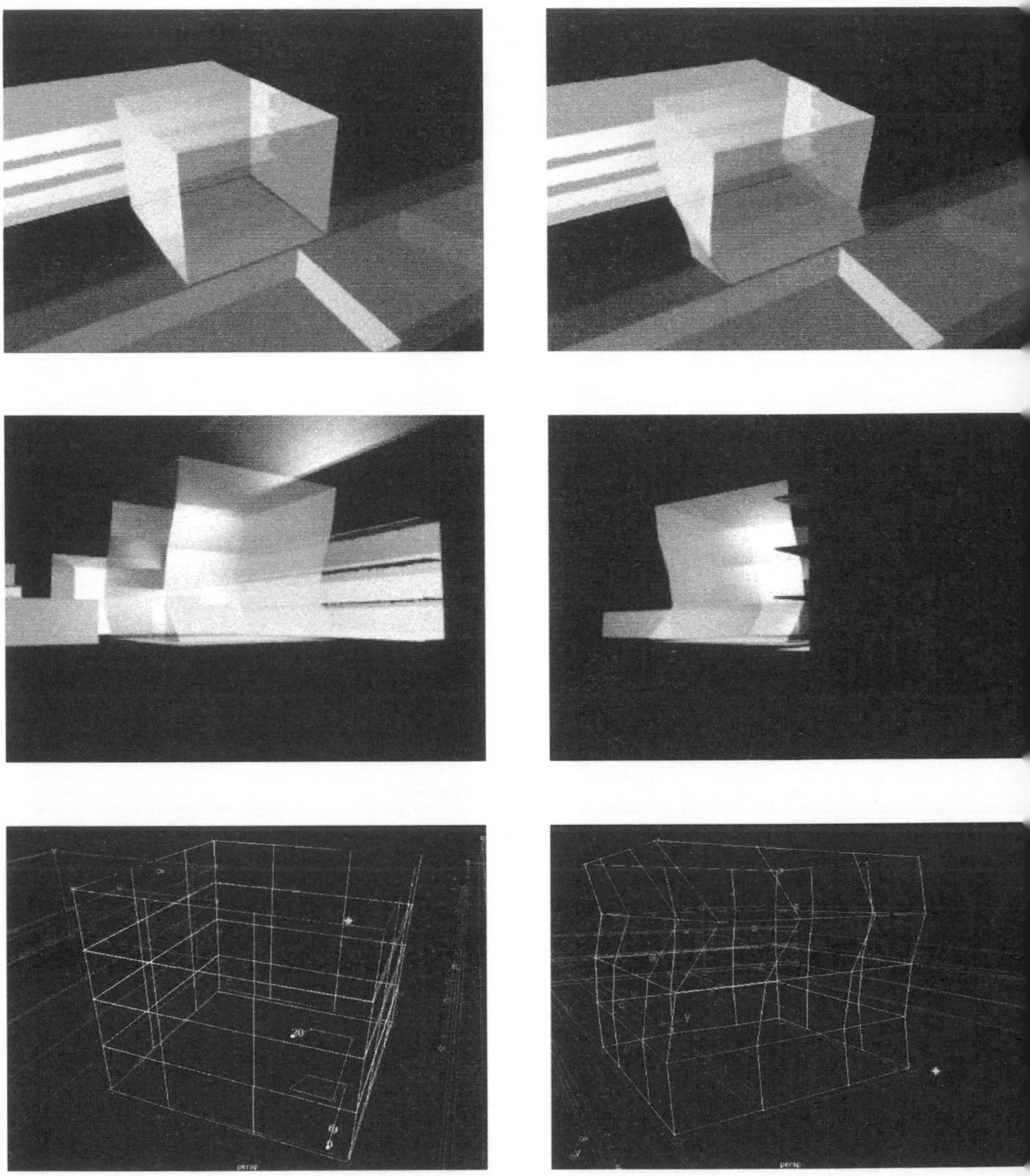

Digital deformation (as in a wind tunnel)

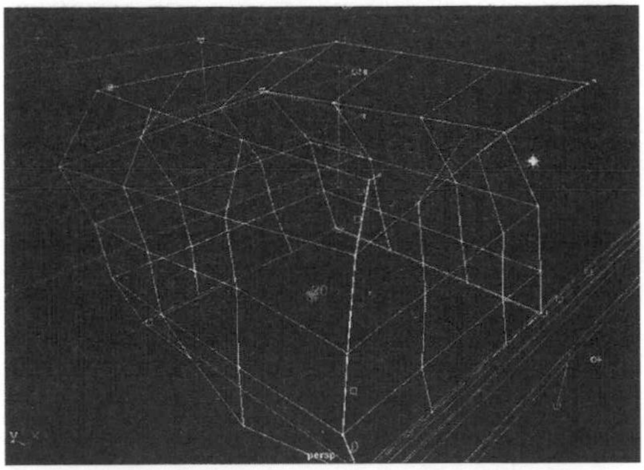
persp

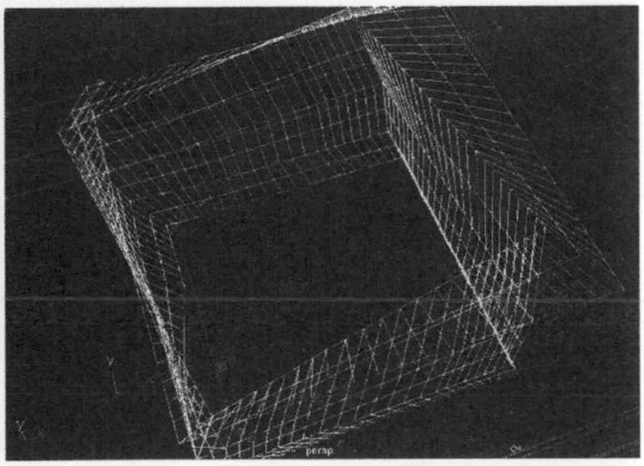
persp

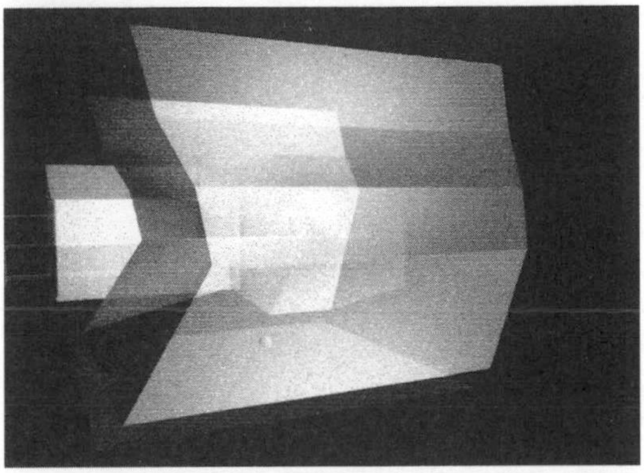

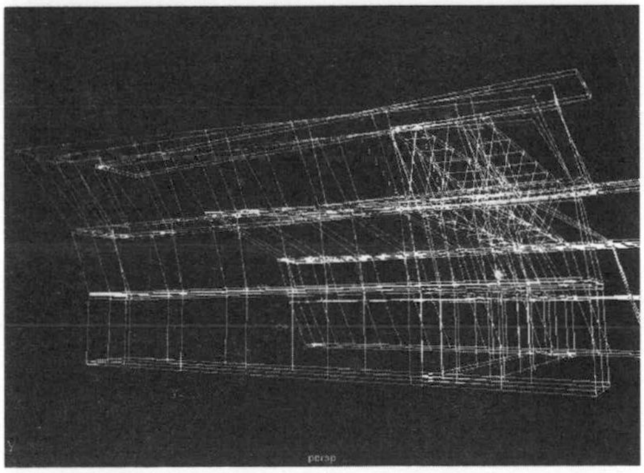
persp

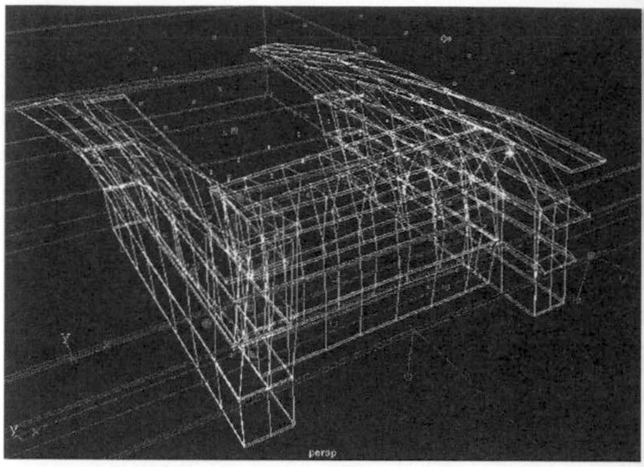
persp

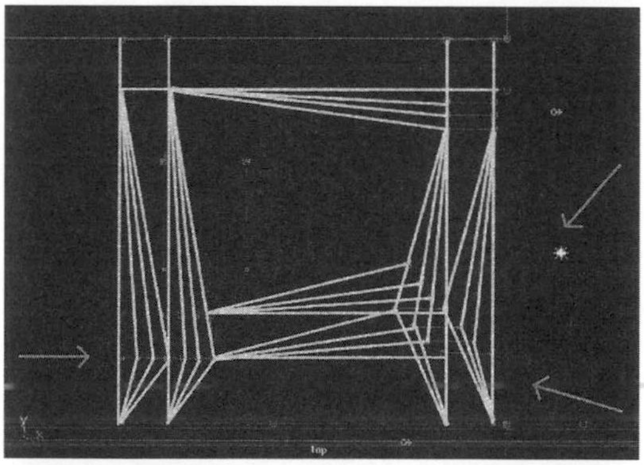
top

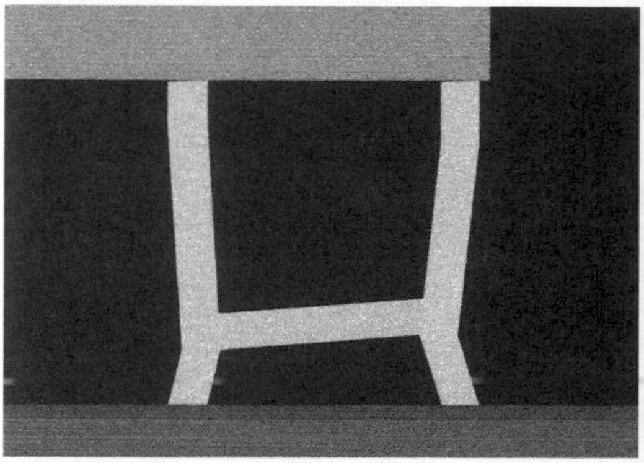

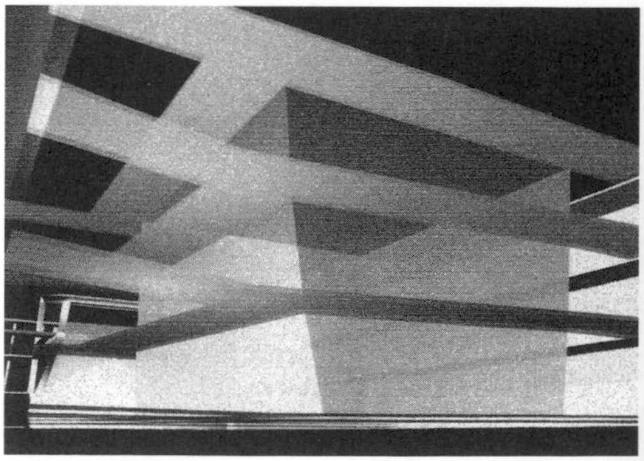

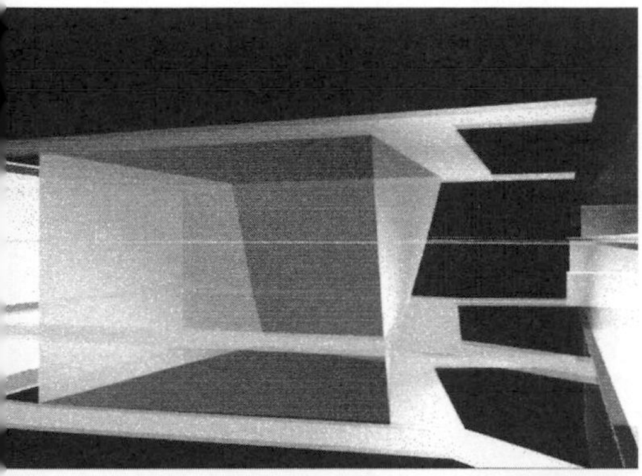

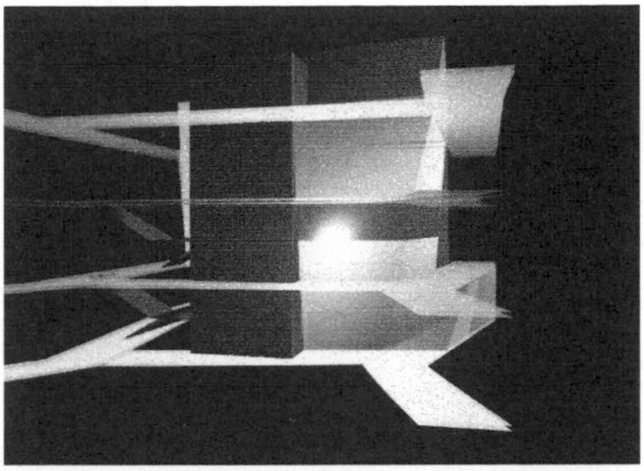

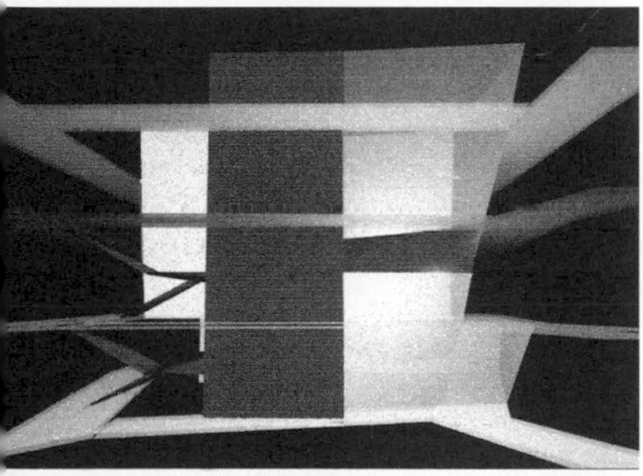

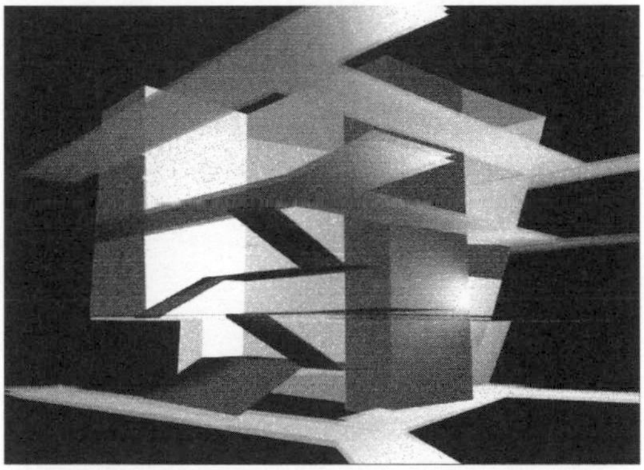

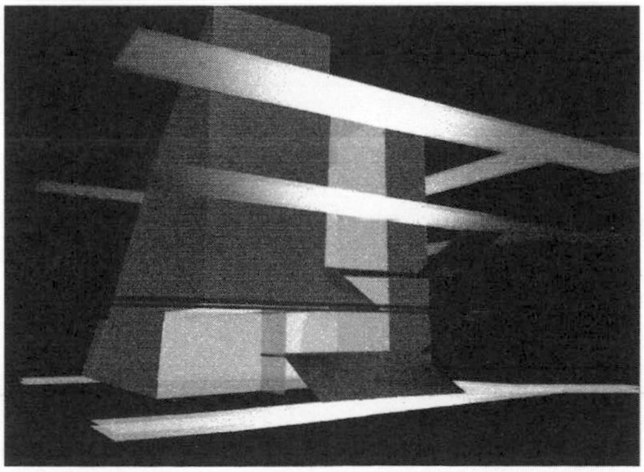

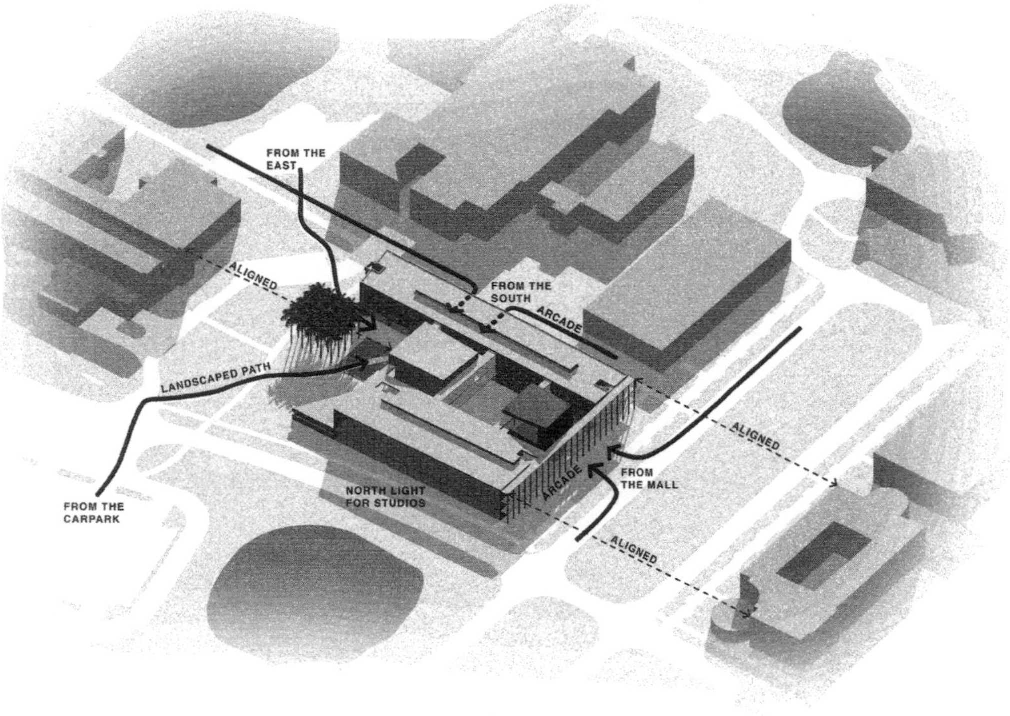

Campus movement patterns all merge into the school's main social spaces: the courtyard, the stairs, the auditorium

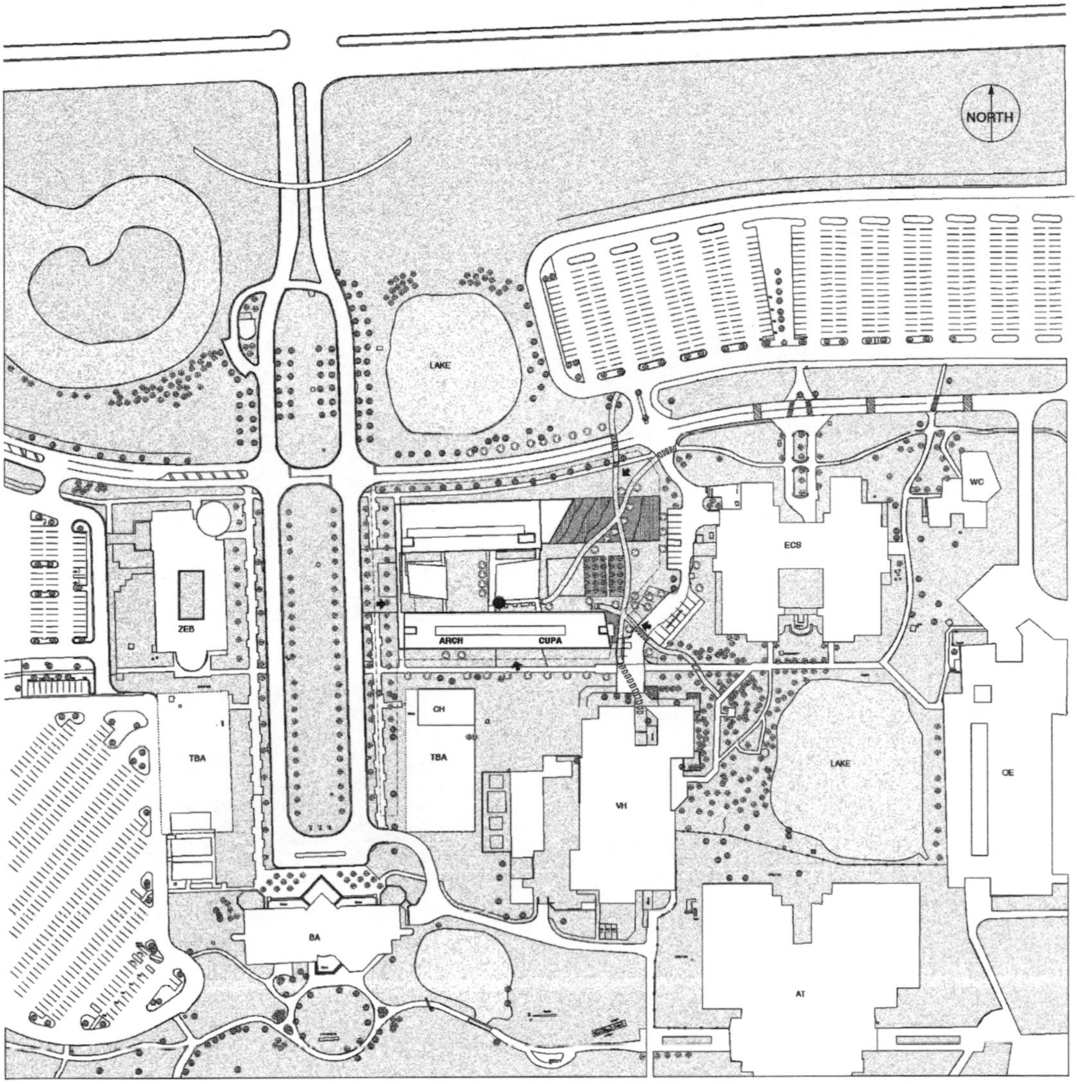
NORTH
LAKE
WC
ECS
ZEB
ARCH
CUPA
CH
TBA
TBA
LAKE
OE
VH
BA
AT

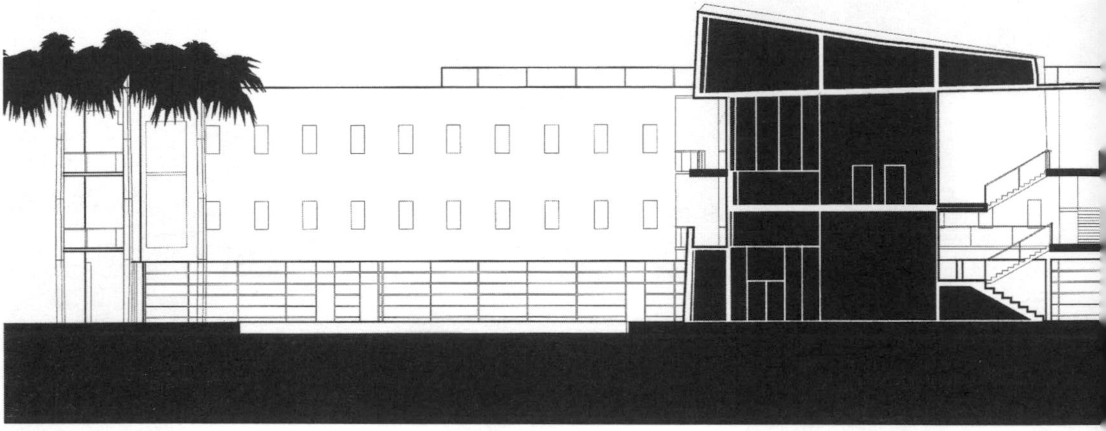

The generators become the place of difference: a specific program, a specific envelope

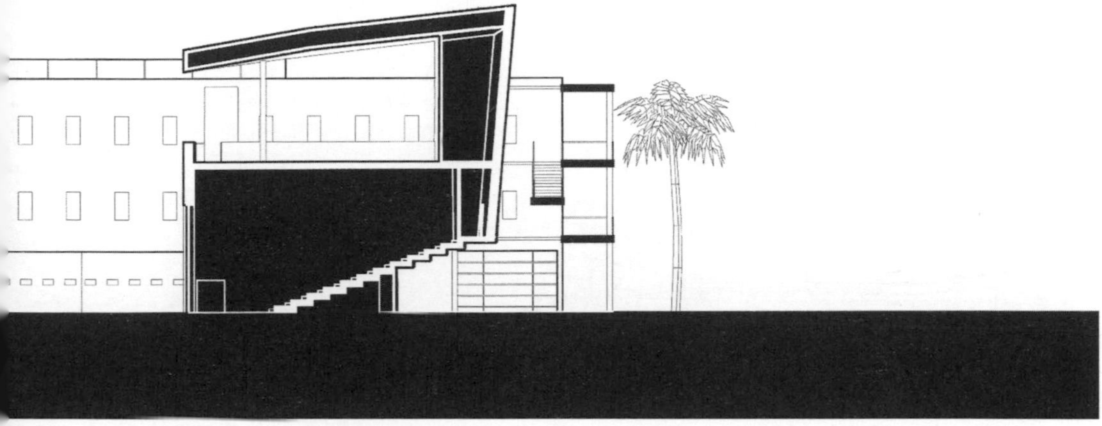

Generators also gather together the more public activities as social condensers

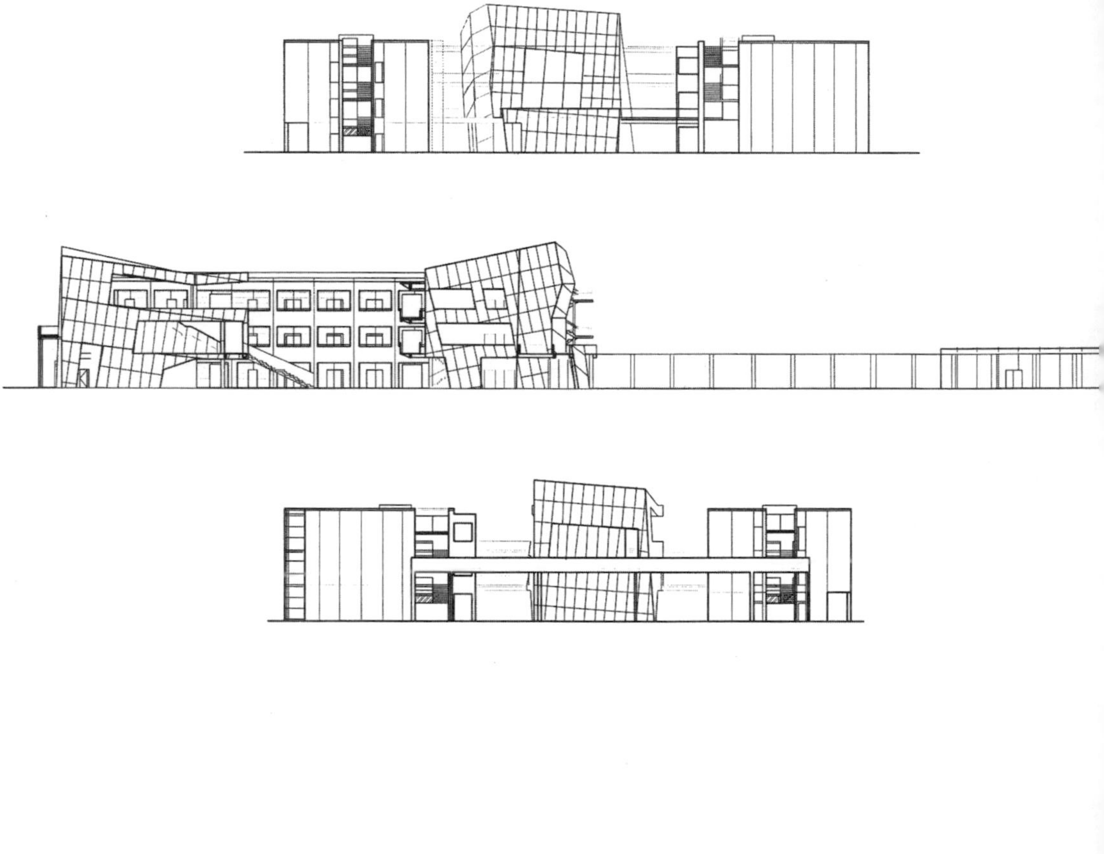

Never about formal homogeneity, but about tension between two material expressions—generic pre-cast concrete vs. warped ceramic surfaces

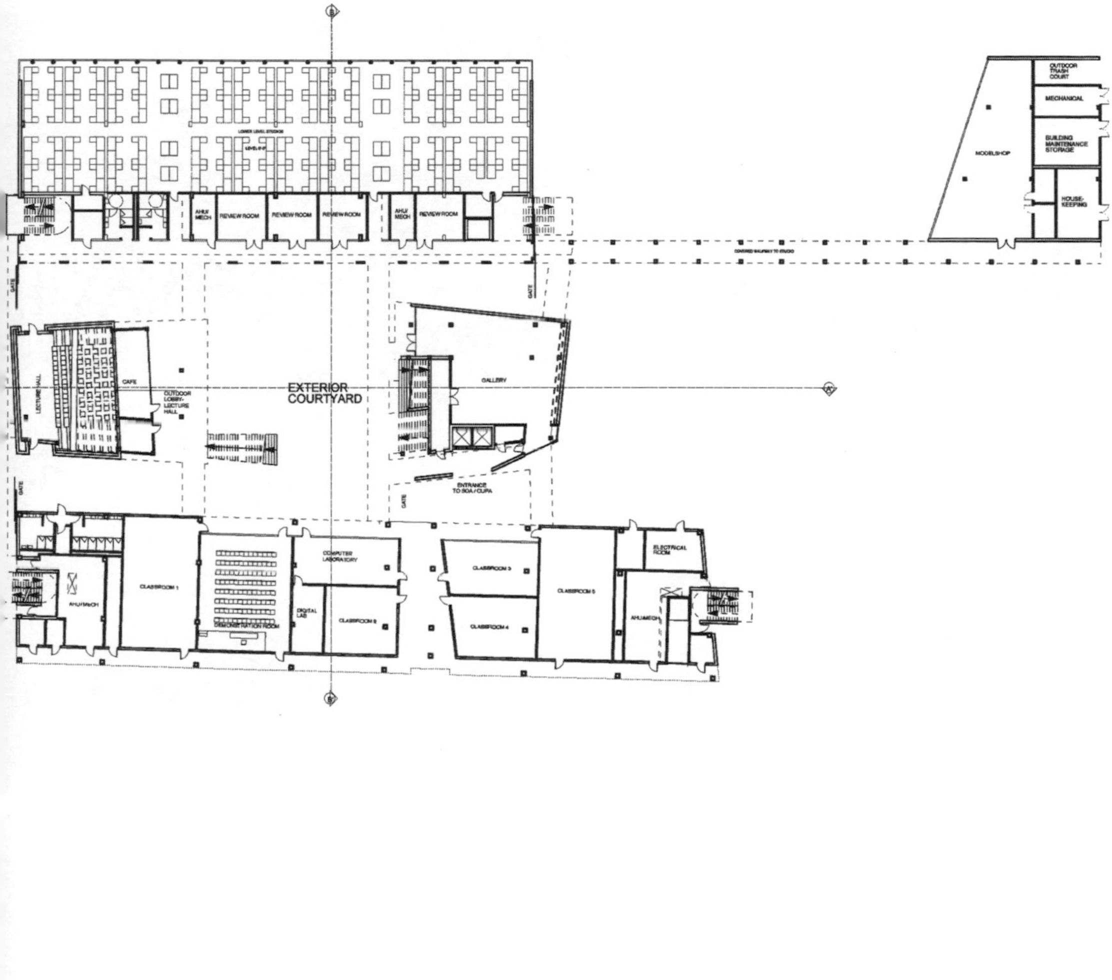

Programmatic intermingling (ground floor): lower studios and review rooms extend into courtyard. Classrooms and auditorium, together with library open stairs, open onto the courtyard

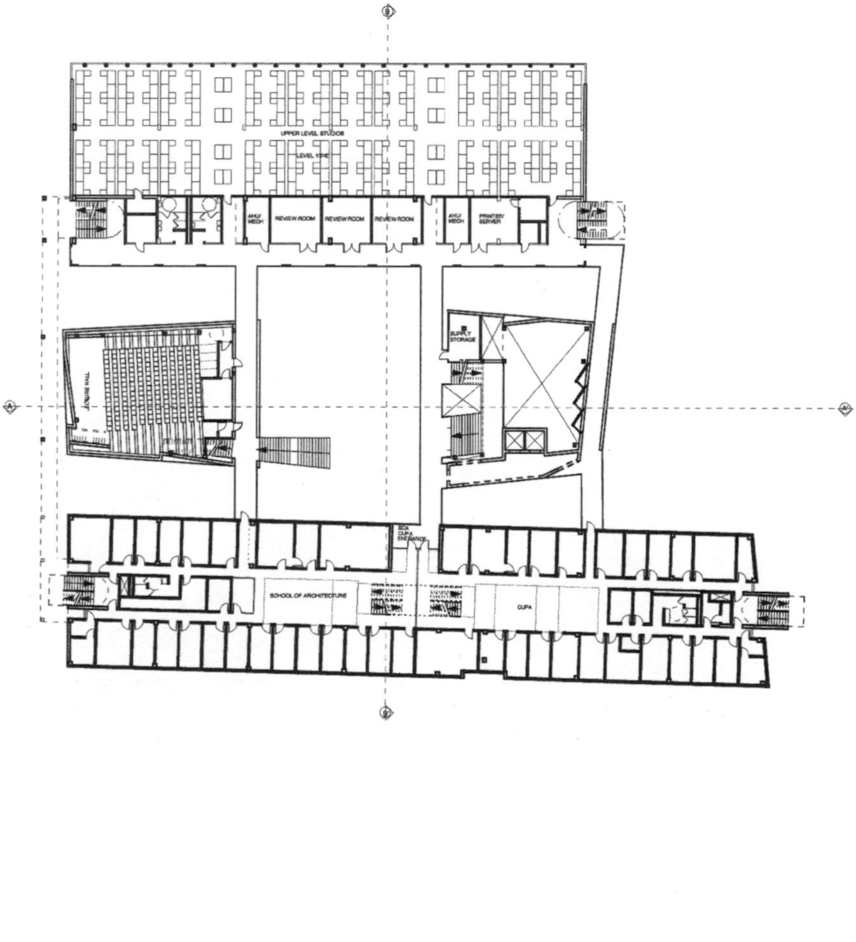

Second floor plan Spatial intermingling (generic upper floors): upper studios have a double height and offices open onto double-height interior court

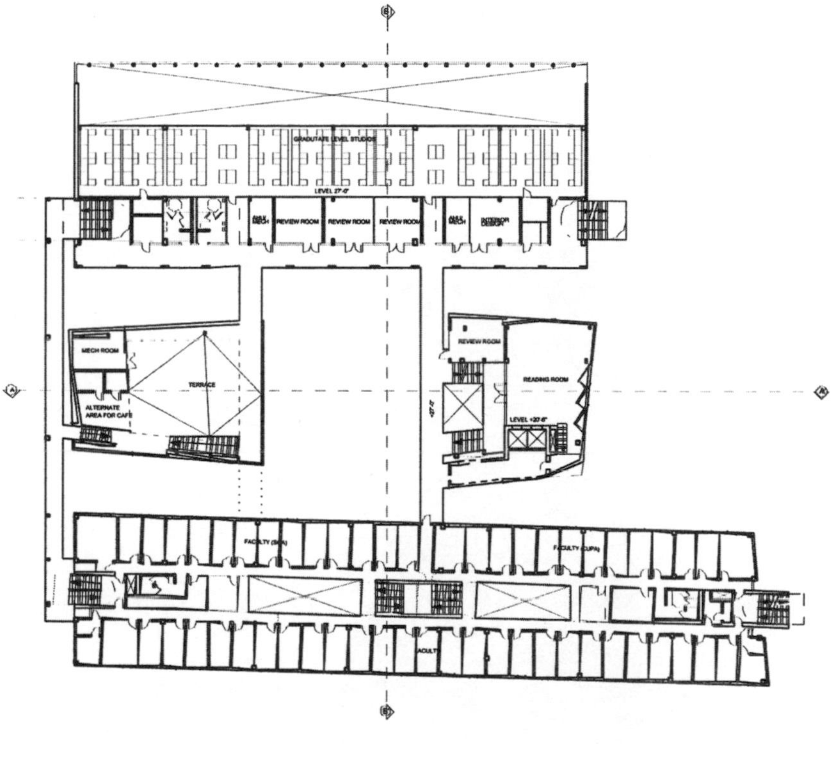

Third floor plan Oppositions between generic and specific, between repetition (the studios and offices) and difference (the generators)

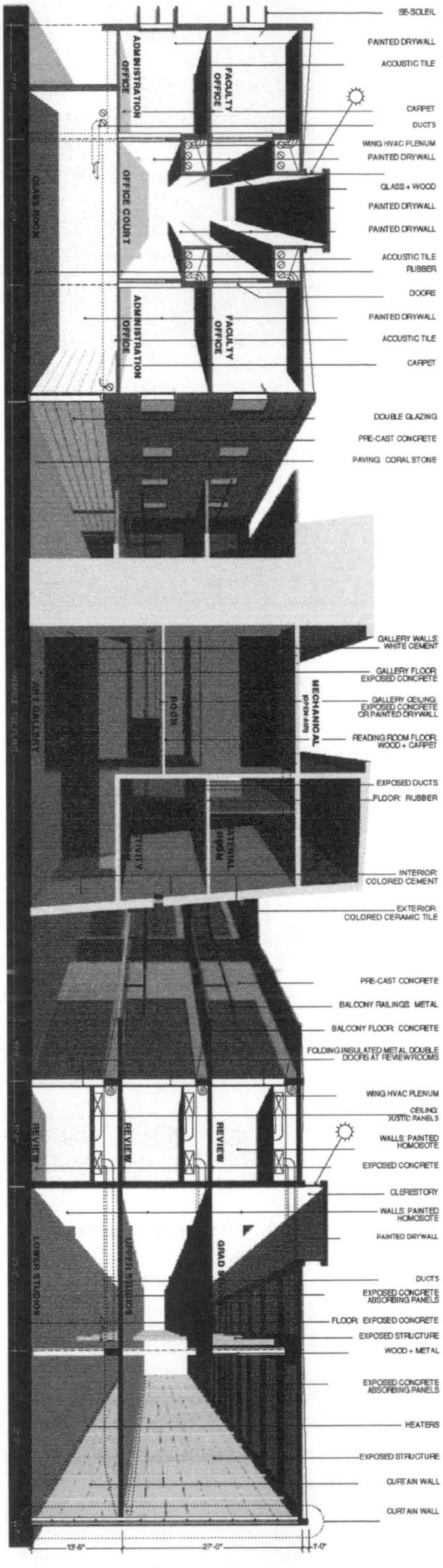
SE-SOLEIL
PAINTED DRYWALL
ACOUSTIC TILE
CARPET
DUCTS
WING HVAC PLENUM
PAINTED DRYWALL
GLASS + WOOD
PAINTED DRYWALL
PAINTED DRYWALL
ACOUSTIC TILE
RUBBER
DOORS
PAINTED DRYWALL
ACOUSTIC TILE
CARPET
DOUBLE GLAZING
PRE-CAST CONCRETE
PAVING: CORAL STONE
GALLERY WALLS: WHITE CEMENT
GALLERY FLOOR: EXPOSED CONCRETE
GALLERY CEILING: EXPOSED CONCRETE OR PAINTED DRYWALL
READING ROOM FLOOR: WOOD + CARPET
EXPOSED DUCTS
FLOOR: RUBBER
INTERIOR: COLORED CEMENT
EXTERIOR: COLORED CERAMIC TILE
PRE-CAST CONCRETE
BALCONY RAILINGS: METAL
BALCONY FLOOR: CONCRETE
FOLDING INSULATED METAL DOUBLE DOORS AT REVIEW ROOMS
WING HVAC PLENUM
WALLS: PAINTED HOMOSOTE
EXPOSED CONCRETE
CLERESTORY
WALLS: PAINTED HOMOSOTE
PAINTED DRYWALL
DUCTS
EXPOSED CONCRETE ABSORBING PANELS
FLOOR: EXPOSED CONCRETE
EXPOSED STRUCTURE
WOOD + METAL
EXPOSED CONCRETE ABSORBING PANELS
HEATERS
EXPOSED STRUCTURE
CURTAIN WALL
CURTAIN WALL
ADMINISTRATION OFFICE
FACULTY OFFICE
OFFICE COURT
ADMINISTRATION OFFICE
FACULTY OFFICE
MECHANICAL
REVIEW
REVIEW
REVIEW
LOWER STUDIOS
UPPER STUDIOS
13'-6"
27'-0"
1'-0"

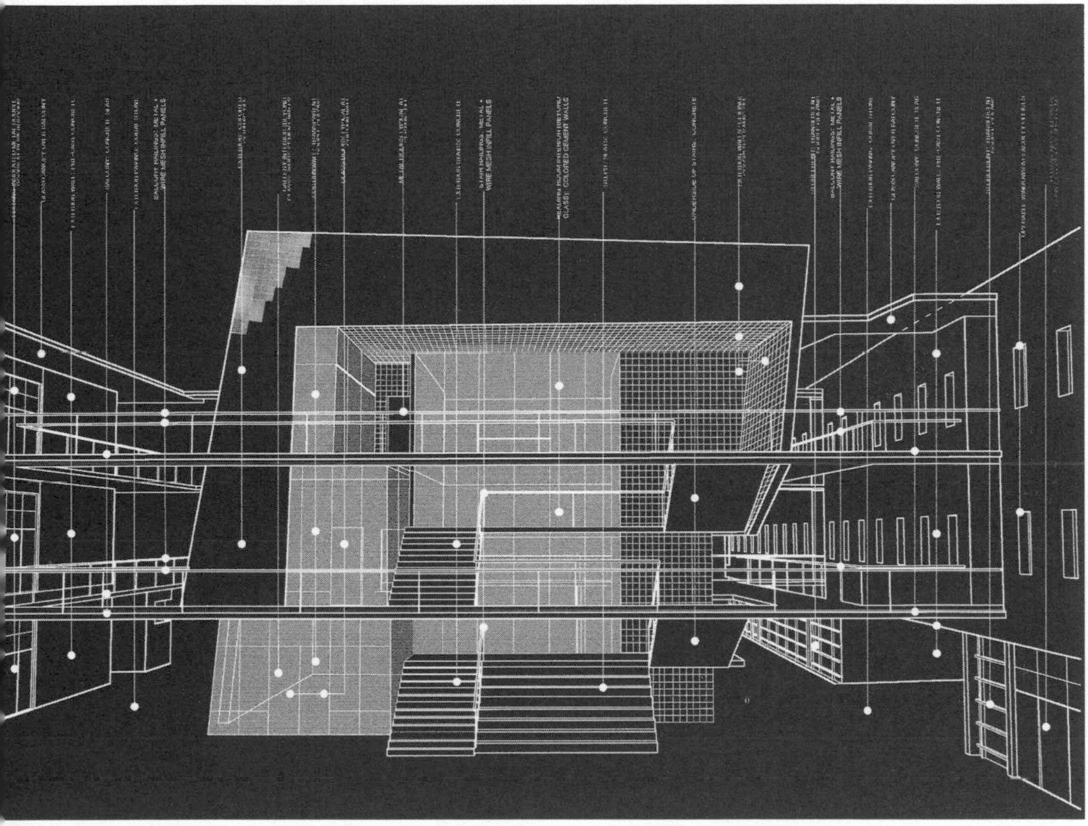

Generators: a colorful ceramic skin qualifies their specificity, from red to yellow and even to green (the Royal Palm Basilica)

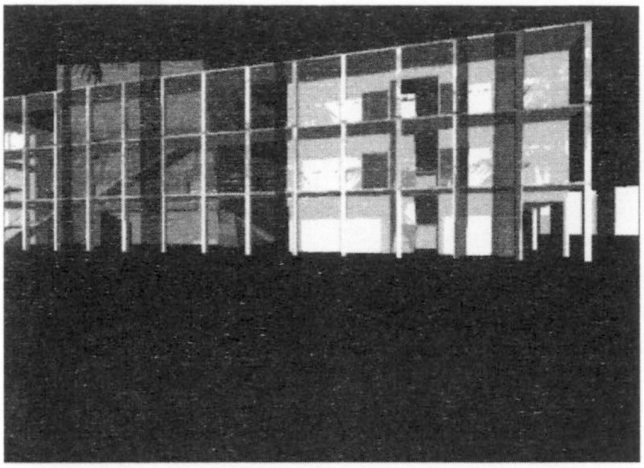

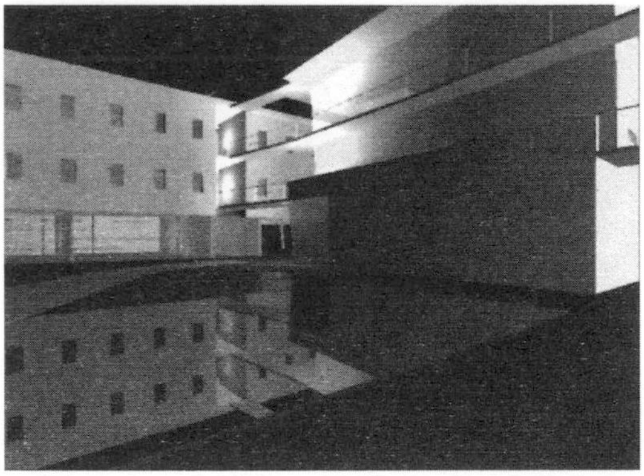
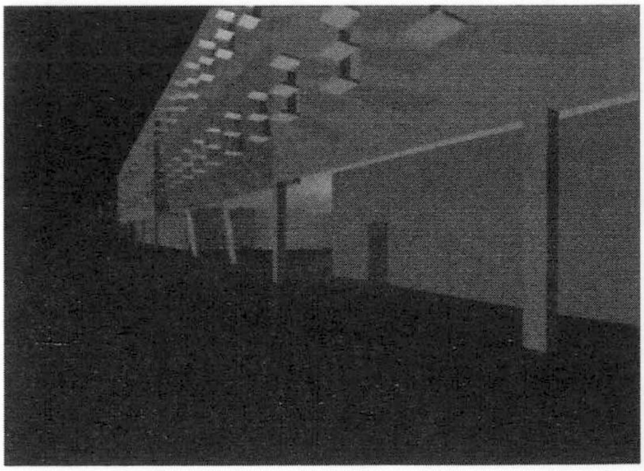

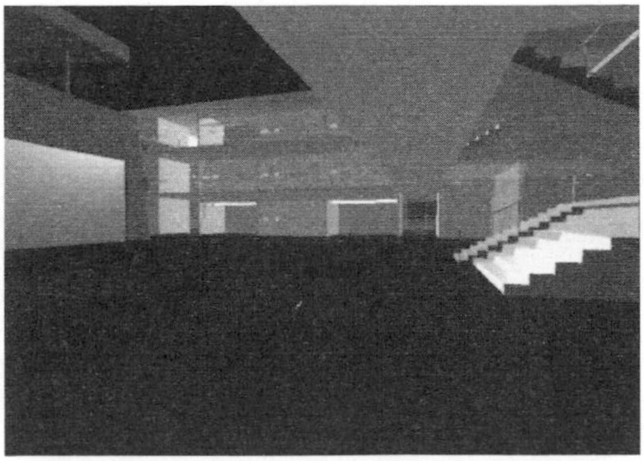

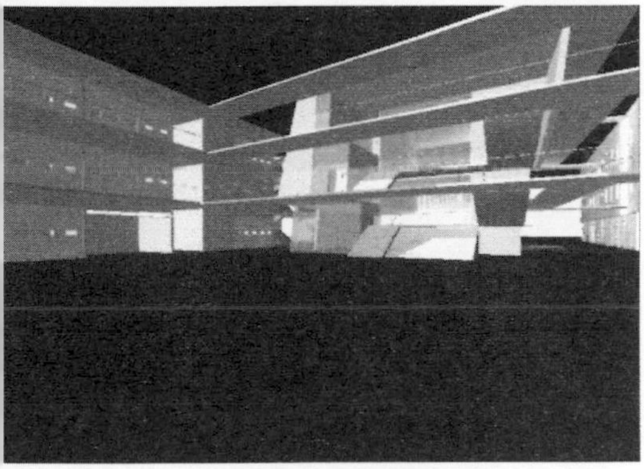

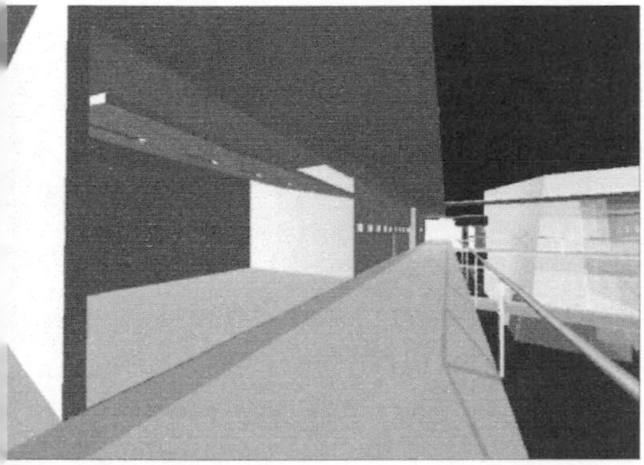

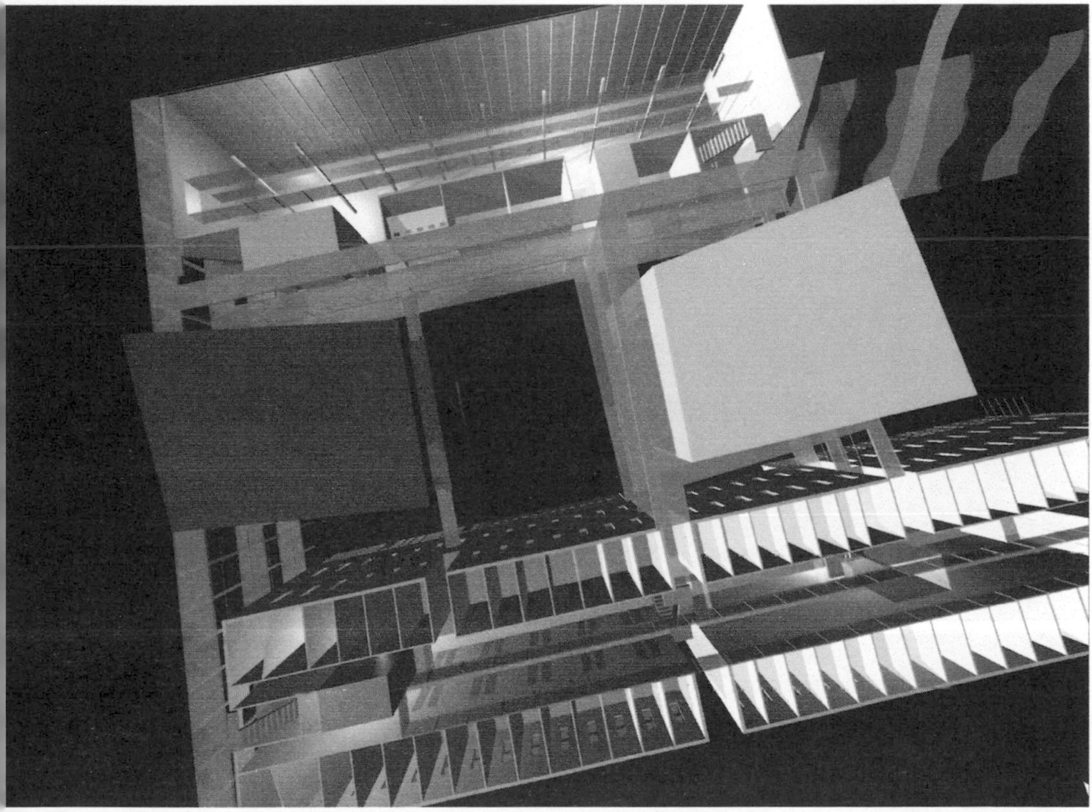

E.
Envelopes

Architecture also can be defined by surfaces, whether continuous or discontinuous, amorphous or obsessively articulated. The very large public assembly space at Rouen is conceived as two envelopes, two event-spaces, one inside the other. Within the inner envelope, the auditorium is programmed according to various venues (music, entertainment, politics). Between the two envelopes is the access area, much like the old foyer of conventional theater. This “in-between” is conceived as a large public space, activated by various circulation routes.

Rouen, Concert Hall and Exhibition Complex, 1998-

Between Two Skins

PARC

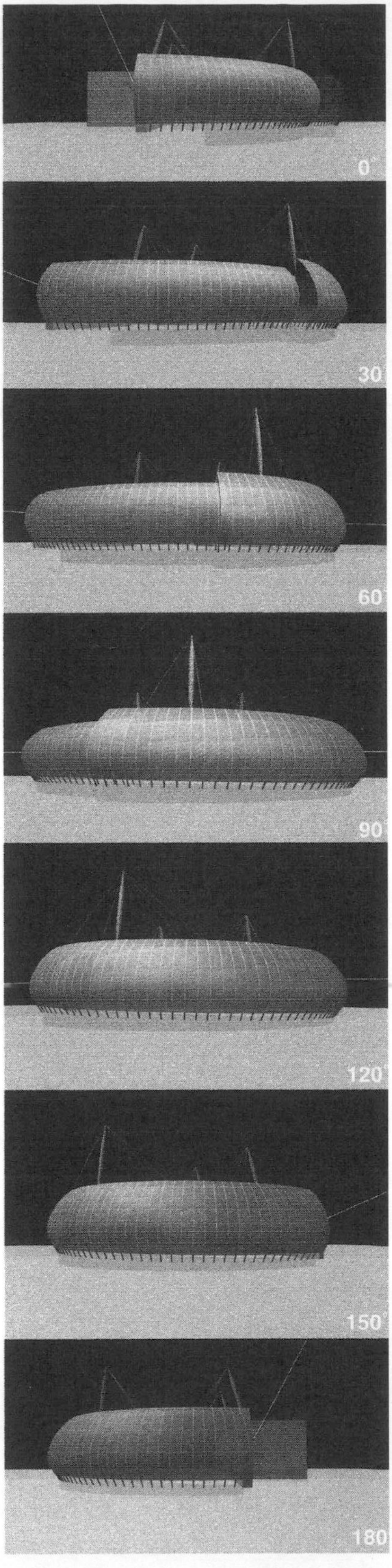
0°
30°
60°
90°
120°
150°
180°

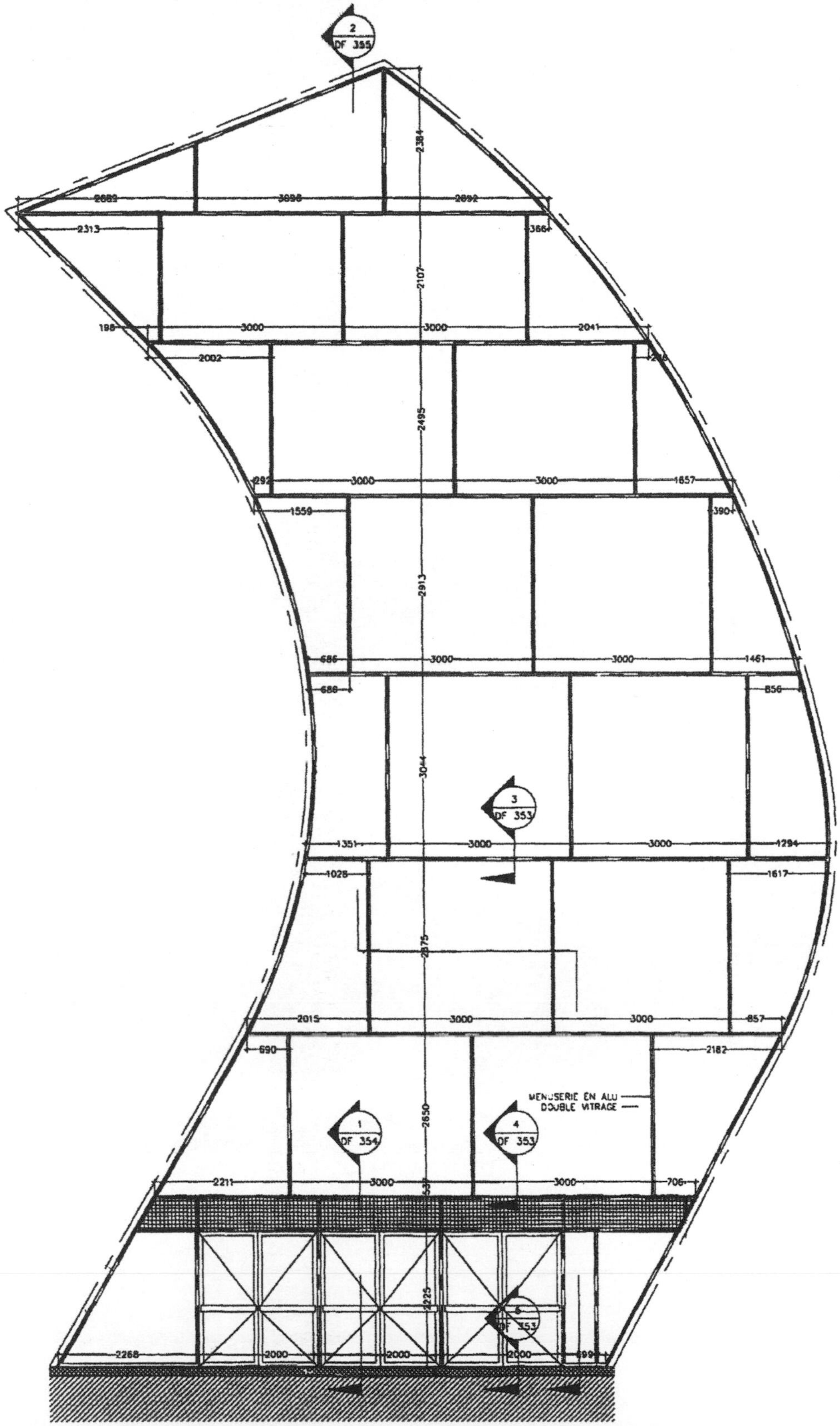
2
DF 355
2384
2883
3098
2892
2313
366
2107
198
3000
3000
2041
2002
2495
292
3000
3000
1657
1559
390
2913
686
3000
3000
1461
686
856
3044
3
DF 353
1351
3000
3000
1294
1028
1617
2875
2015
3000
3000
857
690
2182
MENUSERIE EN ALU
DOUBLE VITRAGE
1
DF 354
2650
4
DF 353
2211
3000
3000
706
2225
2268
2000
2000
2000
699

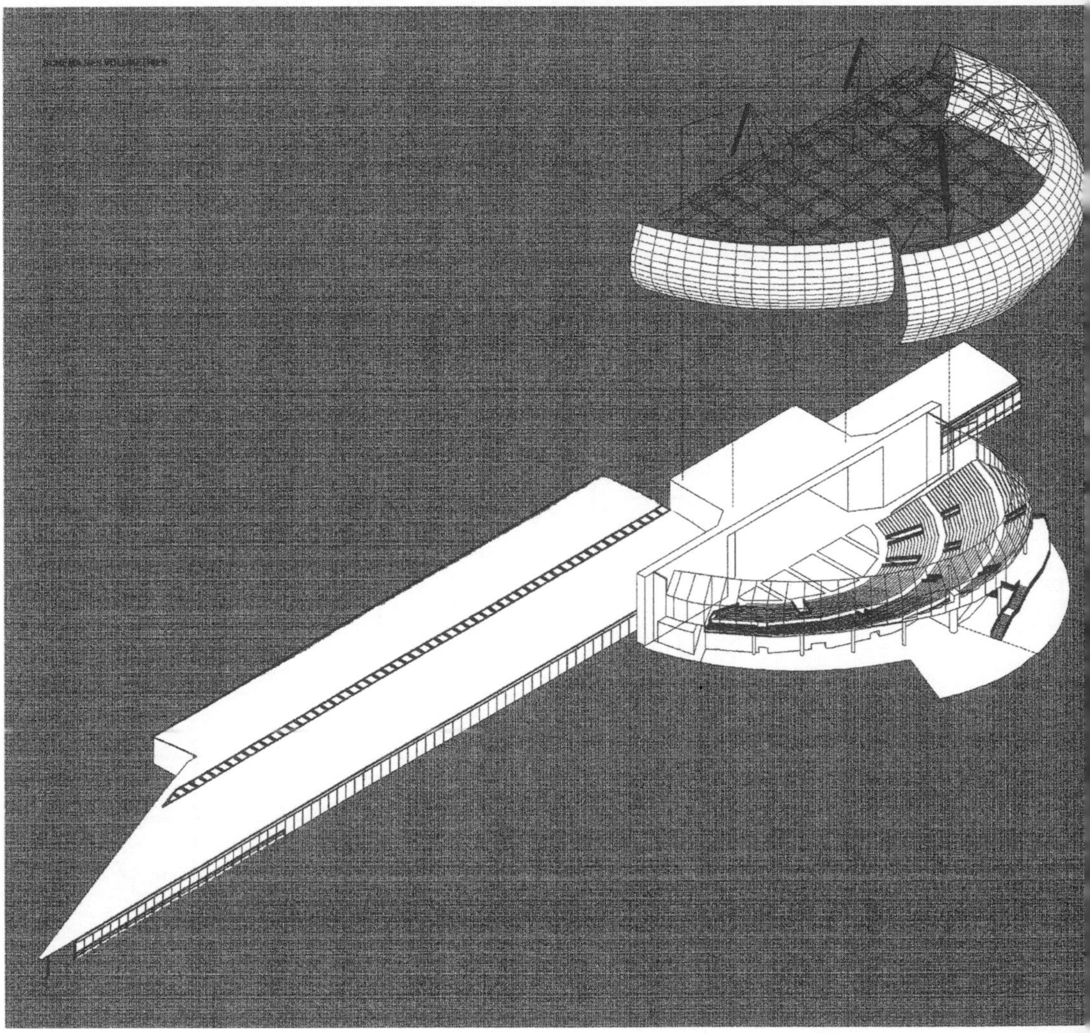

Issue: the question of large envelopes

At the start of the 21st century, to create a tool capable of fostering both the economic expansion and cultural development of the Rouen district: these are the stakes of the project. This double economic and cultural function provides the program's interest; the site, currently banal (an abandoned airfield), but filled with potential, is well located at the entry to Rouen and less than an hour and a half from Paris. As seen from National Route 138, the 7000-seat concert hall (for rock concerts, political meetings, and varied forms of entertainment), the square or plaza, and the new 70,000-square-foot exhibition hall are to be placed on the 70 acres of a site structured by a grid of plantings and lighting.

We located the plaza and the new exhibition hall parallel to Route 138N, and designed the concert hall to be seen with equal interest when heading towards or away from Rouen on the highway. The plaza can also accommodate shows, exhibitions or other open-air events.

The plaza opens towards the respective entrances of the exhibition hall and the concert hall. An opening in the structure allows the public to be welcomed into the spaces of these two buildings without disrupting their structural logic.

The two buildings are conceived to offer a certain degree of polyvalency. The new exhibition hall allows a diversity of layouts so as to accommodate conventions for large crowds or trade fairs for limited groups of professionals. The concert hall accommodates musical events as well as sporting events. Political conventions, summer schools, or theatrical shows are also possible. The 700-foot-long exhibition hall is conceived as a simple structure, its roof slightly vaulted; the overriding horizontality contrasts with the curvature and the guy-wired masts of the concert hall.

For the 350-foot-diameter concert hall, we transformed the typology of the classic concert hall by developing a slight asymmetry in the audience seating so as to lend more spontaneity to the ambience of popular music. This asymmetry also provides functional advantages, allowing the possibility of reconfiguring the theater into three smaller volumes and accommodating the off-center entry.

The structural system of the roof permits both an economical long span and long-distance visibility, due to the three masts, illuminated on concert evenings. Tension cables hold the middle of the long spans, allowing a lighter truss system.

Acoustical concerns led to a complete double envelope surrounding the concert hall. The inner skin and concrete stepped seating are doubled by the exterior, the broken torus of insulated corrugated metal. The space between the structural / acoustical envelope and the weather / security envelope can be described as an "in-between." Its size makes it a major space in the project, animated by the various routes to the hall itself.

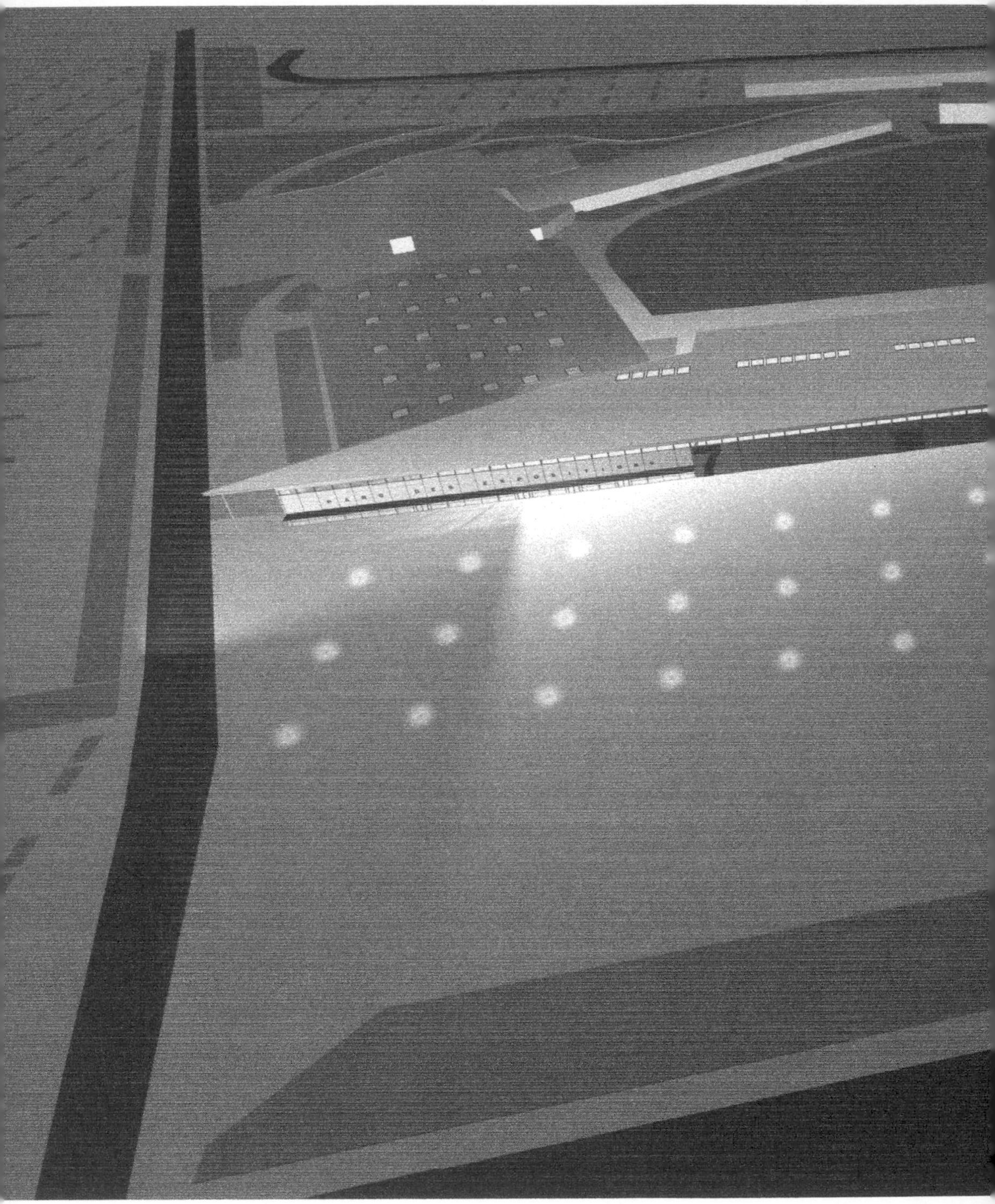

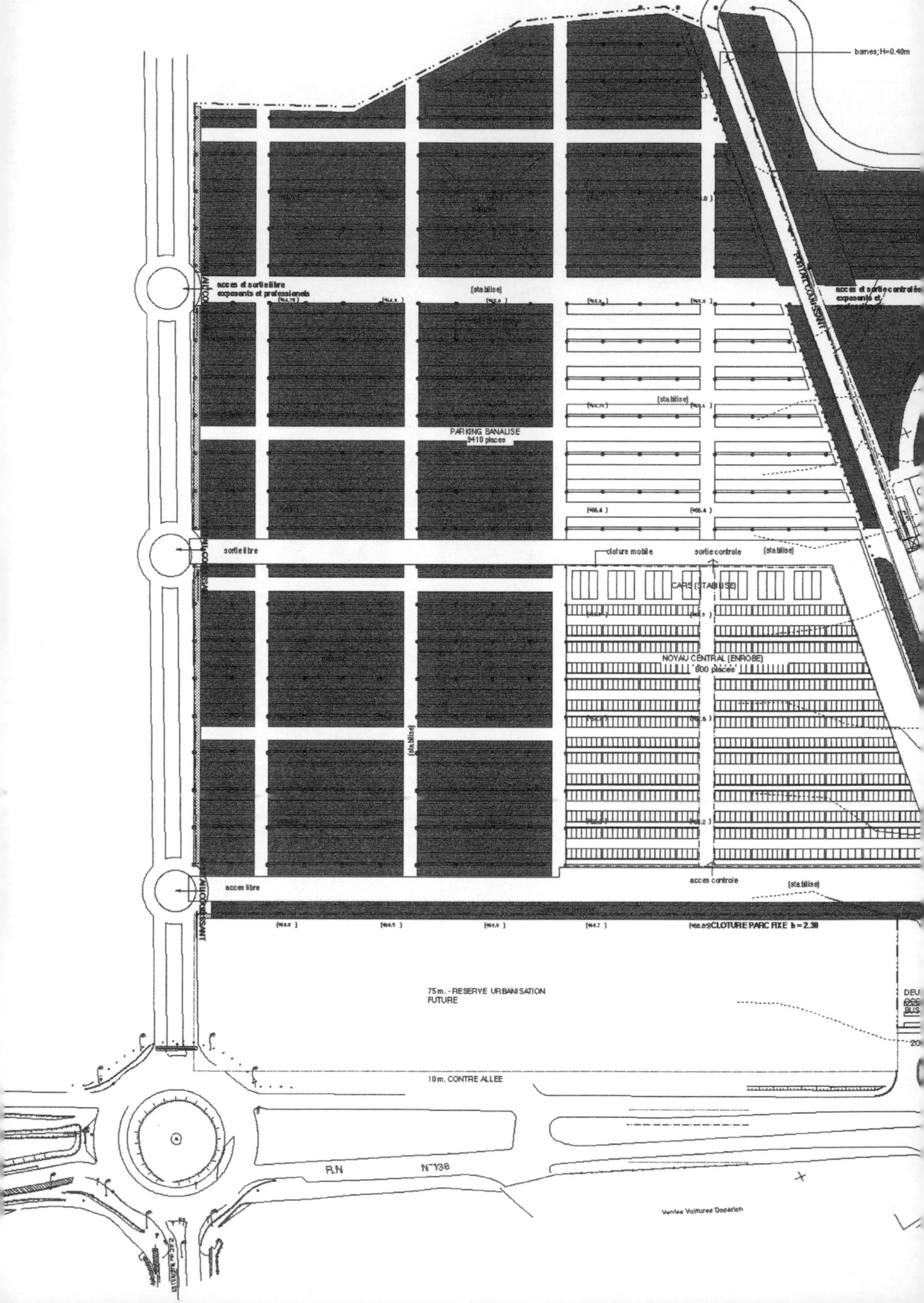
bornes; H=0.40m
acces et sortie libre
exposants et professionels
(stabilise)
acces et sortie controlés
exposants et professionels
PARKING BANALISE
3410 places
sortie libre
cloture mobile
sortie controle
(stabilise)
CARS (STABILISE)
NOYAU CENTRAL (ENROBE)
800 places
(stabilise)
acces libre
acces controle
(stabilise)
CLOTURE PARC FIXE h = 2.30
75m. - RESERVE URBANISATION
FUTURE
10m. CONTRE ALLEE
R.N
N°138
Ventes Voitures Occasion

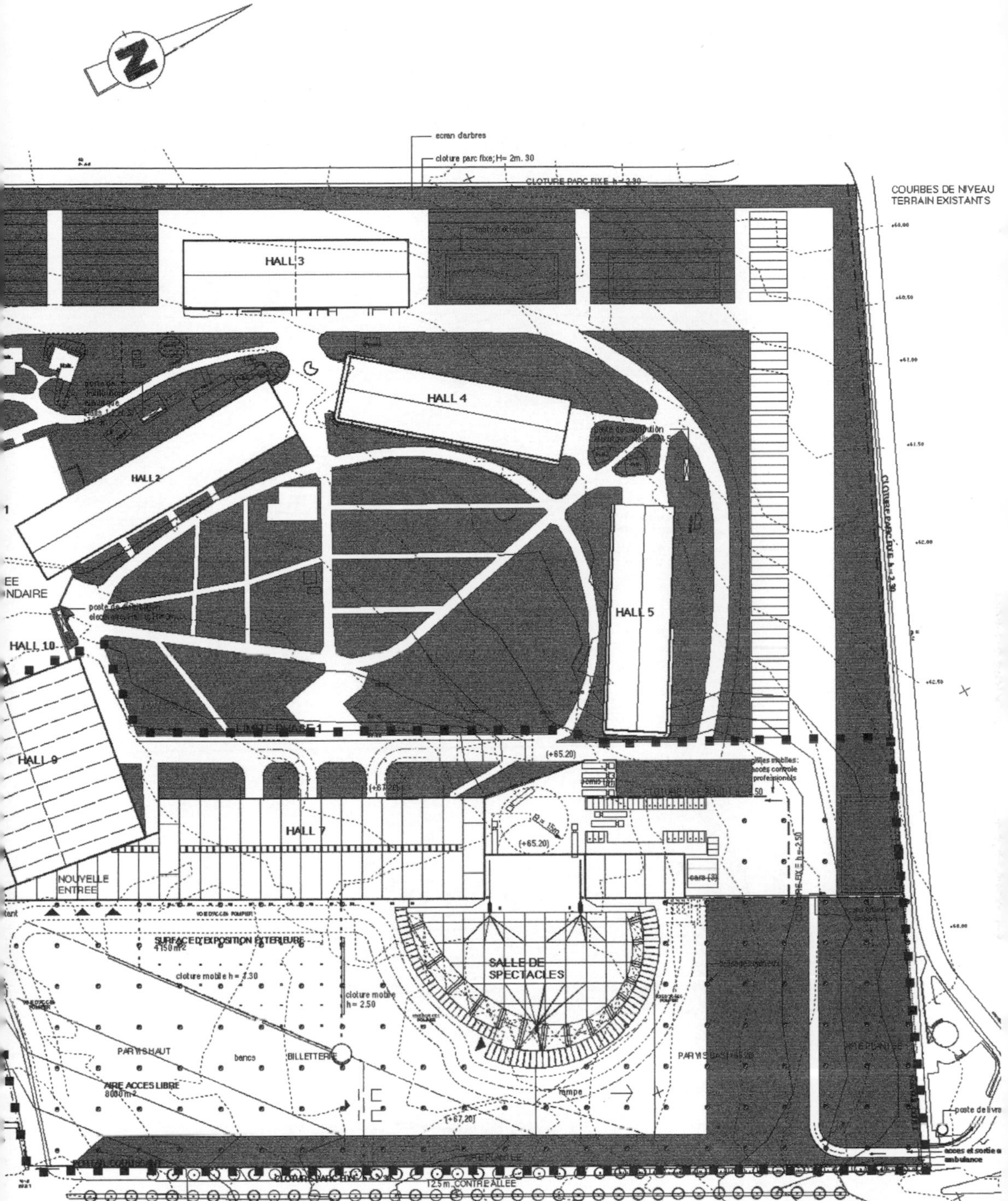

N
ecran d'arbres
cloture parc fixe; H= 2m. 30
COURBES DE NIVEAU
TERRAIN EXISTANTS
HALL 3
HALL 4
HALL 2
HALL 5
HALL 10
HALL 9
HALL 7
(+65.20)
(+67.20)
NOUVELLE
ENTREE
cars (3)
SURFACE D'EXPOSITION EXTERIEURE
4150 m2
cloture mobile h= 2.30
cloture mobile
h= 2.50
SALLE DE
SPECTACLES
PARVIS HAUT
bancs
BILLETTERIE
AIRE ACCES LIBRE
8000 m2
rampe
(+67.20)
12.5 m. CONTRE ALLEE
ROUTE N 138
acces et sortie
ambulance

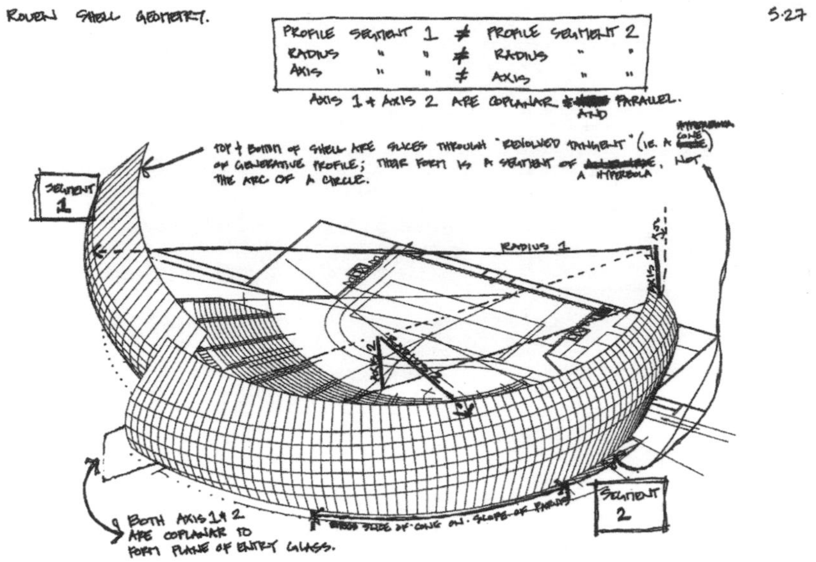

ROUEN SHELL GEOMETRY.
5.27
PROFILE SEGMENT 1 ≠ PROFILE SEGMENT 2
RADIUS " " ≠ RADIUS " "
AXIS " " ≠ AXIS " "
AXIS 1 + AXIS 2 ARE COPLANAR AND PARALLEL.
TOP + BOTTOM OF SHELL ARE SLICES THROUGH "REVOLVED TANGENT" (IE. A CONE) OF GENERATIVE PROFILE; THEIR FORM IS A SEGMENT OF A HYPERBOLA, NOT THE ARC OF A CIRCLE.
SEGMENT 1
RADIUS 1
BOTH AXIS 1 + 2 ARE COPLANAR TO FORM PLANE OF ENTRY GLASS.
SIDE OF CONE ON SLOPE OF PARVIS
SEGMENT 2

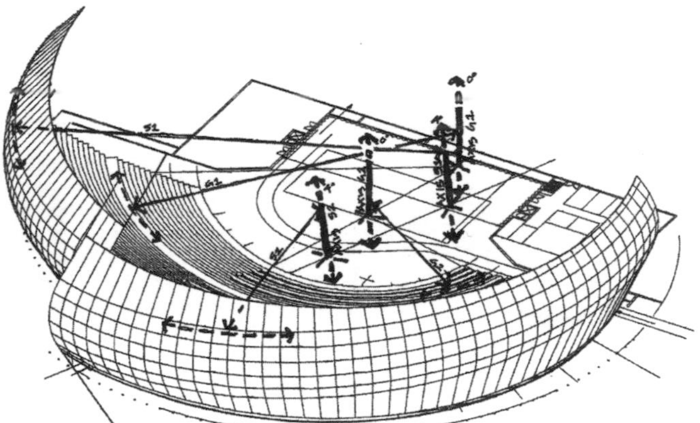

Not a structural shell, but a thin, taut metal skin, coupled with an insulating membrane

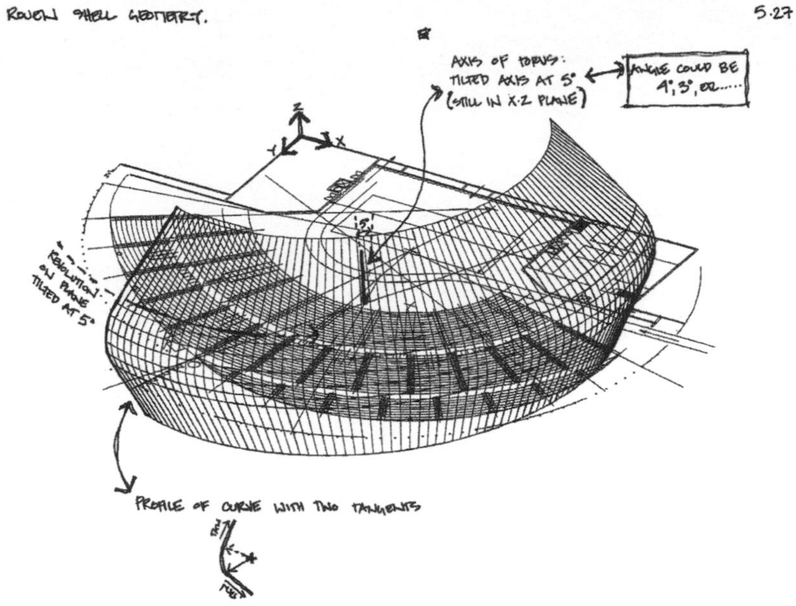

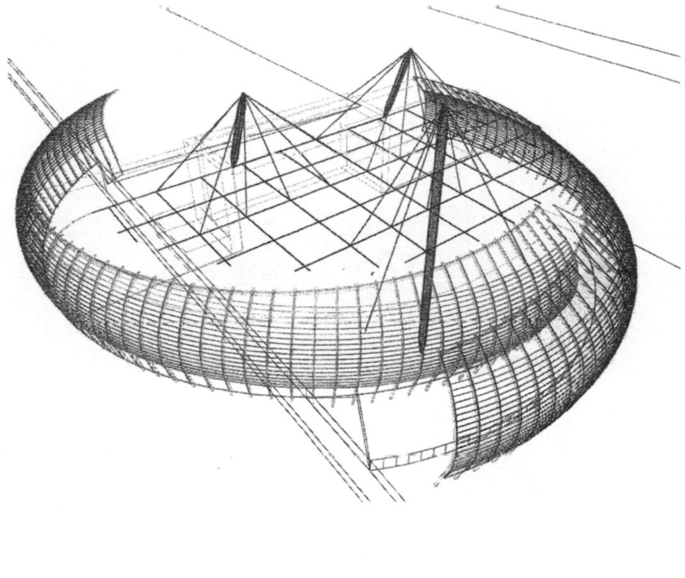

A hybrid structure: long span *and* suspended. The masts also act as signals from a distance

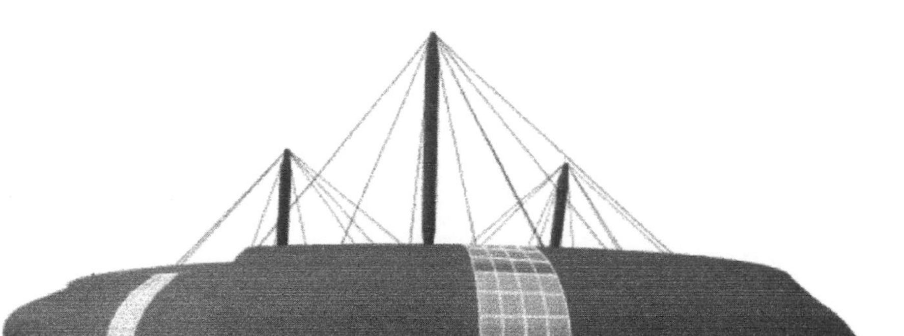

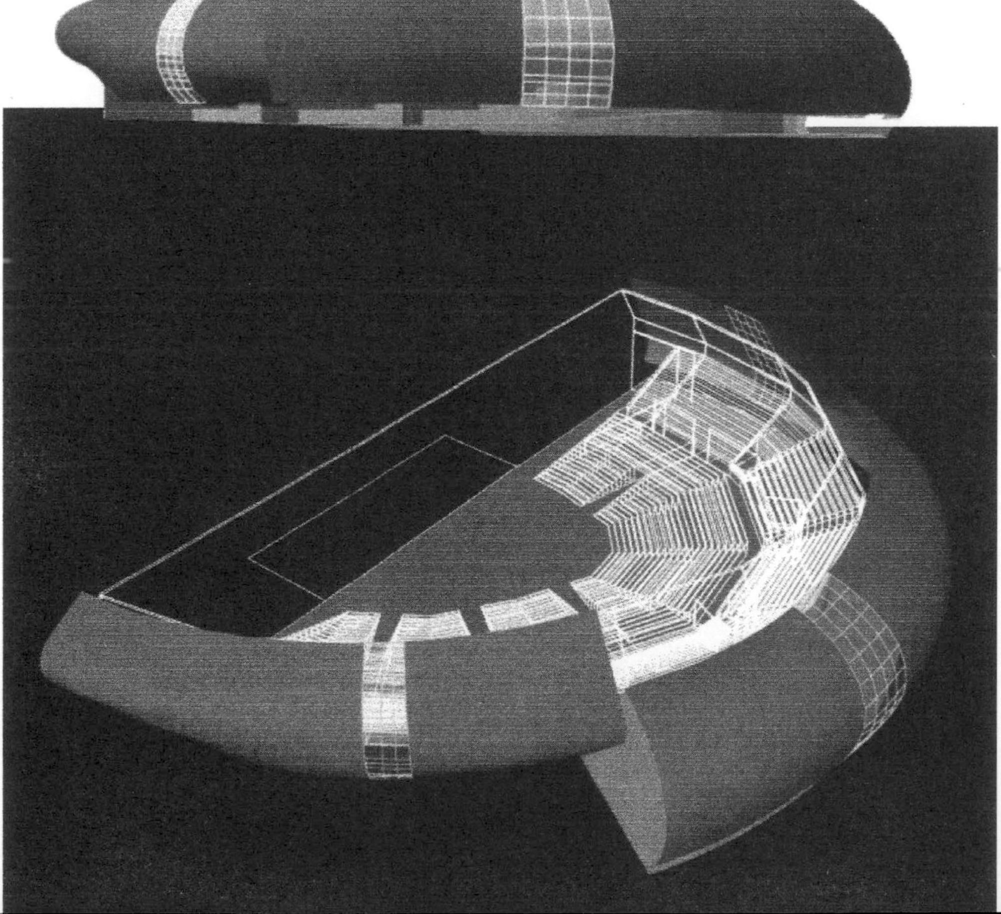

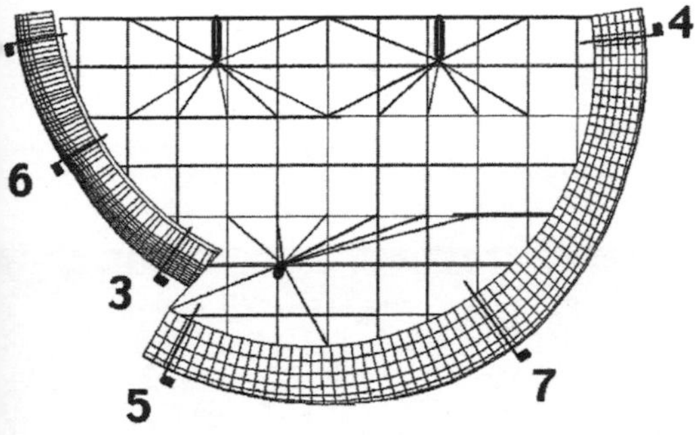
4
6
3
5
7

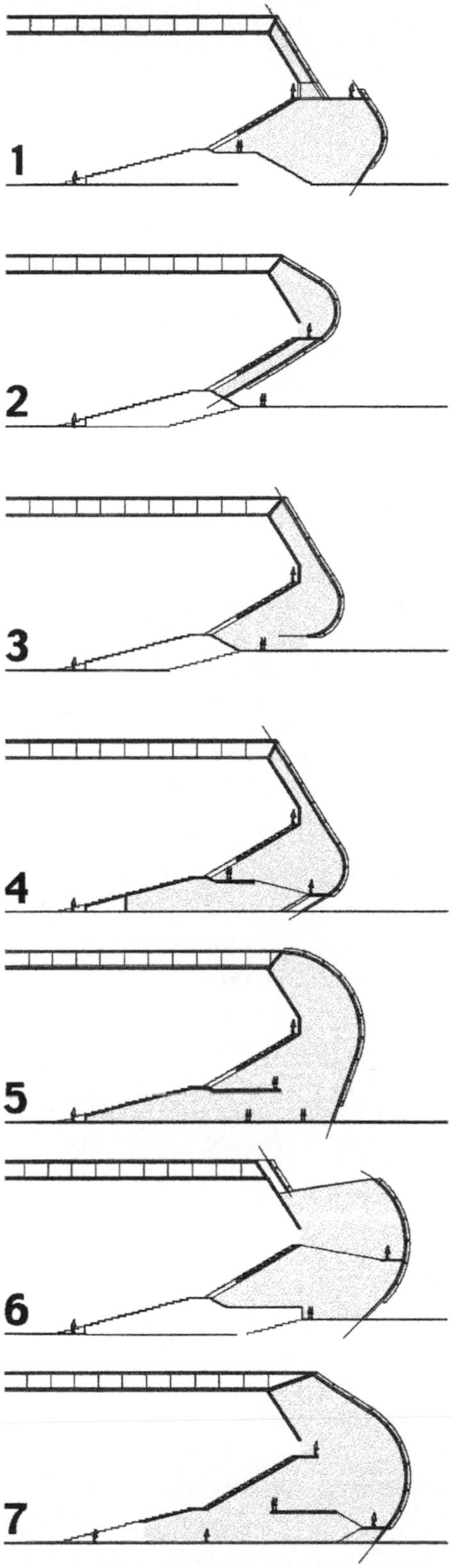
1
2
3
4
5
6
7

The two skins define an in-between: the place of movement ("activating the in-between")

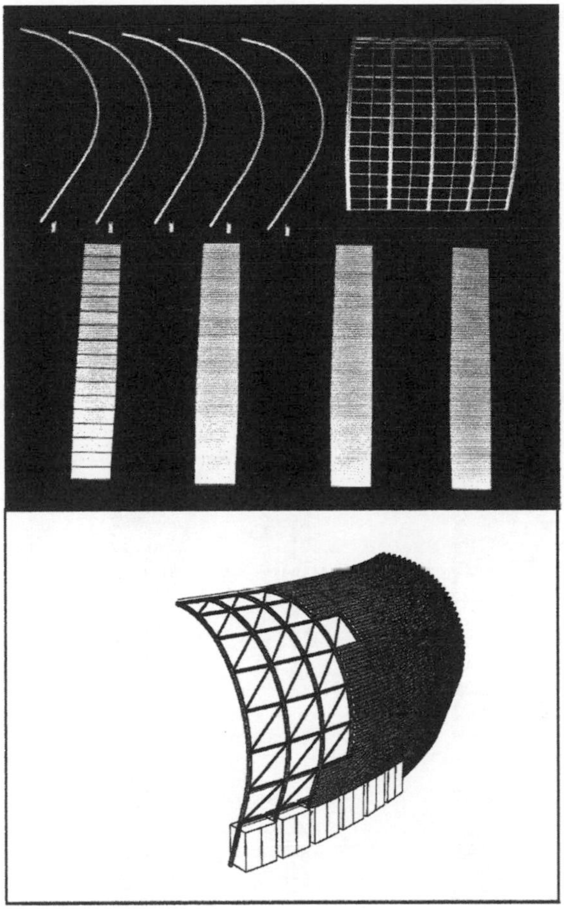

Materials: concrete floor, acoustical insulation, concrete angled curved wall, steel tubing, corrugated steel

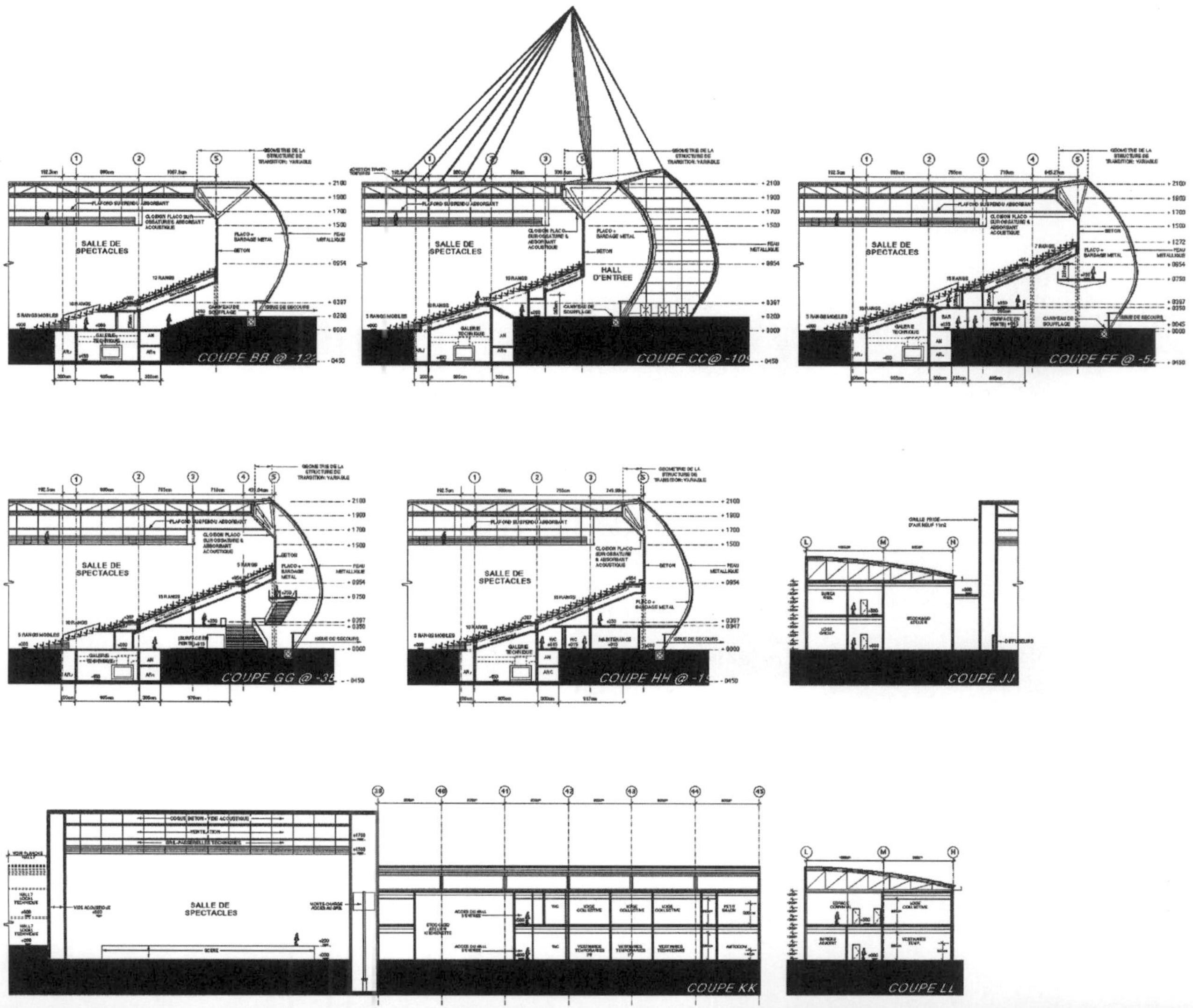
SALLE DE SPECTACLES
COUPE BB @ -122
HALL D'ENTREE
COUPE CC@ -105
COUPE FF @ -54
COUPE GG @ -35
COUPE HH @ -19
COUPE JJ
COUPE KK
COUPE LL

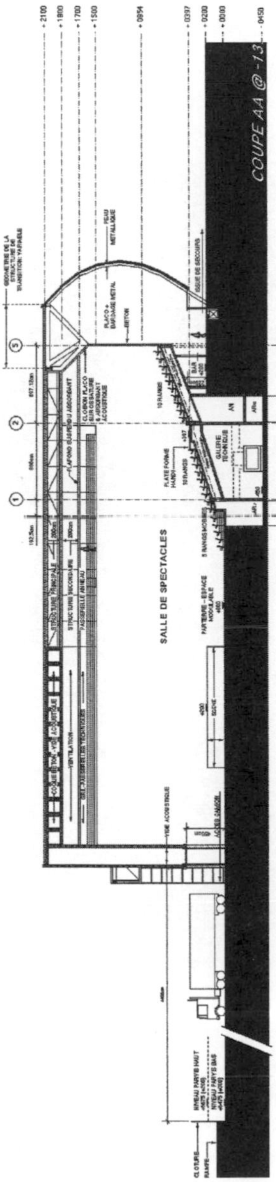
SALLE DE SPECTACLES
GALERIE TECHNIQUE

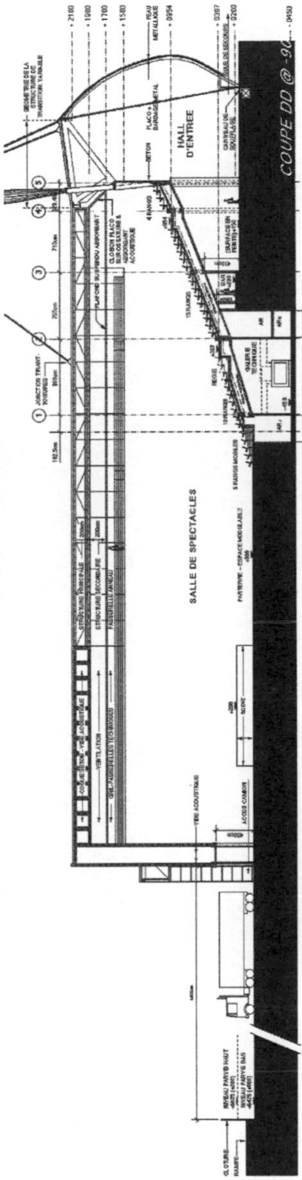
SALLE DE SPECTACLES
HALL D'ENTREE
GALERIE TECHNIQUE

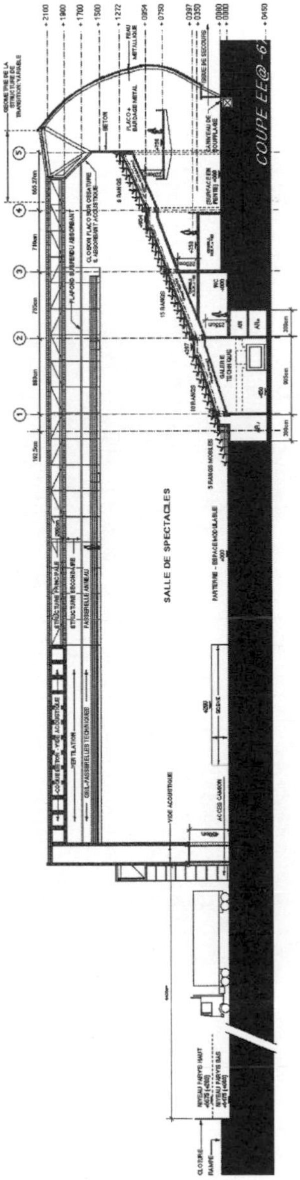
SALLE DE SPECTACLES
GALERIE TECHNIQUE

Architecture as a means to give identity: marking one of the city's major entrances

Envelope: a) an enclosure (e.g., a membrane or shell)
b) a curve tangent to each of a family of curves

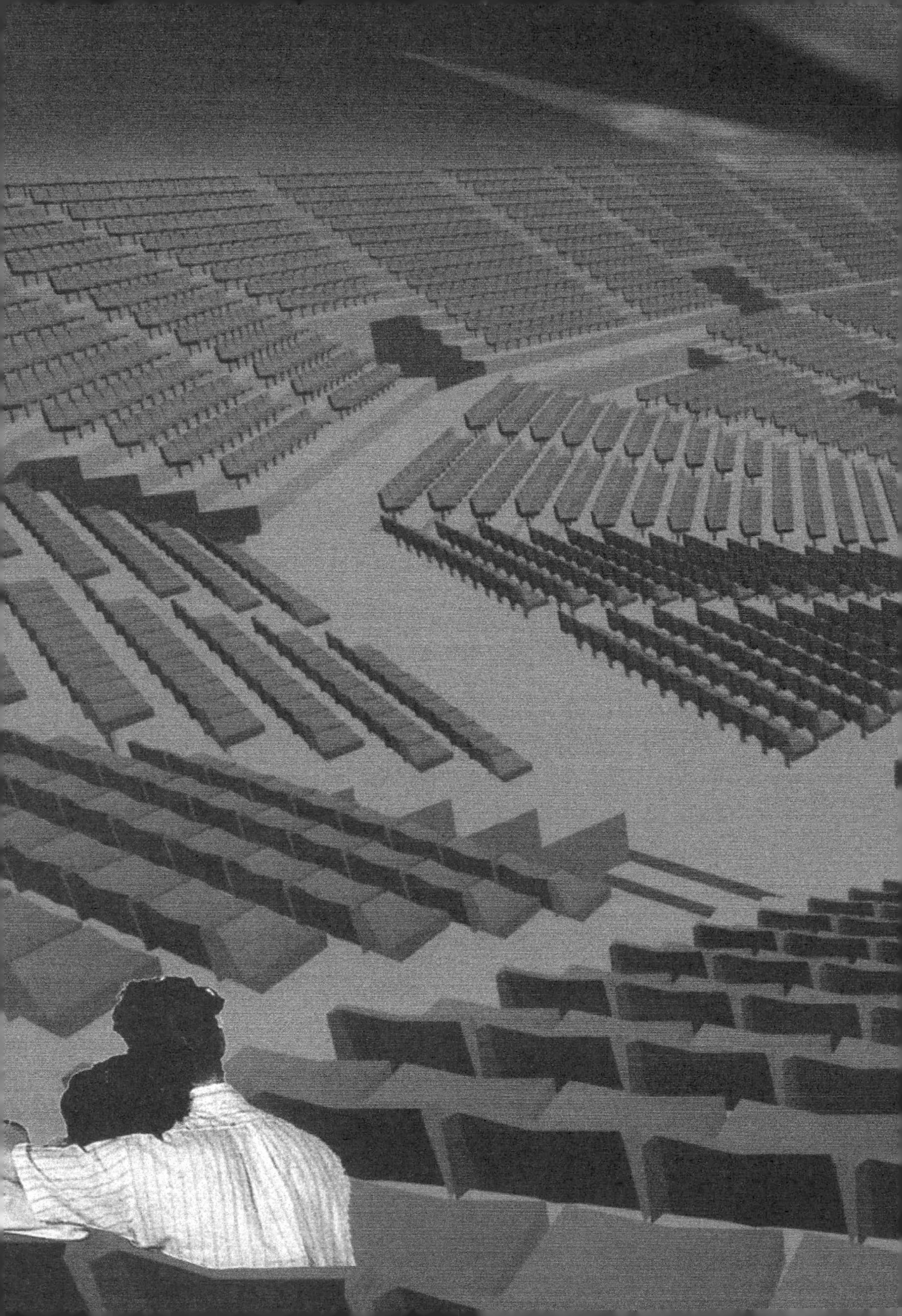

Questioning elitist programs: not a concert hall for a classical repertoire, but a hall for rock, popular music, or even political meetings. Not a museum, but a multipurpose exhibition hall for trade fairs, antique markets, dog shows

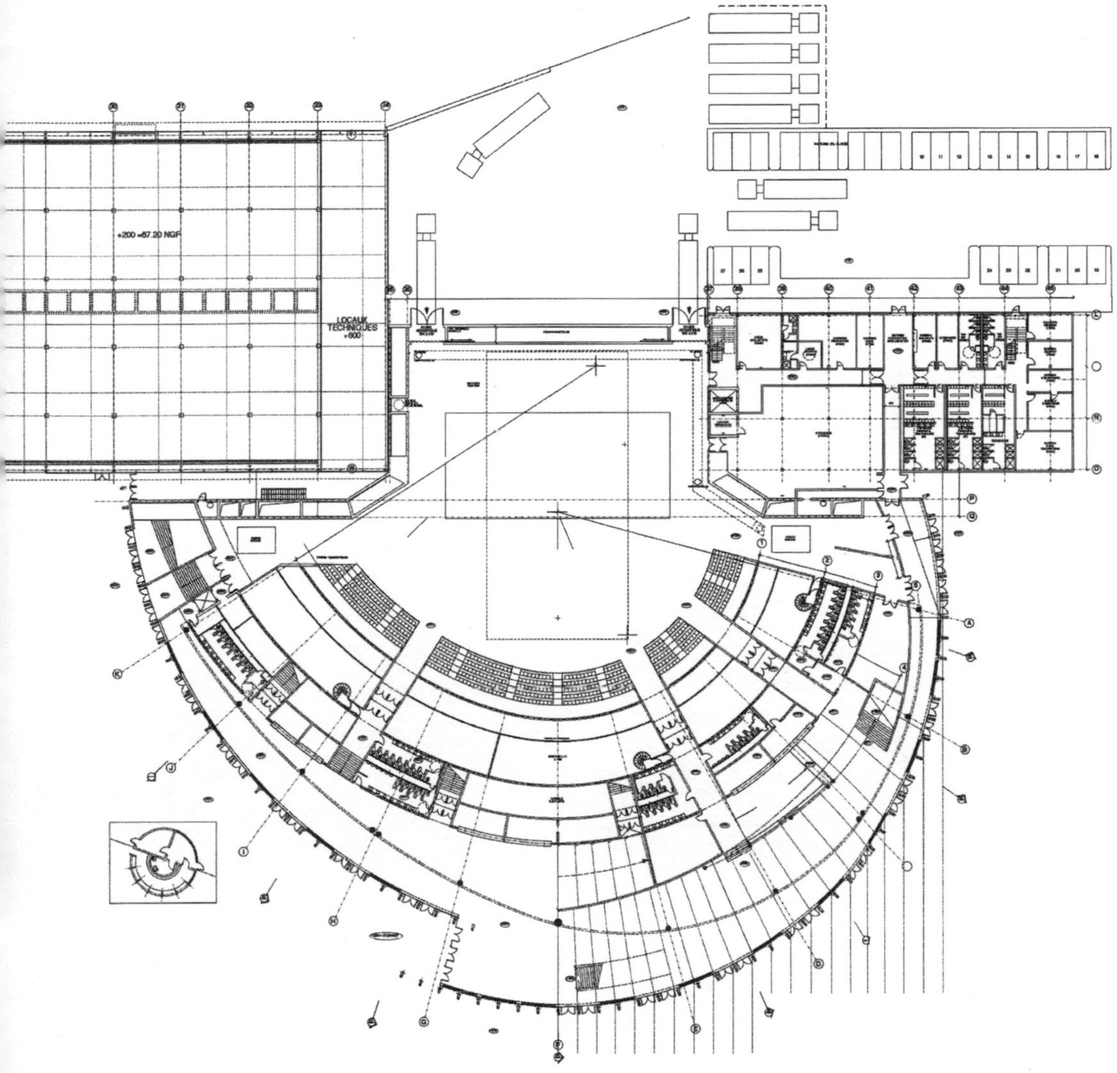

Ground floor

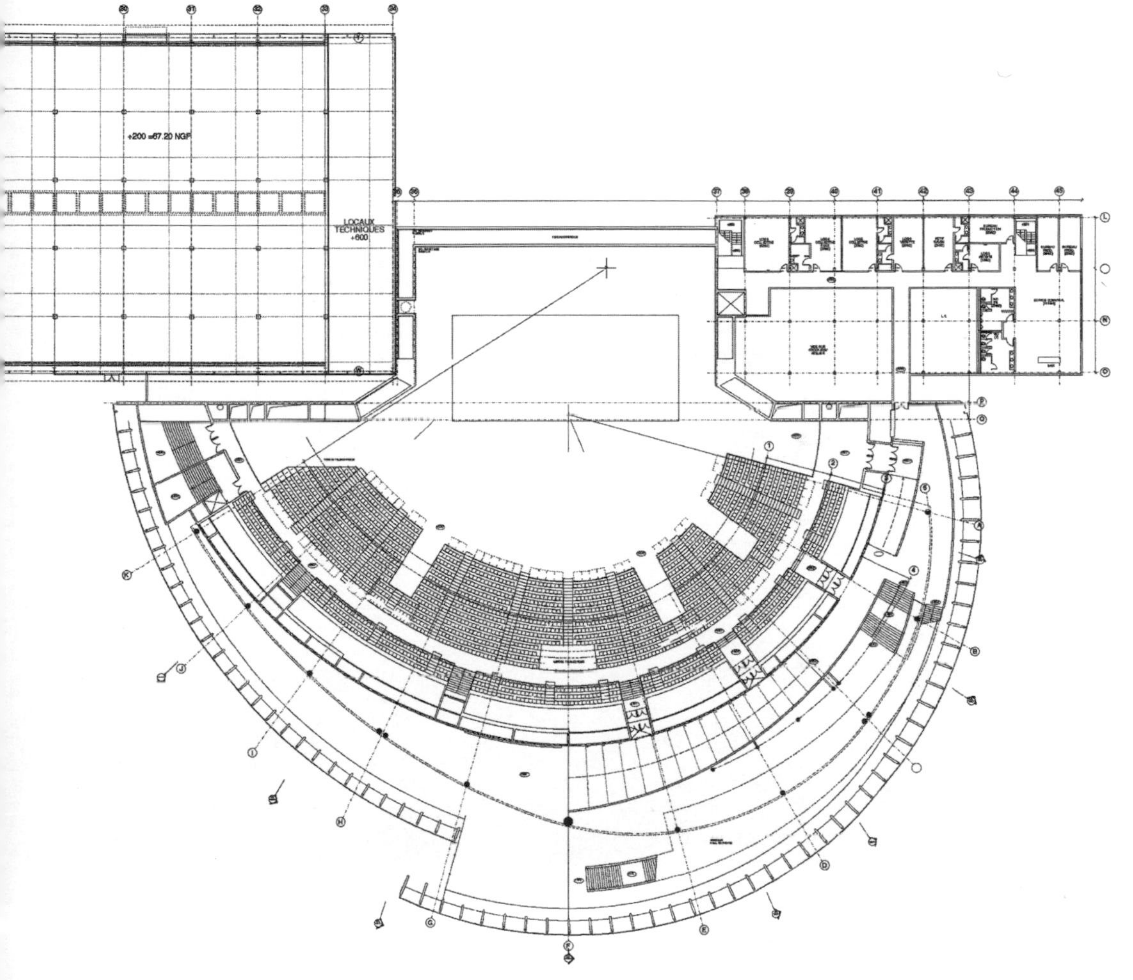

+4.0 meters

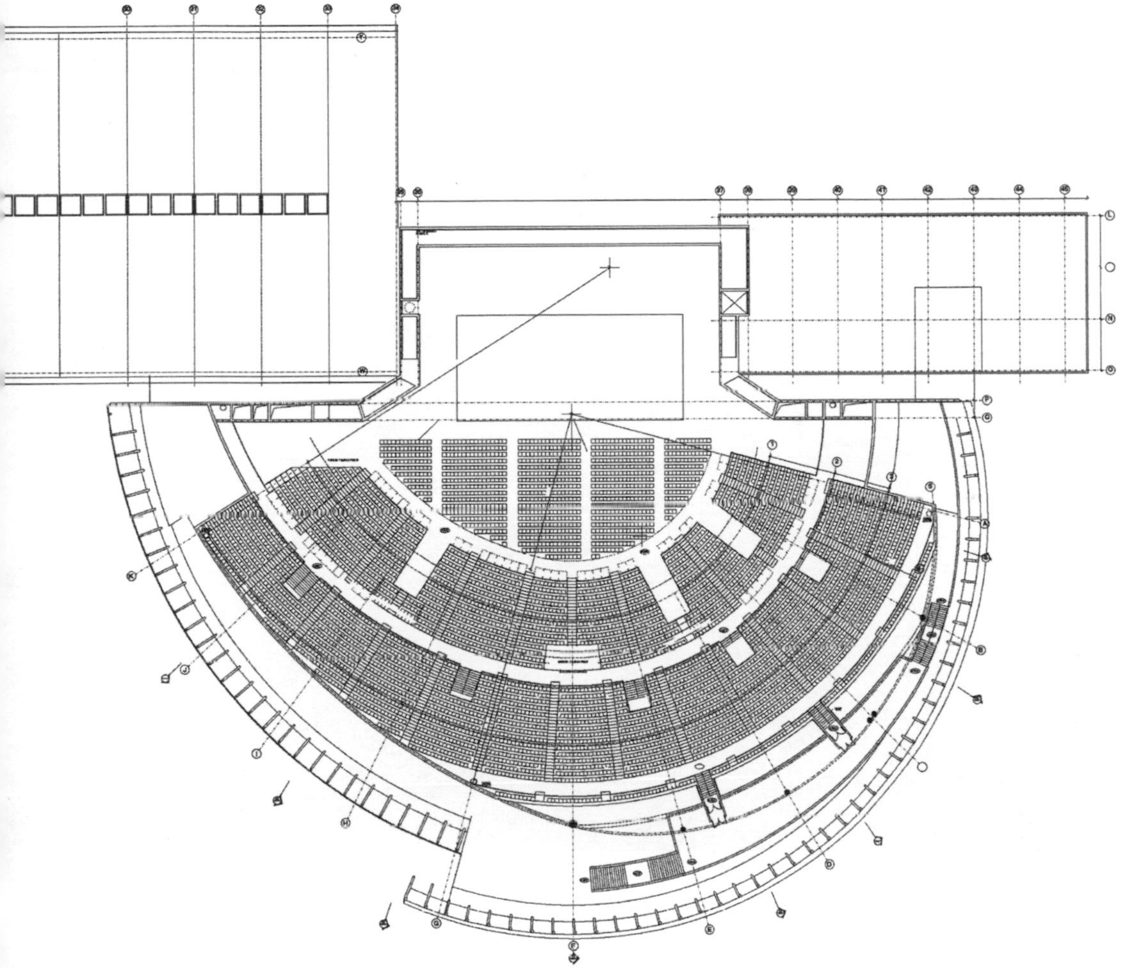

+9.5 meters

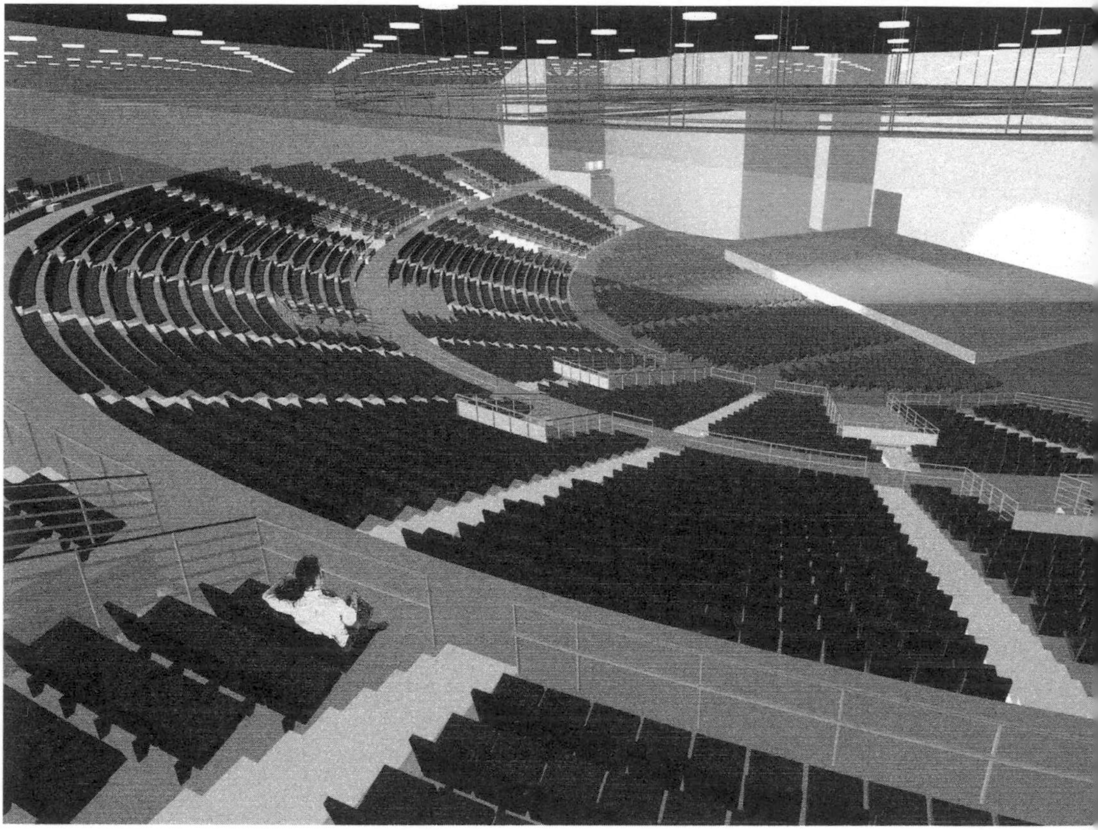

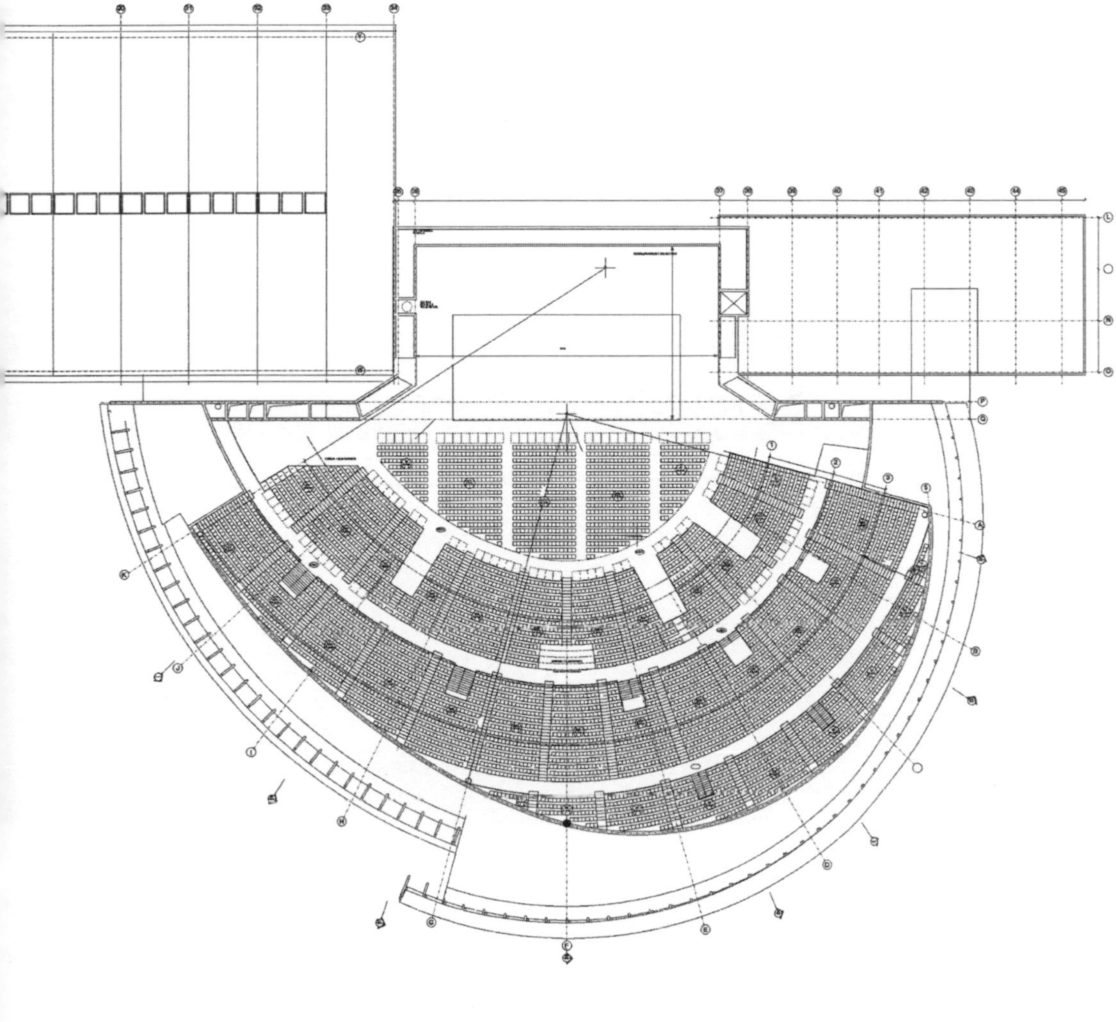

+13 meters

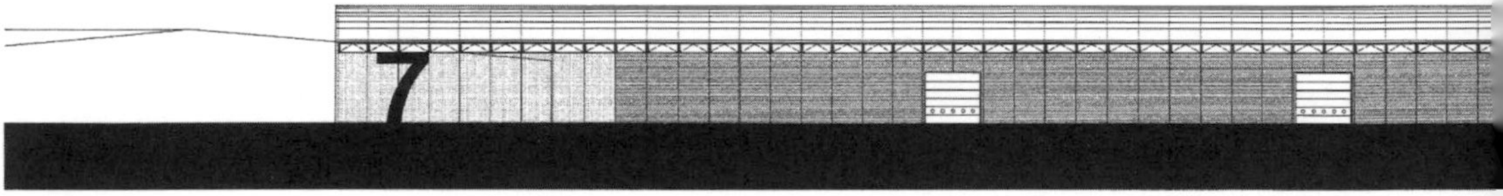

The exhibition hall: a stream-lined shed. The auditorium: a double skin, one acoustical, the other for weather protection

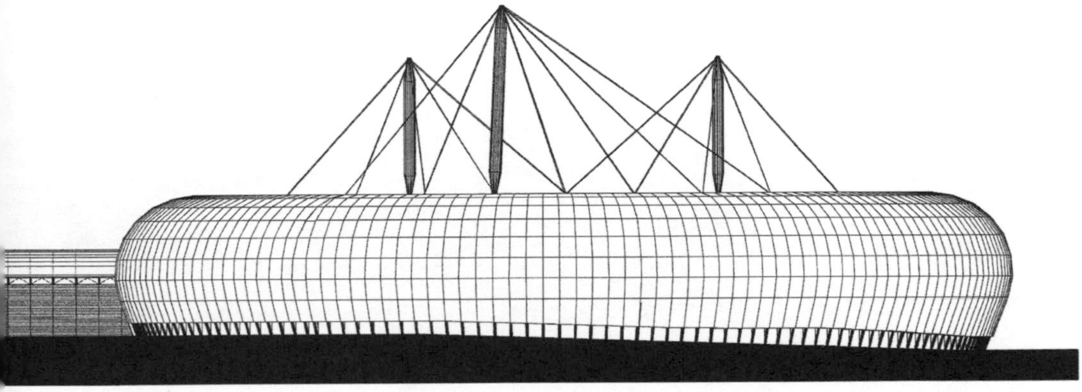

Masts: illuminated signals, color-coded according to the calendar
(red / white / blue for Bastille Day, etc.)

P A R C D E S E X P O S I T I O N S
7

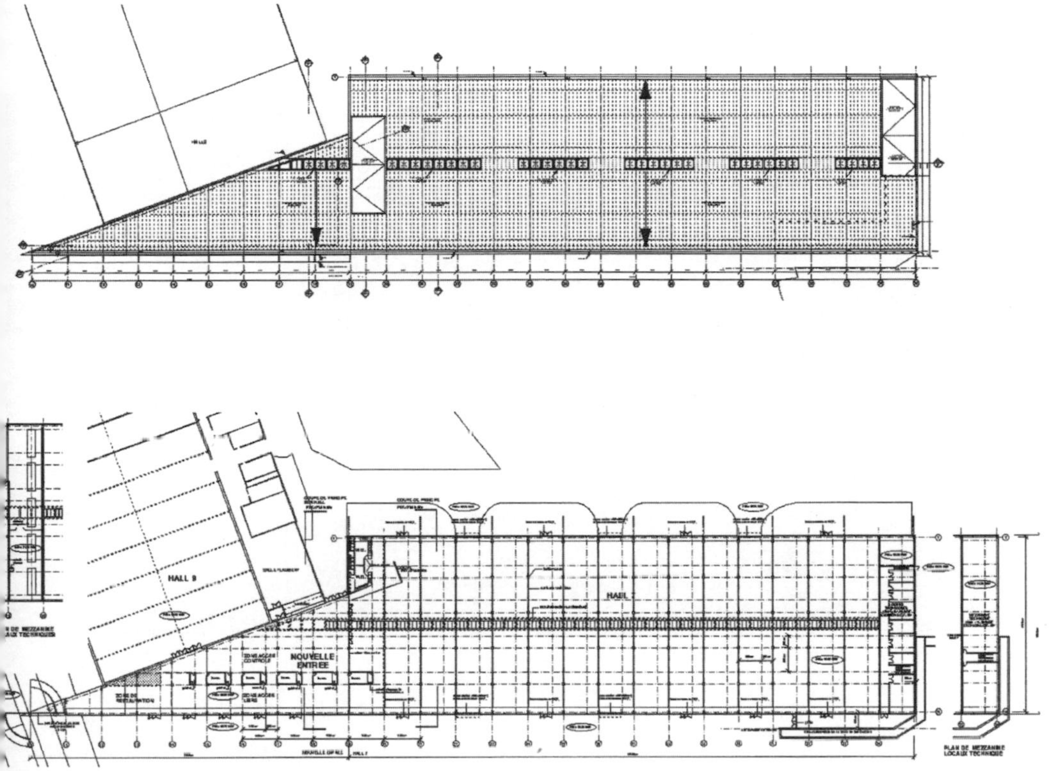

Ground and roof plans of Hall 9, Hall 7, and new entrance

Exhibition hall: fairs, antiques, electronics, dog shows, flower shows

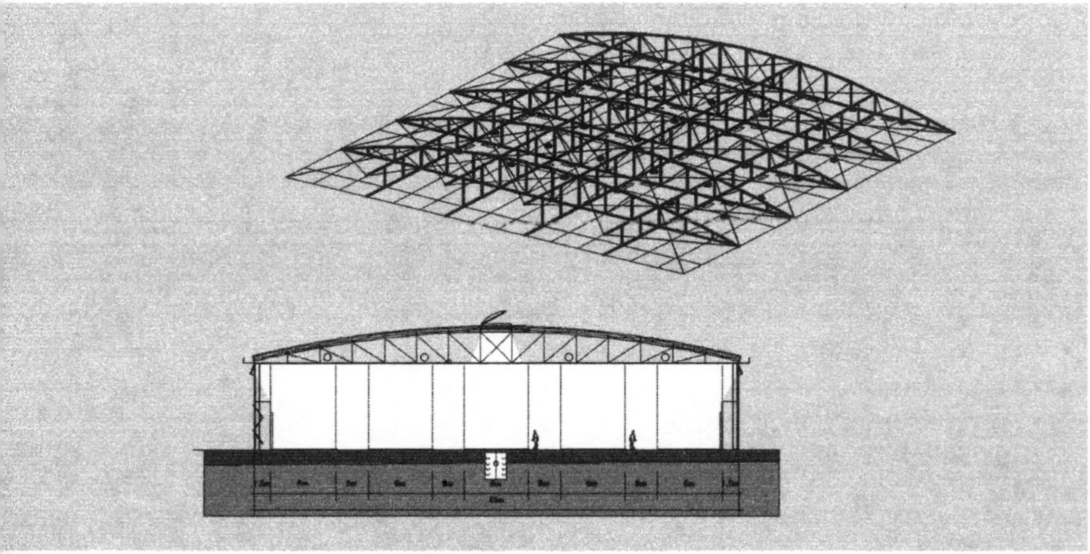

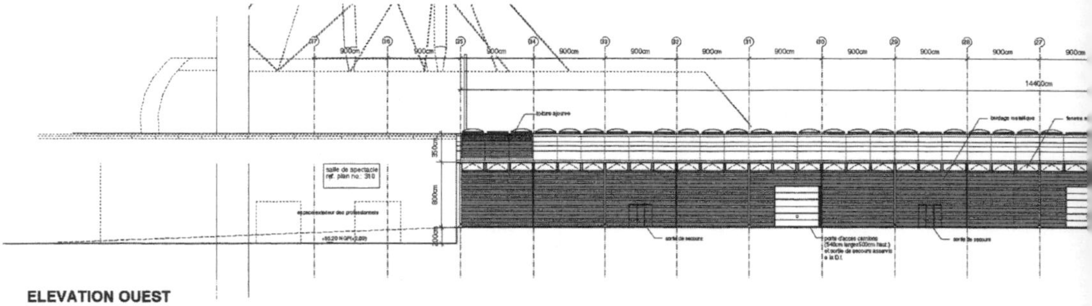

ELEVATION OUEST

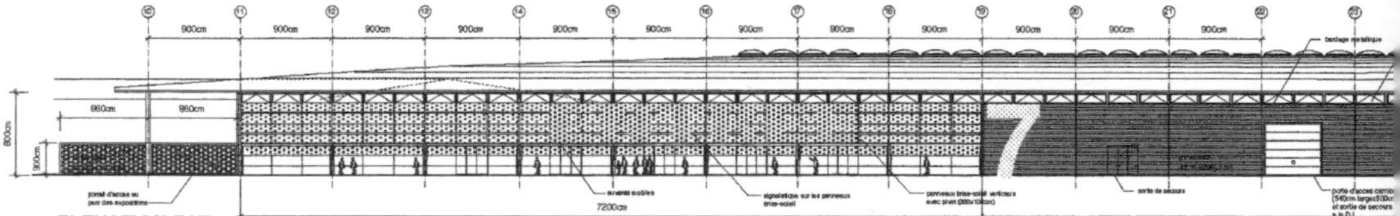

ELEVATION EST

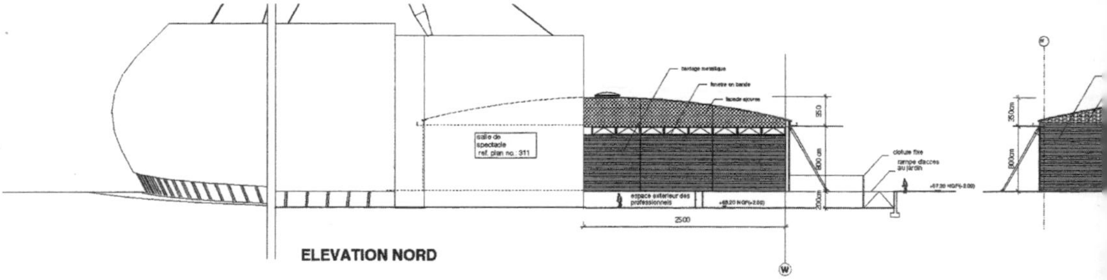

ELEVATION NORD

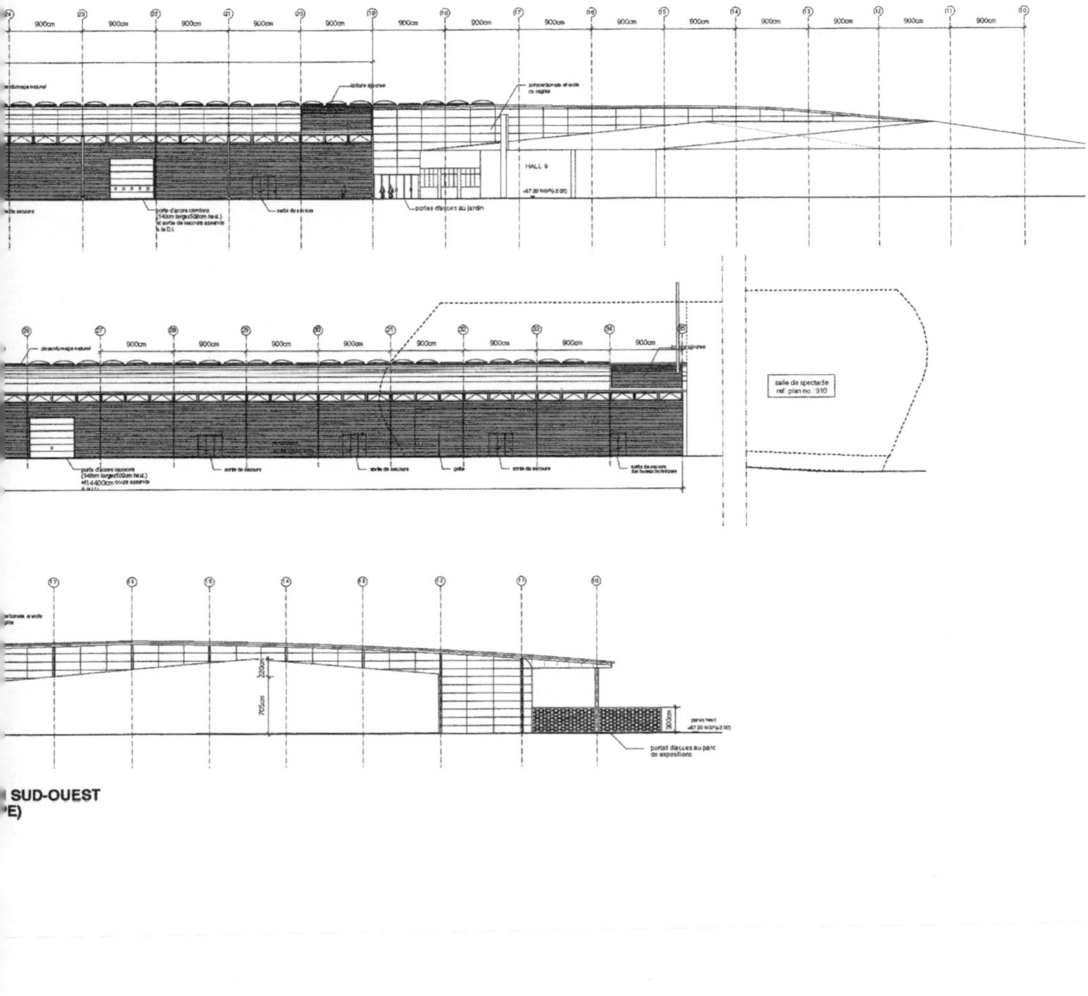
900cm
HALL 9
portes d'accès au jardin
salle de spectacle
ref. plan no.: 310
sortie de secours
portail d'accès au parc
de expositions

SUD-OUEST
E)

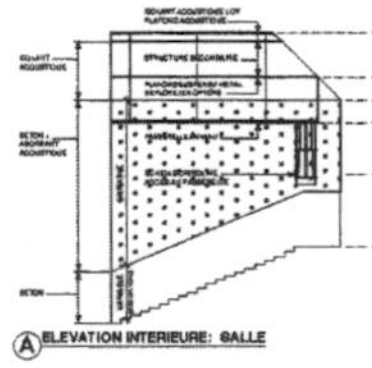

(A) ELEVATION INTERIEURE: SALLE

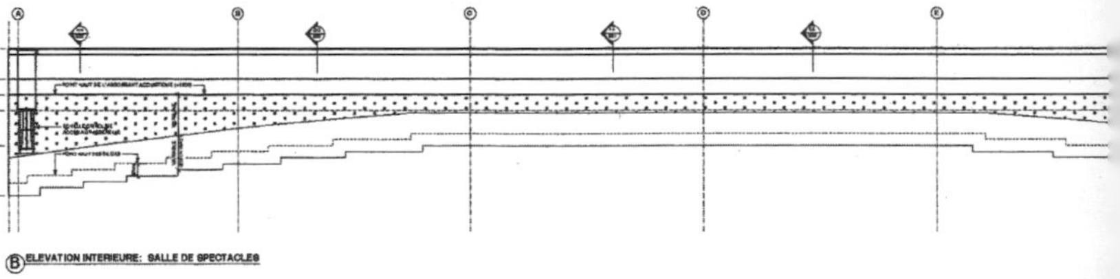

(B) ELEVATION INTERIEURE: SALLE DE SPECTACLES

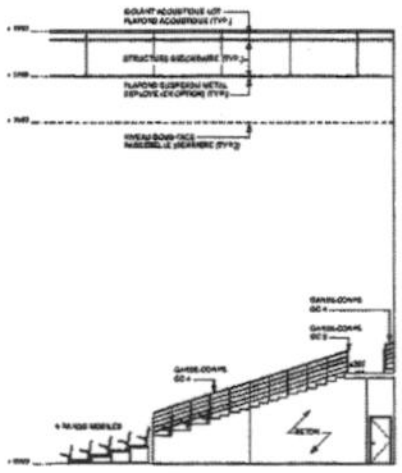

(D) ELEVATION INTERIEURE: SALLE

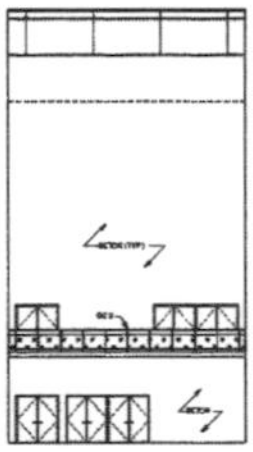

(E) ELEVATION INTERIEURE: SALLE

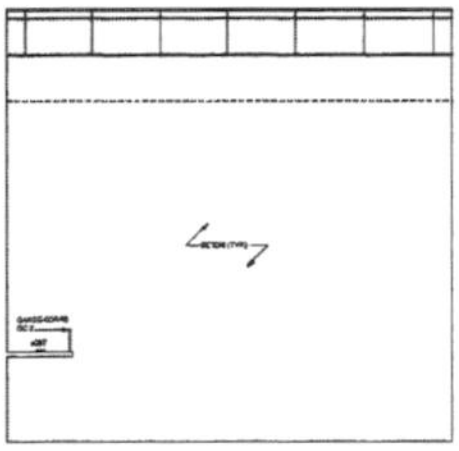

(F) ELEVATION INTERIEURE: SALLE

(G) ELEVATION INTERIEURE: SALLE

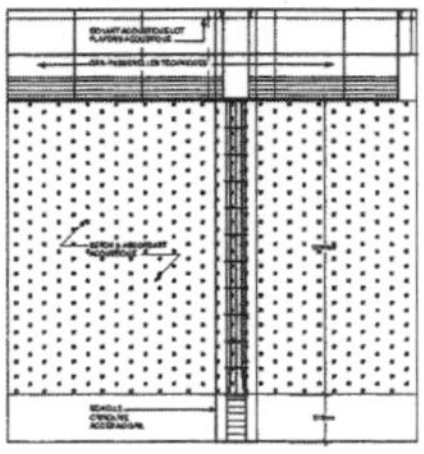

(H) ELEVATION INTERIEURE: SCENE

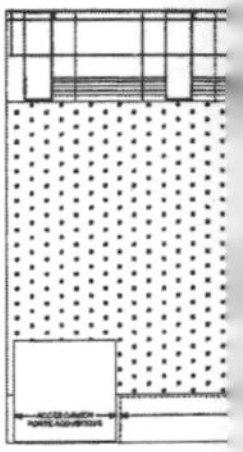

(I) ELEVATION

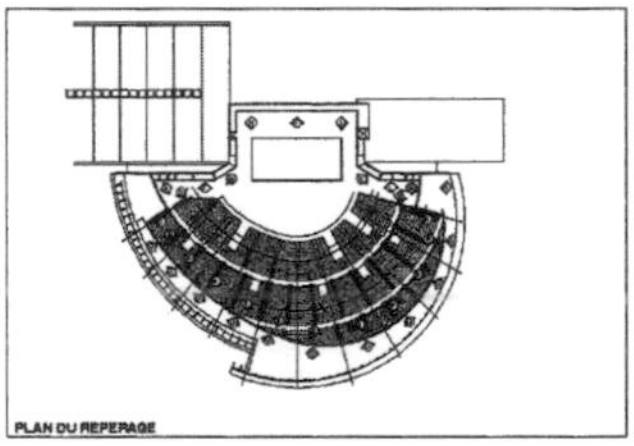

PLAN DU REPERAGE

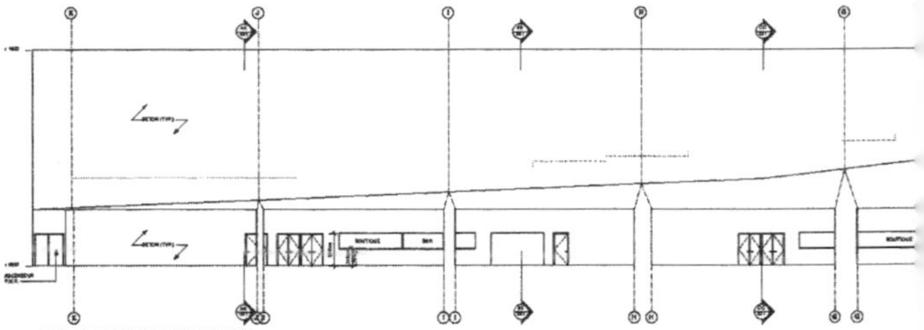

(O) ELEVATION INTERIEURE: HALL D'ENTREE

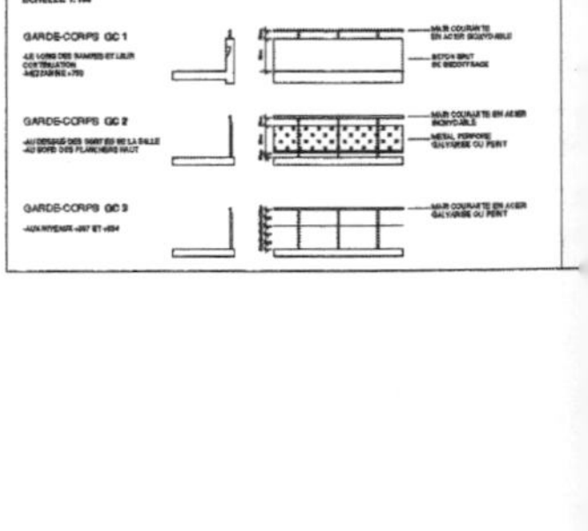

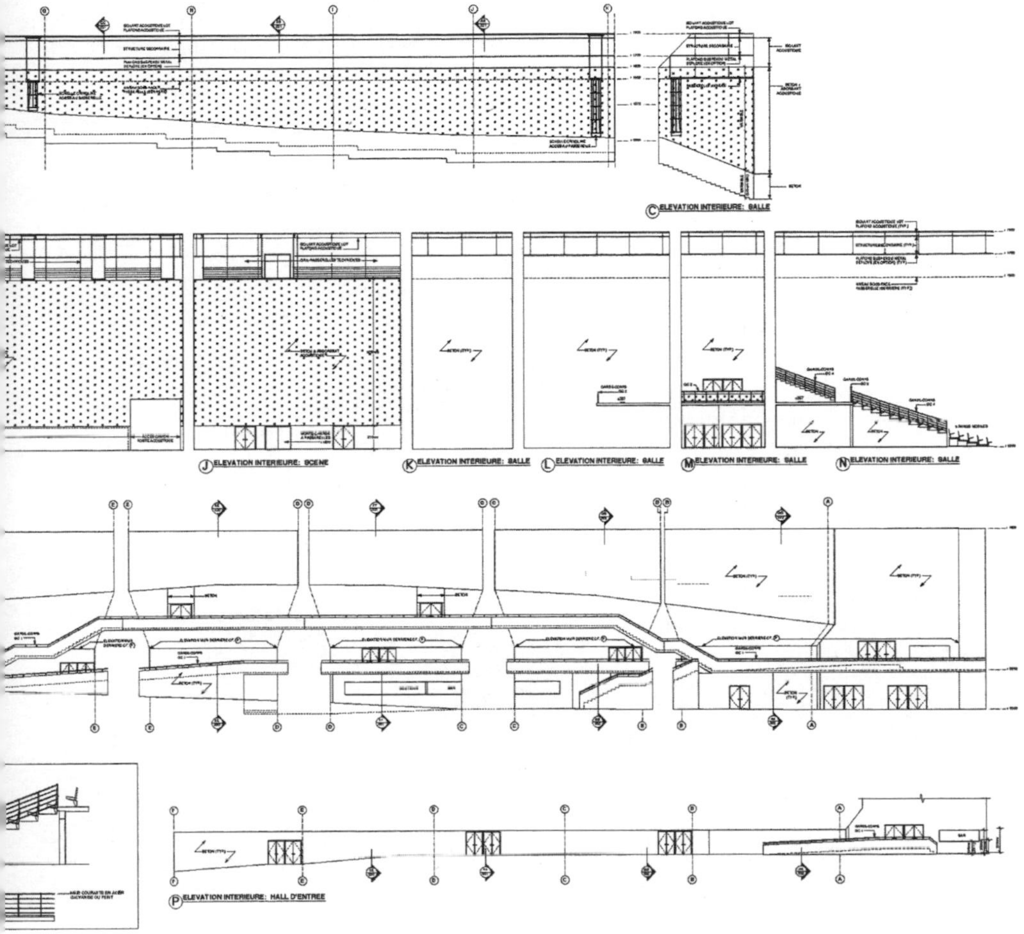

Interiors: only major construction materials, no finishes.
In French: "pas de second oeuvre, seulement du gros oeuvre"

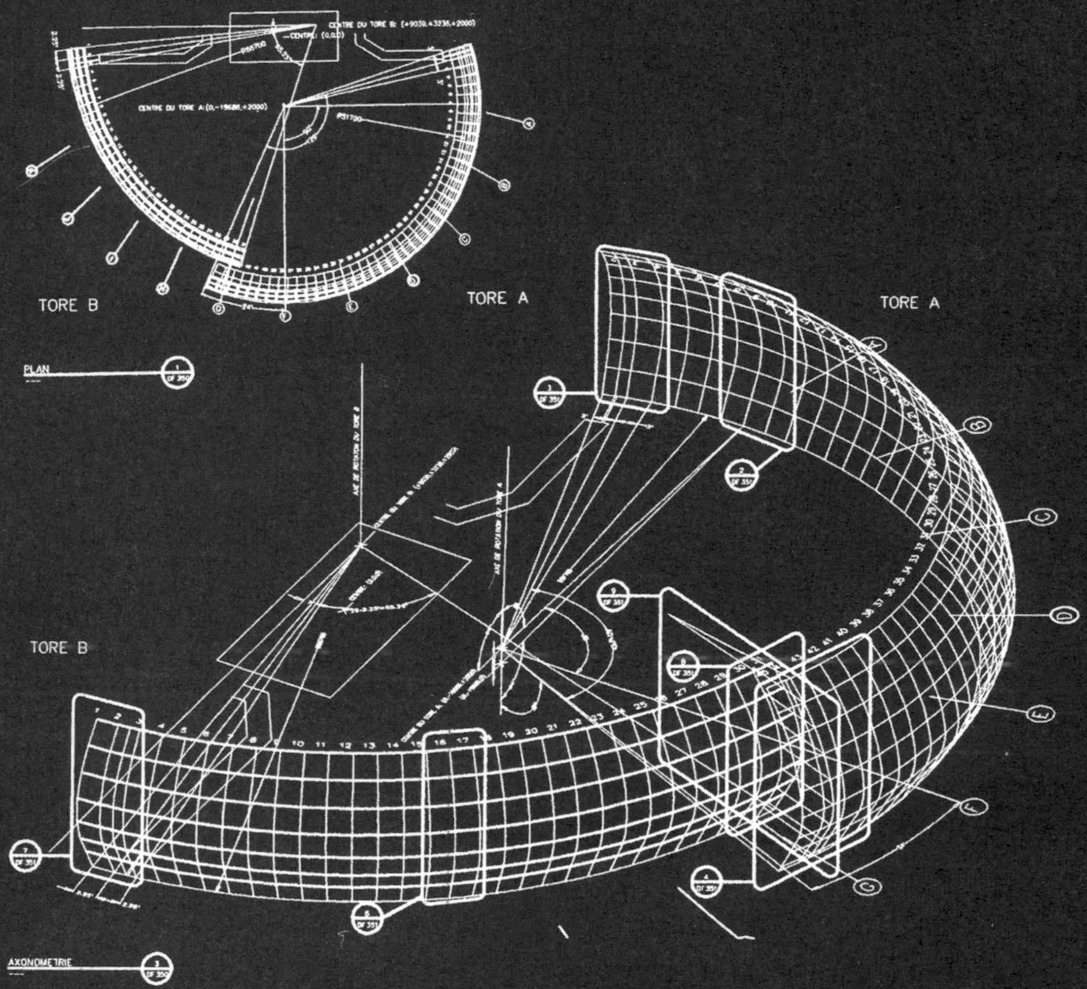

CENTRE DU TORE B: (+9039,+3236,+2000)
CENTRE DU TORE A:(0,-19686,+2000)
TORE B
TORE A
TORE A
PLAN
TORE B
AXONOMETRIE

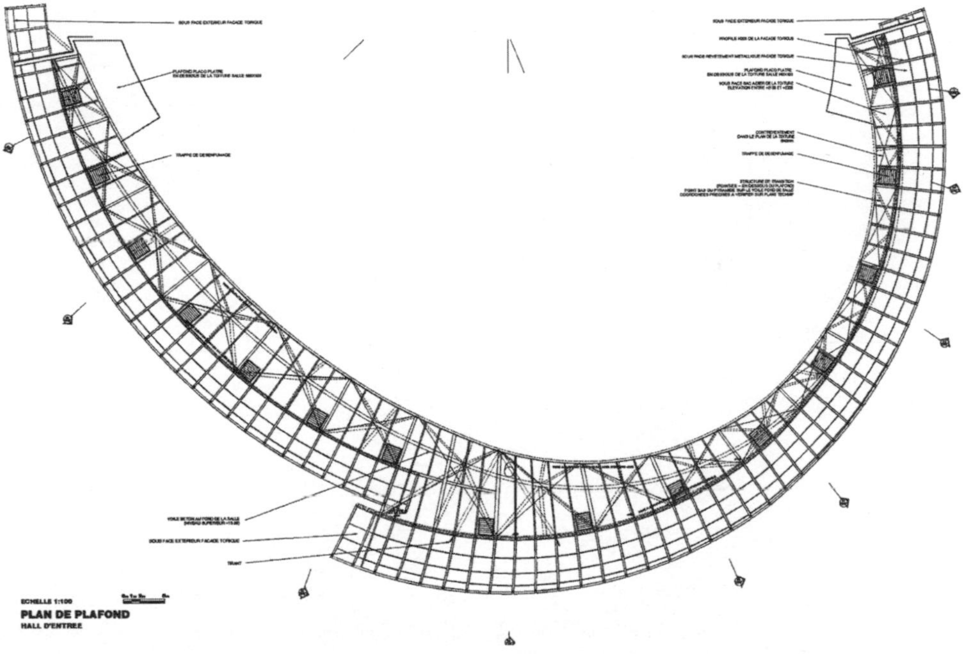

Roof plan Architecture is the materialization of concepts.
The moment of the concept can be the place of technological invention

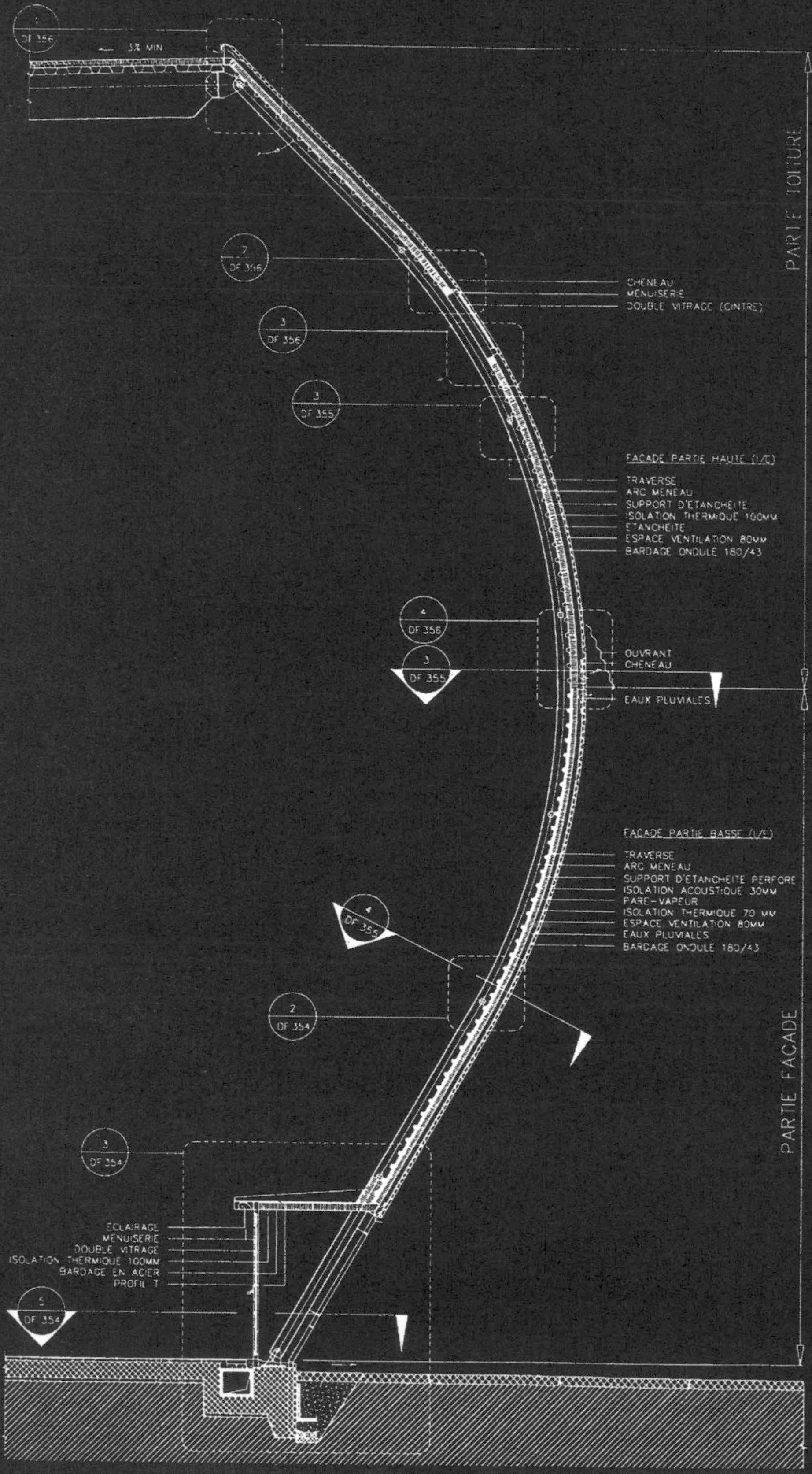
1 DF 356
3% MIN
2 DF 356
CHENEAU
MENUISERIE
DOUBLE VITRAGE (CINTRE)
3 DF 356
3 DF 355
FACADE PARTIE HAUTE (1/E)
TRAVERSE
ARC MENEAU
SUPPORT D'ETANCHEITE
ISOLATION THERMIQUE 100MM
ETANCHEITE
ESPACE VENTILATION 80MM
BARDAGE ONDULE 180/43
4 DF 356
OUVRANT
CHENEAU
3 DF 355
EAUX PLUVIALES
PARTIE TOITURE
FACADE PARTIE BASSE (1/E)
TRAVERSE
ARC MENEAU
SUPPORT D'ETANCHEITE PERFORE
ISOLATION ACOUSTIQUE 30MM
PARE-VAPEUR
ISOLATION THERMIQUE 70 MM
ESPACE VENTILATION 80MM
EAUX PLUVIALES
BARDAGE ONDULE 180/43
4 DF 355
2 DF 354
PARTIE FACADE
3 DF 354
ECLAIRAGE
MENUISERIE
DOUBLE VITRAGE
ISOLATION THERMIQUE 100MM
BARDAGE EN ACIER
PROFIL T
5 DF 354

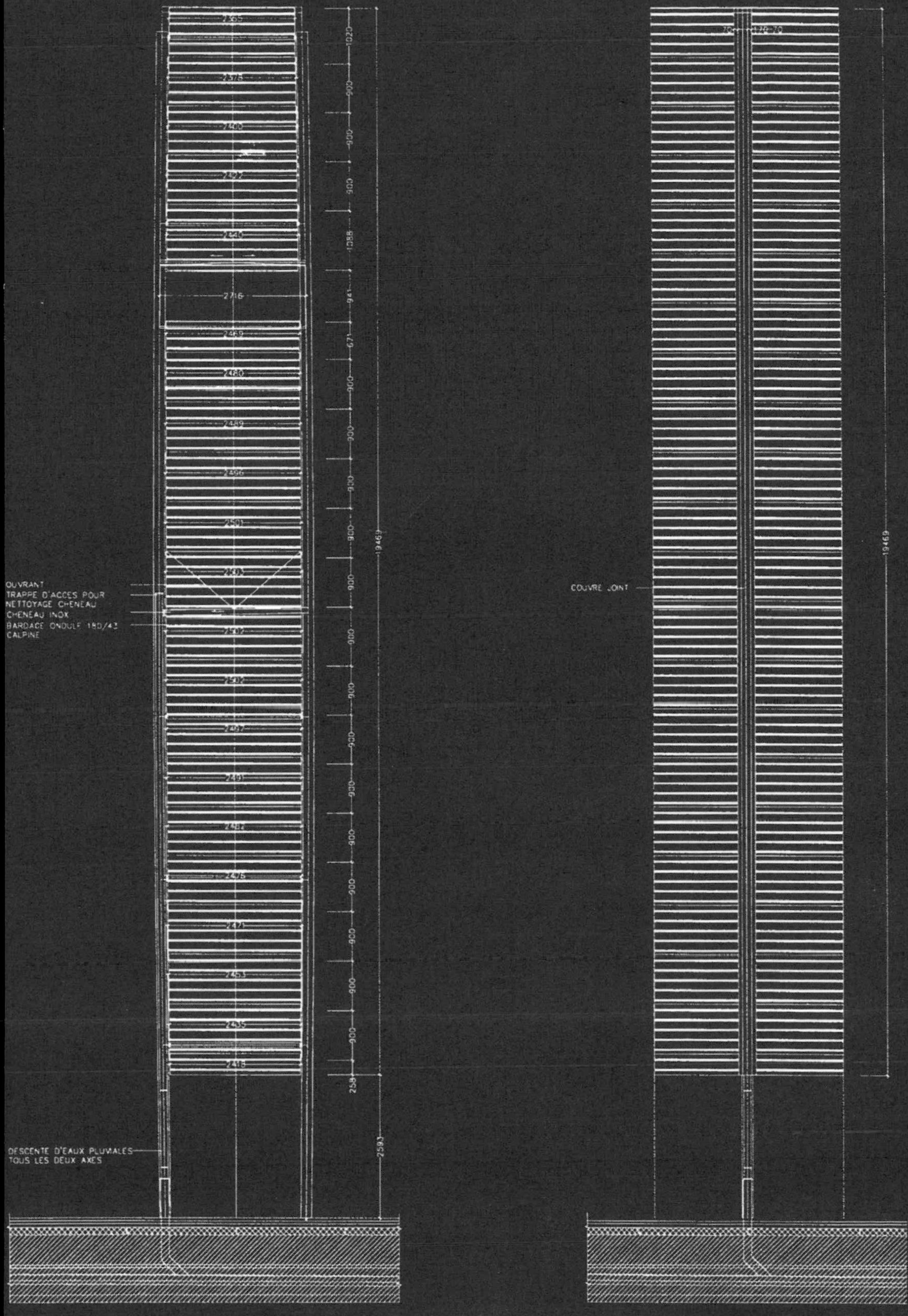
OUVRANT
TRAPPE D'ACCES POUR
NETTOYAGE CHENEAU
CHENEAU INOX
BARDAGE ONDULE 180/43
CALPINE
DESCENTE D'EAUX PLUVIALES
TOUS LES DEUX AXES
COUVRE JOINT
19469
2593
19469

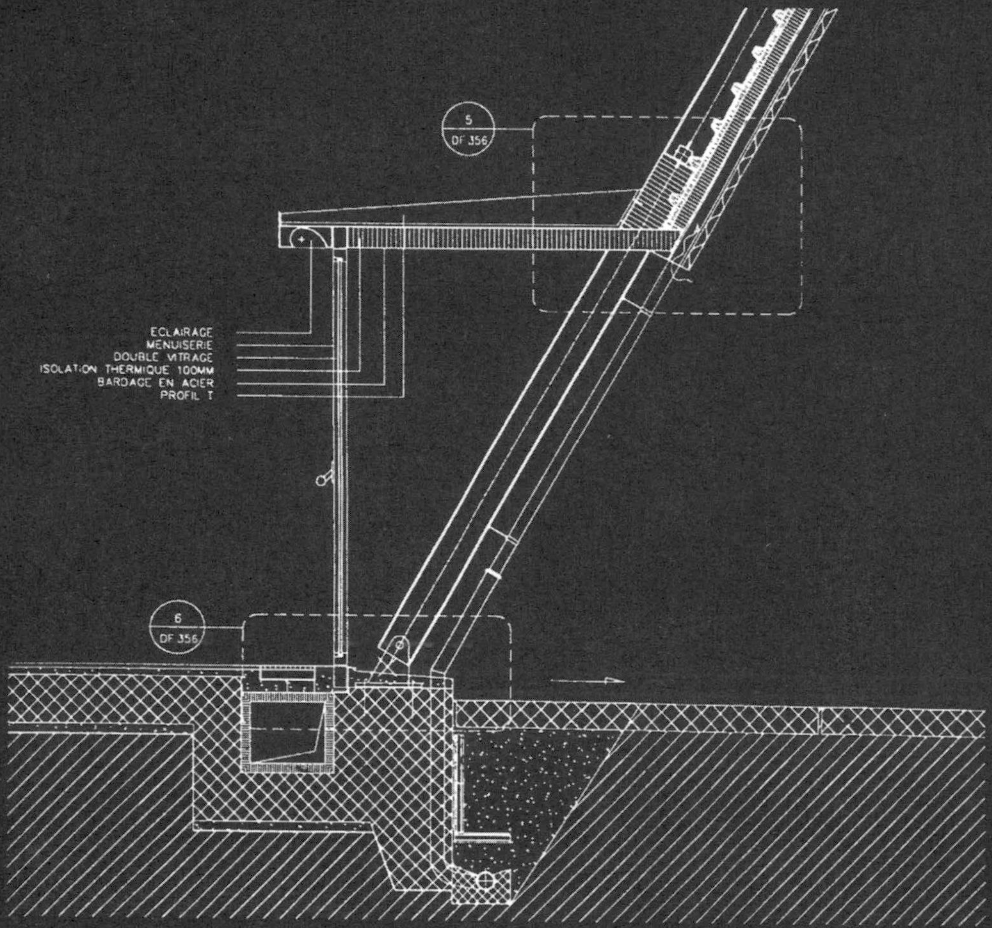
5
DF 356
ECLAIRAGE
MENUISERIE
DOUBLE VITRAGE
ISOLATION THERMIQUE 100MM
BARDAGE EN ACIER
PROFIL T
6
DF 356

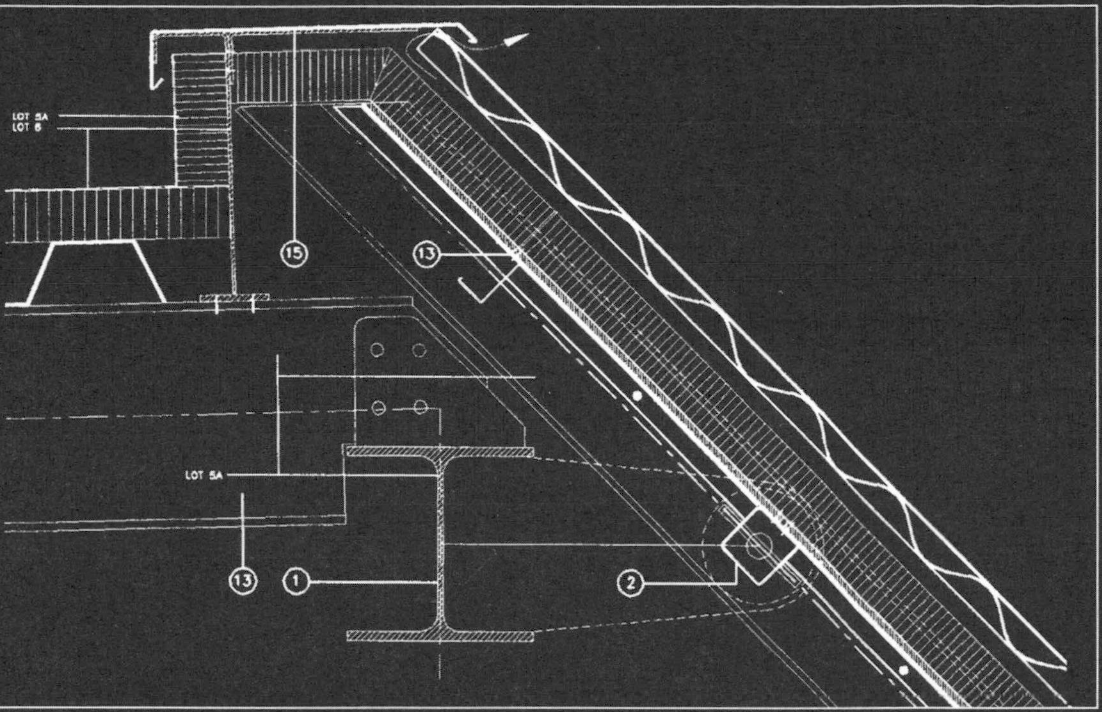
LOT 5A
LOT 6
15
13
LOT 5A
13
1
2

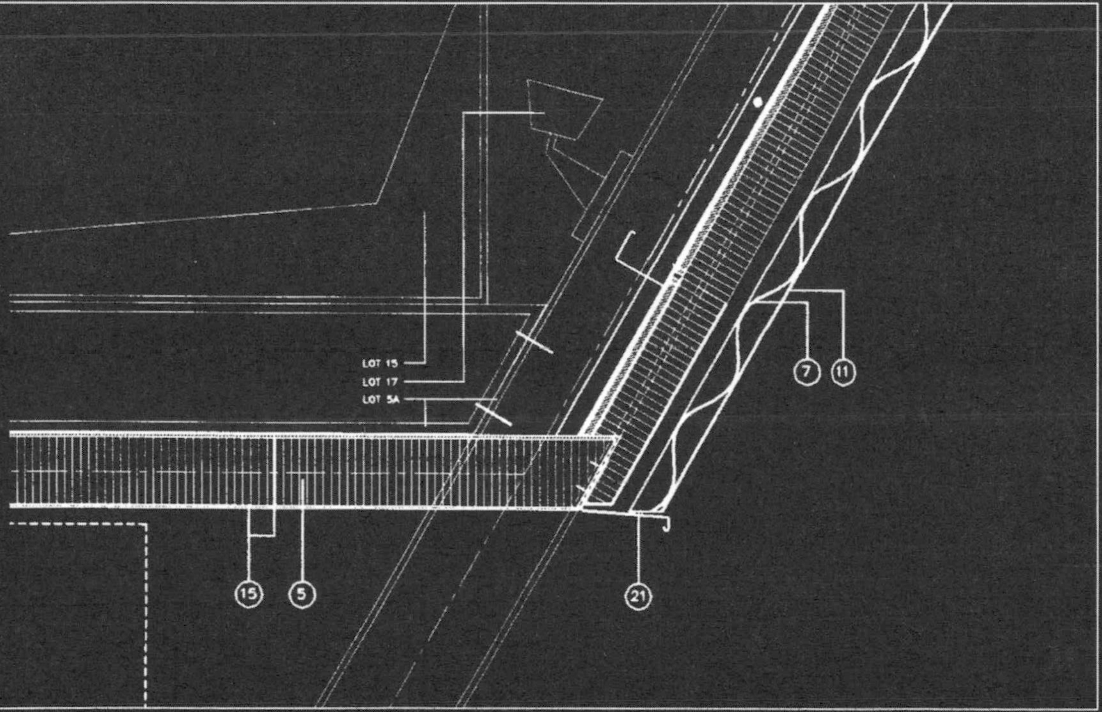
LOT 15
LOT 17
LOT 5A
7
11
15
5
21

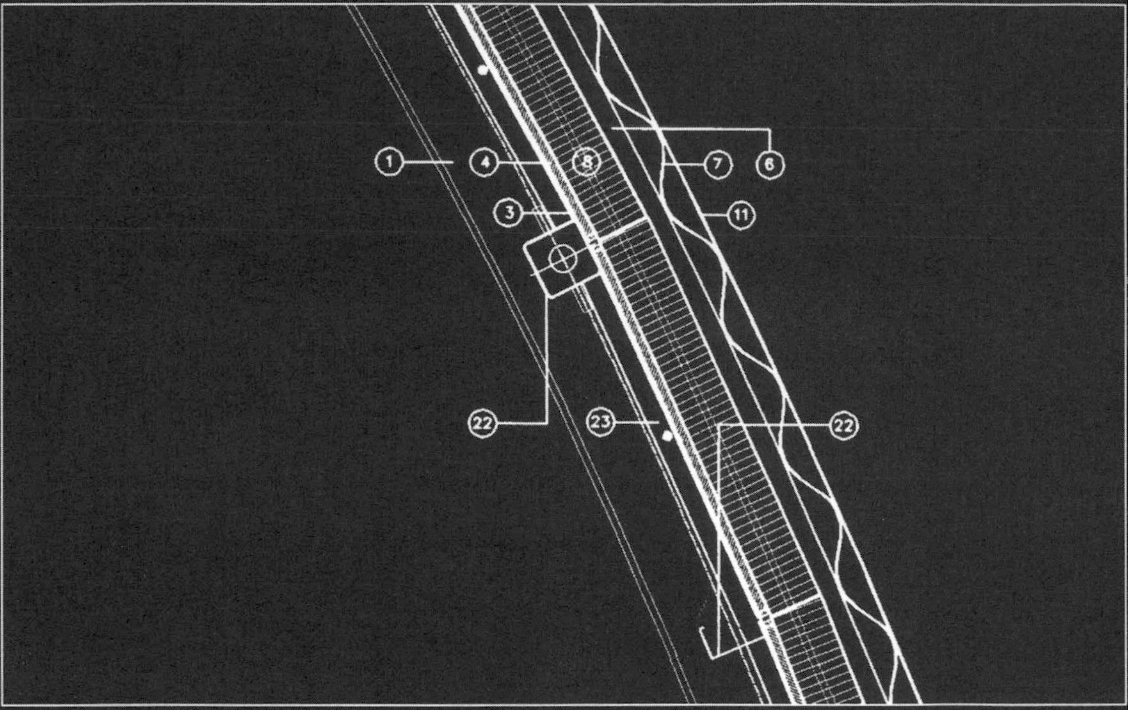

1
4
8
7
6
3
11
22
23
22

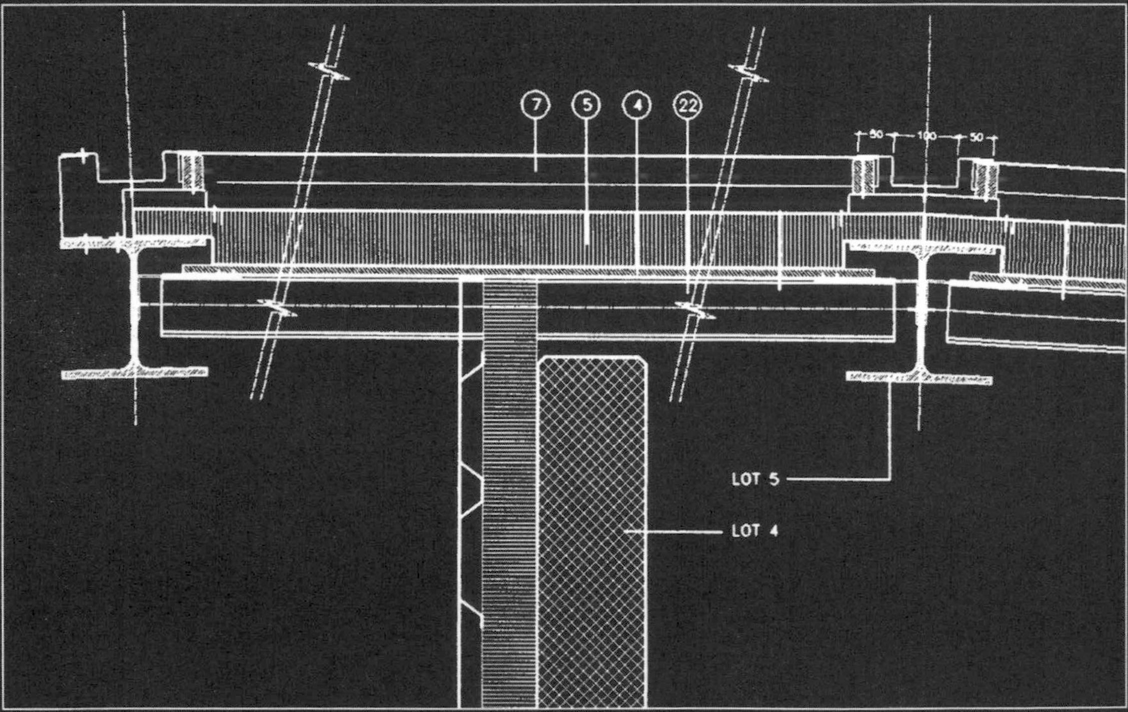

7
5
4
22
50
100
50
LOT 5
LOT 4

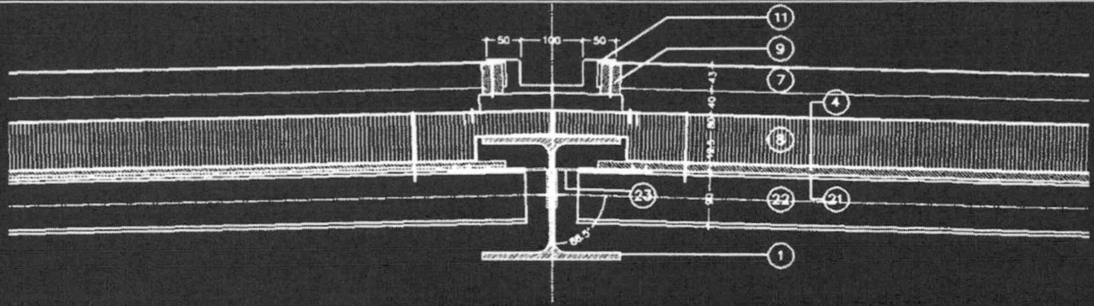

COUPE HORIZ. TYPE TORE A
1:5
2
DF 355

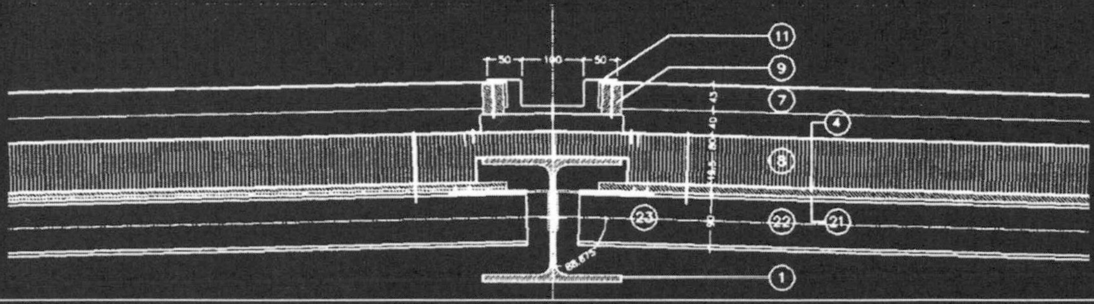

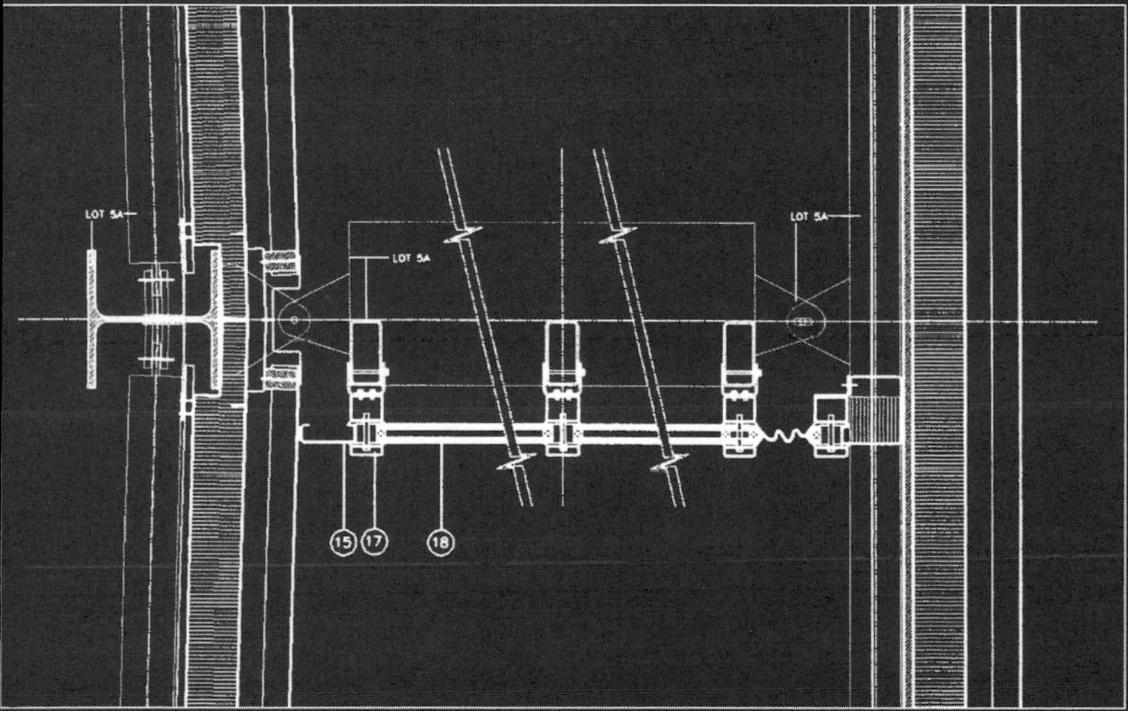

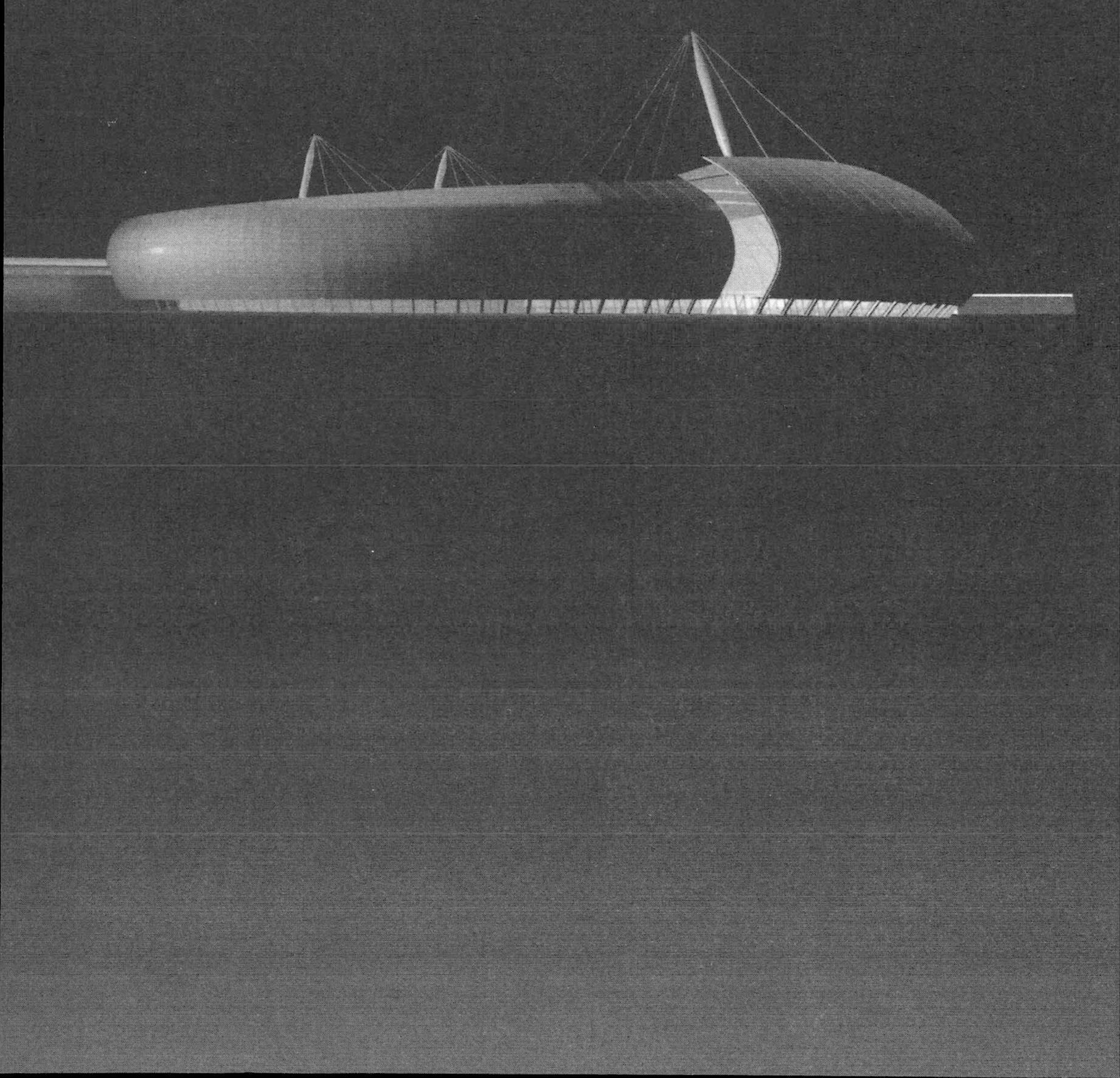

Project Teams

Rituals
Bernard Tschumi

Paris, Parc de la Villette
Competition: Bernard Tschumi, Luca Merlini, Alexandra Villegas, Luca Pagnamenta, Galen Cranz, Phoebe Cutler, William Wallis, Jon Olsen, Thomas Balsley
Project: Bernard Tschumi, Jean-François Erhel, Alexandra Villegas, Ursula Kurz, Luca Merlini, Christian Biecher, Marie-Line Luquet, Neil Porter, Steve McAdam, Luca Pagnamenta, Jean-Pierre Nourry, Didier Pasquier, Kathryn Gustafson, Renzo Bader
Consultants: *Planning*: Colin Fournier; *Landscape* : Setec-TP; *Interiors:* Tschumi-Erhel Architects Associés; *Structural*: Peter Rice (RFR, Bridge and Gallery structures), Hugh Dutton, Setec-Batiment; *Mechanical*: Setec-Batiment

Zurich, K-polis Department Store
Bernard Tschumi, Gregory Merryweather, Niels Roelfs, Ruth Berktold, Tom Kowalski, Mark Haukos, Kevin Collins

Geneva, Organisation Mondiale Météorologique Headquarters
Bernard Tschumi, Luca Merlini, Robert Young, Tom Kowalski, Emmanuel Ventura

Lausanne, Interface-Flon Bus / Railway Station
Bernard Tschumi, Luca Merlini, Emmanuel Ventura, Gregory Merryweather, Kevin Collins, Rhett Russo, Peter Cornell

New York, Lerner Hall Student Center—Columbia University
Project Team: Bernard Tschumi Architects: Bernard Tschumi, Tom Kowalski, Mark Haukos, Ruth Berktold, Megan Miller, Kim Starr, Richard Veith, Galia Solomonoff, Yannis Aesopos, Anthony Manzo, Peter Cornell, Jordan Parnass, Frederick Norman
Project Team: Gruzen Samton Architects: Peter Samton, Tim Schmiderer, David Terenzio, Ken Hutchinson, Jerzy Lesniak, Scott Broaddus, Liane Williams-Liu, Geoff Doban, Nick Lombardo, John Mulling, Nicholas Hedin, Rogelio Escarcega, Cameron Lory, Jo Goldberger
Consultants: Steel Structure: Severud Associates; *Mechanical Engineers:* Ove Arup & Partners, New York; *Special Structures Engineering (suspended ramps & glass wall)*: Ove Arup & Partners, New York with Hugh Dutton (HDA), Paris; *Theater:* David Harvey Associates, New York with Peter George Associates, New York

New York, Franklin Furnace Gallery
Bernard Tschumi, Mark Haukos

Nantes, FRAC Art Center
Bernard Tschumi, Véronique Descharrières, Megan Miller, Ruth Berktold

New York, Expansion of The Museum of Modern Art
Bernard Tschumi, Kevin Collins, Gregory Merryweather, Peter Cornell, Rhett Russo, Frederick Norman, Ruth Berktold, Tom Kowalski, Kim Starr, Jimmy Miyoshi, Tyson Godfrey, John Cleater, Fiona Whitton, Megan Miller
Consultants: *Facade:* Hugh Dutton (HDA), Paris; *Structural Engineers:* Ove Arup & Partners, New York; *Art:* Kate Linker; *Model:* Kennedy Fabrications, New York and BTA New York

Lausanne, EPFL Extension
Bernard Tschumi and Luca Merlini with Richter and Rocha Architects, Lausanne; François Gillet, Yannis Aesopos, Henning Ehrhardt, Tom Kowalski, Emmanuel Ventura, Robert Young, Peter Korner

Paris, Renault Ile Seguin Master Plan
Bernard Tschumi, Luca Merlini, Véronique Descharrières, Emmanuel Ventura, Jordan Parnass, Kevin Collins

Marne-la-Vallée, School of Architecture
Competition: Bernard Tschumi, Kevin Collins, Yannis Aesopos, Véronique Descharrières, Robert Young, Tom Kowalski, Mark Haukos, Stéphanie Bayard, Jordan Parnass, Grace Cheung
Project: Bernard Tschumi, Véronique Descharrières, Alex Reid, Kevin Collins, Gregory Merryweather, Rhett Russo, Frederick Norman, Cristina Devizzi, Laurane Ponsonnet
Consultants: *Facade:* Hugh Dutton (HDA), Paris; *Structures:* RFR; *MEP:* Choulet; *Acoustics:* CIAL; *Landscape:* Ursula Kurz; *Infrastructures:* Setec-TP

Miami, FIU School of Architecture
Bernard Tschumi Architects: Bernard Tschumi, Johanne Riegels Oestergaard, Anne Save de Beaurecueil, Roderick Villafranca, Valentin Bontjes Van Beek, Andrea Day, Kim Starr, Peter Cornell, Tom Kowalski, Kevin Collins
Bruno-Elias & Associates: Bruno Elias Ramos, Gustavo Berenblum, Susan Laredo

Rouen, Concert Hall and Exhibition Complex
Bernard Tschumi, Kevin Collins, Peter Cornell, Véronique Descharrières, Alex Reid, Megan Miller, Joel Rutten, Kim Starr, Roderick Villafranca, Robert Holton, Cristina Devizzi, Laurane Ponsonnet
Consultants: *Facade:* Hugh Dutton (HDA), Paris; *Structures / MEP:* Technip Seri Construction; *Theater:* 2ème Acte; *Acoustics:* Cabinet Cial

Project List

1999

- School of Architecture, Miami, Florida International University *(competition: first prize)*
- Water Treatment Plant, Alençon, France *(competition: first prize)*
- Tour Perret Exhibition Center, Amiens, France *(competition)*
- International Sports Center, Metz, France *(competition)*
- World Sea Memorial—Submarine Base, Lorient, France *(competition)*

1998

- Concert Hall and Exhibition Complex, Rouen, France *(competition: first prize)*
- Contemporary Arts Center, Cincinnati, Ohio *(competition: one of three finalists)*
- French Embassy, Pretoria, South Africa *(competition)*

1997

- Expansion of The Museum of Modern Art, New York *(competition: one of three finalists)*
- FRAC Art Center, Nantes, France *(competition)*
- Virtual Architecture Exhibition, Tokyo, Japan
- NAi Exhibition, Rotterdam, Holland

1996

- Biennale VI International Exhibition, French Pavillion, Venice, Italy

1995

- Interface Railway Station, Lausanne, Switzerland *(competition 1988: first prize)*
- K-polis Department Store, Zürich, Switzerland *(competition)*

1994

- School of Architecture, Marne-la-Vallée, France *(competition: first prize, completed)*
- Lerner Hall Student Center—Columbia University, New York, New York *(completed)*
- Franklin Furnace Gallery, New York, New York *(study)*
- Renault Ile Seguin Master Plan, Paris, France *(study)*

All projects and bibliographical information prior to 1994 are included in the first volume of *Event-Cities.*

Books, Catalogs, and Selected Articles by Bernard Tschumi

1994

Architecture and Disjunction. Cambridge and London: The MIT Press, 1994.

"Architecture of the Event." In Cynthia C. Davidson, ed., *Anyway.* New York: Anyone Corp. and Rizzoli, 1994, pp. 76-83.

Bernard Tschumi 1983-1993. A+U (Tokyo), March 1994. (Special issue)

Event-Cities. Cambridge and London: The MIT Press, 1994.

The Manhattan Transcripts (revised and enlarged edition). London and New York: Academy Editions / St. Martin's Press, 1994.

1995

"Discussion I: The Province of Architecture in Thought." In Cynthia C. Davidson, ed., *Anyplace.* New York and Cambridge: Anyone Corp. and The MIT Press, 1995, pp. 40-43. (Also contains Bridge-City, Lausanne project, pp. 56-63)

"One, Two, Three: Jump." In Martin Pearce and Maggie Toy, eds., *Educating Architects.* London: Academy Editions, 1995, pp. 24-25.

"Urban Pleasures and the Moral Good." *Assemblage,* no. 25, pp. 6-13.

1996

Architecture and Disjunction (Japanese edition). Tokyo: Kajima Institute Publishing, 1996.

"City and Void." In *Architectural Associations: The Idea of the City* (in celebration of Alvin Boyarsky). London: Architectural Association, 1996, pp. 136-43.

1997

"Architecture in a Non-Linear Age: The Unceasing Flow of Change." *Inter-Communication* (Tokyo), pp. 243-62. (Special issue: Arata Isozaki)

Bernard Tschumi: Architecture In/Of Motion. Rotterdam: NAi Publishers, 1997. (Introduction by Jos Bosman)

Bernard Tschumi. Architectural Profile (Bangkok), vol. 1, no. 4 (January-February, 1997).

Bernard Tschumi: GA Document Extra, no. 10. Tokyo: GA (A.D.A. Edita), 1997.

1998

"Through a Broken Lens." In Cynthia C. Davidson, ed., *Anyhow.* New York and Cambridge: Anyone Corp. and The MIT Press, 1998, pp. 236-241.

1999

"Diasync." In Cynthia C. Davidson, ed., *Anytime.* New York and Cambridge: Anyone Corp. and The MIT Press, 1999, pp. 168-175.

"On the Museum of the Twenty-First Century: An Homage to Italo Calvino's *Invisible Cities.*" *Daedalus*, vol. 128, no. 3, pp. 333-337.

Tschumi Le Fresnoy: Architecture In/Between. New York: The Monacelli Press, 1999. (Includes essays by Joseph Abram, Sylviane Agacinski, Véronique Descharrières, Alain Fleischer, Alain Guiheux, Sylvia Lavin, Alain Pélissier, Dominique Rouillard, and Bernard Tschumi)

Selected Criticism and Reviews on Bernard Tschumi

1994

Allen, Stanley. "Bernard Tschumi at The Museum of Modern Art." *Newsline* (New York), March-April 1994, p. 2.

Ambroise-Rendu, Marc. "Le site de La Villette attire déjà autant de visiteurs qu'Euro Disney." *Le Monde* (Paris), December 2, 1994.

Cohn, David. "El MoMA Expone a Tschumi." *Arquitectura Viva* (Madrid), no. 36 (May-June 1994), pp. 64-65.

"Competition Projects for the New Congress Centre, Salzburg: Bernard Tschumi." *Zodiac* (Milan), vol. 10 (September 1993-February 1994), pp. 162-171.

Doutriaux, Emmanuel. "Etude Lumineuse pour l'Ecole du Fresnoy." *L'Architecture d'Aujourd'hui* (Paris), no. 292 (April 1994), pp. 62-63.

Giovannini, Joseph. "Tschumi Exhibit at The Museum of Modern Art." *Architecture* (New York), vol. 83, no. 6 (June 1994), pp. 30-33.

—. "More Than One Way to See Art." *The New York Times* (New York), November 13, 1994, p. H48.

Girot, Christophe. "Learning from La Villette." *Documents* (New York), vol. 2, no. 4/5 (Spring 1994), p. 23.

Hine, Thomas. "The Radically Useless Building." *The New York Times Book Review* (New York), April 24, 1994, p. 9.

Kwon, Miwon. "Looking at Parc de la Villette." *Documents* (New York), vol. 2, no. 4/5 (Spring 1994), p. 23. Also includes "Interview with Bernard Tschumi," pp. 25-30, and Bernard Tschumi, "Looking Back at Parc de la Villette: Some Comments," pp. 42-45.

Melhuish, Clare. "Rocking the Foundations." *Building Design* (London), November 18, 1994, p. 18.

Merrill, Bertram. "Installations at the Edge." *Oculus* (New York), vol. 56, no. 10 (June 1994).

Muschamp, Herbert. "Urban Dreams, Urban Realities." *The New York Times* (New York), April 21, 1994, p. C26.

Oppici, Fabio and Enrique Walker. "Entre Vista a Bernard Tschumi." *Diseno* (Santiago), March-April 1994, pp. 97-103.

Ouroussoff, Nicolai. "Architecture's Radical Without Risks." *The New York Observer* (New York), April 24, 1994, p. 15.

Pascucci, Ernest. "Arrested Development." *Documents* (New York), vol. 2, no 4/5 (Spring 1994), pp. 46-56.

Patterson, Richard. "Seductive Argument." *Building Design* (London), November 18, 1994, p. 18.

Tabor, Philip. "Impossible Moment." *Architectural Review* (London), October 1994, pp. 104-105,

1995

Aesopos, Yannis. "Bernard Tschumi's Metropolitan Pleasures." *Ntizaïn* (Athens), Autumn 1995, n.p..

"Bernard Tschumi: Le Fresnoy Center for Art and Media." *GA Document* (Tokyo), 43 (April 1995) (GA International '95), pp. 100-103.

"Bernard Tschumi: New York Loft, 1988." In Anatxu Zabalbeascoa, ed., *The House of the Architect.* Barcelona: Gustavo Gili, 1995, pp. 150-51.

Bonami, Francesco. "Bernard Tschumi. The Schizophrenic Side of Architecture." *Flash Art* (Milan), October, pp. 83-86. (Interview)

Bouman, Ole. "Architecture for Lazarus." *Archis* (Rotterdam), no. 6/95 (June 1995), pp. 53-59.

— and Hans van Dijk. "I Find the Affirmation of Process Intensely Desirable: An Interview with Bernard Tschumi." *Archis* (Rotterdam), no. 6/95 (June 1995), pp. 60-67.

Castellano, Aldo. "Prassi, Città, Eventi: Three Reading Keys." *L'ARCA* (Milan), September 1996, pp. 10-21.

Chantre, Pierre-Louis. "Le Parc de la Villette fait la nique à Disney." *L'Hebdo* (Lausanne), April 6, 1995, pp. 80-84.

Coates, Nigel. "La Biblioteca di Bernard Tschumi" and "Identità e differenze: I racconti dell' abitare." In *Abitare*. Milan: Segesta Cataloghi, 1995, pp. 122-23. (Proceedings of symposium, Milan Triennale, 1994)

Frampton, Kenneth. "Tschumi, Cinétique et Architecture." *L'Architecture d'Aujourd'hui* (Paris), no. 302 (December 1995), p. 24.

Fromond, Françoise. "Ecole, étude de cas." *L'Architecture d'Aujourd'hui* (Paris), no. 302 (December 1995), pp. 10-13.

"Jardin d'Entreprises." *Zodiac* (Milan), vol. 13 (June 1995), pp. 128-133.

Mead, Andrew. "Bernard Tschumi: Architecture of Movement." *The Architect's Journal* (London), June 15, 1995, p. 24.

Melhuish, Clare. "Au revoir, Ecole des Beaux-Arts." *Building Design* (London), February 10, 1995, p. 8.

Ozkan, Suha. "Tschumi: Yeni-Modernizm ile arasinda." *Arredamento Dekorayson* (Turkey), February 1995, pp. 67-71. Also contains Yildoz Salman, "Bernard Tschumi, ile oylesi," pp. 72-73, and interview with Sulan Kolatan, pp. 74-82.

Péllissier, Alain. "Le Programme comme Projet." *Techniques et Architecture* (Paris), July 1995, pp. 35-37.

Pichler, Irene. "Die Stadt der Architektur / Konzept für eine Architekturschule in Marne-la-Vallée." *Architektur* (Vienna), November 1995, pp. 12-14.

Rambert, Francis. "Contre les Chapelles, une Cathédrale?" *D'Architecture* (Paris), no. 53 (March 1995), pp. 10-11.

Widder, Lynnette. "Haus ohne Eigenschaften (Building without Qualities)." *Daidalos* (Berlin), August 1995, pp. 104-9.

1996

"Bernard Tschumi: Letzipolis, Zürich." *Archithese* (Zurich), no. 2/96 (March-April 1996), pp. 36-37.

Bretler, Marc. "Les passages de Bernard Tschumi." *Archimade* (Lausanne), no. 54 (December 1997), pp. 7-31. (Also includes interview and presentation of four projects)

Fleischer, Alain. "Grandes Lignes d'un Grand Projet." *Jardin des Modes* (Paris), no. 193 (Winter 1996), pp. 48-51.

Hendrix, John. "The Dean of Deconstruction." *Manhattan Mirror* (New York), January 31, 1996, p. 14.

La Villette. Vis à Vis (Paris), no. 3 (Winter 1996). (Special issue on Parc de la Villette)

"Le Fresnoy National Studio for Contemporary Arts, Tourcoing, France." *Zodiac* (Milan), no. 15, pp. 150-59.

Migayrou, Frederic. *Bloc: Le Monolithe Fracturé*. Catalogue for French Pavillion Exhibition, Venice Biennale, 1996, pp. 138-145.

Ouroussoff, Nicolai. "Tschumi Abstracts McKim, Mead & White's Plan for Columbia University." *Architectural Record* (New York), January 1997, p. 11.

Rappaport, Nina. "Center of a New Era." *Oculus* (New York), March 1996, p. 3.

Rouand, Jean. *Promenade à la Villette*. Paris: Editions d'Art Somogy, Paris.

"School of Architecture, Marne-la-Vallée, France." *Zodiac* (Milan), no. 15, pp. 160-166.

Widder, Lynnette. "The Margins of Error: A Media Center in Le Fresnoy and the Souks of Beirut." *Daidalos* (Berlin) no. 59 (March 1996), pp. 122-27.

Wiseman, Carter. "Get Real or Be Gone." *ARTnews* (New York), September 1996, pp. 119-123.

Yum, Di Lou. "Bernard Tschumi: Architecte d'Art et d'Essai." *Jardin des Modes* (Paris), no. 193 (Winter 1996), pp. 52-55.

1997
"An Interactive Station: School of Architecture, Marne-la-Vallée, France." In Ken Sakamura and Hiroyuki Suzuki, eds., *The Virtual Architecture.* Tokyo: Tokyo University Digital Museum, 1997, pp. 122-27.

"Arts of Memory: Center of Contemporary Arts Tourcoing." *Arquitectura Viva Monographs* (Madrid) no. 65 (May/June 1997), pp. 92-99.

"Bernard Tschumi: Le Fresnoy Center for Contemporary Arts." *Quaderns* (Barcelona), no. 218 (1997), pp. 28-39.

Boyer, Charles-Arthur. "Le Fresnoy, un Bauhaus New Age." *Art Press* (Paris), no. 228 (October 1997), pp. 49-55.

Davis, Douglas. "MoMA Looks to the Future." *Art in America* (New York), October 1997, pp. 33-35.

de Roux, Emmanuel. "La Villette, l'étrange alchimie d'un poumon vert qui fut un abattoir." *Le Monde* (Paris), January 1997, p. 28.

Decker, Andrew. "The New MoMA." *ARTnews* (New York), October 1997, pp. 130-135.

Devinat, François. "L'Art à Nouvelle Ecole." *Libération* (Paris), November 25, 1997, pp. 32-33.

"Die Strategie des 'Dazwischen.' Kulturzentrum Le Fresnoy." *Arch+* (Berlin), no. 138 (October 1997), pp. 40-44.

Dunlap, David W. "Alma Mater Gets a Makeover." *The New York Times* (New York), November 16, 1997, Section 11, p. 1.

Ellis, Charlotte. "Creative Umbrella." *The Architectural Review* (London), September 1997, pp. 40-43.

Fleischer, Alain. "Le Fresnoy: Une Ecole." *L'Architecture d'Aujourd'hui* (Paris), no. 314 (December 1997), pp. 52-55.

Giovannini, Joseph. "Back to the Box." *The New Yorker* (New York), May 12, 1997.

—. "Finalists Announced for MoMA Expansion" *Architecture* (New York), vol. 86, no. 5 (May 1997), pp. 46-47.

Huxtable, Ada Louise. "Redefining the Modern." *The Wall Street Journal* (New York), May 8, 1997, p. A20.

Jacobs, Karrie. "Rough Drafts." *New York Magazine* (New York), May 26, 1997, pp. 18-19.

"La región intermedia: Centro de Arte Contemporaneas Le Fresnoy, Tourcoing." *Arquitectura Viva* (Madrid), no. 57 (November-December 1997), pp. 46-53.

Lavin, Sylvia. "Inter-objective Criticism: Bernard Tschumi and Le Fresnoy." *ANY* (New York), no. 21, pp. 32-35.

"L'entre-deux: de l'espace à l'événement et de l'événement à l'espace." (Interview by Yves Dessuant) In *Le Lieu, la Scène, la Salle, la Ville. Etudes Théâtrales* (Louvain-la-Neuve, Belgium), no. 11-12 (1997), pp. 46-54.

"Le Fresnoy Center for the Arts and Media." *Architecture* (New York), vol. 86, no. 1 (January 1997) (Progressive Architecture Awards issue), pp. 96-97.

Le Garrec, Ivan. "Figure de l'entre-deux." *Techniques et Architecture* (Paris), pp. 18-23.

"Lerner Student Center." *A+U* (Tokyo), no. 324 (September 1997), pp. 10-29. (Essays by Bernard Tschumi with text by Hugh Dutton)

Loriers, Marie-Christine. "Projects in France: Between Two Roofs." *Archis* (Rotterdam), August 1997, pp. 60-67.

Merwood, Joanna. "Ten Projects for the MOMA." *Lotus International* (Milan), no. 95 (December 1997), pp. 26-49.

Michel, Florence." Le toit en folie." *Architecture Intérieure Crée* (Paris), no. 279 (December 1997), pp. 46-53.

Muschamp, Herbert. "Architects' Visions of How the Modern May One Day Appear." *The New York Times* (New York), May 3, 1997, pp. C15, 20.

Ouroussoff, Nicolai. "Up on the Roof at New Film School." *Los Angeles Times* (Los Angeles), December 2, 1997.

Perret, Florence. "De la vallée du Flon aux vallons de Manhattan." *L'Hebdo* (Lausanne), December 31, 1997, p. 43.

— and Arianne Dayer. "Oui, C'est La Ville Absolue." *L'Hebdo* (Lausanne), December 31, 1997, pp. 42-43.

Phillips, Christopher. "Tschumi-Designed Arts Center Opens." *Art in America* (New York), December 1997, p. 25.

Rambert, Francis. "Quand l'architecture se prête au jeu du cinéma." *Connaissance des Arts* (Paris), no. 542 (September 1997), pp. 95-105.

—. "Dossier: L'Architecte en mutation." *D'Architecture* (Paris), no. 77 (October 1997), pp. 17-20.

Rappaport, Nina. "Interview." *SI+A* (Schweizer Ingenieur und Architekt) (Zurich), February 6, 1997, pp. 4-9.

Robert, Jean-Paul. "Dossier" and "Le Fresnoy: Un Lieu." *L'Architecture d'Aujourd'hui* (Paris), no. 314 (December 1997), pp. 34-51.

—. "Samplen met gebouwen." *de Architect* (The Hague), no. 28 (September 1997), pp. 33-47.

Rodermond, Janny. "Faking or Making the Future." *de Architect* (The Hague), no. 28 (September 1997), pp. 36-38.

"Ruptures, Bernard Tschumi." *Techniques & Architecture* (Paris), no. 429 (January 1997), pp. 50-52.

Ryan, Raymund. "Remaking MoMA." *Blueprint* (London), June 1997, p. 12.

—. "The Intelligent Roof." *Blueprint* (London), September 1997, pp. 42-44.

"School of Architecture, Marne-la-Vallée, France." In Andreas Papadakis, ed. *New Architecture* (London), no. 1 (August 1997), pp. 24, 62-69.

Singmaster, Deborah. "Tschumi finds spatial gap for Lille culture." *The Architects' Journal* (London), October 9, 1997, pp. 10-11.

Terranova, Antonino. In Claudio Roseti, *La Decostruzione e il Decostruttivivismo.* Gangemi Editore, pp. 207-218.

Uddin, M. Saleh. *Composite Drawing: Techniques for Architectural Design Presentation.* New York: McGraw-Hill Publishers, 1997.

Urbach, Henry. "Picks and Plans." *Artforum* (New York), June 1997.

Vidler, Anthony. "MoMA's and Magmas." *Lotus International* (Milan), no. 95 (December 1997), pp. 24-25.

1998

Arnaboldi, Mario Antonio. "Concert Hall in Rouen." *L'ARCA* (Milan), no. 132 (December 1998), pp. 12-17.

"Autopilot" and "Bernard Tschumi '81: The Manhattan Transcripts." *ARCH+ 30 Yahre (Architektur und Städtebau seit 1968)* (Berlin), no. 139/40 (January 1998), pp. 119, 122-23.

Beck, Haig and Jackie Cooper, eds. "Bernard Tschumi: Le Fresnoy National Studio of Contemporary Arts, Tourcoing, France." *UME* (Melbourne), no. 7 (March 1998), pp. 38-45.

Beret, Chantal. "The Once and Future MoMA." *Art Press* (Paris), no. 237 (July-August 1998), pp. 54-57.

Bonami, Francesco. "Bernard Tschumi: L'architettura schizofrenia." *Intervista* (Milan), no. 13 (March-April 1998), pp. 32-34.

Bretler, Marc, ed. "Conversation: Zaha M. Hadid, Wolf Prix, Bernard Tschumi." *A+U* (Tokyo), no. 334 (July 1998), pp. 4-11.

—. "Performance Hall and Exhibition Center in Rouen, France." *A+U* (Tokyo), no. 334 (July 1998), pp. 12-23.

Byard, Paul Spencer. "Pickling the Past." *Architecture* (New York), February 1998, pp. 58-63.

—. *The Architecture of Additions: Design and Regulation.* New York and London: W.W. Norton, 1998, pp. 175-176.

Dawson, Jessica Barrow. "Project Portfolio: Bernard Tschumi Architects." *Architecture* (New York), April 1998, pp. 45-47.

Edelmann, Frédéric and Michel Guerrin. "Le Fresnoy, multimédia pour artistes de demain." *Le Monde* (Paris), January 30, 1998, p. 26.

Elderfield, John, ed. *Imagining the Future of The Museum of Modern Art.* New York: The Museum of Modern Art and Harry N. Abrams, Inc., 1998, pp. 254-339.

Flanagan, Barbara. "Umbrella of Tourcoing: Where Imagination Finds Shelter." *The New York Times* (New York), April 16, 1998, p. F3.

Foster, Hal, with Denis Hollier, Silvia Kolbowski, and Rosalind E. Krauss. "The MoMA Expansion: A Conversation with Terence Riley." *October* (New York), no. 84 (Spring 1998), pp. 3-30.

Fuchigami, Masayuki. *Crosscurrents: Fifty-One World Architects.* Tokyo, 1998, pp. 182-85.

Graaf, Vera. "Der Querdenker...." *Architektur & Wohnen* (Berlin), no. 2/98 (April-May 1998), pp. 146-50.

Holt-Damant, Käthi. "Space and Time in the Architecture and Theory of Bernard Tschumi." *UME* (Melbourne), no. 7 (March 1998), pp. 48-51.

Jodidio, Philip. *Contemporary European Architects, vol. VI.* Cologne: Taschen, 1998, pp. 27-32, 172-83.

Nuridsany, Michel. "Le Fresnoy, utopie multimédia." *Le Figaro* (Paris), January 27, 1998, p. 23.

Papathanassiou, Marilia. "Bernard Tschumi." *Gynaika* (Athens), June 21, 1998, pp. F12-13.

Pawley, Martin. "Tschumi's City in the Sky." *Architecture Today* (London), no. 85 (February 1998), pp. 16-23. Also contains "Forum: 'The Space Between'" (editorial), p. 2.

Pelkonen, Eeva-Liisa. "Bernard Tschumi Ereignis-Raum." *Daidalos* (Berlin), no. 67 (March 1998), pp. 82-85.

Rambert, Francis. "Bernard Tschumi: 'Le Montage cinématographique m'a inspiré.'" *Le Figaro* (Paris), Tuesday, January 27, 1998, p. 23.

—. "Cinema as the Motor of Architecture." *Architektur Aktuell* (Vienna), no. 214 (April 1998), pp. 48-61.

Safran, Yehuda. "Le Fresnoy National Studio for Contemporary Arts, Tourcoing, France." *Domus* (Milan), no. 801 (February 1998), pp. 10-17.

Stein, Karen D. "Sheltering the Arts: Bernard Tschumi Builds at Le Fresnoy." *Architectural Record* (New York), January 1998, pp. 86-95.

Thomsen, Christian W. *Sensuous Architecture: The Art of Erotic Building.* Munich: Prestel Verlag, 1998, pp. 12-13, 36, 171.

Vernes, Michel. “Les Modernes contre l’aventure.” *Archicrée* (Paris), no. 284 (September 1998), pp. 44-51.

1999

“Alfred Lerner Hall.” *Praxis* (New York), vol. 1, no. 0 (Fall 1999), pp. 66-81.

Arenson, Karen. “On Campus.” *The New York Times* (New York), July 28, 1999, p. B8.

Barron, James. “An Architect With a Film Director’s Eye.” *The New York Times* (New York), October 5, 1999, p. B2.

“Best Design of 1999.” *Time* (New York), International Edition, December 20, 1999, pp. 44-45.

Brand, Ulrika and Suzanne Trimel. “Bernard Tschumi: International Architect Makes His American Debut with Lerner Hall” and “Introducing Alfred Lerner Hall.” *Columbia University Record* (New York), September 17, 1999, pp. 1, 6-8.

Bressi, Todd. “Going Public: Lerner Hall.” *Oculus.* (New York), vol. 62, no. 4 (December 1999), p. 7.

Campbell, Robert. “Alfred Lerner Hall, Columbia University.” *Architectural Record* (New York), November 1999, pp. 94-101.

“Concepts Materialized: A Conversation with Bernard Tschumi.” *Praxis* (New York), vol. 1, no. 0 (Fall 1999), pp. 56-65.

Croft, Catherine. “Filmic Inspiration.” *Building Design* (London), September 10, 1999, p. 23.

Ebony, David. “State-of-the-Art Student Center for Columbia.” *Art in America.* (New York), December 1999, pp. 25.

“Guide to Alfred Lerner Hall.” *Columbia Daily Spectator* (New York), August 31, 1999, pp. 1-8. (Supplement)

“Hague Villa.” In Terence Riley, *The Un-Private House*, New York: The Museum of Modern Art and Harry N. Abrams, Inc., 1999, pp. 68-71 and passim.

Henninger, Paul. “Alfred Lerner Hall in New York by Bernard Tschumi.” *de Architect* (The Hague), no. 30 (November 1999), pp. 70-75.

“Lerner Student Center.” *Domus* (Milan), no. 816 (June 1999), pp. 35-38.

“Lerner Student Center.” *Zodiac* (Milan), no. 20 (May 1999), pp.104-11.

Litke, Ronald. “Building a Dream.” *University Business* (New York), vol. 2, no. 9 (November 1999), pp. 40-44.

Litt, Steven. “Lerner’s New York Triumph.” *The Plain Dealer* (Cleveland), October 17, 1999, p. I-4.

Muschamp, Herbert. "Echoes of '68 on Columbia's Campus." *The New York Times* (New York), October 24, 1999, Section 2, pp. 40-41.

"Parc de la Villette." *Domus* (Milan), no. 817 (August 1999), pp. 8-17.

Pelkonen, Eeva. "In Context: Tschumi at Lerner Hall." *Praxis* (New York), vol. 1, no. 0 (Fall 1999), pp. 82-87.

"Performance Hall and Exhibition Center, Rouen, France." In *Sci-Fi Architecture. Architectural Design* (London), vol. 69, no. 3/4 (March-April 1999), pp. 10, 62-65.

Powell, Kenneth. "Le Fresnoy." In *Architecture Reborn: The Conversion and Reconstruction of Old Buildings*. London: Laurence King, 1999, pp. 134-141.

Rattenbury, Kester. "Clear as Daylight." *Building Design* (London), October 29, 1999, p. 22.

Rocco, Alessandro. "X-files. Unidentified Objects on Planet Architecture." *Lotus* (Milan), no. 100 (Spring 1999), pp. 36-38.

"Rouen Concert Hall and Exhibition Complex." *GA Document* (Tokyo), 58 (GA International '99), pp. 96-99.

Ruby, Andreas. "Burrowing through MoMA: Interview with Bernard Tschumi." *Daidalos* (Berlin), no. 71 (June 1999), pp. 38-47.

—. "En attendant Tschumi: Die neue Architekturschule in Marne-la-Vallée." *Bauwelt* (Berlin) no. 40/41 (October 1999), pp. 2246-2253.

Rutkowski, Roman. "Le Fresnoy: A XXI Century Art School." *Architektura & Biznes* (Krakow), vol. 6, no. 83, pp. 12-17.

Ryan, Raymond. "Re-made in America." *Blueprint* (London), no. 165 (October 1999), pp. 44-47.

Sandler, Linda. "Schools Build Luxury Hangouts." *The Wall Street Journal* (New York), April 28, 1999, p. B14.

"Short Takes: Tschumi Le Fresnoy." *Time* (New York), vol. 153, no. 25 (June 28, 1999), p. 72.

Stuart, John. "More than a Campus Icon: A New Facility for FIU's Architecture Program." *Competitions* (Louisville, KY), vol. 9, no. 2 (Summer 1999), pp. 16-27.

Uddin, M. Saleh. *Digital Architecture*. New York: McGraw Hill Publishers, 1999, pp. 194-197.

Vidler, Anthony. "Take One." *Architecture* (New York), vol. 88, no. 12 (December 1999), p. 81.

von Fischer, Sabine. "Lerner Student Center." *Bauwelt* (Berlin), no. 40/41 (October 1999), pp. 2232-2233.

Biographical Notes

Bernard Tschumi was born in 1944 in Lausanne, Switzerland and lives in New York and Paris. He has French and Swiss nationalities and is a permanent resident of the United States. Tschumi studied in Paris and at the Federal Institute of Technology (ETH) in Zurich, Switzerland, from which he received his degree in 1969. He taught at the Architectural Association in London (1970-79), the Institute for Architecture and Urban Studies in New York (1976), Princeton University (1976 and 1980) and the Cooper Union (1981-3). Since 1988 he has been Dean of the Graduate School of Architecture, Planning and Preservation at Columbia University in New York. Tschumi is a member of the Collège International de Philosophie and, as the recipient of distinguished honors, is Chevalier in the Légion d'Honneur and Officier in the Ordre des Arts et Lettres in France. He was awarded France's Grand Prix National d'Architecture in 1996 and received England's Royal Victoria Medal, as well as awards from the American Institute of Architects and the National Endowment for the Arts. Tschumi is a member of the American Institute of Architects and the Ordre des Architectes in France. He is principal of Bernard Tschumi Architects, New York and Paris.

Photography Credits

p. 40/41 Sophie Chivet **p. 82** J.M. Monthiers **p. 92-93** Sophie Chivet **p. 122** Peter Mauss / Esto **p. 126** Peter Mauss / Esto **p. 130** Peter Mauss / Esto **p. 138** Peter Mauss / Esto **p. 146** Peter Mauss / Esto **p. 150** Sophie Chivet **p. 154** J.M. Monthiers **p. 158** Peter Mauss / Esto **p. 166** Peter Mauss / Esto **p. 170** J.M. Monthiers **p. 174** J.M. Monthiers **p. 178** J.M. Monthiers **p. 182** Jan Derwig **p. 186** Jan Derwig **p. 190** J.M. Monthiers **p. 196** Peter Mauss / Esto **p. 198** Peter Mauss / Esto **p. 200** Peter Mauss / Esto **p. 202** Peter Mauss / Esto **p. 206/207** Arnaud Legrain / EPPY **p. 214** J.M. Monthiers **p. 220** Peter Mauss / Esto **p. 222/223** J.M. Monthiers **p. 344** Peter Mauss / Esto **p. 354/355** Peter Mauss / Esto **p. 360** Peter Mauss / Esto **p. 362** Hugh Dutton **p. 370** Lydia Gould **p. 372/373** Peter Mauss / Esto **p. 390/391** Alfred Hitchcock, film, *Spellbound* **p. 404/405** George Cukor, film, *What Price Hollywood?* **p. 484/485** John Cromwell, film, *Since You Went Away* **p. 500/501** Jacques Marie **p. 512** Peter Mauss / Esto **p. 582/583** Peter Mauss / Esto **p. 618/619** Murray Spivack **p. 672/673** John Cromwell, film, *Since You Went Away*. All other photographs by Bernard Tschumi Architects.